Tropentag 2016

Tropentag 2016

International Research on Food Security, Natural Resource Management and Rural Development

Solidarity in a competing world - fair use of resources

Book of abstracts

Editors: Bernhard Freyer & Eric Tielkes

Reviewers/scientific committee: Folkard Asch, Tina Beuchelt, Patrick van Damme, Frank Hartwich, Christian Hülsebusch, Irmgard Jordan, Brigitte Kaufmann, Ulrich Köpke, Günter Langergraber, Margareta Lelea, Willibald Loiskandl, Reinfried Mansberger, Andreas Melcher, Hycenth Tim Ndah, Andreas de Neergaard, Daniel Neuhoff, Zbynek Polesny, Fred Rattunde, Regina Rößler, Stefan Sieber, Christian R. Vogl, Eva Weltzien, Florian Wichern, Stephan Winter, Maria Wurzinger

Editorial assistance: Anne Siegmeier

Impressum

Bibliografische Information der Deutschen Nationalbibliothek
Die Deutsche Nationalbibliothek verzeichnet diese Publikation in der Deutschen Nationalbibliografie; detailierte bibliografische Daten sind im Internet über http://dnb.ddb.de abrufbar.

Tropentag 2016: Solidarity in a competing world - fair use of resources, Freyer, B. & E. Tielkes (eds.) 1. Aufl. - Göttingen: Cuvillier, 2016

© CUVILLIER VERLAG, Göttingen
  Nonnenstieg 8, 37075 Göttingen
  Telefon: 0551-54724-0
  Telefax: 0551-54724-21
  http://www.cuvillier.de

Gedruckt auf umweltfreundlichem, säurefreiem Papier aus nachhaltiger Forstwirtschaft.

ISBN: 978-3-7369-9341-9
eISBN: 978-3-7369-8341-0

Online-Version: http://www.tropentag.de/

Preface

The annual *Tropentag*, the largest European interdisciplinary conference on research in Tropical and Subtropical Agriculture and Natural Resource Management, rotates between universities and research institutes in Berlin, Bonn, Göttingen, Hohenheim, Kassel-Witzenhausen, Prague, and since 2016 Vienna, where this year's Tropentag is hosted by the University of Natural Resources and Life Sciences Vienna (Universität für Bodenkultur Wien).

Regular organisational support for the event is provided by the Council for Tropical and Subtropical Research (ATSAF e.V.), the German Institute for Tropical and Subtropical Agriculture (DITSL) in Witzenhausen, and the GIZ Advisory Service on Agricultural Research for Development (BEAF) on behalf of the German Federal Ministry for Economic Cooperation and Development BMZ. Since 2015, additional financial support is provided by the German Federal Ministry of Education and Research BMBF and the German Federal Ministry of Food and Agriculture BMEL in collaboration with the Federal Office for Agriculture and Food BLE, both hosting additional thematic sessions. Unique is the organisation of a common workshop of BMEL with the Austrian Federal Ministry of Agriculture, Forestry, Environment and Water Management (BMLFUW). The *Tropentag* 2016 also profits from the participation of the Austrian Development Agency ADA and the United Nations Industrial Development Organization UNIDO, each with an own workshop. Again with us is our longstanding supporter, the *fiat panis* foundation represented by Dr. Andrea Fadani. New on board is the "Bäuerliche Erzeugergemeinschaft Schwäbisch Hall" represented by Rudolf Bühler, which took over the award for the best conference poster.

The *Tropentag* has become the most important international conference on development-oriented research in the fields of food security, natural resource management and rural development in central Europe and provides a unique platform for scientific and personal exchange for students, junior and senior scientists, development experts and funding organisations from several countries together with their international partner institutions. Approximately 1000 participant registrations from 74 countries underline the importance of interdisciplinary scientific exchange to address the challenges ahead of us.

The *Tropentag* 2016 is organised by the University of Natural Resources and Life Sciences (BOKU), Vienna, Austria from September 18. - 21. It has been developed by several Departments and Divisions of BOKU, Eric Tielkes from DITSL, Witzenhausen, and supported by several sponsors.

The theme of 2016 is "Solidarity in a competing world - fair use of resources". While on the one hand, one part of the world is profiting from natural resources, the other part of the world is suffering with hunger, malnutrition, human diseases, low income, violence and lately is also challenged through climate change. There is need to rethink and engage in a fair share of all resources between the continents and nations. This includes huge engagement into the management of natural resources to solve the long list of environmental threats expressed through ongoing erosion, loss of soil fertility and loss of biodiversity, and topped by climate change having strong impact on the productivity in agriculture, fishery and forestry, and the use and quality of water and of energy in the South.

Natural sciences are able to contribute to sustainable use of natural resources through all kind of strategies today discussed under terms like sustainable intensification, organic farming or bioeconomy, but have to keep in mind that their success is highly dependent from learning and training processes that are sensitive to the cultural, social and religious as well as socio-economic and political environments. Gender and generation sensitive participatory and governance structures are to develop which secure the integration of stakeholders along the whole value chains. Thus the broad field of social sciences takes over a crucial role for identifying and understanding the needs and strategies for implementing solidary and fair solutions for the future use of global resources. In this context, besides excellent disciplinary approaches, inter- and transdisciplinary research takes over a key role to bring the potential of different disciplines together toward an added value in a process of mutual knowledge production of scientists and stakeholders.

The *Tropentag* 2016 theme will be critically introduced and further discussed in a panel discussion by six renowned international keynote speakers. In 28 oral sessions including specific contributions by the ministries, 34 guided poster sessions and 16 workshops, participants present and discuss their research ideas and findings of the theme. A special session featured by CGIAR Center Bioversity International will underline the role of biodiversity and the CGIAR on tropical trees and forests conservation and crop diversity under climate change.

We wish to thank all participants for their scientific contributions, our colleagues, supporting the conference through reviewing more than 1000 abstracts and acting as session and poster chairs. Special thanks are given to Eric Tielkes, who gave us guidance and strong support in organising the conference. Finally we thank the donors for their financial, and food and drinks contributions that allow us to offer the conference affordable for participants with lower income.

We welcome you from different parts of the world at the *Tropentag* Conference 2016 in Vienna and wish you an inspiring and enriching event with lots of discussions and exchange of knowledge and experiences, and finally learning steps.

On behalf of the local organising team of *Tropentag* 2016

Univ.Prof. Dr. Bernhard Freyer (BOKU)

and

Anna Porcuna (local coordinator - special thanks to you) and the organising team with Ass.Prof. DI Dr. Michael Hauser, Priv.-Doz. DI Dr. Günter Langergraber, Univ.Prof. Dr. Willibald Loiskandl, Max Manderscheid, Ass.Prof. DI Dr. Reinfried Mansberger, Tamara Piniel, Ao.Univ.Prof. Dr. Harald Vacik, Priv.-Doz. Dr. Maria Wurzinger

Vienna, September 2016

Contents

Plenary speeches

How the Equitable Sharing of Benefits from Genetic Resources Can Contribute to Fairness and Innovation

M. ANN TUTWILER

Bioversity International, Office of the Director General, Italy

The Sustainable Development Goals (SDGs) take a holistic approach, recognising that human and environmental wellbeing are inextricably linked. SDG 1 – No poverty – expands the vision of poverty reduction to go beyond economic resources and include also the natural resources on which the poor depend. Agricultural biodiversity is one natural resource pool that poor farmers have always relied on‰in fact farmers are the people who developed the thousands of crop varieties we know today, which provide nutritious diets and support low-input farming systems. Even though farmers developed these genetic resources, and depend upon them, their rights over them and the traditional knowledge associated with them are not always recognised and the ensuing benefits are not always shared fairly and equitably.

Two SDG targets directly address fair and equitable sharing of benefits from genetic resources and traditional knowledge: 2.5 Zero hunger, and 15.6 Life on land. Additionally, several international treaties govern the use of agricultural genetic resources: The International Treaty on Plant Genetic Resources for Food and Agriculture, the Nagoya Protocol of the Convention on Biological Diversity, and the International Union for the Protection of New Varieties of Plaunts (UPOV) Convention. National governments also have their own laws.

Into this mix, farmers and private sector companies bring their own perspectives and interests of what is fair, what is equitable and what is necessary to spur agricultural innovation. In some cases, different views about what fair and equitable treatment means divide actors who should be working together. But there are also examples of where heightened emphasis on promoting equity and fairness has contributed to successful outcomes. My remarks will discuss how to bring successful local practices to national and international levels; how to bring international legal commitments on access and benefit sharing to local levels; and how to engage the private sector at the local, national and international levels.

Contact Address: M. Ann Tutwiler, Bioversity International, Office of the Director General, Via Dei Tre Denari 472/a Maccarese, 00057 Rome, Italy, e-mail: a.tutwiler@cgiar.org

ID 1173

Solidarity in a Competing World and Food Security Challenge

POONPIPOPE KASEMSAP

Kasetsart University, Thailand

Collaboration is probably one of the most important success factors for development. However, a combination of both competition and collaboration may be needed for sustainable development, especially under a number of current world challenges. Global climate change and increasing population challenges are forcing us to be more innovative in using scare natural and non-renewable resources much more efficiently and fairly, in order to achieve food and nutrition securities. Our greatest challenge may be to adopt more of the demand side management measures such as shifting diets and reducing food waste. Finally, cases on collaboration between the North and the South on food and nutrition security issues will be presented: (1) horticulture innovation lab and (2) dual/joint master degree in food security and climate change.

Contact Address: Poonpipope Kasemsap, Kasetsart University, Bangkok, Thailand, e-mail: agrppk@ku.ac.th

Sharing Benefits of Hindu Kush Himalayan Waters

DAVID MOLDEN

International Centre for Integrated Mountain Development (ICIMOD), Nepal

The Hindu-Kush Himalayas (HKH), the water tower of Asia, serve directly and indirectly 1.5 people through 10 major river basins. However, mountains and their resources are under pressure from climate change and various other socio-ecological transformations rapidly taking place such as outmigration and increasing energy and food demands. For sustainable mountain development, a key question is how to obtain and share benefits from critical resources like water. For HKH waters this benefit sharing must take place at different scales, from community to the entire region. Six of the 10 great rivers of the HKH are transboundary in nature, and there is growing demand for the water for food and energy across countries, yet great uncertainty about future flows. Collaboration and knowledge sharing will help countries to share benefits. In addition, countries can also learn a lot from how communities manage to share water and its benefits, and how they derive local solutions. The paper will provide two cases, one of benefit sharing from local hydropower development, and a second case on how communities manage to maintain and share water from traditional water supplies in the Kathmandu valley. In doing so, this presentation will touch upon issues of equitable distribution of benefits and conflicts that emerge when these benefits are not fairly distributed among affected people. It will also discuss various mechanisms through which individuals and communities enter into negotiation with the state and private actors for a fair and equitable share of local water resources.

Contact Address: David Molden, International Centre for Integrated Mountain Development (ICI-MOD), Kathmandu, Nepal, e-mail: David.Molden@icimod.org

Resource Competition, Degradation and Recovery in Urbanizing Landscapes

JOSIANE NIKIEMA

International Water Management Institute (IWMI), Ghana

Urbanisation is the pre-eminent global phenomenon of our time. Already today, urban areas account for 75 % of the world's natural resource consumption, while producing over 50 % of the globe's waste on just 2—3 % of the earth's land surface. There is a growing international focus on fair resource allocation and governance between sectors. With resource flows being more and more determined by urban demands, peri-urban areas are becoming hot spots for farming system intensification in view of urban demands but also resource degradation, competition and depletion. The SDGs support rural-urban linkages and closed loop processes to address these challenges.

Contact Address: Josiane Nikiema, International Water Management Institute (IWMI), Accra, Ghana, e-mail: J.Nikiema@cgiar.org

Sustainable Management of Natural Resources as Key to Rural Livelihoods: Challenges and Opportunities Within a Context of Climate Change

EDITH FERNANDEZ-BACA

National Agrarian University - La Molina, Peru

Natural resources have always been closely linked to human development. Both urban and rural livelihoods depend on the provision of ecosystem services. In Latin America, a resource-rich region, the relationship between nature and society provide opportunities and challenges for the achievement of more fair, equitable and sustainable development especially within a context of climate change. This is evident in the Andes sub-region, considered as highly vulnerable to the adverse effects of climate change due to the fragility of ecosystems and the population. In Peru, the social and demographic characteristics found in the Andes, including persisting inequalities faced by communities largely disconnected from Peru's recent economic growth, as well as unsustainable land use practices and resource degradation, limit their capacities to manage the natural environment and the services it provides. Nevertheless, there are opportunities to better manage existing resources and help improve the provision of needed services to adapt, diversify and sustain rural livelihoods within a context of climate change. This presentation looks at an example of how this is being done in Peru through the use of an ecosystem based-adaptation approach.

Contact Address: Edith Fernandez-Baca, National Agrarian University - La Molina, Lima, Peru,
e-mail:

Regenerative Organic Agriculture Can Increase Yields with Renewable Resources

ANDRE LEU

IFOAM - Organics International, Australia

Most farming systems use non-renewable resources such as synthetic fertlizers and pesticides. Regenerative organic farming systems prioritise the recycling of organic matter to build soil health and fertility. Eco-functional Intensification, using functional biodiversity and agroecological methods can ensure that the inputs for soil nutrition and pest, disease and weed control can be generated on farm or sourced locally. Most of these regenerative systems are renewable and solar powered through the efficient use of photosynthesis. Published scientific studies show that organic systems can have higher yields under conditions of climate extremes such as drought and heavy rain events. Organic practices based on ecological science have been shown to increase yields in traditional farming systems. A report by the United National Conference on Trade and Development and the United Nations Environment Programme that reviewed 114 projects in 24 sub-Saharan African countries, covering 2 million hectares and 1.9 million farmers, found that organic practices increase yields on average by 116 per cent (range: +54 % to +176 %). The combination of higher yields, resilient biodiverse production systems and lower production costs can achieve both food and income security for farmers as well as good environment outcomes.

Contact Address: Andre Leu, IFOAM - Organics International, Daintree, Australia, e-mail: andreleu.al@gmail.com

Plants

Cropping systems

Improvement of Agronomic Practices in Sugarcane Production by Designing Homogeneous Management Zones

MARCOS ALBERTO LANA, ANGELIKA WURBS, DENNIS MELZER, CLAAS NENDEL

Leibniz Centre for Agricultural Landscape Research (ZALF), Germany

Site specific management has the potential to change the way fields are currently managed. The advent of the popularisation of global positioning systems (GPS), together with a range of different on-board sensors (harvest sensors, soil conductivity, reflectance, etc.) allows for continuous increase of data availability. Among the different concepts of precision farming application is the use of spatially similar field sub-units that require the same management, designated homogeneous management zones (HMZ). A HMZ is a sub-region of a field that expresses a relatively homogeneous combination of yield-limiting factors, in any scale. Many techniques are already available for annual crops, and they can basically be divided in terms of output data: a) factors that can influence yield, like variability of soil parameters or topographic properties and b) variability of the yield, assuming that yield is a product of different sites properties. The objective of this work is to test different HMZ delineation procedures for sugarcane, a semi-perennial crop playing a major role in sugar and bioethanol production, which only recently is being effectively included in precision farming systems. Field data from four crop seasons (2011–2014) included soil chemical and physical parameters collected from 122 sampling points, so as yield maps from a 50 ha experiment in the Campinas region, Brazil. Yield maps were linearized and filtered to remove sensor failures and discrepant values. Fuzzy clustering (c-means) and multivariate regressions were applied to different parameters in order to identify which are the factors that are more spatially correlated with sugarcane yield. The majority of the parameters presented low correlation with yield. The parameter with higher yield correlation was soil pH (0.31), which could then be correlated with other parameters such as extractable Aluminum and soil organic matter content. The investigation is still being conducted in order to identify i) which parameters effectively influence the yield of sugar cane and ii) which procedure is more adequate for sugarcane homogeneous management zones delineation, as the actually available methods are designed for annual crops and therefore not adequate for semi-perennial species. Finally, a method for HMZ delineation for sugarcane fields will be presented.

Keywords: Management efficiency, precision farming, sugarcane, zoning

Contact Address: Marcos Alberto Lana, Leibniz Centre for Agricultural Landscape Research (ZALF), Land Use Systems, Eberswalder Str. 84, 15374 Müncheberg, Germany, e-mail: lana@zalf.de

ID 950

Conservation Agriculture in the Mt Elgon Highlands of Kenya and Uganda: Successes and Limitations

JAY NORTON, URSZULA NORTON, DENNIS ASHILENJE

University of Wyoming, Dept. of Ecosystem Science and Management, United States of America

Degradation of soil resources underlies yield gaps and nutritional deficiencies in sub Saharan Africa (SSA) and is a principle barrier to sustainable intensification (SI) of agricultural production. Proper management of soil resources is key to SI, increasing options for diverse crop-livestock systems, but there are many persistent barriers to adoption of soil-building farming practices. Results of a five-year study that utilised co-design and co-innovation frameworks toward participatory research indicate that conservation agriculture systems (which utilise reduced disturbance, soil cover, and crop rotation) can effectively improve yields and soil quality in the densely populated Mt. Elgon border region of Kenya and Uganda. Systems evaluated included maize-bean intercropping with a cover crop relay in maize inter rows following bean harvest and a strip-intercrop system in which maize, beans, and a cover crop are grown in monocultural strips narrow enough for advantageous interactions such as light interception and complementary root growth. Each system was planted using three tillage approaches: conventional moldboard plow, minimum tillage, and no tillage. Using *Mucuna* as the cover crop, both systems performed well agronomically under all tillage approaches, with similar or greater grain yields than conventional maize-bean intercropping. Structured focus group discussions with participating farmers, their neighbours, ag technicians, and others familiar with the project revealed a preference for the strip-intercrop system combined with minimum tillage. Reasons for preferring minimum tillage over no till included more options for weed control than herbicides alone and decreased labor/traction needs compared to conventional tillage. Reasons for preferring the strip intercrop system included higher yields in the monocrop rotations, particularly for maize following *mucuna*, easier management of single-crop strips with cultivation or herbicides, and the observation that cash and labour outlays for maize could be concentrated on one-third of the area, increasing yields and reducing labour. The discussions made it clear that knowledge of fundamental crop and soil fertility management concepts is a primary need. Proper fertilisation of smaller plots could maintain overall maize yields while reducing labour and creating space for soil building cover or forage crops.

Keywords: Conservation agriculture, fertiliser management, soil organic matter

---

Contact Address: Jay Norton, University of Wyoming, Dept. of Ecosystem Science and Management, 1000 E. University Avenue, 82071 Laramie, United States of America, e-mail: jnorton4@uwyo.edu

Climate-Smart Manure Management Practices in Smallholders Crop-Livestock Systems

Daniel Ortiz Gonzalo[1], Victor Suarez Villanueva[1], Todd Rosenstock[2], Myles Oelofse[1], Andreas de Neergaard[1], Philippe Vaast[3]

[1] University of Copenhagen, Dept. of Plant and Environmental Sciences, Denmark
[2] World Agroforestry Centre (ICRAF), Kenya
[3] CIRAD Montpellier, France & ICRAF Nairobi, Kenya

Among endogenous resources in smallholder farming systems, animal manure has a remarkable potential to improve farm nutrient cycling efficiencies (NCE) and soil fertility. However, major challenges are encountered to reduce nitrogen losses through direct and indirect greenhouse gas emissions (GHG) during manure handling processes. The objective of our study is to identify those affordable manure management practices which improve manure quality while reducing GHG emissions in the Central Highlands of Kenya. We combined social and natural science methods in order to: 1) Characterize manure management systems in the Central highlands of Kenya; 2) Quantify NCE and GHG emissions through a field experiment mimicking the systems of the area; 3) Identify and discuss the main barriers for climate-smart practices adoption. Four manure management systems (MMS) were identified among 107 farms in Murang'a County: Unmanaged systems (UNM), heaps (HEAP), pits (PIT) and biodigestors (BIO). The collection phase, or manure retention time in the cowshed, ranged from 1 ± 0.5 days in BIO to 59 ± 36 days in UNM. The storage phase or heaping process ranged from 36 ± 30 days in BIO to 80 ± 50 days in HEAP. The use of concrete as an improved cowshed floor increased from UNM (0 %) to BIO (100 %). On the other hand the use of bedding followed an opposite trend with a higher number of farmers performing this practice in UNM than in PIT, HEAP or BG systems. The field experiment showed a higher dry matter loss in the solid storage forms (UNM and HEAP) than in the liquid forms (PIT and BIO). Affordable treatments such as covering the manure with banana leaves reduced these losses significantly. However, manure storage time was the only variable affecting both N conservation and GHG emissions in the form of nitrous oxide (N_2O). Lastly, high costs of sophisticated technologies such as biodigestors, knowledge gaps on manure handling and labour demand are identified as main barriers for adoption of climate-smart practices. The emergence of low-cost affordable options and improved extension mechanisms may bring a shift to the accessibility and embracement of best manure management practices.

Keywords: Affordable options, climate-smart agriculture, greenhouse gas, Kenya, manure management systems, smallholder farming systems

Contact Address: Daniel Ortiz Gonzalo, University of Copenhagen, Dept. of Plant and Environmental Sciences, Thorvaldsensvej 40, 1871 Frederiksberg C, 1871 Copenhagen, Denmark, e-mail: gonzalo@plen.ku.dk

ID 1083

Understanding Yield Constraints to Guide Climate Change Adaptation for Arabica Coffee on Mt. Elgon, Uganda

ALEJANDRA SARMIENTO[1], ERIC RAHN[2], DAVID MUKASA[3], SOPHIE GRAEFE[4], LAURENCE JASSOGNE[3], PIET VAN ASTEN[3], PHILIPPE VAAST[5]

[1] *Georg-August-Universität Göttingen, Crop Production Systems in the Tropics, Germany*
[2] *ETH Zurich, Institute of Terrestrial Ecosystems, Switzerland*
[3] *International Institute of Tropical Agriculture (IITA), Uganda,*
[4] *Georg-August-Universität Göttingen, Tropical Silviculture and Forest Ecology, Germany*
[5] *CIRAD Montpellier, France & ICRAF Nairobi, Kenya*

Coffee (*Coffea arabica*) is the most important exported crop in Uganda. Almost 90 % of coffee production originates from small farms (< 1 ha), and the livelihoods of approximately one million smallholders depend on this activity. Average coffee yields in Uganda are low (<700 kg ha^{-1} year^{-1}), reaching only 20 - 30 % of those obtained in high-yielding regions, such as Latin American and Vietnam. On top of low productivity, the scarcity of land due to population growth and the impacts of climate change (i.e. rising temperature and changing rainfall patterns), increase the vulnerability of farmers' households and threaten the long-term sustainability of the coffee sector. Therefore, increasing resilience to climate change while improving coffee yield is one of the top priorities over the coming years. To achieve this, it is necessary to identify major production constrains and their effects on yield gaps. This study aims to investigate Arabica yield gaps and identify limiting production factors in three altitude ranges on the slopes of Mount Elgon, eastern Uganda. A total of 173 farmers distributed homogenously in each altitude class were interviewed about their management practices and presence of pests and diseases, and asked to recall yields of three consecutive years (2013, 2014 and 2015). Moreover, their farms were inventoried to determine the vegetative structure (coffee and shade tree density, shade tree species and canopy coverage), soil and foliar nutrients. Furthermore, coffee yields were estimated in the field, and environmental parameters (i.e. rainfall, soil moisture, temperature, relative humidity) were monitored during two years (2014 and 2015) in a subsample of 27 farms. Coffee yield gaps were investigated using boundary functions for each production factor per altitude class. We found that production constrains vary along the altitudinal gradient. Structural variables such as canopy closure and density of coffee trees have higher impact on yield at lower altitudes, whereas soil fertility problems (P and N deficiency) become more prominent with increasing altitude. Our results reinforce that management recommendations, which aim to increase yield and adapt to climate change need to be site-specific, adjusted to local needs and available resources, instead of being generalised for a whole region.

Keywords: Boundary functions, climate change, coffee, productivity, yield gap

Contact Address: Alejandra Sarmiento, Georg-August-Universität Göttingen, Crop Production Systems in the Tropics, Göttingen, Germany, e-mail: asarmie@gwdg.de

Liebig's Law – Increase and Stabilise Tanzanian Maize Yields by Combining Different Crop Modelling Approaches

CHRISTOPH GORNOTT, FRED HATTERMANN, FRANK WECHSUNG

Potsdam Institute for Climate Impact Research (PIK), Climate Impacts and Vulnerabilities, Germany

For Tanzania food security is an important challenge, which will increase for the next decades. In Tanzania, maize (*Zea mays* L.) is the most planted food crop. Due to limited extendable arable land, maize yields (per hectare) must increase to achieve a sufficient food production. Besides the average yield level, yield stability is also crucial for food security. Despite a low average actual maize yield of 1.3 t ha^{-1}, yield variability is relatively high (standard deviation: ±0.8 t ha^{-1}). For increasing and stabilising maize yields, crop models can contribute to optimising agronomic management practices. In our study, we analyse the yield impact of actual and optimal fertilisation and separate the weather-related yield variability for micro-insurance purposes. With the process-based model SWIM (Soil and Water Integrated Model), we compute impacts on crop yields of actual and optimal fertilisation. The statistical model IRMA (Interregional Regression Model for Agriculture) captures variability of weather, agronomic management, and socio-economic influences on farm maize yields. The model allows decomposing these effects. The use of those two crop models improves the robustness of both model outputs and enables yield assessments on different production levels. For entire Tanzania, we find a yield gap of 6.2 t ha^{-1} between actual and optimally-fertilised yields. Thus, actual yields are only 17 % of optimally-fertilised yields (7.5 t ha^{-1}). Such higher yields are more sensitive to weather impacts, because nutrient supply is no longer yield limiting (which is the major constraint of actual yields). To enhance the implementation of sufficient fertiliser supply in Tanzania, micro crop insurances can contribute indemnifying smallholder farmers for the increased yield variability. Since SWIM is only partly able to assess the inter-annual yield variability, we utilise IRMA to capture the remaining yield variability. By separating weather-related yield variability, IRMA provides insights of socio-economic impacts on maize yields. These IRMA results are directly useable to calculate micro-insurance claims, which might contribute to stabilise smallholder farmers' income.

Keywords: Food security, maize, process based and statistical crop models, risk assessment, Tanzania

---

Contact Address: Christoph Gornott, Potsdam Institute for Climate Impact Research (PIK), Climate Impacts and Vulnerabilities, Telegraphenberg A 62, 14412 Potsdam, Germany, e-mail: gornott@pik-potsdam.de

ID 887

How Reliable Are Microbial Inoculants in Agriculture for Improving Nutrient Use Efficiency and Growth Promotion? A Meta-Analysis of Field Studies from 1981 to 2015

LUKAS SCHÜTZ[1], ANDREAS GATTINGER[2], MATTHIAS MEIER[2], ADRIAN MÜLLER[2], MATHIMARAN NATARAJAN[1], PAUL MAEDER[2], THOMAS BOLLER[1]

[1]*University of Basel, Environmental Sciences, Switzerland*

[2]*Research Institute for Organic Agriculture (FiBL), Dept. of Soil Sciences, Switzerland*

Application of microbial inoculants, so-called "biofertilisers", is a promising technology for sustainable agriculture. Rhizosphere microorganisms have evolved together with the plants and represent a valuable resource for improving plant growth and health. Many of them can be utilised to take advantage of their beneficial effects, as they are able to fix nitrogen, help to mobilise soil nutrients, increase water availability or improve plant health. Poor soils are most promising for an application of biofertilisers, and most studies in this area come from tropical and subtropical countries. Centers of research are in India, Iran, Egypt and Argentina. However, soils are highly variable in their composition and soil biota, and the success of inoculation is difficult to predict. We have conducted a meta-analysis to quantify benefits in terms of yield increase, as well as nitrogen and phosphorus use efficiency. Peer-reviewed articles and cross-references published between May 2015 and February 2016 in Web of Science by Thomson Reuter, Scopus by Elsevier and Google scholar were searched with the following keywords: "biofertiliser", "biofertiliser" and "microbial inoculants". A total of 544 studies were identified, and 174 studies proved to be eligible for meta-analysis. All data was extracted and integrated into the data matrix. For gap filling of mineral N mineralisation from soil, we employed the nitrogen flux model. These calculations enabled a comprehensive analysis of the influence of biofertiliser technology on nitrogen balance. We found biofertiliser application to be a viable technology to be applied in tropical and subtropical soils. Newly available tools for the analysis of microbial communities will further optimise this technology.

Keywords: Biofertiliser, microbial inoculants, nutrient use efficiency

Contact Address: Lukas Schütz, University of Basel, Environmental Sciences, Hebelstr. 1, 4056 Basel, Switzerland, e-mail: lukas.schuetz@gmx.de

How Does Grazing Work in Semiarid Savannahs? – Responses of Desirable Perennial Grasses to Clipping and Water

KATJA GEISSLER, LISA SCHRADE, EVA OSTERTAG, NIELS BLAUM

University of Potsdam, Plant Ecology and Nature Conservation, Germany

Semi-arid savannahs of southern Africa have been used for cattle grazing for decades. In many areas, unsustainable high stocking rates have led to severe shrub encroachment. The increase of woody shrubs at the cost of palatable plant species causes a significant reduction in economic value and can be considered a threat to livelihoods. It also leads to habitat loss for many species and fragmentation with major implications for biodiversity dynamics and functions. Therefore, alternative sustainable grazing regimes must be developed together with an understanding of how desired perennial grasses respond to different patterns of grazing and drought.

At a commercial cattle farm in the southern Kalahari we designed a 20 times replicated clipping-experiment using *Stipagrostis uniplumis* and *Aristida stipitata* which are two of the main palatable perennial grass species in the area. Grass tussocks were clipped at four different heights in combination with watering. Re-growth was determined after 6 weeks. In particular, we analysed accumulated green biomass and number of tillers. Independent of species, at low clipping height the simulated grazing resulted in up to 95 % reduced aboveground biomass compared to a non-clipped control. The grass individuals were not able to reach the initial average weight during the 6 weeks period. Only the growth rate significantly increased. In contrast, at moderate clipping heights the simulated grazing resulted in an obvious compensation or even overcompensation of aboveground biomass. Additional water had no stimulating effect. We conclude that the recovery of palatable grasses is possible in a short period of 6 weeks even under drought conditions, but strongly depends on grazing height.

Keywords: Aboveground biomass, compensational growth, grazing, perennial grasses, rangelands, savannah

Contact Address: Katja Geissler, University of Potsdam, Plant Ecology and Nature Conservation, Am Mühlenberg 3, 14476 Potsdam, Germany, e-mail: kgeissle@uni-potsdam.de

    ID 1068

Bee Pollination Increases Yield and Quality of Cash Crops in Burkina Faso, West Africa

KATHARINA STEIN[1], DRISSA COULIBALY[2], SOULEYMANE KONATÉ[2],
DETHARDT GOETZE[3], STEFAN POREMBSKI[3], KARL-EDUARD LINSENMAIR[1]

[1] *University of Wuerzburg, Theodor-Boveri-Institute of Bioscience, Dept. of Animal Ecology and Tropical Biology, Germany*

[2] *University Nangui Abrogoua, Dept. of Research in Ecology and Biodiversity, Ivory Coast*

[3] *University of Rostock, Inst. of Biological Sciences, Dept. of Botany and Botanical Garden, Germany*

Insect pollination constitutes an ecosystem service of global importance, providing significant economic benefits to human society alongside vital ecological processes in terrestrial ecosystems. A growing human population especially in developing countries induce a rising demand for food and income security under rapidly changing environments. Seventy-five per cent of all agricultural crop species rely, to some degree, on animal pollination. Bees are the most important pollinators worldwide; a complete loss of their pollination service could reduce crop yields by ca. 40 %. The study aimed to investigate the contribution of pollination by bees for yield and quality in cotton and sesame. Field research was carried out in 2015 in south-west Burkina Faso. Pollination experiments were conducted to determine the rate of self-compatibility. On 11 fields for each crop pollinator exclosure and outcrossing experiments were conducted on 50 flowers per field. Efficiency of various bee pollinator species for fruit set and quality was investigated. Germination experiments with seeds resulting from self or outcross pollination were conducted to test for seed quality in terms of inbreeding depression. Honey bees and one wild bee species were the most effective pollinators. The exclusion of bees led to a reduction in fruit set of ca. 11 % in cotton and ca. 26 % in sesame. Pollinators significantly increased the number of intact seeds and seed mass in both species. Bees increased the economically most important fibre mass of cotton by ca.62 % in comparison to flowers where pollinators were excluded. In sesame fruit weight was enhanced by ca. 63 % when pollinated by bees. The germination rate of seeds resulting from self-pollination decreased significantly in both species, which is a clear sign of inbreeding depression and economical important, since the seeds are used for the next sowing season. The gratis pollination service by bees was thus beneficial, contributing to cotton and sesame production by enhancing the quantity and quality of these major cash crops in Burkina Faso.

Keywords: Bees, Burkina Faso, cotton, pollination, quality, sesame

Contact Address: Katharina Stein, University of Wuerzburg, Theodor-Boveri-Institute of Bioscience, Dept. of Animal Ecology and Tropical Biology, Josef-Martin-Weg 52, 97074 Wuerzburg, Germany, e-mail: katharina.stein@uni-wuerzburg.de

Effects of Wildlife Crop Raiding on Livelihoods of Khumaga, Boteti-Sub District, Botswana

KENALEKGOSI GONTSE, JOSEPH E MBAIWA, OLEKAET THAKADU

University of Botswana, Okavango Research Institute, Botswana

Human wildlife interaction in Boteti District, Botswana is critical. Wild animals destroy agricultural products and threaten human lives. This paper, therefore, assessed the effects of wildlife crop raiding on livelihoods of Khumaga, Boteti-Sub District, Botswana. A total of 119 arable farmers were interviewed using open and close-ended structured questionnaires. Key informant interviews were also conducted with purposively selected officials at the Department of Wildlife and National Park, the Department of Crop Production and with village leaders. Findings indicate that arable farmers at Khumaga face challenges of crop depredation by wildlife. Elephant (*Loxodonta africana*), hippo (*Hippopotamus amphibious*), porcupine (*Hystrix africaeaustralis*), monkey (*Cercopithecus aethiops*), duiker (*Sylvicapra grimmia*), jackal (*Canus mesomelas*), and kudu (*Tragelaphus strepsiceros*) were all considered by respondents to be problem wildlife. Wild animals destroy agricultural production at Khumaga leading to food insecurity; sometimes farmers can lose the entire field as in elephant crop raiding. In relation to crop production and loss due to wildlife crop raiding, costs incurred by arable farmers at Khumaga were also assessed. Findings indicated that crop raiding has resulted in some of the arable farmers abandoning crop farming at Khumaga village. In conclusion, decision-makers should ensure that farmers at Khumaga are protected against wildlife to improve arable farmer's livelihoods and conservation efforts at Khumaga village in Botswana.

Keywords: Conservation, crop raiding, human wildlife interaction, livelihoods, wildlife

Contact Address: Kenalekgosi Gontse, University of Botswana, Okavango Research Institute, Sexaxa, 00000 Maun, Botswana, e-mail: kgontse@ori.ub.bw

Growth and Resource Use of Young Rubber (*Hevea brasiliensis*) on Hillsides in Northern Thailand

NUTTAPON KHONGDEE[1], WANWISA PANSAK[1], THOMAS HILGER[2]

[1]*Naresuan University, Dept. of Agricultural Science, Thailand*

[2]*University of Hohenheim, Inst. of Agricultural Sciences in the Tropics (Hans-Ruthenberg-Institute), Germany*

In the past decade, rubber production largely expanded into the uplands of northern Thailand, substituting primary forests. Without proper soil conservation, monocropping of rubber generates soil loss in the magnitude of 14 Mg ha^{-1} in upland areas. Growing rubber together with either annual crops and/or cover crops is a way to decrease such environmental impacts. The objective of this study was to evaluate rubber growth, soil and leaf nutrient content of two soil and water conservation systems. The study was conducted during 2013 and 2015 on a rubber plantation established in 2011 at Wang Thong District, Phitsanulok province, Thailand (16° 55'N, 100° 32'E), using clone RRIM 600. The slope gradient ranged from 12 to 30 %. The experiment was set up as a randomized complete block design with three replications. The treatments were: (i) rubber sole cropping, (ii) rubber plus maize, and (iii) rubber plus maize and legume. Results show that the girth expansion used as proxy for growth performance was highest in rubber intercropped with maize. Across all treatments, C, N, C/N ratio, P, K, Ca, Mg, K/Mg, K/Ca, and Mg/Ca ratios of soil were 1.18-1.26 %, 0.13-0.14 %, 8.89-9.17, 2.74-3.16 mg kg^{-1}, 387-466 mg kg^{-1}, 76-93 mg kg^{-1}, 203-245 mg kg^{-1}, 1.67-2.22, 4.47-5.26, 2.44-2.72, respectively. Soil organic carbon and exchangeable potassium concentrations under sole rubber and intercrop treatments were higher than the optimum ranges for premature rubber trees. Leaf C, N, C/N ratio, P, K, Ca, Mg K/Mg, K/Ca, and Mg/Ca ratio of all treatments were in the ranges of 47.7-48.2 %, 2.87-3.11 %, 15.6-16.9, 0.17-0.24 %, 0.21-0.24 %, 0.09 %, 0.35-0.45 %, 0.48-0.87, 2.72-3.65, and 4.95-5.75, respectively. Leaf Mg concentration showed an optimum level as recommended by standard values for rubber, while leaf C, N, C/N ratio, K, Ca, and K/Mg, ratio values represented low levels of rubber requirements. The soil conservation systems tested indicate a fair resource use, improve farmers' economy during juvenile growth of rubber where tapping is not possible, and avoid negative environmental impacts. Rubber intercropping with annual crops is, hence, a viable alternative cropping option for the target region.

Keywords: Growth performance, *Hevea brasiliensis*, premature rubber, soil and leaf nutrients, soil conservation

---

Contact Address: Wanwisa Pansak, Naresuan University, Dept. of Agricultural Science, 65000 Phitsanulok, Thailand, e-mail: wanwisapa@nu.ac.th

Effect of Soil Surface Roughness and Crop Cover on Runoff and Soil Loss under Potato Cropping Systems, Kenya

SHADRACK NYAWADE[1], CHARLES GACHENE[1], NANCY KARANJA[2], ELMAR SCHULTE-GELDERMANN[2]

[1]*University of Nairobi, Dept. of Land Resource Management and Agricultural Technology (LARMAT), Kenya*

[2]*International Potato Center - sub Saharan Africa (CIP-SSA), Integrated Crop Management, Kenya*

Potato production is majorly carried out in sole stands in East African Highlands. This is despite the fact that the production of this crop entails a lot of soil disturbance associated with hilling which changes the soil surface roughness thereby concentrating surface runoff flow which induces soil erosion. A field study was carried out using runoff plots during the short (October to February) and long (March to September) rainy seasons of 2014/15 respectively at the University of Nairobi Upper Kabete Farm, Kenya. The objective was to assess the effect of soil surface roughness and crop cover on soil loss and runoff under sole and mixed potato cropping systems. The treatments comprised of Bare Soil (T1); Potato + Garden Pea (*Pisum sativa*) (T2); Potato + Climbing Bean (*Phaseolus vulgaris*) (T3); Potato + Dolichos (*Lablab purpureus*) (T4) and Sole Potato (*Solanum tuberosum*) (T5). Soil surface roughness and crop cover were monitored at a two weeks interval throughout the growing seasons. The amount of soil loss and runoff recorded in each event differed significantly between treatments ($p < 0.05$) and were consistently highest in T1 and lowest in T4. Mean cumulative soil loss reduced by 6.4, 13.3 and 24.4 t ha^{-1} from T2, T3 and T4 respectively compared to sole potato plots (T5), while mean cumulative runoff reduced by 8.5, 17.1 and 28.3 mm from T2, T3 and T4 respectively when compared with the sole potato plots (T5) indicating that T4 plots provided the most effective cover in reducing soil loss and runoff. Both runoff and soil loss related significantly with soil surface roughness and percent cover (R^2=0.83 and 0.73 respectively, $p < 0.05$). Statistically significant linear dependence of runoff and soil loss on surface roughness and crop cover was found in T4 ($p < 0.05$) indicating that this system was highly effective in minimizing soil loss and runoff. This study shows the need to incorporate indeterminate legume cover crops such as Dolichos lablab into potato cropping systems. These crops provide sufficient protective cover which can interact with soil surface roughness to minimize soil loss and runoff.

Keywords: Crop cover, cropping systems, runoff, soil erosion, soil loss, soil surface roughness

Contact Address: Shadrack Nyawade, University of Nairobi, Dept. of Land Resource Management and Agricultural Technology (LARMAT), P.O. Box 29053, 00625 Nairobi, Kenya, e-mail: shadnyawade@gmail.com

ID 688

Economic Analysis of Tropical Forages in Livestock Systems in the Eastern Plains of Colombia

KAREN ENCISO, STEFAN BURKART, JHON FREDDY GUTIERREZ SOLIS, MICHAEL PETERS

International Center for Tropical Agriculture (CIAT), Colombia

70 % of the Colombian livestock production are characterised by extensive production systems, which usually show low productivity levels, low land use efficiency and often lack environmental sustainability. This is related to native grasses and degraded pastures that generate limited forage supply, both in volume and quality, especially in the dry season. The International Center for Tropical Agriculture (CIAT) is working on the development of improved forages able to adapt to various adverse soil and climatic conditions of the lower tropics, while increasing productivity levels and reducing the environmental impact of livestock production. However, the establishment of these new forage technologies implies higher investment and management costs for the producer, which limits in many cases their adoption.

This paper evaluates the financial viability of the implementation of new forage technologies, in this case of improved pastures and scattered trees in livestock systems, and compares them to the traditional production system with native pastures. The developed model is based on a cash flow analysis and a Monte Carlo simulation, and includes uncertainty factors in the variables identified as critical (e.g., meat price, productivity). Research took place in 2015 in the Casanare Department in the Eastern Plains of Colombia.

The results indicate that investment in improved pastures is profitable with an incremental net present value (NPV) of US$ 45 and an internal rate of return of 18%. The system in association with scattered trees was not profitable due to the high initial investment costs and time expectations for achieving improvements in production parameters. Both evaluated alternatives were only evaluated for livestock income, not taking into account additional income that might arise from the trees (e.g., fruits, wood). The feasibility of investment is highly sensitive to changes in the selling prices of the meat and expected returns. The technologies evaluated in this study showed to be an alternative to improve production efficiency and profitability of livestock farms. However, strategies and / or incentives need to be developed that aim at reducing the high initial costs of systems in association with scattered trees.

Keywords: Improved forages, Monte Carlo simulation, profitability analysis, risk analysis, silvo-pastoral systems

Contact Address: Stefan Burkart, International Center for Tropical Agriculture (CIAT), Tropical Forages Program, Km 17 Recta Cali-Palmira, Cali, Colombia, e-mail: s.burkart@cgiar.org

Irrigated Crop Production in a Floodplain River Oasis of the Mongolian Altay Mountains

GRETA JORDAN, BAIGAL ULZIISUREN, SVEN GOENSTER-JORDAN,
ANDREAS BUERKERT

University of Kassel, Organic Plant Production and Agroecosystems Research in the Tropics and Subtropics, Germany

In the Mongolian Altay Mountains, the transformation of traditional transhumance systems to sedentary ones was driven by the promise of job opportunities and benefits of social services. During this process, new cropping opportunities played a subordinated role. However in recent years, numerous efforts to reduce the dependence of Mongolia on vegetable imports from China and as part of herders' risk minimisation strategy, irrigated crop and hay production is gaining importance, notwithstanding the limited water availability. This study aimed to quantify water use for irrigated crop and hay production in the river oasis of Bulgan sum center in Western Mongolia.

In the framework of the IFAD-funded project WATERCOPE (grant I-R-1284), a total of 98 semi-structured questionnaires were used to assess water management and discharge, remote sensing was applied to determine the extent of agriculturally used areas and, a participatory rural appraisal, facilitated the estimation of irrigation water use across the river oasis.

During the 4-months growing season, on a total irrigated agricultural area of 7.69 km^2, hay was grown on 71 % of the area and potatoes as a staple food on 3 %. Miscellaneous fruit trees (15 %), sea buckthorn (6 %), vegetables (2 %), melons (2 %), and cereals (1 %) played a minor, but economically important role in these systems. Average plot sizes were 3.3 ha for hay and 0.27 ha for crops. With only 23 % of the harvest being sold, all cropping systems were subsistence-oriented. On average, all fields were flood irrigated 13 times per growing season and the irrigation water used per unit land ranged from 292 (hay) to 2763 (vegetable) m3 ha^{-1} year^{-1}, leading to water consumption between 1.64 (cereals) to 0.18 (melons) m^3 kg^{-1} fresh matter.

The low water use efficiency and the increasing competition for limited water resources calls for crop- and season-specific irrigation management strategies.

Keywords: Central Asia, flood irrigation, land use map, PRA, water use efficiency

Contact Address: Andreas Buerkert, University of Kassel, Organic Plant Production and Agroecosystems Research in the Tropics and Subtropics, Steinstraße 19, 37213 Witzenhausen, Germany, e-mail: buerkert@uni-kassel.de

ID 791

Challenges and Prospects for Transitions to Conservation Agriculture in Iran

SOMAYE LATIFI[1], HOSSEIN RAHELI[1], MICHAEL HAUSER[2]

[1]*University of Tabriz, Dept. of Extension and Rural Development, Iran*
[2]*University of Natural Resources and Life Sciences (BOKU), Centre for Development Research (CDR), Austria*

In Iran, conservation agriculture (CA) has become a national strategy for the agricultural sector to decrease soil erosion, combat the emerging water crisis, and to reduce the high cost associated with conventional agricultural production. CA involves minimum soil disturbance, permanent soil cover through crop residues or cover crops, and crop rotations. It has emerged as a management practice with the potential of increasing the sustainability of soil and water, reducing the cost of production and improving efficient use of resources. Despite its promotion for nearly one decade, CA is not widely adopted by farmers throughout Iran. Only an estimated 1.5 million ha of land is managed through CA. In this paper we present the status of CA in Iran, and the barriers farmers face during the transition from conventional agriculture to CA. We used qualitative social science methods for establishing the status of CA in Iran. Based on 32 expert exploratory interviews carried out in 9 provinces, we have prioritised the most important factors impeding and supporting the transition from conventional agriculture to CA. Our findings show that the dissemination of CA technology is slow. Moreover, farmers abandoned CA due to lack of or insufficient access to machinery and equipment for CA; limited access to credits to purchase CA machines and inputs; poor economic benefits during early phases of CA practices; lack of knowledge and experience of residue supply and management; and management and control of weed, pest and diseases. At policy level, the lack of knowledge about CA among key decision makers hinders its promotion; but also a weak set of special formal organisational structures, rules and informal norms (institutional framework); lack of strategic long-term plans and low investments in agricultural credit, infrastructure, and markets for its development are the main reasons for CA not spreading faster in Iran. Therefore, an enabling government policy and institutional environment are needed for the development of CA.

Keywords: Conservation agriculture, Iran, technology, transitions

Contact Address: Somaye Latifi, University of Tabriz, Dept. of Extension and Rural Development, No 7, Tohid Alley, Qiam Alley, Shahid Zamani Blv , 6517779369 Hamedan, Iran, e-mail: somaye.latifi84@gmail.com

Evaluation of the Effect of Planting Date and Density on Germination and Vigor of Soybean Seed

HOSSEIN SADEGHI, SHEIDAEI SAMAN

Seed and Plant Certification and Registration Research Institute, Iran

Environmental conditions such as high temperature during seed set and seed filling stage can reduce yield and seed quality. It is supposed that different planting dates have different influence on soybean seed quality and yield. In order to evaluate the effect of different planting dates and densities on soybean seed quality, an experiment was conducted as a split factorial based on completely randomised block design in three replications at two locations including: the seed and plant certification and registration institute of Karaj and the agricultural and natural resources center of Moghan, in 2013. The evaluated factors were planting date (5th of May, 5th of June and 5th of July), plant density (300, 400 and 500 thousand plants per ha) and soybean varieties (Williams and L17). The results of standard germination test showed that, the highest normal seedling percentage (92.1 %) in Moghan area was obtained on fifth of June and in Karaj area it (96.2 %) was gained on fifth of July. In addition, it was observed that cv. L17 in Moghan and cv. Williams in Karaj had the highest normal seedlings percentage. The results of accelerated aging test indicated that the normal seedlings percentage in Karaj was more than in the Moghan area and it showed that the seed quality of produced seeds in Karaj was better than produced seeds in Moghan. There was no significant difference between areas in 300 and 400 thousand plants per ha, but a significant difference was observed in normal seedlings percentage after accelerated aging test between Karaj (77.6 %) and Moghan (58 %) in density of 500 thousand plants per ha. The highest seedling vigor index (11.75) was obtained at 400 thousand plants per ha sown on fifth of July in Karaj area and the lowest rate of (5.41) was observed using 300 thousand plants per ha sown on fifth of June in Karaj area.

Keywords: Rainfall, reproductive growth, seed filling, seed quality, temperature

Contact Address: Hossein Sadeghi, Seed and Plant Certification and Registration Research Institute, Sohrevardi corner, Nabovat BLV., Karaj, Iran, e-mail: sadeghi_spcri@yahoo.com

ID 974

Optimising Growth and Yield of Maize and Pigeon Pea in Kongwa and Kiteto Districts, Tanzania

ELVIS JONAS[1], ANTHONY KIMARO[2], MARTHA SWAMILA[2], EZEKIEL MWAKALUKWA[1], L.L. LULANDALA[1], PATRICK OKORI[3]

[1] Sokoine University of Agriculture, Forest Biology, Tanzania

[2] World Agroforestry Centre (ICRAF), Tanzania Country Programme, Tanzania

[3] International Crops Research Institute for the Semi-Arid Tropics (ICRISAT), Malawi

Low crop yields and limited supply of high-quality livestock feeds are among the main development challenges facing farmers in semi-arid Tanzania. To address these problems, farmers under the Africa RISING project in Kongwa and Kiteto Districts are integrating maize, pigeon pea and *Gliricidia sepium*. Pigeon pea is a fairly new legume crop in these Districts, requiring both adaptability and agronomic studies to guide farmers on the best technology options, which can optimise farm productivity. We employed the participatory variety selection approach to identify adaptable pigeon pea varieties. These were then tested on farms under various intercropping arrangements with maize (Pure stands, 1:1, 1:2 and 2:1) and/or *G. sepium* (Pure stands, Maize+Pigeon pea, Maize+Pigeon pea+*Gliricidia*) to assess options for optimising growth and yields of crops and fodder supply. Two pigeon pea varieties (ICEAP 0057 and ICEAP 0054) were selected by farmers based on superior growth and grain yield. Maize grain yield ranged from 1.20–2.04 t ha^{-1} in Mlali and from 1.24–3.25 t ha^{-1} in Chitego, reflecting higher potential in the latter site. Relative to monoculture, yield of maize was reduced (28–40 % in Mlali and 2–62 % in Chitego) with the highest reduction noted for with increasing pigeon pea proportions. At 1:1 ratio, the most common ratio, reduction was modest and ranged from 30–40 % in both sites. Similar trend was noted for pigeon pea grain yield. As expected, the decline in maize and pigeon pea yields with increasing ratio of a companion crop reflects interspecific competition. However, the competition did not reduce other overall farm production because the Land Equivalent Ratio (LER) was above 1 in all cropping combinations (ratios), suggesting that intercropping was more efficient in utilising land resources for sustained productivity. The LER revealed that increasing the proportions of pigeon pea in maize based systems was more beneficial to farmers in less potential sites (LER = 1.53) than in high potential sites (1.15) at 1: 2 ratio of Maize and pigeon pea intercropping. At higher potential sites, farmers can benefit more by having larger proportion of maize than pigeon pea (1.06 versus 1.71). Thus, pigeon pea intercropping at the appropriate proportions based on local site conditions is necessary and a promising strategy to optimise yields in mixture.

Keywords: Intercropping, LER, sustainable intensification

Contact Address: Anthony Kimaro, World Agroforestry Centre (ICRAF), Tanzania Country Programme, P.O. Box 6226, Dar-es-Salaam, Tanzania, e-mail: a.kimaro@cgiar.org

Crops and Cropping Strategies to Maintain Food Security under Changing Weather Conditions in Papua New Guinea

Tai Kui[1], Dominik Ruffeis[2], Birte Nass-Komolong[1],
Willibald Loiskandl[2]

[1]*National Agricultural Research Institute (NARI), Soils and Water Management, Papua New Guinea*

[2]*University of Natural Resources and Life Sciences (BOKU), Institute of Hydraulics and Rural Water Management, Austria*

Papua New Guinea's climate varies considerably from year to year due to the effect of the El Niño-Southern Oscillation (ENSO). This cyclic variation leads to two extreme climatic conditions; the El Niño and La Niña. El Niño can lead to severe drought conditions and La Niña is associated with excessive rainfall causing flooding, water logging and erosion of food gardens. El Niño conditions occur approximately every 10 to 15 years resulting in reduction of almost 75 % of mean annual precipitation. Thus, important tuber crops such as sweet potato, yam and taro which provides almost 80 % of food energy for PNG's population, produce low yields and/or even fail to yield, leaving affected communities food insecure. Currently, there is lack of information on soil available water capacity for PNG soil types and crop water requirement (ETc) under different climatic extremes, which would form the basis for recommendations on suitable crop management practices. This study addressed the lack of availability of weather data in PNG and investigated potential impacts of ENSO events and future climate change on crop production through generation of past, current and future climatic scenarios, determination of soil moisture retention characteristic curves, and calculation of ETc for the main staple crops across different agro-ecological zones in PNG based on generated climatic scenarios. The tools and methods used for meteorological data generation and climate scenario development were evaluated for their applicability in the PNG context. The used tools for simulation of climatic and weather data clearly show that not all give accurate results. Results highly depend on the quality of downscaled climatic data based on selected emission scenarios of CSIRO-Mk3.6.0 GCM model, high topographic variations between interpolated data points and the type of tools used. Results showed that ETc for all food crops may increase in the future due to rising temperature; however this effect might be compensated through increased annual rainfall and cloud cover. Dry spells, droughts and changing weather patterns will make it necessary for farmers to adjust their cropping calendars and apply improved farming technologies to adapt to the changing conditions according to local soil water storage capacities and agro-ecological zones.

Keywords: Climate change, crop water requirement, soil water storage capacity

Contact Address: Tai Kui, National Agricultural Research Institute (NARI), Soils and Water Management, NARI-HRC Aiyura, 444 Aiyura, Papua New Guinea, e-mail: tai.kui@nari.org.pg

ID 1137

Resource Use in Abaca (*Musa textilis*): A Versatile Smallholder Fiber Crop from the Philippines

CATHERINE MEYER, THOMAS HILGER, GEORG CADISCH

University of Hohenheim, Inst. of Agricultural Sciences in the Tropics (Hans-Ruthenberg-Institute), Germany

Abaca is economically important for the Philippines. Its fibre is highly demanded by the pulp and paper industry as it is an important resource for specialty papers, e.g. tea bag papers. Currently, Catanduanes Island of the Philippines is the world's largest producer of abaca fibres, being an important smallholders' income source. Traditionally, they grow abaca as a cash crop in secondary forest areas of mountainous regions throughout humid areas of the Philippines. Farmers maintain fields over decades without application of any external inputs. Little is known on the impact of that on soil fertility and nutrient balances in abaca cropping. We hypothesized that the traditional way of harvesting leads to a concentration of nutrients close to the tuxying place within a field, whereas areas distant to it deplete in nutrients. This study aimed to (i) assess the impact of the abaca harvesting on soil nutrient availability, (ii) appraise the spatial distribution of the nutrients along the slope in abaca cropping systems, and (iii) provide understanding of the dynamics and loss of nutrients due to harvesting and handling of crop residues after fibre extraction. Therefore, we determined the aboveground biomass of abaca at three positions along the slope at two typical abaca field on Cantanduanes Island. We analysed pseudostem, leaf and fibre samples for nitrogen, phosphorus, potassium and carbon content at the same positions. These results were combined with nutrient analysis of the soil, litter and natural vegetation of the monitored plots of each field site. Furthermore, we measured photosynthetically active radiation and soil cover at each plot. Results show that the amount of nutrients in the cropping system strongly depended on the field management. Especially the amount of phosphorus in the cropping systems was highly impacted by the crop waste treatment ($P = 0.0009$, a=0.05). Nutrient distribution shows a high heterogeneity within fields at the level of the soil, litter, natural vegetation and abaca. However, no apparent trend in the nutrient distribution along the hill slope was found, suggesting erosion and leaching was minimised due to the abundance of natural vegetation providing enough soil cover (85-98 %) in combination with the broadleaved abaca.

Keywords: Fibre yield, minor crop, *Musa textilis*, nutrients, resource use, smallholder

Contact Address: Catherine Meyer, University of Hohenheim, Inst. of Agricultural Sciences in the Tropics (Hans-Ruthenberg-Institute), Garbenstrasse 13, 70593 Stuttgart, Germany, e-mail: catherine.meyer@uni-hohenheim.de

Influence of Altitude and Management System on Coffee Quality in Mt. Elgon, Uganda

ANNA LINA BARTL[1], DAVID MUKASA[2], ALEJANDRA SARMIENTO[3], SOPHIE GRAEFE[1], LAURENCE JASSOGNE[2], PHILIPPE VAAST[4], PIET VAN ASTEN[2]

[1]*Georg-August-Universität Göttingen, Tropical Silviculture and Forest Ecology, Germany*
[2]*International Institute of Tropical Agriculture (IITA), Uganda,*
[3]*Georg-August-Universität Göttingen, Crop Production Systems in the Tropics, Germany*
[4]*CIRAD Montpellier, France & ICRAF Nairobi, Kenya*

The intrinsic quality of a cup of coffee is largely determined by farm level factors. Besides the influence of cultivation and harvest management, also environmental parameters are important. Climate change in Uganda will result in different environmental conditions, which not only influence yield, but also coffee quality, and can negatively affect the income of farmers.

The present study aimed to identify drivers of coffee quality, in order to develop recommendations that help farmers to keep or even improve coffee quality under harsher environmental conditions. For our quality measurements three altitude levels (<1400 m, 1400–1700 m, >1700 m) and three types of management system ('coffee open sun', 'coffee banana', 'coffee tree') were differentiated in the research area of Mount Elgon in eastern Uganda. This area is one of the most important regions for Arabica coffee cultivation in the country. Through physical bean characteristics and cupping data of coffee samples, we determined relationships between altitude, management levels and coffee quality. There was a clear trend of a better quality with increasing altitude. On the other hand, the influence of management system on quality was not that strong. Interviews with farmers allowed characterising current post-harvest processing, and additionally some farmer-processed samples were analysed for quality parameters, to identify if there is a gap between current and optimal processing. Our results allow the development of recommendations towards an optimal post-harvest processing that secure coffee quality in the context of climate change. Two important aspects for a better coffee quality are floating before pulping and the improvement of drying conditions. Resulting recommendations should allow for more secured livelihoods of coffee farmers and to sustain the reputation of Uganda as an important exporter of high quality coffee.

Keywords: Coffee, management systems, quality, Uganda

Contact Address: Sophie Graefe, Georg-August-Universität Göttingen, Tropical Silviculture and Forest Ecology, Göttingen, Germany, e-mail: sgraefe@gwdg.de

ID 519

Evaluation of Potato (*Solanum tuberosum* L.) Nutrient Use Efficiency under Legume Intercropping Systems

HARUN SAMUEL[1], CHARLES GACHENE[1], NANCY KARANJA[1], ELMAR SCHULTE-GELDERMANN[2]

[1] *University of Nairobi, Dept. of Land Resource Management and Agricultural Technology (LARMAT), Kenya*
[2] *International Potato Center - sub Saharan Africa (CIP-SSA), Integrated Crop Management, Kenya*

A field study was carried out to assess the effect of potato - legume intercropping on a number of nutrient use efficiency indices, i.e. nitrogen use efficiency (NUE), nitrogen uptake efficiency (NUpE) and nitrogen harvest index (NHI) and yield. The experiment was laid in a randomised complete block design (RCBD) with four replicates at Upper Kabete Campus field station, University of Nairobi during the 2014 short (October-December) and 2015 long (March to June) rainy seasons. Treatments comprised of Sole Potato (CS1) and Potato intercropped with either climbing bean (*Phaseolus vulgaris* L.) (CS2) garden pea (*Pisum sativum*) (CS3) or dolichos (*Dolichos lablab*) (CS4). A basal $200\,kg\,ha^{-1}$ of 17N:17P:17K fertiliser was band applied at planting and an equivalent quantity of CAN (27 % N) as a top dress to potato crop only at tuber initiation stage. The indices differed significantly among treatments ($p < 0.05$) during the two seasons. In season one, CS4 and CS2 had the highest, lowest total nutrient uptake (Mg ha^{-1}) at 0.062 and 0.045 respectively, while in season two, CS1 and CS3 had the highest (0.12) and lowest (0.05) respectively. Tuber dry matter yield, which reflected the NUE followed the significant trend CS4 > CS3 > CS1 > CS2 and CS1 > CS4 > CS3 > CS2 in season one and two respectively ranging between 0.018 Mg ha^{-1} and 0.030 Mg ha^{-1}. Only in the second season did the NHI (proportion of nitrogen retained in the tubers to the total plant uptake) showed a significant trend (CS3 > CS4 > CS1 > CS2) ranging from 50 % – 65 %. In terms of tuber yield, CS4 and CS2 recorded the highest (26.63 Mg ha^{-1}) and lowest (18.31 Mg ha^{-1}) respectively in the short rains and CS1 with 39.32 Mg ha^{-1} and CS1 with 36.91 Mg ha^{-1} in the long rains season. *Dolichos lablab* (CS4) was the most effective intercrop and could be recommended for integration into potato cropping systems to improve NUE and productivity.

Keywords: Nitrogen harvest index, nitrogen uptake efficiency, nitrogen use efficiency, tuber yield

Contact Address: Harun Samuel, University of Nairobi, Land Resource Management and Agricultural Technology (LARMAT), University of Nairobi -Cavs, 00625 Nairobi, Kenya, e-mail: hgitari@gmail.com

Crop Choice and Planting Time for Upland Crops in Northwest Cambodia

STEPHANIE MONTGOMERY[1], ROBERT J. MARTIN[1], CHRIS GUPPY[1], GRAEME WRIGHT[1], RICHARD J. FLAVEL[1], SOPHANARA PHAN[2], SOPHOEUN IM[2], VAN TOUCH[1], MATTHEW TIGHE[1]

[1]*University of New England, Agronomy and Soil Science, Australia*
[2]*Maddox Jolie-Pitt Foundation, Agriculture, Cambodia*

Crop yields are declining in Northwest Cambodia and crop failure in the pre-monsoon season is commonplace with 70 % of farmers surveyed stating that drought is a constraint to production. Farmers currently lack knowledge to adopt more sustainable farming practices. A trial was conducted in Samlout District, Battambang Province, Northwest Cambodia to investigate the feasibility of a sowing time two months later than typical local practices. The aim of the shift in sowing time was to increase crop yield and reduce crop failure due to heat and drought stress throughout the season. A secondary aim was to compare sequences of continuous maize, and maize in rotation with peanut, sunflower, sorghum, cowpea or mungbean. The trial was undertaken for four cropping seasons over two years, during which time the maize-sunflower sequence produced the highest gross margins. Maize-sunflower returns were $514 per hectare per annum more than the typical planting of continuous maize, and over $1100 per hectare per year higher than the other maize-legume and maize-sorghum rotations. Continuous maize produced the most stable yields across the four seasons and maize-sunflower produced the second highest mean yield. Results from modelling of soil moisture suggest that a shift in sowing time may avoid the extreme heat and align crop growth stages with periods of more reliable rainfall. Site specific surface soil moisture data and rainfall was entered into the APSIM model to predict the soil profile moisture throughout the growing season. The results from both modelling and on-farm research resulted in high crop yields compared with traditional practices and expectations, and a low probability of crop failure. Crops of maize, sunflower and sorghum grew well from an early October sowing date into the post monsoon season and produced good yields on stored soil water with low plant stress due to mild seasonal conditions. This may prove to be the best option for farmers in the Northwest upland, achieved by a simple shift of sowing dates.

Keywords: Legume, maize, peanut, planting window, sorghum, Southeast Asia, sunflower

Contact Address: Stephanie Montgomery, University of New England, Agronomy and Soil Science, Department of Agronomy and Soil Science, 2351 Armidale, Australia, e-mail: smontgom@myune.edu.au

ID 1112

Soil fertility and nutrient management

Posters

Plant Residue-Derived Organic Carbon Input into Soil in African Indigenous Vegetable Production Systems

ENOS ONYUKA[1], GODFREY NAMBAFU[1], HOLGER BESSLER[1], ANNA ADAM[1], DARIUS O. ANDIKA[2], JOSEPH PATRICK GWEYI-ONYANGO[3], SAMUEL MWONGA[4], CHRISTOF ENGELS[1]

[1] *Humboldt-Universität zu Berlin, Albrecht Daniel Thaer-Institute of Agricultural and Horticultural Sciences (ADTI), Germany*

[2] *Jaramogi Oginga Odinga University of Science and Technology, Dept. of Plant, Animal and Food Sciences, Kenya*

[3] *Kenyatta University, Dept. of Agricultural Science and Technology, Kenya*

[4] *Egerton University, Dept. of Crops, Horticulture and Soils, Kenya*

Food production in sub Saharan Africa is constrained by low soil fertility, whereby soil organic matter (SOM) is key factor regulating many soil functions that determine the yielding ability of soils. SOM content is influenced by the mass and quality of organic carbon input into soil. In smallholder farming systems manure and composts are scarce, and only small fractions are allocated to soil amendment due to alternative use as feed and fuel. Therefore, organic matter input into soil is often restricted to plant residues remaining in the field. In this study, we quantified the effects of species and harvesting method on the mass and quality of plant-derived carbon input into soil with the aim to improve soil fertility management in African indigenous vegetable (AIV) production systems.

Five AIV species (amaranthus - *Amaranthus cruentus*, cowpea - *Vigna unguiculata*, African kale - *Brassica carinata*, African nightshade - *Solanum scabrum*, spider plant - *Cleome gynandra*) and common kale (*Brassica oleracea acephala*) were grown in a field experiment. Plants were harvested by two different methods, which are both commonly used in Kenya: Plants were either pulled out with some coarse roots adhering to the stems or cut about 5 cm above the soil surface. Leaf litter, above-ground plant residues and below-ground residues (coarse root, fine roots in 0–0.3 m and 0.3–0.6 m soil depth) were quantified and analysed for C content. The humification efficiency of plant residues was determined in incubation studies under controlled conditions.

Input of plant residue-derived organic carbon into the soil significantly differed among species with minimum of $0.3\,kg\,C\,m^{-2}$ for cowpea and maximum of $0.8\,kg\,C\,m^{-2}$ for amaranthus. In all species, input with leaf litter was negligible, while the contribution of fine roots to C input varied between about 40 % in spider plant and 80 % in cowpea. Pulling out instead of cutting plants reduced carbon input by 14 % in cowpea and nearly 60 % in African kale and spider plant.

It is concluded that in AIV production systems with low availability of organic fertilisers species selection and harvesting method are important determinants for soil C dynamics and fertility.

Keywords: Coarse roots, fine roots, harvest method, humification, leaf litter, stubble

Contact Address: Christof Engels, Humboldt-Universität zu Berlin, Albrecht Daniel Thaer-Institute of Agricultural and Horticultural Sciences (ADTI), Berlin, Germany, e-mail: christof.engels@agrar.hu-berlin.de

Nitrate Reductase Activity as Potential Indicator for Biological Nitrification Inhibition in *Brachiaria humidicola*

MARC-ANDRÉ SPARKE[1], HANNES KARWAT[1], JACOBO ARANGO[2], JONATHAN NÚÑEZ[2], DANILO MORETA[2], IDUPULAPATI RAO[2], GEORG CADISCH[1]

[1]*University of Hohenheim, Inst. of Agricultural Sciences in the Tropics (Hans-Ruthenberg-Institute), Germany*
[2]*International Center for Tropical Agriculture (CIAT), Colombia*

"Biological Nitrification Inhibition" (BNI) is a naturally occurring process by which soil nitrogen (N) is conserved in the less mobile form of ammonium (NH_4^+) resulting in a reduction of nitrate (NO_3) leaching losses and N_2O emissions. The pasture grass *Brachiaria humidicola* (Bh) is currently the most prominent species showing potential to naturally inhibit nitrification. This research aimed to identify *in situ* plant physiological indicators for BNI activity and to evaluate Bh accessions for their BNI potential with a rapid and reliable methodological approach under field conditions, proposing a direct linkage between nitrification deriving NO_3 in soil and nitrate reductase activity (NRA) in plants. *In vivo* NRA in leaf was determined after N fertilisation and synchronised with soil sampling to test the relationship between soil nitrification rates and NRA. Soil $N\text{-}NO_3$ was determined *in situ* to facilitate correlation analysis. The genotypes tested included two *B. humidicola* CIAT germplasm accessions (CIAT 16888 and CIAT 26146) as controls and four *B. humidicola* hybrids that were preselected based on greenhouse evaluation of BNI activity in soil. Beforehand enzyme substrate (NO_3) inducibility was clearly verified and plant leaves turned out to be the main tissue of NO_3 reduction (roots vs. leaves). The high BNI Bh accession (CIAT 16888) showed the lowest NRA, whereas the low BNI accession (CIAT 26146) showed highest NRA among all the tested materials. Previously, Bh-08–679 and Bh-08–675 were identified as high BNI and low BNI hybrids, respectively. The NRA assay confirmed these previous observations. Two Bh hybrids (Bh-08–700 and Bh-08–1149) showed an intermediate level of BNI potential. Methodological comparison (soil nitrification rates vs. *in vivo* NRA) resulted in discrepancies concerning ranking of BNI capacity. NRA in plant tissue correlated well with soil $N\text{-}NO_3$ concentration ($R^2 = 0.81$, $p < 0.05$). This significant positive correlation between NRA vs. $N\text{-}NO_3$ concentration in the soil indicates that plant tissue NRA can be a potential indicator of BNI in soil. Further research is needed to estimate to what extent the high BNI Bh hybrids can contribute to N conservation in soil to benefit resource-poor smallholders in the tropics where synthetic nitrification inhibitors are expensive and less effective.

Keywords: Forages, nitrogen cycle, tropical grasslands

Contact Address: Marc-André Sparke, University of Hohenheim, Inst. of Agricultural Sciences in the Tropics (Hans-Ruthenberg-Institute), 70593 Stuttgart, Germany, e-mail: marc.sparke@sparke-wohnbau.de

ID 460

Biochar-Based Inoculum of *Bradyrhizobium* Improve Plant Growth and Yield of Lupin (*Lupinus angustifolius* L.) under Drought Stress

DILFUZA EGAMBERDIEVA, MORITZ RECKLING, STEPHAN WIRTH

Leibniz-Centre for Agricultural Landscape Research (ZALF), Germany

The legume-Rhizobium symbiosis is known as the most efficient system for biological nitrogen fixation (BNF) through nodulation in legume roots. Drought stress is a major abiotic impact on the symbiotic performance of legumes, inhibiting plant growth, and decreasing yields. Biochar is a fine-grained substrate rich in organic carbon that is produced by pyrolysis or by heating biomass in a low oxygen environment and has been used worldwide as a soil amendment to increase soil fertility and plant growth. It is also considered as a suitable carrier material for bacterial inoculants. We have evaluated the potential of a biochar for suitability as a carrier for *Bradyrhizobium* sp. (Lupinus) under irrigation and drought conditions. The three types of char were used as carrier material for bacteria: (i) hydrochar (HTC) from maize silage (ii) pyrolysis biochar from maize (MBC), and (iii) pyrolysis biochar from wood (WBC). A field experiment was conducted at the experimental field station of Leibniz Centre for Agricultural Landscape Research (ZALF), Müncheberg, Germany. In the pot experiment survival of *Bradyrhizobium* sp. (BR) populations were higher in HTC-char carrier material as compared to pyrolysis biochar from maize (MBC), and pyrolysis biochar from wood (WBC). The HTC based *Bradyrhizobium* sp. inoculant (HTC-BR) significantly enhanced plant growth, uptake of N and P, and nodulation of lupin under drought compared to inoculation with BR strain. The survival of BR was more competent at drought stress condition, when introduced as HTC-based inocula compared to a direct inoculation. The result of field experiment showed, that the HTC-BR inoculant was effective in lupin growth promotion, and pod formation of lupin under both irrigated and drought conditions in comparison to the un-inoculated control. From our study, we conclude in general that HTC as carrier substrate increased survival of *Bradyrhizobium* sp. inoculum, improving plant growth, nutrient uptake and symbiotic performance of lupin under drought stress. Our results imply that biochar based microbial inoculants are a promising practical approach to improve growth of legumes under hostile conditions.

Keywords: Extreme conditions, grain legumes, hydrochar, inoculation, water scarcity

Contact Address: Dilfuza Egamberdieva, Leibniz-Centre for Agricultural Landscape Research (ZALF), Inst. for Landscape Biogeochemistry, Eberswalder Str. 84, 15374 Müncheberg, Germany, e-mail: Dilfuza.egamberdieva@zalf.de

Enhancing Phosphorus Fertiliser Use Efficiency of Wheat via Controlled Release of Microbes by Coating Alginate Loaded Bacteria on Diammonium Phosphate

Muhammad Yaseen, Muhammad Zahir Aziz, Muhammad Naveed

University of Agriculture Faisalabad, Inst. of Soil and Environmental Sciences, Pakistan

Efficiency of applied phosphatic fertilisers on calcareous soil is very low i.e. 10–25 %. This is mainly because phosphorus (P) fertiliser granule in soil is subjected to a series of primary and secondary solution reactions with Ca^{2+} and Mg^{2+} which substantially retard P availability to plants by fixation. Saving of P granule from these reactions and solubilising the fixed P is in fact improving its availability to plant. Coating granules of diammonium phosphate (DAP) fertiliser with alginate-loaded bacteria can improve availability of P and deliver microbe in rhizosphere for improving P use efficiency and crop production. A series of experiments including laboratory and wire house were conducted to investigate the efficacy of alginate coated DAP bioaugmented with endophytic bacteria on growth, yield and P use efficiency of wheat (*Triticum aestivum* L.). Pre-isolated endophytic strain *Enterobacter* sp. MN17::gusA and alginate was used for experiments. In laboratory experiment, best concentration of alginate viz 0.5, 1.0 and 1.5 % and organic amendment (OA) glucose (G) 1 %, glycerol (Gly) 1 % and both together was screened out on the basis of microbial survival. After, screening best concentration of polymer/organic amendment along with microbe were coated on DAP. Microbial survival after coating on fertiliser granule and P released pattern in soil was determined under control conditions and its subsequent effect on wheat growth and PUE was evaluated under wire house conditions. Results revealed that maximum microbial survival was 12×10^7 CFU ml^{-1} up to one month in alginate concentration 1.5 % with OA (G+Gly) coating on fertiliser. Further, incubation results showed that microbe number and P released from granules was 80×10^8 CFU g^{-1} soil and 79 % in soil after one month. Similarly, data of pot trial revealed that wheat growth, yield, physiological parameters and P use efficiency was improved and successfully delivery of microbes in rhizosphere was achieved by fertiliser granules coated with alginate-loaded microbes. So, it can be summarised that DAP fertiliser coated with alginate-loaded microbe is a novel approach and it can effectively improve growth, yield, P use efficiency of wheat and target site delivery of microbes.

Keywords: Alginate, diammonium phosphate, *Enterobacter* sp., phosphorus fertiliser, wheat

Contact Address: Muhammad Yaseen, University of Agriculture Faisalabad, Institute of Soil and Environmental Sciences, Faisalabad, Pakistan, e-mail: dr.yaseen@gmail.com

ID 972

Climate-Smart Crop-Livestock Systems for Smallholders in the Tropics: Regulation of Nitrification in Soil by *Brachiaria humidicola* Hybrids

JACOBO ARANGO[1], DANILO MORETA[1], JONATHAN NÚÑEZ[1], ASHLY AREVALO[1], HANNES KARWAT[2], MANABU ISHITANI[1], JOHN MILES[1], MARGARET WORTHINGTON[1], MICHAEL PETERS[1], JOE TOHME[1], MARIO CUCHILLO HILARIO[1], STEFAN BURKART[1], NGONIDZASHE CHIRINDA[1], GLENN HYMAN[1], JESUS MARTINEZ[1], JEIMAR TAPASCO[1], MICHAEL SELVARAJ[1], PAOLA PARDO[1], MAURICIO EFREN SOTELO CABRERA[1], REIN VAN DER HOEK[3], MARTÍN MENA[3], ALVARO RINCÓN[4], REYNALDO MENDOZA[5], MARC-ANDRÉ SPARKE[2], KONRAD EGENOLF[2], GUNTUR SUBBARAO[6], GEORG CADISCH[2], IDUPULAPATI RAO[1]

[1] *International Center for Tropical Agriculture (CIAT), Colombia*

[2] *University of Hohenheim, Inst. of Agricultural Sciences in the Tropics (Hans-Ruthenberg-Institute), Germany*

[3] *International Center for Tropical Agriculture (CIAT), Nicaragua*

[4] *Corporación Colombiana de Investigación Agropecuaria (Corpoica), Colombia*

[5] *Univesidad Nacional Agraria, Suelos, Nicaragua*

[6] *Japan International Research Center for Agricultural Sciences (JIRCAS), Japan*

Poor management of nitrogen (N) applied as fertiliser to agricultural systems results in massive loss of N due to a rapid nitrification process in soil, posing serious environmental and economic constraints. The N is lost in the form of nitrate through leaching which contaminates water and in the form of nitrous oxide (N_2O) to the atmosphere causing global warming. Tropical forage grass, *Brachiaria humidicola* (Bh), exudates from its roots chemical compounds that inhibit nitrification in soil and this characteristic is known as Biological Nitrification Inhibition (BNI). The BNI technology represents a smart alternative to mitigate climate change by using N more efficiently in agro-pastoral systems and this technology was the centre of focus for a four years (March 2012 to December 2015) interdisciplinary project work in Colombia and Nicaragua funded by GIZ-BMZ (Germany) and led by the International Center for Tropical Agriculture (CIAT) in collaboration with the University of Hohenheim, Corpoica and the University of Llanos in Colombia and MIS-UNA consortium in Nicaragua. The major findings of this project were: 1) Using phenotyping methods developed for the BNI trait, high genetic diversity was found among Bh hybrids suggesting BNI as a quantitative trait; 2) High saturated linkage maps were developed and minor QTLs identified for BNI using a bi-parental mapping population; 3) Through participatory agronomic evaluation with farmers in Colombia and Nicaragua, promising Bh hybrids were identified that combine the BNI capacity with superior forage production and nutritional quality; 4) The residual BNI effect in soil was evaluated in

Contact Address: Jacobo Arango, International Center for Tropical Agriculture (CIAT), Tropical Forages, A A 6713, NA Cali, Colombia, e-mail: j.arango@cgiar.org

maize as subsequent crop, observing an improvement in the N use efficiency as well as an increase in maize grain yields; and 5) Using a modelling approach (EcoCrop model), potential areas to use the BNI technology around the world were identified and an economic analysis of this technology was made for its use in agro-pastoral systems. Results obtained from this project together with previous research highlight the potential of Bh as a climate-smart forage grass with several desirable attributes (e.g., adaptation to problem soils and climate variability; deep and vigorous root system to accumulate large amounts of carbon in soil).

Keywords: *Brachiaria humidicola*, climate change, Livestock, nitrogen, nitrogen use efficiency

Conservation Agriculture Practices in Smallholder Farming of Western Kenya: Nutrient Cycling and Greenhouse Gas Fluxes

URSZULA NORTON[1], JUDITH ODHIAMBO[1], JAY NORTON[2]

[1]*University of Wyoming, Plant Sciences and Program in Ecology, United States of America*

[2]*University of Wyoming, Dept. of Ecosystem Science and Management, United States of America*

Conservation Agriculture (CA) encompasses a set of practices designed to improve crop yields and soil quality. In Kenya, CA is gaining acceptance not as an alternative, but rather necessity to increase food production by food insecure smallholder farmers. Limited understanding of short-term agroecosystem response during transition to CA can impede the process of adoption. The objective of this study was to explore short-term impacts of selected CA practices on soil nitrogen (N), greenhouse gas (GHG) fluxes, weed population dynamics and crop performance at two locations in western Kenya: low altitude with two annual cropping seasons (Bungoma) and high altitude with one annual cropping season (Trans-Nzoia). Three tillage practices (conventional, minimum and no-till) were combined with three cropping systems (continuous maize intercropped with common beans; maize intercropped with common beans relayed with *mucuna* cover crop after beans harvest; and maize, common beans and *mucuna* planted in strip cropping arrangement). Herbicides were used in no-till, shallow hand hoeing and herbicides were used in minimum till and deep hoeing with no herbicides was used in conventional till. In general, Bungoma demonstrated high GHG fluxes, soil N mineralisation but significantly lower yields compared with Trans-Nzoia. Transitioning to minimum-till or no-till-based CA practices at both locations and forgoing second-season cropping in Bungoma will reduce soil disturbance and C and N losses to mineralisation, GHG emissions and potential leaching. Even though evidence of early accrual of soil benefits associated with CA practices may take longer than the timeframe of this research, farmers noticed immediate reduction in weed competition, which is one of the leading causes of yield loss in Kenya. Weed density of grass and forb species declined significantly under minimum till and no-till in Trans-Nzoia and of grass species only in Bungoma. Transitioning to CA systems resulted in a decline of four out of five most dominant weed species. Corresponding costs of weed management were reduced by $148.40 ha^{-1} in minimum till and $149.60 ha^{-1} in no-till compared with conventional tillage.

Keywords: Bimodal precipitation, Bungoma, carbon dioxide, farmer adoption, methane, nitrous oxide, sub-Saharan Africa soil mineral nitrogen, Trans-Nzoia

Contact Address: Urszula Norton, University of Wyoming, Plant Sciences and Program in Ecology, Dept 3354 1000 E. University Ave, 82070 Laramie, United States of America, e-mail: unorton@uwyo.edu

Fertiliser Derived from Fecal Sludge in Sri Lanka: Analysis of Plant Nutritional Value and Heavy Metal Contamination

FELIX GRAU[1,2], NIKITA DRECHSEL[2], DIETER TRAUTZ[1], JAYANTHA WEERAKODY[3], BADULA RANAWEERA[4]

[1] University of Applied Sciences Osnabrueck, Fac. of Agricultural Sciences and Landscape Architecture, Germany

[2] International Water Management Institute, Resource Recovery & Reuse, Sri Lanka,

[3] Wayamba University of Sri Lanka, Department of Plantation Management, Sri Lanka

[4] Wayamba University of Sri Lanka, Horticulture & Landscape Gardening, Sri Lanka

Urban and rural areas in developing countries face major challenges in closing the nutrient and carbon resource loop. To address this issue, IWMI implemented a resource recovery treatment scheme to recycle fecal sludge and organic municipal solid wastes by jointly co-composting input materials from these two waste streams. The implementation took place in Ghana initially and resulted in a commercially available fertiliser. Sri Lanka was chosen to be one of the countries for further implementation and evaluation where the current focus is on the safe production of co-compost, agricultural application, economical viability of compost plants, value chain development and demand analysis. The data presented in this paper aim to link research findings of the pellet production process with options and potentials for agricultural application. Therefore, different types of compost and co-compost have been analysed for macro- and micro plant nutrients, organic matter, pH-value, electric conductivity and heavy metals. While composted fecal sludge from septic tanks (FS) displays like farmyard manure high levels of some micronutrients-cum-heavy metals, the co-composts with rice husk (FS-RH) or organic municipal solid waste (FS-MSW) show all levels in the desired range. The process of co-composting allows to create a nutrient and organic carbon rich agricultural resource, which can further be enriched according to crop demands or ease of handling through mineral enrichment or pelletizing. Results reveal that pelletizing e.g. FS and MSW maintains the chemical properties while enhancing product value, e.g. for storage, transport and controlled field application. Based on the obtained results, it can be concluded that an enriched and pelletized FS-MSW co-compost presents an interesting alternative to conventional fertiliser and soil amendments, especially in Sri Lanka where there is a strong political push for organic fertilisers. Ongoing research is addressing farmers' demand and other potential contaminants targeting its certified organic agricultural use.

Keywords: Compost, fecal sludge, heavy metal, plant nutrient

Contact Address: Felix Grau, University of Applied Sciences Osnabrueck, Fac. of Agricultural Sciences and Landscape Architecture, Osnabrueck, Germany, e-mail: leifgrau@gmail.com

 ID 287

Crop and Soil Response on Fecal Sludge Derived Fertiliser in the Intermediate Climate Zone of Sri Lanka

FELIX GRAU[1,4], JAYANTHA WEERAKODY[2], BADULA RANAWEERA[3], NIKITA DRECHSEL[4], INDIKA KARUNARATHNE[5], VOLKER HÄRING[6], DIETER TRAUTZ[1], PRIYANGA DISSANAYAKE[7]

[1] *University of Applied Sciences Osnabrueck, Fac. of Agricultural Sciences and Landscape Architecture, Germany*

[2] *Wayamba University of Sri Lanka, Department of Plantation Management, Sri Lanka*

[3] *Wayamba University of Sri Lanka, Horticulture & Landscape Gardening, Sri Lanka*

[4] *International Water Management Institute, Resource Recovery & Reuse, Sri Lanka,*

[5] *Wayamba University of Sri Lanka, ICT Centre, Sri Lanka*

[6] *Ruhr-Universität Bochum, Inst. of Geography, Soil Science and Soil Ecology, Germany*

[7] *Regional Agriculture Research & Development Centre, Makandura, Sri Lanka*

Trials in Ghana and Sri Lanka showed that co-composted fecal sludge (FS) and organic municipal solid waste (MSW) revealed high potential to be used as an agricultural resource. Besides options for cost recovery in waste management, closing the nutrient and carbon cycles between urban and rural areas, substitution of mineral fertilisers, reduced pollution and the restoration of degraded arable land are possible benefits. In order to enhance their properties, MSW compost and FS-MSW co-compost were enriched with ammonium sulphate to 5 % total N and rice flour was added to enable faster disintegration and pelletized. Two field experiments were conducted to assess the effect of nine different treatments in terms of several phenological parameters, plant nutrition and short-term effects on the soil properties (Luvisol) in intermediate zone of Sri Lanka. The application amount of each treatment was based on local Nitrogen recommendations for farmers, which served as control. In addition, a poultry litter treatment was used as cheapest available organic alternative. All inputs were analysed on their plant nutritional values and possible contaminants. As a short term crop *Raphanus sativus* 'Beeralu rabu' was cultivated for 50 days using a randomised complete block design (RCBD). Similarly, the second field trial, *Capsicum annuum* 'CA-8', was planted as RCBD, using the same treatments, for a cultivation period of 120 days. The results of these trials are currently analysed and will be presented at the conference. The trials will be followed by others, including plantation crops to assess long term effects of crop production and soil fertility.

Keywords: Capsicum, compost, crop response, fecal sludge, field experiment, pelletizing, plant nutrient, radish, soil response

Contact Address: Felix Grau, University of Applied Sciences Osnabrueck, Fac. of Agricultural Sciences and Landscape Architecture, Osnabrueck, Germany, e-mail: leifgrau@gmail.com

Effects of Water Restriction on Quality of Goat Manure

MWANAIMA RAJAB RAMADHAN[1], STEFFI APPENBURG[1], OSMAN MAHGOUB[2], EVA SCHLECHT[1]

[1]University of Kassel / Georg-August Universität Göttingen, Animal Husbandry in the Tropics and Subtropics, Germany

[2]Sultan Qaboos University, College of Agricultural & Marine Sciences, Dept. of Animal and Veterinary Sciences, Oman

Water scarcity is a major challenge affecting agriculture in tropical and subtropical drylands. Since agriculture is the backbone of the majority of countries in these regions, it is important to make wise use of locally available sources of water and nutrients when aiming at optimising resource use efficiency. Thus our objective was to determine the effects of restricted drinking water intake of goats, known to be tolerant to such limitation, on the quality of their faeces and the consequences for utilisation of such manure as soil amendment in crop production.

Two trials were conducted at Sultan Qaboos University, Muscat, Oman, during summer (August-October) 2013 and 2014. Set up as a complete Latin Square Design, each trial included six adult male Batinah goats subjected to three regimes: drinking water offered *ad libitum* (100 %), water restricted to 85 % and to 70 % of individual *ad libitum* consumption. During three 7-day experimental periods preceded each by three weeks of adaptation, faeces were quantified and analysed for concentrations of dry matter (DM), nitrogen (N), neutral detergent fibre (NDF) and acid detergent fibre (ADF) following standard protocols. The mixed model procedure in SAS was used to conduct ANOVA with year, period and treatment as fixed effects and animal as random effect.

Water restriction decreased the quantitative DM excretion in both years but increased the DM concentration of faeces. Quantitative and qualitative NDF excretion decreased when water was restricted, whereas no change occurred with respect to the amount and concentration of faecal N, indicating a slight shift of N excretion from urine to faeces. In 2014, quantitative and qualitative ADF excretion was higher ($p < 0.05$) in water restricted than in unrestricted goats. Since this fraction consists of slowly decomposable organic carbon (C), faeces of water-restricted goats may stabilise soil organic matter when applied as manure, which is very relevant for heavily weathered or sandy tropical and subtropical soils. As recalcitrant organic C fosters short-term N immobilisation in the soil, immediate N-losses, which often occur directly after manure application, may also be reduced in manure obtained from water-restricted goats.

Keywords: Desert conditions, nutrient cycling, small ruminants, water restriction

Contact Address: Eva Schlecht, University of Kassel / Georg-August-Universität Göttingen, Animal Husbandry in the Tropics and Subtropics, Steinstraße 19, 37213 Witzenhausen, Germany, e-mail: tropanimals@uni-kassel.de

ID 233

Effects of Modified Biochars on the Growth of Maize (*Zea mays* L.)

CHARLOTTE CHRISTINA DIETRICH[1], MD. ARIFUR RAHAMAN[2,1], KIATKAMJON INTANI[2], SAJID LATIF[2], JOACHIM MÜLLER[2], NICOLAI DAVID JABLONOWSKI[1]

[1] *Forschungszentrum Jülich GmbH, Inst. of Bio-and Geosciences, IBG-2: Plant Sciences, Germany*

[2] *University of Hohenheim, Inst. of Agricultural Sciences in the Tropics (Hans-Ruthenberg-Institute), Germany*

The application of biochar as a soil amendment is becoming a viable option against depleting soil resources and fertility. Especially in the context of an increasing demand for agricultural land, biochar-based organic fertilisers have the potential to improve soil fertility and production in otherwise unsuitable soils. Recent studies however, indicate that the interaction between biochar applications and certain environmental components such as climate, soil type and fertilisation are highly variable and might not substantially increase crop yield. Thus, modifying biochars to fit certain soil characteristics is the necessary first step in sustainably increasing long-term soil fertility on low-yielding soils. In the present study, the growth of *Zea mays* L. on sandy, marginal substrate was evaluated in a greenhouse experiment. We applied untreated maize cob biochar, biochar washed with ethanol or hydrochloric acid, as well as biochar incubated in digestate, a nutrient-rich by-product of the anaerobic digestion of organic feedstock. These modifications were designed to either remove pollutants and alter the biochars' surface properties or load it with additional nutrients. Maize plants were harvested 21, 28 and 35 days after germination. The results indicated that the biochars had varying effects on soil parameters, shoot and root biomass production, plant growth and plant specific leaf area over the course of the three harvests. Biochar incubated in digestate had the most pronounced positive effect, while biochar washing resulted in negligible variations of the biomass production when compared to the untreated biochar. This study underlines the importance of modifying biochars and serves as a basis for future studies incorporating mixtures of variously treated organic fertilisers in a bid to increase crop yields on marginal soils.

Keywords: Biochar, biogas digestate, crop yield, maize cob, soil amendment

Contact Address: Sajid Latif, University of Hohenheim, Inst. of Agricultural Sciences in the Tropics (Hans-Ruthenberg-Institute), Garbenstr. 9, 70599 Stuttgart, Germany, e-mail: s.latif@uni-hohenheim.de

Modelling Effects of Residual Biochar, Rice Husk and Rice Straw on Productivity of Maize (*Zea mays* L.) for Sustainable Soil Fertility Restoration in the Guinea Savannah Zone

ISRAEL K. DZOMEKU[1], OSMAN ILLIASU[1], PETER T. BIRTEEB[2], STELLA OBANYI[3], TARA WOOD[3]

[1] *University for Development Studies, Dept. of Agronomy, Ghana*

[2] *University for Development Studies, Dept. of Animal Science, Ghana*

[3] *Internation Fertilizer Development Center (IFDC), Integrated Soil Fertility Management, Ghana*

The International Fertiliser Development Center's (IFDC) concept and approach to integrated soil fertility management as a set of agricultural practices adapted to local conditions to maximise the efficiency of nutrient and water use and improve agricultural productivity on poor fertility soils in the Sudan and Guinea savannah zones of West Africa is innovative to the rural communities. A field experiment was conducted at Nyankpala, near Tamale during the 2014 cropping season and continued during 2015, to investigate the residual effects of available indigenous organic materials (Biochar - partially burnt rice husk, rice husk and rice straw) in combination with supplementary mineral fertiliser N on yield components and grain yield of drought and *Striga* tolerant maize varirty "Wang Data". It was a $3 \times 3 \times 3+1$ experiment consisting of the 3 organic materials at 3 rates (2.5, 5 and 7.5 t ha^{-1} on dry matter basis) and 3 N fertiliser rates (0, 45 and 90 kg ha^{-1}) plus a pure control laid out in a randomised complete block design with four replicates. Results showed increased maize growth and grain production on residual organic material nutrients required supplementary mineral N fertilisation. Best growth parameters, early days to 50 % flowering and highest cob length, cob weight and stover weight, 100 seed weight and grain yield were obtained with 2.5 to 7.5 t ha^{-1} Biochar + 45-90 kgN ha^{-1}; 5 to 7.5 t ha^{-1} rice husk + 45-90 kgN ha^{-1} and 7.5 t ha^{-1} rice straw + 90 kgN ha^{-1}. Biochar provided the least quantitative input of 2.5 t ha^{-1} + 45 kgN ha^{-1} for maximum maize production and most efficient soil fertility management system. Correlation analysis showed good relationship between grain yield and leaf count (r=0.5699), plant height (r=0.5340), and height of cob attachment (r=0.5164) and cob weight accounted for 69 % of the grain yield. The best prediction model (Eqn. 4) for using Biochar was grain yield = -1414 + 177 (leaf count at 9 WAS) + 5.76 (plant height at 9 WAS).

Keywords: Biochar, maize, mineral N fertiliser, rice husk, rice straw

Contact Address: Israel K. Dzomeku, University for Development Studies, Dept. of Agronomy, Box Tl 1350, Tamale, Ghana, e-mail: ikdzomeku2009@yahoo.com

Effect of Biochar and Wastewater Irrigation on Crop Production in Urban Horticulture of Tamale, Ghana

Edmund Kyei Akoto-Danso[1], Delphine Manka'abusi[1], Steffen Werner[2], Volker Häring[2], Christoph Steiner[1], George Nyarko[3], Pay Drechsel[4], Andreas Buerkert[1]

[1] *University of Kassel, Organic Plant Production and Agroecosystems Research in the Tropics and Subtropics, Germany*

[2] *Ruhr-Universität Bochum, Inst. of Geography, Soil Science / Soil Ecology, Germany*

[3] *University for Development Studies, Fac. of Agronomy, Ghana*

[4] *International Water Management Institute (IWMI), Water Quality, Health and Environment, Sri Lanka*

Little is known about the effects of biochar in wastewater irrigated urban vegetable production of West Africa. We therefore established a two-year field experiment comprising 12 crops in Tamale, Ghana, on an area underlain by a petroplinthic combisol. A split block design with four treatments (Farmer Practise (FP), NFP + biochar, biochar, and an unfertilised control) were factorially combined with two water qualities (clean water and untreated wastewater) and two water quantities (usual irrigation quantity and two-thirds of the usual volume). The 16 treatment combinations were replicated four times on plots of 8 m^2. At the onset of the experiment, rice husk biochar was applied at a rate of 20 t ha^{-1} at 0–20 cm depth.

Biochar increased dry matter yield of the vegetables grown in the first four cropping cycles in both clean water and wastewater irrigated plots whereby the effect of wastewater was more pronounced. During the dry season, wastewater increased crop dry matter yields of unfertilised plots between 10 to 20 fold compared with a four-fold increment in the wet season. For fertilised plots, this increment was 1.5-fold for the wet and two-fold for the dry season. This was explained by the higher concentration of nutrients and the more frequent irrigation during the dry season. Biochar tended to increase yields in the first year (16 % on fertilised plots), but effects were not statistically significant in any year. Fertigation with wastewater contributes significantly to plant nutrition and efficient resource use.

Keywords: Biochar, Ghana, Tamale, wastewater

Contact Address: Edmund Kyei Akoto-Danso, University of Kassel, Organic Plant Production and Agroecosystems Research in the Tropics and Subtropics, Steinstr. 19, 37213 Witzenhausen, Germany, e-mail: Kydanso07@yahoo.com

Agronomic Benefits of Biochar after its Use as Wasteater Filtration Media in a Sudano-Sahelian Soil

STEFFEN WERNER[1], KORBINIAN KÄTZL[2], BERND MARSCHNER[1], MARC WICHERN[2], ANDREAS BUERKERT[3], CHRISTOPH STEINER[3]

[1] *Ruhr-Universität Bochum, Inst. of Geography, Soil Science / Soil Ecology, Germany*

[2] *Ruhr-Universität Bochum, Inst. of Urban Water Management and Environmental Engineering, Germany*

[3] *University of Kassel, Organic Plant Production and Agroecosystems Research in the Tropics and Subtropics, Germany*

Urban agriculture is contributing significantly to food security and diversity in developing countries. It is characterised by the use of untreated wastewater for irrigation of vegetable crops and consequently causes health risks for farmers and consumers. Carbonaceous materials are frequently used for water purification. Biochar, the solid residue of pyrolysis, is able to retain pathogens and harmful substances during filtration and researchers reported nutrient accumulation in water filters. In this study, we tested the hypothesis that biochar after its use in water filters has specific properties and therefore may have different effects on plant growths.

To test this hypothesis a water filter with biochar made from rice husks was constructed and fed with untreated wastewater for three month. After filtration, total nutrient and carbon content, pH and electrical conductivity were assessed and compared with untreated biochar. Subsequently, a six weeks pot experiment with a sandy soil from Niger was carried out and biomass production of summer wheat, nutrient uptake, plant available phosphorus (Bray I) and mineral nitrogen in soil were measured after the experiment. As treatments we used the original biochar, filterchar (20 t ha^{-1}, each) and untreated soil as control. All treatments were tested in a fertilised and unfertilised variant and replicated five times.

The data showed a reduction of nutrients, especially phosphorus (P), during the filtration but, nitrogen (N) remained unchanged. Biomass production was highest in biochar treatment (+72 %) while filterchar (+37 %) produced lesser biomass but still higher than the control. The plants uptake of P was increased but N uptake was reduced on biochar treated soil. The soils with biochar and filterchar had higher available phosphorus content (+106 % and +52 %) but showed lower mineral N content after the experiment. Data suggested that in our study biochar effects on biomass production were likely due to a direct P fertilising effect. The fertiliser value of filterchar was reduced after filtration but still yielded higher biomass than control treatment. Field experiments should be carried out to assess filterchar effects on other soil processes such as nutrient leaching.

Keywords: Biochar, nutrient cycles, water treatment

Contact Address: Steffen Werner, Ruhr-Universität Bochum, Inst. of Geography, Soil Science / Soil Ecology, Universitätstr. 140, 44801 Bochum, Germany, e-mail: steffen.werner@rub.de

ID 727

Rock Dust as Agricultural Soil Amendment: A Review

PHILIPP SWOBODA

Karl-Franzens University Graz, Institute of Systems Sciences, Innovation and Sustainability Research (ISIS), Austria

The declining quality and quantity of soils, climate change and increasing drawbacks of chemical fertilisers are among the top threats for present and future food security. Agricultural rock dust application constitutes a agrogeological technique which could positively contribute to all of the outlined areas. Soils are formed by weathering of primary rocks and from the 18 elements essential for higher plant growth, expect nitrogen, all are derived from naturally occurring rocks and minerals. These nutrients contained in the rocks are however not readily plant available, but have to be released through weathering. Subsequently, the continuous weathering of rock dust can remineralise the soil with a wide range of micro and macro nutrients over the long term, whilst commercial fertilisers mainly supply soluble forms of N, P and K.

Results derived from a comprehensive review of the contradictory and limited literature indicate a positive tendency with a wide scope of potential agronomic benefits. Especially in tropical regions, where chemical fertiliser use is limited economically and by the fact that the highly weathered soils cannot retain the soluble nutrients, rock dust has proven to be a suitable soil amendment. The geochemical status is improved and plant yields are similar to synthetic equivalents. When the rock dust is reused from the mining industry, where it is disposed in ample amounts as a problematic by-product, the eco-environmental costs are furthermore decreased. Other benefits include improved disease resistance, reduction of GHG emissions during the composting process and fixation of CO_2 by weathering and subsequent precipitation of Ca- and Mg-carbonates. Examples from Brazil reveal additional socio-economic advantages over the long term and the strengthening of local food networks.

However, the complex interaction of several factors and the lack of consistency in terms of the design of individual trials is limiting comparison and extrapolation. Inter- and transdisciplinary research is thus needed to understand weathering mechanisms and find appropriate rock dust applications for the respective environment.

Keywords: CO_2 fixation, rock fertiliser, soil remineralisation, waste reuse, weathering

Contact Address: Philipp Swoboda, Karl-Franzens University Graz, Institute of Systems Sciences, Innovation and Sustainability Research (ISIS), Leonhardstraße 6, 8010 Graz, Austria, e-mail: philipp.swo@gmx.at

Economic Profitability of Organo-Mineral Fertilisation in Cotton Farming System in Northern Benin

DANSINOU SILVERE TOVIGNAN, ZAKARI F. TASSOU, RAOUL ADEGUELOU

Universty of Parakou, Fac. of Agronomy, Benin

The promotion of organic materials (OM) in cotton production constitutes an important challenge for a sustainable soil fertility management in West Africa. Farmers face problems such as the availability of sufficient OM and their transportation. Some attempts to overcome these constraints, rescue to combinations of mineral fertilisers (MF) and OM. Considering that OM are from various sources, one important question is what types of OM optimise the output and profitability in cotton farming? This study assesses the economic profitability of organo-mineral fertilisation consisting of combinations of mineral fertiliser (MF) and organic fertilisers such as manure, crop residues and legumes in cotton farming system in northern Benin.

Survey data from 198 cotton farmers randomly selected is used (including 110 for MF and 88 combining mineral and organic fertilisers). Analysis methods combine the calculations of net margin, return on family labour, return on capital and variance analysis.

The findings show higher profitability indicators for organo-mineral combinations than the use of MF except for the integration with legumes. For example, the returns to capital are respectively 0.48, 0.49, 0.57 and 0.63 for combined MF with legumes, MF alone, MF and crop residues and MF and manure. These suggest that manure and crop residues improve cotton farmer's profitability whereas legumes reduce it. Moreover, the variance analysis indicates that there is no significant difference between mean values of profitability indicators for the use of MF and its integration with crop residues and legumes but the mean difference is significant between MF and its integration with manure. Thus, manure constitutes the best option of organic fertilisers to increase cotton farmer's profitability in northern Benin. This implication is consistent with earlier economic analyses which showed that manure was more productive and profitable for farmers than mineral fertiliser.

Based on findings, combination of manure and mineral fertilisers is recommended, and we suggest more sensitisation of farmers about the role of manure in the soil and to improve policy support needed for enhancing manure uptake in cotton farming system. Like most West African governments subsidise MF, similar policy can be recommended to promote private sector investments to develop OM market.

Keywords: Crop residues, legumes, manure, Benin, organo-mineral, profitability

---

Contact Address: Dansinou Silvere Tovignan, University of Parakou, Faculty of Agronomy, Parakou, Benin, e-mail: tsilvere@yahoo.fr

  ID 886

Identification of Potato (*Solanum tuberosum*) Yield Limiting Nutrients in Kenya

JAMES MUGO[1], NANCY KARANJA[2], ELMAR SCHULTE-GELDERMANN[1], CHARLES GACHENE[2], KLAUS DITTERT[3]

[1] *International Potato Center, Kenya*

[2] *University of Nairobi, Dept. of Land Resource Management and Agricultural Technology (LARMAT), Kenya*

[3] *Georg-August-Universität Göttingen, Dept. of Crop Sciences, Germany*

Due to continuous cultivation with limited application of nutrient fertiliser and manure by Kenyan potato farmers, the ability of the soils to supply adequate nutrient for potato yield potential is not known. The aim of the study was to identify limiting nutrients to potato productivity in selected sites. A total of 198 soil samples were collected from farmers' fields in Meru and Nyandarua and chemical properties determined Samples of recently mature leaves (4th leaf) of potato crop at flowering stage were taken from same points where soils were sampled and analysed for their nutrient contents. Nutrient sufficiency for soil (nitrogen (N) (25–80 ppm), phosphorous (P) (30–80 ppm), potassium (K) (70–250 ppm), sulphur (S) (4.5 ppm), calcium (Ca) (175–300 ppm), magnesium (Mg) (30–60 ppm),copper (Cu) (0.2–1 ppm), zinc (Zn) (0.6–2 ppm), boron (B) ($>$1 ppm) and pH (5.5–6.5)) and leaf nutrient (P (0.25–0.5 %), K (3.9–5.5 %), S (0.3–0.5 %), Ca (0.9–2.5 %), Mg (0.25–0.5 %), Cu (5–30 ppm), Zn (20–50 ppm) and B (25–60 ppm)) levels were used to cluster farms into low, optimum or high. In soil chemical results, 46 and 85 % of the farms in Meru and Nyandarua were found to be low in P, 66 and 20 % in N, 67 and 31 % in S and 87 and 80 % in B, respectively. For soils from Nyandarua, 18 and 51 % were low in K and Cu respectively. Results from potato leaf samples showed that 22 and 15 % of farms in both Meru and Nyandarua had low K content while 17 and 55 % were low in B content. Soil pH was found to be below 5.5 in 54 % and 86 % of the farms in Meru and Nyandarua, respectively. In both regions pH had significant ($p < 0.05$) positive correlation with soil P, K, B, Ca and Mg and negative correlation with Cu. There was significant positive correlations between soil and plant P, K, Ca and Cu. In conclusion, N, P, K, S and B were limiting in a number of farms thus a new fertiliser recommendation is required. Liming should be considered for soils with low pH.

Keywords: Chemical characteristics, limiting nutrients, pH, potato, soil fertility

Contact Address: James Mugo, International Potato Center, 25171, Nairobi, Kenya, e-mail: jnjeru30@gmail.com

Nutrient Requirements of Cassava under Different Management Systems in South-Kivu, D.R. Congo

WIVINE MUNYAHALI[1,3], RONY SWENNEN[2], ROEL MERCKX[3]

[1] Université Catholique de Bukavu (UCB), DR Congo

[2] KU Leuven / IITA / Bioversity International, Belgium

[3] KU Leuven, Dept. of Earth and Environmental Sciences, Belgium

Previous works have shown that cassava is highly responsive to fertiliser additions and benefits from improved management. Yet the yield responses of cassava to mineral fertilisers often remain highly variable and are not always clearly related to soil fertility levels. The objective of this study was to investigate and understand factors limiting yield responses of cassava to mineral fertilisers and their interactions with the different agricultural management practices in South-Kivu. Two types of experiments were carried out in multi-locational participatory farmer trials during two consecutive seasons (LR2014 and LR2015): The first type consisted of macronutrient (N, P or K) omission experiments including a manure treatment (FYM) as well as a full NPK, NPK+FYM and NPK+Ca-Mg-S-Zn treatments, to evaluate possible limiting nutrients to cassava growth and yield, and they were established with an improved cassava variety (sawasawa). A control and NPK+FYM treatments with a local variety (nambiyombiyo) were also included for comparison; The second type were leaf management trials with two factors including leaf harvesting effect as the main factor with 3 levels (no leaf harvesting, harvesting every 2 weeks, or 4 weeks, from 4 months after planting) and fertilisation effect (with or without fertiliser application) as the second factor. Fertiliser application significantly affected cassava growth and yields in the two types of experiments. NPK+FYM treatment was the best treatment as it gave the tallest plants throughout the growing period and significantly increased cassava root yield at harvest. Its fresh root yield increment was 26 % on average. The improved variety positively affected growth and yield of cassava with 52 % on average of root yield increment. Harvesting of leaves at 2-week interval reduced root yield relative to the control and 4-week interval treatments. In LR^{2}015, leaf harvesting at 4-week interval significantly increased both cassava fresh biomass and root yields when fertiliser was applied (82 % and 40 % of yield increment compared with the control and the 2-week interval treatment, respectively). Results from compositional nutrient diagnosis (CND) approaches will be performed to determine nutrient disorders in cassava in the study area and their suitability to assess optimal nutrient conditions for cassava growth and yields.

Keywords: Cassava yield, leaf harvesting, mineral fertiliser, nutrient balances, organic input

Contact Address: Roel Merckx, KU Leuven, Dept. of Earth and Environmental Sciences, Kasteelpark Arenberg 20 / P.O. Box 2459, 3001 Leuven, Belgium, e-mail: roel.merckx@kuleuven.be

Assessment of Nutrient Imbalances Limiting Maize (*Zea mays*) Production in Western Kenya

Ruth Njoroge[1], Abigael Otinga[2], Mary Pepela[2], John Okalebo[2], Roel Merckx[1]

[1] *KU Leuven, Dept. of Earth and Environmental Sciences, Belgium*
[2] *University of Eldoret, Soil Science, Kenya*

Poor maize response to N, P and K fertiliser applications in western Kenya results in low grain yields far below the potential. However, the extent and causes of this poor response are still unclear. Nutrient imbalances expressed either in deficiencies and/ or excess are speculated to limit the maize response to fertiliser. To investigate this, a multi-locational trial comprising of 52 sites across Bungoma and Busia counties of western Kenya was conducted during the long rainy season of 2014.The study identified 20 % out of the total experimental sites as poorly responsive to fertiliser application characterised by an average value cost ratio ranging between 0.5 and 1.65. Further, a total of 312 maize ear leaf samples were analysed for macro- (N, P, K, S, Ca, Mg) and micronutrients (B, Cu, Zn, Mn) and related to their corresponding maize grain yield using the Compositional Nutrient Diagnosis (CND) procedure. This led to the determination of maize nutrient sufficiency ranges that ranked the frequencies of either deficiency or excessive nutrient concentration occurrences across sites. Beforehand, the determined nutrient sufficiency ranges were compared with published references to ensure their relevance. The sufficiency ranges expressed in % for N (2.60–2.90), P (0.26–0.29), K (2.5–2.80), S (0.19–0.22) and Mg (0.20–0.22) were in agreement with the published references but Ca (0.70–0.80 %) deviated by 36 % above the references indicating sufficiency variations in different environments. All the micronutrients expressed in mg kg $^{-1}$ for B (7.8–8.33), Cu (8.86–9.99), Zn (16.39–18.26) and Mn (67.24–74.93) were within the published sufficiency ranges. Despite the application of N and P, results indicated that the two nutrients alongside Ca, Mg, Zn and S had the largest frequencies of being deficient, ranging between 75–100 % across all the sites. Cu, K, B and Mn followed with moderate deficiency frequencies ranging between 50 and 74 %. The occurrence of excess nutrient concentrations was much less frequent, led by Mn ranging between 25 and 49 %. Other nutrients were rarely present in excess with frequency ranges less than 20 %. Not surprisingly, P was never in the excess nutrient category confirming its unrelenting importance for maize production in western Kenya.

Keywords: Deficiency, excess, maize, nutrient imbalances, poor response, sufficiency ranges

Contact Address: Ruth Njoroge, KU Leuven, Dept. of Earth and Environmental Sciences, Kasteelpark Arenberg 20, 3001 Heverlee, Belgium, e-mail: ruth.njoroge@kuleuven.be

Effect of Mineral and Organic Fertilisers on Maize Productivity in an Inland Valley in Uganda

SIMON ALIBU[1], DANIEL NEUHOFF[2], KALIMUTHU SENTHILKUMAR[3], MATHIAS BECKER[4], ULRICH KÖPKE[2]

[1]National Agricultural Research Organisation (NARO), National Crops Resources Research Institute (NaCRRI), Uganda

[2]University of Bonn, Inst. of Organic Agriculture, Germany

[3]Africa Rice Center (AfricaRice), East and Southern Africa, Tanzania

[4]University of Bonn, Inst. Crop Sci. and Res. Conserv. (INRES) - Plant Nutrition, Germany

We carried out field experiments in three hydrological zones along the gradient of an inland valley in Namulonge, Uganda to compare the effects of organic and mineral nitrogen fertilisers on productivity of maize (Longe-10 Hybrid). The maize was sown in December 2014 and 2015 (after the long rainy season) at a plant spacing of 0.45 m by 0.45 m. Two organic N rates equivalent to 60 and 120 kg (N) ha^{-1} season^{-1} using chicken manure and green manure were tested in comparison to equivalent mineral N rates and an N-free control. Plots were arranged in a randomised complete block design with four replications. Maize grain yield, total biomass at physiological maturity and harvest index were measured, and subjected to ANOVA. Total biomass averaged for all treatments in the first season was highest (10.42 t ha^{-1}) in the centre and lowest (4.80 t ha^{-1}) in the fringe zone, while the mid-slope zone produced 5.80 t ha^{-1}. Correspondingly, grain yields were significantly higher in the centre (4.86 t ha^{-1}) than in the middle (2.30 t ha^{-1}) and fringe (1.47 t ha^{-1}). Likewise, maize in the centre had a significantly higher harvest index than in the fringe and middle zones. In contrast, grain yield response of maize to mineral N fertilisation was low in the centre, with a maximum 22 % increase compared with the standard reference. No clear response to mineral nitrogen was found in the fringe zone. Application of green manure (Sesbania rostrata) only tended to increase grain yield in the middle zone, while chicken manure did not affect grain yield. These results suggest that the greatest potential for maize production in the dry season lies in the centre zone of inland valleys, albeit with low resource use efficiency of intensive production systems.

Keywords: Chicken manure, green manure, hydrological zone, wetlands

Contact Address: Simon Alibu, National Agricultural Research Organisation (NARO), National Crops Resources Research Institute (NaCRRI), Namulonge, Kampala, Uganda, e-mail: simoalibu@hotmail.com

ID 832

Analysis of N Use Efficiency of Maize to Optimise N Fertiliser Application under Weed Competition

SAEID SOUFIZADEH[1], MAJID AGHAALIKHANI[2], MOHAMMAD BANNAYAN[3], ESKANDAR ZAND[4], AHMAD M. MANSCHADI[5], GERRIT HOOGENBOOM[6]

[1]*Shahid Beheshti University, Dept. of Agroecology, Environmental Sciences Research Institute, Iran*

[2]*Tarbiat Modares University, Dept. of Agronomy, Iran*

[3]*Ferdowsi University of Mashhad, Dept. of Agronomy, Iran*

[4]*Plant Pests and Diseases Research Institute, Weed Research, Iran*

[5]*University of Natural Resources and Life Sciences (BOKU), Dept. of Crop Sciences, Austria*

[6]*University of Florida, Agricultural and Biological Engineering, United States*

Analysis of nitrogen (N) use efficiency of maize plants may enhance the understanding of the mechanisms governing the N status of maize under weed competition and thus will help with the optimisation of N fertiliser application. The goal of this study was to optimise N fertiliser application rate in maize under weed-free and weed-infested conditions in order to minimise the overuse of N in maize agroecosystems. In this study experiments were conducted in 2008 and 2009 at the experimental field of Tarbiat Modares University, in Iran, in which maize cv. OSSK 602 competed with two different weed species at two densities and under different N fertiliser levels. The experimental levels included N fertiliser rates at 138, 184 and 230 kg N ha^{-1}), two weed species (proso-millet and redroot pigweed), and low and high densities of each weed species. Low and high densities of proso-millet were 7.5 and 37.5 plants m^{-2} while for redroot pigweed they were 5 and 25 plants m^{-2}. Proso-millet was less responsive to the application of N fertiliser compared to the redroot pigweed. Competition with weeds significantly reduced maize grain yield, total biomass and N use efficiency (NUE). At high densities of both proso-millet and redroot pigweed an increase in the N application from 138 and 230 kg N ha^{-1} reduced maize grain yield, N content, and NUE from 44 % to 52 %. It was found that maize was more sensitive to nitrogen uptake efficiency (NUpE; the ratio between N taken up by the crop to the soil N at planting) than nitrogen utilisation efficiency (NUtE; the ratio between grain N content to the total plant N) so that weed competition mainly affected maize NUE through reducing its NUpE component (up to about 43 %). The greater role of NUpE on NUE may suggest a more important role of below-ground competition in weed-infested maize fields compared to above-ground competition.

Keywords: Biomass N, grain N, nitrogen uptake efficiency, nitrogen utilisation efficiency, proso-millet, redroot pigweed

Contact Address: Saeid Soufizadeh, Shahid Beheshti University, Dept. of Agroecology, Environmental Sciences Research Institute, Evin, Tehran, Iran, e-mail: s_soufizadeh@sbu.ac.ir

Nutritive Value and Biomass Production of *Brachiaria humidicola* Hybrids with Divergent Biological Nitrification Inhibition Activity

MARIO CUCHILLO HILARIO[1,2], DANILO MORETA[2], JACOBO ARANGO[2], JOHANNA MAZABEL[2], PAOLA PARDO[2], STIVEN QUINTERO[2], MAURICIO EFREN SOTELO CABRERA[2], MARGARET WORTHINGTON[2], IDUPULAPATI RAO[2], JOHN MILES[2], MICHAEL PETERS[2]

[1]*National Institute of Medical Sciences and Nutrition 'Salvador Zubirán' (INCMNSZ), Animal Nutrition Department, Mexico*

[2]*International Center for Tropical Agriculture (CIAT), Colombia*

Tropical land areas utilised for feed production are under continuous pressure to provide sufficient feed in terms of biomass and nutrient quality. Also, some *Brachiaria humidicola* (Bh) genotypes have been identified with high Biological Nitrification Inhibition (BNI) activity. The BNI trait may reduce the rate of transformation of ammonia into nitrate in soils and could contribute to mitigation of climate change by avoiding the formation of nitrate and later moderating nitrous oxide emission during denitrification. Twelve intraspecific hybrids of Bh with contrasting BNI activity were classified into 1) high (0.58–0.96 mg NO_3 kg^{-1} soil day^{-1}), 2) intermediate (1.27–1.62 mg NO_3 kg^{-1} soil day^{-1})) and low (1.84–2.49 mg NO_3 kg^{-1} soil day^{-1})) activity. Five Bh genotypes from CIAT's forage germplasm collection (CIAT 679, CIAT 26146, CIAT 26149, CIAT 26159, CIAT 16888) were employed as controls. Seventeen plots ($4 \times 4m^2$) with three replications were use to allocate the experimental units. Each single plot was divided into eight subplots (0.5×0.5 m^2). Rising-plate-meter (RPM, 30 cm diameter) was used to measure successively the compressed sward height (CSH) of pasture on each subplot at 0, 7, 14, 21, and 28 days after pasture height homogenisation. Eight RPM-heights were taken on each subplot and were averaged. Biomass was collected at two points below the disc (one sample under and one sample above CSH average) of the RPM to ground level after CSH measurement. Biomass was dried for 48 hours at 60°C and ground (1mm) for further analysis. Near infrared spectroscopy (Foss 6500) was used to calculate crude protein (CP), neutral detergent fiber (NDF), NDF digestibility (NDFd), acid detergent fiber (ADF), and in-vitro dry matter digestibility (IVDMD). Ten percent of the samples were randomly assessed by wet chemistry for NIRS validation. The randomised complete block design was employed for data analysis (SPSS-v20). Bh hybrids with intermediate BNI activity had the largest biomass production (3208 kg DM ha^{-1}) and which differed from that of the hybrids with either high of low BNI activity (2916 or 2800 kg DM ha^{-1}, respectively). In contrast, no differences among the BNI groupings were observed for CP, NDF, ADF, NDFd, or IVDMD. Further evaluations across seasons, years, and locations, are recommended to confirm and extend these findings.

Keywords: BNI, *Brachiaria humidicola*, nitrous oxide, tropical grasses

Contact Address: Mario Cuchillo Hilario, National Institute of Medical Sciences and Nutrition 'Salvador Zubirán' (INCMNSZ), Animal Nutrition Department, Mexico City, Mexico, e-mail: mario.cuchilloh@incmnsz.mx

ID 388

Brachiaria humidicola Grass Reduces Soil Nitrous Oxide Emissions from Bovine Urine Patches under Tropical Conditions

JONATHAN NÚÑEZ[1], RYAN BARNES[2,1], LAURA ARENAS[1], IDUPULAPATI RAO[1], CATALINA TRUJILLO[1], CAROLINA ALVAREZ[3,1], NGONIDZASHE CHIRINDA[1], JACOBO ARANGO[1]

[1]*International Center for Tropical Agriculture (CIAT), Colombia*
[2]*University of California, Dept. of Land, Air and Water Resources, United States of America*
[3]*INTA EEA, Argentina*

The generally high levels of nitrogen (N) in bovine urine result in the formation of soil nitrous oxide (N_2O) emission hotpots when bovine urine is deposited in grazed pastures. High spatial variability in the distribution of urine patches makes mitigation of N_2O emission challenging. Previous studies have reported that the roots of tropical forages such as *Brachiaria humidicola* (Bh) exude organic molecules that can inhibit the activity of soil microbial nitrifiers (biological nitrification inhibition-BNI), thus reducing ammonia oxidation and, consequently, nitrate and N_2O production. We hypothesised that N_2O emissions from soils under forages with BNI capacity are lower than from soils under forage species without BNI capacity. To test this hypothesis, field plots with two forage cultivars, *Brachiaria* Hybrid Mulato (BHM) and Bh 679 which, correspondingly, have low and high BNI capacity, were selected from a long-term field experiment (10 years) at the International Center for Tropical Agriculture in Colombia. Soil nitrification rates and denitrification potential were evaluated through laboratory assays conducted using soils from the selected field plots. Soil N_2O emissions from simulated urine and water patches were monitored using the static chamber technique over a 30 day period. Concurrently, soil variables such as mineral N and moisture were monitored. Results from the laboratory assays show a suppression of both nitrification and denitrification in soils from plots with Bh 679 than those BHM. Cumulative N_2O fluxes were higher from soils under BHM (155 mg N_2O-N per m^2) compared to those under Bh 679 (60 mg N_2O-N per m^2). N_2O emissions were not related to N input. We conclude that tropical forages with BNI capacity can play a key role in mitigating N_2O emissions from bovine urine deposited on grazing pastures.

Keywords: Biological nitrification inhibition, climatic change mitigation, denitrification, nitrification, nitrous oxide, urine patches

Contact Address: Jacobo Arango, International Center for Tropical Agriculture (CIAT), Tropical Forages, A A 6713, NA Cali, Colombia, e-mail: j.arango@cgiar.org

Economic Analysis of Maize Production and Nitrogen Use Efficiency in Rotation with *Brachiaria humidicola*

STEFAN BURKART[1], KAREN ENCISO[1], HANNES KARWAT[2], DANILO MORETA[1], JACOBO ARANGO[1], GEORG CADISCH[2], MICHAEL PETERS[1]

[1] *International Center for Tropical Agriculture (CIAT), Colombia*

[2] *University of Hohenheim, Inst. of Agricultural Sciences in the Tropics (Hans-Ruthenberg-Institute), Germany*

Among the essential macro elements for maize production, nitrogen (N) is the one limiting growth and yield the most. To maintain desired production levels, substantial amounts of N are required, mainly obtained through nitrogen fertiliser, a significant cost driver in maize production (13–18 %). However, much of this fertiliser is lost after nitrification through leaching and denitrification processes. Fertiliser not used by the crop produces considerable environmental damage (e.g. water pollution, emission of greenhouse gases) and generates economic loss to the producers. The International Center for Tropical Agriculture (CIAT), in collaboration with the University of Hohenheim and Corpoica, have conducted research on the phenomenon of biological nitrification inhibition (BNI) present in permanent plots of *Brachiaria humidicola* (Bh) (≥ 10 years established) to quantify the residual effects of BNI on subsequent maize cultivars. This residual effects of BNI result in greater nitrogen use efficiency (NUE) and therefore in higher maize grain yields. The trial was planted at the Research Center Corpoica-La Libertad, located in the eastern Plains of Colombia, during a period of three years (2013–2015). This article aims to evaluate the profitability of maize production on plots previously used for Bh and compares the results to conventional maize production (M). The analysis focused on measuring indicators of technical and economic efficiency with respect to NUE, yields and costs associated with each plot. Subsequently, profitability indicators were defined and a sensitivity analysis was performed to identify changes in yields, prices and expected costs. The results show that maize production on plots previously used for Bh (with residual BNI effect) is more profitable, with yields exceeding the ones obtained on conventional maize plots (no residual BNI effect) by up to 62 %. This is accompanied by an increased technical and economic efficiency in NUE, lower unit costs (75 %) and a superior cost-benefit ratio. However, the results are highly sensitive to variations in expected returns, and to some extent to maize sales prices and increased production costs. In general, crop rotation of *Brachiaria humidicola* and maize is an alternative to improve production efficiency and profitability, resulting from the residual effects of BNI related to Bh.

Keywords: Biological nitrification inhibition, *Brachiaria humidicola*, economic efficiency, improved forages, resource efficiency, rotation systems

Contact Address: Stefan Burkart, International Center for Tropical Agriculture (CIAT), Tropical Forages Program, Km 17 Recta Cali-Palmira, Cali, Colombia, e-mail: s.burkart@cgiar.org

ID 433

Performance of Soybean (*Glycine max* L.) as Influenced by Different Rates and Sources of Phosphorus Fertiliser

AMUDALAT OLANIYAN[1], ENOOBONG UDO[2], AYODEJI AFOLAMI[1]

[1] *University of Ibadan, Dept. of Agronomy, Nigeria*
[2] *International Institute of Tropical Agriculture (IITA), Maize Improvement Programme, Nigeria*

Low yields of soybean in Nigeria are attributed to many factors among which are declining soil fertility and use of low yielding soybean varieties. Phosphorus is a soybean plant growth-limiting nutrient; therefore, application of phosphorus fertiliser at optimum level is essential. *Tithonia diversifolia* and poultry manure have been previously identified as good organic fertiliser sources. Two experiments were carried out in the screen house of the Department of Agronomy, University of Ibadan, Nigeria to estimate the optimum P requirement for soybean and to investigate the response of soybean to different sources of P fertiliser applied at the optimum rate. The treatment in the first experiment were two soybean varieties (TGX 1987–10F and TGX 1987–62F) and single superphosphate (SSP) fertiliser applied at five rates: $0\,kg\,P\,ha^{-1}$, $20\,kg\,P\,ha^{-1}$, $40\,kg\,P\,ha^{-1}$, $60\,kg\,P\,ha^{-1}$ and $80\,kg\,P\,ha^{-1}$. The treatments in the second experiment were: SSP, Tithonia compost (TC), poultry manure (PM), TC+PM, SSP+TC, SSP+PM applied at optimum P rate obtained from Experiment 1 and control. Data were collected on morphological parameters, grain yield and nutrient uptake. The data were subjected to analysis of variance and the significantly different means were separated using least significant difference at 0.05 level of significance. Results showed that TGX1987–62F ($1.96\,Mg\,ha^{-1}$) produced significantly higher grain yield than TGX1987–10F ($1.26\,Mg\,ha^{-1}$). Application of SSP at 40 kg P ha^{-1} produced tallest plants (104.9 cm), highest number of leaves/plant (19.0), number of pods/plant (19.4), and grain yield ($2.28\,Mg\,ha^{-1}$) across the two varieties. Highest K-uptake was observed in plants treated with TC+SSP ($6.1\,mg\,pot^{-1}$) while highest P-uptake was observed with application of SSP ($2.6\,mg\,pot^{-1}$), significantly higher than the control. The combination of *Tithonia* compost and SSP at 40 kg P ha^{-1} produced highest number of flowers per plant (35.6), number of pods/plant (38.7) and grain yield ($3.9\,Mg\,ha^{-1}$). A combination of *Tithonia* compost (an abundant under-utilised weed) and SSP applied at 40 kg P ha^{-1} will increase seed yield of soybean in southwestern Nigeria.

Keywords: Nigeria, phosphorus fertiliser, soybean varieties, SSP, *Tithonia* compost

Contact Address: Enoobong Udo, International Institute of Tropical Agriculture (IITA), Maize Improvement Programme, Idi-ose, Ibadan, Nigeria, e-mail: enoobong_udo@yahoo.com

Strategies of African Indigenous Vegetables to Cope with Phosphorus Deficient Soils

GODFREY NAMBAFU[1], ENOS ONYUKA[1], HOLGER BESSLER[1], NICOLAI HOEPPNER[1], DARIUS O. ANDIKA[2], JOSEPH PATRICK GWEYI-ONYANGO[3], SAMUEL MWONGA[4], CHRISTOF ENGELS[1]

[1] *Humboldt-Universität zu Berlin, Albrecht Daniel Thaer-Institute of Agricultural and Horticultural Sciences (ADTI), Germany*

[2] *Jaramogi Oginga Odinga University of Science and Technology, Dept. of Plant, Animal and Food Sciences, Kenya*

[3] *Kenyatta University, Dept. of Agricultural Science and Technology, Kenya*

[4] *Egerton University, Dept. of Crops, Horticulture and Soils, Kenya*

Food production in smallholder farming systems of sub-Saharan Africa is often constrained by low soil contents of plant-available phosphorus (P). An option to increase food production is cultivation of species with high P efficiency. Plant strategies to improve growth and P acquisition on low P soils include root foraging strategies to improve spatial soil exploitation, P mining strategies to enhance desorption, solubilisation or mineralisation, and improving internal P utilisation efficiency.

The aim of this study was to measure plant responses to low P availability in soil and to determine if there is variation among African indigenous vegetables (AIV) in their ability to use organic phosphate and sparingly soluble P forms.

Six AIV species (Spider plant *Cleome gynandra*, African nightshade *Solanum scabrum*, Amaranthus *Amaranthus cruentus*, Cowpea *Vigna unguiculata*, African kale *Brassica carinata*, Common kale *Brassica oleracea*) were cultivated under controlled conditions in pots on a low P substrate. The substrate was amended with P using four different forms (highly soluble K_2HPO_4, sparingly soluble $FePO_4$ or phosphate rock, phytate). Measurements included biomass and P concentration in shoots and roots, morphological root traits (root length and diameter, root hair density) and substrate characteristics (pH, content of soluble P) after harvest. The AIV species significantly differed in morphological root traits and rhizosphere pH, and in the responses of morphological root traits to different P treatments. For example in average of all P levels rhizosphere pH varied from 3.9 in Amaranthus to 6.0 in African kale. All species were able to use P from phytate as effectively for biomass formation as P from K_2HPO_4. The efficiency for utilisation of sparingly soluble P forms (either $FePO_4$ or rock phosphate) was low in African nightshade and Spider plant, and high in Amaranthus and African kale. Cowpea was efficient in utilisation of P from rock phosphate but not from $FePO_4$.

The data indicate large variation among AIV species in root traits relevant for P acquisition and their ability to use soil P from different sparingly soluble P forms. This information may be used for site-specific recommendation of species best adapted to low P soils.

Keywords: P acquisition, phosphate rock, phytate, rhizosphere pH, root morphology

---

Contact Address: Christof Engels, Humboldt-Universität zu Berlin, Albrecht Daniel Thaer-Institute of Agricultural and Horticultural Sciences (ADTI), Berlin, Germany, e-mail: christof.engels@agrar.hu-berlin.de

ID 831

Effects of Different Sources of N on Pearl Millet Growth and Yield in P-limited Environments of West Africa

FRANCESCA BEGGI, ANDREAS BUERKERT

University of Kassel, Organic Plant Production and Agroecosystems Research in the Tropics and Subtropics, Germany

Pearl millet (*Pennisetum glaucum* L.) is the major food crop in West African Sahel and largely contributes to food security of 50 millions farmers. Its adaptation to soil phosphorus (P) deficiency at early seedling stages is crucial for its final yield. Plant-based strategies, such as long roots, and efficient P fertiliser application are fundamental, being P resources limited. Evidence from pot trials in 2011 indicated that the addition of NH_4^+ to P can stimulate early root growth more than other N sources.

To test this hypothesis in field-like conditions, an innovative experiment was set in Niger, ICRISAT research station, in 2012. Twenty-four lysimeters were cut, rearranged with a longitudinal plexiglass surface and filled with P-deficient soil (Bray P1<5). Millet plants from a genotype known as tolerant to low soil P were grown until yield. Three treatments were applied at sowing: +P, +P + NH_4^+ and +P + NO_3, with 8 repetitions. We measured: root length at 2, 3, 4 and 5 weeks after sowing (WAS), plant growth, final yield, transpiration (twice a week). Roots were hand marked on a plastic removable surface on the plexiglass, scanned and analysed through WinRhizo. Root length correlated with root biomass (r=0.7).The addition of NH_4^+ decreased the flowering time and increased grain yield, while NO_3 increased the vegetative biomass. At early stage, roots in the upper 40 cm soil of treatment 2 were longer than roots in treatment 3 and 1 (at 4 WAS: 129.3 cm, 83.6 cm and 54.3 cm, respectively). Throughout the season, the root system developed more in treatment 3 than in treatment 2 and 1 (40.87 g, 26.4 g and 13.8 g, respectively), mainly due to higher solubility of NO_3. At a given root length at 5 WAS, plants in treatment 2 produced the highest total yield. They transpired more water than plants in treatment 3, despite being smaller, probably because of the higher cost of grain production versus overall biomass. Our results suggest that the choice of N source to add to P can be critical to differential development of reproductive/vegetative organs, probably due to a mechanism during early root growth.

Keywords: Nitrogen, pearl millet, phosphorus, root length

Contact Address: Francesca Beggi, CIM Expert, Bioversity International, Delhi Office, Nasc Complex Pusa Campus, 110012 New Delhi, India, e-mail: f.beggi@cgiar.org

Sesbania rostrata (Bremek and Oberm.) as Biological Nitrogen Fixator for Sustainable Lowland Rice Production

MOUDJAHID AKORÉDÉ WABI[1], KAAT VERZELEN[1], PASCAL HOUNGNANDAN[2], WOUTER VANHOVE[1], GLÈLÈ KAKAÏ ROMAIN LUCAS[3], PATRICK VAN DAMME[1]

[1] *Ghent University, Dept. of Plant Production, Belgium*

[2] *University of Abomey-Calavi, Laboratory of Soil Microbiology and Microbial Ecology, Benin*

[3] *University Abomey-Calavi, Laboratory of Applied Ecology, Benin*

Nitrogen plays a crucial role in rice cultivation. It is usually supplied as chemical fertiliser (urea). However, rice monocropping without fallow and loss of urea-N through leaching often lead to decreased soil fertility, decline in soil organic matter and environmental pollution. As a result, rice yield decreases and this is predicted to worsen by climate change. This may affect food security especially in view of the continuing rise in human populations, particularly in sub-Sahara Africa. New and alternative nitrogen resources should be explored to sustainably supply rice crop needs and to reduce the adverse environmental effects of current urea-N use in rice.

Biological Nitrogen Fixation (BNF) by legumes is a promising and friendly mechanism that can be used to convert atmospheric di-nitrogen into valuable substances such as fertilisers for agriculture. As such, BNF could contribute to sustainable traditional rice production with its current low productivity figures. In this respect, *Sesbania rostrata*, which is native to Africa, is one of the best nitrogen-fixating plant species because of its nodulation on both stem and roots, fast growth, high nitrogen-fixation rates and tolerance of waterlogged soils. *S. rostrata* is often used as green manure between rice crops in lowland. The plant, when plowed under at 34–42 days after sowing, can add 90 to 150 kg N ha^{-1} and 7.4 t ha^{-1} of biomass to the soil. It has been found that *S. rostrata* supplied as green manure can double rice yields after one rice cultivation cycle. Findings further reveal a 35 % residual effect of the same green manure application on grain yield in a second rice cultivation cycle. It may thus easily be the cheapest alternative nitrogen source to smallholder farmers. This paper reviews the potential and challenges of using its green manure to sustain lowland rice system in developing countries.

Keywords: Agro-ecology, climatic change, farming systems, green manure, smallholder farmers' income, soil fertility

Contact Address: Patrick van Damme, Ghent University, Dept. of Plant Production - Lab. for Tropical Agronomy, Coupure links 653, 9000 Ghent, Belgium, e-mail: patrick.vandamme@ugent.be

Crop diversity and plant breeding

Tropical Forage Genetic Resources – A Global Strategy for Conservation and Utilisation

Bruce Pengelly[1], Brigitte L. Maass[2], Charlotte E. Lusty[3]

[1]*Pengelly Consultancy, Australia*
[2]*Georg-August-Universität Göttingen, Crop Sciences, Germany*
[3]*Global Crop Diversity Trust, Germany*

Tropical and sub-tropical forages (TSTF) are critically important for livestock feed and environmental benefits in extensive and intensive livestock systems of developed and developing countries. There has been focussed collection and conservation of forage genetic resources (GR), and research on their diversity, adaptation and use for the past 60 years. That work through the late 20th century laid the foundations for the impacts TSTF have had, and continue to have. However since 1995, there has been a global scale reduction in forage science investment, new knowledge and capability, which has strangely coincided with the rapid growth in demand for livestock products globally. The decline in capacity and knowledge must be urgently reversed if the tropical systems are to benefit from the best genetic material and knowledge. Relying on 20th century knowledge and capability is unsustainable, and it ensures that the livestock systems of rural communities in developing countries cannot reach their potential regarding efficiency and productivity. In 2015, the Global Crop Diversity Trust initiated the development of a strategy to overcome some of the major barriers to TSTF conservation, research and utilisation. That strategy was developed with input from across the TSTF-GR community and aims to build a strong, functional network of national, regional and international GR centres, introducing efficiencies, and enabling genebanks to improve their role as knowledge managers and advisors for research and development programs. The main objectives are:

1. Rebuilding the community of TSTF genebanks and genebank users to develop closer collaboration and trust;
2. Ensuring more efficient and rationalized conservation within and among genebanks;
3. Actively supporting utilisation by anticipating germplasm needs and responding to users' requests for information and seeds.

That strategy, now in the early stages of implementation, depends on the buy-in and cooperation of international and national genebanks to make changes in management and use, and the long-term engagement of partner countries and the donor community. Without this commitment, 60 years of knowledge and expertise will likely have to be rebuilt and generations of farmers and others will not realise the production and environmental benefits of well-adapted and sustainably managed improved forages.

Keywords: Conservation, forage utilisation, genetic resources, strategy

Contact Address: Brigitte L. Maass, Georg-August-Universität Göttingen, Crop Sciences, Grisebach-str. 6, 37077 Göttingen, Germany, e-mail: Brigitte.Maass@yahoo.com

ID 616

Genetic Diversity of *Parkia biglobosa* (African Locust Bean) and its Implications for Conservation Strategies

DJINGDIA LOMPO[1], HEINO KONRAD[2], JÉROME DUMINIL[3], HANNES GAISBERGER[3], BARBARA VINCETI[3], MOUSSA OUEDRAOGO[1], THOMAS GEBUREK[2]

[1] *National Tree Seed Center, Burkina Faso*
[2] *Federal Research and Training Center for Forests, Natural Hazards and Landscape, Dept. of Forest Genetics, Austria*
[3] *Bioversity International, Italy*

Parkia biglobosa is an African Savannah tree with a wide range from Senegal to Uganda between the latitudes 5° and 15° in the North of equator. It is well-known as an agroforestry tree but also as a medicinal and food tree. Seeds, barks, roots, leaves and flowers are used to treat more than 80 diseases and complaints while fermented seeds and pulp of fruits have highly nutritional and commercial values.

Understanding the level and distribution of genetic diversity of a widespread species such *P. biglobosa* is crucial for its conservation and sustainable utilisation. The genetic diversity and population structure were investigated using height nuclear microsatellites developed for the species. The sampling included 84 populations from twelve countries in West and Central Africa. The height microsatellite loci were highly polymorphic and did not show evidence of null alleles. A total of 217 alleles were revealed among the 1,610 genotypes of *P. biglobosa*. The number of alleles per locus was ranged from 17 to 50 with an average of 27 alleles per locus. The estimates of genetic diversity were moderate for the populations of extreme West Africa and Central Africa and were high to populations in the centre of West Africa. Individual-based assignment using admixture model with correlated allele frequencies revealed strong genetically structured populations across *P. biglobosa* range in West and Central Africa. The clustering analysis showed five most plausible subpopulations for the biogeographic study in West and Central Africa. Analysis of molecular variance partitioned the molecular variation 9.10% among groups, 2.71% among populations within groups and 88.19% within populations. Overall, the genetic differentiation among populations was moderate ($FST=0.118$; $P < 0.001$). In regard to the distribution of intraspecific diversity, we also discussed the implications for conservation and sustainable use of the species.

Keywords: Agroforestry, conservation, genetic diversity, *Parkia biglobosa*

Contact Address: Djingdia Lompo, National Tree Seed Center, Ouagadougou, Burkina Faso, e-mail: ldjingdia@gmail.com

Participatory Multi-Environmental Trials (MET) Identified Promising Durum Wheat Landraces in Northern Ethiopia

DEJENE KASSAHUN MENGISTU[1], AFEWORK Y. KIROS[1], JEMAL N. MOHAMMED[1], CARLO FADDA[2]

[1]Mekelle University, Dept. of Dryland Crop and Horticultural Sciences, Ethiopia

[2]Bioversity International, Agrobiodiversity and Ecosystem Services Programme, Kenya

Participation of farmers in research process from early stage has been gaining ground in breeding research. Participant farmers can provide very valuable scientific evaluation of genotypes that can be used for effective discrimination of useful varieties easily adopted by similar farmers. Participatory varietal selection (PVS) is a powerful tool in identifying crops varieties with high acceptance probability in marginal environments because participant farmers evaluate the genotypes not only from yield perspective but also from stress tolerance perspective. Here we present a participatory MET conducted in four locations to select durum wheat landraces for larger scale production in the areas. In all four locations, 36 genotypes (31 landraces plus 5 improved varieties) were tested for two cropping seasons and evaluated by both researchers and farmers groups. In each location, a total of 30 farmers (15 female and 15 male) and five breeders critically evaluated the each variety for earliness, spike quality, drought tolerance and overall performance on scale of 1 to 5, traits defined by the farmers themselves. 1 stands for bad and 5 for excellent performance. Researchers have collected data for three phenological traits and seven agronomic traits and analysis was conducted to see preference matching between researcher data and farmers score data.

The results show clearly that farmers are capable to discriminate genotypes reasonably though their discrimination power varies from location to location. The discrimination by breeders was consistent across locations. Very high significant ($p < 0.01$) association was established between farmers visual score and researchers collected grain yield data and days to maturity in all locations with some exceptions for maturity date. Genotypes ranking for grain yield based on researchers collected data and farmer scoring matched about 80 % in the 10 top performing genotypes.

In conclusion:

• Participatory varietal selection could bridge the problem of variety adoption by complementing farmers and breeders preferences.

• Farmers are keen in evaluating genotypes and have reasons for rejecting or accepting varieties.

• There was good agreement between farmers score and objectively collected data in identifying the 10 top performing genotypes.

Participatory MET could be a reliable approach for fast technology development and dissemination as it considers the involvement of end users from the very beginning.

Keywords: Ethiopia, landraces, multi-location trial, participatory, promising

Contact Address: Dejene Kassahun Mengistu, Mekelle University, Dept. of Dryland Crop and Horticultural Sciences, Main campus, airport road, 251 Mekelle, Ethiopia, e-mail: dejenekmh@gmail.com

Horticultural Crops Diversity and Cropping in the Smallholders Home Gardens in the Transitional Area of Yayu Coffee Forest Biosphere Reserve, Ethiopia

EDOSSA ETISSA, TADESSE WELDEMARIAM, AKALU TESHOME, TECHANE GONFA ABEBIE

Environment and Coffee Forest Forum (ECFF), Ethiopia

Yayu Biosphere Reserve (YBR) is part of the Eastern Afromontane Biodiversity hot/-spot located in Illu-Adbabor, Ethiopia. This reserve is a centre of coffee genetic resources and the origin of many other indigenous horticultural crops. The YBR has three parts with the central Core, followed by Buffer and the external Transitional area. The Transitional area covering 70.5 % of the YBR is dominated by smallholders with different land-use systems. This smallholders grow coffee, horticultural crops and other crops together. Our survey was conducted in home gardens to identify diversity and crop combinations of horticultural crops cultivation and utilisation. Multistage sampling was used, first selection of two districts- Yayu and Hurumu, followed by selection of two villages in each district to arrive at a total of 40 sample gardens bordering the YBR. A detailed data on the crops diversity, combinations, utilisation and cropping systems were collected. The survey results also showed that many horticultural crops grow in all home gardens and a total of economically 25 fruit, 20 vegetable, 15 root and tuber crops, nearly 25 spices, herbs and oil bearing plants, 3 stimulants and many hundreds of African indigenous fruits, vegetables, root and tuber, spices and herbs were recorded in the sample home gardens. This clearly showed that food source diversification and smallholder income generation are an untapped potential that could substantially contribute to nutrition security including low livelihood status of almost all smallholders in the area. Diversity of cropping systems such as double cropping, inter cropping, multistory cropping and others were observed in most gardens. However, all farmers replied that there are no improved technologies for horticultural crop production. Almost all farmers use local varieties with unimproved management practices obtaining very low yields and quality. Thus research should give attention on adding value to potential crops and the home garden cropping system in the area should also be further investigated with the identification of smallholder development interventions so that social development in parallel with resource conservation can be achieved.

Keywords: Biosphere, crop diversity, home gardens, smallholder farmers

Contact Address: Edossa Etissa, Environment and Coffee Forest Forum (ECFF), Addis Abeba, Ethiopia, e-mail: edossa.etissa@gmail.com

Agrobiodiversity: The Key to Food Security, Adaptation to Climate Change and Resilience

FRIEDERIKE KRAEMER, ALBERTO CAMACHO

GIZ, Sustainable Agriculture, Germany

In many tropical regions of the world people depend of what nature can provide: Food, medicine, fodder for their animals as well as construction and burning material. At the same time there is an increasing pressure on natural resources by a growing population and changing consumption patterns. Agrobiodiversity is the outcome of the interactions between genetic resources, the environment and the management systems and practices used by farmers and herders. It has developed over millennia, as a result of both natural selection and human interventions. The conservation and sustainable use of agrobiodiversity is essential for the survival of humankind. Besides its supporting role in risk-management for smallholder farmers in developing countries by assuring their survival and livelihood, agrobiodiversity holds important keys for the future adaptation of agriculture to a changing environment. Greater genetic diversity contributes to reducing climatic and disease-related risks and increases resilience.

However, in the last few decades agrobiodiversity has decreased at an alarming rate and these losses are still increasing rapidly, especially in developing countries where agricultural biological diversity is often very rich. The extinction of traditionally cultivated crop species and varieties as well as local animal breeds has many causes. Essential approaches in slowing down the present rate of loss of agrobiodiversity are the active involvement of the rural population in *in situ* (on farm) conservation, considering the vital role of women, smallholders and pastoralists in the conservation process, traditional knowledge and local innovation.

Therefore GIZ with its partners is working with integrated, mulit-sectoral and multi-level approaches, ranging from village interventions and capacity-building to providing policy advice and mainstreaming agrobiodiversity at local, national and international levels.

Keywords: Agrobiodiversity, developing countries, food security, genetic resources, German development cooperation, resilience, smallholder farmers, sustainable agriculture

Contact Address: Friederike Kraemer, GIZ, Sustainable Agriculture, Dag-Hammarskjöld-Weg 1-5, 65760 Eschborn, Germany, e-mail: friederike.kraemer@giz.de

ID 404

Peru, Ten Years Later: Medicinal Plant Species from Piura

ISABEL MADALENO

The University of Lisbon, National Museum of Natural History and Science, Portugal

The world has scarcer natural resources as time goes by. Humans are by far the most demanding species on earth, in competition for food, health and shelter with the other living beings. Therefore, women and men are addressing the scarcity of plant species in their environment that results from excessive and uncontrolled exploration of our forests and bushlands. Peru is one of the most biodiverse countries in South America, integrating altogether extensive Amazon rainforest areas, Andean terraced farming lands, and coastal arid and semi-arid urbanised territories. In 2006, at the service of the Tropical Research Institute of Lisbon, we have conducted a survey to the markets and fairs of Lima, looking for plants used for therapeutic purposes. We collected sixty different species then, mostly native, some endemic. The standing curiosity was that chamomile, a European herb, was the most consumed plant, a mild sedative. Ten years later, we decided to go back to Peru, in order to conduct a similar sample in another littoral and dry environment, using the same methodology. Results show that chamomile is again the preferred species, even though native plants continue to be dominant in consumption, most of them collected in Andean, Amazon or semi-arid tropical environments. A total of 150 plants were collected in this survey, 99 of which have medicinal uses. This finding demonstrates that in ten years there is increase in natural remedies consumption in Peru. About 49 species encountered in Piura, the northern city investigated, coincide with the ones collected in Lima, ten years ago. Current research registered the existence of an international project focusing the reforestation of local semi-arid lands using a native tree, algarrobo, aimed at improving research, learning processes and fair use of this cherished resource, in cooperation between European institutions and Peru, meaning, between the North and the South. The seed is antioxidant and anti-anemic, which feeds a good number of local businesses that make oil, bread, cookies, algarrobina syrup, and powdered algarrobo (a coffee alternative). Another Piura project, supported by the United Nations and the regional government, replants ceibos, palo santo, guayacán and hualtaco, in mountainous environments.

Keywords: Algarrobo, biodiversity, evolution, medicinal, Peru, Piura, solutions

Contact Address: Isabel Madaleno, The University of Lisbon, National Museum of Natural History and Science, Rua Andrade, 8-2ºE, 1170-015 Lisbon, Portugal, e-mail: isabel-madaleno@museus.ulisboa.pt

Marker-Assisted Selection of Disease and Pest Resistant Mungbean Lines Using Cel-I Genotyping

JO-YI YEN[1], THU GIANG BUI[2], ROLAND SCHAFLEITNER[1], CHEN-YU LIN[1], SHU-MEI HUANG[1], LONG-FANG CHEN[3], RAMAKRISHNAN NAIR[1]

[1]*AVRDC - The World Vegetable Center, Taiwan*

[2]*Plant Resources Center, Agro-Biodervisity Division, Vietnam*

[3]*Academia Sinica, Insitute of Plant and Microbial Biology, Taiwan*

Mungbean (*Vigna radiata*) is cultivated on about 6 million hectares worldwide. Short duration varieties are highly attractive as a rotation crop in cereal farming systems in South and Southeast Asia. Mungbean is consumed as grains or sprouts, and the green pods are eaten as a vegetable; the grains are processed into a variety of products such as noodles, sweets or drinks. Major constraints for mungbean yield and profitability are diseases caused by Mungbean yellow mosaic virus (MYMV) and damage from bruchid beetles (*Callosobruchus* sp.), a storage pest. Quantitative trait loci analyses in populations segregating for Mungbean yellow mosaic virus and bruchid resistance have led to the identification of markers linked with resistance genes. Single nucleotide polymorphic (SNP) markers mapping to chromosomes 3, 4 and 5 showed strong association with bruchid resistance, while markers on chromosomes 2, 5, 7, 9 and 10 were found associated with MYMV resistance. Selection based on these markers facilitates breeding of disease- and pest-resistant varieties. However, genotyping SNP markers in the absence of specialised equipment requires their conversion into polymerase chain reaction (PCR)-based markers. Often, SNP markers are converted to cleaved amplified polymorphic markers (CAPS) by including a restriction enzyme digestion step specific for the SNP base. Alternatively, tetra markers can be developed that use two allele-specific primers in addition to locus-specific PCR primers. Efficient conversion of SNP markers to PCR markers depends on the sequence context; not all SNPs can be successfully transformed into CAPS or tetra markers. To overcome this limitation, we have adopted a CEL-I nuclease-based SNP genotyping method, which detects SNPs independent of the sequence context at low cost. CEL-I nuclease can be easily purified from fresh celery. It cuts the DNA double strand at single-stranded mismatch sites and is used in mutation detection. We have shown that this nuclease can also be applied for SNP detection. The method has been successfully tested for genotyping mungbean breeding lines for presence and absence of MYMV and bruchid resistance alleles. The technique requires only very simple equipment and therefore is well suited for marker-assisted selection in breeding programs that lack access to sophisticated laboratories.

Keywords: Marker-assistant selection, mungbean, SNP genotyping

---

Contact Address: Jo-Yi Yen, AVRDC - The World Vegetable Center, 60 Yi Min Liao Shanhua, 74151 Tainan, Taiwan, e-mail: joyce.yen@worldveg.org

ID 516

Genetic and Genomic Resources for Amaranth Breeding to Improve Income and Nutrition of Resource-Poor Farmers

ROLAND SCHAFLEITNER[1], HOA THI LE[2], RAY-YU YANG[1], YUN-YIN HSIAO[1], YEN-WEI WANG[1], ANDREAS GRAMZOW[3], FEKADU DINSSA[3]

[1] AVRDC - The World Vegetable Center, Biotechnology and Molecular Breeding, Taiwan

[2] Plant Resources Center, Vietnam

[3] AVRDC - The World Vegetable Center, Eastern and Southern Africa Regional Office, Tanzania

Amaranthus species are used as grain and vegetable crops. As a C4 plant, amaranth is more tolerant to heat and drought than many other vegetables. The extraordinary nutritional properties of the plant – the seed and leaf protein of amaranth has a composition comparable to milk protein – make it a valuable addition to human diets, particularly in countries where the population has limited access to animal protein sources. Production of this high-value crop can increase the income and improve the livelihoods of resource-poor smallholder farmers. The broader use of amaranth is constrained by the lack of improved cultivars combining disease resistance with high market and eating quality. Little is known about the breeding potential and sustainable use of different *Amaranthus* species. AVRDC–The World Vegetable Center holds a diverse collection of 800 amaranth accessions and has started to mine this collection for genotypes with farmer- and consumer-desired traits for breeding. The most important traits sought are abiotic stress tolerance, disease and pest resistance, high nutrient and low antinutrient concentrations. Selected genotypes serve as founder lines for a multi-parent advanced generation intercross (MAGIC) population of genotypes displaying new trait combinations. The MAGIC population is an ideal genetic resource for research and breeding, with the final aim of developing new improved cultivars. In parallel, molecular markers for germplasm diversity analysis and for monitoring amaranth crosses have been developed. Rapid wilting of harvested shoots is a major obstacle for marketing vegetable amaranth. Tetraploid genotypes of this otherwise diploid crop have been generated and individuals with waxy leaves have been selected. Agronomic and nutritional properties as well as eating quality of slow wilting polyploid lines are currently being analysed and will be presented. This amaranth improvement initiative will accelerate variety development. Complementary research targeting variety uptake, marketing and consumption is currently planned with partners from developing countries in Africa. The combination of germplasm enhancement and breeding with nutritional and socioeconomic research to increase marketing and consumption of amaranth will maximise the potential of this crop for mitigating poverty and malnutrition.

Keywords: Amaranthus, genetic resources, nutrition, vegetable

Contact Address: Roland Schafleitner, AVRDC - The World Vegetable Center, Biotechnology and Molecular Breeding, Tainan, Taiwan, e-mail: roland.schafleitner@worldveg.org

Assessment of New Yacon (*Smallanthus sonchifolius*) Genotypes Obtained via Indirect Somatic Embryogenesis

STACY HAMMOND, IVA VIEHMANNOVÁ, PETRA HLÁSNÁ ČEPKOVÁ, DUONG HANG

Czech University of Life Sciences Prague, Fac. of Tropical AgriSciences, Dept. of Crop Sciences and Agroforestry, Czech Republic

Yacon [*Smallanthus sonchifolius* (Poepp. and Endl.) Robinson] is a perennial root crop belonging to the *Asteraceae* family, and originating in the Andean regions. It is cultivated for its edible roots that contain fructooligosaccharides (FOS) of inulin type with low caloric value. The aim of this study was to evaluate morphologically and chemically four new yacon genotypes, obtained via indirect somatic embryogenesis within a previous research carried out by Viehmannova et al. (2014). These new somaclones were classified as B8, E1, E9 and F5, and were obtained from an octoploid plant classified as ECU 41, which was also used as the control plant in our study. Five plants from each genotype were transferred *ex vitro*. After acclimation of plants in the greenhouse, the plants were planted to the trial plots. At the end of the vegetation, plant height, number of nodes, tuberous root production, weight of rhizomes and the content of fructooligosaccharides were evaluated. Significant differences among genotypes were found for some morphological characteristics and FOS content in tuberous roots. Overall, the most promising results provided genotypes E1 and F5 producing plants comparably high as control, with similar number of nodes and yields, however with significantly higher FOS content in tuberous roots. On the contrary, genotypes B8 and E9 provided in most characteristics the lowest values of all studied genotypes. Surprisingly, all the new genotypes produced rhizomes with higher weight than the control plant. Based on these results can be concluded that genotypes E1 and F5 demonstrated promising improvements when compared to the control plant and they might be used for further breeding of yacon. Moreover, mass production of new somaclones followed by thorough selection might represent an effective tool for breeding of yacon.

Keywords: Fructooligosaccharides, plant morphology, regenerants, somaclonal variation

Contact Address: Stacy Hammond, Czech University of Life Sciences Prague, Fac. of Tropical Agri-Sciences, Dept. of Crop Sciences and Agroforestry, Kamycka 129, 165 21 Prague 6, Czech Republic, e-mail: hammondstacy9@gmail.com

ID 796

Morphological Diversity and Performance of *Cleome gynandra* (L.) Briq. an African Leafy Vegetable Germplasm Collection

EMMANUEL OMONDI[1], THOMAS DEBENER[2], MARCUS LINDE[2], MARY ABUKUTSA-ONYANGO[3], FEKADU DINSSA[4], TRAUD WINKELMANN[1]

[1] *Leibniz Universität Hannover, Woody Plant and Propagation Physiology, Germany*
[2] *Leibniz Universität Hannover, Inst. for Plant Genetics, Molecular Plant Breeding, Germany*
[3] *Jomo Kenyatta University of Agriculture and Technology (JKUAT), Dept. of Horticulture, Kenya*
[4] *AVRDC - The World Vegetable Center, Vegetable Breeding, Tanzania*

Cleome gynandra L., known by the common names spider plant or cat's whiskers is among other African leafy vegetables making a huge nutritional contribution to daily diets in many sub-Saharan Africa countries. Market demand for the vegetable is on the rise. However, its production is still based on low yielding farmers' cultivars. This is due to little research attention on the crop especially until very recently, hence scarce information regarding the extent of phenotypic variation within and among populations to enable genetic improvement programmes. This study, therefore, assessed the level of genetic diversity of the crop using 30 accessions obtained from six African countries based on phenotypic markers under field conditions in Jomo Kenyatta University of Agriculture and Technology in Kenya between October 2015 and February 2016. A randomised complete block design was used with four replications. The accessions were characterised for 24 variables – eight qualitative and 16 quantitative traits. These included stem, leaf and flower characteristics, plant height, primary branch number, internodes number, number of leaflets per leaf, fresh and dry stem mass, fresh and dry leaf mass, days to germination, days to flowering, days to silique formation, silique weight and number of seeds per silique. There were significant differences ($p = 0.05$) among the accessions from the same country and also from different countries different locations in all the traits measured except for silique weight, and four main morphotypes were identified. Phenotypic variability was also observed within and among accessions. Significant correlations were found for some traits enabling the reduction of scored parameters in future trials. The hierarchical cluster analysis mainly revealed tendency of grouping of accessions from the same country with some accessions from different countries mixing. In view of the variations in the traits of accessions from different countries and also within accessions, these accessions could be used for future breeding and conservation programmes.

Keywords: Accessions, *Cleome gynandra*, genetic diversity, phenotypic variation

Contact Address: Emmanuel Omondi, Leibniz Universität Hannover, Woody Plant and Propagation Physiology, Herrenhaeuser Str. 2, 30419 Hannover, Germany, e-mail: eomondi2008@gmail.com

High-Density Molecular Characterisation and Association Mapping in Ethiopian Durum Wheat Landraces Reveals High Diversity and Potential for Wheat Breeding

Dejene Kassahun Mengistu[1], Yosef Gebrehawaryat Kidane[2], Marcello Catellani[2], Elisabetta Frascaroli[3], Carlo Fadda[4], Mario Enrico Pè[2], Matteo Dell'Acqua[2]

[1] Mekelle University, Dept. of Dryland Crop and Horticultural Sciences, Ethiopia

[2] Sant'Anna School of Advanced Study, Life Science, Italy

[3] University of Bologna, Agrarian Science, Italy

[4] Bioversity International, Agrobiodiversity and Ecosystem Services Programme, Kenya

Durum wheat (*Triticum turgidum* subsp. *durum*) improvement and adaptation to emerging environmental and climatic threats is hampered by the limited amount of allelic variation included in its elite breeding pool. It is therefore a priority to identify adaptive traits by exploring germplasm from different parts of the world, particularly centres of origin or diversity. Here we report the extensive molecular and phenotypic characterisation of hundreds of Ethiopian durum wheat landraces and improved lines, with the underlying assumption that new allelic diversity will provide novel loci to international wheat breeding through quantitative trait loci (QTL) mapping. We score 30,155 single nucleotide polymorphisms and use them to survey the structure and molecular diversity available in the panel. We report the uniqueness of Ethiopian germplasm using a siding collection of Mediterranean durum wheat accessions. We phenotype the Ethiopian panel for ten agronomic traits in two highly diversified Ethiopian environments for two consecutive years, and use this information to conduct a genome wide association study. We identify several loci underpinning agronomic traits of interest, both confirming loci already reported and describing new promising genomic regions. These loci may be efficiently targeted with molecular markers already available to conduct marker assisted selection in Ethiopian and international wheat. We show that Ethiopian durum wheat represents an important and mostly unexplored source of durum wheat diversity. We propose this panel as a novel resource for accumulating QTL mapping experiments on the superior diversity of Ethiopian durum wheat, providing the initial step for a quantitative, methodical exploitation of untapped diversity in producing a better wheat.

Keywords: Association mapping, durum wheat, Ethiopia, QTL

Contact Address: Matteo Dell'Acqua, S. Anna School of Advanced Studies, Life Science, Piazza Martiri della Liberta', 56127 Pisa, Italy, e-mail: m.dellacqua@sssup.it

Which Wheat for Smallholder Ethiopian Farmers? Joining Traditional Knowledge with Metric Phenotypes

CHIARA MANCINI[1], YOSEF GEBREHAWARYAT KIDANE[1], DEJENE KASSAHUN MENGISTU[2], MARIO ENRICO PÈ[1], CARLO FADDA[3], MATTEO DELL'ACQUA[1]

[1] Sant'Anna School of Advanced Studies, Life Science, Italy
[2] Mekelle University, Dept. of Dryland Crop and Horticultural Sciences, Ethiopia
[3] Bioversity International, Agrobiodiversity and Ecosystem Services Programme, Kenya

Africa hosts approximately 33 million smallholder farms, which account for 80 % of the continent's farming system. Subsistence farming systems face highly variable climatic conditions that threaten locally-adapted, low-input agriculture. For the near future, they are among the most seriously affected by changing climatic conditions, posing additional risks to these systems. The benefits of modern breeding benefits may fail to reach small farming communities when broadly adapted material does not address specific local requirements. To date, participatory variety selection has only scratched the surface of the exploitability of farmers' knowledge in breeding. Yet, considering that over 80 % of the farmers receive seeds from informal systems, making sure that well adapted material is available in production systems, seems to be a reasonable solution to quickly affect a large populations. Ethiopia is one of the most populous countries in Africa, with more than 96 million inhabitants, 80 % of whom are engaged in small-scale agriculture, and often subsistence farming. We involved 60 smallholder farmers in two locations in Ethiopia to evaluate traits of their interest in 400 wheat accessions, producing 230,400 data points. We couple this information with metric measurements of 10 agronomic traits, breaking down farmers' preferences on quantitative phenotypes. We found that the relative importance of wheat traits is gender- and locality- dependent, and produced a ranking of the 400 varieties identifying the combination of traits most desired by farmers. The study scale and methods lead to a better understanding of smallholder farmer needs, broadening the discussion for the future of local, sustainable breeding efforts accommodating farmers' knowledge.

Keywords: Climate change, decentralised breeding, participatory variety selection, traditional knowledge

---

Contact Address: Carlo Fadda, Bioversity International, Agrobiodiversity and Ecosystem Services Programme, Nairobi, Kenya, e-mail: c.fadda@cgiar.org

Genome Wide Association Studies for Exploring Salt Tolerance in Barley

Oscar Nnaemeka Obidiegwu[1], Rajiv Sharma[2], Benjamin Kilian[2], Willmar L. Leiser[3], Folkard Asch[1]

[1] *University of Hohenheim, Inst. of Agricultural Sciences in the Tropics (Hans-Ruthenberg-Institute), Germany*

[2] *Leibniz-institute of Plant Genetics and Crop Plant Research (IPK), Genome Diversity, Germany*

[3] *University of Hohenheim, Inst. of Plant Breeding, Seed Sciences and Population Genetics, Germany*

Salt stress poses an increasing threat to barley production. Salt is taken up passively and distributed within the crop via its transpiration stream. Thus uptake of salt is directly related to stomatal responses to vapour pressure deficit (VPD) perceived as atmospheric drought signal. Due to the variability in the timing and severity of salt stress in addition to less reliable seasonal patterns associated with climate change, salinity effects on the crop may increase at several development stages of the crop. Salt tolerance is a complex trait characterised by interactions between genes and their environment. Consequently genotypes grown in varying VPD environment tend to respond differently to salt stress. Hence identifying patterns of polymorphism in the genome that are suggestive of the effect of the risk enhancing or protective alleles has been a major challenge in the quest to develop salt tolerant crop varieties. This research aims at understanding the genetic basis for genotypic adaptation in barley to combinations of salt and VPD stress at different crop development stages. A diverse set of 216 spring barley accessions of worldwide origin (constituting of six row and two row spike morphology types) were screened at emergence and early seedling stage at 250 mM NaCl concentrations and control. Subsequently, these genotypes were grown on hydroponics within a phenotyping platform and were exposed to varying VPD levels (0.73 and 1.85 kpa) in addition to salt level of 200 mM NaCl. Using genome wide association studies (GWAS) employing 9K SNP markers (iSelect assay), we explore the genetic variation for salt tolerance in barley for traits such as seed germination rate, mobilisation efficiency of endosperm reserves, biomass accumulation and partitioning, tiller number, leaf area and leaf ion balance (Na^+, K+) for the aforementioned stress combination. We observed broad genetic variation for salt stress tolerance. Relative responses due to salt and VPD stresses will be presented and the potentials for efficient screening for salt tolerance will be discussed. Findings on QTLs would be validated with previous research and reported.

Keywords: Association mapping, *Hordeum vulgare*, QTL, salt tolerance, SNP

Contact Address: Oscar Nnaemeka Obidiegwu, University of Hohenheim, Inst. of Agricultural Sciences in the Tropics (Hans-Ruthenberg-Institute), Garbenstr. 13, 70599 Stuttgart, Germany, e-mail: oscaro@uni-hohenheim.de

ID 1023

Advance in Grain Legumes Genetic Transformation: The Case of GM Pea and Cowpea

ALEMAYEHU TERESSA NEGAWO[1], FATHI HASSAN[2], EDGAR MAISS[3], HANS-JÖRG JACOBSEN[2]

[1]*International Livestock Research Institute (ILRI), Forage Diversity, Ethiopia*
[2]*Leibniz Universität Hannover, Inst. of Plant Genetics, Germany*
[3]*Leibniz Universität Hannover, Inst. of Plant Diseases and Plant Protection, Germany*

Grain legumes are socio-economically important crops playing a substantial role in providing dietary protein for millions of households in the world. As multipurpose crops, they are used for different purposes such as food and feed. They also fix atmospheric nitrogen contributing to the sustainability of farming system by enriching soil fertility and maintaining the productivity of agricultural land. However, different production factors, such as insect pests and diseases, have limited the productivity of grain legumes both in field and during the storage and are impacting their contribution to nutrition security and poverty reduction. Furthermore, in the current trend of climate change, there is an increasing pressure on plant breeders to develop climate-smart varieties of crops with multiple traits against the different production factors. In order to enhance the economic and social contribution of grain legumes, genetic transformation approaches have been used to develop transgenic lines with new traits such as resistance to insects and diseases as well as tolerance to drought. In this paper, the experience and result of pea and cowpea Agrobacterium-mediated transformation will be presented. Special emphasis will be given to the success and challenges of transgenic insect resistance and its importance in these two important grain legumes. Based on insect bioassay tests, the level of insect resistance in some of the transgenic lines will be presented against that of none transgenic lines. Finally, recommendation will also be discussed for future genetic transformation to develop climate-smart variety of transgenic grain legumes.

Keywords: Agrobacterium, cowpea, genetic transformation, grain legume, pea, transgenic

Contact Address: Alemayehu Teressa Negawo, International Livestock Research Institute (ILRI), Forage Diversity, Box 5689 Addis Ababa, Ethiopia, e-mail: alemayehu_teressa@yahoo.com

Quantitative Genetic Variation of Autofertility in Faba Bean (*Vicia faba* L.)

WINDA PUSPITASARI, WOLFGANG LINK

Georg-August Universität Göttingen, Department of Crop Sciences, Germany

Faba bean, a grain legume, is an important crop which provides rich protein nutrition for human and animal. The reproductive mode of faba bean is a partially allogamous, which means both self- and cross-fertilisation occur. However, faba bean has a constraint in potential yield due to lack of autofertility combined with lack of pollinators. Autofertility is the ability of a plant to self-fertilise without pollinators and without manual stimulus of fertilisation. The purposes of the current experiment are to study the genetic variability of autofertility in-detail and to identify QTLs (Quantitative Trait Loci) which are responsible for this trait in faba bean. 189 homozygous lines of Göttingen winter faba bean population together with 11 control lines were used in the experiment. The study was carried out using tripped and un-tripped treatment in bee-isolation green foil house. Tripping was conducted as mechanical stimulus to assist fertilisation which in the experiment was manually conducted by hand. The trial was randomised by lattice design experiments with 2 replicates in three years of experiment. Rate of fertilisation and some reproductive characters were observed in the study. Genotyping was conducted using 1322 polymorfic markers of AFLP and SNP. The results showed that tripping significantly increased the rate of fertilisation. The genotypes were varied in some reproductive characters for tripped and un-tripped treatment. Large variation of rate of fertilisation which found in un-tripped treatment indicates that each genotype has its own ability in self-fertilisation. Several significant putative markers for QTL connected to reproductive characters were identified.

Keywords: Autofertility, faba bean

Contact Address: Winda Puspitasari, Georg-August Universität Göttingen, Department of Crop Sciences, Von-Siebold-Str. 8, 37075 Göttingen, Germany, e-mail: winda.puspita@gmail.com

Seed Systems of Rice and Finger Millet in Nepal, Between Formality and Informality

RAHEL WYSS[1], DOMINIQUE VINCENT GUENAT[1], ISABEL LOPEZ NORIEGA[2], DEVENDRA GAUCHAN[3], DEEPAK UPADHYA[4]

[1] Bern University of Applied Sciences, School for Agricultural, Forest and Food Sciences (HAFL), Switzerland
[2] Bioversity International, Policy Unit, Italy
[3] Bioversity International, National Project Management, Nepal
[4] World Wildlife Fund for Nature, Social Science, Nepal

In Nepal, more than 90 % of cereal seed flows from informal systems and there are regions and groups of farmers that are not connected at all to any seed networks with external seed supply. Nepal's agricultural policies and formal institutions are promoting the development of the formal seed system. However, knowledge gaps exist on the opportunities and challenges for smallholder farmers when formal seed systems are becoming accessible. This study identified impacts of different seed systems on agrobiodiversity, seed value chains and livelihood of smallholder farmers in Ghanpokhara, a mid-hill region of Nepal.

A survey was conducted in 40 farm households (rice and finger millet), numerous key informants and experts involved in Nepal's seed systems were interviewed and extensive literature review was done. Four different seed systems were identified: the formal system, the intermediary system, the informal system and the no seed supply system (except local seeds). The latter was found in Ghanpokhara for rice and finger millet. Although (seed and crop) markets can be found not too far away, farmers in the study site appear to be locked off from the formal seed system. Their interest to purchase new seed seems to be high, but their awareness about potential benefits of quality seed is low, and they have limited access to information and new seed. The present research also found that varietal diversity along the continuum of seed systems is highest in informal seed systems. Besides numerous benefits, increasingly formal seed systems bear also disadvantages (and risks) for small-holder farmers: higher costs of input, dependency from formal seed sources and changes in crop genetic diversity, among others.

The recommendations derived from this study are: extension service should be promoted in remote areas, more resources should be made available for farmers' training on seed production, selection and storage techniques. Furthermore, the organisation in farmer groups for seed production should be facilitated (socially inclusive) in order to produce good quality seed of farmer preferred varieties locally and in sufficient quantity.

Keywords: Agrobiodiversity, food security, formal seed systems, improved varieties, informal seed systems, Nepal, seed policy, seed security, traditional varieties, value chain analysis

Contact Address: Rahel Wyss, Bern University of Applied Sciences, School for Agricultural, Forest and Food Sciences (HAFL), Bern, Switzerland, e-mail: rahel.wyss@bfh.ch

How Would Ethiopian Farmers Like to Access Hybrid Maize Seeds? Evidence from a Choice Experiment on the Attributes of Seed Distribution Systems

Tilahun Woldie Mengistu, Saurabh Gupta, Regina Birner

University of Hohenheim, Inst. of Agricultural Sciences in the Tropics (Hans-Ruthenberg-Institute), Germany

Ensuring access to high-quality seeds for smallholder farmers has remained a challenge in many African countries. In Ethiopia, the maize seed system has, until recently, been highly centralised and controlled by state-sponsored cooperatives. This was, in particular, the case for the marketing and distribution of hybrid maize seeds. Inefficiencies in this state-controlled system have been identified as one of the main reasons for the lack of growth and productivity in Ethiopia's maize sector. However, important changes in the seed distribution policy introduced in 2013 have ended the monopoly of cooperatives and made direct seed marketing by both public and private enterprises possible. As farmers can now choose between different seed providers, the question arises as to how they prefer to access hybrid maize seeds. Which attributes of seed distribution systems do they prefer most? These research questions are addressed in the proposed paper. A choice experiment focusing on seed purity, quantity, group formation, sales outlet number, credit and price attributes was conducted with 325 randomly selected maize farmers located in the two maize belt areas of Oromia and Amhara regions. A Latent Class Model (LCM) identified three classes of farmers. LCM estimation demonstrates a significant heterogeneity of preferences to the distribution attributes within classes and between study areas. Diversity of actors engaged in seed distribution, asymmetry in implementing the new distribution system in the two areas, access to irrigation, age, family size and distance to seed collection points are factors that account for heterogeneity of preferences between and within study areas. In spite of the uniformity of the prescribed approaches to resolve the challenges of seed distribution, farmers preferences to distribution attributes are quite different, implying that 'one size doesn't fit all'. Furthermore, the results underline the role of contextual factors for choice of the distribution attributes, and the cost of ignoring them. The study, therefore, suggests that policy makers should carefully consider sources of preferences heterogeneity in relation to distribution attributes. It is important to re-orient the seed distribution approaches to suit the local contexts as well as the identified preference differentials before scaling up to the country level.

Keywords: Choice experiment, Ethiopia, hybrid maize seed distribution, latent class model, maize farmers, preferences, socioeconomic contexts

Contact Address: Tilahun Woldie Mengistu, University of Hohenheim, Inst. of Agricultural Sciences in the Tropics (Hans-Ruthenberg-Institute), Wollgrasweg 43, 70599 Stuttgart, Germany, e-mail: tilahun.mengistu@uni-hohenheim.de

ID 570

Comparative Investigation of Farmer's Criteria for Cowpea Varieties via Farmers' Participatory Varietal Selection in Niger and Burkina Faso

HARUKI ISHIKAWA[1], ISSA DRABO[2], CHRISTIAN FATOKUN[1], BOUKAR OUSMANE[1], SATORU MURANAKA[3]

[1] *International Institute of Tropical Agriculture (IITA), Grain Legume, Nigeria*
[2] *Institut National d'Environnement et des Recherches Agricoles (INERA), Burkina Faso*
[3] *Japan International Research Center for Agricultural Sciences (JIRCAS), Tropical Agriculture Research Front, Japan*

Cowpea (*Vigna unguiculata*) is an important crop for promoting the food security, livelihood, and cash income of farmers. Various improved cowpea varieties have been developed and released by the breeding programs in many national agricultural research systems in sub-Saharan African countries. However, the reports on farmers' selection criteria and acceptability of improved cowpea varieties are still limited. Further, these acceptability are sometimes complicated by the fact that the selection criteria employed by farmers vary by region. Thus, in order to better understand the preferences and selection criteria employed by farmers, farmer participatory varietal selection activities were undertaken in different regions in Niger and Burkina Faso. A total of 1,134 farmers (224 farmers in Niger, 910 farmers in Burkina Faso) were invited to the demonstration fields with 37 genotypes in 12 villages (7 villages in Niger and 5 villages in Burkina Faso). The survey revealed that the most important criterion for farmers was grain yield. Interestingly, the difference of farmer's preferences in both countries was in the second and third criteria. The second most important trait was "fodder yield" in Niger, and "early maturity" in Burkina Faso. In addition, farmers in Niger were concerned with "*Striga* resistance" of the variety. On the other hand, farmers in Burkina Faso were interested in "seed colour". Furthermore, this study also clarified regional and gender differences among farmers' preferences. Details of their preferences will be discussed in the presentation. These regional differences of preferences for cowpea varieties should be taken into account when developing improved varieties with better acceptability.

Keywords: Cowpea, farmers preference, FPVS, improved variety

Contact Address: Haruki Ishikawa, International Institute of Tropical Agriculture (IITA), Grain Legume, Oyo Road, PMB5320 Ibadan, Nigeria, e-mail: h.ishikawa@cgiar.org

Environmental impact on soil and crop health

Microbiological Analysis of Contamination Risks in Urban and Peri-Urban Vegetable Production of Ouagadougou, Burkina Faso

JULIANE DAO[1], PHILIP AMOAH[2], KATHRIN STENCHLY[1], ANDREAS BUERKERT[1]

[1]*University of Kassel, Organic Plant Production and Agroecosystems Research in the Tropics and Subtropics (OPATS), Germany*

[2]*International Water Management Institute (IWMI), Ghana*

The production of vegetables in and around urban open space areas of Ouagadougou (Burkina Faso) supplies city residents with fresh vegetables all year round, and contributes to food security. As in most of West Africa, the economic opportunities offered especially by exotic vegetable production in and around cities are significant, moving famers above the poverty line. The absence of environmental safeguard policies and food safety standards may pose health risks for producers and consumers, as irrigation water for vegetable production is often taken from raw or diluted sewage.

The purpose of this study was to analyse to which degree irrigation water and lettuce plants of ten production areas with either sewage polluted channels (n=4) or wells (n=6) as water source for irrigation was contaminated by total and fecal coliforms. A particular focus was placed on *Escherichia coli* and tracking of bacteria loads on lettuce leaves along the food supply chain (from field to fork).

The results show that lettuce irrigated with channel water had a similar load of faecal bacteria as lettuce irrigated with well water. Well water was also polluted by coliforms and channel water was cleaner than expected. At three locations (n=10) irrigation water met the health based target for lettuce of less than 10^3 *Escherichia coli* per 100 ml irrigation water. Irrespective of the source, contamination of irrigation water varied between 3.6×10^3 and 1.87×10^7 total coliform per 100 ml. This wide range is also reflected in the crop contamination at the farm gate, where lettuce had on average a load of 5.03×10^5 total coliforms per g (n=10). Postharvest data showed that regardless of the lettuce treatment along the marketing chain *Escherichia coli* and total coliform rates increased on average by one log unit until the final sales point. Additional experiment showed that appropriate postharvest handling could prevent such increase in total coliforms. We concluded that inappropriate lettuce handling after harvest constitutes a major source of risk for produce contamination in Ouagadougou.

Keywords: *Escherichia coli*, lettuce, peri-urban, total coliform, urban

Contact Address: Juliane Dao, University of Kassel, Organic Plant Production and Agroecosystems Research in the Tropics and Subtropics (OPATS), Steinstrasse 19, 37213 Witzenhausen, Germany, e-mail: dao@uni-kassel.de

Assessing Meteorological Risk Factors for Aflatoxin Contamination of Maize Dried on Small Farms in Kenya

ISAIAH ETEMO MUCHILWA, OLIVER HENSEL

University of Kassel, Agricultural Engineering, Germany

Kenya lies within the Equatorial tropics of East Africa and is renowned globally as a world hot-spot for aflatoxins, i.e. toxic and carcinogenic compounds associated with fungal colonisation of foods. Contrary to the general belief that there is enough "sunshine" in the equatorial tropics to dry foods, farmers in Kenya are struggling with delayed and insufficient dehydration that accounts significantly for the high prevalence of mycotoxins in maize supplies. All the major outbreaks of acute aflatoxicosis in Kenya have occurred during recurrent El Niño episodes arising from sea surface temperature anomalies in the tropical pacific. El Niño in Kenya has historically been associated with intensification of the October, November, December rains, often extending to February and thereby coinciding with most of the country's maize harvest across the different agroecological zones.

The prevalence of pre-and postharvest aflatoxins is skewed both locally and globally, stemming from locational differences in the altitude and latitude at which maize is grown. Generally, high outdoor night temperatures exceeding 22oC are considered high risk for pre-harvest aflatoxins in maize. In this study, psychrometric data was obtained from 14 different weather stations located within maize growing zones, i.e. 10 stations in Kenya (equatorial-East Africa), 1 in Ghana (equatorial-West Africa), 2 in the USA and 1 in Germany (locations outside the tropics). The elevations of the stations varied from 55 m to 2115 m above sea level. The assessed data included hourly recordings of relative humidity, dry bulb, wet bulb and dew point temperatures and descriptions of relative cloud cover and occurrence of thunderstorms, rains, frosts and fog, taken for the month of November 2015, to coincide with a peak in extreme wet weather presented by the latest El Niño episode in Kenya. The results associated higher risks for pre-harvest aflatoxin contamination of maize dried under extreme weather with the equatorial lowlands, where typical indoor conditions occur outdoors at night. Fumonisins and not aflatoxins were observed to be the bigger threat for pre-harvest in the cooler equatorial highlands. Heavy rains and the associated build-up of clouds impede sun-drying and investment in artificial driers is inevitable to mitigate mycotoxins in Kenya's maize.

Keywords: Aflatoxins, maize, mycotoxins, sensor-psychrometrics, sun-drying

---

Contact Address: Isaiah Etemo Muchilwa, University of Kassel, Agricultural Engineering, Nordbahnhofstr. 1a, 37213 Witzenhausen, Germany, e-mail: imuchilwa@yahoo.co.uk

ID 1026

Response of Common Bean to Rhizobia Inoculation, Nitrogen and Phosphorus Across Variable Soils in Zimbabwe

VONGAI CHEKANAI[1], REGIS CHIKOWO[2], KEN GILLER[3], FRED KANAMPIU[4]

[1] University of Zimbabwe, Crop Science Department, Zimbabwe
[2] Michigan State University, Plant Soil and Microbial Sciences, United States of America
[3] Wageningen University (WUR), Dept. of Plant Sciences, The Netherlands
[4] International Institute of Tropical Agriculture (IITA), Kenya

Soil fertility depletion ranks as the most important drawback to crop productivity in sub-Saharan Africa. Three on-farm experiments were conducted to explore the effect of nitrogen (N), phosphorus (P) and rhizobia inoculation on common bean productivity in Eastern Zimbabwe. Two common bean cultivars readily available on the market were tested in a split-plot arranged in randomised complete block design. The main plot was the combination of N (0 and $60\,kg\,ha^{-1}$) and P (0 and $20\,kg\,ha^{-1}$) and the sub-plot were cultivar (Gloria and NUA 45) and inoculation (+/- inoculum). Both N and P were applied at $20\,kg\,ha^{-1}$ at planting and an extra $40\,kg\,ha^{-1}$N top dressing. Number of nodules, active nodules and pods were significantly increased by N and P application. On a degraded site with 0.32 % SOC, none of the factors significantly increased grain yields ($p > 0.05$). Yields for control were a paltry $0.21\,t\,ha^{-1}$ compared to $0.45\,t\,ha^{-1}$ with N, P and rhizobia. Analysis of variance of grain yield for the two sites that had SOC > 0.6 % resulted in significant simple effects of N and P, and NP interaction ($p = 0.03$). Grain yields significantly increased from $0.49\,t\,ha^{-1}$ (control) to $1.56\,t\,ha^{-1}$ at $60\,kg\,ha^{-1}$N and $20\,kg\,ha^{-1}$P.

These results suggest that farmers can invest in both N and P for common bean production, but not in acutely degraded soils. Improved common bean cultivars currently on the market barely respond to the local rhizobia inoculum.

Keywords: Common bean, nitrogen, phosphorus, rhizobia, Zimbabwe

Contact Address: Vongai Chekanai, University of Zimbabwe, Crop Science Department, 5319 Budiriro 3, Harare, Zimbabwe, e-mail: vchekanai@gmail.com

Will Climate Change Threaten Temperate Fruit Trees in Warm Growing Regions?

Eike Luedeling[1], Haifa Benmoussa[2], Sebastian Saa[3], Liang Guo[4], Michael Blanke[5], Jens Gebauer[6], Johann Martinez-Lüscher[7]

[1] World Agroforestry Centre (ICRAF) and Center for Development Research (ZEF), Germany

[2] National Agronomic Institute of Tunisia and Olive Institute, Tunisia

[3] Pontificia Universidad Católica de Valparaíso, Escuela de Agronomía, Chile

[4] Northwest A&F University, China

[5] University of Bonn, INRES - Horticultural Science, Germany

[6] Rhine-Waal University of Applied Sciences, Fac. of Life Sciences, Germany

[7] University of Reading and East Malling Research, United Kingdom

Many important growing regions of fruit and nut trees of the temperate zone are warmer than the regions of origin of the respective species. Almonds, walnuts, pistachios, peaches, apples, apricots and many other species thrive in California, Chile, Australia, India, China and the Mediterranean region. They are even found in the highlands of Oman, Ethiopia, Kenya and Vietnam. In all these places, growers must carefully select appropriate species and cultivars to ensure that the trees' mandatory chilling requirements are met. If this is not the case, trees can display delayed and protracted bloom, develop growth anomalies and produce yields that are economically unsatisfactory in terms of quantity and quality. Climate change is a concern to growers of temperate trees in warm locations, because increasing temperatures could reduce chill to insufficient levels, putting large investments and many livelihoods at risk. Despite their central importance in fruit production, systematic studies of chilling requirements and temperature responses of trees along climate gradients are scarce. While many growers monitor chill, most of them use outdated models that have long been proven inaccurate.

We have developed methodologies to extract information on temperature responses from long-term bloom records of fruit and nut trees. These procedures are based on Partial Least Squares regression and have been published in an open-source analysis package (chillR for R language). Here we present results from applying these techniques across a wide range of climates, using data from California, China, Tunisia, Germany and the United Kingdom. We show that the response of tree phenophases to warming depends on temperatures during the chill accumulation phase. In cold-winter climates, winter warming advances spring phases, as has been reported for many species. In the warmest locations in our dataset, however, warm winters delayed spring phenology, leading to concerns that additional warming might threaten the productivity of many orchards. We also provide evidence for the inadequacy of commonly used chill models, highlight the currently most reliable model and propose strategies for developing more accurate models. Progress in this field is urgently needed to prepare growers of temperate trees for the impacts of global warming.

Keywords: Chilling requirement, climate change, dormancy, fruit trees, physiology

Contact Address: Eike Luedeling, World Agroforestry Centre (ICRAF) and Center for Development Research (ZEF), Walter-Flex-Str. 3, 53113 Bonn, Germany, e-mail: e.luedeling@cgiar.org

ID 470

Linking Stocks and Flows: New Emission Factors for Managed Tropical Histosols

Louis Verchot[1], Kristell Hergoualc'h[2]

[1] International Center for Tropical Agriculture (CIAT), Colombia
[2] Center for International Forestry Research (CIFOR), Peru

Quantifying greenhouse gas (GHG) emissions from managed tropical histosols was one of the major gaps in the 2006 revision of the IPCC National Greenhouse Gas Inventory Guidelines. Since the Guidelines were published, several studies suggested that emissions from these soils were high when they were drained and converted to agriculture. In 2011 IPCC began an effort to provide better guidance for the inclusion of these lands in national GHG inventories. Estimates of these emissions remain controversial because of methodological limitations and incompleteness of many studies. For most types of tropical agriculture emission factors were based chamber measurements, but data availability remained a major constraint. Tropical agricultural emissions ranged from of 1.5 to 14 Mg C ha^{-1} y^{-1} for different types of croplands. Developing the emission factor for oil palm and short rotation forestry posed a challenge as data were available for both chamber and subsidence measurements. For short rotation plantations, data were available form a limited geographic range (22.1 and 17.7 Mg C ha^{-1} y^{-1} for subsidence and flux approaches, respectively). For oil palm, the two methods produced results that were not significantly different (8.9 and 12.2, respectively). Results of the two approaches were averaged to produce the final emission factors of 20 and 11 Mg ha^{-1} y^{-1} for short rotation plantations and oil palm, respectively. Since the publication of these results, new data has confirmed the emission factors. New emission factors were also produced for non-CO_2 GHGs. Soil N_2O emissions between 0 and 5 kg N_2O-N ha^{-1} y^{-1}, but these factors are also based on few data. New data suggests that emissions may be considerably higher than these values, particularly in highly fertilised oil palm plantations. Emissions of CH4 are also high in several types of production systems, ranging from 0 to 140 kg CH4 ha-1 y-1, and they are extremely high from drainage ditches (>2500 kg CH_4 ha^{-1} y^{-1}). We conclude with some recommendations for improving measurement efforts to better constrain emissions from managed tropical histosols.

Keywords: Greenhouse gas emissions, IPCC, palm oil plantation, tropical soils

Contact Address: Louis Verchot, International Center for Tropical Agriculture (CIAT), Dept de Suelos Km 17 Recta Clai-Palmira Aptd. Aereo 6713, 763537 Cali, Colombia, e-mail: l.verchot@cgiar.org

Mechanisms of Resistance and Alteration of Chemical Compositions of the Potential Cash Crop *Halophyte leptochloa Fusca* L. Kunth under Salinity Stress

Sayed Eisa[1], Nasr El-Bordeny[2], Ahmed Abdel-Ati[3], Mohamed Eid[4], Sayed Hussin[1], Safwat Ali[5], Abdalla Masoud[2], Abd-El-Rahman El-Naggar[1]

[1]*Ain Shams University (ASU), Dept. of Agricultural Botany, Egypt*
[2]*Ain Shams University (ASU), Dept. of Animal Production, Egypt*
[3]*Desert Research Center, Plant Production Dept., Egypt*
[4]*Ain Shams University (ASU), Dept. of Soil Science, Egypt*
[5]*Ain Shams University (ASU), Dept. of Agricultural Biochemistry, Egypt*

Fresh water resources both for domestic and agriculture use are constantly depleting and crop yield suffer from a steady increase in water salinity, particularly in arid and semi-arid regions. Climate change is expected to lead to reductions in water supply worldwide and to major concern for prospective development. A burgeoning population in most developing countries is a further threat not only to sustained food supply but also affect other resources like fodder and fuel wood. Hence efforts are needed to find alternate solution to utilising saline lands and water for economic benefits. Cash halophyte crops can grow using land and water unsuitable for other conventional crops and provide food, fodder, fuel, medicines, landscaping. One of these plants is Kallar Grass (*Leptochloa fusca* L. Kunth). It is a fast growing, perennial herbaceous, and can be utilised as forage, bioreclamation of saline soil, phytoremediation and carbon sequestration. A sustainable use of *Leptochloa fusca* at high salinity cannot be predicted without a detailed knowledge about its mechanisms of resistance and they closely depend on the ability to cope with (I) water deficit due to a low water potential of the soil, (II) restriction of CO_2, (III) avoidance of ion- toxicity and ion-deficiency. Therefore osmotic potential, Na and K contents, transpiration rate, stomatal conductance, were determined of plants irrigated with nutrient solution containing 0, 20 %, 40 %, 60 %, 80 %, 100 % sea-water-salinity (sws). Increasing NaCl significantly decreased shoot growth yield. The transpiration rate and stomatal conductance showed a linearly reduction by rising salinity levels and that was associated with decreasing of leaves osmotic potential. Concerning chemical compositions of shoot, salinity led to an obvious increase in protein, ash, fat and carbohydrates contents, while fiber content was decreased as compared to non-saline treated plants.

Keywords: Chemical compositions, Halophytes, *Leptochloa fusca*, osmotic potential, salinity, stomatal conductance, transpiration rate

Contact Address: Sayed Eisa, Ain Shams University (ASU), Dept. of Agricultural Botany, 68 Hadyke Shubra, 12244 Cairo, Egypt, e-mail: sayed_eisa@hotmail.com

Effect of Temperature on Crop Water Use Efficiency: Case Study in the Northeast of Iran

ALIREZA KOOCHEKI, MEHDI NASSIRI MAHALLATI, ZARE HOSSEIN, SARA ASADI

Ferdowsi University of Mashhad, College of Agriculture, Department of Agronomy, Iran

Water scarcity is one of the main challenging issues for supplying sufficient food in most part of the world. Moreover, water supply is under pressure from climate change. Therefore, it is essential to identify drivers for improving agro-ecosystem water use efficiency (WUE). This paper aims to estimate WUE for wheat, alfalfa, sugar beet and tomato in northeast part of Iran for a 20 years period (1990–2010) and evaluate the effect of temperature on WUE. Crop water use (CWU) was estimated based on potential evapotranspiration (Penman-Monteith) and crop coefficient. WUE was calculated as production per unit of water used by evapotranspiration. To simulate the effect of temperature on WUE three scenarios were supposed: 1, 2 and 3 °C increase in air temperature during observation period. Eventually, to evaluate WUE changes, WUE was scattered against the CWU. Results showed that WUE varied from 0.2 to 0.8 kg grain yield per m^3 water used for wheat, 0.4 to 1.4 kg above ground dry matter per m^3 for alfalfa, from 1.5 to 4.5 kg fresh root per m^3 for sugar beet and 1 to 5 kg fresh fruit per m^3 water for tomato. A polynomial model was fitted to show WUE trend against CWU. The highest WUE was obtained around 490, 850, 880 and 780 mm water used for wheat, alfalfa, sugar beet and tomato, respectively. To define upper and lower WUE variation, two boundary lines were fitted based on the model. Different agronomic managements are responsible for the gap between upper and lower boundary lines. Temperature increment up to 1 °C did not affect WUE of any models derived from the boundary lines for all the crops. Although 3 °C increase in temperature had a negligible impact on WUE in higher boundary line, WUE in lower boundary line decreased dramatically. Alfalfa was the most sensitive and sugar beet was the most tolerant crop to temperature increase in terms of WUE. Our results illustrated that by temperature increment, WUE gap widens and agronomic management will play an important role in this case.

Keywords: Climate change, evapotranspiration, food security, water use efficiency gap

Contact Address: Zare Hossein, Ferdowsi University of Mashhad, College of Agriculture, Department of Agronomy, 9177948974 Mashhad, Iran, e-mail: hossein.zr84@gmail.com

Pollution of Heavy Metals (Cadmium, Nickel & Lead) in some Farms of Torbat Jam, East of Khorasan Razavi Province, Iran

Majid Jamialahmadi[1], Alireza Pourkhabbaz[2], Bent-Olhoda Sangak Sani Sangak Sani[1]

[1] University of Birjand, Fac. of Agriculture, Dept. of Agronomy, Iran

[2] University of Birjand, Fac. of Natural Resources and Environment, Dept. of Environmental Science, Iran

The purpose of this research was to determine cadmium (Cd), nickel (Ni) and lead (Pb) concentrations in melon (*Cucumis melo* var. inodorus), sugar beet (*Beta vulgaris*) and corn (*Zea mays*), and also in water and soils of some farms in Torbat Jam, and to examine whether the chemical fertilisers can be a source of heavy metals contamination of soil and groundwater, or not. Some samples were taken from the soil and water of each farm, both before fertiliser application and after final harvest (combined sample), as well as the most commonly used fertilisers (triple superphosphate, urea and potassium sulfate). Also during growth season, root (all crops), fruit (melon) and total shoot (corn forage) of all crops were sampled separately in each farm. The soil, plants and fertilisers samples were prepared by acid digestion and their heavy metals content, along with water samples, were measured by atomic absorption. Results showed that heavy metals concentrations in groundwater and soil were lower than adopted global standards. The only exception, among fertilisers, was Cd in triple superphosphate fertiliser, which its content was higher than California Department of Food and Agricultural Standards. The total Cd had increased to a greater extent in the soil of melon, sugar beet and corn farms in the region, in compare to Pb. The total Pb concentration in soils of corn farms showed a greater increase during season than melons and sugar beet farms. This is probably due to greater use of potassium fertiliser, which contains more Pb than other fertilisers, in corn farms. Lead had the highest transfer coefficient among all the metals studied. In general, it is likely that current farm management practices and the excessive use of chemical fertilisers will lead to more pollution and the loss of soil quality. Therefore, in addition to optimal use of fertilisers and control their quality, using other agricultural methods such as crop rotation, crop residues, green manure, organic fertilisers, and biological control could be assessed in order to mitigate the harmful effects of chemical fertiliser and to approach agricultural sustainability.

Keywords: Cadmium, corn, fertiliser, lead, melon, nickel, sugar beet

Contact Address: Majid Jamialahmadi, University of Birjand, Fac. of Agriculture, Dept. of Agronomy, Birjand, Iran, e-mail: mja230@yahoo.com

ID 351

The Nutritional Treasure of Leafy Vegetable – *Perilla frutescens*

NIKOLINA GRBIC, KERSTIN PASCHKO, INA PINKER, MICHAEL BÖHME

Humboldt-Universität zu Berlin, Horticultural Plant Systems, Germany

The quantity of consumed fresh herbs is increasing in Europe. In this respect there is also rising interest on use of exotic, especially Asian vegetables in restaurants and at home too. Most of the Asian leafy vegetables and herbs have culinary, nutritional and medicinal importance but intensive cultivation systems are rarely investigated. *Perilla frutescens* (L.) Britt. (Lamiaceae) is an Asian herbaceous plant, native to mountainous areas from India to China, but mainly cultivated and consumed in Korea, Japan, Thailand and Vietnam. Except for culinary use, its fresh leaves and seeds are well-known for a range of beneficial medicinal properties and therefore used in traditional medicine for treatments of various diseases like tumour, heart disease, diabetes, anxiety, depressions, infections and intestinal disorders. The health promoting effects of *Perilla* have been attributed to its high content of secondary metabolites such as polyphenols, flavonoids and anthocyanins. The possibility to cultivate *Perilla* in greenhouse in temperate regions was already shown in previous studies. The aim of the experiments was to investigate the influence of different growing conditions, in particular light intensity and light spectra on plant growth, development of different plant parameters and growth rate. Furthermore, the influence of the light conditions on the content of secondary metabolites as polyphenol, flavonoid, anthocyanin, and the antioxidant activity has been examined. In this study effects of natural light with additional blue, green and red light emitting diodes (LEDs), providing 7–12 μmolm^{-2}s^{-1}, have been investigated. Results showed, that use of additional LED lighting had a significant effect on the plant parameters as height and fresh matter of *Perilla*. The different LED light spectra did not influence synthesis of anthocyanins, polyphenols and its antioxidant activity, with exception of flavonoids in green LED treatment, which concentration was 74.26 % higher than those found in control. However, concentration of investigated secondary metabolites found in control was comparable to other studies with *Perilla*, thus its cultivation in temperate region could be possible without negative impact on bioactive compounds.

Keywords: Greenhouse, health improving herbs, light spectra, *Perilla frutescens*, secondary metabolites

Contact Address: Michael Böhme, Humboldt-Universität zu Berlin, Dept. Horticultural Plant Systems, Lentzeallee 75, 14195 Berlin, Germany, e-mail: michael.boehme@cms.hu-berlin.de

Preliminary Characterisation of Soybean Nodulating Rhizobia from Ethiopian Soils

YIFRU ABERA[1], FASSIL ASSEFA[1], THUITA MOSES[2], CARGELE MASSO[2]

[1]*Addis Ababa University, Cellular, Microbial and Molecular Biology, Ethiopia*
[2]*International Institute of Tropical Agriculture (IITA), Kenya*

Soybean (*Glycine max* (L.) Merrill) is one of the most important crops in the world today. It is considered to be a miracle crop as it is extraordinarily rich in protein (40 %) and oil (20 %). However, it is a relatively new crop for smallholder farming communities in most African countries, gaining popularity as a consequence of the increasing need for food and fodder. The introduction of soybean to Ethiopia dated back to 1950s, but it was soon abandoned due to low yields. The real production was started later in the 1970s with the introduction of high yielding soybean varieties from Europe and the USA. However, the national average yield (1.4 t ha^{-1}) is very low compared to the potential yield of the crop. This may be due to several reasons of which poor soil fertility or lack of compatible rhizobia could be one. Previous studies showed that soybean response to rhizobia inoculation is very high in many locations. However, knowledge about the diversity and symbiotic efficiency of rhizobia nodulating soybean in Ethiopian soils is scanty. Soybean rhizobia were trapped using two soybean varieties; Awassa-95 and Clark-63K and one cowpea variety (Bole) from major soybean growing soils in Ethiopia. These isolates were characterised on the basis of colony morphology, tolerances to extremes of temperature, salt and pH, ability to grow on different carbon and nitrogen sources and resistance to different heavy metals and antibiotics. The majorities of the isolates were slow growers and produced alkaline reaction in YEMA medium containing bromothymol blue. The isolates were diverse with respect to their physiological and biochemical properties as well as their symbiotic effectiveness. The majority of the isolates were sensitive to salinity and unable to tolerate more than 0.8 % NaCl which is a characteristic of slow growers. Most isolates were able to grow at pH ranging from 4 to 9.5 and grew at a maximum temperature between 35 and 40 °C. Some of the isolates with an outstanding symbiotic performance were identified, and will be tested under field conditions in a search for efficient and competitive strains for use in commercial inoculants in Ethiopia.

Keywords: Biochemical characterisation, Ethiopia, rhizobial isolates, slow growers, symbiotic efficiency

Contact Address: Yifru Abera, Addis Ababa University, Cellular, Microbial and Molecular Biology, Addis Ababa, Ethiopia, e-mail: yifrua@yahoo.com

ID 545

Effects of High Temperature and Drought Stress Around Anthesis on Wheat

AMIRHOSSEIN MAHROOKASHANI, STEFAN SIEBERT, HUBERT HÜGING, FRANK EWERT

University of Bonn, Inst. Crop Sci. and Res. Conserv. (INRES), Germany

High temperature and drought stress are projected to reduce crop yields and threaten food security. While effects of heat and drought on crop growth and yield have been studied separately, little is known about the combined effect of these stressors. Thus pot experiments were laid out to study the effects of high temperature, drought stress and combined heat and drought stress around anthesis on yield and its components for three wheat cultivars originating from Germany and Iran in 2014 and 2015. We found that effects of combined heat and drought on the studied physiological and yield traits were considerably stronger than those of the individual stress factors alone but the magnitude of the effects varied for the specific traits. All stress treatments in this study significantly reduced grain number, single grain weight and grain yield while heat stress did not significantly decrease single grain weight across cultivars in both years. In 2014 single grain weight was reduced for the three varieties under drought stress by 13–27 % and under combined heat and drought stress by 43–83 % while in year 2015 single grain weights were reduced by 11–34 % for drought and 27–41 % under combined heat and drought stress. Heat stress significantly decreased grain number by 14–28 %, 10–22 % and grain yield by 16–25 %, 6–20 % in 2014 and 2015 respectively. We conclude that heat and drought stress affect different processes and sink-source relationships resulting in distinct impacts on yield components and that the magnitude of the responses to heat and drought is cultivar specific.

Keywords: Combined heat and drought stress, drought stress, high temperate, wheat, yield

Contact Address: Amirhossein Mahrookashani, University of Bonn, Inst. Crop Sci. and Res. Conserv. (INRES), Katzenburgweg 5, 53115 Bonn, Germany, e-mail: amahru@uni-bonn.de

Qualitative Assesment of *Portulaca oleracea* under Water Deficit Stress, Different Nutritional Systems and Mycorrhizal Symbiosis

HOSSEINZADEH MOHAMMAD HADI[1], GHALAVAND AMIR[1], MASHHADI AKBAR BOOJAR MASOOD[2], SEYED ALI MOHAMMAD MODARRES-SANAVY[1]

[1] *Tarbiat Modares University, Dept. of Agronomy, Iran*

[2] *Kharazmi University, Dept. of Biology Science, Iran*

Medicinal plants have many different uses in various fields of medical, industry, agriculture and food. Nutrients are a vital part of sustainable agriculture that must be available for the optimal plant growth in appropriate amounts and at the right time. The combined use of chemical, organic and biological fertilisers improves soil physical and chemical conditions. Purslane (*Portulaca oleracea* L.) is listed by the World Health Organisation as one of the most used medicinal plants and termed a "global panacea". Purslane leaves are a rich source of omega-3 and omega-6 fatty acids, which prevents heart attacks and strengthens the immune system. A field experiment was conducted during 2015 using a factorial split in a randomised complete block design with three replications in order to evaluate the effects of different nutritional systems and mycorrhizal symbiosis under water deficit stress on qualitative characteristics of Purslane. Factors include two water deficit stress: S1: with no stress: irrigation at 70 % of FC and S2: stress: irrigation at 50 % of FC after the establishment of the plant and two treatments of mycorrhizal fungus (*Glomus intraradices*) including: M1 no inoculated and M2 inoculated, as main plots. The subplots consisted of six fertilisation treatments which were a combination of a mixture of manure (sheep and chicken) and nitrogen chemical fertilisers. F1 with no manure and no nitrogen fertiliser, F2 with 100 % manure and no nitrogen fertiliser, F3 with 75 % manure and 25 % nitrogen fertilisers, F4 with 50 % manure and 50 % nitrogen fertilisers, F5 with 25 % manure and 75 % nitrogen fertilisers, F6 with no manure and 100 % nitrogen fertilisers. Results showed that treatments with mycorrhizal fungi + 25 % manure and 75 % nitrogen fertiliser, increased linoleic acid, linolenic acid, total antioxidant capacity, phosphorus and nitrogen in the leaves and water deficit stress decreased these. Impacts of water deficit stress (S2) on malondialdehyde and proline were increased by treatment F1 (no manure and no nitrogen fertiliser), and S2 increased also mucilage in leaves.

Keywords: Fatty acids, manure, mycorrhizal fungus, purslane, water deficit stress

---

Contact Address: Hosseinzadeh Mohammad Hadi, Tarbiat Modares University, Dept. of Agronomy, Jalal-Al-Ahmad, 1411713116 Ttehran, Iran, e-mail: m-hosseinzadeh@modares.ac.ir

Suitability of Simulation Models for Crop Growth and Development in West African Sudan Savannah

Kokou Adambounou Amouzou[1,2], Jesse B. Naab[2], John Lamers[1], Mathias Becker[3]

[1] *University of Bonn, Center for Development Research (ZEF), Germany*
[2] *West African Science Service Center for Climate Change and Adapted Land Use (WAS-CAL), Burkina Faso*
[3] *University of Bonn, Inst. Crop Sci. and Res. Conserv. (INRES) - Plant Nutrition, Germany*

Increased food security and livelihoods in West African Sudan Savannah can be gained through sustainable cropping systems. In the region, rain-fed agriculture remains the dominant source of food production systems, typified as deficient in organic matter, nitrogen, and phosphorus. Changing climate and agricultural land use dynamics challenge the future of these systems because warming will alter nutrient use efficiency. Quantification of nitrogen and phosphorus dynamics versus crop responses within production systems are in its infancy, but could make a major step forward towards sustainable intensification when using suitable deterministic models. Obviously, crop models needs to be parameterised and validated before a systematic use can be envisaged. This study examined how and to what extent CERES-Maize and Sorghum, CROPGRO-Cotton and Cowpea models of DSSAT v4.6 package can capture crop growth and development in the Sudan Savannah agro-ecological zone of Benin. The models were parameterised and calibrated with data set of researcher-managed field trials carried out under non limited nutrient and water-stress conditions on Gleyic Alisols in 2014. The calibrated models were validated with data set of 2015. The models simulated accurately anthesis and maturity with normalised root mean square error (nRMSE) of 1–15 % for *Zea mays*, *Sorghum bicolor*, *Vigna anguiculata* and *Gossypium hirsutum*. The CERES-Maize simulated final grain yields with nRMSE of 7 % while CERES-Sorghum reproduced the yields with nRMSE of 21 %. The CROPGRO-Cowpea and Cotton predicted the grain yields with nRMSE of 36 % and 13 % respectively. The nRMSE between observed and simulated final biomass were 3–17 % in CERES and CROPGRO. The CERES-Maize reproduced the time series above ground biomass (AGB) with a Modelling efficiency (EF) of 0.93 and Index of agreement (d) of 0.98. The CERES-Sorghum showed a goodness of fit, evidenced by EF of 0.92 and d of 0.98. The CROPGRO accurately represented the AGB with EF of 0.60–0.95 and d of 0.91–0.99. The CERES and CROPGRO models accurately predicted crops components within the acceptable thresholds of the lowest nRMSE, EF $\geq$0 and d $\geq$0.75. These models could be used for further assessment of their capability in simulating N and P dynamics in soil-plant systems.

Keywords: CERES and CROPGRO models, crop growth and yields, models validation, production systems

Contact Address: Kokou Adambounou Amouzou, University of Bonn, Center for Development Research (ZEF), Walter-Flex-Straße 3, D-53113 Bonn Bonn, Germany, e-mail: amouzoutg@yahoo.com

Water Use and Efficiency of Cereal and Oil Crops in Tanzania: A Case Study from Makutupora, Tanzania

ANGELA SCHAFFERT, ALEXANDRA SCHAPPERT, JÖRN GERMER, FOLKARD ASCH

University of Hohenheim, Inst. of Agricultural Sciences in the Tropics (Hans-Ruthenberg-Institute), Germany

Water is the major limiting factor for crop growth in seasonally drought prone areas in East Africa. Although the total amount of rainfall is often sufficient to bring the crops to maturity, the yield is often low because of poor rainfall distribution. The aim of this study is to assess the potential of productivity increase for pearl millet (*Pennisetum glaucum* (L.) R.Br.), sorghum (*Sorghum bicolor* (L.) Moench), upland rice (NERICA 4) and sunflower (*Helianthus annuus* L.) within the seasonal variability of the Trans-SEC study regions Dodoma and Morogoro, Tanzania. The focus lies on exploring the effects of different water availabilities and drought events on the crop growth. Phenological development, biomass production and partitioning, yield determining processes and grain yield are analysed as a function of changing water input, soil water availabilities and climatic factors (crop × environment interactions). The crop water requirements in order to achieve a certain desired yield are defined for different environments. This involves examining the timing and depth of its application with regard to the crop growth stages.

The experiments were conducted at the Agricultural Research Institute Makutupora in the central zone of Tanzania between April 2014 and November 2015. Field trials were implemented both in the dry season and with a slightly different set up in the rainy season. During the dry season, precipitation patterns of the Dodoma and Morogoro region were simulated with an installed drip irrigation system. Drought scenarios were integrated, varying in their onset and duration. Within the rainy season rainfed treatments were compared with life saving irrigation. For all seasons one treatment was irrigated according to the crop water requirements.

The gained dataset is expected to serve as a basis for the planning of using external water sources (supplemental irrigation) in order to mitigate the effects of drought events. In addition, the outcomes are expected to facilitate a climate sensitive selection of crops in regions where unpredicted rainfall occurs, to explore the suitability of alternative crops and to validate current crop water models.

Keywords: Crop water requirements, crop × environment interactions, phenological development, soil water

Contact Address: Angela Schaffert, University of Hohenheim, Inst. of Agricultural Sciences in the Tropics (Hans-Ruthenberg-Institute), Stuttgart, Germany, e-mail: a.schaffert@uni-hohenheim.de

ID 1013

Crop biotic stresses (DPG session)

Anti-Oomycete Activity of some Fungal Root Endophytes in the Potato-*Phytophthora infestans* System

Grace Ngatia, Abbas El-Hasan, Barbara Kaufmann, Ralf T. Voegele

University of Hohenheim, Phytopathology, Germany

The oomycete *Phytophthora infestans* (Mont.) de Bary is the most important pathogen of potato in Kenya and requires an integrated approach for effective management. The use of endophytes in disease control has received gaining interest as they are resident potential antagonists, confer abiotic stress tolerance, and may promote plant growth. The antagonistic activity of 354 root-endophytic fungi isolated from four solanaceous species obtained from Kenya was screened *in vitro* against *P. infestans*. 60 isolates were selected and further evaluated in dual culture assays. The results revealed that mycelial growth of *P. infestans* was differentially affected by the tested endophytes. *Trichoderma harzianum* (positive control) along with two endophytes (KB1S2–4 and KA1S1–1) suppressed mycelial growth of the pathogen by 84.5 %, 78.2 %, and 76.5 %, respectively. Other endophytes (KB1S1–4, KB2S2–15, and KA2S1–42) showed their inhibitory activity in a different way. 25 μl of crude extracts from culture filtrates of KB2S2–15 and KA2S1–42 completely (100 %) inhibited sporangia germination while extracts from KB1S1–4 significantly decreased sporangia germination (>72 %) and elongation of germ tubes ($p > 0.0001$). *In vivo* assays on detached potato leaflets revealed that treatment with 25 μl of crude extracts from KB1S1–4, or KA2S1–42, or 2.5 μl of KB2S2–15 completely suppressed necrotic symptoms elicited by *P. infestans*. Additional *in vivo* investigations showed that isolates KB2S2–15 and KA2S1–42 significantly increased tuber yield and leaf dry weight of potato. By contrast, isolate KA2S1–42 had a negative influence on tuber yield, while other fungi tested showed no significant differences of growth parameters compared to the control. Confocal microscopy studies revealed extensive colonisation of potato roots by isolates KA2S1–42 and KB2S2–15. In addition, scanning electron microscopy studies showed that isolate KA2S1–42 colonized potato tissue intracellularly. Interestingly, the ribosomal gene sequences of endophytic fungi KB1S1–4, KB2S2–15 and KA2S1–42 showed no significant similarities to known fungal species in the NCBI database. Identification of these endophytes is still in progress.

Keywords: Antagonism, fungal endophytes, *Phytophthora infestans*

Contact Address: Grace Ngatia, University of Hohenheim, Phytopathology, Stuttgart, Germany, e-mail: grace_ngatia@yahoo.co.uk

Agro-Ecological Niche of Bacterial Wilt (*Xanthomonas campestris* pv. *musacearum*) of Enset (*Ensete ventricosum* (Welw.) Cheessman) in Gamo Highlands of Ethiopia

SHARA SABURA[1], RONY SWENNEN[2], JOZEF DECKERS[3], RUDI AERTS[1], FELEKE WELDEYES[4], GIRMA ABEBE[5], ALEMAYEHU HAILEMICHAEL[4], FANTAHUN WELDESENBET[4], GUY BLOMME[6], KAREN VANCAMPENHOUT[3]

[1]*KU Leuven, Dept. of Microbial and Molecular Systems, Belgium*
[2]*KU Leuven / IITA / Bioversity International, Belgium*
[3]*KU Leuven, Earth and Environmental Sciences, Belgium*
[4]*Arba Minch University, College of Natural Science, Ethiopia*
[5]*ESGPIP, Livestock Department, Ethiopia*
[6]*Bioversity International, Ethiopia*

In Ethiopia, nearly 20 million people depend on Enset (*Ensete ventricosum* (Welw.) Cheessman) for food, animal feed and fibre. Most of its cultivation is concentrated in the South and South-Western parts of the country. Enset based farming system is common in the Gamo highlands, with 11, 150 ha currently covered by it. Enset is supplemented with the cultivation of cereals, pulses and other root and tuber crops. Diverse high yielding clones of different ages are available all year round and can withstand dry spells, making Enset the most important food security crop in these densely populated highlands. Despite its relevance, Enset remains very poorly studied. One of the most important problems is Bacterial Wilt disease caused by *Xanthomonas campestris* pv. *musacearum*, destructive to Enset at all growth stages and present in all Enset growing areas of the country. As a plant takes up to 8 years to mature, an attack of Bacterial Wilt can leave a family vulnerable to famine for years. It is most likely spread by infected farm tools, harvesting knives, plant debris and repeated transplanting of corms. Adoption of the control package by farmers has been less effective and all known varieties are susceptible, putting a great challenge on controlling the epidemic. Despite being present in the entire Enset belt, the severity of a Bacterial Wilt infection varies greatly from region to region. Hence, this study aims at correlating the distribution and severity of the disease to environmental factors such as soil type, fertility, climate and altitude, and to the socio-economical status of the farm households. A better knowledge of the influence of these factors would help in developing more targeted measures to control the disease.

Keywords: Ecological niche, Enset, management constraints, Xanthomonas wilt

Contact Address: Karen Vancampenhout, KU Leuven, Dept. of Earth and Environmental Sciences, Celestijnenlaan 200E, 3001 Leuevn, Belgium, e-mail: karen.vancampenhout@kuleuven.be

 ID 1121

The Biocontrol Agent *Fusarium oxysporum* F.sp. *strigae* – Its Impacts on Beneficial Indigenous Prokaryotes in a Maize Rhizosphere

MARY MUSYOKI, JUDITH ZIMMERMANN, GEORG CADISCH, FRANK RASCHE

University of Hohenheim, Inst. of Agricultural Sciences in the Tropics (Hans-Ruthenberg-Institute), Germany

Integrating resistant crop varieties and *Fusarium oxysporum* f.sp. *strigae* (Fos) as biocontrol agents (BCAs) was shown to be effective in controlling the *Striga hermonthica* weed which parasitizes on several tropical cereals. Effects of Fos on beneficial microbial rhizosphere communities has however not been observed so far, although it is a prerequisite for prospective field application. Hence, our objectives were (1) to assess the potential impact of Fos on indigenous nitrifying abundance and proteolytic enzymatic activity prokaryotes in a maize rhizosphere cultivated on two distinct tropical soils (sandy Ferric Alisol versus clayey Humic Nitisol) in a rhizobox study, and (2) to evaluate potential effects of Fos versus those of soil properties (i.e. pH and texture), seasonality and crop growth stage on the abundance and diversity of nitrifying prokaryotes from two contrasting agroecological sites in western Kenya (Homabay and Busia). Fos-BCA "Foxy-2" was applied as model organism via seed coating of a *S. hermonthica* tolerant maize variety to the four soils. Nitrifying prokaryotes and proteolytic enzyme activity in the rhizobox study was followed at 14, 28 and 42 days after experiment start while for the field study nitrifying prokaryotes abundance and community structure was determined at early leaf development (EC30), flowering stage (EC60) and senescence stage (EC90). Two significant influence factors were considered: (1) presence of *S. hermonthica* plants, and (2) application of *Tithonia diversifolia* residues as nitrogen source for "Foxy-2", and the indigenous microbes. The rhizobox study revealed a stimulating effect of "Foxy-2" and *S. hermonthica* on abundance of archaeal nitrifiers, while bacterial counterparts and proteolytic enzyme activity remained unaffected. Proteolytic abundance revealed a transient decline which was compensated by *Tithonia diversifolia* application. The field study demonstrated that soil properties, seasonality and crop growth stages exerted a strong influence on abundance and community structure nitrifying prokaryotes compared to "Foxy-2" inoculation effects. In conclusion, we showed that "Foxy-2" did not pose a negative effect on indigenous nitrifiers and that application of high quality organic input *Tithonia diversifolia* compensates minor "Foxy-2" effects on pro teolytic abundance. To strengthen our findings, we recommend plant-microbiome interaction studies to better understand the action mechanisms of "Foxy-2".

Keywords: Biocontrol, Foxy-2, indigenous prokaryotes, rhizosphere

Contact Address: Mary Musyoki, University of Hohenheim, Inst. of Agricultural Sciences in the Tropics (Hans-Ruthenberg-Institute), Garbenstrasse 13, 70599 Stuttgart, Germany, e-mail: marykamaa2002@yahoo.com

The Influence of Banana Cultivars on Pathogenic and Non-Pathogenic *Fusarium oxysporum*

PAULINE DELTOUR, SORAYA FRANÇA, MONICA HÖFTE

Ghent University, Dept. of Crop Protection: Phytopathology Laboratory, Belgium

Fusarium oxysporum f. sp. *cubense* (Foc) is a devasting soil-borne pathogen of banana. Monocultures are often blamed for the widespread epidemics of Foc. One option to reduce the vulnerability caused by genetic uniformity could be the use of banana cultivar mixtures. The use of different cultivars can have a positive effect if they curtail inoculum pressure or foster beneficial microorganisms, such as non-pathogenic *Fusarium oxysporum* (np-Fox). We studied the influence of four banana cultivars with different levels of Foc resistance on Foc race 1 (FocR1) and np-Fox strains. Cultivar (cv.) Silk (AAB) is highly susceptible to FocR1, cv. Prata (AAB) is moderately susceptible, and cvs. Ouro Colatina (AA) and Dwarf Cavendish (AAA) are both resistant. Tissue culture plantlets were grown in autoclaved soil inoculated with (1) the pathogen, (2) a combination of three np-fox strains or (3) the pathogen combined with the np-fox strains. After 65 days, root colonization by the different strains was quantified by qPCR, while the soil population was assessed by dilution plating. Root colonization by FocR1 of the highly susceptible cv. Silk was higher than of the other cultivars. Likewise, only cv. Silk provoked an increase of FocR1 population in soil. Cv. Prata, although showing internal symptoms similar to those of cv. Silk, did not increase FocR1 in soil and had lower root colonization by FocR1. Cv. Ouro Colatina had the lowest root colonization by FocR1, and, when inoculated with np-Fox, was the only cultivar that caused an increase of np-Fox in soil. The presence of np-Fox delayed the disease and reduced root colonization by FocR1 in all cultivars. This study suggests that inoculum pressure in soil could be reduced by the use of different cultivars. Also additional traits, such as the stimulation of np-Fox in soil by cv. Ouro Colatina, could be useful to manage the disease. Further research is needed to reveal if the positive effect on inoculum pressure and np-fox can be observed when the cultivars are planted in a mixture.?

Keywords: Banana, cultivars, *Fusarium oxysporum* f. sp. *cubense*, non-pathogenic *Fusarium oxysporum*

Contact Address: Pauline Deltour, Ghent University, Dept. of Crop Protection: Phytopathology Laboratory, Coupure Links 653, 9000 Ghent, Belgium, e-mail: pauline.deltour@ugent.be

ID 1005

Reducing Spatial Variability of Soybean Response to Rhizobia Inoculants in Siaya County of Western Kenya

THUITA MOSES, BERNARD VANLAUWE, EDWIN MUTEGI, CARGELE MASSO

International Institute of Tropical Agriculture (IITA), Kenya

Soybean grain yields in sub-Saharan Africa have remained approximately 50 % below those attained in South America despite numerous efforts. Variability in yields related to soil fertility remain a major challenges towards development of integrated soil fertility management packages for use with rhizobia inoculants. A study was conducted in Siaya County (western Kenya) involving 107 farmers with soils of different fertility status. The main objective was to test two inoculants (Legumefix and Biofix) and nutrient source (Minjingu and Sympal) combinations to raise soybean grain yields in the soils of variable fertility. Inoculation was done using Legumefix (*Bradyrhizobium japonicum* strain 532c) or Biofix (*Bradyrhizobium diazoefficiens* strain USDA110) with and without Minjingu or Sympal in a factorial design with each farmer acting as a replicate. Widespread potassium, nitrogen, phosphorus deficiency and soil acidity was observed in most soils. Inoculation and phosphorus+ sources resulted in increased nodulation, nodule occupancy and grain yields in most sites. The yield response varied from farmer to farmer with increases in grain yield and no response in other farms reported. Higher grain yields (3000–4000 kg ha^{-1}) were obtained with Legumefix+ Sympal (12 % of the farmers testing it). The formulation of the nutrient source (Sympal or Minjingu) was important to meet other nutrient deficiency in most of the soils. Determination of value cost ratio (VCR) showed that inoculants alone are the most profitable with VCR of 47.5 (Legumefix) and 11.4 (Biofix). However for sustainable yields Legumefix + Sympal, Legumefix +Minjingu and Biofix + Sympal were recommended with VCR of 6.3, 5.1 and 3.9 respectively.

Keywords: Biological nitrogen fixation, nodule occupancy, soil fertility gradient, soybean inoculants

Contact Address: Thuita Moses, International Institute of Tropical Agriculture (IITA), Nairobi, Kenya, e-mail: M.Thuita@cgiar.org

How Much Do Farmers Care about Pesticide Externalities?
A Choice Experiment among Thai Vegetable Farmers

Suwanna Praneetvatakul[1], Pepijn Schreinemachers[2],
Prasnee Tipraqsa[1]

[1] *Kasetsart University, Dept. of Agricultural and Resource Economics, Thailand*
[2] *AVRDC - The World Vegetable Center, Agricultural Economics, Taiwan*

Agricultural pesticides are widely used to control pests globally in market-oriented farming systems especially in vegetable production. High and incorrect use has led to high external costs to ecosystems and human health. This paper aims to explore farmers' choice preference for alternative pest management methods, ranging from environmentally harmful to benign. External costs of pesticides were reviewed and alternative pest management practices were studied for selected vegetables in Thailand. Farmers' preference for certain pest management methods and outcomes were investigated using a choice experiment. About 300 vegetable farmers were sampled in three sub-urban provinces of Bangkok, including Ratchaburi province, Nakorn Pathom province and Pathum Thani province. Attributes of pest management methods and outcomes included farm ecosystems, human health, eco-labeling, market opportunities, training in integrated pest management, and the additional farm cost. A mixed logit model was employed in order to investigate the effect that each attribute can have on the respondents' preferences for the pest management practices and outcomes and to estimate farmers' marginal willingness to pay for each attribute. Levels of pesticide use in vegetable production were found to be high as farmers tried to protect their investment from a wide range of pests and diseases. Alternative methods were not widely available and used in an *ad-hoc* manner to complement pesticides rather than substitute them. Biological control products available in Thailand need improvement to better meet farmers' preferences. To make vegetable farming in Thailand more environmentally friendly, alternative pest management practices need to be disseminated in combination with intensive farm-level training.

Keywords: Agricultural pesticides, choice model, integrated pest management, sustainable agriculture

Contact Address: Suwanna Praneetvatakul, Kasetsart University, Dept. of Agricultural and Resource Economics, Paholyothin Road, 10900 Bangkok, Thailand, e-mail: fecoswp@ku.ac.th

Aphids: A Major Threat to Cabbage Production in Ghana

KEN FENING[1], ETHELYN FORCHIBE[2], FRANCIS WAMONJE[3], IBRAHIM ADAMA[4], KWAME AFREH-NUAMAH[5], JOHN CARR[3]

[1] *University of Ghana, Soil and Irrigation Research Centre, School of Agriculture, College of Basic and Applied Sciences, Ghana*

[2] *University of Ghana, African Regional Postgraduate Programme in Insect Science (ARP-PIS), Ghana*

[3] *University of Cambridge, Plant Sciences, United Kingdom*

[4] *Council for Scientific and Industrial Research - Crops Research Institute, Plant Health Division, Ghana*

[5] *Universiy of Ghana, Forest and Horticultural Crops Research Centre, Ghana*

Cabbage (*Brassica oleraceae* L. var. *capitata*) is a popular leafy vegetable consumed by many households in Ghana. It serves as a good source of vitamins and minerals, especially for malnourished children and pregnant women. Cabbage cultivation offers income to the rural, peri-urban and urban farmers and market women. In spite of its importance, insect pest damage contributes to high yield losses in cabbage production. Aphid attack can result in over 70–90 % loss in cabbage yield. A field trial was undertaken during the major and minor seasons in 2015 at Kpong and Kumasi in Ghana to study the infestation of aphids on cabbage, the species involved and a description of their damage and management. Ten cabbage leaves were randomly sampled weekly per treatment plot into 70 % alcohol and the total number of aphids were counted. Five pesticides were also applied weekly, namely Chlorpyrifos, Lambda-cyhalothrin, hot pepper fruit extract, neem seed extract, solution of local soap (alata samina) and water, as control. DNA barcoding using cytochrome oxidase sequences revealed two species of aphids, the mustard aphid, *Lipaphis erysimi* Kalt, which is the most abundant, and the generalist aphid, *Myzus persicae* (Sulzer), all occurring on cabbage at both locations. Aphid infestation was associated with sooty mold formation, leaf curling, mosaic, yellowing, browning, wilting and death of the plant; effects likely due to a mixture of direct feeding damage and transmission of pathogens, potentially including virus(es). Leaf samples from symptomatic plants are being tested for the presence of RNA and DNA viruses using RT-PCR and PCR, respectively, with universal primers for the different genera of viruses known to attack cabbage. The incidence and severity of aphid infestation on the cabbage was high with or without insecticide protection, except for plots sprayed with neem. A peak count of 1092 and 669 *L. erysimi*, and 495 and 199 *M. persicae* per leaf were obtained in the major and minor seasons, respectively. The least number of aphids, the highest yield and marketability was recorded in the neem-treated plots than the insecticide treated plots for both seasons.

Keywords: Aphids, cabbage, DNA barcoding, management, pesticides, viruses

Contact Address: Ken Fening, University of Ghana, Soil and Irrigation Research Centre, School of Agriculture, College of Basic and Applied Sciences, P. O. Box LG. 68, 233 Accra, Ghana, e-mail: kenof2@yahoo.com

Phytotoxic Effect of Soil-Incorporated Dried Leaf Residue of *Euphorbia golondrina* L.C.Wheeler on Tomato Growth and Yield

NDAM LAWRENCE MONAH[1], MATHIAS AFUI MIH[1], AARON SUH TENING[2], AUGUSTINA G. NWANA FONGOD[2], YOSHIHARU FUJII[3], NKEGUA TEMENU[4]

[1] *University of Buea, Dept. of Botany and Plant Physiology, Cameroon*
[2] *University of Buea, Dept. of Agronomy, Cameroon*
[3] *Tokyo University of Agricultural Sciences, International Environmental and Agricultural Sciences, Japan*
[4] *ABA Home Health Care Inc., Nursing, United States of America*

There is convincing evidence that the allelopathic attribute of alien invasive plant species plays a major role in agricultural and natural ecosystems by determining vegetation pattern, plant dominance, succession and biodiversity, preventing seed decay, causing seed dormancy and yield loss. Studies on allelopathy have led to using this phenomenon to reduce reliance on chemical herbicides for weed control. *Euphorbia golondrina*, an annual native to Central America, is now reported in Cameroon where it is a nuisance in subsistent farming systems. This study was designed to evaluate the phytotoxic effects of *E. golondrina* soil-incorporated dried leaf residue at varied concentrations on growth and yield of tomato in the Greenhouse of the University Buea, Cameroon. Incorporation of the leaf residue to the soil showed chlorosis, necrotic lesions and wilting of tomato under treatments 30 g and 50 g at 2 WAP. The number of leaves, leaf area, dry shoot and root weight of tomato grown in the soil-leaf mixtures were also significantly reduced. The inhibition percentages due to the addition of the three concentrations of *E. golondrina* dried leaf residue on the dry shoot weight at 4 WAP were 42.1 g, 49.6 g and 75.9 g for tomato. Similarly, declines in the dry root weight of 62.4, 83.1 and 84.5 % were registered under amended soil treatments. Further, the dry fruit yield and shoot weight of tomato under the treatments 20 g, 30 g and 50 g reduced with increase in leaf residue concentrations. The reductions in the fruit yield and fresh head weight caused by treatments 30 g and 50 g were 54.2 and 71.4 % respectively. The mineral contents in the leaves of tomato showed significant differences in the uptake of N, Mg, Na, Cu and Fe by the tomato plants. However, the P content was relatively constant in the leaves of tomato at 4 and 12 WAP. At 12 WAP, the Fe content in soils with treatments 30 g and 50 g was markedly enhanced in comparison with the other nutrients. Hence, under the greenhouse experiment, *Euphorbia golondrina* has been shown to contain some phytotoxic chemical compounds in its leaf materials.

Keywords: Allelopathy, Cameroon, *Euphorbia golondrina*, invasive plants, leaf residue, tomato

Contact Address: Ndam Lawrence Monah, University of Buea, Dept. of Botany and Plant Physiology, Molyko, 63 Buea, Cameroon, e-mail: nlmonah@yahoo.com

   ID 1038

Development of the Different Population of *Heterodera schachtii* in *Arabidopsis thaliana*

JENISH NAKARMI, FLORIAN M. W. GRUNDLER

University of Bonn, Inst. Crop Sci. and Res. Conserv. (INRES), Germany

Plant parasitic nematodes are obligate and biotrophs. Cyst nematodes of the genus *Heterodera* are economically most important plant parasitic nematodes worldwide. Among them, *Heterodera schachtii*, the beet cyst nematode, is a major pest for sugar beet production but also has wide host range covering the family Brassicacae. The second stage juveniles (J2) attack the roots of the plants after hatching from the cysts and induce the formation of specialised feeding sites which become their permanent source of nutrition during all of their sedentary life stages. Cyst nematodes result in a substantial damage to the yield with symptoms such as wilted leaves resulting in retarded growth and small sized beets bodies. *Arabidopsis thaliana* is a model plant which is commonly used to study various aspects of plant-nematode interaction. In this study, *A. thaliana* (Col-0) has been used to study the variation in the development of the populations of *H. schachtii* compared with a laboratory stock culture. This stock culture of *H. schachtii* is maintained on mustard roots for many years in *in-vitro* conditions. The samples of *H. schachtii* populations were collected from seven different locations of Germany i.e. Holle, Hildesheim, Harsum, Rommerskirchen, Boslar, Wolfenbüttel and Münster. The number of established males and females of these populations were compared with the control. The study revealed differences between the populations of the same species especially in virulence to the host. As a result, the establishment of the adult nematodes was strongly reduced in all samples compared to the stock culture. The female sizes and syncytia sizes were also used as important parameters to know the extent of infection. There were no differences in the female sizes and syncytia sizes between the populations and the stock culture. The different populations of *H. schachtii* were able to penetrate the roots of *A. thaliana* (Col-0) but were less successful in establishing parasitism compared to the stock culture. We conclude that the different populations are less virulent; the basis of this reduced virulence is a matter of further studies.

Keywords: *Arabidospsis thaliana*, *Heterodera schachtii*, plant-nematode interaction, population, virulence

Contact Address: Jenish Nakarmi, University of Bonn, Agriculture and Resource Management, Pariser Str.54, 53117 Bonn, Germany, e-mail: zen_jadoo@hotmail.com

Effect of Soil Management on Suppressions of *Rhizoctonia solani* in Agroecosystems of Santa Clara, Cuba

HÉCTOR PABLO HERNÁNDEZ ARBOLÁEZ[1], STEFAAN DE NEVE[2], MONICA HÖFTE[3], EDITH AGUILA ALCANTARA[1]

[1] *Universidad Central Marta Abreu de Las Villas, Faculty of Agricultural and Animal Sciences, Cuba*

[2] *Ghent University, Dept. of Soil Management, Belgium*

[3] *Ghent University, Dept. of Crop Protection: Phytopathology Laboratory, Belgium*

Disease suppression can be seen as a feature to determine healthy soil. From an ecological standpoint, soil health implies ecosystem stability, diversity, functional connectivity and resilience in response to a disturbance or stress. Previously suggested indicators to evaluate soil health and disease suppression have been mainly lists variables that correlate with the more or less disturbed soils (ranging from conventional and organic agricultural soils) or favourable conditions to eradicate the disease. This paper suggests that indicators of soil health and disease suppression could be found by monitoring the responses of *Rhizoctonia solani* in common bean and nutrient availability for the application of a disturbance or stress. Generally these results show a greater impact on systems (state and private) conventional handling and less impact on those systems had an agro-ecological management. This approach illustrates the responses of this fungus with respect to soil management in calcareous soils brown, after incorporation of a crop on this soil. In this research, the incidence was higher when incorporated into the soil more of external products and disturbances in the soil was higher, depending on these soil management in each of the evaluated systems. Rot caused by *Rhizoctonia solani* was less severe in agroecological systems compared to conventional systems which showed most affected although all soils tested cobdujeron disease greater or lesser degree. These results suggest that the proposed finding indicators of soil health and disease suppression and resistance to disturbance or stress approach is promising.

Keywords: Beans, disease, manage, *Rhizoctonia solani*, suppression

Contact Address: Héctor Pablo Hernández Arboláez, Universidad Central Marta Abreu de Las Villas, Faculty of Agricultural and Animal Sciences, Street A Between 2da and 4ta #8 Lizardo Proenza Neighborhood, 50100 Santa Clara, Cuba, e-mail: hectorha@uclv.edu.cu

ID 479

Managing Bacterial Wilt (*Ralstonia solanacearum*) of Potato (*Solanum tuberosum*) Using Indigenous Biological Control Agent

JOYCE AGUK[1], NANCY KARANJA[2], ELMAR SCHULTE-GELDERMANN[3], CHRISTIAN BRUNS[1]

[1] *University of Kassel, Dept. of Organic Farming and Cropping, Germany*

[2] *University of Nairobi, Dept. of Land Resource Management and Agricultural Technology (LARMAT), Kenya*

[3] *International Potato Center - sub Saharan Africa (CIP-SSA), Integrated Crop Management, Kenya*

The study was aimed at developing effective indigenous biological control agents (BCAs) isolated from Kenyan soils for use in managing bacterial wilt (BW) caused by *Ralstonia solanacearum* on potato. #300 rhizobacteria were locally isolated from potato rhizosphere and their antagonistic activity tested against BW *in vitro*. Promising isolates were then screened in the greenhouse using semi-sterilized soil through soil solarisation and inoculated with BW having 107 CFU. Those treatments that were most effective in control of BW were in consortium (mixtures) and included; *Bacillus* spp. + *Azotobacter* spp., *Pseudomonas spp.*+ *Bacillus* spp. and *Pseudomonas spp.* + *Bacillus* spp.+ *Azotobacter* spp. with area under disease progress curve ranging from 40–28 compared with the control having 2052–2900. A field study to evaluate these best performing BCAs was conducted for two seasons in 2015. During the first season (March to June), three experiments were established at three locations which were, two highly infected farms with soils containing BW of 10^3 CFU and an artificially inoculated field located at a research quarantine station with different BW inoculum concentration of 10^3, 10^5 and 10^7 CFU. Tolerant (Shangi) and susceptible (Tigoni) potato cultivars were used in this study. The second season experiment was established during the short rains (October– December) and was carried out only at the quarantine station where BW inoculation (10^6 CFU) was done and only the susceptible potato cultivar was used.

In the first season all the fields had few wilted plants from 1–3 observed across all the treatments including control hence there was no effect of the BCAs on yield. In the second season, there was no significant difference ($P \leq 0.05$) on tuber number and weight of BCAs compared to control despite them having high number of wilted plants ranging from 12–21 compared to the control with 8. Under controlled conditions the BCAs were effective in controlling BW however in the fields there was no effect. Further studies need to be undertaken on the mode of delivery of the BCAs to determine if this will enhance their performance in managing BW.

Keywords: *Azotobacter*, *Bacillus*, bacterial wilt, *Pseudomonas*, Rhizobacteria

Contact Address: Joyce Aguk, University of Kassel, Dept. of Organic Farming and Cropping, Witzenhausen, Germany, e-mail: joycaguk@yahoo.co.uk

Surveying Cassava Mosaic Disease (CMD) and *Sri Lankan Cassava Mosaic Virus* (SLCMV) in Four Provinces of Cambodia

Monica Carvajal-Yepes[1], Jenyfer Jimenez[1], Sophearith Sok[2], Sreng Cheaheng[3], Pou M3[3], Kris Wyckhuys[4], Stef de Haan[4], Wilmer Cuellar[1]

[1]*International Center for Tropical Agriculture (CIAT), Virology Unit, Colombia*

[2]*International Center for Tropical Agriculture (CIAT), Cambodia*

[3]*Provincial Department of Agriculture (PDA), Cambodia*

[4]*International Center for Tropical Agriculture (CIAT), Vietnam*

Cassava growers in Asia account for 30 % of world production. Its production, processing and marketing contributes to social and economic development in Asia. Cassava in Cambodia is the second most produced commodity after rice. Over the past 10 years, their cassava output has grown from 330 thousand tonnes in 2003 to 8 million tonnes in 2013 (FAOSTAT). Early this year, Wang et. al. reported a disease outbreak of cassava mosaic disease (CMD) observed in May 2015 in the province of Ratanakiri, Cambodia. The causal agent was identified as *Sri Lankan cassava mosaic virus* (SLCMV) (Wang et al. 2016). A study was conducted through a survey to determine the status of CMD and SLCMV in farmers' fields in four provinces: Ratanakiri, Tbong Khmum, Pursat and Battambang in February 2016 in Cambodia. To monitor the disease and the virus, collection of samples from the field was done through walking in the field using a "W" pattern. A total of 30 plants were assessed per field. SLCMV detection was done by ELISA and by PCR using primers designed to SLCMV. The study reveals that cassava mosaic disease was present only in Ratanakiri with a prevalence of 51.4 % at the Holley Eco-Industrial Co., Ltd fields. Interestingly, no symptoms of CMD were observed in any other cassava plot inspected around the location of the company or in other provinces of Cambodia. However, PCR results readily indicated that although the disease is contained to a limited region in Ratanakiri, the virus is already present in other provinces of Cambodia. Sequencing results confirmed the identity of the virus in all these provinces as SLCMV (>99 % identity in nucleotide sequence of the capsid protein to other isolates of SLCMV). The ELISA tests could detect the virus only in samples displaying symptoms of the disease and were associated to high levels of virus accumulation in symptomatic plants. PCR test sensitivity was significantly higher than ELISA. These results confirmed the presence of SLCMV and its wide distribution in other cassava growing regions in Cambodia. Monitoring and management strategies need to be done to control and prevent yield losses in the region.

Keywords: Cambodia, cassava mosaic disease, *Sri Lankan cassava mosaic* virus

Contact Address: Monica Carvajal-Yepes, International Center for Tropical Agriculture (CIAT), Virology Unit, Cali, Colombia, e-mail: monicarva@gmail.com

Influence of Plant Functional Groups on Microbial Residue Accumulation Process in two Different Soil Types

Rajasekaran Murugan[1], Sanjay Kumar[2]

[1] University of Kassel, Dept of Soil Biology and Plant Nutrition, Germany

[2] University of Agricultural Sciences, Regional Rice Research Station, India

In this study, influence of plant functional groups on specific contribution of microbial residues to soil organic C (SOC) was evaluated in a tropical Eucalyptus forest ecosystem with different plantation age and soil types. The treatments were stem girdling (SG), understory removal (UR) and control (CO). The amino sugars glucosamine and muramic acid were used as biomarkers for fungal and bacterial residues, respectively. Removal of plant functional groups significantly decreased the total amino sugar concentrations, especially in the SG treatment, followed by the UR. This suggests a negative effect of SG and UR on the accumulation of microbial residues in soil. The highest bacterial residues were observed in the SG treatment, which could be attributed to reduction in belowground carbon input and increased N availability. The SG and UR treatment recorded significantly lower concentrations of fungal residues, fungal C/bacterial C ratio and microbial residue C/soil organic C compared to the control. Accumulation of fungal residues as indicated by the fungal C/bacterial C ratio was in sandy loam soils with a high C/N ration and low pH. In contrast, the microbial residue C/soil organic C ratio was higher in clay loam soil. The fungal C/bacterial C ratio was higher in 5-year-old than in 15-year-old plantation. Our results highlight the ecological importance of plant functional groups and their effects on microbial residue build-up in different soil type. The use of the two ratios (fungal C/bacterial C and microbial residue C/soil organic C) reflects different dynamics of fungal and bacterial contribution to soil organic C sequestration. The different patterns of individual amino sugars suggest a change in the quality of microbial-derived soil organic matter.

Keywords: Amino sugars, bacteria, Eucalyptus, fungi, microbial community structure, soil organic matter

Contact Address: Rajasekaran Murugan, University of Kassel, Dept of Soil Biology and Plant Nutrition, Nordbahnhof Straße 1a, 37213 Witzenhausen, Germany, e-mail: raja.murugan15@gmail.com

Organic Soil Amendments: A Potential Bacterial Wilt Control in Potato

BRUCE OCHIENG OBURA[1], MONICA L. PARKER[1], CHRISTIAN BRUNS[2], MARIA
RENATE FINCKH[2], ELMAR SCHULTE-GELDERMANN[1]

[1]*International Potato Center (CIP), Intergrated Crop Management, Kenya*
[2]*University of Kassel, Ecological Plant Protection, Germany*

Potato bacterial wilt (BW) disease caused by *Ralstonia solanacearum* is one of the most destructive bacterial diseases of potato production. Control of BW is very difficult as there are no effective chemical control measures available. The presented study aimed at investigating the effect of soil amendment (SA) and inoculum density on the subsequent development of (BW) in field conditions over two seasons. Eight SA used included compost 10 mm sized particles (C10) at three application rates of $5\,t\,ha^{-1}$, $2.5\,t\,ha^{-1}$ and $1.25\,t\,ha^{-1}$, Neem kernel cake (N) at three application rates of $1\,t\,ha^{-1}$, $0.25\,t\,ha^{-1}$ and $0.125\,t\,ha^{-1}$, a combination of C10 at $1.25\,t\,ha^{-1}$ + N $0.125\,t\,ha^{-1}$, Plantmate (an organic fertiliser consisting of 25 beneficial microorganisms and macronutrients, probiotics, enzymes, amino acids, and growth promoting substances) and a control without SA, two inoculum densities used were 3.26×10^3 $CFU\,ml^{-1}$ and 2.9×10^5 $CFU\,ml^{-1}$. The experimental layout was a split plot design with four replications, inoculum density as main plot and SA as sub plots. The field was inoculated three days before treatment application in each season with 200 ml per unit area of bacterial suspension. Potatoes were planted in all the two consecutive seasons and treatments were applied to the same plots before planting. BW population were quantified 48 hours before SA application and at the end of every season, weekly observations of disease incidences were recorded. The findings showed significant reduction of BW by 75 % and 65 % in Plant mate at 10^3 $CFU\,ml^{-1}$ and 10^5; $CFU\,ml^{-1}$ respectively and 60 % and 40 % in (N) at 10^3 $CFU\,ml^{-1}$ and 10^5 $CFU\,ml^{-1}$ respectively against Control. Yields losses in these treatment were low with average yields of $34\,t\,ha^{-1}$ at 10^3 $CFU\,ml^{-1}$ for both Plant mate and (N) as compared to $1\,t\,ha^{-1}$ in the control and $29\,t\,ha^{-1}$ and $27\,t\,ha^{-1}$ at 10^5; $CFU\,ml^{-1}$ for Plant mate and (N) respectively as compared to only $1\,t\,ha^{-1}$ in the control. This study shows that Plant mate and (N) had a great potential in reducing losses caused by BW. Further studies on the mode of action particularly of the SA are currently underway.

Keywords: Compost, Neem kernel cake, potato, *Ralstonia solanacearum*

Contact Address: Bruce Ochieng Obura, International Potato Center - sub-Saharan Africa (CIP-SSA), Intergrated Crop Management, Old Naivasha Road Off Waiyaki Way, Nairobi, Kenya, e-mail: b.ochieng@cgiar.org

ID 920

Rice

Rice Yield Variability in West Africa and its Determinants

ABIBOU NIANG[1,2], MATHIAS BECKER[1], KAZUKI SAITO[2], FRANK EWERT[1]

[1] *University of Bonn, Inst. Crop Sci. and Res. Conserv. (INRES) - Plant Nutrition, Germany*

[2] *Africa Rice Center (AfricaRice), Benin*

Rice is staple food in West Africa but farmers' production does not satisfy consumption demands. Rice farmers' yields are low contributing to a large yield variation between and within major production systems and climatic zones. The objectives of this study are to quantify spatial variability of on farm yields in the three main rice production systems (irrigated lowland, rainfed lowland and rainfed upland) across the three main climatic zones (semi-arid, sub-humid and humid) in West Africa, and to identify yield-affecting factors. This study analysed data on yield, climate, soil, and crop management practices collected in 1305 farmers' fields in 22 sites in 11 West African countries over 2012 to 2014. A boundary function approach was used to evaluate the maximum yield response in relation to solar radiation and rainfall during rice growing period. Random forest method was used to identify factors affecting variation in difference between the maximum yield derived from the boundary curves and on-farm yield. Rice yields ranged from 0.3 to 8.0 Mg ha^{-1} with mean yields of 4.1, 2.0, and 1.5 Mg ha^{-1} and maximum yield of around 8, 6, and 4 Mg ha^{-1} in irrigated lowland, rainfed lowland, and rainfed upland rice production systems, respectively. Rice yield was higher in semi-arid zone in irrigated and rainfed lowland rice, whereas there was no large difference among the three zones in upland rice. Nitrogen application rate and herbicide use were major contributors to the yield variation in irrigated lowland rice. Bunding, variety used, N fertiliser application rate, weeding frequency and soil pH affected variation in the yield differences in rainfed lowland rice. Bird control, bunding and variety used were the major determinants in rainfed upland rice. We conclude that improved crop management strategies will enhance on-farm rice yield in West Africa. Improving access to inputs and their use efficiencies in irrigated lowland rice and dissemination of local-specific crop management practices in rained lowland rice are likely to be key areas for rice research and development in this region.

Keywords: Climatic zones, management practices, *Oryza sativa*, yield gaps

Contact Address: Abibou Niang, University of Bonn, Inst. of Crop Science and Resource Conservation (INRES), Katzenburgweg 5, 53115 Bonn, Germany, e-mail: abibou.niang@cgiar.org

Effects of Water Management on the Performance of NERICA 4 in Semi-Arid Areas, Tanzania

ALEXANDRA SCHAPPERT, ANGELA SCHAFFERT, JÖRN GERMER, FOLKARD ASCH

University of Hohenheim, Inst. of Agricultural Sciences in the Tropics (Hans-Ruthenberg-Institute), Germany

In semi-arid areas in Africa soil degradation and droughts are reducing agricultural productivity. In order to counteract the yield reduction soil and water conservation methods need to be applied. The aim of this study is to analyse the potential of growing upland rice, one of the most important stable crops, in seasonal drought prone areas in Tanzania. Three water management techniques are identified and evaluated: modifying the soil surface to collect and save water, adding a minimum amount of water in case of drought events and to decrease evaporation by adapted weeding management.

Experiments were conducted near Dodoma, Tanzania during the wet season from January until May in which an average precipitation of 430 mm is recorded. The upland rice variety NERICA 4, which is well adapted to the African environment, was used for investigating the potential for growing NERICA 4 upland rice under following management practices: i) rainfed, ii) rainfed in combination with tied-ridging, iii) tied-ridging with additional irrigation to keep soil moisture above the permanent wilting point of the soil (life saving irrigation), iv) life saving irrigation without tied ridges and v) under irrigation (full crop water requirements). Those options were combined with time based weeding strategies. This study explores the effects of these water management methods on the soil water status and the performance of the crop in terms of leaf area, specific leaf area (SLA), biomasspartitioning, yield determining components like number of productive tillers and spikelets, grain yield, harvest index (HI), yield loss and water use efficiency (WUE) were investigated. Tied ridges did not improve irrigated cropping systems. The competitiveness of weeds led to changed soil moisture values and microclimate within the canopy, caused development delay and reduced grain yields up to 45 %. The poor rainfall distribution in the growing season 2015 provoked total crop failure of all rainfed treatments without irrigation and caused yield loss and thus low water use efficiencies for the treatments with life saving irrigation. In that context possibilities for growing upland rice successfully under rainfall limited conditions will be discussed.

Keywords: Deficit irrigation, tied ridges, upland rice variety NERICA 4

Contact Address: Alexandra Schappert, University of Hohenheim, Inst. of Agricultural Sciences in the Tropics (Hans-Ruthenberg-Institute), Stuttgart, Germany, e-mail: alexandraschappert@web.de

ID 1033

Growth Dynamics and Yield Formation Related to Flag Leaf Photosynthesis and PSii Fluorescence in Rice

MARC SCHMIERER, OLIVER KNOPF, FOLKARD ASCH

University of Hohenheim, Inst. of Agricultural Sciences in the Tropics (Hans-Ruthenberg-Institute), Germany

The world population is predicted to reach 10 billion people in 2030, requiring a yearly increase in world rice production of more than 1 %. Since urbanisation and land degradation will lead to a severe reduction in growing area in the coming decades, more rice must be produced on less land. On a physiological level, rice yield is determined by the number of reproductive organs per unit ground area and their size. Consistently, most approaches to increase yield target on minimising the difference between the potential and the realised sink size of the plant. While there is a wide agreement in the literature that a high nitrogen content in meristem cells during the early reproductive phase will lead to a greater panicle size, the relation between growth rates during different stages of the reproductive phase and eventual sink size is still unclear. In order to address this question, we conducted a climate chamber experiment comprising 54 rice plants. Growth rates after panicle initiation were manipulated by different levels of irradiance and nitrogen. Destructive samplings and photosynthesis measurements on flag leaves, including fluorescence measurements as well as carbon and light reaction curves were performed at early, mid and late reproductive phase. While growth rates during the early reproductive phase were positively correlated with final yield and yield components, this relation consistently disappeared during later development phases. Correspondingly, correlation between fluorescence and photosynthesis parameters and final sink size was highest when measured pre-heading. Finally, our data indicates that the non-regulated PSII heat-dissipation of flag leaves measured shortly before heading is a promising predictor for constricted sink dimensioning. Remarkably, this is not an effect of stress or N-deficiency induced downregulation of photosystems as will be demonstrated by analysis of supplemental fluorescence and photosynthesis parameters.

Keywords: Non-regulated PSII heat-dissipation, rice, sink dimensioning

Contact Address: Marc Schmierer, University of Hohenheim, Inst. of Agricultural Sciences in the Tropics (Hans-Ruthenberg-Institute), Stuttgart, Germany, e-mail: marc.schmierer@gmail.com

Phenological Response of Lowland Rice Genotypes to Environmental Conditions - Case of Ambohibary, Madagascar

Arisoa Rajaona[1], Elke Vandamme[2], Kalimuthu Senthilkumar[2], Pepijn Van Oort[3], Kazuki Saito[3]

[1]Africa Rice Center (AfricaRice), Sustainable Productivity Enhancement, Madagascar
[2]Africa Rice Center (AfricaRice), Tanzania
[3]Africa Rice Center (AfricaRice), Benin

Rice is the most important cereal in the world and one of the main staple foods for millions of people in sub-Saharan Africa. It constitutes a strong component of food security and poverty alleviation in Africa. However, Africa's rice production has not been able to meet the increasing in demand and there is a huge gap between consumption and local production. AfricaRice and its partners have developed a decision-support tool called "RiceAdvice" to improve farmers' decision making in irrigated and rainfed lowland rice production systems. RiceAdvice provides users with information on best-bet cropping calendars; with emphasis on good agricultural practices in general, in particular soil fertility management. To incorporate rice phenology as a function of varietal choice, air temperature and day length into the current version of RiceAdvice, detailed physiological field experiments, so called "Rice Garden Trials" are conducted in Ambohibary, in Central West Madagascar. This area, at high altitude (1500 m asl) is prone to cold stress and climatic hazard. Therefore, data collected will be used to estimate growth duration and timing of specific development stages for each variety, as well as expected yield loss due to cold and heat stress, through use of crop simulation models. Rice Garden trials were established using existing and new cold-tolerant varieties, some popular varieties grown in different countries across Africa, and some new varieties developed by AfricaRice (ARICA's). 100 genotypes are selected including: 5 check and 95 test varieties. They were sown in November 2015, January and February 2016. For each sowing month, an augmented design with 5check cultivars and 5 replicate blocks was installed. Each plot is 1.92 m^2 large, with a density of 25 hills m^{-2}. Besides phenological observation during the crop cycle, yield and its components were measured, and spikelet sterility was determined. The main results: (i) Crop duration of lowland rice cultivars changes at different sawing dates; (ii) Genotype and sowing dates are contributing to observed variability in crop duration and grain yield (iii) Morpho-physiological traits contributing to cold tolerance that should be used to improve rice phenological and growth models (RiceAdvice) and adapt cropping calendars.

Keywords: Cold sterility, cropping calendars, decision-support, food security

Contact Address: Arisoa Rajaona, Africa Rice Center (AfricaRice), Sustainable Productivity Enhancement, Antisrabe, Madagascar, Madagascar, e-mail: a.rajaona@cgiar.org

ID 506

'New Roots for Rice Production': Root Research in the Low-Input Systems of Sub-Saharan Africa

PIETERJAN DE BAUW[1], ELKE VANDAMME[2], ROEL MERCKX[1]

[1]*KU Leuven, Dept. of Earth and Environmental Sciences, Belgium*
[2]*Africa Rice Center (AfricaRice), Tanzania*

In large parts of sub-Saharan Africa (SSA), rice serves as an important staple crop. The rice consumption in SSA is steadily rising and population growth drastically increases the demand. As net rice importers, several countries in SSA face a critical socio-economic situation which endangers their food security. Rice production in SSA needs to increase, despite several biophysical limitations such as drought and low soil fertility. More specifically related to the latter, low soil phosphorus (P) availability is a key limitation. The uptake of water and P by roots is strongly related and different root traits or root characteristics have synergistic or antagonistic effects on water and P uptake.

High crop yields in 'high-input systems' are mostly sustained by intensive use of fertilisers and irrigation. However, conventional breeding strategies focusing on above ground features did neither lead to sustainable solutions nor to significant yield increases in low-input systems on which many resource-poor, smallholder farmers rely. In search for sustainable and resilient solutions to increase rice production in SSA, it is important to unravel the 'belowground opportunities' of the rice crop. The acquisition of soil resources by plant roots is of major importance to establish reasonable agricultural outputs in low-input systems. In this perspective, we need to understand the root responses of contrasting rice cultivars in situations that face combined drought and low P stresses.

In this study, both pot and field trials are established in Tanzania, whereby combined P and water treatments are imposed. During rice development, roots are excavated and washed out for root system and root morphology characterisation. The corresponding responses of roots and the genotypic variation among different cultivars will be evaluated and discussed.

The expected outcome is the selection of breeding traits that contribute to higher P- and/or water uptake-efficiency of rice. Using these traits, rice breeders could develop 'stronger' and 'more resilient' varieties that survive and reasonably produce in these constrained environments. This would have a substantial contribution to improving food security and root system research could hence contribute to a 'brown' revolution (from 'soil' and 'roots') in the resource poor agricultural systems of SSA.

Keywords: Drought stress, low phosphorus availability, rice, sustainable and efficient root systems

Contact Address: Pieterjan De Bauw, KU Leuven, Dept. of Earth and Environmental Sciences, Kasteelpark Arenberg 20 - Box 2459, 3001 Leuven, Belgium, e-mail: pieterjan.debauw@ees.kuleuven.be

Soil Attributes and Grain Yield of Upland Rice as Affected by Cover Crops

ADRIANO STEPHAN NASCENTE, ANNA CRISTINA LANNA, MARTA CRISTINA CORSI FILIPPI

Brazilian Agricultural Research Corporation (EMBRAPA), Rice and Beans, Brazil

Better understanding of the use of cover crops in no-tillage systems (NTS) in upland rice crop could contribute to an increase in grain production. In the soil, $N-NO_3^-$ and $N-NH_4^+$ are the main forms of N available to plants, and in aerobic soils nitrate prevails in relation to ammonium. Most plants absorb both nitrate and ammonium. However, upland rice plants in the early stages of development have a reduced capacity for uptake, storage and/or metabolising $N-NO_3^-$. Some researchers bring up the principal hypothesis that rice seedlings present low activity of nitrate reductase (NR) enzyme. The use of cover crops can change the relation between the mineral forms of N in soils, providing larger amounts of $N-NH_4^+$, and may so enable a better development of crops that absorb more this form of N, such as upland rice. The aim of this study was to determine the effect of pearl millet intercropped with other cover crops on mineral forms of N and urease activity in soil, nitrate reductase activity in the leaves of the follow-up rice crop, as well as the yield components of this rice crop. The experiment was performed in the year 2012/2013 at two locations of the Brazilian Cerrado. The experimental design was a complete randomised block with eight replications. The treatments consisted of four types of cover crop [1. Pearl millet (*Pennisetum glaucum*) - control, 2. Pearl millet + *Crotalaria spectabilis*, 3. Pearl millet + *Brachiaria ruziziensis*, 4. Pearl millet + *C. spectabilis* + *B. ruziziensis*]. The results allowed us to conclude that among the cover crops evaluated intercropping with the cover crops pearl millet + *C. spectabilis* provided higher nitrate content in the soil than with pearl millet alone or combined with *B. ruziziensis*. However, no differences were found for the ammonium content and urease in the soil after intercropping, neither for the nitrate reductase activity in the rice leaves, nor for the yield components of the rice crop in a no-tillage system. Nevertheless, our results indicate that the evaluated cover crops could be an important option to be considered for upland rice crop when aiming for higher rice grain yield.

Keywords: Ammonium, *Brachiaria ruziziensis*, *Crotalaria spectabilis*, nitrate, nitrate reductase, *Oryza sativa*, *Pennisetum glaucum*, urease

Contact Address: Adriano Stephan Nascente, Brazilian Agricultural Research Corporation (EMBRAPA), Rice and Beans, P.O. Box 179, Highway 462, km 12, 75.375-000 Santo Antônio de Goiás, Brazil, e-mail: adriano.nascente@embrapa.br

ID 21

Rice Affected by Seed Treatment, Soil Compaction and Nitrogen at No-Tillage and Conventional Tillage

ADRIANO STEPHAN NASCENTE, VENERALDO PINHEIRO,
LUIS FERNANDO STONE

Brazilian Agricultural Research Corporation (EMBRAPA), Rice and Beans, Brazil

Rice is included in the diet of half of the world's population. Mostly of this cereal is grown on irrigated land. However, available water for growing irrigated rice by flood irrigation has been reduced because of the competing demands of industry and population. As a result, we are looking for alternatives that allow greater efficiency of water use. Some alternatives include growing rice under upland conditions, such as at a no-tillage system (NTS). The objective of this study was to determine the best combination of management options for upland rice production: seed treatment, N management and soil compaction in zero and conventional tillage methods. We conducted two field trials, one in NTS and another at conventional tillage (CT) (one plowing and two disking). For each trial, experimental design was a randomised block design in a factorial scheme. The treatments consisted of a combination of five rice cultivar (BRS Caçula, BRS Serra Dourada, BRS Primavera, BRS Sertaneja, and BRS Esmeralda) with two compaction pressures on the sowing furrow (25 kPa or 126 kPa), two types of seed treatment (with or without pesticide) and two types of N management (all amount of N at sowing or all amount of N at topdressing). Application of N at sowing instead of at topdressing was effective to allow higher grain yield at NTS. Under this system, upland rice genotypes had higher grain yield with higher compaction pressure. Seed treatment with pesticide provided higher grain yield for BRS Sertaneja at NTS, and for all genotypes at CT. BRS Esmeralda at NTS, and BRS Esmeralda and BRS Primavera at CT, were the most productive genotypes. Our results show that it is possible to produce upland rice under NTS, however the farmers should pay attention to some factors, such as the genotype more adapted for this condition, application timing of N, and compaction pressure on the sowing furrow. At CT, seed treatment is an important practice to improve upland rice grain yield.

Keywords: Aerobic rice, early N fertilisation, fipronil, pesticide, termite

Contact Address: Adriano Stephan Nascente, Brazilian Agricultural Research Corporation (EM-BRAPA), Rice and Beans, P.O. Box 179, Highway 462, km 12, 75.375-000 Santo Antônio de Goiás, Brazil, e-mail: adriano.nascente@embrapa.br

Rice Grain Yield as Affected by Grain-Producing Cover Crops in Cabo Delgado, Mozambique

ADRIANO STEPHAN NASCENTE[1], JOSÉ DAMBIRO[2]

[1]Brazilian Agricultural Research Corporation (EMBRAPA), Rice and Beans, Brazil
[2]Aga Khan Foundation (Mozambique), Agricultural Manager, Mozambique

Rice is considered a staple food for countries worldwide. Specifically in Mozambique, this grain can contribute to reduce poverty of 3.1 million people directly dependent of rice grains production and 20 million Mozambicans indirectly dependents. However, the rice grain yield in this country is very low, ranging from 970 kg ha^{-1} to 1170 kg ha^{-1}. The main reasons are the use of rudimentary techniques, limited knowledge, inefficient management of water and infrastructure, which keeps rice production in Mozambique, and in several African countries, in family subsistence levels. The inclusion of cover crops before rice cultivation besides providing benefits to the environment such as soil protection, release of nutrients, moisture maintenance and weed control, can increase rice production. The aim of this study was to evaluate the production of biomass and grain cover crops, yield components, and grain yield of rice in Mozambique. The study was conducted in two sites located in the province of Cabo Delgado, in Mozambique. The experimental design was a randomised block in a factorial 2×6, with four repetitions. Treatments were carried out in two locations (Cuaia and Nambaua) and 6 vegetation covers: Millet (*Pennisetum glaucum* L.); namarra bean (*Lablab purpureus* (L.) Sweet), velvet beans (*Mucuna pruriens* L.), oloco beans (*Vigna radiata* (L.) R. Wilczek), cowpea (*Vigna unguiculata* L.), and fallow. The cover crops *Lablab purpureus*, *Vigna unguiculata*, and *Mucuna pruriens* stood out in the production of biomass, being better for soil protection and for cycling nutrients. All covers provided similar results for rice grain production. The cover crop *V. unguiculata* showed to be the best as it had the highest grain production (1793 kg ha^{-1}). Rice grain yield in Nambaua (2594 kg ha^{-1}) was two times greater than average of Mozambique, while in Cuaia the grain yield (4509 kg ha^{-1}) was four times higher than the average grain yield of rice in Mozambique (1160 kg ha^{-1}).

Keywords: Conservation agriculture, grain production, legumes, sustainability

Contact Address: Adriano Stephan Nascente, Brazilian Agricultural Research Corporation (EMBRAPA), Rice and Beans, P.O. Box 179, Highway 462, km 12, 75.375-000 Santo Antônio de Goiás, Brazil, e-mail: adriano.nascente@embrapa.br

ID 29

Effects of Soil and Foliar Applied Micronutrients on Productivity and Profitability of Rice in Tanzania

KALIMUTHU SENTHILKUMAR[1], FITTA SILAS SILLO[1], BONAVENTURE JANUARY TESHA[1], IBNOU DIENG[2], JONNE RODENBURG[1], KAZUKI SAITO[2], ELKE VANDAMME[1], CHRISTIAN DIMKPA[3]

[1]*Africa Rice Center (AfricaRice), Tanzania*
[2]*Africa Rice Center (AfricaRice), Benin*
[3]*Virtual Fertiliser Research Center (VFRC), United States of America*

Rice production in sub-Saharan Africa is largely nutrient-limited, hence application of micronutrients along with NPK is often needed to boost and sustain yields. Foliar and soil application of micronutrients could be efficient, however, few studies have simultaneously compared the efficiency and effectiveness of foliar vs soil-applied fertilisers, and the results have been inconclusive. This study, therefore, assessed the productivity and profitability of different soil- and foliar-applied micronutrients in 30 on-farm trials during the wet season of 2015, in Tanzania. Five representative, locally-available foliar formulations were tested following two NPK-fertiliser treatments (N:P:K@80:17:33 kg ha^{-1} vs no-NPK), under three growing conditions (irrigated lowland, rainfed lowland and rainfed upland) against two reference treatments (control; and soil application of micronutrients (SMN) – B:Zn:S:Mg @ 2:3:7.5:10 kg ha^{-1}). Grain yield, yield attributing characteristics and benefit: cost (B:C) ratio were assessed for all treatments. In rainfed lowland conditions, application of NPK alone increased yield from 2.7 to 5.0 t ha^{-1} while additional SMN further increased the yield to 6.8 t ha^{-1}. With NPK, two of the five foliar products increased yield significantly, while none increased yield significantly under the no-NPK conditions. The highest B:C ratio (14) was achieved for SMN, being between 4 and 11 for the five foliar products. In irrigated lowland conditions, NPK increased yield from 3.1 to 4.1 t ha^{-1}, while additional SMN increased yield further to 4.6 t ha^{-1}. With NPK, no significant yield increase was observed for the foliar products, except for one product under no-NPK. The B:C ratio for SMN was 4, and between 1 to 5 for foliar products for both NPK and no-NPK conditions. In upland conditions, no significant yield increase was observed with NPK, SMN and the five foliar products, with yields ranging from 1.3 to 2.7 t ha^{-1}. The efficiency and economic benefits of micronutrients is variable across rice growing conditions. Application of small doses of micronutrients increased yields significantly under rainfed and irrigated lowland conditions; however, its effectiveness was not evident in upland conditions.

Keywords: Cost benefit analysis, fertiliser products, food security, sub-Saharan Africa

---

Contact Address: Kalimuthu Senthilkumar, Africa Rice Center (AfricaRice), East and Southern Africa, Avocado Street, 33581 Dar es Salaam, Tanzania, e-mail: k.senthilkumar@cgiar.org

Soil Management Options for Improving Nitrogen Use Efficiency of Rice in the Kilombero Flood Plains

JULIUS KWESIGA[1], DANIEL NEUHOFF[1], KALIMUTHU SENTHILKUMAR[2], MATHIAS BECKER[3], ULRICH KÖPKE[1]

[1]University of Bonn, Inst. of Organic Agriculture, Germany

[2]Africa Rice Center (AfricaRice), East and Southern Africa, Tanzania

[3]University of Bonn, Inst. Crop Sci. and Res. Conserv. (INRES) - Plant Nutrition, Germany

Rice is an important staple food crop in East Africa and its production needs to be increased to meet the increasing demand. East African wetlands provide opportunities to meet the demand if managed efficiently. On-farm experiments to evaluate different soil management options that can improve the nutrient use efficiency of lowland rice under rain-fed conditions are ongoing in the Kilombero flood plain of Tanzania. Three on-farm experiments have been completed since 2014 under three hydrological zones called 'Fringe', 'Middle', and 'Center'. Treatments included inorganic fertiliser (urea), organic fertilisers (cow manure (Cm)) and green manure (*Lablab purpureus*). Urea applied at three levels 0, 60 and 120 kg N ha^{-1}. Cm was applied at rates equivalent to 60 kg N ha^{-1} while a 6-week old Lablab was grown and incorporated *in-situ* before transplanting. Lowland rice variety SARO 5 was used in the experiment. The management practices ranged from farmers practice to best management practice. Plant samples were taken at different growth stages for biomass and nutrient use efficiency analysis. Nitrogen uptake (NP), physiological efficiency (PE), agronomic efficiency (AE) and Nitrogen use efficiency (NUE) have been evaluated at 30 and 50 DAT and yield assessed at harvest. Preliminary results show that the middle zone has a higher PE and AE compared to the fringe zone. Organic amendments produced better PE compared to the inorganic amendments (Lablab > Cm > 60 kg > 120 kg N ha^{-1}) at 50 DAT. AE was high in the order of Lablab > 60 kg N > 120 kg N > Cm. NP was significantly higher in the treatments receiving mineral N compared with all other treatments. There were no significant differences on the NUE at 30 and 50 DAT. However, differences are expected after full bloom and harvest lab data analysis is completed. 120 kg N ha^{-1} obtained the highest grain yield (9.9 t ha^{-1}) as an average for Fringe and Middle which is 6.7 t ha^{-1} higher than what is obtained on farmers' practice (3.2 t ha^{-1}). So far the different responses to NUE in the hydrological zones of the flood plain are in line with the needed optimisation of crop yield and recommendation for the most appropriate management strategies.

Keywords: Agronomic efficiency, fertilisers, lowland, N uptake, nutrient use efficiency, on-farm, rainfed, SARO5

Contact Address: Julius Kwesiga, University of Bonn, Inst. of Organic Agriculture, Bonn, Germany, e-mail: kwesigajulius@yahoo.com

ID 787

Seasonal Nitrogen Dynamics in Lowland Rice Cropping Systems in Inland Valleys of Northern Ghana

MICHAEL ASANTE[1], MATHIAS BECKER[2], CARLOS ANGULO[2]

[1] *Savannah Agricultural Research Institute (CSIR), Soil Fertility, Ghana*

[2] *University of Bonn, Inst. Crop Sci. and Res. Conserv. (INRES) - Plant Nutrition, Germany*

Rainfed lowland rice farmers in the inland valleys of northern Ghana are challenged with N deficiency as a major production constraint. With extremely low use of external inputs, there is a need to efficiently use systems' internal resources such as native soil N. Largest soil nitrate-N losses are expected to occur during the transition between the dry and wet season (DWT) when the soil aeration status changes from aerobic to anaerobic conditions. Technical options avoiding the build-up of nitrate are expected to reduce N losses and may thus enhance the yield of rice. A field study in the moist savannah zone of Ghana assessed the *in-situ* mineralisation of native soil N, the contribution of nitrate to the valley bottom by sub-surface flow from adjacent slopes, and the effects of crop and land management options during DWT on seasonal soil N_{min} dynamics and the yield of lowland rice. Large amounts of nitrate were accumulated during DWT with a peak of $58\,kg\,ha^{-1}$ in lowland soils, of which $32\,kg\,ha^{-1}$ was contributed from the adjacent upland slope. Most of this nitrate disappeared at the onset of the wet season, possibly by leaching and denitrification upon soil flooding. While the incorporation of rice straw (temporary immobilisation of soil N in the microbial biomass) had little effect on soil N conservation, growing a crop during DWT conserved 22–$27\,kg$ of soil N ha^{-1} in the biomass and *Crotalaria juncea* supplied an additional $43\,kg\,N\,ha^{-1}$ from biological N_2 fixation. Farmers' practice of bare fallow during DWT resulted in the lowest rice grain yield that increased from 1.3 to 3.9 Mg ha^{-1} in case of the transition season legume. Growing a pre-rice legume during DWT appears a promising option to manage N and increase lowland rice yields in the inland valleys of northern Ghana.

Keywords: *Crotalaria juncea*, moist Savannah zone, nitrate, *Oryza sativa*

Contact Address: Michael Asante, Savannah Agricultural Research Institute (CSIR), Soil Fertility, Tamale, Ghana, e-mail: mkasante08@yahoo.co.uk

Research on Water-Saving System for Paddy Field in Thai Highland Communities

JANJIRA RUNGCHAROEN[1], SIRIPONG HUNGSPREUG[1], SUTHAT PLEUMPANYA[2], NUTTAYA SURIYAWONG[1], SATHIT MITHARN[1], SIRODE PRAKUNHUNGSIT[1], BOONLUE KACHENCHART[3]

[1] *Highland Research and Development Institute, Thailand*
[2] *Royal Project Foundation, Thailand*
[3] *Mahidol University, Thailand, Thailand*

Rice cultivation in the Thai highlands is usually on terraced paddy fields that are rain-fed and often flooded, but flooding can cause water loss. Climate variability often results in insufficient rainfall at the beginning of rainy season, which can delay field preparation and transplanting. The objectives of this research were: (1) to investigate the volume of water usage on rice fields under the non-flooded and flooded soil condition; and (2) to monitor the emission of greenhouse gases on rice fields on non-flooded and flooded soil. The experiment was conducted in Chiang Mai province in 2014–2015. Two treatments were imposed: 1) flooded, which used irrigation water to maintain water depth from 3 to 10 cm; and 2) non-flooded, which used irrigation to maintain a water depth of 3 cm until 3 weeks after transplanting, followed by alternate drying and rewetting: when irrigation was applied water depth was up to 5 cm. Results showed that in 2014, local variety San-Pa-Tong1 yielded 3,925 kg ha^{-1} when grown under non-flooded conditions and 3,600 kg ha^{-1} under flooded conditions. The irrigated water volume of non-flooded was 4,504 m^3 ha^{-1} and 6,947 m^3 ha^{-1} under flooded soil condition, which is a 35% water savings in the non-flooded treatment. In 2015, the non-flooded treatment 4,581 kg ha^{-1} and the flooded treatment yielded 4,147 kg ha^{-1}. The non-flooded treatment used 9,015 m^3 ha^{-1} of irrigation water, which was 56% less water than the flooded treatment, which used 20,462 m^3 ha^{-1}. The cumulative methane emissions in the non-flooded treatment was 12.2 kg CH$_4$ ha^{-1}, which was 75% less than the 50.4 kg CH$_4$ ha^{-1} emitted in the flooded treatment. Cumulative nitrous oxide emission was 2.69 kg N$_2$O ha^{-1} in the non-flooded treatment, which was 14% less than the 3.13 kg N$_2$O ha^{-1} emitted in the flooded treatment. Combined, non-flooded produced 46% less carbon equivalents than the flooded treatment. Thus, non-flooded conditions with alternate wetting and drying cycle increased crop yields and efficiency of water use while reducing greenhouse warming potential. If farmers adopt this water-saving system of non-flooded rice production in highland areas, they can conserve water for production of further crops.

Keywords: Greenhouse gases, rice, terraced paddy field, Thai highland, water-saving system

---

Contact Address: Janjira Rungcharoen, Highland Research and Development Institute, 65 Moo 1 Suthep Road Chiangmai, 50200 Chiang Mai, Thailand, e-mail: puntase@hotmail.com

Biological Nitrification Inhibition (BNI) in Rice (*Oryza sativa* L.) for Contrasting Piedmont Llanos Soils of Colombia

ASHLY AREVALO, JONATHAN NÚÑEZ, YOLIMA OSPINA, CECILE GRENIER, JACOBO ARANGO

International Center for Tropical Agriculture (CIAT), Colombia

Within the nitrogen cycle, nitrification is the oxidation of ammonium (NH_4^+) to nitrate (NO_3) and is mediated by microorganisms. Nitrate is an inorganic form of nitrogen (N), susceptible to being lost by leaching and denitrification resulting in the loss of N fertiliser (around 70%). These losses of applied N fertiliser have negative socio-economic and environmental impacts. One strategy to prevent the loss of N in agricultural systems, is the inhibition of nitrification. Certain plants are able to release chemicals from their roots that inhibit nitrification in the rhizosphere, this process is called Biological Nitrification Inhibition (BNI). BNI function has been characterised in *Brachiaria humidicola* (Bh) tropical grass, and identified as the species with the greatest BNI activity. This study evaluated the residual BNI effect of Bh in a simulation of a Bh-upland rice rotation system for contrasting Piedmont Llanos soils from Santa Rosa, department of Meta, Colombia. In soils from Santa Rosa the BNI potential of different lowland and upland rice genotypes was explored, with comparisons made between varieties, breeding lines and commercial cultivars. The methodologies used were those developed for the determination of BNI in Bh and sorghum, including bioluminescence assay (bioassay) with the recombinant ammonia-oxidising bacteria (AOB) *Nitrosomonas europaea* strain, and the incubation of rhizosphere soil for the determination of nitrification rates. Yield differences were found among the rice lines with greater yields obtained from those that grew in the soil where Bh was previously planted. In terms of BNI activity (determined by bioassay) of root exudates, significant differences ($P \leq 0.05$) were identified between rice genotypes expressed as allylthiourea units per gram of dry root (ATU g^{-1}) in a range of 3.27 to 31.75. Moreover, soil nitrification rates expressed as mg NO_3-N kg^{-1} soil day^{-1} ranged from 3.06 to 7.63. For lowland rice genotypes there was a 50% of relation ($r^2 = 0.52$) between the root exudates and nitrification rates. Altogether, these results indicate that some rice genotypes have the ability to reduce nitrification in soil. Additionally the Bh-rice rotation system should be further evaluated and implemented in the field to increase rice yields and N use efficiency.

Keywords: Agro-pastoral systems, bioluminescence assay, nitrification inhibition, nitrogen, rice yield

Contact Address: Jacobo Arango, International Center for Tropical Agriculture (CIAT), Tropical Forages, A A 6713, NA Cali, Colombia, e-mail: j.arango@cgiar.org

Genome-Wide Association Study to Understand the Genetics of Manganese Toxicity Tolerance in Rice

Asis Shrestha[1], Ambrose Kwaku Dziwornu[1], Michael Frei[2]

[1] University of Bonn, Agricultural Sciences and Resource Mangement in Tropics and Subtropics, Germany

[2] University of Bonn, Inst. Crop Sci. and Res. Conserv. (INRES) - Plant Nutrition, Germany

Manganese is a transition metal occurring in different oxidative states. Rice (*Oryza sativa* L.) is mostly cultivated in anaerobic soil conditions where micro-organisms use redox active metals such as manganese as final electron acceptors to complete their energy metabolism. In this process, Mn^{4+} ions are reduced to Mn^{2+} ions leading to high levels of plant available manganese. Therefore, flooded rice fields are often characterised by high levels of manganese in soil solution, which can become toxic when taken up by the plants. Here, we discuss a genome-wide association study (GWAS) to identify candidate loci conferring manganese toxicity tolerance in rice. A diversity panel of 288 rice genotypes representing indica and japonica sub-populations was screened. 12 days old rice seedlings were grown in hydroponics at 5ppm manganese concentration for three weeks to induce toxicity effects. Manganese toxicity significantly affected several biomass traits with reduction of 29 % in root weight, 21 % in shoot weight, 9 % in root length, 4 % in shoot length and 18 % in tiller numbers when averaged over all genotypes. Association mapping based on more than 30,000 single nucleotide polymorphism (SNP) markers produced 11 significant markers throughout the genome (significance threshold of $p < 0.0001$). Linkage disequilibrium blocks associated with significant markers in chromosome 6 yielded 58 candidate genes. The candidate region comprises genes coding for proteins like receptor kinase, transposon protein, RING-H2-finger protein, retrotransposon protein, F-box domain and LRR containing protein, resistance LR10 protein and coffeoyl-CoA O-methyltransferase protein. Sequence variation in contrasting haplotypes will be determined to test the validity of candidate genes found on target locus on chromosome 6. This study indicates significant natural variation in rice to high level of manganese and possibility of using GWAS to unfold the genetic factors responsible for manganese toxicity tolerance.

Keywords: GWAS, manganese, rice

Contact Address: Asis Shrestha, University of Bonn, Agricultural Sciences and Resource Mangement in Tropics and Subtropics, Lennestr. 26-28, 53113 Bonn, Germany, e-mail: asis.shrestha@gmail.com

Animal science

Livestock systems, animal health and ruminants

Closing the Feed Gap in Drylands for Enhanced Livestock Productivity and Efficient Resource Use

BARBARA ANN RISCHKOWSKY[1], SERKAN ATES[2], JANE WAMATU[1], MUHI EL-DINE HILALI[2], SOUHEILA ABBEDDOU[3], AZIZ NURBEKOV[4]

[1]*International Center for Agricultural Research in the Dry Areas (ICARDA), Ethiopia*
[2]*International Center for Agricultural Research in the Dry Areas (ICARDA), Jordan*
[3]*ETH Zurich, Institute of Plant, Animal and Agroecosystem Sciences, Switzerland*
[4]*International Center for Agricultural Research in the Dry Areas (ICARDA), Central Asia and the Caucasus-Office, Uzbekistan*

Livestock is the world's fastest-growing highest-value agricultural sub-sector already accounting for about 40 % of agricultural GDP globally. By 2050 massive increases over 2005/7 amounts of cereals, dairy and meat will be needed: an extra of 2–3 Gt cereals, 0.66–1 Gt dairy products and 258–460 Mt meat. To meet this demand, large productivity increases are required as expansion of animal numbers and croplands is no longer an option. Hence, food and feed production will compete for land and water resources, particular in the drylands. These trends have to be seen against the background of widespread and growing land degradation and the additional challenge of climate change and variability. As one of the most extensive agents of land degradation, grazing pressure has already resulted in a significantly reduced contribution of rangelands to feed supply. E.g. in Near East – North Africa region this is only 10 to 25 % of livestock needs. This scenario clearly calls for research on resource-efficient feed production optimally integrated with food production. The International Center for Agricultural Research in the Dry Areas (ICARDA) and its partners have been exploring resource-efficient options to increase feed quantity and quality, among others addressing inefficiencies in feeding systems through balanced rations and smart supplementation; replacing expensive food grains in animal diets by agro-industrial by-products without jeopardising product quality; breeding for full purpose crops which includes selecting for food-feed cultivars in grain legumes and barley, and harvesting green forage from winter cereals in early growth stages; and intensifying cropping systems by replacing summer fallows with short duration legume crops which contribute to feed supply and soil health. This presentation will give examples of these research areas in dryland countries.

Keywords: Feed supply, livestock

Contact Address: Barbara Ann Rischkowsky, International Center for Agricultural Research in the Dry Areas (ICARDA), P.O. Box 5466, Addis Ababa, Ethiopia, e-mail: b.rischkowsky@cgiar.org

Land Use Change and Intensification, and Family Farmers in Uruguay: The Crop/Cattle Dilemma

PABLO MODERNEL[1], SANTIAGO DOGLIOTTI[2], VALENTIN PICASSO[3], WALTER ROSSING[1], MARC CORBEELS[4], PABLO TITTONELL[5]

[1] *Wageningen University and Research Centre, Farming Systems Ecology, The Netherlands*

[2] *Universidad de La República, Facultad de Agronomía, Uruguay*

[3] *University of Wisconsin-Madison, Agronomy Department, United States of America*

[4] *Centre de Coopération Internationale en Recherche Agronomique pour le Développement (CIRAD), France*

[5] *National Institute for Agricultural Technology (INTA), Natural Resources and Environment Program, Argentina*

The land use change process occurred in Uruguay between the years 2000 and 2013 has had a profound impact in the country. In this period, soybean and forest crops have increased by 100,000 and 40,000 ha per year, respectively. Changes in farming structure and access to resources between 2000 and 2010 endangered the livelihood of 57 % of family farmers in Uruguay; most of them cattle keepers on native grasslands, and 25 % of them have abandoned the activity in the last 10 years. This has been fuelled by low productivity and incomes, higher cost of access to land, insecure land tenure and the loss of 2 million ha from local farmers to anonymous societies (mostly foreign companies). Soybean has advanced mostly in areas of mix farming where sown pastures and crops coexisted for more than 30 years, shifting from crop-livestock systems into continuous cropping, increasing the risk of soil erosion and the vulnerability of the farming systems to market and climate variability. Parallel to crop and forest expansion, livestock systems have intensified through the use of external feedstuffs, whose imports have steadily grown in the last 10 years. This process is linked with the growth in number and size of feedlots, associated with risks of water eutrophication, higher use of fossil fuels and pesticide contamination. Research has shown that livestock productivity can be improved on native grasslands without increasing costs, resulting on 30–40 % increase in family income. Such promising models of meat production on native grasslands can improve the conservation of the highly species-rich grasslands along with benefits in terms of climate change mitigation, soil conservation and nutrient cycling.

Keywords: Ecosystem services, family farming, livestock

Contact Address: Pablo Modernel, Wageningen University and Research Centre, Farming Systems Ecology, Droevendaalsesteeg 1 Building 107, 6708 PB Wageningen, The Netherlands, e-mail: pablomodernel@gmail.com

ID 1025

Organisation of Smallholder Goat Breeding under Low Input Agricultural Systems of Ethiopia

TATEK WOLDU, ANDRÉ MARKEMANN, CHRISTOPH REIBER, ANNE VALLE ZÁRATE

University of Hohenheim, Inst. of Agricultural Sciences in the Tropics (Hans-Ruthenberg-Institute), Germany

Understanding the enabling environment for livestock genetic improvement is a pre-requisite to design and implement functional breeding programs under smallholder conditions. The present study aimed at identifying major organisational elements of goat breeding and highlighting possibilities to link them with goat community-based breeding programs (CBBPs) to be implemented in three districts of Ethiopia. The study defined organisation of smallholder goat breeding as part of a system, which is affected by institutions and other organisational elements at different levels. Accordingly, focus group discussion with 68 farmers, key informant interview of public and private institutions and social network analysis (SNA) were conducted in Abergele, Konso and Meta Robi districts of Ethiopia. Own and village flocks were the major sources of breeding goats in all districts. In Abergele, however, NGOs and research centres also supplied breeding goats to farmers. Farmer organisations such as marketing cooperatives, farmer development groups, farmer networks and informal farmer associations, which could be linked with the CBBPs were identified. Farmer organisations in Abergele were actively involved in goat production and marketing in contrast to those in Konso and Meta Robi districts. Key informants of the investigated agricultural research institutes indicated that a majority (80 %) of the current goat breeding research topics focused on crossbred goats, while limited emphasis was given to improve local goats by within breed selection schemes. The SNA indicated that public actors such as extension officers had the highest average centrality (73.0 %) and closeness (77.5 %) values indicating their prominent role in goat production and marketing networks, while private actors such as traders and export abattoirs had the lowest centrality and connectedness values. Key actors such as research institutions and NGOs were missing in social networks of Meta Robi district. Extension officers should play a major role in the establishment and operation of the CBBPs due to their key position in the social network structures. Moreover, agricultural research institutions should rather contribute to the success of CBBPs by providing continuous technical backstopping and allocating infrastructures for multiplication of selected breeding goats from the CBBPs than putting too much effort in promotion of insignificant number of exotic goats.

Keywords: Breeding organisations, goat, production systems, social networks

Contact Address: Tatek Woldu, University of Hohenheim, Inst. of Agricultural Sciences in the Tropics (Hans-Ruthenberg-Institute), Garben Str. 17, 70599 Stuttgart, Germany, e-mail: tatekwbelete@yahoo.com

Effects of Feeding Tropical Forage Legumes on Nutrients Digestibility and Performance of Dairy Cows

JOAQUÍN CASTRO-MONTOYA[1], RAVINDRA GOWNIPURAM[1], ELMER COREA GUILLEN[2], UTA DICKHOEFER[1]

[1] University of Hohenheim, Inst. of Agricultural Sciences in the Tropics (Hans-Ruthenberg-Institute), Germany
[2] University of El Salvador, El Salvador

In El Salvador, most dairy farms rely on sorghum or maize silage as basal diet. These forages are low in protein, so that cattle are commonly supplemented with expensive human-edible protein feeds such as imported soybean. Hence, in this study two legumes, jackbean (*Cannavalia ensiformis*) silage and cowpea (*Vigna unguiculata*) hay, were studied as alternative protein sources for dairy cows to reduce farmers' dependency on imported protein sources.

Eight crossbred cows (451 $\pm$ 50.7 kg body weight; 9.4 $\pm$ 2.60 kg milk d^{-1}; 125 $\pm$ 50.6 days in milk) were used in a replicated 4×4 latin square design with four periods (14 days adaptation + 7 days sampling).

Four sorghum silage-based diets differing in their main Nitrogen source were tested: Soybean meal (control), jackbean silage, cowpea hay, or urea. A concentrate mixture was supplemented to create iso-proteic (125 g crude protein kg^{-1} dry matter (DM)) and iso-energetic (8.7 MJ metabolisable energy kg^{-1} DM) diets with a forage to concentrate ratio of 70:30 (DM basis). Feed intake, apparent total tract nutrients digestibility, energy corrected milk yield (ECM) and composition, and cost-benefit ratio were studied.

Dry matter intake increased when feeding jackbean (14.8 kg d^{-1}) and cowpea (14.6 kg d^{-1}) compared with the control diet (13.6 kg d^{-1}) without affecting ECM (ranging from 8.8. to 9.2 kg d^{-1}). There were no differences in apparent DM and nitrogen digestibility (ranging from 0.52 to 0.58) across all diets. Legumes did not change fat, protein, or lactose contents of milk ($P > 0.10$). Even though not statistically different, cost-benefit ratio was 0.18 US$ higher with the jackbean diet compared with the Control, which might still be an incentive for farmers. Furthermore, ECM relative to human-edible protein intake (*i.e.* from cereals and soybean) was higher when legumes were fed compared with the Control diet; however, compared with the diet containing urea, only the cowpea diet showed a higher ratio of ECM to human-edible protein intake. The results suggest that these legume forages, as alternative protein sources, may also reduce competition in resource use for feed or food production.

Keywords: Legume silage, milk, protein, tropical dairy

Contact Address: Uta Dickhoefer, University of Hohenheim, Inst. of Agricultural Sciences in the Tropics (Hans-Ruthenberg-Institute), Fruwirthstr. 31, 70599 Stuttgart, Germany, e-mail: Uta.Dickhoefer@uni-hohenheim.de

ID 747

Improving Productivity in Kenyan Smallholder Dairy Systems through Selective, Intensive Education and Supported Adoption

JOHN GOOPY[1], JESSE GAKIGE[1], KLAUS BUTTERBACH-BAHL[2,1]

[1] *International Livestock Research Institute (ILRI), Kenya*
[2] *Karlsruhe Institute of Technology, Institute for Meteorology and Climate Research, Atmospheric Environmental Research, Germany*

Improving productivity in Kenyan smallholder dairy systems is perceived as having the potential to greatly improve the supply of milk to processors and make substantial improvements in rural incomes by doing so. Surveys recently commissioned by GIZ in Western Kenya indicated that milk yield was between 1.8–3 l/cow/d (depending on county). Poor milk yield is often attributed to poor genetics, but we discovered that frequently production is constrained by a lack of knowledge, particularly with regard to husbandry, feeds and feeding practice. Much has already been done in these areas by NGOs, but training is frequently short-term, focused on a narrow area and participant selection is untargeted.

In the framework of a BMZ funded project we are working with NGOs, dairy cooperatives and GIZ to assess the potential of farmers to implement new technologies that will further improve their operations. We are specifically aiming at early adopters as those are likely to continue and thus, might serve as role models. We are currently identifying innovators in a number of communities in Western Kenya and will provide them with an 18d intensive course covering husbandry, animal nutrition, forage/crop agronomy and business analysis skills. On completion we will support each farmer to implement knowledge and technology in his/her community. These farmers should be able to adapt the skill set and learned technologies to their own situation, but also act as a focal point and exemplar to their own community.

The presentation will outline the training concept, selection procedure of farmers, and summarise first results on knowledge implementation in the communities following the return of the trainees.

Keywords: Dairy, education, Kenya, smallholder

Contact Address: John Goopy, International Livestock Research Institute (ILRI), Nairobi, Kenya, e-mail: j.goopy@cgiar.org

Brucellosis in Ruminants in two Counties of Yunnan, China and the Use of an Integrated Approach for Effective Control

FRED UNGER[1], YANG SHIBAO[2], LI WENGUI[3], YANG XIANGDONG[4], YANG GUORONG[5]

[1] *International Livestock Research Institute (ILRI), Vietnam*

[2] *Yunnan Animal Science and Veterinary Institute, Kunming, China,*

[3] *Yunnan Agricultural University, Kunming, China,*

[4] *Yunnan Institute of Endemic Disease Control and Prevention, China*

[5] *Yunnan Academy of Grassland and Animal Science, Kunming, China*

Brucellosis is an increasing production and public health concern in many countries of Asia including China. Challenges for an effective control include lack of collaboration between sectors or uncontrolled animal movement (among others). Yunnan might be at particular risk as ruminants are increasingly introduced from other parts of China e.g. Inner Mongolia, a known high prevalence area in a response to a higher demand for milk. To face this challenges, new integrated approaches are needed such as Ecohealth to support transdisciplinary collaboration versus silo thinking, the latter rather common in the top down animal health control system of China. In the presented research, which was part of an IDRC funded ILRI-Ecozd project, veterinary, public health, animal science experts from five provincial institutions, practitioners from the project sites, and policy authorities worked together to achieve a more effective control of brucellosis. The research was carried out between 2011 and 2013 in two counties of Yunnan, Mangshi and Yiliang and consisted of a historical data review, biological sampling (milk) in herds/households with dairy ruminants and people at risk (serum). Questionnaires were used to collect management data (N=192) from farmers; focus group discussions (villagers) and in depth interviews (village vets and human doctors) gained information on perception and awareness on zoonoses in general and more specifically on the targeted disease. Results from the biological sampling indicate brucellosis as an existing and potentially emerging public health concern depending on the production system. Risk factors for the spread of brucellosis were reported and included risky handling of aborted fetus among others. Awareness and perception on zoonoses (including brucellosis) of all interviewed groups was in general low. The use of a "learning by doing" EcoHealth approach led to improve team member's capacity on Ecohealth and its practical realisation in a field study, e.g. by building up collaboration between those institutions but also stakeholders. Crucial was the support by the Agriculture Department and Health Department of Yunnan. Outcome mapping indicated a change of behaviour in the targeted groups in particular on zoonoses knowledge and willingness to share of information between sectors (vet and public health).

Keywords: Brucellosis, EcoHealth, Yunnan

Contact Address: Fred Unger, International Livestock Research Institute (ILRI), 17 A Nguyen Khang, Hanoi, Vietnam, e-mail: f.unger@cgiar.org

Balanced Feeding Could Improve Productivity of Cross-Breed Dairy Cattle in Smallholder Systems (Tigray, Northern Ethiopia)

ALEMAYEHU TADESSE[1], MOSES MATOVU[2], YAYNESHET TESFAY[3], MARK BREUSERS[4], VEERLE FIEVEZ[5]

[1]Mekelle University, Animal, Rangeland and Wildlife Sciences, Ethiopia
[2]Ghent University, Food Safety and Food Quality, Belgium
[3]International Livestock Research Institute (ILRI), Ethiopia
[4]KU Leuven, Faculty of Social Sciences, IARA, Belgium
[5]Ghent University, Animal Production (Lanupro), Belgium

This study was conducted to assess the feed baskets of lactating Holstein Friesian crossbred cows and to formulate suggestions for optimisation of the ration to balance crude protein and metabolisable energy (ME) supply for optimal milk production under smallholder dairy farming in Agula and Hagereselam districts of Tigray region, northern Ethiopia. A total of 60 smallholder dairy farmers (30 from each district) who owned 1–5 lactating cows were involved in the study during the months of July and August 2015. Feed intake and milk production were recorded. Weende and Van Soest analysis was done on representative feed samples from which ME content was assessed. The observed diets offered to lactating cows of both study sites were grouped into five categories based on the inclusion rate of wheat and barley straw (WBSM), noug seed cake (NSC) and atella (local brewery by-product). The average ration composition in the groups were: group 1 (60.4 % WBSM, 30.8 % wheat bran (WB) and 8.7 % atella), group 2 (49.8 % WBSM, 21.8 % WB, 17.5 % NSC and 10.8 % atella), group 3 (53.5 % WBSM, 24.5 % WB, 13.3 % NSC and 8.7 % atella), group 4 (40.7 % WBSM, 24 % WB, 13.1 % NSC and 22.2 % atella) and group 5 (49.8 % WBSM, 21.8 % WB, 17.5 % NSC and 10.8 % atella). The potential milk yield was calculated based on ME and crude protein (CP) intake from the rations of each group. Protein and ME supply only seemed balanced in group 5 (18 % of the farms). In the other groups imbalanced diets were fed, of which 26 % were protein deficient (group 1), whereas (surprisingly) 56 % of the farms included more than 10 % NSC in their diet, which resulted in an excessive protein supply. The milk yield of group 1 potentially could be increased by 114 % with an additional supplement of 1.6 kg of NSC. Overall, NSC could be an excellent protein corrector, when included at a proportion of about 10 % in the diet in combination with 43–58 % WBSM, 23–31%WB and 9–20 % atella.

Keywords: Crude protein, metabolisable energy, milk yield, Noug seed cake, small scale dairy farming

Contact Address: Alemayehu Tadesse, Mekelle University, Animal, Rangeland and Wildlife Sciences, Mekelle University Endayesus Campus, 231 Mekelle, Ethiopia, e-mail: alextmu@yahoo.com

Intensification of Smallholder Livestock Production through Utilisation of Crop Residues for Livestock Feed in Tanzania

BEN LUKUYU[1], GREGORY SIKUMBA[1], JOB KIHARA[2], MATEETE BEKUNDA[3]

[1]*International Livestock Research Institute (ILRI), ASSP, Kenya*
[2]*International Center for Tropical Agriculture (CIAT), Tropical Soil Biology and Fertility (TSBF), Kenya*
[3]*International Institute of Tropical Agriculture (IITA), Tanzania*

Poor feed utilisation and seasonal feed availability are considered contributory factors leading to less-than-optimal livestock productivity on smallholder farms in Babati, Tanzania. Cereal and legume crop residues, such as dry or green maize stover and bean haulms, are commonly fed to livestock but are also of low quality and they are poorly used by farmers. Improving the efficiency with which the crop residues can be used as animal feed appears the first step towards solving critical feed shortage. Studies on maize crop residue uses and trade-offs on smallholder crop-livestock farmers have proven on an economic perspective that it is logical to prioritise its use for feed over soil fertility management . A study was conducted to assess availability of types, quantity and quality of crop residues and other feed resources for livestock on farms. The study aimed to understand how cereal and legume crop residues are harvested, stored, processed and used in different farms. It also aimed to identity gaps in managing crop residues in intensified systems and factors that may affect adoption. Post-harvest forage processing technologies such as feed choppers offer potential to enhance use of crop residues for livestock feeding. This not only reduces feed wastage but also enhances feed intake and quality . It also has potential to improve quantity and quality of manure. Following the study a feed chopping technology to enhance utilisation was introduced to farmers. The findings showed that the average household tropical livestock unit (TLU) is 3.8 (se = 0.15). Crop residues are the major contributor to livestock diet in the dry season. The most dominant cereal crop residues are maize stover (57 %) and rice straw (20 %) while the most common legumes straws are pigeon pea (4 %); bean (12 %), groundnut (5 %) and cowpea (2 %) haulms. On average the maize stover yield on farms is 9.3 t ha^{-1} (se = 0.28). There is a lot of feed waste on farms due to chopping by using a machete. Yield of maize stover from a hectare of land can sustain one TLU of livestock for 247 days.

Keywords: Cereal and legume crop residues, crop livestock systems, livestock feed, maize stover

Contact Address: Ben Lukuyu, International Livestock Research Institute (ILRI), Animal Sciences for Sustainable Productivity Program, PO Box 30709, 00100 Nairobi, Kenya, e-mail: b.lukuyu@cgiar.org

ID 364

Digestibility and Metabolisable Energy Concentrations of Tropical Feeds as Estimated *in vitro* or by Prediction Equations

ALICE ONYANGO[1], UTA DICKHOEFER[1], KLAUS BUTTERBACH-BAHL[2,3], JOHN GOOPY[3]

[1] *University of Hohenheim, Inst. of Agricultural Sciences in the Tropics (Hans-Ruthenberg-Institute), Germany*

[2] *Karlsruhe Institute of Technology, Institute for Meteorology and Climate Research, Atmospheric Environmental Research, Germany*

[3] *International Livestock Research Institute (ILRI), Kenya*

In vivo determination of digestible organic matter (dOM) and metabolisable energy (ME) concentrations of feeds is laborious and expensive, whereas analysis of their nutrient contents is routinely performed. Prediction equations based on the chemical composition of feeds can be a compromise. This study compared dOM and ME estimates of tropical feeds derived from selected equations (Yan and Agnew, 2004; Stergiadis et al., 2015a; Stergiadis et al., 2015b; AFRC, 1993) with those determined by the *in vitro* gas production method (Menke and Steingass, 1988). Samples of supplement feedstuffs (n = 12) and the herbaceous and ligneous vegetation on native pastures (n = 12) were collected in Lower Nyando, Kenya, over two seasons of one year. Samples were analysed for dry matter (DM; in % of fresh matter), crude ash, crude protein, ether extract, neutral and acid detergent fiber (NDF, ADF) (all in % of DM). Gross energy was determined by calorimetry.

Nutrient concentrations varied across all samples with $8.5 - 87.9\%$ DM, $5.2 - 16.8\%$ crude ash, $36.7 - 74.1\%$ NDF, $25.5 - 39.4\%$ ADF, $3.2 - 14.2\%$ crude protein, and $0.6 - 4.5\%$ ether extract. The gross energy, *in vitro* dOM, and ME concentrations were $14.5 - 18.8\,\mathrm{MJ\,kg^{-1}}$ DM, $26.3 - 54.5\%$, and $3.8 - 8.4\,\mathrm{MJ\,kg^{-1}}$ DM, respectively. Compared with the *in vitro* method, all nutrient-based equations overestimated dOM ($p < 0.001$), whereas ME estimated from *in vitro* gas production was similar to that derived from the AFRC equation ($p > 0.5$). Nutrient-based equations do not sufficiently account for differences in nutrient availability, an aspect better simulated *in vitro*. Further development and/or validation of nutrient-based equations might be needed to more accurately predict dOM and ME of tropical feeds.

AFRC. 1993. Wallingford: CAB International.

Stergiadis et al. 2015a. J Dairy Sci, 98(5), 3257–3273

Stergiadis et al 2015b. Brit J Nutr, 113(10), 1571–1584.

Yan and Agnew. 2004. J Anim Sci., 82, 1367–1379.

Keywords: Digestibility, metabolisable energy, prediction, tropical feedstuff

Contact Address: Uta Dickhoefer, University of Hohenheim, Inst. of Agricultural Sciences in the Tropics (Hans-Ruthenberg-Institute), Fruwirthstr. 31, 70599 Stuttgart, Germany, e-mail: Uta.Dickhoefer@uni-hohenheim.de

Immune Response and Milk Production of Ewes Fed Salt Tolerant Forages as a Replacement of Berseem Hay

Amr Salah Morsy[1], Mohamed M. Eissa[2], Mohamed M. Anwer[2], Hesham Ghobashy[2], Sobhy M.A. Sallam[3], Yosra Soltan[3], Adel M Saber[2], El-Saeed A. El-Wakeel[2], Wailed M. Sadik Mohamed[2]

[1] City of Scientific Research and Technological Applications (SRTA-City), Arid Lands Cultivation Research Institute, Livestock Research Department, Egypt

[2] Agriculture Research Centre, Animal Production Research Institute, Sheep and Goats Research Department, Egypt

[3] University of Alexandria, Faculty of Agriculture, Dept. of Animal Production, Egypt

The comparative evaluation of different, less-well researched forages will yield promising candidates to overcome the limitations of feed sources in most sub-tropic areas during drought and may enhance the immune response and milk production as well. Diets substitution of berseem (*Trifolium alexandrinum*) hay by leaves of cassava (*Manihot esculenta*), acacia (*Acacia saligna*) or atriplex (*Atriplex nummularia*) were evaluated using forty late pregnant Barki ewes (43.2 ± 1.1 kg body weight). Ewes were divided into four experimental diets (n=10 each): control (per kg DM 600 g concentrate and 400 g berseem hay) or substitute forage diets (per kg DM 600 g concentrate and 400 g leaves of cassava, acacia or atriplex). Samples of dam colostrum and their lamb blood serum were taken at 2, 6, 12, and 24 h after parturition while milk production composition and serum biochemical parameters were measured at one week postpartum and lasted for 8 weeks. Cassava based diet increased ($p < 0.05$) colostrums IgG and IgM concentrations compared with control. Atriplex and cassava based diets enhanced ($p < 0.01$) the concentrations of lamb serum IgM compared with control. Colostrum and lamb serum IgG and IgM concentrations were synchronised recorded the highest ($p < 0.01$) levels at 2 h after parturition then decreased dramatically ($p < 0.01$) to reach the lowest concentrations after 24 h for all treatments. Milk yield was enhanced ($p < 0.01$) by cassava diet and milk protein, lactose, density, ash and solid not fat were increased ($p < 0.05$) by substitute forage diets compared with control. Either acacia or atriplex decreased ($p < 0.01$) glucose concentrations while cassava had greater ($p < 0.05$) serum total protein and the lowest triglycerides concentration when compared to control. Cassava increased ($p < 0.05$) lambs weaning weights and daily weight gain compared to other treatments. It could be concluded that cassava, atriplex and acacia are valuable alternatives to berseem hay in lactating Barki ewe diets without compromising immunity and milk production, among the experimental forages, cassava was more effective than acacia and atriplex.

Keywords: Immune response, lamb performance, milk yield, salt tolerant forages

Contact Address: Amr Salah Morsy, City of Scientific Research and Technological Applications (SRTA-City), Arid Lands Cultivation Research Institute, Livestock Research Department, Universities and Research Centers District New Borg El-Arab City, 21934 Alexandria, Egypt, e-mail: amrsalah277@hotmail.com

ID 83

Sustainable Beef Production with Forage Associations in the American Tropics

JHON FREDDY GUTIERREZ SOLIS, MAURICIO EFREN SOTELO CABRERA, BELISARIO HINCAPIE, MICHAEL PETERS, STEFAN BURKART

International Center for Tropical Agriculture (CIAT), Colombia

Grass-legume forage associations are an alternative to address seasonality in feed supply in livestock systems, as they provide benefits in the production of biomass as well as in terms of diet quality and productivity. At the same time, they contribute to achieving sustainability of livestock production in the American tropics and thus play an important role in addressing national sustainability plans and strategies such as the Colombian Strategic Plan for Livestock Production (PEGA 2019) aiming at a reduction of the total area under pasture.

Under a completely randomised block design, three treatments with three repetitions were sown and evaluated for daily animal live weight gains in 2015: 1) the grass *Brachiaria brizantha* cv. Toledo as monoculture, 2) *Brachiaria brizantha* cv. Toledo associated with the legume *Canavalia brasiliensis*, and 3) *Brachiaria brizantha* cv. Toledo associated with *Canavalia brasiliensis* and *Leucaena diversifolia*. This resulted in a trial with a total of 9 experimental plots on 3.0 hectares. Once established, rotational grazing started with 15 commercial animals (male Zebu, 5 per treatment, initial live weight of 200 kg) and data was obtained for measuring daily live weight gains in relation to each treatment.

Results demonstrate that the animals with highest individual weight gains were the ones grazing *Brachiaria brizantha* cv. Toledo associated with the legume *Canavalia brasiliensis*, showing daily gains of 380 g, 125 g more than those grazing *Brachiaria brizantha* cv. Toledo only. With regard to overall productivity of each treatment, animals grazing grass-legume associations (treatment 2 and 3) showed higher per area live weight gains (554 and 526 kg y^{-1}) than those grazing *Brachiaria brizantha* cv. Toledo only (371 kg y^{-1}). The higher per area productivity of grass-legume associations is related to both forage quantity and quality. The results show that associations could be a valuable option for livestock producers in the tropics, for achieving higher productivity levels but also for sustainable intensification of livestock production systems and thus can contribute to compliance with national sustainability plans and strategies.

Keywords: Forage associations, live weight gain, sustainable intensification, tropical beef production, tropical forages

Contact Address: Stefan Burkart, International Center for Tropical Agriculture (CIAT), Tropical Forages Program, Km 17 Recta Cali-Palmira, Cali, Colombia, e-mail: s.burkart@cgiar.org

Community-Based Goat Breeding Programs in Malawi: Set-Up and First Experiences

WILSON NANDOLO[1], MARIA WURZINGER[2], GÁBOR MÉSZÁROS[2], CURT VAN TASSELL[3], TIMOTHY GONDWE[4], HENRY MULINDWA[5], DOREEN LAMUNO[2], JOHANN SÖLKNER[2]

[1]*Lilongwe University of Agriculture and Natural Resources, Animal Science, Malawi*

[2]*University of Natural Resources and Life Sciences (BOKU), Dept. of Sustainable Agricultural Systems, Austria*

[3]*USDA, United States of America*

[4]*University of Malawi, Bunda College of Agriculture, Animal Science, Malawi*

[5]*National Agricultural Research Organisation (NARO), Uganda*

Goats are a very important animal genetic resource in Malawi, and their improvement has been identified as one of the available sustainable ways of improving the livelihoods of farmers. Traditionally, the approach of improvement of goat genetic resources in Malawi has been through the introduction of exotic goat breeds for crossbreeding or complete breed replacement. Most of these improvement programmes have not produced the expected positive results, mostly due to problems with genotype and environment interactions as well as lack of organised recording schemes. Recently, animal breeders have resorted to use of within-breed selection as a tool for sustainable breed improvement. However, Malawian goat farmers have small flock sizes, so that goat selection by individual farmers is not easy. Most farmers allow their flocks to graze together on communal grazing areas, leading to larger virtual flocks in a mixed crop-livestock production system. Community-based goat breeding programmes have been identified as a possible avenue for improvement in such production systems, and this presentation explains how such breeding programs have been set up in two regions of Malawi. We outline the conceptualisation of the breeding programme; stress the role of the linkages and collaborations between the implementing partners and local stakeholders in all stages of implementation; and highlight the philosophy of the current approach in the implementation of community-based breeding programmes: simplicity and sustainability. The design and implementation timeline is outlined, and preliminary results of the initial selection activities are discussed. Challenges that have been encountered in the implementation of the programs, and the lessons learnt from the management of these challenges are explained. For successful implementation, there is need to pay close attention to the specific circumstances of the community and the local environment.

Keywords: Breeding programme, community, goats, Malawi, sustainability

Contact Address: Maria Wurzinger, University of Natural Resources and Life Sciences (BOKU), Dept. of Sustainable Agricultural Systems, Gregor Mendel Straße 33, 1180 Vienna, Austria, e-mail: maria.wurzinger@boku.ac.at

ID 945

The Use of System Dynamics Modelling Methodologies in Sheep Breeding Programs and Management Systems

KAHSA TADEL GEBRE[1], MARIA WURZINGER[2], SOLOMON GIZAW[3], AYNALEM HAILE[4], BARBARA ANN RISCHKOWSKY[4], JOHANN SÖLKNER[2]

[1] *Mekelle University, Dept. of Animal, Rangeland and Wildlife Sciences, Ethiopia*
[2] *University of Natural Resources and Life Sciences (BOKU), Dept. of Sustainable Agricultural Systems, Austria*
[3] *International Livestock Research Institute, Ethiopia*
[4] *International Center for Agricultural Research in the Dry Areas (ICARDA), Ethiopia*

System dynamics modelling approach has been widely used in the agriculture sector to describe livestock production systems, livestock health and natural resource management. However, its application in modelling livestock breeding programs and systems is limited. Therefore, this study explores the utility of system dynamics modelling in evaluation of sheep breeding programs and management systems in the Ethiopian highland. A community-based sheep breeding programme was modeled using STELLA software. A weather and resource driven stochastic herd model was developed to evaluate the effect of genetic improvement and change in management system on herd dynamics and profitability. The baseline model was developed using historical rainfall and temperature data. Performance data was extracted from the herd-book of the breeding programme and additional input data were obtained from various sources. The model accounts for pasture growth, nutrient requirement and seasonal variation in animal performance, physiological status and aging chain of the herd. Economic analysis was also done considering the returns and costs of the system. The baseline model was further expanded to account for genetic selection of body size, fattening strategies and alternative management systems to evaluate their effect on herd dynamics and profitability. Technical evaluation and extensive logic testing during the building phases was conducted. The model results were compared to independent calculations to determine whether the model was matching expectations, and to help clarify the relationships between variables. The model demonstrates that balancing the feed supply and demand is crucial. Genetic selection for large body size has resulted in decrease of herd size and higher income. Fattening of young animals has increased the farm income. Increase feed supply by producing improved forage plants increased herd size and farm income. For more economic benefit genetic improvement programs should be coincide with appropriate fattening strategies and resource availability. Overall, system dynamics modelling tools are useful to describe breeding programs and management systems by building simple, flexible and usage driven simulation models.

Keywords: Breeding programs, Ethiopia, sheep, STELLA, system dynamics

Contact Address: Johann Sölkner, University of Natural Resources and Life Sciences (BOKU), Department of Sustainable Agricultural Systems, Gregor Mendel Str. 33, A-1180 Vienna, Austria, e-mail: soelkner@boku.ac.at

Genomic Selection for Growth, Reproductive and Conformation Traits in Zebu Brahman in Colombia

RODRIGO MARTÍNEZ[1], GÁBOR MÉSZÁROS[2], DIEGO BEJARANO[1], Y. GOMEZ[1], J. RAMIREZ [1], J. FERNANDEZ[1], N. POLANCO [1], ARIEL JIMENEZ[3], GAËL EVEN[4], JOHANN SÖLKNER[2]

[1] Colombian Corporation of Agricultural Research, Colombia
[2] University of Natural Resources and Life Sciences (BOKU), Dept. of Sustainable Agricultural Systems, Austria
[3] National Association of Zebu Brahman Breeders ASOCEBU, Colombia
[4] Genes Diffusion, France

Colombia is the fourth largest producer of beef cattle in Latin America. The meat production is based on Zebu breeds and their crossbreeds, with about 80 % of the population residing in tropical lowlands. Currently the selection process is based solely on pedigree, without consideration of inbreeding, which can subsequently threaten the genetic variability. These developments motivated the establishment of the genomic selection programme in Colombia. The aim of this work was to estimate the increase of breeding value accuracies compared the more traditional pedigree scheme. Pedigrees and production phenotypes from about 120,000 animals from 35 farms, distributed in the three main Colombian regions were used for the analysis. The weight traits were evaluated in different age groups: at birth, at four months, at weaning, at 12 months and at 18 months. For the reproductive traits age at first calving (AFC) and calving interval (CI) were considered. Finally conformation traits loin eye area (LEA) and dorsal fat (DF) were evaluated by ultrasound. Genotypes from 4,250 animals were used as the reference population when estimating genomic breeding values and their accuracies with single step Genomic BLUP. A substantial increase of accuracy was shown in growth traits, where the accuracies were on average 32 % higher when genomic information was used, compared to an estimation without genotypes. This increase was the highest for the weight measurements at four months (around 66 %) and the lowest for the measurements at 18 months (9–18 %). For reproductive traits the accuracy increased by 22 % for AFC and by 13 % for CI. The additive genetic variance was also the lowest for these traits. For the conformation traits our results showed an increase of 18 % for LEA and 19 % for DF. In conclusion, the use of genomics resulted into a substantial increase breeding value accuracies. This increase was higher in growth traits, where the additive variance was also higher. This study also confirms the importance to consider genomic data in the modern breeding programs, such as the one for Colombian Zebu Brahman cattle, in order to obtain higher accuracy breeding values with a subsequent increase in genetic gain.

Keywords: Accuracy, breeding values, Colombia, genomic selection, Zebu Brahman

Contact Address: Gábor Mészáros, University of Natural Resources and Life Sciences (BOKU), Dept. of Sustainable Agricultural Systems, Gregor-Mendel Str.33, 1180 Vienna, Austria, e-mail: gabor.meszaros@boku.ac.at

ID 584

Phenotypic Body Measurements as Predictors of Body Weight in Butana Cattle Ecotype under Field Conditions in Sudan

AHMED MUSA[1], MOHAMED KHAIR ABDALLA AHMED[2], NAHID IDAM[3], KHALID ELAMIN[2]

[1] University of Gezira, Genetics and Animal Breeding (Molecular Genetics), Sudan
[2] University of Khartoum, Animal Genetics and Breeding, Sudan
[3] University of Gezira, Animal Physiology and Biochemistry, Sudan

Data on body weight (Bwt) and phenotypic body measurements; heart girth (HG), Body length (BL) and height at withers (HTWs) were individually collected from mature (N = 200, males (n) = 50 and females (n) = 150) Butana cattle ecotype that thrive under field conditions in Butana area of Sudan between October and March 2013. The aims of the study were to: (1) determinate certain phenotypic body measurements, (2) evaluate the effect of sex on the body weight and phenotypic body measurements, (3) establish associations between body weight and phenotypic body measurements and (4) predict body weight from phenotypic body measurements in Butana cattle ecotype by statistical analysis models. Data collected were subjected to least squares analysis using general linear model procedures when phenotypic body measurements (cm) and animal body weight (kg) were outcome variables and animal sex as input variable, simple linear Pearson's correlation and regression analysis were performed. Findings indicated that males showed higher values for body weight and phenotypic body measurements ($P < 0.05$) than females, the correlation coefficients (r) between body weights and heart girth measurements (r = 0.90 for males and 0.98 for females) were strong, positive in direction and significant ($P < 0.001$). Simple linear regression models were fitted ($P < 0.05$) with body weight as dependent variable and heart girth as independent variable. Body weight had a linear relationship with heart girth ($R^2 = 0.81$ and 0.96) for males and females respectively. The coefficient of determination indicated that heart girth measurement succeed to describes more variation in body weight. Thus, heart girth taken with a tape is the phenotypic body measurement that is most appropriate for prediction of body weight more accurately in Butana cattle ecotype under field conditions in Sudan. Results obtained in present study would also be valuable, useful and helpful to animal breeder and farmers under field conditions who are involved in cattle breeding.

Keywords: Butana cattle, correlations, phenotypic measurements, prediction, Sudan

Contact Address: Ahmed Musa, University of Gezira, Genetics and Animal Breeding (Molecular Genetics), Elgamaa, Wad Medani, Sudan, e-mail: ahmed.musa12@yahoo.com

Performance of Camels and Cattle Kept Extensively on East African Rangelands

Paul Leparmarai[1], Michael Kreuzer[1], Ilona Gluecks[2], Mwangi Miano[3], Svenja Marquardt[1]

[1] ETH Zurich, Inst. of Agricultural Sciences, Switzerland
[2] Vétérinaires sans Frontières Suisse, Kenya
[3] Kenya Agricultural and Livestock Research Institute Agriculture, Kenya

Camels (Camelus dromedarius) and local cattle breeds (Bos indicus) are among the preferred livestock species kept in the arid and semi-arid regions of the Horn of Africa as they play an important role in providing milk and meat. In addition, they are adapted to utilising forage from extremely dry land areas. The present study aimed at comparing dairy camels with two dairy cattle breeds (local "Pokot" cattle and Boran × Guernsey crossbreds) with regard to their performance. All genotypes were subjected to two different supplementation treatments: no supplementation (NO) vs. supplementation with rumen-degradable protein ad lib (PS). Measurements were performed in the rainy season (R; May/June 2015) and a more dry transition period (T; September/October 2015) (36 days each). The animals were all accompanied by calves and grazing in rangeland during the day. Milk yield and composition were assessed daily, the latter by using a portable ultra-sonic milk analyser (Lactoscan SA-L, Milkotronic Limited, Nova Zagora, Bulgaria). The values measured were adjusted by regressions using lab values from Swiss cows. The Mixed procedure of the SAS programme (version 9.3) was used for analysis of variance separately per genotype. The mean values obtained per period for each animal were used and a covariable (milk yield and composition recorded before supplementation) was included. The milk amount recorded did not include the amount suckled by calf. Supplementation ($p > 0.05$) had no effect on milk yield in the two cattle genotypes and in the camels. Period had a strong effect ($p < 0.01$) on milk yield in both Pokots and crossbreds. The milk yield of the camels did not differ ($p > 0.05$) between periods suggesting better coping strategies of the camels than the cattle to the changing climatic conditions in the arid and semi-arid areas of East Africa. By contrast, there was no comparative advantage of the Pokot against the exotic crossbreds.

Keywords: Camelus dromedarius, milk yield, Pokot, season, supplementation

Contact Address: Paul Leparmarai, ETH Zurich, Institute of Agricultural Sciences, Universitätstrasse 2, 8092 Zurich, Switzerland, e-mail: lepapaul@yahoo.com

ID 994

Characteristics of Indonesian Cattle Breed Based on Morphology Indeces

SULASMI[1], ASEP GUNAWAN[1], JOHAR ARIFIN[2], CECE SUMANTRI[1], RUDI PRIYANTO[1]

[1]*Bogor Agricultural University, Dept. of Animal Production and Tecnology, Indonesia*
[2]*Padjajaran University of Indonesia, Animal Science, Indonesia*

Bos Indicus (zebu) and *Bos javanicus* (banteng) have contributed to Indonesian cattle breed (Pasundan, Madura, and Peranakan Ongole) and Bali cattle. Those cattle have the power of adaptation to marginal environments, are resistant to tropical diseases and to conditions of limited and low quality feed. Characterisation is the first steps for the development of cattle. One effort of characterisation can be done through the identification of linear body measurements. Linear measurements have been used as prediction of weigth and as indicator of type and function of beef cattle using a morphology indeces. The aims of this study were to identify weigth and characteristics of body size using a morphology index for Pasundan, Madura, Peranakan Ongole and Bali cattle. The total number of cattle used in this study were 490 consisting of 162 bulls and 328 cows. The body parts measured are withers height, rumpt height, body length, chest width, chest depth, hearth girth, crotch width, hip width and crotch length. Data were analysed using analysis of variance and tukey test. The results showed that the general morphology index of Pasundan cows is higher ($P < 0.05$) as compared with Madura, Peranakan Ongole and Bali cattle except for the length index and cumulative index. Bali cattle have a higer cumulative index ($P < 0.05$) than Pasundan, Madura and Peranakan Ongole cattles.

Keywords: Indonesian cattle breed, linear body measurement, morphology index

Contact Address: Sulasmi, Bogor Agricultural University, Dept. of Animal Production and Tecnology, Dramaga Bogor, Bogor, Indonesia, e-mail: sulasmi.kisman@gmail.com

Integrating Gender Analysis in Understanding Dual-Purpose Cattle Breeding Practices in Nicaragua

JULIE OJANGO[1], MARTIN MENA URBINA[2], MARIA ALEJANDRA MORA[2], ROLDAN CORRALES[3], EDWIN OYIENG[1], ALESSANDRA GALIÈ[1], MARIA WURZINGER[4], REIN VAN DER HOEK[2]

[1] International Livestock Research Institute (ILRI), Kenya

[2] International Center for Tropical Agriculture (CIAT), Central America, Nicaragua

[3] National Agrarian University (UNA), Integral Systems of Animal Production, Nicaragua

[4] University of Natural Resources and Life Sciences (BOKU), Dept. of Sustainable Agricultural Systems, Austria

Dual purpose cattle production in mixed farming systems of Nicaragua is predominantly based on permanent grazing of naturalized grasslands, introduced pastures and crop residues. Milk production and animal offtake rates are low. Information to guide gender responsive interventions to improve livestock production is being generated through a collaborative project by the International Livestock Research Institute (ILRI), the International Center for Tropical Agriculture (CIAT), the National Agrarian University of Nicaragua (UNA), and the University of Natural Resources and life Sciences in Austria (BOKU). Gender disaggregated data on milk production of 447 animals on 59 farms from Camoapa in central Nicaragua have been collected over 8 months. The data shows that more than 40 % of the households keep Brown Swiss crosses, however, male headed households keep significantly more Brahman and Holstein crosses than female headed households. The average daily milk production per animal is also significantly lower in female headed households (3.54 ± 1.55 kg) than in male headed households (4.14 ± 1.87 kg). Farmers are conversant with Artificial Insemination (AI), however the technology is not widely adopted. Reasons mentioned for low adoption include: high costs of service, need for repeat services, and unavailability of semen from desired breed-types (e.g. Brahman × Brown Swiss). Gender analysis revealed that the need for repeated services, which increased the costs of AI, is caused by a time mismatch between the animals' heat and the AI provision. These delays are in turn determined by the gender division of labour in livestock management: women are in charge of identifying when animals come into heat but have to wait for the men to call the AI service providers. Women head of households have difficulty accessing AI services and information altogether as they are less involved in cooperative groups and training on technologies related to cattle production. This reduces the effectiveness of AI in both male and female headed households. Practical training programs are required on reproductive management and the use of AI designed with gender responsive approaches.

Keywords: Artificial insemination, dual purpose cattle, gender

Contact Address: Julie Ojango, International Livestock Research Institute (ILRI), Nairobi, Kenya, e-mail: j.ojango@cgiar.org

ID 805

Potential Impacts of Increased Napier Cultivation in Lushoto, Tanzania

BIRTHE PAUL[1], STIJN HEEMSKERK[2], JULIUS BWIRE[3], BEATUS NZOGELA[1], PABLO TITTONELL[4], JEROEN C.J. GROOT[2]

[1] *International Center for Tropical Agriculture (CIAT), Tropical Forages Program, Kenya*
[2] *Wageningen University (WUR), Farming Systems Ecology, The Netherlands*
[3] *Tanzania Livestock Research Institute (TALIRI), Tanzania*
[4] *National Institute for Agricultural Technology (INTA), Natural Resources and Environment Program, Argentina*

In Tanzania, 21.3 million cattle (1 million crossbred dairy, 10.3 East African Zebu) are reared by estimated 1.7 million smallholder farmers, with Tanga being one of the most important dairy production regions. Inadequate feed resource base and low quality of natural pastures are among the main reasons for poor livestock productivity. Forage technologies have been promoted in Tanzania for sustainable intensification of crop-livestock systems, but there is a lack of research that quantifies the potential impacts and trade-offs of these technologies on livelihoods of smallholder farmers.

Therefore, a study was initiated in Lushoto district in Tanga region. Household surveys, feed and milk analyses, and geo-referenced soil sampling were conducted at 20 farms participating in an Innovation Platform to improve livestock productivity in Ubiri village. A participatory scenario development workshop was conducted to identify the preferred livestock feeding strategy. Livestock, crop and whole-farm simulation models were then linked to compare bio-economic performance, trade-offs and synergies of business as usual to the forage intensification scenario.

Currently, farmers were found to feed only half of the quantity that is required for crossbred cows, resulting in low average milk production per animal of 4.8 L day^{-1}. An average 31 % of all on-farm labour is used for livestock feeding, especially for cutting from far-away natural pastures. Total income including own farm production was low with an average of 772 USD year^{-1}. Increased Napier grass (*Pennisetum purpureum*) cultivation on homestead plots for cut and carry was identified as the preferred livestock feeding intensification strategy, together with maize bran supplementation. The scenario shows potential for substantial improvement compared to the baseline in terms of milk production, net cash income and labour demands. However, attention needs to be paid to soil fertility and risk of nutrient mining when substituting forage collection from public (wet)lands with on-farm forage cultivation as less nutrients are imported to the farm. Also, long establishment time of Napier grass in the Lushoto mountainous climate would diminish potential returns in the first year.

Keywords: Bio-economic modelling, *ex-ante* impact assessment, farming systems

Contact Address: Birthe Paul, International Center for Tropical Agriculture (CIAT), Tropical Forages Program, Nairobi, Kenya, e-mail: b.paul@cgiar.org

Balancing Extensive Goat Production and Conservation Interests in the Caatinga Rangeland Resource

CHRISTOPH REIBER, MIRA SIEMANN, KARIN STOCK DE OLIVERIA SOUZA, GUILHERME AMORIM FRANCHI, ANNE VALLE ZÁRATE

University of Hohenheim, Inst. of Agricultural Sciences in the Tropics (Hans-Ruthenberg-Institute), Germany

Extensive livestock production is an important livelihood strategy in the semi-arid NE Brazil. However, recent studies indicated that mismanagement, high stocking rates and exploitation of resources coupled with frequent droughts threaten the sustainability of the farming and eco-systems. In the frame of the BMBF-Research Program "Sustainable Land Management", the "Innovate" project addresses the interplay and interdependencies of land management, climate change and the services provided by ecosystems. This study aims at revealing farmers' and experts' perceptions of livestock impacts on the vegetation and biodiversity of the Caatinga rangeland and adaptation strategies in order to co-develop measures for an improved management of natural resources. Data collection methods comprised interviews with 135 small ruminant keepers and 10 experts from agricultural institutions and cooperatives.

Growing goat and sheep populations, despite of the drought in 2012 and 2013, indicate that small ruminant production is a drought-robust strategy for farmers. Average stocking rates of 3 to 5 goats per ha Caatinga and a general low feed supplementation level revealed excessive pressure on the vegetation. 85 % and 80 % of farmers perceived that in the past density and biodiversity in the Caatinga, respectively, were higher or much higher compared to today. Drought was perceived as main reason for Caatinga degradation followed by deforestation, whereas overgrazing was considered irrelevant by farmers. In contrast, 70 % of experts perceived that extensive livestock production affects Caatinga degradation.

While the majority of farmers stated not to know any Caatinga management strategies, experts suggested to improve grazing management, increase forage production and conservation, stop deforestation and establish Caatinga protection areas. As an outcome of project interventions, legal status of a Caatinga conservation area has been achieved. It is recommended to adapt goat stocking rates to specific conditions, considering the carrying capacity and its simultaneous use by wild or feral animals. Communication and collaboration between local stakeholders, scientists and policy makers needs to be enhanced further in order to develop feasible, fair and site-adapted solutions for sustainable land management.

Keywords: Adaptation strategy, Caatinga rangeland, conservation, drought

Contact Address: Christoph Reiber, University of Hohenheim, Inst. of Agricultural Sciences in the Tropics (Hans-Ruthenberg-Institute), Garbenstrasse 17, 70599 Stuttgart, Germany, e-mail: C_Reiber@uni-hohenheim.de

ID 317

Participatory Evaluation of Cattle Fattening Innovations of Smallholder Farmers in Gamogofa Zone of Southern Ethiopia

YOSEPH MEKASHA, AZAGE TEGEGNE, TESFAYE DUBALE

International Livestock Research Institute (ILRI), Ethiopia

The study was conducted in Gamogofa zone, southern Ethiopia, located 445–505 km south of Addis Ababa. The area is semi-arid lowland with altitudes ranging from 746 to 1450 m asl and mean temperature ranges from 22 to 25°C. The dominant farming system is mixed crop-livestock. Cattle, goats and poultry are the major livestock species, while maize, sorghum, teff, banana and mango are the major crops. Cattle fattening is an important undertaking and source of livelihoods. However, the fattening system is traditional low-input-low-output and producers are not benefiting much from the sector. This study evaluated the challenges and constraints, and cattle fattening innovations introduced through the participation of stakeholders in the study area. The study used focus group discussion, key informants interview, livestock commodity platforms and questionnaires for data collection. The major challenges and constraints identified are; a) feed and feeding related - lack of improved fodder and poor utilisation, lack of fodder conservation practices, poor natural grazing lands management and energy loss due to long distance grazing; lack of access for concentrate feed; b) cattle related - inappropriate cattle type for fattening; c) production related - long cycle fattening (> 8 months), poor housing and poor cattle management; d) market related - unorganised cattle marking, dominance of local markets with brokers which makes producers price takers, lack of market linkage; e) capacity related - lack of knowledge and skill on improved cattle fattening by producers, input providers and livestock extension staff. The following interventions were introduced: a) capacity related, which includes skill based training and coaching & mentoring of producers and livestock extension staff on improved cattle fattening, improved reproductive management and artificial insemination; b) fattening innovations which includes stall feeding instead of grazing, short cycle (3–4 months) multiple fattening per annum, improved on farm fodder production, improved fodder utilisation through chopping, fodder conservation through bag silage making & proper harvesting and storage of crop residues, initiation of commercial concentrate feed supplying business and use of concentrate supplementation, better animal selection from the market and deworming before fattening, establishment of fattened cattle marketing groups, and marketing linkage with buyers.

Keywords: Capacity development, improved fodder, short cycle fattening

Contact Address: Azage Tegegne, International Livestock Research Institute (ILRI), LIVES Project, P.O. Box 5689, Addis Ababa, Ethiopia, e-mail: a.tegegne@cgiar.org

The Effect of Adopting an Improved Dairy Cattle Breed on Livelihoods of Ethiopian Smallholder Farmers

TAMIERATE DEBELE[1], JIREWAN KITCHAICHAROEN[2], UTA DICKHOEFER[1]

[1] *University of Hohenheim, Inst. of Agricultural Sciences in the Tropics (Hans-Ruthenberg-Institute), Germany*

[2] *Chiang Mai University, Agricultural Economics and Agricultural Science, Thailand*

The adoption of improved cattle breeds is one of the means to improve smallholder dairy production and to thereby increase the self-sufficiency of agricultural households (HH) in Ethiopia. Hence, this study aimed at assessing the effects of adopting crossbred Holstein Friesian dairy cattle on (physical, human, economic, and social) capital of smallholder farmers, while investigating the challenges and opportunities of adopting this breed. The study was conducted in West Shewa zone, Oromiya regional state, Ethiopia. Multi-stage sampling techniques were employed to determine the sample households (N=138). Primary data were collected using a structured questionnaire in randomly selected HH that either had adopted (N = 69) or not adopted (N=69) the improved cattle breed. A semi-structured check-list was employed in two focus group discussions with randomly selected HH that either adopted (N=8) adopter or not adopted (N=12) the breed. The preliminary results show that the average daily milk production ($\pm$ standard deviation (SD)) is higher in adopter (28 $\pm$ 8.43 l/HH) than the non-adopter group (7.34 $\pm$ 2.53 l/HH; P< 001). Similarly, mean per-capita income ($\pm$ SD) from dairy cattle husbandry in adopter and non-adopter HH were 7984 $\pm$ 5217 and 5243 $\pm$ 3190 Ethiopian Birr per year, respectively (P< 001). Moreover, the average herd size, income from cattle sale, and average cost per cow per year were 28.8 %, 24.2 %, and 65 % higher in the adopter than the non-adopter HH, respectively ($p < 0.001$). Results also indicate that access to credit, lack of market information on price of dairy products, and access to animals of the improved breed are impeding factors, whereas access to veterinary service favours the improved livestock production system in the study area. These initial results suggest that introducing crossbred Holstein Friesian dairy cattle to the smallholder herds may improve farmers' livelihoods, provided that extension services offer assistance on appropriate management practices for this breed.

Keywords: Cattle, dairy, Ethiopia, improved breed, smallholder

Contact Address: Uta Dickhoefer, University of Hohenheim, Inst. of Agricultural Sciences in the Tropics (Hans-Ruthenberg-Institute), Fruwirthstr. 31, 70599 Stuttgart, Germany, e-mail: Uta.Dickhoefer@uni-hohenheim.de

 ID 756

Indigenous Milk Hygiene and Preservation Techniques by Maasai Too Valuable to Lose

JOHN LAFFA[1], CAMERON MCCULLOCH[1], DAGMAR SCHODER[2,1]

[1] Veterinarians without Borders Austria, Austria
[2] Vetmed University Vienna, Inst. of Milk Hygiene, Austria

The indigenous Parakuyo Maasai communities of Tanzania are traditional pastoralists who depend on fresh cow's milk as a staple food. However, the arid climate and a lack of clean water challenge milk production and conventional milk hygiene practices. Instead, the internal surfaces of empty, naturally occurring calabashes used for milk storage are smoke-treated by burning a variety of select local plant materials and this significantly prolongs milk keeping qualities, despite high temperatures. We sought to explore this sustainable and poorly understood innovation further by making enquiries throughout eight Parakuyo Maasai regions and 13 districts. By conducting informational interviews with 120 knowledgeable pastoralists, we sought to identify the key indigenous plants preferred and establish their traditional manner of use. A semi-structured questionnaire was designed to: (i) determine the plants used, (ii) the parts used, (iii) methods of preparation and utensil smoking, (iv) therapeutic applications and associated health benefits of these plants, and (v) alternative uses; that may suggest why they are used and preferred. Twenty plants were identified as being the most valuable, comprising predominantly hard wood trees and shrubs with strong aromas and astringent tastes suggestive of a role played by secondary metabolites. The most frequently mentioned plants, in order of preference, were: *Zanthoxylum chalybeum* (prickly ash; overall preference 26.6 %), *Olea europaea* subsp. *africana* (African wild olive; 11.9 %), *Combretum molle* (velvet bush willow; 11.4 %), *Cordia ovalis/monoica* (satin saucer berry; 9.5 %) and *C. sinensis* (oldoroko; 7.3 %). Many of these plants are also used medicinally by these pastoralists for a variety of infectious diseases, suggesting possible antimicrobial properties. Plant choices also tended to vary by local geography and the purpose to which the calabashes were assigned, e.g. old or new calabashes and milk stored for children or mothers. Nevertheless, the expertise of selecting these plants and their innovative applications is transmitted solely by the oral tradition. Further, climatic change is adversely affecting herbaceous habitats in these regions and inter-tribal territorial strife and land-grabs necessitate that the pastoralists remain nomadic. Unless we document and attempt to understand this old indigenous and sustainable hygiene know-how, it may be too late.

Keywords: Maasai, milk hygiene, pastoralist, plants, smoke

Contact Address: Dagmar Schoder, Vetmed University Vienna, Inst. of Milk Hygiene, Veterinärplatz 1, 1210 Vienna, Austria, e-mail: dagmar.schoder@vetmeduni.ac.at

Association of On-Farm Animal Feeds Handling Practices with Growth of Mycotoxin Producing Molds in Feeds on Smallholder Dairy Farms in Nakuru, Kenya

CAROLINE MAKAU[1], JOSEPH MATOFARI[1], BOCKLINE BEBE[2]

[1]*Egerton University, Dept. of Dairy, Food Science and Technology, Kenya*
[2]*Egerton University, Dept. of Animal Science, Kenya*

Practices used by smallholder dairy farmers for handling of animal feeds at the farm pose a risk of mycotoxins to dairy animals and dairy products, hence a public health concern. The aim of the study was to document the on-farm practices of handling animal feeds used by these farmers and how they influence the growth of mycotoxin producing fungi together with prevailing extrinsic conditions. The study involved the use of structured questionnaires to interview smallholder dairy farmers (n=120) on on-farm feed handling practices and collection of feed samples (n=97) for microbial analysis of the mycotoxin producing molds. The mold counts were interrelated with the feed handling practice and therefore a measure of its impact. Results found out that rural dairy system was characterised by practice of free range grazing unlike peri-urban system practice that had semi-intensive stall feeding. As a result rural system farmers predominantly fed their cows on pasture and crop residues while in peri-urban fed predominantly on commercial dairy meals and crop residues. Though most farmers in both systems had storage facilities for animal feeds, they were in poor condition. Storage facilities in 18 % of farmers' homes were poorly constructed for use of storage of animal feeds with 12 % of farmers keeping animal feeds on the floor under humid conditions. Results showed that *Aspergillus* spp. (77 %) and *Fusarium* spp. (70 %) were the main toxigenic fungi. The highest mold counts were observed in commercial dairy feeds of $4.39 \pm 1.0 \, \text{cfu} \, \text{g}^{-1}$ as compared to forages and hence are of high risk for mycotoxin contamination. Feed contamination on- farm at rural and peri-urban sub-value chains with mycotoxic fungi is primarily due to poor storage facilities exposing feed to environmental conditions that favour growth of mold.

Keywords: Animal feeds, *Aspergillus*, *Fusarium*, smallholder farms

Contact Address: Caroline Makau, Egerton University, Dept. of Dairy, Food Science and Technology, P.O. Box 536, Nakuru, Kenya, e-mail: makau.carol@gmail.com

ID 814

Assessing and Improving Animal Welfare on Mexican Dairy Farms

RAHEL ZIEGLER[1], JAN GRENZ[1], PEDRO ROGELIO AGUIRRE JOCHIN[2]

[1]*Bern University of Applied Sciences (BFH), School of Agricultural, Forest and Food Sciences (HAFL), Switzerland*

[2]*Nestlé, Group Mexico, Mexico*

Livestock husbandry depends on the wellbeing of the animal to be productive. Through technical industrialisation in agriculture this initial concept was levered and not questioned by society and politics until the 1960s, when the concept of the five freedoms arose and built the base for animal protection laws in many countries. This is also the case in Switzerland and Mexico. Switzerland has one of the strictest animal protection laws worldwide and can therefore serve as a benchmark for a Swiss dairy processor willing to improve farm animal welfare of their Mexican dairy suppliers. This is the objective of our study. For the investigative survey, 61 farms throughout all Mexican climate zones were visited and assessed during the rainy season. Data collection was done using a structured questionnaire and the evaluation was mainly descriptive. Main animal welfare concerns were found with regard to (1) structural or input-based indicators concerning (a) lack of sun protection (shelter), (b) poor state of the underground especially during the rainy season, (c) risk locations, where cattle can get hurt, and (d) qualitative and quantitative issues about drinking water supply; (2) animal-based indicators or behavioural expressions showing poor animal welfare concerning (e) feeding (selecting feed), (f) resting (too many cows standing around, i.e. not wanting to lie down), (g) locomotion (indicating poor claw health), and (h) lesions (neck, fewer hocks). Overall, farmers claimed that animal welfare was important for them. However it was not possible to make a statement on whether the detected issues concern all dairy farms selling their milk to the Swiss milk processor. Nevertheless, there are some more or less simple and cheap and therefore mostly feasible solutions for the dairy farmers to encounter the mentioned concerns.

Keywords: Dairy production, farm animal welfare, Mexico, sustainability

Contact Address: Rahel Ziegler, Bern University of Applied Sciences (BFH), School of Agricultural, Forest and Food Sciences (HAFL), Geissfluhweg 2, 4600 Olten, Switzerland, e-mail: rahel.ziegler@gmx.ch

Seasonal Behaviour of Criollo-Chaqueño Compared to Crossbreds Kept in the Chaco Dry Forests of Bolivia

SVENJA MARQUARDT[1], NELSON JOAQUIN[2], MICHAEL KREUZER[1]

[1]*ETH Zurich, Inst. of of Agricultural Sciences, Switzerland*

[2]*Universidad Autónoma Gabriel Rene Moreno, Fac. de Ciencias Veterinarias, Bolivia*

In the Bolivian Chaco local cattle breeds such as Criollo Chaqueño (*Bos taurus*) are kept extensively in the dry forests throughout the year. However, crossbreeding of local cattle with exotics like Brahman (*B. indicus*) is increasingly common. Local cattle are assumed to better cope with the challenging conditions of rainy seasons with good and dry seasons with marginal forage on offer. This hypothesis was tested in a behaviour study where Criollo Chaqueño (C) were compared with Brahman × Criollo Chaqueño (B×C) within three periods (dry (D) and rainy season (R) and transition period (T)). The animals (n=12 per genotype, bodyweight 328 ± 22 and 399 ± 52 kg in C and BxC, respectively) were kept on two fenced Chaco rangelands of 175 ha each. Their behaviour in terms of eating (grazing, browsing, gleaning), resting (standing or lying) and walking was recorded during 24 days per season using direct observations and scan sampling with 1 min of data recording every 3–4 min. One animal per day was observed during daytime hours. There was a daily switching between genotypes. The time between 10 am and 3 pm (6000 s) was used for statistical analysis by SAS 9.3., resulting in n=6 to 8 replicates per period and genotype. Data were analysed separately per period with genotype as fixed effect using either ANOVA or the non-parametric Kruskal-Wallis Test. Overall resting was the main activity. No statistical differences were found in the behaviour of the two genotypes during T. In D, C spent more time (s) browsing as compared to B×C (176 vs. 20, respectively, $p < 0.01$). Also the walking time was increased in C compared to BxC ($p < 0.01$). Resting time did not differ between the genotypes in D, but C spent more of this time standing and BxC were lying more (both $p < 0.001$). The same resting patterns were found in R. It is an indication for a better adaptation of C to the Chaco dry forests that they spent more time browsing during D and thus partially switched to woody forages during feed scarcity. The differences in the resting behaviour between the two genotypes need further analysis.

Keywords: Activity pattern, browsing, extensive system, grazing

Contact Address: Svenja Marquardt, ETH Zurich, Inst. of of Agricultural Sciences, Universität-strasse 2, 8092 Zurich, Switzerland, e-mail: svenja.marquardt@inw.agrl.ethz.ch

ID 895

Semen Characteristics and Freezing Capability of Madura's Cattle

MARLENE NALLEY[1], IIS ARIFIANTINI[2], EROS SUKMAWATI[3]

[1] *University of Nusa Cendana, Animal Reproduction, Indonesia*

[2] *Bogor Agricultural University, Dept. of Veterinary Clinic, Reproduction and Pathology, Indonesia*

[3] *Artificial Insemination Centre, Indonesia*

Madura cattle are a stable, inbred hybrid of Zebu and Banteng (*Bos javanicus*). They originated on the island of Madura near northeastern Java, where the original cattle population was Banteng, very similar to Bali cattle. Nowadays, Madura cattle frozen semen in Indonesia is produced by two National Artificial Insemination (AI) centres. The information of semen characteristics and the freezing capability of this semen is limited. This research aimed to study the characteristics of Madura fresh semen and its freezing capability from one National AI centre. Five Madura bulls belonging to National Lembang AI centre were used for this research. In total 185 ejaculates were collected in 2015 using artificial vagina and subsequently evaluated macro- and microscopically according to AI centre procedures. Semen were diluted with skim milk egg yolk extender, packed into ministraws (0.25 ml), equilibrated at 5/textdegree C for 4 hours and frozen using an automatic freezing machine. The colour of the ejaculates ranged from milky white to creamy, the mean semen volume ranged from 5.2 ± 1.04 to 6.0 ± 1.39 ml per ejaculation. Progressive motility and sperm concentration were 70.0 to $71.9 \pm 2.94\%$ and 746.6 to $1{,}305.52 \times 10^6$ sperm, respectively. Post thawing motility varied among bulls. All bulls showed moderate post thawing motility which was only $40.0 \pm 1.76\%$ to $42.9 \pm 3.93\%$. This result was lower than found for other native breed. In conclusion, the presented results indicate that there is variability of sperm concentration among individuals and Madura sperm has a moderate freezing capability.

Keywords: Freezing capability, Madura cattle, semen characteristics

Contact Address: Marlene Nalley, University of Nusa Cendana, Animal Reproduction, Perumahan Kupang Sejahtera Regency B11 Tdmoebufu Kupang Ntt, 85111 Kupang, Indonesia, e-mail: nalleywm@yahoo.co.id

The Spread of East Cost Fever in South Sudan - Results of a Baseline Study

Sylvester Okoth[1], Nicoletta Buono[2], Tinega Ong'ondi[1], Cornelia Heine[1]

[1] *Vétérinaires sans Frontières Germany, Germany*
[2] *Vétérinaires Sans Frontières Germany, Kenya*

East Coast Fever (ECF) is of the most important livestock diseases in Africa caused by the protozooan parasite *Theileria parva*. Although formerly prevalent in Central, Eastern and Western Equatorial states only, ECF has been spreading to other states after the Peace Agreement, with resulting high mortalities/morbidities. In recognition of the high importance of cattle ownership in South Sudan, both economically and socially, the Food and Agriculture Organisation (FAO) funded a study to investigate the epidemiology of the recent ECF spread in the states of Lakes States, Jonglei State, Western and Eastern Equatoria State. Data collection was based on literature review, interviews and sample collection for laboratory diagnosis, based on a two stage herd level sampling, with a sample size of 5 % per herd, and consisted of an analysis of disease morbidity, herd movements, vector distribution and and the level of vector infection with *Theileria parva*. Non-migrant calf samples were used as controls.

In total 721 animals were tested and 95 ticks (*Rhipicephalus appendiculatus (R.a.)*) collected. *R.a.* was found in 90 % of the tested herds out of which 36,7 % were ECF-positive whereas 0 % to 66.7 % of the tested herds were sero-positive for ECF. The study found that livestock movements with associated mutual grazing grounds of infected and non-infected animals that compete in search of grazing land, water and salt is the key factor in the spread of ECF. It may be concluded that cattle that do not migrate extensively, are more prone to ECF infections, probably due to accumulation of *R.a.* in the environment of animals which do not move significantly. However, traditional quarantine mechanisms have proved pivotal on the control of the disease. Also, traditional cattle grooming practices, such as using cow dung ash /urine were found to demonstrate significant potential for reducing the tick burden on cattle.

The study established areas considered ashigh ECF risk location- Guthum and Golo where further research is needed to support the observation. A key recommendation as result of the study is to place cattle owners at the centre of any ECF control strategy and undertake a countrywide tick collection and identification.

Keywords: East coast fever, migration, pastoralism, ticks

Contact Address: Cornelia Heine, Vétérinaires Sans Frontières Germany / Tierärzte Ohne Grenzen e.V., Marienstr. 19/20, 10117 Berlin, Germany, e-mail: cornelia.heine@togev.de

ID 513

Genetic Variation of the Alpha-Lactalbumin Gene in Sudanese Goat Breeds

SIHAM RAHMATALLA[1], AMMAR SAID AHMED[2], MONIKA REISSMANN[3], GUDRUN A. BROCKMANN[2]

[1] University of Khartoum, Dept. of Dairy Production, Sudan

[2] Humboldt-Universität zu Berlin, Breeding Biology and Molecular Genetics, Germany

[3] Humboldt-Universität zu Berlin, Albrecht Daniel Thaer-Institute of Agricultural and Horticultural Sciences (ADTI), Germany

The gradual disappearance of Sudanese indigenous goat breeds in numbers over the last years is due to the displacement by other breeds, cross-breeding with exotic breeds or with other indigenous breeds. To prevent the irreversible loss of Sudanese indigenous goat breeds which are well adapted to the local environment, breeding improvement and conservation strategies for these breeds should be based on a combination of phenotypic and genetic characteristics. Therefore, milk protein genetic variations are useful functional markers for characterising breeds. The objective of this study was to assess the allelic variation of alpha-lactalbumin (LALBA) gene of Sudanese goat breeds including Nubian, Desert, Taggar and Nilotic goat breeds. The α-lactalbumin is a subunit of lactose-synthase, an enzyme responsible for lactose production, a disaccharide that influences milk production.

Twenty Sudanese goats (five animals per breed) were sequenced for all exons and flanking intronic sequences of the LALBA gene. The obtained sequences were compared with the *Capra hircus* reference sequence at National Center for Biotechnology Information (NCBI): NC_022297.1. We identified seventeen single nucleotide polymorphisms (SNPs) in Sudanese goat breeds compared to the reference sequence at NCBI. Among these SNPs seven in the promoter region, six synonymous, three in the 3 prime UTR and one intronic SNPs. In this study, four SNPS were novel, three synonymous SNPs in Exon 2 (A>G) and one SNP in intron 2 (A>C). Identification of different variants in the LALBA gene can be used for the improvement and conservation of Sudanese local goat breeds. However, more research will be required to assess the functional effects of the genetic variation and association with milk production traits.

Keywords: Alpha lactalbumin gene, milk protein genes, Sudanese goat

Contact Address: Siham Rahmatalla, University of Khartoum, Dept. of Dairy Production, Khartoum, Sudan, e-mail: sihamerwa76@yahoo.com

Herd Growth and Population Development in Camels (*Camelus dromedarius*) - A Neglected Research Agenda

HORST JÜRGEN SCHWARTZ[1], ANAS SARWAR QURESHI[2]

[1] *Humboldt-Universität zu Berlin, formerly Institute of Animal Science, Dept. of Livestock Ecology, Germany*

[2] *University of Agriculture Faisalabad, Anatomy, Pakistan*

The scientific interest in camels (*Camelus dromedarius*) has been increasing dramatically in the past three decades as the steeply rising number of publications on this subject demonstrates. Parallel the camel has gained economic importance in many African and Asian countries with large arid and semi-arid areas which lend themselves to efficient exploitation through camel husbandry. Furthermore new, intensive camel production systems are emerging and new camel products are becoming of interest for certain high price markets. This raises the interest in the expansion of camel populations. One of the key constraints to faster expansion of camel herds is the well documented slow reproduction. Consequently considerable research effort has been successfully expended on the biology of camel reproduction ranging from behavioural, hormonal, physiological, histological and medical aspects to the adoption of modern breeding techniques such as artificial insemination and embryo transfer. However, not much of this research was carried out under field conditions or with larger numbers of animals and the impact of its results on the vast majority of camel herds existing in marginal and remote areas has remained minimal. We discuss the effects of other than the inherent biological constraints of camel reproduction arising from the management systems applied, the prevalent production objectives, the degree of commercialisation of production and market integration, and from the seasonal and annual fluctuations of environmental conditions. We formulate relevant research needs with specific emphasis on applicability in production environments. We outline possible research project approaches and we examine potential benefits to camel producers.

Keywords: Camels, herd growth, non-biological reproduction constraints, research needs

Contact Address: Horst Jürgen Schwartz, Humboldt-Universität zu Berlin, formerly Institute of Animal Science, Dept. of Livestock Ecology, Asternplatz 2a, 12203 Berlin, Germany, e-mail: schwartzhj@gmail.com

ID 865

Women Headed Farmer's Participation in Sheep Fattening at Rural Small Holder in Ethiopia

SAMUEL KIFLAY[1], JANE WAMATU[2], YESHAMBEL MEKURIAW[1], GETACHEW ANIMUT[3], ASHRAF ALKHTIB[4], BARBARA ANN RISCHKOWSKY[2]

[1]*Bahir Dar University, Animal Production and Technology, Ethiopia*
[2]*International Center for Agricultural Research in the Dry Areas (ICARDA), Ethiopia*
[3]*Haramaya University, Dept. of Animal Science, Ethiopia*
[4]*University of Damascus, Dept. of Animal Production, Syria*

The purpose of the study was to evaluate women's participation in sheep fattening at small holder level in rural areas of Ethiopia in four different regions; Amhara, Tigray, SNNPR and Oromia. Three woredas were selected based on AEZ, per every region. Within every woreda, three kebeles were selected on purpose based on the fattening experience, sheep population, distance from urban markets and infrastructure availability of the area. Twelve respondents were selected per every kebele, from both sexes at random sampling. The total number of respondents was 432. Data was collected using primary sources by semi structured questionnaire and group of farmers and secondary data sources, using records of government offices and cooperatives. The result of the study shows that Sex ratio of the total respondents was 14.4 % for women and 85.6 % for men headed farmers. There was significant difference ($p > 0.05$) in sheep fattening experience between the female (6.95 years) and the male headed farmers (6.55 years). There was no significant difference ($p < 0.05$) between sexes in educational status except in diploma holding that the female headed farmers were higher. There was significant difference ($p > 0.05$) in sheep possession between the two sexes that the men headed farmers owned (8.49 +0.45) higher than the women headed farmers (7.84 +0.45). The men headed farmers were significantly ($p > 0.05$) higher in areas for grazing and for cultivated fodder, (0.01+0.01, 0.07+0.01) than the women headed farmers (0.043+0.01), respectively. There was significant difference ($p > 0.05$) in sheep fattening performance in age and weight that the women headed farmers were better. Higher gross profit was achieved by men, 1095.61ETB, than women headed farmers, 1070.65 ETB. The men headed farmers were dominant over the female headed once. Major constraints for women headed farmers were double responsibility in the house, social acceptance and lack of time. It was a profitable business to both genders. But women headed farmers should be supported and followed up.

Keywords: Ethiopia, farmer, rural, sheep fattening, smallholder, women headed

Contact Address: Jane Wamatu, International Center for Agricultural Research in the Dry Areas (ICARDA), Addis Ababa, Ethiopia, e-mail: j.wamatu@cgiar.org

Live-Bird-Selling in Greater Hanoi - The Case for Socially Equitable Solutions in Animal Disease Control

TILMAN REINHARDT[1], THI THANH THUY NGUYEN[2], NGAN GIANG VO[2], ASTRID TRIPODI[3]

[1]*Humboldt-Universität zu Berlin, Georg-Simmel-Center for Metropolitan Studies, Germany*

[2]*Food and Agriculture Organisation (FAO), Vietnam*

[3]*Food and Agriculture Organisation (FAO), Italy*

Every day up to 150.000 birds are delivered into the expanding megacity of Hanoi for meat consumption. Most of this poultry is sourced from small farms in rural provinces, where livelihoods critically depend on livestock-income. This poses a giant intermediation challenge. Value-chains are complicated and often extend far into the hinterland. Starting at improvised hatcheries they involve multiple intermediaries and a complex, uncontrollable urban retail-infrastructure: Birds are distributed through a small number of giant wholesale-markets, before being retailed by small vendors on over 1.000 street-markets. Under these conditions live-bird-selling is a crucial tool to ensure market-efficiency. It responds to the consumer's desire for freshness without a cold-chain. It protects retailers from miscalculations of demand. Most importantly, it allows for a differentiated projection of quality, with price-variations >100% amongst different chicken-varieties. However, live-selling also plays a major part in spreading Avian Influenza. Street markets bear the risk of bird-to-human-infection. The aggregation process increases the risk of bird-to-bird-infection. Especially the large wholesale-markets act as reservoirs, where virus-strains are sustained and circulate freely among the poultry. Vehicles and wastewater transmit the virus back to small farms, critically endangering the livelihood of the rural poor. Despite their economic and epidemiological significance, wholesale markets lack adequate governance and often operate in legal grey-areas. For over a decade the international community has tried to assist Vietnam in containing Avian Influenza by emphasising restrictions on live-bird-selling and promoting a "western" pattern of large-scale-production, industrial slaughter and supermarket vending. These efforts have largely failed, mainly due to severe negligence of the underlying socio-economics. Whilst the economic significance of Avian Influenza for the rural poor is recognised, almost no attention has been paid to the impact of the proposed interventions on the tens of thousands intermediaries, slaughterers and vendors along the value chain. Interventions have also ignored urban consumers, 50% of which could for example not enter supermarkets because of prohibitively high motorbike-parking-fees. Our presentation highlights the importance of rural-urban-linkages and socio-economics in the combat of emerging zoonotic diseases. It critically asses the effectiveness of current international-response-mechanisms and emphasises the need for socially equitable solutions in animal disease control.

Keywords: Emerging pandemic threats, food security, nutrition transition, urban-rural linkages

Contact Address: Tilman Reinhardt, Humboldt-Universität zu Berlin, Georg-Simmel-Center for Metropolitan Studies, Mohrenstraße 41 , 10117 Berlin, Germany, e-mail: tilman.reinhardt@hu-berlin.de

ID 770

Mobile dryland pastoralism

Analyzing the Use of ICT in Demand and Access to Information and Services for Pastoralists

DUNCAN KHALAI, RUPSHA BANERJEE, ANDREW MUDE

International Livestock Research Institute (ILRI), Kenya

Index Based Livestock Insurance in the Arid and Semi-Arid Land (ASALs) of northern Kenya and southern Ethiopia is being implemented by the International Livestock Research Institute (ILRI), as a drought coping mechanism, anchored on the belief that development of an insurance scheme for livestock in a pastoral setting could be an effective risk-management strategy. The contracts are designed using low cost, accessible and reliable satellite data; Normalized Differenced Vegetation Index (NDVI). The payouts ensure that the animals are kept alive instead of providing payouts to replace / restock potentially dead animals. One of ILRI's commercial partners, Takaful Insurance of Africa (TIA) uses community shop agents in the distribution of the IBLI product. This approach is based on an agency model for providing financial services such as micro- insurance. Accurate, reliable and timely information, enable pastoralists to make better decisions on the kinds of feeds, animal health and marketing decisions; particularly where to sell and buy animals and negotiate better prices. Though ICT in developing countries have become a major means of disseminating information, both pastoralists and organisations working in the ASALs of Kenya have not yet fully taken advantage of the available cutting edge scientific techniques. This study therefore sought to understand how mobile technology through an agency model can be leveraged for crowd-sourcing and dissemination of information important for marketing livestock, livestock products and services. Key informant interviews and focused group discussions were carried out with the different actors from the private sector, public sector and the pastoralists. Isiolo County was chosen as the study site. Some of the key findings suggest that most efforts to use ICTs in collection and dissemination of information have failed in contexts that have no other support mechanisms around the pastoralist. Secondly, an agent in the form of drought monitors, food monitors, Community Animal Health Workers and Government administrators', are vital support to phone based approaches in collection and dissemination of information. Further investigations are needed to understand how these entities can be used to implement an effective ICT based market information system, leading to sustainable and food secure livelihoods in the ASALs.

Keywords: ASALs, ICT, market information, pastoralists, service provision

Contact Address: Rupsha Banerjee, International Livestock Research Institute (ILRI), Livestock Systems and Environment, Nairobi, Kenya, e-mail: B.Rupsha@cgiar.org

ID 743

The Economic and Ecological (Side-)Effects of Index Insurance for East African Pastoralists

FELIX JOHN[1], RUSSELL TOTH[2], KARIN FRANK[1], BIRGIT MÜLLER[1]

[1] *Helmholtz Centre for Environmental Research (UFZ), Ecological Modelling, Germany*
[2] *University of Sydney, School of Economics, Australia*

Currently, microinsurance is considered a promising tool to combat hunger and extreme poverty in the developing world. During their 2015 summit, G7 declared their intention to increase the number of people with access to microinsurance from 100 to 500 million people by 2020. Weather-index insurance constitutes one important form of microinsurance, especially for people living in arid and semi-arid lands (ASALs). In these regions, mobile pastoralism is very common and frequently seen as the way best adapted to use the sparse and heterogeneous lands. Yet the ASALs are very vulnerable to drought. And pastoralists for whom animal husbandry is the most important income source run the risk of becoming destitute when hit by extreme droughts. While there is evidence for the immediate positive economic effects of insurance, its (long-term) ecological effects are not yet well understood. We argue that insurance can have a negative impact on the rangelands since it reduces the natural resting period that would normally occur after a drought.

To test this hypothesis, we developed a social-ecological agent-based model (ABM) that is adapted from the Borana pastoral land use system in Kenya/Ethiopia. Our model depicts the feedbacks between herders' mobility decisions and rangeland dynamics. It is spatially implicit, includes stochastic rainfall and is based on quarterly time steps that account for dry and rainy seasons.

Our results corroborate the hypothesis that insurance cushions the immediate economic impact of a drought. Yet they also show that it can degrade the ecosystem in the long run. With insurance, animal numbers decrease less after a drought and pastures get less resting time. For ecosystems of low resilience (i.e. where grazing has a strong impact on the pasture), this effect can trigger a phase transition towards a long-term degradation. We conclude that pasture characteristics have to be considered when designing the insurance contract. Additionally, changes in land use (e.g. the expansion of agriculture) can further aggravate the situation.

Keywords: Agent-based modelling, drought, livestock, pastoralism, social-ecological systems, weather-index insurance

Contact Address: Felix John, Helmholtz Centre for Environmental Research (UFZ), Ecological Modelling, Permoserstr. 15, 04318 Leipzig, Germany, e-mail: felix.john@ufz.de

Ninety Years of Pastoralists Land Use Change - A Case Study from Northern Kenya

Horst Jürgen Schwartz[1], Neal W. Sobania[2], Markus G. Walsh[3]

[1] Humboldt-Universität zu Berlin, formerly Institute of Animal Science, Dept. of Livestock Ecology, Germany

[2] Pacific Lutheran University, Dept. of History, United States of America

[3] Columbia University, New York, United States of America

We use three different data sets to reconstruct land use patterns of the Rendille pastoral people in Marsabit District, Kenya, for the past ninety years. The first is extracted from an oral history record of seasonal migrations of eight Rendille settlement units (gobs) between 1927 and 1978. The second results from nine aerial surveys of South-Western Marsabit District carried out 1979–1980. The third stems from the analysis of Digital Globe images (Google Earth) of Marsabit District recorded between 2012 and 2014. The oral history record allows the placement of settlement sites within a 10 by 10 km grid, the aerial survey allows a 5 by 5 km grid, and the satellite image analysis uses accurate geo-referencing. All data sets facilitate, albeit with different accuracy, estimation of frequency and distance of seasonal movements of the gobs. The two more recent ones also permit counting of household numbers per gob as well as estimating size and number of animal enclosures, differentiated into those for small-stock, camels and others. Some striking changes in the land use patterns occurred during the period under observation: 1) the overall home range of the Rendille people shrunk by about two thirds since the 1940s; 2) migration distances and migration frequencies as an important aspect of pasture management diminished significantly; 3) distinct clustering of gobs in very small areas has become common; 4) the gobs became smaller in average, i.e. having lower number of households. We interpret these developments against environmental parameters such as rainfall, range condition, vegetation types, land degradation, and others which have been mapped during the 1980s for the Range Management Handbook of Kenya and with recently recorded corresponding results from remote sensing exercises carried out under AFSIS, and we present what the analyses show.

Keywords: Long-term land use change, migration patterns, Kenya, pastoralists

Contact Address: Horst Jürgen Schwartz, Humboldt-Universität zu Berlin, formerly Institute of Animal Science, Dept. of Livestock Ecology, Asternplatz 2a, 12203 Berlin, Germany, e-mail: schwartzhj@gmail.com

ID 354

Relationships of Mobility and Markets in Different Pastoralist Hotspots

ANDREAS JENET[1], NICOLETTA BUONO[2], KOEN VAN TROOS[1], STEFANO MASON[3], SARA DI LELLO[4], RITA SAAVEDRA[5], MARGHERITA GOMARASCA[1]

[1] *Vétérinaires Sans Frontières International, Belgium*
[2] *Vétérinaires Sans Frontières Germany, Kenya*
[3] *Agronomes et Vétérinaires Sans Frontières, France*
[4] *Società Italiana di Veterinaria e Zootecnia Tropicale - Veterinari Senza Frontiere, Italy*
[5] *Veterinarios sin Fronteras, Spain*

Concerns about increased marginalisation of pastoralist communities have led institutions such as International Fund for Agricultural Development to put pastoralism on the agenda. A consultation process to evaluate the global political integration and the enabling environment of pastoralists was carried out in 26 countries distributed over 5 subcontinents and was subsequently analysed in 8 selected pastoralist hotspots. On aspects of enabling environment, a minimum of 3 interlocutors per country were interviewed, whereas 315 pastoralists have been surveyed in the hotspots in respect to their employed practices. Multiple comparisons of means were carried out using Scheffe function of SPSS statistical package. Mobility is a critical livelihood feature that enables pastoralists to adapt to harsh conditions. Results revealed that Afar (East Africa, annual migration distance 85 km ±14.1), Arkhangai (Asia, 67 km ±13.4), Chaco (South America, 55 km ±12.7) and Altiplano (67 km ±8.1) were characterised by limited mobility, while pastoralists in Tiris Zemmour (North Africa, 100 km ±13.3), Gourma (West Africa, 168 km ±14.1) and Wagadou (105 km ±14.1) reported migrations from significant higher distances and were only exceeded by pastoralists from the East African Chalbi territory reporting 345 km (±14.1) annual herd migration. Impeded mobility was probably the reason why in this survey migration and herd splitting were only mentioned by 50 % and 29 % of the pastoralist when asked about drought adaptation mechanisms, whereas selling of livestock even at low prizes was the main coping mechanism during periods of stress for 62 % of the pastoralists. It is remarkable that pastoralists chose distressful coping mechanisms which require longer periods to recover over adaptive mechanisms that with seemingly less disadvantages. Perhaps there are constraints that limit full mobility? If mobility played a decreasing role as coping mechanism, market access becomes important. More than half of the interviewed pastoralists perceived that policy harmonisation efforts amongst the ministries and agencies were low. Improved information exchange amongst ministries and towards the pastoralist communities was a prioritised plea. For the consulted pastoralist, development is not only about enabling access to information and knowledge, but also about rights and participatory decision making.

Keywords: Coping mechanisms, livestock migration, markets, pastoralism

Contact Address: Andreas Jenet, Vétérinaires Sans Frontières International, Av Paul Deschanellaan 36-38, 1030 Brussels, Belgium, e-mail: a.jenet@alumni.ethz.ch

Income and Asset Poverty among Pastoralists in Northern Kenya

SAMUEL MBURU[1], ALFONSO SOUSA-POZA[1], STEFFEN OTTERBACH[1],
ANDREW MUDE[2]

[1] *University of Hohenheim, Dept. of Household and Consumer Economics, Germany*
[2] *International Livestock Research Institute (ILRI), Livestock Systems and Environment,*

The Kenyan drylands, which make up about 84 % of Kenya's total land surface, support about 8 million Kenyans with animal husbandry as the main source of livelihood. The livestock subsector in these dry areas accounts for over 70 % of local family income, as well as 10 % of the country's gross domestic product (GDP) and 50 % of its agricultural GDP (Government of Kenya, 2012). Yet despite this sector's significant contribution to the economy, these dryland areas, especially in northern Kenya, have been undermined by systematic marginalisation, poor infrastructure and services, and persistent community conflicts and raids. At the same time, the threats from persistent droughts have escalated, with Northern Kenya recording 28 major droughts in the past 100 years and 4 in just the last 10 years, and given the changing global climate, this trend is likely to continue or even worsen. These recurrent droughts and lack of supporting infrastructure have resulted in increased loss of livestock, leading to income loss that has rendered the pastoralists vulnerable to poverty. In this study, we use five waves of household panel data collected in the Marsabit district of northern Kenya, to analyse the patterns of livelihood sources and poverty among pastoralists in that area. We estimate income poverty using imputed household income relative to the adjusted poverty line and asset poverty using a regression-based asset index and tropical livestock units (TLU) per capita. Our results indicate that keeping livestock is still the pastoralists' main source of livelihood, although there is a notable trend of increasing livelihood diversification, especially among livestock-poor households. The majority of households (over 70 %) are both income and livestock poor with few having escaped poverty within the five-year study period. Disaggregating income and asset poverty also reveals an increasing trend of both structurally poor and stochastically nonpoor households. Food aid plays only a minor role in alleviating poverty.

Keywords: Asset index, Kenya, livestock, pastoralists, poverty

Contact Address: Samuel Mburu, University of Hohenheim, Dept. of Household and Consumer Economics, 70599 Stuttgart, Germany, e-mail: mburusam@yahoo.com

ID 389

Borana Cattle Reproductive Performance and Modelled Herd Development under Different Restrictions of Mobility

MAREIKE AUFDERHEIDE, HUSSEIN WARIO, CHRISTIAN HÜLSEBUSCH, BRIGITTE KAUFMANN

German Institute for Tropical and Subtropical Agriculture (DITSL), Germany

Mobile pastoralism on communal grazing land in arid and semi-arid regions strategically exploits spatial and temporal variability of pasture resources. Since decades, Borana pastoralists in southern Ethiopia employ seasonal mobility to match livestock nutritional requirements with available grazing resources at any given time, and have developed sophisticated short and long term grazing itineraries. In recent times, however, seasonal mobility is decreasing drastically due to population growth, land privatisation, and governmental regulation. Livestock is the only asset under the pastoralists' full managerial control. The herd is an autopoietic system, renewing itself within the production cycle. At the same time, it is the pastoralists' capital asset, which transforms grazing into surplus and potential offtake, generating return on capital investment often as high as 20 %. The generated products, goods, and services are traded (monetary income), bartered, and serve home consumption. Livestock reproductive performance being at the base of this, the present study aimed at analysing Borana cattle reproductive performance and demography under different restrictions of mobility.

Progeny history questionnaires were used in three regions of the Borana rangelands (n = 169 Dirre, n = 126 Malbe and n = 110 Golbo) to derive mortality and culling rates, age at first parturition, parturition interval, and litter size as determinants of herd development. Data were analysed to gain information on cattle reproductive performance and demography using Excel, LiDaSt and the bio-economic herd model PRY/HerdLife.

Significant differences were found between the regions. The most viable population of cattle of the three regions is in Malbe compared to Golbo as a medium and Dirre as the most difficult area of cattle keeping. Modelling herd development revealed the same trend and showed a potential annual herd expansion rate of 8.5 % for Dirre, 11.4 % for Golbo and 13.4 % for Malbe. Cattle reproductive performance has decreased compared to earlier findings from other studies. Since mobility is most restricted in Dirre due to high population density and regulations, we conclude that reduced seasonal mobility has a decisive share in the decrease of reproductive performance and potential herd growth.

Keywords: Cattle, modelling, pastoral, PRY, reproductive performance

Contact Address: Mareike Aufderheide, German Institute for Tropical and Subtropical Agriculture (DITSL), Witzenhausen, Germany, e-mail: mareike@calluna-naturgarten.de

Modelling Boran Cattle Populations under Climate Change and Varying Carrying Capacity in Borana Rangelands

SAMUEL TUFFA KAWO, ANNA C. TREYDTE

University of Hohenheim, Inst. of Agricultural Sciences in the Tropics (Hans-Ruthenberg-Institute), Germany

Cattle populations in semi-arid rangelands are currently facing severe threats due to erratic rainfall and increasing drought frequencies, leading to poor vegetation quality and overgrazing. However, little is known how the particular sex and age cohorts respond to these threats and how population trajectories develop under these stochastic environmental conditions. In the Borana rangelands, southern Ethiopia, much detailed information is available on the Boran cattle (*Bos indicus*) population demographics, a special breed which is highly adapted to the prevailing environmental conditions. We generated stochastic models and assessed the future development of the cattle population under different drought scenarios. We analysed changes in age- and sex-cohorts of Boran cattle populations by introducing different drought frequencies (scenarios 1 to 4, i.e., one drought every 20-year and 5-year, respectively) and their effect on vital rates, carrying capacity and market demands. We calibrated the cattle model on the basis of 12-year data sets of the Borana zone. Model validation yielded R^2 values of 0.86, 0.94, 0.79 and 0.99 for scenarios 1, 2, 3 and 4 models, respectively. In our population model, sale of mature cows affected population trajectories most strongly (77 %) under stochastic environmental conditions. Model outcomes were most sensitive to sale rates of mature cows, young cows, and juvenile females compared to vital rates and male sale rates of the population. Hence, through monitoring of demographic and environmental factors, we can improve predictions of cattle population development over time under different climate change scenarios. Further management should focus on lowering female sale rates through increasing sale of mature males that increases feed availability to females during drought years in the Borana Rangelands. This cows feeding strategy, through reserved grazing or supplemental feeding, further reduces calf mortality by increasing milk yield. Otherwise, the supplemental feeding during drought emergency will keep the population artificially high, which will negatively influence the carrying capacity that increases overgrazing and herd-crash in the following drought. Therefore, supplemental feeding should focus female animals than the whole herd to minimise herd-loss when drought happens.

Keywords: Drought frequency, modelling, stochasticity

Contact Address: Samuel Tuffa Kawo, University of Hohenheim, Inst. of Agricultural Sciences in the Tropics (Hans-Ruthenberg-Institute), 70593 Stuttgart, Germany, e-mail: satukada@gmail.com

ID 173

Application of Scaling Frameworks to the Scaling of Grazing Exclosures in Ethiopia

JASON SIRCELY

International Livestock Research Institute, Livestock Systems and Environment, Ethiopia

Grazing exclosures are a cost-effective means of restoring or enhancing the productivity of communal lands in Ethiopia. An extension of the traditional practice of excluding grazing from communal areas to enable regeneration of vegetation, exclosures provide much needed livelihood and environmental benefits. The success of the exclosure approach faces several challenges to their scaling by government and civil society, including inequity and competition within and among communities, rates of economic return, and individualisation of the commons. First, success factors in exclosure management are identified for exclosures in general, as well as along gradients in social (e.g., strength of community institutions, market access, and cultural precedents), ecological (e.g., climate and soils), and socio-ecological conditions (e.g., watershed and agricultural development stages). The status of grazing exclosures is then conceptualised within documented scaling processes in drylands in Ethiopia and elsewhere. Next, to identify possible pivots in the scaling process, two scaling frameworks are applied to address constraints and opportunities for sustainable management of grazing exclosures for inclusive and economically sustainable benefits. These frameworks include consideration of up-scaling (vertical or hierarchical) versus out-scaling (horizontal) approaches to expansion of exclosures. The past, current, and potential roles of the state (district, regional, and federal government), civil society (local and international organisations), and farming communities are analysed to explore the contributions of various stakeholders to effective scaling. Knowledge gaps and learning opportunities in exclosure management and policy solutions are identified to draw attention to possible 'blind-spots' and 'win-win' solutions that may affect the widespread success of exclosures in Ethiopia and elsewhere. Finally, the roles of scientists and researchers and incentives for their involvement are assessed to illustrate how scientists can help effectively facilitate the scaling of exclosures and other sustainable land management practices.

Keywords: Exclosure, grazing, restoration, scaling

Contact Address: Jason Sircely, International Livestock Research Institute, Livestock Systems and Environment, Gurd Shola Po Box 5689, Addis Ababa, Ethiopia, e-mail: j.sircely@cgiar.org

The Integration of Stakeholder Knowledge – How Do Namibian Farmers Perceive Natural Resources and their Benefits?

JENNY BISCHOFBERGER[1], STEFAN LIEHR[1], CHRISTIAN REUTTER[2], OLIVER SCHULZ[1]

[1]*Inst. for Social-Ecological Research, Dept. of Water Resources and Land Use, Germany*
[2]*Georg-August Universität Göttingen, Dept. of Physical Geography, Germany*

In Namibia 45 per cent of the national land area can only be used as rangeland. Directly or indirectly, its natural resources provide the livelihoods for the majority of Namibians. Yet, the rangelands are increasingly threatened by degradation. Sustainable management of these ecosystems is challenging due to the complex interactions between irregular climate patterns, vegetation and water dynamics and land use intensity. Research aiming for a better understanding of these systems can assist in finding optimal management strategies for natural resources. However, when scientific assessments require realistic management scenarios and when information is needed for decision making and the subsequent implementation of locally optimised management, users of resources as well as policy advisors should from an early stage be involved in the process. This ensures the joint production of knowledge among users, policy advisors and scientists, and helps to identify hindrances to sustainable management practices for different stakeholders. Findings on local knowledge and preferences can point to suitable approaches for management and the development of an adequate ecosystem response and ensure better communication between stakeholders and scientists. Within the transdisciplinary project OPTIMASS we focus on management options available to commercial livestock farmers in Namibia. In order to merge scientific and applied user knowledge we use the conceptual frame of Ecosystem Services (ESS). This framework lends itself to visualise the aims which are motivating management decisions meant to achieve benefits from an improved ecosystem functioning as perceived by stakeholders. Based on interviews conducted with cattle farmers and other experts, data on management options, the perception of ESS, expected benefits and environmental variability on farms were collected. To use their resources more sustainably, one important management option for farmers could be the de-bushing of their farms as a response to the encroachment of bushes. Further options are the adaptation of the rotational grazing system and the sowing of perennial grasses for restoration of the grass layer. We will present our results on management options with regard to grazing and water management. This study is aiming to contribute to progress in the management of natural resources by identifying the underlying motivations for management decisions and their impact on the ecosystem.

Keywords: Namibia, natural resources management, Savannah

Contact Address: Jenny Bischofberger, Inst. for Social-Ecological Research, Dept. of Water Resources and Land Use, Hamburger Allee 45, 60486 Frankfurt, Germany, e-mail: bischofberger@isoe.de

ID 1134

Multiple Scale Consultation in Pastoral Development Depicts Deficient Knowledge Management as Impediment to Decentralisation

ANDREAS JENET[1], CORNELIA HEINE[2], NICOLETTA BUONO[2], KOEN VAN TROOS[1], STEFANO MASON[3], SARA DI LELLO[4], RITA SAAVEDRA[5], MARGHERITA GOMARASCA[1]

[1] *Vétérinaires Sans Frontières International, Belgium*
[2] *Vétérinaires Sans Frontières Germany / Tierärzte Ohne Grenzen e.v., Germany*
[3] *Agronomes et Vétérinaires Sans Frontières, France*
[4] *Società Italiana di Veterinaria e Zootecnia Tropicale - Veterinari Senza Frontiere, Italy*
[5] *Veterinarios sin Fronteras, Spain*

Crisis and increased marginalisation has led international institutions to put pastoralism on the political agenda. Government decentralisation processes, changed development narratives and supportive advocacy are among the first signs of progress towards supporting policies for pastoralism. But is it enough and what must change? A multiple-scale consultation process to evaluate the level of political integration and the effectiveness of services provided to pastoralists was carried out in 26 countries and 8 selected pastoralist hotspots. In each country, a minimum of 3 interlocutors from central government, public and private service delivery, local decision makers were interviewed, whereas in the hotspots 315 pastoralists have been surveyed in respect to their practices. Many pastoralists were found to be associated to social networks, such as market-, religious-, and rangeland groups. However, in order to link with local government authorities (LGA), pastoralists showed their preference for leaders' councils (35 % of respondents) and animal health networks (31 % of respondents). Government extension workers were the principal source of information for 49 % of the respondents, followed by nearby pastoralists (37 %). Traditional group meetings were seen by 45 % to be the most appropriate information technology, together with local radio (31 %) and mobile phone (31 %). Throughout our survey, pastoralist demanded improved knowledge access and communication with public bodies, but stressing the importance of LGA for being main motor for basic services, education, veterinary, information and knowledge exchange. Local capacities for inclusive territorial development are required and must be built, in order to assume responsibilities, act autonomously and take decentralised decisions. However, the perceptions on the transparency of decision making and publicly available procedures of agencies and ministries illustrates a comparative low level character. On the contrary, pastoral civil society organisations are seen by the vast majority of the pastoralists as transparent organisations. Working with 'change agents' i.e. topics such as veterinary service, that connect multiple scales along pastoralist households, community leaders, civil society groups, LGA and national authorities could constitute an important learning process when building territorial capacities. Pastoral development is then possible when territorial decisions are taken jointly.

Keywords: Multiple-scale consultation, pastoralism, territories

Contact Address: Andreas Jenet, Vétérinaires Sans Frontières International, Av Paul Deschanellaan 36-38, 1030 Brussels, Belgium, e-mail: a.jenet@alumni.ethz.ch

Relationships of Ecosystem Services in Pastoral Economy

ANDREAS JENET[1], CORNELIA HEINE[2], NICOLETTA BUONO[3], KOEN VAN
TROOS[1], STEFANO MASON[4], SARA DI LELLO[5], RITA SAAVEDRA[6],
MARGHERITA GOMARASCA[1]

[1]*Vétérinaires Sans Frontières International, Belgium*
[2]*Vétérinaires Sans Frontières Germany / Tierärzte Ohne Grenzen e.V., Germany*
[3]*Vétérinaires Sans Frontières Germany, Kenya*
[4]*Agronomes et Vétérinaires Sans Frontières, France*
[5]*Società Italiana di Veterinaria e Zootecnia Tropicale - Veterinari Senza Frontiere, Italy*
[6]*Veterinarios sin Fronteras, Spain*

Pastoral market integration has been encouraged with different levels of success. Using the
community capitals framework, we assessed direct and indirect ecosystem service (ES) fluxes
between natural capital, human well-being (HWB) and market economy in order to better understand which ES can be transformed. Through a survey involving 315 households in 8 pastoralist territories, pastoralist practices, ES and services from the HWB towards the natural
capital, have been categorised and partly quantified. Indirect ES, those which are being transformed once entering the economy as marketable product (milk, meat, charcoal), are competing in a pastoral economy with free accessible direct ES. To which extent a pastoral economy
would be elastic to substitute direct with indirect ES and at which point value addition would
become economically efficient? The pastoral system is characterised by low degrees of dependency towards external inputs. From the assessed pastoralists, 51 % did not have a livestock
market nearby, while 27 % had between 2–6 sales outlets for their animals. While livestock
itself was not frequently sold, other livestock commodities, such as cheese, milk, or ghee, were
more frequently traded. Although 12 % of the pastoralist did not trade livestock products, the
bulk (75 %) sold their animal products in 2 to 7 outlets. The majority of the households sold
their produce in rural markets, with exception of butter, ghee and cheese which was sold in urban markets, showing that urban markets are accessed with livestock products including value
addition.
The framework assists to recognise that the interaction of humans and natural capital is the
basis of pastoralists livelihood: there are plenty of ES that supply the HWB system, while
HWB is providing services to protect the nature. Indirect ES, transformed in market economy,
are sometimes opportunistically used, were economic efficiency and elasticity proofs to have
an advantage. This occasions are not frequently found, since opportunity costs are often not
favourable. In the case of ghee, cheese, however, pastoralist found niches that are increasingly
exploited. In order to pursue and support pastoralist integration, we recommend an economic
analysis on efficiencies and trade-offs of various promising ES based commodities.

Keywords: Community capitals framework, ecosystem services, market integration, pastoralism, trade

Contact Address: Andreas Jenet, Vétérinaires Sans Frontières International, Av Paul Deschanellaan 36-
38, 1030 Brussels, Belgium, e-mail: a.jenet@alumni.ethz.ch

ID 631

Constraints and Solutions to Increased Productivity in two Pastoral Communities of Moroto and Samburu

GEORGE GITAO[1], DAGMAR SCHODER[2], PEACE MUSIIMENTA[3]

[1] *The University of Nairobi, Dept. of Microbiology, Parasitology and Pathology, Kenya*
[2] *Vetmed University Vienna, Inst. of Milk Hygiene, Austria*
[3] *Makerere University, School of Women and Gender Studies, Uganda*

In sub-Saharan Africa, mobile pastoralism has evolved over many years as the most efficient system as it involves movement of people and livestock according to the shifting availability of water and pasture. The dry and pastoral lands of East Africa occupy 70 % of the horn of Africa which ranges from more than 80 % in Kenya and 60 % in Uganda. While Kenya is home to 4 million (10 % of the population) pastoralists, Uganda has 5.5 million (22 %) pastoralists mainly dependent on livestock. Currently, years of neglect, resource scarcity and climate variability has reduced the ability of many pastoralists to maintain a sustainable livelihood. This bleak situation, however, affords an opportunity to design and implement development models that can substantially improve livelihoods. In the first phase of an APPEAR funded project, the prevailing circumstances were examined in a study conducted between Dec 2015 and Jan 2016 in Moroto District, Karamajong region of Uganda and Opiroi, Samburu county. The constraints were determined through participatory focus group discussion with use of semi-structured interview as the main tool. These were followed by transect walks across the manyattas and discussions with key informants. In both places access to domestic water was the main challenge but in Samburu, there was in addition lack of pasture due to extensive environmental degradation. In both places, camel keeping has become very popular due to degraded environmental conditions. Other alternative livelihoods include beekeeping and poultry keeping especially for the women. The main livestock diseases in both places were foot and mouth, anaplasmosis, peste des petits ruminants, CCPP, lumpy skin disease and CBPP mange in that order of priority. In both places, men own the livestock while women perform daily chores. Ninety percent of school going age were at home some tending to livestock. In both places, community elders placed heavy penalties on cutting of trees. The proposed interventions will be undertaken by both social and natural scientists from Makerere, University of Nairobi and University of Vienna. These interventions will involve design, trial and implementation of successful models in livestock trade, diseases, energy utilisation, natural conservation, alternative livelihoods, water conservation and purification.

Keywords: Constraints, East Africa, pastoralism, poverty reduction

Contact Address: George Gitao, The University of Nairobi, Dept. of Microbiology, Parasitology and Pathology, Nairobi, Kenya, e-mail: cggitao@gmail.com

Pastoral Households' Livelihood Diversification Strategies: Evidence from Afar Region, Northern Ethiopia

Tagesse Melketo[1], Michelle Bonatti[2], Martin Schmidt[2], Stefan Sieber[2], Jonas Koche[2]

[1] *Wolaita Sodo University, Rural Development and Agricultural Extension, Ethiopia*
[2] *Leibniz-Centre for Agricultural Landscape Research (ZALF), Germany*

Animal husbandry is the major economic activity for pastoralists. Though it plays an important role in the pastoral livelihood, livestock on its own is not providing sustainable and sufficient basis of living for the nomadic society. Evidences indicate that pastoralism in Afar continues to be affected by uncertain and variable climate situations as well as land use changes. One of the phenomena which is gaining prominence in the pastoral development literature is the promotion and support of diversification of non-pastoral income activities to meet consumption needs and prepare them against shocks such as drought. This research, therefore, is interested on an intervention project designed by Engineers without Borders, Germany, which intends to enhance the livelihood resilience of Afar people (Mille, Arsis) through challenging water scarcity and land management practices. The study attempts to answer the following research questions: a) What is the vulnerability situation of households who are under pressure arising from both policy-related and natural challenges? b) What are their livelihood patterns? c) What are the potential opportunities and constraints for the livelihood diversification of pastoral households? Data were gathered from sample of 98 households who are randomly selected out of the project participants. Household questionnaire, focus group discussions, key informant interviews and grey literature were used for the data collection. Key results of the scoping study are that livestock and livestock related activities, either as sales of animal products or direct consumption, are the dominant drivers of livelihoods. Household income portfolios witness the prevalence of poor livelihood diversification strategies. Key challenges to overcome at production level are lack of water both for human and for livestock, and rural finance institutions are least developed. Loss of grazing land, poor pasture and low productivity are major manifesting features.

Keywords: Afar, climate variability, livelihood diversification, pastoral development

Contact Address: Tagesse Melketo, Wolaita Sodo University, Rural Development and Agricultural Extension, Wolaita Sodo, Ethiopia, e-mail: tageabo@gmail.com

ID 295

Could Cheese Be the Missing Hard, Stable Currency to Fortify Self-Sufficiency of Pastoralist Communities?

DAGMAR SCHODER[1], JOHN LAFFA[2]

[1] Vetmed University Vienna, Inst. of Milk Hygiene, Austria

[2] Veterinarians without Borders Austria, Austria

Traditional pastoral existence in Africa has always necessitated close, sustainable interaction with a harsh natural environment. However, growing pressures from climate change, modern economies and land-grabs are forcing many to abandon self-sufficiency for the big cities. One such group are the indigenous Parakuyo Maasai of Tanzania, who traditionally depend on fresh cow's milk as a staple. They are among the few African ethnic groups that still live as small, socially intact associations close to nature. Their life-style thereby places great value on cattle, land for grazing and excess milk that they may be exchanged for other goods. Unfortunately fresh milk is difficult to store and inevitably times of plenty fluctuate with the times of hunger that threaten cultural retreat. Milk storage is particularly challenging in an arid climate without refrigeration and at such times survival takes precedence over prosperity. We describe an ongoing pilot project that has attempted to address these hardships, facilitate traditional subsistence and the economic autonomy of the Parakuyo Maasai. We proposed that a simple solution is cheese production. The "Maasai-cheese" project (www.vsf.at) was implemented in 2011 and instructs sustainable cheese production on the Maasai boma using locally sourced assets, combining Austrian experience of cheese production with Maasai experience of arid dairy farming.

Anticipated gains for the Maasai are becoming realised. These can be grouped as follows:

(i) Family incomes can be assured during hardship. During the dry season Zebu cattle do not produce enough milk that can be sold or exchanged. However, cheese produced and matured earlier can be sold at this time;

(ii) Antibiotic abuse in cattle can be drastically decreased. When cheese is a valuable commodity there is a strong disincentive to treat cattle with antibiotics, which prevent fermentation.

(iii) Cheese is a sought-after commodity in Africa. This pilot initiative is being well received as the demand for cheese in Africa is enormous. In particular, technical know-how has been a limiting factor until now.

We are encouraged that projects of this nature may continue to support and reintegrate traditional African cultures sustainably, without handouts, and foster fair use of natural resources.

Keywords: Antibiotic abuse, Maasai, milk, pastoralism, poverty reduction

Contact Address: Dagmar Schoder, Vetmed University Vienna, Inst. of Milk Hygiene, Veterinärplatz 1, 1210 Vienna, Austria, e-mail: dagmar.schoder@vetmeduni.ac.at

The Prevalence of Mycotoxin Contamination of Animal Feeds and Implications on Milk Safety in Kenya

CAROLINE MAKAU[1], JOSEPH MATOFARI[1], PATRICK MULIRO[1], BOCKLINE BEBE[2]

[1] Egerton University, Dept. of Dairy, Food Science and Technology, Kenya

[2] Egerton University, Dept. of Animal Science, Kenya

Mycotoxins are metabolites of fungal contamination of animal feeds as a result of poor feed storage or on-field infestation during plant growth. These mycotoxins are subsequently excreted in milk when dairy animals consume such feeds and therefore posing a safety risk of public health concern. The aim of this study was to conduct a risk assessment in milk from small-scale farms that form the informal dairy sub-value chains in rural system in Olenguruone and peri-urban system in Bahati, both in Nakuru County, by determining the prevalence and quantifying levels of mycotoxins in animal feed and milk. A total of 74 animal feed samples from actors in informal dairy value chain and 120 milk samples from individual cows were simultaneously collected. Feed samples were analysed for Aflatoxin B1 (AFB1) and Deoxynivalenol (DON) while milk samples were analysed for Aflatoxin M1 (AFM1). Mycotoxin concentration level was determined using commercial enzyme linked immune sorbent assay (ELISA). Results showed that 56 % of all animal feeds had AFB1 above European Union (EU) limits of $5\,\mu g\,kg^{-1}$ while 63 % had DON. Levels of AFB1and DON in animals feed was significantly ($p < 0.05$) high and was determined by the type of feed which was either concentrate or forage and the source of the feed which was either commercial or farm-sourced. The farm-sourced concentrates being used in the peri-urban dairy system reported the highest AFB1 and DON contamination. Forages used in rural dairy system had the lowest AFB1 and DON below the EU limits. Only milk samples from the peri-urban dairy system had AFM1 contamination levels that exceeded the EU limits of $0.05\,\mu g\,L^{-1}$. Therefore there was a higher public health risk of AFM1 in peri-urban system. The results obtained from this study indicate that the peri-urban dairy system which is intensive faces the challenge of quality feed and one contributing factor is the on-farm production and handling of animal feeds.

Keywords: Aflatoxin B1, animal feeds, deoxynivalenol and aflatoxin M1, milk

Contact Address: Caroline Makau, Egerton University, Dept. of Dairy, Food Science and Technology, P.O. Box 536, Nakuru, Kenya, e-mail: makau.carol@gmail.com

Milk Handling Practices and Microbial Contamination Sources of Raw Milk in Rural and Peri-Urban Farms in Nakuru, Kenya

JOY DEBORAH ORWA, JOSEPH MATOFARI, PATRICK MULIRO

Egerton University, Dept. of Dairy, Food Science and Technology, Kenya

Milk contamination begins the moment it leaves the udder. Milk contamination if not prevented will lead to milk losses along the dairy value chain. The objective of this study was to identify the risk factors associated with contamination of milk with spoilage microorganisms and to quantify these losses along the dairy sub value chain. A survey was carried out to identify the risk factors followed by microbiological analysis of the sources of contamination identified, and milk along the sub value chain. Contamination sources sampled from were; the udder, milking hands, milking and bulking containers which provided 560 samples. Milk samples along the sub value chain were 461 from the udder, farm gate, transporters and at the cooling centres. Microbiological analysis included total viable counts (TVC), Coliform counts (CC), Thermophillic bacteria counts (ThBC) and Psychrophilic bacteria counts (PBC). The survey showed that only 11 % of rural farmers practiced hand and udder drying compared to 50 % in peri-urban. Regression of risk factors versus farm gate milk from viable colony counts, showed that udder swabs were the highest source of contamination of milk (r =2.73). Losses due to microbiological quality were determined based on the KEBS standards (2×10^5 CFU ml^{-1}). Transporters node at peri urban location recorded the highest percentage (30%) of probable losses. It is evident from the results that effective udder cleaning and observation of high hygiene may reduce the risk of microbial contamination and milk losses along the dairy sub value chains.

Keywords: Handling practices, probable losses, peri-urban, risks, rural

Contact Address: Joseph Matofari, Egerton University, Dept. of Dairy, Food Science and Technology, Box 536-20115, Nakuru, Kenya, e-mail: jmatofari@gmail.com

Quality of Pasteurised Market Milk in Kenya

Samuel Nato[1], Joseph Matofari[1], Bockline Bebe[2], Christian Hülsebusch[3]

[1] Egerton University, Dept. of Dairy, Food Science and Technology, Kenya
[2] Egerton University, Dept. of Animal Science, Kenya
[3] German Institute for Tropical and Subtropical Agriculture (DITSL), Germany

Milk pasteurisation is a heat treatment of milk which aims at destroying all pathogenic and vegetative spoilage microorganisms. Unexpired pasteurised milk is therefore supposed to be safe for human consumption. The aim of this study was to investigate the quality conformance of whole pasteurised milk sold on the Kenyan market to East African Standard (EAS) requirements. Forty, 500 ml of unexpired whole pasteurised milk packed in polythene pouches and representing four brands were bought from supermarkets in Nakuru, Kenya in February 2016. The milk was tested for proximate composition, microbial quality and degree of pasteurisation. None of the milk brands met all the EAS requirements. For all the milk sampled, butterfat had a mean of $3.21 \pm 0.33\%$ with 60% below EAS requirement of $>3.25\%$. In one brand, the mean butterfat was $2.80 \pm 0.05\%$ and none of the samples met the quality requirement while in another brand, the mean was $3.66 \pm 0.09\%$, and all the samples met the quality requirement. The mean Milk-Solid-Non-Fat (MSNF) and density for all the milk sampled was $7.25 \pm 0.18\%$ and 1.026 ± 1.02 g/ml respectively with no sample meeting the requirement of $>8.5\%$ for MSNF and >1.028 g ml^{-1} for density. The mean Total Viable Count was $\log_{10} 5.65 \pm 3.19$ cfu ml^{-1} with 7% not meeting the requirement of $<\log_{10} 4.48$ cfu ml^{-1} while the mean Coliform Count (CC) was $\log_{10} 1.02 \pm 2.6$ cfu ml^{-1} with 15% of samples failing the requirement of $<\log_{10} 1$ cfu ml^{-1}. In addition, 22% of the milk failed the pasteurisation test. In one brand, milk was properly pasteurised but failed the quality requirement for CC. Processors need to assess microbial quality of milk by quick methods such as methylene blue dye reduction test to increase the severity of the pasteurisation regime if microbial quality of milk is poor. Proper cleaning and sterilisation of plant equipment and surfaces, and observing aseptic packaging is necessary to avoid milk post-pasteurisation contamination. Processors also need to provide incentives to milk suppliers such as quality based payment to encourage delivery of good quality milk for processing. Finally, processors should take responsibility for sale of good quality milk to the consumers.

Keywords: East African Standard, milk quality, pasteurised milk

Contact Address: Samuel Nato, Egerton University, Dept. of Dairy, Food Science and Technology, P.O Box 536-20115, Egerton, Kenya, e-mail: nato@tum.ac.ke

ID 523

Characteristics of Farm-Level Practices Attributed to Postharvest Milk Losses in Smallholder and Pastoral Systems in Kenya

BASOLE OLIVIER KASHONGWE[1], BOCKLINE BEBE[1], JOSEPH MATOFARI[2]

[1] Egerton University, Dept. of Animal Science, Kenya

[2] Egerton University, Dept. of Dairy, Food Science and Technology, Kenya

This study characterised milk production, handling and marketing practices in sample herds from three production systems: smallholder rural, smallholder peri-urban and pastoral camel in Kenya. These practices, when not adequately applied, contribute to reduction in milk production and quality. Postharvest milk losses, occurring as a result of reduced quality, quantity and economic value of milk can be minimized through proper practices. A cross sectional survey followed by laboratory analysis of milk and feed samples was conducted. Data was analysed using descriptive, inferential statistics and regression models. Pre-milking hygiene and handling procedures were implemented most herds in rural (90 %) and peri-urban (71 %) but not in pastoral herds due to insufficient access to water. This resulted in higher $Log_{10}SCC$ (somatic cell count) level in camel milk (7.4 cells ml^{-1}) compared to cows' milk in smallholder system (5.4 cells /ml). Smallholder peri-urban herd tended to have higher $Log_{10}SCC$ (5.4 cells ml^{-1}) than rural (5.3 cells ml^{-1}). Intensification of production in peri-urban herds may be the reason since hygienic constraints for the milking environment are higher. In rural, aluminium containers were predominantly used for milking (63 %) and milk storage (62 %), and plastic containers for bulking and transportation (68 %). Rural farmers predominantly practiced free grazing (83 %), while peri-urban practiced diversified feeding, integrating Napier grass (28 %) and crop residues (18 %). This led to higher nutritive value of rations for rural farmers compared to peri-urban reflected in milk (12 kg herd^{-1} d^{-1} vs 9 kg herd^{-1} d^{-1}). Feed composition did not meet cows' requirements in both systems. Feeding in pastoral was matched to available feed resources including shrubs in the rangelands and *Euphorbia tirucalli* in the peri-urban town. Morning milk was mostly sold through formal market in rural (80 %), peri-urban (59 %) and pastoral herds (97 %). The prominence of small traders in marketing morning milk in smallholder peri-urban (35 %) was also noted. Evening milk was mostly sold to informal market (63 % and 92 % in rural and peri-urban respectively). Milk market participation was based on quantity rather than quality and price negatively influenced participation to formal markets. Therefore reinforcing training in milk hygiene, handling and feeding will improve quality, thus reduce postharvest milk losses.

Keywords: Feeding practices, milk market outlets, on-farm milk handling practices, pastoral systems, postharvest milk losses, smallholder

Contact Address: Basole Olivier Kashongwe, Egerton University, Dept. of Animal Science, Egerton, Njoro, Kenya, e-mail: okashongwe@yahoo.fr

Quality of Milk and Dairy Products under Traditional Smallholder System in Northern Ethiopia

Muhi El-Dine Hilali[1], Barbara Szonyi[2], Bekahgn Wondim[3], Minister Birhanie[4], Aynalem Haile[5], Barbara Ann Rischkowsky[5]

[1] Intentional Center for Agricultural Research in the Dry Areas (ICARDA), Sustainable Intensification and Resilience of Production Systems Program (SIRPS), Jordan

[2] International Livestock Research Institute (ILRI), Ethiopia

[3] Sekota Dryland Agriculture Research Center, Ethiopia

[4] Tigray Agricultural Research Institute, Ethiopia

[5] International Center for Agricultural Research in the Dry Areas (ICARDA), Ethiopia

In Ethiopia, goats represent an important component of the farming system. In Abergelle, goats make the highest contribution to farmers' livelihoods, compared with other agricultural enterprises. Processing of traditional dairy products is an important activity by women that contribute to the nutrition and livelihood of the family. The main products are Kibe; local butter, Ergo; local fermented milk and Arera. However, hygienic conditions are often poor and milking practices are conducive to contamination.

Farmers' local knowledge on traditional processing methods were assessed through a survey conducted in eight villages in Abergelle regions using a structured questionnaire aiming to collect data on milk production, processing and hygienic practices, to develop a safer, low-cost processing technologies.

In total 375 households were surveyed. It was found that Ergo is mainly consumed by the family whereas Kibe is the main sold product for 44 % households. However, processing Kibe is labour intensive 12 %. Moreover, farmers are facing problems related to product quality. Due to hygiene conditions, product spoilage was observed in 28 % of the farms. Product taste is attributed to proper cleaning and fumigation of the milk container with Ekema wood 43 %, and 6 % of households reported a problem of appearance due to elevated acidity of Ergo.

Moreover, 91 samples of goat milk and milk products were collected. Analysis of milk components showed a big variation in composition. Fat content that is important for butter production was varying from 2.8–9.9 %. Almost 60 % of analysed milk samples tended to become acidic due to high microbial load. In addition, alkaline milk was observed in some farms indicating mastitis, which is confirmed by elevated values of electric conductivity, up to $7.3\,mS/cm$.

Samples found to have a prevalence of 5.4 % of *Staphylococcus aureus* and 8.7 % of *E. coli*. The standard plate count for 79 % of the samples was $\geq 10^6$, indicating a serious deficiencies in production hygiene.

The quality of raw milk is a challenge for milk processing, and there is a need to focus on goat husbandry and management to produce healthy milk. Improving processing practices and hygiene is crucial to overcome constraints and enhance the livelihood of households.

Keywords: Ergo, fermented milk, goat milk, Kibe, quality

Contact Address: Muhi El-Dine Hilali, Intentional Center for Agricultural Research in the Dry Areas (ICARDA), Sustainable Intensification and Resilience of Production Systems Program (SIRPS), P.O. Box 950764, 11195 Amman, Jordan, e-mail: m.hilali@cgiar.org

ID 829

Shelf Life of Raw Milk Based on Storage Containers

FAITH NDUNGI, PATRICK MULIRO, ABDUL FARAJ, JOSEPH MATOFARI, RUTH MOMANYI

Egerton University, Dairy, Food Science and Technology, Kenya

Deterioration of milk quality contributes to high milk post-harvest losses. One of the factors that leads to this deterioration is the type of containers used to store and transport milk to collection centres after milking. The commonly used containers are plastic containers, mazzi cans (the recommended food grade containers), aluminum cans and stainless steel cans. The utilisation of the mazzi cans may be hindered by some factors like transporters' preference, road terrain and container carrying capacity. The utilisation of plastic containers has been reported to increase deterioration of milk quality compared to the other containers. Farmers and operators of milk collection centres have reported that milk rejection is higher for milk stored in plastic containers. This study therefore aimed at determining the shelf-life (keeping quality) of raw milk stored in the four commonly used containers. A liter of milk was stored in each of the containers and transported using a motorbike from the farm to the laboratory at Olenguruone cooperative in Nakuru County. Titratable acidity, alcohol test and resazurin test were carried out on the milk and monitoring done until it failed the tests. The experiment was repeated with the containers of milk stored outside the laboratory. Results indicate that milk in the plastic cans failed all the tests in less than 24 hours unlike the mazzi, stainless steel and aluminum cans that took 30, 32 and 28 hours respectively. With the containers stored in the open, the milk in the plastic can still took the least time to fail the tests. It was concluded that the use of plastic containers contributed to quick milk quality deterioration. It is recommended that the concerns by the transporters about containers used are addressed by the respective regulatory bodies in the dairy sector. There should also be proper enforcement of laws regarding use of the recommended milk containers.

Keywords: Mazzi can, plastic can, raw milk, shelf-life

Contact Address: Faith Ndungi, Egerton University, Dairy, Food Science and Technology, 536, 20115 Egerton, Njoro, Kenya, e-mail: faith.ndungi@gmail.com

Utilisation of High Acid Milk at Rural and Peri-Urban Milk Value Chain Systems in Nakuru County, Kenya

Faith Ndungi, Patrick Muliro, Abdul Faraj, Joseph Matofari

Egerton University, Dairy, Food Science and Technology, Kenya

Developed acidity in milk results from microbial activity as it is being transported from farms to collection centres or stored under uncontrolled temperature. The resulting high acid milk is considered of low quality and rejected at the centres based on failed alcohol test. Milk rejection contributes to post-harvest losses at farm level which can be a significant amount of total production. The contribution of rejected milk to post-harvest losses is documented however its utilisation is not. This study therefore determined the utilisation of high acid milk that is rejected at collection centres. It sought knowledge on any products developed from this kind of milk as well as the products' processing steps. Using a semi-structured researcher administered questionnaire, Focus Group Discussions (FGDs), observation checklist and Key Informant Interviews (KIIs), data was collected from peri-urban and rural milk value chain systems, that is, Dundori and Olenguruone respectively in Nakuru County. Results reveal insufficiency of milk quality control at the collection centres therefore leading to disposing of high acid milk that can be utilised. It was noted that the most common quality control tests performed across the collection centres, were the alcohol test and lactometer test. Several volumes of milk failed these tests per month resulting to milk post-harvest losses. Frequency of milk rejection was higher during rainy season compared to the dry. Naturally fermented milk was the most common product developed from rejected high acid milk. Other farmers mentioned the disposal of this milk while others fed it to animals and/or sold it to neighbours. The study concludes that once safety and physico-chemical quality of high acid milk is determined, appropriate technologies for processing it can be developed. Minimal industrial (processing) infrastructure that can be accessed by small-scale processors can be used.

Keywords: Milk post-harvest losses, high acid milk, milk collection centres

---

Contact Address: Faith Ndungi, Egerton University, Dairy, Food Science and Technology, 536, 20115 Egerton, Njoro, Kenya, e-mail: faith.ndungi@gmail.com

ID 785

Physiochemical Properties of Camel Milk Samples Collected from Farms and Sale Points in Khartoum State, Sudan

Lemya M. Warsma, Ibtisam El Zubeir

University of Khartoum, Dept. of Dairy Production, Sudan

The camel (*Camelus dromedarus*) is of significant socioeconomic importance in many arid and semi-arid parts of the world and its milk constitutes an important component of human diets in these regions. Sudan has the second highest camel population worldwide, which is produced under four management systems that include traditional nomadic system, semi-nomadic system, sedentary system and the intensive system. This study was conducted to evaluate the compositional quality of camel milk supplied to consumers in Khartoum State from intensive and semi–intensive systems during winter and summer seasons. Fifty raw milk samples (n=50) were collected and evaluated for the physiochemical properties (fat, solids not fat; SNF; density, protein, lactose and acidity). Twenty five samples each were collected from farms and sale points. The average of fat content of raw camel milk was higher ($3.7 \pm 0.16\%$) during winter season, while SNF, lactose and density were high during summer season ($8.5 \pm 0.15\%$, $4.5 \pm 0.0 \pm 8\%$ and $1.030\,\mathrm{g\,cm^{-3}}$, respectively). Protein and acidity revealed similar values during different seasons. Fat content of camel milk samples collected from dairy farm was higher ($3.1 \pm 0.1\%$) than that collected from the sale points. Whereas, SNF, density, protein and lactose of camel milk samples collected from different sources revealed similar values ($8.3 \pm 0.15\%$, $1.02 \pm 0.0\%$, $3.2 \pm 0.0\%$, and $4.4 \pm 0.08\%$, respectively). The data revealed non significant ($P \geq 0.05$) variations between the samples from both sources and during different seasons. The performance of she camel at semi-intensive system was better in comparison to that from the other management system; therefore initiations of the semi–intensive system should be encouraged.

Keywords: Camel milk, composition, management systems, season

Contact Address: Lemya M. Warsma, University of Khartoum, Dept. of Dairy Production, P.O. Box 321, Khartoum, Sudan, e-mail: areejwarsmaq3@gmail.com

Strategies and Technologies for Camel Milk Preservation and Utilisation of Non-Marketed Milk in Pastoral Regions

JACKLINE AKINYI OGOLLA[1], CHRISTIAN DEDE[1], MICHAEL WANDAYI OKOTH[2], OLIVER HENSEL[1], BARBARA STURM[3,1]

[1] *University of Kassel, Agricultural Engineering, Germany*

[2] *University of Nairobi, College of Agriculture and Veterinary Sciences, Dept. of Food Science, Nutrition and Technology, Kenya*

[3] *Newcastle University, School of Agric., Food and Rural Developm., United Kingdom*

Information on seasonal variation of camel milk production, strategies and preservation technologies for camel milk loss reduction exists. However, a knowledge gap exists on the utilization of non-marketed milk in different seasons and on uptake of these strategies and preservation technologies in arid and semi-arid areas of Africa.

A mixed method study was conducted from July to September 2015. Both quantitative and qualitative data collection tools were used to obtain information from the participants. For the quantitative study, data was collected from 216 camel milk value chain actors (farmers, traders, transporters), using a structured questionnaire and document review check list while qualitative data was collected through participant observations (POs), expert interviews and focus group discussions (FGDs) involving the camel milk value chain actors. Descriptive and inferential analysis were conducted for quantitative data, whereas thematic analyses was used for qualitative data. Camel milk production, sales, consumption, rejects and spillages were higher ($p < 0.01$) in the wet season than in the dry season, increasing by 45.5 %, 42.1 %, 40 %, 81 % and 79.1 %, respectively.

Non-marketed camel milk utilization varied with season as 31.6 % and 10 % of this milk was disposed-off while 32.2 % and 19 % processed into fermented milk in the wet and dry seasons respectively. Maintenance of hygienic practices (88 % producers, 61 % traders), smoking of the milking and jerry cans (68 % producers, 10 % traders), simple cooling (13 % producers), milk filtration (10 % traders), and boiling (8 % producers) were indicated as the main strategies for milk loss reduction by the respondents. According to the traders, milk preservation technologies depended on electricity (62.7 %) for cooling, firewood (27.5 %) and charcoal (7.8 %) for smoking and boiling of the camel milk. Approximately 95 % of the camel milk was smoked while 5 % was refrigerated during transportation. The emerging themes from qualitative data indicated that high cost and technical feasibility limited the utilization of these technologies. Thus, in the study area non-marketed milk is either disposed-off in wet or processed for home consumption in dry season. These findings show the need for appropriate milk preservation technologies for longer shelf life milk products in arid and semi-arid areas.

Keywords: Non-marketed camel milk, preservation technologies, reduction strategies, seasonal dependency

Contact Address: Jackline Akinyi Ogolla, University of Kassel, Agricultural Engineering, Nordbahnhof Str.1a, 37213 Witzenhausen, Germany, e-mail: ogollajackline@rocketmail.com

Food Safety and Hygiene Knowledge and Practice along the Pastoral Camel Milk Value Chain, Kenya

NICANOR ODONGO[1], JOSEPH MATOFARI[2], PETER LAMUKA[1], GEORGE ABONG'[1]

[1] University of Nairobi, Dept. of Food Science, Nutriton and Technology, Kenya
[2] Egerton University, Dept. of Dairy, Food Science and Technology, Kenya

Camel milk is faced with a number of challenges, especially poor handling practices that contribute to milk post-harvest losses due to poor quality and safety. The handling practices have been associated with poor knowledge and practices on food hygiene and safety among the camel milk handlers along the pastoral value chain. The study aimed at determining the level of knowledge and practices on food hygiene and safety of camel milk actors along pastoral value chain. Structured questionnaire, focused group discussions and key informant interviews were used to collect data on handling practices along the camel milk value chain. The study focused on three points which include herdsmen who do the milking, women at the cooling and collection centres in Isiolo town and those retailing camel milk in Isiolo and its environs. The study established that herdsmen had significantly ($p < 0.05$) lower knowledge than those retailing and bulking milk in Isiolo town with a mean score of $49\% \pm 9\%$. The retailing women in Isiolo scored $62\% \pm 9\%$. The women at the collection centre had the highest knowledge with a score of $69\% \pm 10\%$. The average score along Isiolo camel milk value chain was $60\% \pm 9\%$. Each point showed significant difference ($p < 0.05$) in various questions of knowledge in food safety and hygiene. The respondents showed low knowledge in questions regarding spoilage microorganisms and also effective cleaning of containers. The food safety risk is compounded by consumption of rejected/spoiled milk with 53% of retailers using it. Their was no washing of hands by the herdsmen. Training of the stakeholders can be a way of improving their knowledge on food safety and hygiene

Keywords: Camel milk handlers, food hygiene, food safety, hygiene practices

Contact Address: Nicanor Odongo, University of Nairobi, Dept. of Food Science, Nutriton and Technology, Nairobi, Kenya, e-mail: obieronicanor@yahoo.com

Predisposing Factors for Microbial Loads in Camel Milk along the Dairy Value Chain in Kenya

SAMUEL NATO[1], JOSEPH MATOFARI[1], BOCKLINE BEBE[2], CHRISTIAN HÜLSEBUSCH[3]

[1]Egerton University, Dept. of Dairy, Food Science and Technology, Kenya

[2]Egerton University, Dept. of Animal Science, Kenya

[3]German Institute for Tropical and Subtropical Agriculture (DITSL), Germany

Camel milk contributes greatly to the livelihoods of pastoral communities in Kenya. However, these benefits are reduced by milk spoilage associated with high microbial loads. The aim of this study was to identify predisposing factors for increase in microbial counts in milk along the value chain from Isiolo to Nairobi, Kenya. Data collection was done in August 2015 in both Isiolo county and Nairobi City. Three key informants were interviewed to map the value chain while structured interviews with 89 operators from who milk was sampled were conducted. A total of 216 milk samples were taken along the chain and analysed for total viable counts (TVC) and coliform counts (CC). The camel milk value chain was mapped from production to the market. TVC and CC increased significantly from $\log_{10} 4.91 \pm 1.04 \, \text{cfu ml}^{-1}$ and $\log_{10} 3.68 \pm 1.28 \, \text{cfu ml}^{-1}$ at production respectively to $\log_{10} 7.52 \pm 1.32 \, \text{cfu ml}^{-1}$ and $\log_{10} 6.42 \pm 1.13 \, \text{cfu ml}^{-1}$ in Nairobi respectively. At production, milk quality met the Kenya Bureau of Standards specification for raw camel milk but milk in Nairobi did not. Milking persons neither washed their hands nor cleaned the camels' udder before milking; and non-food grade plastic containers were the only receptacles used for milk along the chain. Microbial counts significantly increased with milk delivery time from production to secondary collection centre in Isiolo town with $p = 0.0045$. However, the relationship between microbial counts and milk temperature; microbial counts and the volume of milk handled; and microbial counts of milk handled by individuals who have had training on milk quality and those who have never been trained, was not significant. Poor milking hygiene, use of non-food grade plastic containers and holding milk at high temperature for long time were implicated for high microbial counts in milk. Training of operators should be complemented by programs for water supply to facilitate hygiene during milking. Access to low cost food grade plastic containers as well as cooling milk within 2hr of milking, and uptake of cost effective milk value addition will increase milk shelf-life enabling access to distant markets.

Keywords: Camel, microbial load, milk, predisposing factors

Contact Address: Samuel Nato, Egerton University, Dept. of Dairy, Food Science and Technology, P.O Box 536-20115, Egerton, Kenya, e-mail: nato@tum.ac.ke

The 'Rhythm´ of Rangeland Management – Rest-Rotation Strategies in Simulated Savannah Vegetation Dynamics

DIRK LOHMANN, ELISE MÜNCH, FLORIAN JELTSCH

University of Potsdam, Plant Ecology and Nature Conservation, Germany

Savannah rangelands are prone to widespread degradation associated with significant losses of important ecosystem services. Numerous studies have addressed this issue especially addressing to what extent different drivers cause this problem (i.e. the loss of perennial grasses and an increase in certain species of woody plants – so called shrub encroachment). Mechanistic simulation models have been successfully used to asses the impacts of land use and global change on the associated changes in vegetation dynamics.

In savannah rangelands promising and frequently discussed management methods consider spatial and temporal patterns of intense use alternating with times of rest. The underlying assumptions are based on the hypothesis that under natural conditions, large herds of ungulate herbivores migrating over vast spatial areas have short term, high intensity impacts on the system intermitted by longer periods of rest. Although of high relevance to actual land users, most rangeland models do not allow for an assessment of such impacts, as they often lack the abovementioned necessary resolution of processes like growth, removal of biomass and interlinked dynamics of above and belowground resources of plants.

We have implemented intra-seasonal herbivore impacts, growth and the dynamics of below-ground reserve biomass in an existing model and successful eco-hydrological of dryland vegetation dynamics. We used this adapted model version to assess different spatio-temporal strategies of rangeland management in semi-arid African savannah systems.

We can show that the sequence of grazing and resting periods has significant impacts on vegetation dynamics. This goes along with mid- and long-term changes of sustainable carrying capacities of these ecosystems for livestock production.

Keywords: *Acacia mellifera*, bush encroachment, eco-hydrological savannah model, livestock grazing, rangeland management, semi-arid savannah

Contact Address: Dirk Lohmann, University of Potsdam, Plant Ecology and Nature Conservation, Am Mühlenberg 3, 14476 Potsdam, Germany, e-mail: dirk.lohmann@uni-potsdam.de

Monogastric livestock

From 'cuy' in South America to 'cavy' in Sub-Sahara Africa: Advancing Development through South-South Cooperation

BRIGITTE L. MAASS[1], LILIA CHAUCA-FRANCIA[2], WANJIKU L. CHIURI[3],
APPOLINAIRE DJIKENG[4], FELIX MEUTCHIEYE[5], BRUCE PENGELLY[6],
CARLOS SERE[7]

[1] Georg-August-Universität Göttingen, Crop Sciences, Germany
[2] Instituto Nacional de Innovacion Agraria (INIA), Peru
[3] University of Laikipia, Kenya
[4] International Livestock Research Institute (ILRI), Kenya
[5] University of Dschang, Cameroon
[6] Pengelly Consultancy, Australia
[7] Bioversity International, Italy

Neglected and underutilised livestock species like 'cuy' or 'domestic cavy' or 'guinea pig' (*Cavia porcellus* L.) play an important role in better nutrition and poverty reduction. Cavy is indigenous in South America and has been introduced to sub-Sahara Africa (SSA), where it has an extensive distribution from Senegal in the West to Tanzania in the East. The remarkable adoption by smallholder farmers and peri-urban dwellers of a simple, apparently suitable technology has not received much international attention. Animals mostly roam freely in the kitchen or house and are kept in a way comparable to the traditional one in South America. In SSA, cavies are a source of meat, a flexible source of cash income – particularly used for schooling expenses – and an appreciated source of manure. In many SSA-countries (e.g., Cameroon, DR Congo and Tanzania), predominantly women and teenage boys engage as cavy keepers and sellers in local markets. Keeping cavies is also used as an alternative to consumption of bushmeat in order to protect wildlife in forest zones; or as part of humanitarian starter kits for displaced people in conflict areas. In Peru, improvement programs of 'cuyes' over the past 60 years have yielded earlier maturing, heavier breeds. Further, improving husbandry and, especially, optimising feeding have led to enhanced 'cuy' production. In most SSA-countries, however, formal knowledge about optimal cavy husbandry is limited. Production systems are simple and animal mortality seems high, partly a negative consequence of inbreeding. Thus, the animal's potential is not realised, and its consumption is not valued in line with its high nutritional value because of certain cultural perceptions of society. Researchers, development agents, practitioners and donors from sub-Sahara Africa, South America, Europe and Australia have come together to further identify opportunities for advancing the use of this resource through enhanced South-South cooperation. While aiming to understand the multiple roles that cavies can have in enhancing livelihoods, paramount differences in cavy culture between the continents must be recognised. The diverse production realities need to be considered, therefore, by conducting socio-economic, cultural, as well as technological research and development to offer producers an array of suitable options.

Keywords: Gender, guinea pig, humanitarian intervention, smallholder agriculture, underutilised species, wildlife conservation, women empowerment, youth participation

Contact Address: Brigitte L. Maass, Georg-August-Universität Göttingen, Crop Sciences, Grisebachstr. 6, 37077 Göttingen, Germany, e-mail: Brigitte.Maass@yahoo.com

Morphometric Differentiation of Indigenous Chicken Populations of Ethiopia Using Discriminant Analysis

KEBEDE KEFENIE KEFELEGN[1,2], BODENA FEYERA[2], AMEHA NEGASSI[2]

[1]*University of Hohenheim, Dept. of Animal Breeding and Husbandry in the Tropics and Subtropics, Germany*
[2]*Haramaya University, School of Animal and Range Sciences, Ethiopia*

Adequate knowledge of diversities within and between chicken populations will not only help in reducing misidentification in poultry husbandry but also aid conservation of many important endangered alleles. In poultry, variability in linear body measurements (LBMs) arises due to genetic and environmental effects, and the magnitude of variability may differ under different management practices and environmental conditions. This study evaluated the usefulness of morphological traits to distinguish three indigenous chicken populations of Ethiopia using discriminant analysis. A total number of 711 matured, traditionally-managed chickens were used for this study. The chickens were sampled from Gobusayo, Bakotibe and Danno districts of western Oromia zone in Ethiopia. Body-weight and LBMs i.e., back-lengths, beak-length, body-length, breast-circumference, comb-height, comb-length, keel-bone-length, neck-length, shank-circumference, shank-length, wattle-length, wattle-width, and wing-span were taken from December 2014 to April 2015 on each bird.

Univariate analysis of the population variability revealed that all the traits showed significant ($p < 0.05$) difference across the districts. The chickens from Danno had for most of the traits the highest LSMEANS value followed by Bakotibe and Gobusayo. Stepwise discriminant analysis indicated that wing-span, breast-circumference, back-length, shank-length, body-weight, comb-height, neck-length, comb-length, wattle-length, wattle-width and beak-length were more effective in that order discriminating the three chicken populations. As revealed by the canonical discriminant analysis, the Mahalanobis distance of the traits found between Gobusayo and Bakotibe chickens was 8.93, between Gobusayo and Danno chickens was 7.85 and between Bakotibe and Danno chickens was 2.05. This was complemented by the results of the nearest neighbour discriminant analysis, where 92.35 % of Gobusayo, 78.02 % of Bakotibe and 73.77 % of Danno chickens were classified into their source population. However, varied percentages of misclassification were observed showing the level of genetic exchange that has taken place between them overtime. This study indicates that discriminant analysis may be used successfully in the field to separate the chicken populations. The successful characterisation will help in selective breeding in future breeding programmes. The present results could be complemented by molecular characterisation using DNA markers; and serve as a basis for further characterisation, conservation and genetic improvement strategies for indigenous poultry.

Keywords: Discriminant analysis, indigenous chicken, morphological traits

Contact Address: Kebede Kefenie Kefelegn, University of Hohenheim, Dept. of Animal Breeding and Husbandry in the Tropics and Subtropics, Garbenstr. 17, 70599 Stuttgart, Germany, e-mail: k_kebede@uni-hohenheim.de

ID 183

Phenotypic Characterisation, Performances and Husbandry Conditions of Local Poultry in (Peri-)Urban Households in Tamale, Ghana

MICHAEL BROWN[1], GABRIEL TEYE[2], BENJAMIN ALENYOREGE[2], REGINA RÖSSLER[1]

[1] University of Kassel / Georg-August Universität Göttingen, Animal Husbandry in the Tropics and Subtropics, Germany
[2] University for Development Studies, Tamale, Ghana.,

The socio-economic importance of urban agriculture continues to rise in Southern countries, due to rapid population growth, rising incomes and urbanisation. Increasing demand for poultry products has led to the growing use of high-performing exotic breeds in poultry production systems worldwide. However, traditional production systems in which local breeds are kept are still relevant in many tropical countries. The frequent mixing of exotic and local birds in such systems raises concerns about genetic losses in local poultry breeds with the number of breeds at risk increasing rapidly. Identifying distinct breed populations through phenotypic characterisation is an important step to provide information for the conservation of animal genetic resources.

Phenotypic traits of adult local chickens (788) and Guinea fowls (394) were assessed and production environments examined in 78 (peri-)urban households in Tamale, Northern Ghana, in 2015. Socio-economic characteristics and preferences for local poultry were also assessed. Reported yearly egg production was 30–50 eggs for chickens and >100 eggs for Guinea fowls. Mean body weights were 0.90 ± 0.19 kg for chickens and 1.19 ± 0.19 kg for Guinea fowls. In both chickens and Guinea fowls, results show different plumage, skin, eye, comb/helmet and earlobe and shank colours. Local breeds are preferred due to their ease of management, adaptability/disease resistance and traditional/religious uses. Households raise chickens and Guinea fowls for home consumption and income. Birds are kept under extensive conditions without the support of technical services. Diseases and poor management are the main challenges of production.

Phenotypic variation of the mentioned qualitative traits points to a genetic diversity, also of quantitative and secondary traits that may be worth conserving for future use. This provides opportunity for selection and improvement of local poultry populations. Utilizing the latter is the best route to their genetic conservation. Therefore production of local breeds of poultry should be given policy and research attention in Ghana.

Keywords: Breeds, conservation, genetic resources, Guinea fowls, traits

Contact Address: Regina Rößler, University of Kassel / Georg-August-Universität Göttingen, Animal Husbandry in the Tropics and Subtropics, Göttingen, Germany, e-mail: regina.roessler@agr.uni-goettingen.de

Spirulina platensis Enhances Nutrient Utilisation and Blood Profile of Broiler Chickens

OLUSESAN FAFIOLU[1], JOEL ALABI[1,2], IFEOLUWA DADA[2], ADERONKE TENIOLA[3], ADEDOTUN ADEGBENJO[1], ABIMBOLA OLADELE OSO[1], ADEBAYO V. JEGEDE[1], OLUSEYI OLUWATOSIN[2]

[1]*Federal University of Agriculture, Abeokuta, Dept. of Animal Nutrition, Nigeria*

[2]*World Bank Centre of Excellence in Agricultural Development and Sustainable Environment (CEADESE), Nigeria*

[3]*Federal College of Animal Health and Production Technology, Animal Health and Production, Nigeria*

Vitamins and minerals are essential for efficient utilisation of bulk nutrients such as protein, carbohydrates and fats in livestock diets. *Spirulina platensis*, a green micro-filamentous algae, contains ample amounts of highly bioavailable vitamins and trace minerals. Therefore, this study investigated the efficacy of resultant diets in which vitamin-mineral premix was replaced by varying levels of *Spirulina platensis*. 300 mixed sexed one-day-old broiler chicks (Marshal) were randomly allocated on weight equalisation basis to 6 dietary groups with 10 birds in five replications. Each group was fed one of the Corn-Soybean meal-based experimental diets which were formulated to meet the NRC (1994) requirements for broiler chickens with no premix (T1), with appropriate premix (T2), with *Spirulina* at 20g (T3), 30g (T4), 40g (T5), and 50g per kg (T6) replacing totally the vitamins and trace minerals in the respective diets for a period of 42 days. Nutrient digestibility and blood profile (haematological indices, serum biochemistry and lipid profile) were determined. Data were subjected to ANOVA in a Completely Randomised Design using General Linear Model procedures of SAS (2007). Results revealed that best ($p < 0.05$) apparent digestibility of dry matter (75.18 %), crude fat (83.75 %), crude protein (85.75 %), crude fibre (73.58 %), ash (84.72 %) and soluble carbohydrates (88.11 %) were obtained in birds fed 50g per kg *Spirulina* while the poorest values were obtained in birds fed diets void of vitamin-trace mineral premix. Inclusion of *Spirulina* in the diets produced significant ($p < 0.05$) effects on blood profile in that highest PCV and reduced WBC, Heterophil: Lymphocyte ratio as well as lowered Low Density Lipoprotein (LDL) were observed in birds fed 30 - 50 g per kg *Spirulina*. It was concluded that *Spirulina platensis* used in place of vitamins and trace minerals improved nutrient utilisation and apparent state of health of experimental birds as indicated by enhanced PCV and lowered serum LDL. Therefore, *Spirulina platensis* holds potential as a viable alternative to use of conventional vitamins and trace mineral premixes (formulated from inorganic salts and vitamin analogues) in nutrition of broiler chickens.

Keywords: Blood indices, broiler chickens, digestibility, *Spirulina platensis*, vitamin-trace mineral premix

Contact Address: Joel Alabi, World Bank Centre of Excellence in Agricultural Development and Sustainable Environment (CEADESE), Federal University of Agriculture, Abeokuta, Ogun State, Nigeria, Livestock Science and Sustainable Environment, 4 Oluwapemi Street Oba-Oke Estate Aregbe, 110001 Abeokuta, Nigeria, e-mail: joelalabi@gmail.com

ID 576

Pig's Diets Containing Fibre-Rich Feedstuff Characterised through *in vitro* Simulation of Small Intestine Digestion and Colon Fermentation

HAI QUAN NGUYEN[1], DUC NGOAN LE[2], PHUNG DINH LE[2], VEERLE FIEVEZ[1]

[1] *Ghent University, Dept. of Animal Production (Lanupro), Belgium*
[2] *Hue University of Agriculture and Forestry, Fac. of Animal Sciences, Vietnam*

Including dietary fibre in pig's diets has been suggested to potentially reduce urinary urea losses, and hence ammonia emissions, through stimulation of the hindgut fermentation. However, protein digestibility in the small intestine might be reduced, resulting in impaired animal productivity. Accordingly, the objective of this *in vitro* study was to screen diets containing one out of nine Vietnamese feed ingredients, rich in fermentable fibre, in terms of apparent ileal crude protein digestibility as well as fermentation capacity and ammonia accumulation in the hindgut. Following nine feed ingredients, rich in fermentable fibre were studied: Banana stem (*Musa acuminata*), Brewery by-product, Cassava (*Manihot esculenta*) leaf and root by-product, Cabbage waste (*Brassica oleracea*), Sweet potato vines (*Ipomoea batatas*), Taro leaves and petioles (*Colocasia esculenta*), Tofu by-product and *Trichanthera gigantean*. All dietary ingredients were analysed for proximate composition, neutral detergent fibre (NDF), lignin, non-starch polysaccharides (NSP), soluble and insoluble fibre and were submitted to a two-steps *in vitro* simulation of the enzymatic hydrolysis in stomach and small intestine followed by microbial fermentation in the colon, using faecal inoculum. The *in vitro* simulation was conducted either for all ingredients separately as well as for complete diets. The latter ten complete diets included a control diet with 15 % NSP and nine experimental diets with 20 % NSP containing one of the fibre-rich feedstuffs which contributed 15 % of the total dietary NSP. Diets were formulated to contain similar amounts of crude protein (160-170 g kg^{-1} DM), metabolisable energy (12.1-12.3 MJ kg^{-1} DM) and ileal digestible protein (120-125 g kg^{-1} DM) based on the chemical analysis and *in vitro* results of the individual feedstuffs. The observed ileal digestible protein of the diet containing *Trichanthera gigantean* was 25 % lower than its corresponding calculated value ($p < 0.05$ based on 95% confidence intervals of both observed and calculated ileal digestibilities), whereas for other diets differences - if any - were smaller. Diets containing Banana stem (p = 0.01), and Cassava leaf (p = 0.021) stimulated hindgut fermentation, as suggested from increased productions of volatile fatty acids as compared with the control diet (T-tests). However, this stimulation did not result in a reduced accumulation of ammonia in the hindgut simulation system.

Keywords: Ammonia, fermentation, ileal digestibility, *in vitro*, large intestine

Contact Address: Hai Quan Nguyen, Ghent University, Dept. of Animal Production (Lanupro), Proefhoevestraat 10, 9000 Gent, Belgium, e-mail: nguyenhaiquan@huaf.edu.vn

Growth and Haematological Assessment of Broiler Chickens Fed Bitter Leaf (*Vernonia amygdalina*) Supplemented Diets

FREDERICK IGENE, KELVIN AIKPITANYI

Ambrose Alli University, Animal Science, Nigeria

In search for alternatives to antimicrobial agents as growth promoters in poultry and other livestock nutrition, researchers are focusing attention on exploitation of non-conventional feed resources and herbal plants. This study was undertaken to assess the growth performance, haematological and serum biochemical indices of broiler chickens fed diets supplemented with graded levels of bitter leaf (*Vernonia amygdalina*) meal (BLM). Ninety (90) Marshal broiler chicks were divided into 5 treatment groups of 18 chicks each with 3 replicates. The chicks were randomly assigned to 5 experimental diets formulated such that diet 1 (negative control) contained no leaf meal nor antibiotics, diet 2 contained 0.10 % oxytetracycline (positive control), while diets 3, 4 and 5 had BLM inclusion at 1, 2 and 3 % respectively. Data generated during the experiment were subjected to a one-way analysis of variance in a completely randomized design and means were seperated by Duncan multiple range test using the general linear model programme of the SPSS computer package. Results on growth performance showed that all parameters were significantly affected by dietary treatments. Total feed intake ranged from $7876\,\text{g bird}^{-1}$ in the 3 % BLM diet to $8145\,\text{g bird}^{-1}$ in the 2% BLM. Final weight gain was least ($3577\,\text{g bird}^{-1}$) in the negative control diet and highest ($3816\,\text{g bird}^{-1}$) in the oxytetracycline diet. Birds on 1 % and 2 % BLM compared favourably with the oxytetracycline birds. Feed conversion and protein efficiency ratios (2.21 and 2.40 respectively) were better in the oxytetracycline diet. On haematological parameters, white blood cell, lymphocytes, monocytes and neutrophils were significantly highest in the negative control diet while values for oxytetracycline and BLM diets were comparable. Haemoglobin, MCH and MCHC values ($14.50\,\text{g dl}^{-1}$, 47.70 pg and $34.80\,\text{g dl}^{-1}$ respectively) were better in the oxytetracycline diet. Other blood parameters namely, red cell distribution width, red blood cell, packed cell volume, mean corpuscular volume, platelet and mean platelet volume were not significantly different. Total protein, albumin and globulin values ($3.55\,\text{g dl}^{-1}$, $1.50\,\text{g dl}^{-1}$ and $2.05\,\text{g dl}^{-1}$ respectively) were least in the oxytetracycline diet. It can be concluded that BLM in the diets of broiler chickens shows a great promise as good alternative to the commonly used oxytetracycline antibiotic growth promoter in Nigeria.

Keywords: Bitter leaf, broiler chickens, growth performance, haematological indices

Contact Address: Frederick Igene, Ambrose Alli University, Animal Science, Benin Express Way, 234 Ekpoma, Nigeria, e-mail: fredogene@yahoo.com

ID 275

Feed Consumption, Carcass Evaluation and Growth Performance of Broiler Rabbits Fed Different Levels and Processing Methods of Milk Thistle (*Silybum marianum*) Supplement

AKHIR PEBRIANSYAH[1], PETRA SILBEROVÁ[2], DANIELA LUKEŠOVÁ[1], ADÉLA DOKOUPILOVÁ[3], KAREL JANDA[3]

[1]*Czech University of Life Sciences Prague, Fac. of Tropical AgriSciences, Dept. of Animal Science and Food Processing, Czech Republic*

[2]*Velaz, S.R.O., Czech Republic*

[3]*Czech University of Life Sciences Prague, Fac. of Agrobiology, Food and Natural Resources, Dept. of Husbandry and Ethology of Animals, Czech Republic*

Milk thistle (*Silybum marianum*) belongs to the family *Asteraceae* which are widely spread in arid and semi-arid areas of Mediterranean regions. This annual plant contains silymarin-flavolignans with hepatoprotective and canceroprotective properties which show positive effects on health and performance of animals. The study aimed to investigate the effect of different level and processing methods of milk thistle (*Silybum marianum*) on feed consumption, carcass composition and growth performance of broiler rabbits. A total of 180 HYLA broiler rabbits, 42 days old, were fed with different concentrations of milk thistle supplement - group III (0.5 % of fermented milk thistle) and group II (1 % non-fermented milk thistle) in comparison with control group I (standard feed ration without any supplementation). Feed and water were available *ad libitum*. The experiment started at 42 days of rabbit age and finished by slaughter when rabbits achieved 2.6 kg of live weight. The weight of the body parts, carcass weight, carcass yield, and growth performance were recorded and calculated. Carcass weight and carcass yield in rabbits fed with 0.5 % fermented milk thistle were significantly higher ($p < 0.05$) than in rabbits of other groups. However, there were no significant differences ($p > 0.05$) between control and experimental groups in the growth performance. Furthermore, daily feed consumption was higher in the treatment group II and group III compared to Control I ($p < 0.05$). The results of this experiment therefore indicated that 1 % non-fermented milk thistle extract supplemented in the feed ration for broiler rabbits is not a suitable supplement for improvement of broiler rabbits´ performance. However, 0.5 % fermented milk thistle could be used to improve the carcass performance.

Keywords: Broiler rabbits, fermented feed, milk thistle, performance

Contact Address: Akhir Pebriansyah, Czech University of Life Sciences Prague, Fac. of Tropical AgriSciences, Dept. of Animal Science and Food Processing, Kamýcká 129, 16521 Prague 6 - Suchdol, Czech Republic, e-mail: avanbenjamin89@gmail.com

Effect of Dietary Inclusion of Tamarind (*Tamarindus indica* L.) Seeds on Broiler Chicken Performance and Carcass Characteristics

MUTAZ MAHMOUD, MOHAMMED OSMAN, ARAFA ELWASEELA, HAMID ALDURRA, LUTFI MOHAMMED ZEN

University of Gezira, Fac. of Animal Production, Sudan

The objective of the study was to measure the effect of dietary inclusion of different levels of raw and processed tamarind seeds on broiler chicken performance and carcass characteristics. The processing implemented for seeds in this trial was boiling. The tamarind seeds were divided into two categories (raw and treated with boiling) and then ground to be included in experimental diets. A total of 180 unsexed one-day broiler chicks (Ross 308) were distributed to 15 pens that were randomly assigned to five treatments. Each treatment was replicated three times (12 birds per pen). In a completely randomised design, the dietary treatments consisted of 5 and 10 % raw (TRS), 5 and 10 % processed (TBS) and 0 % tamarind seeds (control). The experimental diets were formulated iso-nitrogenous and iso-energetic to meet or exceed the requirements of finisher period for broilers (NRC, 1994). At day 42, two birds per replicate were slaughtered to measure the carcass and organs weights. The results showed that tamarind seeds contained 15.98 % protein, 3.77 % fat, 43.5 % ash, 11.4 % fibre, 2.41 % tannin (dry matter) and 13.06 MJ kg^{-1} metabolisable energy. Boiling seeds decreased tannin content by 31 %. All birds fed with diets containing tamarind seeds were better in weight gain and feed conversion ratio than those fed control diets ($p \leq 0.01$).The highest feed consumed were reported with birds fed on control diets. There were no significant differences ($p \geq 0.05$) between different treatments in gizzard, abdominal fat, drumstick and last body weights. The greatest carcass weight was observed with control treatment followed by TBS 5 % treatment ($p \leq 0.01$). The heaviest and the lightest weights of breast were recorded with control and TRS% treatments, respectively. Birds fed on TBS and control treatments had the biggest thigh weights ($p \leq 0.01$). The current study indicated that TRS and TBS scored the best results for broiler growth performance. However, TBS treatments could be the second choice following the control for weights of most edible parts of the carcass. So, tamarind seeds could be used as alternative feedstuff for poultry as protein and energy source specially when treated with boiling.

Keywords: Alternative protein source, boiling treatment, broiler performance

---

Contact Address: Mutaz Mahmoud, University of Gezira, Poultry Production, Elgamaa, Wad Medani, Sudan, e-mail: mutaz_babiker@yahoo.com

ID 137

Carcass Characteristics and Serum Biochemical Indices of Broiler Chickens Fed Diets Containing Natural Additives

AUSAJI AYUK, OLUWATOSIN KENNEDY OKO, FELICIA OKON

Universty of Calabar, Dept. of Animal Science, Nigeria

The study was designed to evaluate the effect of ginger, garlic, bitterleaf and their mixtures used as natural additives on the carcass and serum biochemical characteristics of broiler chickens. A total of 240 broiler chicks were raised for 56 days on eight different combinations of natural additives. Treatment 1 (T1) had no additive and served as control, T2 had $14\,g\,kg^{-1}$ of garlic, T3 had $14\,g\,kg^{-1}$ of ginger, T4 had $14\,g\,kg^{-1}$ of bitterleaf, T5 had $7\,g\,kg^{-1}$ each of garlic and ginger, T6 had $7\,g\,kg^{-1}$ each of ginger and bitterleaf, T7 had $7\,g\,kg^{-1}$ each of garlic and bitterleaf and T8 had $4.67\,g\,kg^{-1}$ each of ginger, garlic and bitterleaf. After eight weeks, the carcass parameters and serum biochemical indices were evaluated. The data were then analysed using One-Way ANOVA for completely randomised designed (CRD). The study revealed that live weight, lungs, gall bladder, breast, wings and intestine were significantly ($p < 0.05$) affected by the inclusion of the additives in the diets of the broiler chickens while other carcass parameters were not. The treatment groups receiving only garlic or ginger or both weighed more than the control diet. Serum biochemical analysis revealed that cholesterol, glucose, Na^+, HDL and urea were significantly different ($p < 0.05$). Furthermore, the combination of both garlic and ginger (T5) was more effective at lowering cholesterol, triglycerides and HDL than either ginger or garlic alone, and all three additives combined together. These findings suggest that using the right combination of both garlic and ginger can be effective at raising broiler with more market value while accumulating lower amount of unhealthy lipids.

Keywords: Bitter leaf, broiler, garlic, ginger

Contact Address: Ausaji Ayuk, Universty of Calabar, Dept. of Animal Science, Etta Agbor, 540001 Calabar, Nigeria, e-mail: yinsaj@yahoo.com

Moringa oleifera Leaf Meal and Differently Processed Seed Meal as Additive in Broiler Diets

ISAAC OLUSEUN ADEJUMO[1], ANTHONY OLOGHOBO[2], CHARLES OLUWASEUN ADETUNJI[3]

[1] *Landmark University, Dept. of Animal Science, Nigeria*
[2] *University of Ibadan, Dept. of Animal Science, Nigeria*
[3] *Landmark University, Dept. of Biological Sciences, Nigeria*

Synthetic antibiotics such as tetracycline have accompanying problems such as non-availability, high cost, resistance and residue in animal products which has made their use in livestock production a concern. This has necessitated the need for sourcing for herbal alternatives which could better replace synthetic antibiotics. *Moringa oleifera* is used in Nigeria for treating several kinds of ailments. Its seeds have been reported to be rich in protein and have been used as source of protein in broiler diet up to 5% without any reported adverse effects on the birds. This study was carried out to investigate the effects of raw and cooked *Moringa oleifera* seed meal and raw *Moringa oleifera* leaf meal as a replacement for synthetic antibiotic (tetracycline) on growth performance and haematological parameters of Arbor Acre starter broilers. The study lasted for 28 days. There were 5 treatments: negative control (D1), positive control (D2), treatments 3, 4 and 5 (D3, D4 and D5) containing 0.25 % raw air-dried *Moringa oleifera* seed meal, 0.25 % cooked air-dried *Moringa oleifera* seed meal and 0.25 % of raw air-dried *Moringa oleifera* leaf meal respectively in a completely randomised design. Each treatment had five replicates of seven one day old birds per replicate. Blood samples for haematological analysis were collected from three birds of similar weight per replicate. The study was conducted in Poultry Unit, Landmark University Teaching and Research Farm, Omu-Aran, Kwara State, Nigeria. Data were analysed using general linear model of analysis of variance. The results of the study revealed that experimental diets compared well with the control diets. There were no significant differences across the treatments for all the parameters measured. Daily body weight gain ranged between $0.5\pm0.05\,\text{g bird}^{-1}$ and $0.6\pm0.02\,\text{g bird}^{-1}$, feed conversion ratio ranged between 2.7 ± 0.11 and 3.1 ± 0.40, packed cell volume (%) ranged between 23.0 ± 0.01 and 27.3 ± 0.02, red blood cell counts ($10^3/\mu\text{L}$) ranged between 3.3 ± 0.15 and 4.6 ± 0.08 while white blood cell counts ($10^6/\mu\text{L}$) ranged between 8.7 ± 0.43 and 12.7 ± 0.02. Inclusion of differently processed *Moringa oleifera* seed meal and leaf meal did not negatively affect growth performance and haematological parameters of starter broilers.

Keywords: Antibiotics, broiler chickens, feeding trial, *Moringa oleifera*

Contact Address: Isaac Oluseun Adejumo, Landmark University, Dept. of Animal Science, P.M.B. 1001, Omu-Aran, Nigeria, e-mail: smogisaac@gmail.com

ID 455

Comparison of Growth and Carcass Characteristics of Thai Native Pigs Fed Curd Milk Supplemented

PILASRAK PANPRASERT, SUNISA ATTANALAI, THARARAT UTILA

Rajamangala University of Technology Isan, Dept. of Natural Resources, Thailand

In Thailand, a population of native pigs, known as Kadon, is found in the North-Eastern areas. Recent studies showed that Kadon pigs fed rice bran as a basal diet gained approximately 200 g per day. The objective of this study was to evaluate the effect of curd milk supplement diets on growth performance and carcass characteristics in Thai native pigs. 24 Thai native pigs (female vs. castrated male) with an average weight of 20 kg were used in a randomised complete design (CRD). The experiment lasted for 170 days. The pigs (8 per group) were assigned to 3 group diets: 1) control diet, 2) 5% curd milk supplemented diet and 3) 10% curd milk supplemented diet. Thai native pigs fed 5% curd milk supplemented diet (groups 2) had a higher average daily gain than pigs fed control diet and diet 3 (10% curd milk supplemented diet). All pigs were slaughtered at a weight of approximatly 55 ± 5 kg for carcass evaluation. There were no differences in weight gain, carcass length, lean and back fat between diet groups. Carcass weight and bone were heavier in pigs fed 10% curd milk supplemented diet group (groups 3). The weight of head, blood, tail, heart, liver, lung, spleen, kidney and large intestine was not different between groups, but the stomach and small intestine were heavier in group 3. This study could show no effect of the different diets on growth rate and carcass weight. It is the first to document reference data for Thai native pigs.

Keywords: Carcass characteristics, curd milk supplement, growth, Thai native pig

Contact Address: Pilasrak Panprasert, Rajamangala University of Technology Isan, Dept. of Natural Resources, Sakon Nakhon Campus, 47160 Phang Kon, Thailand, e-mail: pilasrak.ao@gmail.com

Effects of Dietary Potassium Diformate in Piglets and Fatteners under Tropical Conditions – A Performance Analysis

CHRISTIAN LÜCKSTÄDT

ADDCON, Germany

Dietary potassium diformate (KDF) has been widely applied in pig production for almost 20 years and has been reported in numerous publications and conference contributions for its use in sows, piglets and fatteners. It was the first organic acid salt to be approved as a non-antibiotic growth promoter in pig feed in the European Union, where it has been shown to improve growth performance and feed efficiency in pig production in several efficacy trials. A holo-analysis of all published data on KDF under temperate conditions (n=59) demonstrated that the additive significantly improved feed intake (+3.52 %), weight gain (+8.67 %) and FCR (-4.20 %) compared to negative controls.

As a result of its success in Europe, it has also subsequently been tested under tropical conditions.

This study analysed the average impact from all data collected under tropical conditions on the effect of the additive on the performance parameters weight gain and feed efficiency from commercial and academic trials. The final data-set contained the results of 18 documented studies, comprising 37 trials with KDF-inclusion in piglets and fatteners, at an inclusion rate ranging from 0.2 % to 1.8 %. These studies were carried out between 2003 and 2015 in Australia, Brazil, China, Philippines, Thailand and Vietnam under both commercial and institutional conditions and included more than 3620 pigs. The results are expressed as the percentage difference from the negative control. The average level of dietary KDF from the data-set in all treated pigs was 0.80 %. Daily gain was significantly increased by 11.2 % ($p < 0.001$). Furthermore, the FCR was also significantly improved (6.3%; $p < 0.001$).

In agreement with the findings of the holo-analysis, this study shows that dietary potassium diformate can also significantly improve pig production under tropical conditions, demonstrating that the additive is a valuable tool in reducing reliance on antibiotic growth promoters.

Keywords: Fatteners, feed efficiency, piglet, potassium diformate, weight gain

Contact Address: Christian Lückstädt, ADDCON, Joseph-Schumpeter-Allee 25, 53227 Bonn, Germany, e-mail: christian.lueckstaedt@addcon.com

Dietary Potassium Diformate in Sow Nutrition in Latin America – Impact on Sows and Piglets

CHRISTIAN LÜCKSTÄDT, NICOLAS GREIFFENSTEIN

ADDCON, Germany

Potassium diformate, a double-salt of formic acid, has been shown in numerous trials to improve health and performance in piglets, growing-finishing pigs and sows. Thus, potassium diformate (KDF) has been approved in the European Union as the only non-antibiotic growth promoter for use in swine. The effect of KDF is often described as strong antimicrobial and digestibility enhancing. However, data on its use in sows under tropical conditions are scarce. The objective of the present study was to assess the effect of KDF on feed intake in sows and its impact on the subsequent piglets, under hot and humid conditions in Latin America.

The study was carried out on crossbred sows during late pregnancy. The experiment was conducted at a commercial farm in Caldas, Colombia. In total, 180 Duroc × Large White sows were used. The sows were randomly allotted to 2 treatment groups. Group 1 served as a control in which sows were fed a pelleted corn-soy based feed, without supplemented antimicrobial agents. Sows in group 2 were fed the same diet containing $5\,kg\,t^{-1}$ KDF. Feed and water were available *ad libitum*. Experimental feeding of sows started one week prior to farrowing and finished at weaning, 3 weeks post-partum. Data on feed intake in sows and the piglet weight were recorded and analysed using the t-test. The results are given as mean $\pm$ SD and a confidence level of 95 % was defined for these analyses.

Sows fed potassium diformate at a dosage of $5\,kg\,t^{-1}$ showed no difference in feed intake from 7 days prior to farrowing till farrowing. However, the feed intake in treated sows was significantly increased by $800\,g\,d^{-1}$ from farrowing onwards. Furthermore, the litter weaning weight tended ($p = 0.06$) to be higher at day 21 (63.7 kg vs. 66.0 kg for control and treatment respectively). These results show that the inclusion of potassium diformate into the diet of sows can improve feed intake and the subsequent performance of piglets under tropical conditions. This is in agreement with earlier observations of KDF in temperate climates.

Keywords: Feed intake, piglet weaning weight, potassium diformate, sows, tropical conditions

Contact Address: Christian Lückstädt, ADDCON, Joseph-Schumpeter-Allee 25, 53227 Bonn, Germany, e-mail: christian.lueckstaedt@addcon.com

Evaluation of Rumen Filtrate for Fermentation of Sweet Orange (*Citrus sinensis*) Peel in Rabbit Feed

OLUWABIYI OLUREMI, EJEH AJIH, WINIFRED ANTHONY

Federal University of Agriculture Makurdi, Dept. of Animal Nutrition, Nigeria

Feeding costs account for about 70% of the total cost of non-ruminant animal production in Nigeria. A ninety-one day feeding trial was conducted using thirty (30), 6–7 week old mixed breed weaner rabbits at the Federal University of Agriculture Makurdi, Nigeria from October 10, 2015 to January 9, 2016. The objective was to determine the potential of filtrate from rumen content mixed with water, to improve the nutritive value of Sweet orange (*Citrus sinensis*) peel by fermentation. The filtrate was obtained from the rumen content of cattle and drinking water mixed in equal ratio (1:1). The filtrate was added to 5 kg each of freshly collected sweet orange peel in ratio 1:5 (T1), 2:5 (T2), 3:5 (T3), 4:5 (T4) and 5:5 (T5). Each was mixed thoroughly, put in polythene bags and sealed on top, left under shade of tree to ferment for 24hrs, and thereafter sun-dried. Each of these was milled and used to replace maize in a practical rabbit diet (D) at 30 % level. Five rabbits, individually housed in a rabbit hutch and each serving as a replicate were randomly assigned to and fed diets D, T1, T2, T3, T4 and T5. The experimental diets had significant effect ($p < 0.05$) on the final live body weight and daily body weight gain with rabbits in treatment T5 having superior weights of 1928 g and 15.85 g, respectively. The experimental diets had no significant effect ($p > 0.05$) on percent live weight of liver, kidney, lung, heart and spleen and, on the coefficient of digestibility of dry matter, crude protein, crude fibre, ether extract, nitrogen free extract and total digestible nutrient. Of the carcass yield indicators determined (dressing percentage, fore limb, hind limb and loin), the experimental diets significantly affected ($p < 0.05$) only the loin, with the rabbits in T5 having a comparatively higher weight. The results obtained showed that filtrate obtained from a mixture of the rumen content of cattle and water in ratio 5:5 can be used to ferment sweet orange peel to improve its nutritive value for maize replacement at 30 % in rabbit feed.

Keywords: Orange peel, rabbit, fermentation, filterate, rumen content

Contact Address: Oluwabiyi Oluremi, Federal University of Agriculture Makurdi, Dept. of Animal Nutrition, 972221 Makurdi, Nigeria, e-mail: oiaoluremi@yahoo.com

ID 352

Characterisation and Quantification of Different Indigenous Chicken Production, Feeding and Management Systems in Babati District, Tanzania

LEONARD MARWA, BEN LUKUYU, SAID MBAGA

International Livestock Research Institute (ILRI), Animal Science for Sustainable Productivity (ASSP), Tanzania

The study was done to generate fundamental information for the improved nutritional management in rural chicken production in Tanzania. A survey was conducted aimed at defining the socioeconomic characteristics of the rural chicken production environments in Babati district in Tanzania. The survey included both individual interviews and participatory group discussions. A total of 141 households from four different wards were interviewed. The questionnaire was designed to collect data covering general information on rural chicken production such as socio-management characteristics, production status and population structure. The findings showed that 96.5 % of the chickens kept in Babati district are local strains and they are mostly owned by women. Production of meat and eggs for home consumption is the primary function of chickens in the surveyed areas followed by the sales of both eggs and live birds as source of income. The mean chicken flocksize per household was 5. Most of the village households (53.2 %) were keeping their chickens under scavenging feeding system. The chickens were left to search for their feeds with rare supplementations of handful unbalanced feeds comprised of either maize bran, sorghum or sunflower seed cake. Kitchen left-overs were found to be the dominant supplement throughout the year. Other systems were the semi-scavenging and confinement with fully indoor feeding systems, which were also found to face unbalanced feeding challenge. The sector is then dominated with scavenging nutritional management, absence of vaccination programs and high risk of exposure of chickens to disease and predators. Ultimately, the production system in all geographic sites studied revealed similar characteristics of high mortality rate (60 %) mainly due to malnutrition, diseases, predators and rough environmental conditions such as rainfall. The hens were found producing an average of 13 eggs per clutch with only 3 clutches per year. Price of chickens at village level was also found to fluctuate over the year mainly due to disease incidences and festival seasons such as Christmas and Easter. The results draw a need for interventions in improved strategies on nutritional management of the scavenging chickens to enhance indigenous chicken productivity improvement.

Keywords: Feed resources, management characterisation, production performance, rural chickens

Contact Address: Leonard Marwa, International Livestock Research Institute (ILRI), Animal Science for Sustainable Productivity (ASSP), Africa Rising - Esa Project: IITA Office, Arusha, Tanzania, e-mail: l.marwa@cgiar.org

Improving Livelihoods of the Urban Poor in Kampala City through Kuroiler Chicken Production

Esau Galukande, Justine Alinaitwe, Harriet Mudondo

Kampala Capital City Authority, Uganda

The Kuroiler, a dual purpose hybrid chicken bred in India for village production systems has a potential to contribute greatly to the poultry industry in Uganda because of it fast growth rates and higher egg production as compared to indigenous Uganda chicken. The chicken were introduced in Uganda in 2010.

Focus was laid on the promotion of this chicken in rural areas, however there are indications that the chicken can perform well in an urban setting. The trial was therefore conducted to investigate the performance of Kuroiler chicken in an urban production system where the chicken are confined and fed on market and kitchen waste instead of backyard scavenging as is the case in a rural setting. The trial involved 234 randomly selected farmers from the 5 administrative divisions of Kampala city. Each of the farmers received 20 chicks which were 3 weeks old. The participants in the study were monitored on a weekly basis and at the end of the 4 month period results obtained from a feedback questionnaire indicate that all participants got a higher income per bird reared as compared to other types. Up to 71 % of the farmers preferred the taste of Kuroiler birds compared to local ones and 62 % suggested that these birds were easier to raise than local and exotic birds fetching a higher income while 64 % found Kuroiler more resistant to diseases compared to local or exotic birds. However all farmers noted that the birds had a higher feed intake than other exotic birds. The results indicate that farmers with small production space as is the case in Kampala city, can rear Kuroiler chicken profitably in confinement, however one needs to have a reliable source of clean organic market waste and kitchen leftovers in order to keep the production costs low.

Keywords: Kampala, Kuroiler chicken

Contact Address: Esau Galukande, Kampala Capital City Authority, Directorate of Gender, Community Services & Production, Kampala, Uganda, e-mail: egalukande@kcca.go.ug

ID 766

Ghrelin Receptor (GHSR) Gene Polymorphism in Indonesian Local Chicken and Crossbred Associated with Carcass Composition

ISYANA KHAERUNNISA, JAKARIA JAKARIA, IRMA ISNAFIA ARIEF, CAHYO BUDIMAN, CECE SUMANTRI

Bogor Agricultural University, Graduate School, Animal Production and Technology, Indonesia

Ghrelin receptor (GHSR) gene is candidate gene for growth performance in chicken. This gene modulates growth hormone release from the pituitary by binding to its ligand of ghrelin. Ghrelin gene, or growth hormone secretagogue (GHS) gene, is well known as feed intake and energy homeostasis regulator in mammals and birds. Indonesia has a wide variety of local chickens that play important role in national food security and self-sufficiency. The objectives of this study were to identify the polymorphism of intron 1 GHSR gene in Indonesian local chicken and to evaluate its effects on carcass composition. The gene polymorphism was identified with polymerase chain reaction-restriction fragment length polymorphism (PCR-RFLP) method by using Hin6I restriction enzyme. Effect of genotype on carcass composition was analysed using SAS General Linear Model (GLM) procedure. The genotyping was performed on 343 individuals including 7 Indonesian local chicken and crossbred populations (*Merawang, Pelung, Sentul, Kampung, Cobb* broiler, F1 crossbred of Kampung × Cobb broiler, and F2 crossbred of Kampung × Cobb broiler). All individuals were successfully amplified in GHSR|Hin6I locus, resulting in a fragment with 470 bp PCR product. This locus was polymorphic with two alleles (T and C) and derived three genotypes (TT, CT and CC). The T allele was major allele in *Merawang, Pelung, Sentul, Kampung, Cobb* broiler, F1 crossbred of *Kampung* x *Cobb* broiler, F2 crossbred of *Kampung* x *Cobb* broiler and overall population (0.781, 0.717, 0.944, 0.949, 0.838, 0.869, 0.884 and 0.864, respectively). The TT genotype frequency was found at the highest in *Merawang, Pelung, Sentul, Kampung, Cobb* broiler and overall population (0.596, 0.478, 0.889, 0.918, 0.676, 0.738, 0.768 and 0.741, respectively). Individuals with CT genotype had significantly higher live weight at 26 weeks, carcass weight, commercial cuts weights, and muscles weights than TT genotype in F2 crossbred of *Kampung* × *Cobb* broiler population. Association of GHSR|Hin6I gene polymorphism with chicken carcass composition have been described in Indonesian chicken, providing evidence that GHSR might be an important candidate gene for chicken carcass composition.

Keywords: Carcass composition, GHSR gene, Indonesian local chicken

Contact Address: Isyana Khaerunnisa, Bogor Agricultural University, Graduate School, Animal Production and Technology, Jl. Agatis Kampus Ipb Darmaga, 16680 Bogor, Indonesia, e-mail: isyanakhaerunnisa@gmail.com

Performance Characteristics of Turkeys Fed Full-Fat Soybean or Soybean Meal Based Diets Supplemented with Varying Levels of Protease Enzyme and Related Feed Costs

Avwerosuoghene Okorodudu[1,2], Oluseyi Oluwatosin[1], Olusesan Fafiolu[2], Abdul-Rasaq Adebowale[3], Adebayo V. Jegede[2], Abimbola Oladele Oso[2], Olugbemiga O. Adeleye[4], John Morakinyo[1,2]

[1] World Bank Africa, Centre for Excellence in Agricultural Development and Sustainable Environment, Nigeria

[2] Federal University of Agriculture, Abeokuta, Dept. of Animal Nutrition, Nigeria

[3] Federal University of Agriculture, Abeokuta, Food Science and Technology, Nigeria

[4] Federal University of Agriculture, Abeokuta, Dept. of Animal Production & Health, Nigeria

Full-fat soybean and soybean meal are two major products of soybean processing used in livestock feed formulation. Enzyme-mediated improvement of feed digestibility has a direct effect on the amount of feedstuffs needed to satisfy nutritional requirements of animals, reduce manure output and cost of production. This study sought to evaluate the performance characteristics and cost benefits of turkeys fed either full-fat soybean (FFSB) or soybean meal (SBM) based diets supplemented with a commercial protease enzyme at varying levels. A total of 300 fifty-six day old unsexed British United turkeys were used in this study, they were allotted on weight equalisation basis to 6 treatment groups, 5 replicates of 10 birds each. Two practical diets were formulated according to NRC, 1994 using FFSB or SBM and other conventional feedstuffs to meet the requirements for each phase; protease was supplemented at 3 levels (250 ppm, 500 ppm and 750 ppm). Feed and water were offered ad-libitum during the 56 days feeding trial divided into grower (56-84 days) and finisher (84-112 days) phases. Data analysis was done using ANOVA in a completely randomised design. At the grower phase, feed cost per kg weight gain (N474.43) of birds fed SBM diets was lower than those fed FFSB diets (N497.26), while the reverse was the case at the finisher phase; SBM (N584.44) and FFSB (N517.26). Feed cost per kg diet increased ($P < 0.05$) with enzyme supplementation at both phases. At the grower phase, there was no significant difference between the cost per kg diet of FFSB or SBM while at the finisher phase, SBM diets were more expensive (P<0.05). Birds fed SBM diets had higher daily weight gain (122.65 g) and better FCR (3.14) than those fed FFSB (116.57g: 3.30) at the grower phase. At the finisher phase, turkeys fed FFSB based diets had higher daily weight gain and better FCR (125.07 g: 3.53) compared with those fed SBM based diets (119.52g: 3.91). No significant difference ($P > 0.05$) was observed as a result of varying levels of enzyme supplementation on performance indices. It was concluded that SBM based diets were better for growing turkeys, while FFSB based diets were better for turkeys at the finisher phase as it reduced the feed cost per kg diet and increased the weight gain.

Keywords: Full-fat soybean, protease enzyme, soybean meal, supplementation, turkeys

Contact Address: Avwerosuoghene Okorodudu, World Bank Africa, Centre for Excellence in Agricultural Development and Sustainable Environment, 110001 Abeokuta, Nigeria, e-mail: okorodudurosuo@gmail.com

ID 573

Aquaculture and fisheries

Local Practices vs. Formal Regulations in the Management of Marine Resources

YAZDAN SOLTANPOUR

University of Catania, Agriculture, Food and Environment, Italy

Attentions are directed towards re-engagement of traditional tools in the management of natural resources as the issue of sustainability gets more critical. However, caution has to be taken in this regard due to the complexity of the traditional tools' motivation. We reviewed respective literature in the field of fisheries in order to analyse the motivation of informal regulations and their relative effect in marine resource management. Eventually, incentives which determine the application and effectiveness of local regulations are not conservation of marine resources nor purely economic motivations, but hovers around the maintenance of social relationships. Formal and informal regulations of 12 cases of fisheries management worldwide were reviewed. Also studies from other sectors of common-pool resource management (forestry and pasturing) has been covered (7 cases) to reinforce the findings. The motivation of indigenous practices of each case was analysed from anthropological point of view and the socio-economic drivers of change in the regulation system has been classified. The socio-economic drivers consist of: food consumption change, environmental awareness of stakeholders, competition level of fisheries (considering number and characteristics of fisheries and scarcity of resources).

Benefiting from Ostrom's framework towards common-pool resource management, we will discuss in this study the problems that each, the local practices and formal regulations, address. Local practices mainly seek personal socio-economic stability, while formal regulations impose restrictions in order to stabilise the national economy. We conclude that, although in some cases the outcomes of one party's decision may interest the other party but they are not necessarily, vertically or horizontally, connected. Therefore, one should bear in mind that participatory or bottom-up approaches to policy making in natural resources management is not a simple engagement of natural resources' beneficiaries into the decision making process but it's a negotiation between all stakeholders.

Keywords: Social relationships, sustainability of marine resources, traditional regulations

Contact Address: Yazdan Soltanpour, University of Catania, Agriculture, Food and Environment, Via S.sofia N.100, 95123 Catania, Italy, e-mail: yazdan.soltanpour@gmail.com

Integration of Aquaculture into Egyptian Smallholder Farming Systems: Practical Solution of Fish Farming Seasonality

MOHAMED MEGAHED[1], KHALED AHMED MOHAMED[2]

[1]*National Institute of Oceanography and Fisheries, Aquaculture, Egypt*

[2]*Suez Canal University, Fac. of Agriculture; Animal Production and Fish Resources, Egypt*

As the world faces the huge task of feeding a growing population through more cost-effective farming methods, much can be learned from the experience of thousands of fishers and farmers in Egypt. Scaling up their successes is vital if the world's poor are to have access to the fish they count on. Integrating aquaculture into small-scale farming in Egypt enabled millions to improve their lives and help build a better future for generations to come. Aquaculture is the fastest-growing method of food production, and is providing about half of all fish consumed worldwide. In Egypt as one of the developing countries, there is considerable potential for growth of sustainable aquaculture that suite challenges faced by small-scale farmers. Fish production on Egyptian smallholdings is generally limited by the quantity and quality of inputs to the pond. The seasonality of farm activities results in lower growth rates and yield. This work introduced new farming activities as a potential for improving production and yield through modifications of production schedules to accommodate other farming activities. Limited material inputs among farming system enterprises in Egypt can be better allocated by considering seasonality and adapting the pond and fish farming technology to the farming system. This work is focusing on technology that maximises fish production by adoption of integrated aquaculture by Egyptian smallholder agriculture/aquaculture projects. Farming Systems Research in Egypt is cautiously working to identify opportunities for system improvement for it to be worth supporting as a development intervention. It is essential to mention that water use in small-scale fish farming is quite efficient, as Egyptian farmers learn about and apply water-management strategies that optimise the recycling of pond water to irrigate staple crops and vegetables. This research has revealed that during winter period, small-scale farms integrated into traditional farming operations and become more productive than farms on which integrated aquaculture is not practised.

Keywords: Aquaculture, Egypt, food security, integration, livelihood, nutrition, poverty eradication

Contact Address: Mohamed Megahed, National Institute of Oceanography and Fisheries, Aquaculture, Gulfs of Suez & Aqaba's Branch,, 43511 Attaka, Suez, Egypt, e-mail: aquageimprove@gmail.com

ID 171

The Impacts of Fishery Resource Management Innovation on Nutrition of Households in Plateau State, Nigeria

CHARLES DAWANG[1], SHUKURAT SANNI[2]

[1]*Ahmadu Bello University, National Animal Production Research Institute, Nigeria*
[2]*Ahmadu Bello University, Inst. for Agricultural Research, Nigeria*

The issues of nutrition insecurity and deficiencies of micronutrients consumption among households of rural communities in developing countries is widespread and constitute serious public health problems. This study compared the nutrition impact of participants and non-participants of natural resource management innovation of government regulated (RENLAF) and unregulated (URENLAF) fisheries in Plateau State, Nigeria. We examined nutrition security and technical efficiency of captured fisheries in the wake of the need for adoption of sustainable management of natural resource innovation in the country. Daily fishing observations were made during catch assessment survey (CAS) recorded in a logbook and a seven day food consumption recall. Data were also collected through questionnaire from 80 fishers' randomly selected at four lakes sites of URENLAF and 30 other fishers purposively selected from regulated Pandam Lakes. We analysed and compared the nutrition impacts of RENLAF and URENLAF on fishing households as well as estimated their income and efficiency of fishing. The analyses were carried out using descriptive statistics, food consumption recall record and stochastic frontier function model. Driving on data from both RENLAF and URENLAF fishing families, we show that participation in regulated fishing innovation has significantly positive effects: higher efficiency of harvest (12 %), higher prospects of sustainable fishing and more income by N14,200, while, calorie (energy), Iron, Zinc and Vitamin A consumption among households are also higher by at least 13 %. Also, some observable variables relating to socio-economic characteristics such as extension contact ($p < 0.1$), age ($p < 0.05$) and educational status ($p < 0.1$), were positive and significantly affected by technical efficiency. The major constraints to fishing at both fisheries were hippopotamus and high cost of fishing gears. Transformation for higher nutrition impacts and sustainable fishery management will require the involvement of educated fishers, extension education, gear limit, and setting more RENLAF sites from the existing URENLAF sites by redefinition of property rights.

Keywords: Efficiency, fishing, income, micronutrients, Nigeria, nutrition, stochastic

Contact Address: Charles Dawang, Ahmadu Bello University, National Animal Production Research Institute, Shika Samaru, Zaria, Nigeria, e-mail: dawang4u@yahoo.com

Response of *Tilapia zillii* Juveniles to Different Concentrations of 2,2-Dichlorovinyl Dimethyl Phosphate (DDVP)

MABEL OMOWUMI IPINMOROTI[1], ADAMS OVIE IYIOLA[2], OLUMUYIWA AKANMU[2]

[1]*Osun State University, Osogbo, Dept. of Animal Science and Fisheries, Nigeria*

[2]*Osun State University, Osogbo, Fisheries and Wildlife Management, Nigeria*

Concerns have often been raised about the use of chemicals on cropland, not so much on its use in livestock systems. Domesticated large animals are often bathed against ectoparasites using chemicals. These chemicals often end up in runoff which empty into rivers and streams where they constitute danger to aquatic living organisms. The problem is compounded on integrated farms where crops, animals and aquatic food organisms are jointly raised. The beauty of integrated farming is the recycling of resources among the various components of the farm. More often than not animal bath water and wastewater from chemical treated animals are emptied into drainages which empty into larger pools of water within or outside the farm which are consequently used for fish culture.

This study finds out the lethal concentration of 2,2-dichlorovinyl dimethyl phosphate (DDVP) on juveniles of *Tilapia zillii*. The study was carried out on juveniles of *Tilapia zillii* weighing $0.8 - 1.0$ g raised in a renewable culture facility. Each of the treatments was in three replicates. The bioassay media concentrations were 0.075, 0.15, 0.225 and 0.3 mg litre^{-1} to culture tanks. Fish were stocked at $3l^{-1}$. Physico-chemical parameters of the culture media were measured before and after treatments were added. Data on the fish and water parameters taken were analysed using one way Analysis of Variance (ANOVA), differences between means were separated by LSD. Fish immediately became restive and uncoordinated, restlessness increased with length of exposure and increased concentration of DDVP. LC50 for juvenile T. zillii was after 48 hours at 0.075 mg l^{-1}, 36 hours at 0.15 mg l^{-1} and 24 hours at 0.225 mg l^{-1}. Histological report shows alteration in some of the internal organs. The result indicates that DDVP is highly toxic to *Tilapia zillii*, care should be taken in its use on integrated farms. It should be degraded/detoxified before it is carefully disposed to the environment.

Keywords: Agro-chemical, DDVP, detoxify, integrated farm, *Tilapia zillii*, toxic

Contact Address: Mabel Omowumi Ipinmoroti, Osun State University, Osogbo, Dept. of Animal Science and Fisheries, Osogbo, Nigeria, e-mail: wumsco@yahoo.com

ID 940

Economic Implication of Bycatch Reduction as a Food Security Measure in Nigeria

CLEMENTINA AJAYI

Federal University of Technology, Akure, Dept. of Agricultural and Resource Economics, Nigeria

Aquaculture is very important to rural communities by playing a key role in food security. This is not only for subsistence and small scale fishers who rely on fishery for food, income generation and services but also for consumers who regard it as a source of affordable high quality animal protein. Certainly for many poor households engaged in full-time, seasonal or occasional small-scale fishing activities, such contributions are crucial to individual/household food security. The study is assessing the economic implication of a bycatch reduction as a food security measure in Nigeria. This is achieved by examining the effect of bycatch reduction devices in the equilibrium population of the bycatch species at every level of effort directed at the target species of fish; on cost per unit effort; food security status of fishing households and constraints faced by fishing households. Snowballing was used to select one hundred and eighty (180) artisanal fish farmers across three riverine areas of Lagos, Ondo and Kogi States. Data collected were analysed using descriptive statistics, United States Household Food Security Survey Module (USHFSSM) and Static Fishery Economic Model (SFEM). The study revealed that introduction of a bycatch reduction device raises the unit cost of effort and this cost increase induces a reduction in the profit maximising level of effort and also reduces profit. With food security status of fishing household above average, the constraints faced in bycatch include poor access to information, inadequate capital, poor fishing gears, poor storage facilities and poor value addition. Government should formulate and implement proper policies that would eliminate these constraints by giving attention to the technical, social and regulatory approaches of bycatch; embrace effective bycatch reduction devices at minimum cost and employ well trained extension agents to educate these farmers on importance of bycatch reduction. It is also recommended that small scale fishing credit policy be put in place to help the households; this can be made on the percentage of total agricultural loans to be given to the fishery sub-section.

Keywords: Bycatch, fishing household, food Security, Nigeria, SFEM, USHFSSM

Contact Address: Clementina Ajayi, Federal University of Technology, Akure, Dept. of Agricultural and Resource Economics, School of Agriculture and Agricultural Technology, 34052 Akure, Nigeria, e-mail: coajayi@futa.edu.ng

Age and Growth Based on the Scale Readings of the two Carangid Species *Carangoides bajad* and *Caranx melampygus* from Shalateen Fishing Area, Red Sea, Egypt

ASHRAF MOHAMMED[1], SAHAR MEHANNA[1], USAMA MAHMOUD[2]

[1]*National Institute of Oceanography and Fisheries, Fish Population Dynamics, Egypt*
[2]*Assiut University, Zoology Department, Egypt*

The study of age and growth of individuals in a population is fundamental for understanding the general biology of the species and in particular its population dynamics. Age and growth of two *Carangid* species *Carangoides bajad* and *Caranx melampygus* from Egyptian Red Sea, Shalateen region (Elba National Park, Marine Branch) were studied based on the scale readings using a non-linear back-calculation method. A total of 1103 specimens (145–515 mm in SL) of *C. bajad* and 795 specimens (145–631 mm in SL) of *C. melampygus* were aged and their maximum life span was 8 and 12 years, respectively. The most dominant age groups in the catch were age groups I (22.7 %) and II (36.5 %) for *C. bajad*, while for *C. melampygus*, age group 0 was the most dominant one contributing 28 % of the total collected samples. The von Bertallanfy growth parameters were estimated as L infinity = 575.7 and 699.4 mm for *C. bajad* and *C. melampygus* respectively, while K = 0.24 and 0.17 year^{-1} for the two species respectively. It was found that *C. melampygus* was heavier and characterised by a higher growth rate than *C. bajad* for the same length and age. The higher growth in length rate was observed during the first year of life for both species and decreased gradually with the increase in age. These data are the inputs of the analytical models used to achieve the wise management of this potential fishery. Also, more information about the *Carangid* biology and dynamics is needed to establish an appropriate strategy for their responsible fishery development in the Egyptian Red Sea.

Keywords: *Carangoides bajad, Caranx melampygus*, growth

Contact Address: Ashraf Mohammed, National Institute of Oceanography and Fisheries, Fish Population Dynamics, National Institute of Oceanography and Fisheries. Red Sea Branch, 71515 Hurghada, Egypt, e-mail: ashrafgro@yahoo.com

ID 180

Fish Production in Egypt: Current Status and Future Perspective

AHMED MOHAMMED[1], SAHAR MEHANNA[2]

[1]*Agriculture College, Cairo University, Land Reclamation, Egypt*

[2]*National Institute of Oceanography and Fisheries (NIOF), Fish Population Dynamics, Egypt*

Fish are important as a human food source which can contribute to bridge the food gap of animal protein demand in Egypt. Fish contain as well a large proportion of animal protein, vitamins and minerals, a high proportion of essential amino acids necessary for the body. Despite the improved fish production in Egypt ($\approx$1,500,000 ton in 2013: 25 % from capture fisheries and 75 % from cultured fish), the increasing pressure from growing populations and the desire to increase per capita consumption of fish requires to reorder priorities in order to achieve optimum exploitation of available fish resources. Egypt, as most of the world, needs to focus on fisheries as productive renewable food resources that can contribute to the development or increase national income as well as safeguard food production for coming generations. This will be achieved by the development of capture fisheries and the expansion of aquaculture production especially mariculture. Many problems are facing the development of our natural and artificial fisheries like overfishing, habitat degradation, climate change, illegal fishing practices, pollution, shortage of fresh water. The present work will evaluate the current status of our fishery resources and will discuss and analyse the challenges facing the development of fish production in Egypt (natural resources and aquaculture). The different impacts of these challenges will be illustrated, and finally the study will suggest some practical solutions to overcome these challenges and how to mitigate their negative impacts.

Keywords: Aquaculture, Egypt, fish production, food security, natural resources

Contact Address: Ahmed Mohammed, Agriculture College, Cairo University, Land Reclamation, 14 El-Nour City Faisal, 88888 Suez, Egypt, e-mail: ahmed.nabil2688@yahoo.com

Stock Assessment of the Mediterranean Horse Mackerel, *Trachurus mediterraneus* in the Egyptian Mediterranean Coast Off Alexandria

SAHAR MEHANNA[1], FAHMY EL-GAMMAL[1], MARIA YANKOVA[2]

[1]*National Institute of Oceanography and Fisheries (NIOF), Fish Population Dynamics, Egypt*

[2]*Institute of Oceanology, Marine Ecology and Biology, Bulgaria*

Population parameters such as age, growth, mortality and maturity-at-age are crucial parameters for accurate stock assessment and management plans to ensure the sustainable development of fisheries. Also, they are essential for the calculation of spawning stock biomass (SSB) and equilibrium yield as well as biological reference points. Mediterranean horse mackerel is one of the most important component in the purse-seine fishery along the Egyptian Mediterranean coasts especially Alexandria fishing area. Age and growth parameters were estimated for *T. mediterraneus*, sampled from commercial landings of the purse seine fishery in the Egyptian Mediterranean waters off Alexandria during the period from July 2013 until April 2015. Samples were collected bimonthly. Although there is a closed fishing period, from Mid May until the end of June, this measure is not enforced like the other proposed regulations. Also, the fishing laws in Egypt have many regulatory measurements but unfortunately not enforced. Age and growth study was based on otolith's reading technique. Back calculated lengths were used to estimate the von Bertalanffy growth parameters by applying Ford-Walford plot. Total, natural and fishing mortality rates, exploitation ratio, length-at-50% maturity and the length at first capture were also estimated. These critical lengths are used for determining the optimum mesh sizes of the purse-seine nets in Alexandria fishing ground. SSB analysis showed that the effort reduction is strongly recommended such that fishing mortality is reduced by 40% to rebuild spawner biomass to acceptable levels. Beverton and Holt Per-recruit analysis revealed that fishing mortality should be reduced by about 30% for mackerel to achieve the maximum yield per recruit.

Keywords: Egypt, management, mediterranean horse mackerel, population dynamics

Contact Address: Sahar Mehanna, National Institute of Oceanography and Fisheries (NIOF), Fish Population Dynamics, P.O. Box 182, Suez, Egypt, e-mail: sahar_mehanna@yahoo.com

ID 168

Improve the Productive Performance in Marine Fish Cage Farms in Mariout Valley, Egypt

MOHAMED ESSA, EL-SAID EL-EBIARY, MOHAMED ELOKBY

National Institute of Oceanography and Fisheries, Aquaculture Division, Egypt

Mariout valley (12 thousand acre) in Alexandria Governorate is one of the three promising areas for marine fish culture in Egypt. The most important obstacles to the sustainable development of aquaculture in this area are: lack of sufficient experience, the use of low levels of technology and low quality protein feeds (trash fish) especially for cage culture. Mariculture in Mariout valley is based on two species: gilthead sea bream, *Sparus aurata* and European sea bass, *Dicentrarchus labrax*. As trash fish has a negative impact on the aquatic environment, the present work aimed to improve productive performance in one of the cages guideway farms in Mariout Valley through the use of a balanced pelleted diet (45 % crude protein and 525 kcal gross energy per 100 g diet) at a rate of 3 % of total biomass/day with 2 g kg^{-1} diet prebiotic Bio-Mos®. Sea bream and sea bass fingerlings of mean initial body weight of 57.72±0.78 g fish^{-1} were stocked separately in floating net cages (300 m^3 each) at a density of 3600 fish cage^{-1} and represented in 3 feeding treatments for each species for 7 months fattening period. The results of the present study proved that, adding prebiotic Bio-Mos® to a balanced fish diet improved greatly productive performance parameters for sea bream and sea bass compared with counterpart fed on trash fish only or just balanced diet without Bio-Mos®. The following criteria were improved in sea bream and bass, respectively: 1) the growth rate by 50.69 % and 32. 22 %., 2) the survival percentage by 18.84 % and 15.11 %., 3) feed conversion ratio by 86.88 % and 80.73 %., 4) fish production per cage by 66.96 % and 46.03 %, and 5) economic evaluation parameters (operating ratio, return on sales, return on costs, return on equity). The pre-biotic diet confirmed its ability to bear the burden of increased costs of production by covering the costs resulting in an higher economic surplus than trash fish treatment which achieved lowest fish production and net income.

Keywords: Cages, economic, Mariout Valley, prebiotic, productive, sea bass, sea bream

---

Contact Address: Mohamed Essa, National Institute of Oceanography and Fisheries, Aquaculture Division, Samy Raouf Str. No. 8 from Iskander Ibrahim Miami, Alexandria, Egypt, e-mail: messa51@yahoo.com

Fish and Shrimp as Resources for Livelihood Development of Coastal Fishing Communities in Egypt: DNA Barcoding Application in Fisheries Management, Marine Biodiversity Assessment, Management and Conservation

MOHAMED MEGAHED

National Institute of Oceanography and Fisheries, Aquaculture, Egypt

The future of filling the gap in food and nutrition security in Egypt will rely mainly on coastal water for fishing and aquaculture. Mitochondrial cytochrome c oxidase subunit 1 (COI) gene was suggested as unique barcode region for animals. DNA barcoding has gained worldwide interest as an effective tool for species identification. More than two third of our planet is covered by oceans and this proofs that the future of food and nutrition security will come from the water (capture fisheries and aquaculture). This put responsibility on us to assess and conserve marine biodiversity as a challenging task for future generations. On the one hand, the rapidly increasing global population makes exploitation of marine resources for food and nutrition security an essential task. On the other hand, this puts pressure on the coastal environment and necessitates sustainable management and conservation efforts. The aim of this work is to use DNA barcoding as a useful molecular technique in the assessment of cryptic species and linking the different life cycle stages to the adult which is difficult to accomplish in the marine ecosystem. The second use in this work of DNA barcoding include authentication and safety assessment of seafood, wildlife forensics, conservation genetics and detection of invasive alien species in fisheries grounds in Egypt. Intensive work is going on collection of fish and shrimp samples from fishing grounds in Egypt. Almost 50 % of the commercial fish and shrimp catch has been identified using DNA barcoding. This work proofed that DNA barcoding can serve as an effective and accurate tool in marine fisheries biodiversity assessment, management and conservation.

Keywords: Biodiversity, DNA barcoding, Egypt, fish, fisheries, livelihood, marine ecosystems, shrimp

Contact Address: Mohamed Megahed, National Institute of Oceanography and Fisheries, Aquaculture, Gulfs of Suez & Aqaba's Branch,, 43511 Attaka, Suez, Egypt, e-mail: aquageimprove@gmail.com

ID 170

Natural resource management and ecology

Forestry, agro-forestry

Prosperity Prospects in Contested Forest Areas: Evidence from Community Forestry Development in Guatemala and Nicaragua

DIETMAR STOIAN[1], ALDO RODAS[2], JESSENIA ARGUELLO[3]

[1] *Bioversity International, Healthy Diets from Sustainable Food Systems Initiative, France*
[2] *Ministry of Agriculture and Livestock, Guatemala, Natural Resources and Agrotourism,*
[3] *Independent Consultant,*

Community forestry is carried out under diverse institutional, environmental, and socio-economic conditions. Local communities may have *de jure* rights to forest resources, but *de facto* protection is often weak. This study focuses on 25-year community concessions in the Maya Biosphere Reserve (MBR) in Guatemala and indigenous territories in the North Caribbean Coast Autonomous Region (RACCN), Nicaragua. In both cases, communities are struggling to enforce their rights as powerful external groups seek to expand cattle ranching, cash crops, tourism, and oil exploration. We found evidence that community forestry can generate significant socio-economic benefits that, along with contributions to forest conservation, substantiate the communities' claim for strengthened and extended community forest stewardship. We selected six community forest enterprises (CFEs) along a business development gradient and assessed their context, economic viability, and livelihood benefits among randomly selected CFE members (n=180). Adopting an asset lens, we determined human, social, natural, physical and financial capital endowments at household and enterprise levels. Enterprise assets varied widely, both within and across countries. CFEs were well endowed with natural capital (7,000–54,000 ha of broadleaf forests) but highly dependent on precious woods, such as mahogany (*Swietenia macropylla*) or andiroba (*Carapa guianensis*). Human capital was sufficiently developed for managing forests, but less so for processing wood and doing business. Social capital has been built in Guatemala through internal organisation, bringing CFEs under the umbrella of a regional association, and developing relationships with buyers. In Nicaragua, however, building of social capital has been insufficient for inducing a self-sustaining process of CFE development. Physical capital for logging and wood processing was moderate but, in Guatemala, conditions facilitate significant value adding. CFEs there were profitable, while those in the RACCN struggled to break even. Household assets varied widely but, in the MBR, we found evidence that forest-based income can lift people out of poverty. Our analyses reveal that critical success factors for community forestry to reduce poverty, conserve forests and enhance equity are: secure long-term forest usufruct rights or ownership, efficient business organisation, credible advocacy, a conducive service environment, and differentiated opportunities for women, men and youth.

Keywords: Asset-based approach, community forestry, critical success factors, enterprise development, indigenous territories, livelihood benefits, Maya Biosphere Reserve

Contact Address: Dietmar Stoian, Bioversity International, Healthy Diets from Sustainable Food Systems Initiative, Parc Scientifique Agropolis Ii, 34397 Montpellier - Cedex 5, France, e-mail: d.stoian@cgiar.org

Environmentally Friendly Rubber Plantation in Southern China: Farmers' Awareness and Acceptance

SHAOZE JIN, SHI MIN, HERMANN WAIBEL

Leibniz Universität Hannover, Institute of Development and Agricultural Economics, Germany

With the rapid expansion of rubber farming in the last three decades, Xishuangbanna (XSBN), one of the global hotspots of biodiversity protection in southern China, has emerged serious environmental problems, such as decline of water resource, soil erosion, and loss of biodiversity. A programme named "Environmentally Friendly Rubber Plantation (EFRP)" has been proposed by local researchers and government to mitigate the negative environmental effects of rubber cultivation and improve its sustainability. However, it is still unclear what farmers' attitudes toward the participation in this programme are, due to lacking quantitative information. Hence, the objective of this study is to explore smallholder rubber farmers' interests in and knowledge of EFPR and examine the relationship between their awareness and acceptance to adopt the EFRP. Using the baseline survey data collected in early 2013, we found that although approximate 10 % of farmers were not aware of the negative environmental effects of rubber cultivation, awareness of the negative environmental effects of rubber cultivation was an important driver of farmers' willingness to participate in ecosystem protection measures. Using the follow-up survey data collected in early 2015, we investigated farmers' awareness of EFRP in terms of the suitable growth conditions of rubber, including altitude and slope, cropping systems, and planting place. We examined farmers' willingness to accept these elements and its determinants. Our results show that while smallholders generally lack the knowledge of EFRP, they are aware of more elements of EFRP and are more willing to adopt the practice of EFRP. Moreover, their participation willingness is also determined by the socioeconomic characteristics of household, income sources, and the nature of rubber plantations. Our findings provide important quantitative information for local agricultural extension service and other agencies, and hereby have important policy implications for promoting sustainable development of rubber farming and contribute to environmental conservation in XSBN.

Keywords: Acceptance, awareness, environmentally friendly, rubber plantation

Contact Address: Shaoze Jin, Leibniz Universität Hannover, Institute of Development and Agricultural Economics, Koenigsworther Platz 1, 30167 Hannover, Germany, e-mail: jin@ifgb.uni-hannover.de

ID 776

Cash or Fertiliser – Which Incentive Do Farmers Prefer to Adopt Agroforestry in Malawi and Mozambique?

STEFAN MEYER[1], EDWARD KATO[2], EPHRAIM NKONYA[2], VINCENT H. SMITH[3]

[1] IFPRI, Environment and Production Technology Division, Malawi

[2] International Food Policy Research Institute (IFPRI), United States of America

[3] Montana State University, Department of Agricultural Economics and Economics, United States of America

Despite the benefits for smallholder farmers, adoption rates of sustainable land management practices in Africa South of the Sahara are still low. One of the main barriers for farmers to change from traditional to sustainable practices is the time lag between adaptation and receipt of the benefits. To compensate the initial effort of the farmers and to address the large cost that the severely degraded soils have for the mostly agrarian economies in Africa South of the Sahara, governments should incentivize farmers to adopt sustainable practices. This paper analyses farmer´s perception for different types of incentives for an adoption of agroforestry. In choice experiments, rural participants were asked to state their preferences for a cash transfer or a fertiliser subsidy. The experiments were conducted in two neighbouring districts of Malawi and Mozambique.

The results show that fertiliser is highly valued by rural households, and compared to cash, it is a more efficient incentive for governments to promote the adoption of agroforestry. Thus, adding a sustainable land management condition to Malawi's Farm Input Subsidy Program (FISP) is found to be an ideal adjustment to improve the policy. Additionally, we observe that poorer farmers and households with a lot of obligation for school fees have a stronger preference for cash. Consequently, it would be more efficient for governments to target successful farmers with fertiliser coupons and marginalised households with a cash transfer. Interestingly, the majority of farmers value a fertiliser coupon more than the same amount of cash, because they want to avoid being tempted to spend the cash on immediate needs rather than on fertiliser or other agricultural inputs, which would be more beneficiary in the long run.

Keywords: Agroforestry, conditional subsidy, discrete choice experiment, Malawi, Mozambique

Contact Address: Stefan Meyer, IFPRI, Environment and Production Technology Division, Lilongwe, Malawi, e-mail: s.meyer@cgiar.org

Wildfire Research and Management Supports Local Communities in Mt. Kenya

Kevin Wafula Nyongesa[1], Rhoda Birech[2], John Ngugi Kigomo[3], Harald Vacik[1]

[1] University of Natural Resources and Life Sciences (BOKU), Dept. of Forest and Soil Sciences, Austria

[2] Egerton University, Crops, Horticulture and Soil Chemistry, Kenya

[3] Kenya Forest Research Institute, Dept. of Forest Resource Assessment, Kenya

Human-induced wildfires have caused major loses to forest resources, wildlife and property in Mt. Kenya forest, one of the five water towers of Kenya. The Central Highlands Conservancy covering Mt. Kenya forest has limited and insufficient technical fire management capacities to control the spread of large scale fire events in the recent past. The project FIREMAPS seeks to support wildfire management in Mt. Kenya forest by developing fire danger maps to be used by communities and the government to identify fire hot spots, support fire prevention and firefighting. As wildfire related research and management are multi- and interdisciplinary in nature there is no single organisation that can handle these issues on its own. The project achieves its goal by (i) undertaking a multi-stakeholder participatory engagement of communities around Mt. Kenya forest to identify fire prone areas and causes of wildfires and (ii) analysing records on socio-economic activities, weather data, vegetation types and wildfire data to develop fire danger maps. In this contribution we present the approach for collecting and analysing data on fire events, socio-economic activities, weather data and vegetation types. Questionnaires were used to collect the attitudes and preferences of local people towards fire management. Fire records were digitised and geographically referenced to identify hot spots. Scientific evidence on the fire danger in different forest districts and local knowledge of communities on fire management in Mt. Kenya were combined through an interactive learning approach at community level. This allows making the research relevant to the needs of communities, improving their capabilities, and supporting knowledge and technology exchange. This will enable communities to sustainably use and manage forest resources. The recommendations for monitoring and managing of wildfires will be disseminated to volunteer village fire crews, community leaders and other relevant stakeholders considering the fire danger maps.

Keywords: Fire danger, fire ignition, Kenya, knowledge

Contact Address: Harald Vacik, University of Natural Resources and Life Sciences (BOKU), Department of Forest and Soil Sciences, Peter Jordanstr. 82, 1190 Vienna, Austria, e-mail: harald.vacik@boku.ac.at

ID 845

Challenges and Lessons Learned in Interdisciplinary and Participatory (citizen science) Ethnobotanical Research on Community Conserved Areas in Indigenous Communities in Brazil, Bolivia and Mexico

CHRISTOPH SCHUNKO, CHRISTIAN R. VOGL

University of Natural Resources and Life Sciences (BOKU), Dept. of Sustainable Agricultural Systems, Austria

Practice, knowledge, social organisation, language and world view related to plants allows us better understanding the reality of local people. For a holistic understanding of people's livelihoods and their local knowledge, ethnobiological factors affecting the domains under investigation have to be taken into account. Understanding these factors call for interdisciplinary research. Local people's needs may be included through participatory research approaches such as co-inquiry processes.

We set out to test co-inquiry processes in the EC FP7 COMBIOSERVE project on community-based management of environmental challenges in indigenous communities in Brazil, Bolivia and Mexico. The project involved local Civil Society Organisations and intended to create results for their benefit and the communities involved. The research agenda was developed mainly by local people and included ethnobotanical, ethnobiological and ethnoecological research questions. The themes selected were studied by groups of interested people from the communities together with professional researchers. Research protocols were designed for each group of community researchers and indicated when, how, where and with which tools each investigation was conducted. The community researchers received training in data collection, data processing and applying research tools.

We found that co-inquiry processes are time consuming and may face difficulties of intercultural communication when involving various disciplines and stakeholders. Conflicting interests, short project durations, bureaucratic procedures for documenting project progress and expenses, differing time dynamics, differing distribution of funds and remuneration and differing reliability, commitment and motivation are challenging. In addition the dynamics of professional scientists and their need for publishing in scientific journals causes different needs than those of local stakeholders who expect answering their questions or resolving their needs. Flexibility for the research process is fundamental since each community has particular conditions. The co-design of interdisciplinary and participatory projects and the clear set up of expectations before the start are critical for the success of the project. Enough resources have to be reserved for joint data analysis and report writing.Interdisciplinary and participatory research in ethnobotany may provide many benefits through a holistic understanding of people's livelihoods and through responding to local people's needs but project design and implementation need considerable caution, time and resources.

Keywords: Citizen science, co-inquiry, participatory research, transdisciplinary research

Contact Address: Christian R. Vogl, University of Natural Resources and Life Sciences (BOKU), Dept. for Sustainable Agricultural Systems, Gregor-Mendel-Strasse 33, 1180 Vienna, Austria, e-mail: christian.vogl@boku.ac.at

Oil-Palm: An Amazing Plant as Reforestation Driver in the Tropics Despite its Evil Reputation

HEINZ GATTRINGER

Alchemia-nova Gmbh, Natural Resources & Phytotechnologies, Austria

Oil-palm suffers from negative perception in northern countries as a driver of deforestation in humid lowland tropics. Its "evil" reputation is also emphasised by vegetable oil industries of temperate countries, whom see a formidable competitor in palm oil. While the connection between oil-palm and deforestation currently is undeniable, same will apply to any crop that allows "quick money" schemes in rainforest areas.

A close look at *Elaeis guineensis* reveals an amazing plant with extremely high oil per hectare yields compared to other oil crops. It is a perennial with strong natural resistances, loves associations with N-fixing leguminosae, flowering vegetation, even allows multi-cropping. It requires little crop protection chemicals and is a great provider of employment. Its impressive capacity for biomass accumulation and high evapotranspiration rates help cool surrounding air and stabilise receding yearly rainfalls. It is an excellent crop for high rainfall tropical soils. Under these considerations oil-palm is more sustainable than many tropical crops like bananas, soya, rice, maniok or any short-cycle field-crop, cattle farming, pineapple, maracuja, etc.

It is claimed that oil-palm cropping can be transformed into a reforestation driver, underpinning a surplus oriented industry that can generate foreign exchange. Enough rainforests have been cut down to provide ample space for agricultural activities and even return some areas to reforested states. When cultivated in transition belts between rainforests and deforested agricultural land, intelligently managed, species-diverse oil-palm plantations can serve as "pseudo forests", stabilising rainfall and preventing soil erosion. Areas between forests and the oil-palm plantations can be reforested actively and will benefit from the climate effects of the plantations. After a 20 year cycle the oil palm plantation can be given up and the area further reforested, starting new cycles further away from the forest.

This suggestion will only work with novel "land lease" strategies, where ownership of the land remains with the state, being only leased out in small, medium or even large plots to farmers for defined periods. Existing rainforests must be strict "no-go" areas under severe and effective penalties. Key infrastructure is provided centralised by government contractor companies (like road access and irrigation).

Keywords: Land lease, oil-palm, reforestation, sustainable cropping

Contact Address: Heinz Gattringer, Alchemia-nova Gmbh, Natural Resources & Phytotechnologies, Baumgartenstrasse 93, 1140 Vienna, Austria, e-mail: heinzjos@alchemia-nova.net

ID 76

Climate Change Adaptation with Community Based Management in the Village Common Forest of Bangladesh

MD. ARIF CHOWDHURY[1], SOHAG MIAH[2], PEDRO DANIEL PARDO VILLEGAS[3]

[1] *University of Chittagong, Inst. of Forestry and Environmental Science, Bangladesh*
[2] *Georg-August Universität Göttingen, Fac. of Forest Science and Forest Ecology, Germany*
[3] *Technische Universität Dresden, Fac. of Environmental Sciences, Germany*

This research was conducted in the village common forest - VCF of Komolchari, Khagrachari, by community based management - CBM to assess the adaptation process for climate change. As a framework for the present analysis, the priority themes for climate change adaptation of the FAO (FAO-Adapt) were taken into account: (i) knowledge for impact and vulnerability assessment; (ii) institutions and financing to strengthen capacities for adaptation; (iii) sustainable management of land, water and biodiversity; (iv) practices and processes for adaptation; and (v) disaster risk management. Household and forest surveys were conducted to collect data. For the household surveys, 11 settlers and 30 families from Komolchari village and 30 families from Jaduram Para and Thana Chandra Para villages were selected. Forest surveys consisted of 57 10 m $\times$ 10 m, plots in which the tree species were determined in order to estimate the forest health. In general terms, community people were receptive to the idea of VCF conservation and 87 % of the respondents were willing to get involved in the conservation efforts. The communities report the use and importance of various edible species of flora and fauna, timber species, medicinal plants, animals and birds species, plant species for construction and crafts like cane and bamboo, and some tree species of religious importance like *Ficus religiosa* L. and the *Ficus benghalensis* L., among others. Regarding the forest surveys, the parameters measured provide an idea of the forest health in Komolchari VCF. The tree density (1420 trees ha^{-1}), the Shannon-Weiner Index (2.91), the species diversity Index (50.62), and the index of dominance (0.09) suggest a relative good state of conservation of the forest. This is considered as a result of the creation of the VCF committee and the collaborating programme with a local NGO, which regulates the use of the resources in order to avoid the over-exploitation. Nevertheless, a formal forest management system, the assurance of an alternative income source, and a strong linkage with the government, among other aspects, are required for an effective CBM along with climate change adaptation.

Keywords: Climate change adaptation, community based management, village common forest

Contact Address: Sohag Miah, Georg-August Universität Göttingen, Fac. of Forest Science and Forest Ecology, Albrecht Thaer Weg 14, 37075 Göttingen, Germany, e-mail: miah.sohag2015@gmail.com

Modelling the Carbon Dynamics of Tropical Forest Ecosystem in the Amhara Region of Ethiopia

BEYENE BELAY[1], CHRISTOPHER THURNHER[1], KIBRUYESFA SISAY[1], TESFAYE TEKLEHAYMANOT[2], KHLOT GEBREHANA[2], SIBHATU ABERA[2], HADERA KAHESAY[2], HUBERT HASENAUER[1]

[1]*University of Natural Resources and Life Sciences (BOKU), Inst. of Silviculture, Austria*
[2]*Amhara Agricultural Research Institute, Forestry Research Directorate, Ethiopia*

Improving the current world´s forest carbon sequestration potential through afforestation and reforestation while maintaining the existing forest carbon stock has been given a lot of attention to combat ever-increasing climate change. However, the way to measure the amount of carbon stored through different afforestation initiatives and carbon loss to the atmosphere in deforestation and forest degradation is still a debated issue. Hence, process based models are important in monitoring and reporting and verification (MRV) of forest carbon dynamics and effective implementation of Reducing Emission from Deforestation and forest Degradation (REDD). The purpose of this paper is to adapt the ecosystem model biome-BGC model to mimic Ethiopian forest dynamics and to estimate carbon sequestration potentials in rehabilitation of degraded areas through reforestation and afforestation activities. Thirty-two year daily climate data, physical site parameters (elevation and latitude), soil physical properties (soil texture and soil effective depth), pre-industrial and industrial nitrogen deposition, and evergreen broadleaved ecophysiological parameters were used as drivers and inputs to biome-BGC. For model calibration and validation, above and belowground carbon and terrestrial net primary productivity (NPP) were estimated from vegetation data collected in 156 sample plots of four natural forests (i.e. 56 in Katassi, 33 in Gelawdiwos, 48 in Tara Gedam and 19 in Mahibere Silasse). The above ground carbon stock was derived from the aboveground biomass calculated using an allometric biomass function whereas NPP was determined from core increment samples. The model with default Ecophysiological parameters was found to be limited in explaining Ethiopian forest ecosystem carbon dynamics. It overestimated stem carbon but underestimate the NPP compared to the terrestrial result. Finally, new model parameters were parametrized in a way to predict the Ethiopian forest ecosystem carbon dynamics.

Keywords: BGC model, forest carbon, model validation, parametrisation

Contact Address: Beyene Belay, University of Natural Resources and Life Sciences (BOKU), Forest and Soil Sciences, Peter-Jordan Straße 82, 1190 Vienna, Austria, e-mail: beyene.belay@students.boku.ac.at

ID 319

Socio-Economic Study of an Implemented Agroforestry Project with Small Scale Cocoa Producers in Honduras

KARENT KUPFERSCHMIED[1], INGRID FROMM[1], ARTHUR ROUANET[2]

[1] Bern University of Applied Sciences, School of Agricultural, Forest and Food Sciences, Switzerland

[2] Pur Projet, France

Cocoa cultivation has a long tradition in Honduras. The general knowledge about cocoa, the genetic traits of Honduran cocoa, and the particular environmental conditions of the country has been driving the interest of several organisations and countries to encourage sustainable cocoa production. In October 2014, the Honduran Foundation for Agricultural Research (FHIA) reported 2100 ha of cocoa planted nationwide. The average production area per household is less than 2 ha, at over 200 m asl and under agroforestry systems.

Patuca National Park located in Olancho region is the second biggest protected natural area; nevertheless, it shows the highest deforestation rate in the country. Seeking for environmental and economic alternatives, Helvetas Swiss Intercooperation has strengthened since 2009 the Honduran Association of Organic Cocoa Producers from Olancho (APROSACAO) with private investment from Chocolats Halba Coop Group and the support of PurProjet, an NGO working with them since 2012. The reforestation programme was initiated in order to increase carbon sequestration and ensure the future producers' revenues through the marketing of legal wood.

The main goal of this study was to identify the socio economic impact of the agroforestry programme APROSACAO/PurProjet among cocoa producers. For the purpose of the study, data from 55 producers living in 5 villages in Olancho was collected. The results indicated that there is no direct effect in the income or cocoa yield improvement. Nonetheless, cocoa producers report more income than expenses. In addition, there is a positive influence of the agroforestry programme on food security and cocoa producers' contribution to the environment and future generations. The recommendations from this study are to strengthen trainings towards climate change and women empowerment in the cocoa value chain. Equally, there should be more effort to promote interventions that generate investment capital and sustainable strategies that aim at the future needs of the producers.

Keywords: Agroforestry systems, Honduras, organic cocoa, reforestation program

---

Contact Address: Karent Kupferschmied, Bern University of Applied Sciences, School of Agricultural, Forest and Food Sciences, Laenggasse 85, 3052 Zollikofen, Switzerland, e-mail: kpbermudezv@gmail.com

Evaluation of the Cost of Forest Restoration of Degraded Areas and Legal Reserves in Sinop-Brasil

Katiucia Corrêa Sachet Carauta[1], Marcelo Carauta Montenegro Medeiros de Moraes[1], Wylmor Constantino Tives Dalfovo[2]

[1]University of Hohenheim, Faculty of Agricultural Sciences, Germany
[2]University of the State of Mato Grosso (UNEMAT), Faculty of Economics, Brazil

Throughout the 2000s, the Brazilian federal government implemented several policies in order to inhibit forest deforestation. The main policies are: strengthening monitoring and law enforcement; expanding protected territory; and adopting a conditional rural credit policy. Since 2008, Brazilian landowners are required by law to maintain the Legal Reserve, a mandatory practice instrument which defines a certain share of land (from 20 % to 80 %, depending on the region) that should be left in forest or its native vegetation for biodiversity conservation. Therefore, this study aims to evaluate the costs of implementing several strategies of restoration of degraded areas and legal reserves in the state of Mato Grosso - Brazil. We used Embrapa - Brazilian Agricultural Research Corporation - research field, located in Sinop, Mato Grosso, to collect all the relevant data regarding to all agricultural practices related to first two years. This study presents an economic analysis of ten different forest restoration schemes conducted by Embrapa Agrossilvopastoral. The result shows that the implementation cost varies according to the applied strategy and that they are higher on those strategies that are more labour demanding. On the other hand, those strategies presented a better performance on the forest indicators (better growth and lower mortality rate). If the landowner intended purpose is only to comply with the law, he should choose the cheapest strategy. However, strategies with higher costs are also the ones with greater availability to provide a secondary source of income, such as timber and non-timber forestry products. From 17 different forest species planted in this experiment, we found 44 products which could be economically explored and sold to the market. In this sense, we argue that those non-timber forest products have the potential to generate a new source of secondary income for Mato Grosso landowners and that Brazilian government should support to the establishment of those markets.

Keywords: Brazilian Amazon, deforestation, policies

Contact Address: Katiucia Corrêa Sachet Carauta, University of Hohenheim, Faculty of Agricultural Sciences, Tiefer Weg 40, 70599 Stuttgart, Germany, e-mail: kati.sachet@gmail.com

ID 390

Scaling Sustainable Modernisation in Mountain Agriculture: Agroforestry Experiences in Kaule, Mid-Hills of Nepal

NIELS SCHWAB[1], ALINA SCHICK[2], EVA WIENERS[1], NINA KIESE[3], UDO SCHICKHOFF[1]

[1] *University of Hamburg, CEN Center for Earth System Research and Sustainability, Inst. of Geography, Germany*

[2] *University of Hohenheim, Institute of Crop Science, Germany*

[3] *Karlsruhe Inst. of Technology, Inst. for Geography and Geoecology, Germany*

Modernisation as a transformational strategy towards sustainable development has to promote further improvement of mountain farmers' livelihoods while at the same time ensuring ecological sustainability and inducing social equity. In this context, a multiyear joint project with local farmers was launched in spring 2009 to introduce agroforestry practices in the village Kaule, Nuwakot District, mid-hills of Nepal. Practical components of the project included trainings and workshops on agroforestry, restructuring of terrace fields for conversion to agroforestry, and monthly meetings for open discussions among involved households. The project was accompanied scientifically to analyse socio-economic and ecological impacts. This paper presents scientific findings and summarises the experiences during the transition to sustainable land management from an interdisciplinary perspective, and gives evidence of increased willingness to adopt sustainable agricultural practices, and of the obtainment of environmental benefits and increased livelihood security. Participation of the farmers in the entire process, beginning with the definition of goals, the envisioning of a desired future and the integration of local knowledge, skills and resources was found to be of key importance for the project success. During the transition process, a diversification of marketable crops and additional income generation further enhanced the willingness to adopt new agricultural practices. After the adoption of agroforestry, soil quality and soil productivity have been significantly ameliorated, with positive effects appearing shortly after the conversion from conventional monocropping systems. We also assessed significantly higher species richness, beta diversity and cover of trees and shrubs in the agroforestry system. We conclude that the transition from conventional terrace cultivation to agroforestry practices has the potential to generate significant environmental and socio-economic benefits, thus contributing to sustainable modernisation processes in mountain agriculture.

Keywords: Agriculture, agroforestry, backcasting, innovation diffusion, modernisation, mountain agriculture, soil fertility, sustainability, transition management

Contact Address: Niels Schwab, University of Hamburg, CEN Center for Earth System Research and Sustainability, Inst. of Geography, Bundesstraße 55, 20146 Hamburg, Germany, e-mail: niels.schwab@uni-hamburg.de

Analog Forestry - A Promising Strategy for More Sustainable Agriculture in Tropical Regions

TOMAS SELECKY, SONOKO DOROTHEA BELLINGRATH-KIMURA,
MARCOS ALBERTO LANA

Leibniz-Centre for Agricultural Landscape Research (ZALF), Inst. of Land Use Systems, Germany

Trees play a key function in ecosystems and must be a core part of sustainable food producing systems. They preserve soil fertility, prevent erosion, increase water retention capacity of land and have a dramatic influence on global temperatures as they shade the soil and cool the air by transpiration. The adoption of agroforestry is a promising strategy for more sustainable agriculture, especially in tropical and subtropical regions. In 2010, 43.5 % of the world´s agricultural land had a tree cover greater than 10 %, proving that agroforestry systems do play a significant role in production areas.

This study explores the importance of Analog Forestry as a promising system for sustainable food production. Analog Forestry is an agroforestry system that is seeking to mimic diverse structure of natural forests and employ it in the process of production of marketable products. In comparison with other agroforestry systems, Analog Forestry strives to create food producing systems in advanced stages of succession, managing subclimax or climax plant communities where high niche variability results in high biodiversity and efficient use of resources. Utilizing native as well as exotic plant species, a forest is created that is structurally analogous to a natural forest of the selected area, providing the same ecosystems services, restoring the environment and sustaining local communities. For the establishment of such forests, the driving force of ecological succession must be exploited. Pioneer species, apart from producing marketable goods, create conditions for the successful establishment of climax species.

In this study, we approach the basic principles of Analog Forestry in order to propose establishment of such a system in Amazonian municipality of Tomé-Açu, located in Brazilian state of Pará. During this stepwise design process, the advantages and drawbacks of Analog Forestry will be analysed.

Keywords: Agrobiodiversity, Amazonia, analog forestry, Brazil, successional agroforestry, sustainable agriculture

Contact Address: Tomas Selecky, Leibniz Centre for Agricultural Landscape Research (ZALF), Institute of Land Use Systems, Eberswalder Str. 86, 15374 Müncheberg, Germany, e-mail: tomas.selecky@zalf.de

ID 535

Second-Tier Community Forestry Organisations and Equitable Resource Management in the Maya Biosphere Reserve, Guatemala

NAOMI MILLNER[1], IRUNE PEÑAGARICANO[2], MARIA FERNANDEZ[3], LAURA SNOOK[3]

[1] University of Bristol, Geographical Sciences, United Kingdom

[2] University of Natural Resources and Life Sciences (BOKU), Division of Organic Farming, Austria

[3] Bioversity International, Forest Genetic Resources Programme, Italy

Whilst community forestry programmes have combined sustainable forestry with community empowerment and poverty alleviation since the late 1970s, the role of intermediary organisations in shaping the technical and political capacities of forest user groups has rarely been systematically studied. The long-term durability of community forestry groups has been linked with the congruence between local and national determinations of tenure rights, and the involvement of local communities in determining the 'rules' that govern the management of the forests. However, the role of intermediary organisations in negotiating such rights and rules is of central analytical importance - especially in contexts where pre-existing power and gender relationships influence who makes which decisions and how, and where long-standing conflicts over access to land constantly over-determine the possibilities for upscaling successful projects. As part of an interdisciplinary project on community forestry in Mesoamerica led by Bioversity International, this paper focuses on the case of the Asociación de Comunidades Forestales de Petén [ACOFOP], a second-tier community organisation founded in the mid-1990s to coordinate and represent first-tier organisations that were granted community concessions in the Maya Biosphere Reserve in the Petén region of Guatemala. Drawing on interviews, the outcomes of participative workshops, and a review of key literature, we trace ACOFOP's emergence as a forestry organisation from existing agricultural and non-timber product cooperatives, and its subsequent consolidation as a platform for regional coordination and advocacy. Using a 'Sociology of Knowledge' approach to discourse analysis (SKAD), we highlight three important dimensions of ACOFOP's evolving strategy that facilitate the development of both local autonomies and collective coherence: the mobilisation of concepts of 'environmental justice' and associated international rights frameworks to link local concerns with national governance issues; the elaboration of legal knowledges and mechanisms in these terms to negotiate improved tenure relationships; and a concentration of resources in the development of local leadership with an emphasis on elaborating the fixed 'rules' of forestry management in a manner that is appropriate to each community's individual characteristics. We conclude by highlighting key strategies that may be applied to strengthen community forestry in other regional settings.

Keywords: Community forestry, conservation, forest genetic resources, Guatemala, migration, non-governmental organisations

Contact Address: Naomi Millner, University of Bristol, Geographical Sciences, 4 Oberon Avenue, BS5 7UU Bristol, United Kingdom, e-mail: naomimillner@gmail.com

Contribution of Local Tree Fodder Resources in Smallholder Mixed Production Systems of Central Kenya

AGNES GACHUIRI[1], SAMMY CARSAN[1], PARMUTIA MAKUI[1], SHEM KUYAH[2]

[1]*World Agroforestry Centre (ICRAF), Kenya*
[2]*Jomo Kenyatta University of Agriculture and Technology, Kenya*

Locally available tree fodder resources are seldom considered in livestock feeding strategies in spite of their nutritional potential to supplement grass forages. Knowledge gaps on species utilisation and availability may be responsible for this situation. This study sought to characterise tree fodder species in humid and drier parts of central Kenya to assess available diversity that can be used to supplement present livestock feeding options consisting mainly of nappier grass and crop residues characterised by severe shortages during dry seasons. A survey of 117 farms randomly drawn from humid (Githunguri and Lari) and sub-humid (Kayatta) area was conducted. All the farms surveyed contained 60 fodder tree species, belonging to 27 botanical families - 39 of these species were of indigenous origin. Individually, farms had high indigenous species richness (65 %) but of low individual trees (12 %). Species richness was significantly higher in the sub-humid area of Kayatta (43 species) compared to humid areas of Lari (27) and Githunguri (25). Exotics such as *Grevillea robusta* and *Persea americana* and indigenous species such as and *Acacia tortilis* and *Commiphora eminii* were most frequent across all farms surveyed. Some 46 species were valued during dry season and 15 others are used throughout the year. Indigenous and exotic tree species richness and abundance were positively correlated to farm size, but negatively related to the number of dairy cows per farm. Other results confirmed that the main feed resource used by farmers consists of nappier grass, crop residues, banana stover, dairy meal and hay. Implication of fewer indigenous fodder tree species present in the humid area to support livestock production compared to the more open grazing system of Kayatta are not clear even though it suggests a possible loss of local knowledge on valuable tree fodder resources. Nonetheless, findings show that tree fodder options are available to diversify current feeding options based mainly on grass and crop residues.

Keywords: Abundance, economic value, diversity, species richness, tree fodder

Contact Address: Agnes Gachuiri, World Agroforestry Centre (ICRAF), United Nations Avenue Gigiri, Nairobi, Kenya, e-mail: a.gachuiri@cgiar.org

ID 741

Sustainable Forestry Development through Livelihood Enhancement of Fringe Forest Dwellers: A Case of Gujarat, India

NIDHI SINGH, SUVENDU ROUT

Indira Gandhi National Open University, Social Sciences, India

Since 2007, the Government of Gujarat, India with the support of Japan International Cooperation Agency (JICA), is implementing the Gujarat Forestry Development Project (GFDP) to restore degraded forests through enhancement of livelihoods of people living in and around forest areas. The project focuses on sustainable procurement and value addition of Non Timber Forest Produce (NTFP) such as *Chlorophytum borivilianum, Butea monosperma* and agricultural produce such as turmeric and vegetables. In this light, this paper conducts a detailed analysis of the project under the analysis framework of 'sustainable rural livelihoods' by Ian Scoones (1998). The first part of the paper conducts a literature review of various livelihood enhancement strategies in developing and under-developed nations of the world. It then, focuses on GFDP and uses the Scoones' analysis framework to conclude if the strategies adopted have been able to achieve the desired goals. The analysis finds that the project was able to encourage community participation in conservation and development of degraded forests and enhance livelihood generation capacity of these communities to reduce pressure on forest resources. Joint Forest Management Committees at village level empowered people to take decisions regarding conservation and use of resources. Various capacity development methods and entrepreneurship development through women's groups and producers' groups increased productive capacities and thereby earnings of local tribal communities. This encouraged the communities to protect forests and create new ones. Productive activities were linked to better markets, which meant more revenues for the same effort. Women played an important role in increasing household income through productive activities by self help groups (SHGs) by undertaking value addition to NTFPs and non-farm activities. The project facilitated small entrepreneurs to establish micro-enterprises to add value to local produces, thereby increasing their market value and earning. This paper is a result of extensive qualitative research conducted with GFDP, JICA and tribal communities to gather information.

Keywords: Forest management, rural development, rural livelihoods, self help groups, sustainable development

Contact Address: Nidhi Singh, Indira Gandhi National Open University, Social Sciences, New Delhi, 110018 New Delhi, India, e-mail: nidhi.ns13@gmail.com

Above-Ground Biomass Estimation for Evergreen Broadleaf Forests in Xuan Lien Nature Reserve, Thanh Hoa, Vietnam

THE DUNG NGUYEN, MARTIN KAPPAS

Georg-August-Universität Göttingen, Dept. of Cartography, GIS and Remote Sensing, Germany

The estimation of above-ground biomass (AGB) and carbon sequestration in forests plays a key role in modelling carbon cycle and has a significant concern in addressing the potential areas for carbon credits under Reducing Emissions from Deforestation and Forest Degradation-Plus (REDD+). This study was conducted to estimate the living AGB for evergreen broadleaf forests in Xuan Lien Nature Reserve, Viet Nam with the purpose of providing data for sustainable forest management and baseline data for carbon monioring. These forest stands were classified to four categories by governmental standard basing on standing volume (V), including poor forest (V $\leq$ 100 m^3 ha^{-1}), medium forest (100 $<$ V $\leq$ 200 m^3 ha^{-1}), rich forest (200 $<$ V $\leq$ 300 m^{3}ha^{-1}), and very rich forest (V $>$ 300 m^{3}ha^{-1}). A total of 380 sampling plots were randomly stratified sampled and all trees with DBH $\geq$ 5.0 cm were included for biomass estimation. Values for aboveground biomass were obtained using published allometric equations. The results indicated that the AGB increased from 82.0$\pm$5.3 Mg ha^{-1} in poor forest to 127.3$\pm$10.8 Mg ha^{-1} in medium forest, 184.3$\pm$15.6 Mg ha^{-1} in rich forest, and to 303.2$\pm$21.8 Mg ha^{-1} in very rich forest (95 % confidence interval). The uncertainty for the estimated AGB were low ($<$ 8.5 %) at 95 % confidence level. Trying to test the corelation of AGB with the varying of altitude (from 108 to 1452 m a.s.l) shows that, AGB has a positive relationship with elevation (R^2 = 0.53). It is concluded that tropical evergreen broadleaf forest has significant amount of above-ground carbon stock, and there is strong reductions of above-ground biomass by the degree of human disturbance.

Keywords: Above-ground biomass, carbon stock, evergreen broadleaf forest, uncertainty

Contact Address: The Dung Nguyen, Georg-August-Universität Göttingen, Dept. of Cartography, GIS and Remote Sensing, Goldschmidtstr. 5, 37077 Göttingen, Germany, e-mail: tnguyen4@gwdg.de

ID 830

Using Dendroecology to Determine Growth Rates of Mahogany and Cedar in Community Forestry in Guatemala

ALEX MARTINEZ PRERA[1], BRYAN FINEGAN[1], LAURA SNOOK[2]

[1] *Tropical Agricultural Research and Higher Education Centre (CATIE), Costa Rica*
[2] *Bioversity International, Forest Genetic Resources Programme, Italy*

One of the main technical knowledge gaps for sustainable timber production in tropical forests is the lack of reliable information on tree growth, which is indispensable for defining cutting cycles and estimating harvest volumes. We applied dendroecological methods to measure and model the diameter growth (dbh) of mahogany *Swietenia macrophylla* and cedar *Cedrela odorata* in humid tropical forests of community-managed concessions in the Maya Biosphere Reserve, Petén, Guatemala. The width of growth rings was determined in increment cores from 32 trees of *S. macrophylla* and 27 of *C. odorata* and the annual nature of rings demonstrated using COFECHA software. A standardised chronology derived through comparisons among trees was obtained for 1927–2014 for *S. macrophylla* 1944–2014 in *C. odorata*. Sigmoidal functions were fitted to represent the relationship between stem diameter and tree age. *S. macrophylla* showed a long-term mean annual increment (MAI) of 0.43 cm yr^{-1} and tree ages were 40–184 yr. Based on the age at which the MAI curve crosses the curve of current annual increment (CAI), this species reaches its biological rotation at 92 yr, at 48 cm dbh. Estimated long-term MAI for *C. odorata* was 0.65 cm yr^{-1} and the ages of the trees sampled were 35–110 yr. This species reaches its biological rotation at 85 yr and 65 cm dbh, as compared to the 60 cm minimum cutting diameter. An attempt to correlate the width of growth rings with precipitation and temperature did not reveal an overriding climate signal in the growth data. Statistically significant correlations were found between precipitation measures from the previous year and current growth for *Swietenia macrophylla*, but not for Cedrela. Temperature variables of the previous and current years were both positively and negatively correlated with growth in both species. In conclusion, MAI for *S. macrophylla* is close to the 0.4 cm yr^{-1} used by Guatemalan authorities for harvest planning, but our results show that this MAI underestimates growth and yield of *C. odorata*. Biological criteria for the determination of the rotation time of *S. macrophylla* are not consistent with the official minimum harvesting diameter of 60 cm.

Keywords: *Cedrela odorata*, community forest management, *Swietenia macrophylla*, timber, tropical rain forest, yield

Contact Address: Bryan Finegan, Tropical Agricultural Research and Higher Education Centre (CATIE), Production and Conservation in Forests Programme, 93-7170 Turrialba, Costa Rica, e-mail: bfinegan@catie.ac.cr

Impacts of Uncontrolled Logging on the Miombo Woodlands of the Niassa Reserve in Mozambique

TEREZA ALVES[1], CAMILA SOUSA[1], LAURA SNOOK[2], ROGERIO JAMICE[1], ELIAS FERREIRA[1], LALISA DUGUMA[3], OSCAR CHICHONGUE[1], CHRISTOPH SCHUNKO[4], GEORG GRATZER[5], JUDY LOO[2]

[1]*Instituto de Investigação Agrária de Moçambique (IIAM), Mozambique*

[2]*Bioversity International, Forest Genetic Resources Programme, Italy*

[3]*World Agroforestry Centre, Kenya*

[4]*University of Natural Resources and Life Sciences (BOKU), Dept. of Sustainable Agricultural Systems, Austria*

[5]*University of Natural Resources and Life Sciences (BOKU), Dept. of Forest and Soils Sciences, Austria*

This study evaluated the conservation status of tree populations and the impact of illegal logging in the Niassa National Reserve, a huge protected area in northern Mozambique, bordering Tanzania. The Miombo woodland around 8 villages was sampled on 43 transects laid out from log patios showing evidence of felling. Standing trees and stumps of 8 timber species (*P. angolensis, A. quanzensis, M. sthulmannii, B. africana, C. imberbe, D. melanoxylon, P. angolensis* and *S. madagascariensis*) were identified, quantified and measured. A total of 173 respondents in 12 villages were interviewed about their perception on logging and its benefits. Logging had removed 41 % of the trees above the minimum cutting diameter (20–50 cm dbh, depending on the species). On average, less than 2 m^3ha^{-1} of standing volume of commercial-sized trees remained, of which very few had good form. Pitsaws where trees had been sawn into planks were widespread and large quantities of waste wood were left on the ground. Planks produced had been transported to Tanzania, where they were sold or further processed.

Arrangements for logging were not transparent and villagers complained that they did not receive the benefits accorded by law to communities involved in legal logging (20 % of the profits). Fewer than half of the respondents were in favour of a complete stop of logging; instead, they hoped to obtain greater benefits from it. In return for access, loggers had built schools in two villages, and some local leaders and villagers had received building materials from them. Villagers claimed that people in the area lack forestry skills such as operating chainsaws and transforming timber into products. If required, carpenters have to be brought from Tanzania. Uncontrolled logging has left insufficient volume for future timber harvesting, meaning community forestry is not a feasible livelihood option. Furthermore, tree growth in the reserve is slow (0.25 cm yr^{-1} dbh) and felling is incompatible with the primary management objective of the reserve, which is conservation. The methodology applied here to evaluate the impact of logging could be applied elsewhere to monitor logging and determine whether to issue logging licenses for a specific area.

Keywords: Benefits, conservation, logging, standing volume, sustainability, timber species

---

Contact Address: Tereza Alves, Instituto de Investigação Agrária de Moçambique (IIAM), Maputo, Mozambique, e-mail: tealves@gmail.com

ID 856

Governance Challenges of Community Forestry: The Perspective of Local Actors in Petén, Guatemala and the Miskito Territory, Nicaragua

Mónica Orjuela, Ronnie de Camino Velozo

Agronomical Tropical Center for Research and Higher Education (CATIE), Tropical Forestry Conservation and Managment, Colombia

Governance of community forestry spans from local to national levels and, in cross-border territories, beyond. This study adopted the perspective of local actors to determine enabling conditions that allow governmental entities to renovate and strengthen community forestry agreements in two community forestry concessions in the Maya Biosphere Reserve (MRB), Guatemala and two Forest Management Units in the North Caribbean Coast in Nicaragua. We applied FAO´s Framework for Evaluation and Monitoring of Forest Governance to identify relevant aspects of community forestry governance across three reference frameworks: legal conditions of community forestry, principles, criteria & indicators of the Forest Stewardship Council, and the principles of active territorial governance. From each of these perspectives, community forestry groups have played a crucial role in advancing the sustainable use of the forests in the MBR, along with the social benefits accruing to their members. However, community forestry is threatened by the lack of political will to deal with the dynamics of opening the agricultural frontier, and the institutional and organisational weaknesses of the community groups, puts community forestry in a position of high vulnerability. In both countries, the principal impediment to community forestry is the governments' limited capacity or will to effectively control the illegal usurpation of land earmarked for, or with high potential to initiate, community forestry. The resulting advance of the agricultural frontier by diverse stakeholders, ranging from marginalised, often landless people to powerful interest groups involved in both licit and illicit activities, leaves the communities with limited options to resolve conflicts over land and forest use rights. From a local actors' perspective, an inclusive process of territorial planning appears a viable solution to resolve these conflicts over natural resource governance. We conclude with an outlook on how such an integrated management approach at landscape level could be implemented with high degrees of social legitimacy.

Keywords: Community forestry, governance, Guatemala, local actors, Nicaragua, perspective

Contact Address: Mónica Orjuela, Agronomical Tropical Center for Research and Higher Education (CATIE), Tropical Forestry Conservation and Managment, Avenida 9 No 147-46 Apartamento 808, 57 Bogotá, Colombia, e-mail: monica.orjuela@catie.ac.cr

Farmers' Preferences for Native Bee Conservation Measures after Experiencing a Past Pollination Crisis

MANUEL NARJES, CHRISTIAN LIPPERT

University of Hohenheim, Institute for Farm Management, Germany

The occurrence of localised pollinator crises is not unlikely in Thailand, given its sustained deforestation rates and the four-fold increase of pesticide imports for agricultural application over the past decade. In fact, anecdotal evidence that we collected in Chanthaburi province seems to corroborate reports of past pollinator deficits attributed to pesticide overuse, which forced orchard farmers of this region to manage their crop pollination by renting bee hives or becoming beekeepers themselves. Beekeeping in Thailand, traditionally consisting of farmers capturing wild swarms of the eastern honeybee (*Apis cerana*) and/or colonies of stingless bees, has nevertheless originally mainly benefited farmers with hive products such as honey and with the additional income these products may generate. Thailand's agriculture could thus benefit from a policy that reconciles individual economic incentives of farmers, with the objective of conserving native pollinators and their habitats.

We conducted a discrete choice experiment (DCE) with longan (*Dimocarpus longan*) and rambutan (*Nephelium lappaceum*) farmers of northern and eastern Thailand respectively, to elicit their preferences for different proposed native bee conservation measures and their possible effect on the population of native bees. The coefficient estimates from a generalised mixed logit (GMXL) model suggest that farmers have heterogeneous preferences for the conservation policy attributes. Furthermore, part of that heterogeneity resulted from differences between subsamples of respondents, pertaining the variances of the unaccounted factors that influenced their choices (i.e. hetersocedasticity). In fact, significantly different variances were evidenced between those farmers who engaged in beekeeping and those who did not. Nevertheless, taking heteroscedasticity into account, the results suggest that the subsample of farmers who either engage in beekeeping or believe having experienced an insufficient crop pollination in the past had a higher preference for some of the conservation policy attributes. This result may hint at the possible benefits of warning farmers about the production losses that a pollination crisis may entail: implemented as a preliminary measure, it could increase farmers' willingness to invest in conserving the local pollinating fauna.

Keywords: Conservation, discrete choice experiment, native bees, pollination, Thailand

Contact Address: Manuel Narjes, University of Hohenheim, Institute for Farm Management, Schwerzstraße 44, 70599 Stuttgart, Germany, e-mail: manuel.narjes@uni-hohenheim.de

ID 917

Brachiaria brizantha cv. BRS Piatã Forage Yield under Integrated Crop-Livestock-Forestry Systems in Brazil

Mariana Pereira[1], Sarah Glatzle[2], Valéria Ana Corvalã Dos Santos[3], Maria da Graça Morais[1], Juliana Mara de Freitas Santos[2], Roberto G. Almeida[4]

[1]*Federal University of Mato Grosso do Sul, Animal Science, Brazil*
[2]*University of Hohenheim, Inst. of Agricultural Sciences in the Tropics (Hans-Ruthenberg-Institute), Germany*
[3]*São Paulo State University (UNESP), Animal Science, Brazil*
[4]*EMBRAPA Beef Cattle, Integrated Production Systems, Brazil*

Integrated crop-livestock-forestry (ICLF) systems are increasingly considered for a diversified agricultural production in Brazil. In this study we analysed the forage yield [kg DM ha^{-1}], of *Brachiaria brizantha* BRS cv. Piatã for ICLF demonstration plots at the Brazilian Agricultural Research Corporation - EMBRAPA, located in Campo Grande-MS, Brazil. The analysed plots with four replicates corresponded to three production systems: Two integrated crop-livestock-forestry systems (ICLF1 and ICLF2) and an integrated crop-livestock system (ICL). The trees (*Eucalyptus urograndis*) in the ICLF systems were planted in single rows with 2 m between tress and 14 or 22 m between rows, resulting in 357 trees ha^{-1} (ICLF1) and 277 trees ha^{-1} (ICLF2), respectively. The crop component is soy-bean, planted every 4 years. Grass biomass was sampled monthly in a line of five sampling points at equal distance from each other between tree rows to represent the understory shading gradient. Animal feed intake was considered using the moving cages method. During the dry season (June - October) the forage yields between the different treatments didn't differ significantly from each other (average 5.4 kg DM ha^{-1}). In the rainy season (November - January) the ICLF system had the highest forage yield (ICLF 17.7 > ICL 6.6 kg DM ha^{-1}). Most likely the main reason for these results is due to the management practice. In the dry season the ICLF systems had such a low stocking rate compared to the ICL system, that in the rainy season the ICLF systems were able to exceed the forage production of the ICL system. In the tree plots during the dry season the forage yields along the shading gradient didn't differ significantly (average 5.3 kg DM ha^{-1}). In the rainy season the points with higher shading (near the tree rows) had lower forage yields (9.9 and 11.8 kg DM ha^{-1}, respectively) than the central points (16.1 kg DM ha^{-1}). The microclimate within the tree plots has a great effect on the forage production. During the dry season the shading effect of the trees on the whole area is more evenly distributed resulting in similar forage yields along the shading gradient.

Keywords: Agroforestry, Brazilian savannah, shading, tropical grass

Contact Address: Mariana Pereira, Federal University of Mato Grosso do Sul, Animal Science, Avenida Senador Filinto Muller 2443, Campo Grande, Brazil, e-mail: maripereirazoo@gmail.com

Productivity of Different Cacao Cultivars Depends on the Production Systems

Laura Armengot[1], Erick Lohse[2], Christina Vaccaro[3], Pietro Barbieri[1], Freddy Alcon[4], Victor Soto[4], Joachim Milz[4], Monika Schneider[1]

[1] Research Institute of Organic Agriculture (FiBL), Switzerland
[2] University Mayor de San Andres (UMSA), Bolivia
[3] University of Hohenheim, Germany
[4] ECOTOP, Consulting on Successional Agroforestry, Bolivia

Cacao production systems vary from full-sun monocultures to highly diversified agroforestry systems, which can be both organically or conventionally managed. Agroforestry systems have the potential to improve biodiversity in tropical regions but also farmer's food security by diversifying the crops. However, higher cacao yields are usually reported in monocultures. A proper choise of cacao cultivars might help to improve cacao yields in agroforestry systems. The aim of this study is to identify the most suitable cultivars for organically managed agroforestry systems.

The study was performed in 2015 in a long-term trial established in Bolivia in 2008 within the framework of the SysCom-programme (www.systems-comparison.fibl.org). It comprises monoculture and agroforestry systems under organic and conventional management and one successional agroforestry system with organic management. Twelve cultivars including locally selected trees by the plant breeding programme of EL CEIBO Coopertive, foreign clones (from the Imperial College Selections and Trinidad Selections) and hybrids were planted in each production system. Each system is replicated four times in a randomised block design, i.e. a total of 20 plots, and four trees of each cultivar were evaluated in each plot. Harvest data, i.e. number of pods and fresh weight were collected at tree level. Moreover, the number of cherelle wilt, the physiological abortion of the small pods, was registered for each tree throughout the harvesting season.

The results showed higher yields and number of pods in the monocultures, mainly the ones under conventional farming. No differences between organic and conventionally managed agroforestry systems were detected. Overall, the percentage of pod losses due to cherelle wilt was higher in the agroforestry systems. Interestingly, we found an interaction between the production system and the cultivars for both the cherelle wilt and yield and number of pods. It reveals that some cultivars performed better in some systems than in others, and *vice versa*. Therefore, our results suggest that there is the potential for improving cacao yield in organically managed agroforestry systems by accurately choosing the best performing cultivars in these production systems. The best performing cultivars could be then the base for the selection of improved cultivars for organic agroforestry

Keywords: Agroforestry systems, cacao yields, cherelle wilt, cultivars, full-sun monocultures, organic farming

Contact Address: Laura Armengot, Research Institute of Organic Agriculture (FiBL), Ackerstrasse 113, PO Box 219, Frick, Switzerland, e-mail: laura.armengot@fibl.org

ID 926

Silvicultural Treatments of Exotic and Native Tree Monocultures and Influence on Biodiversity Facilitation in Southern Ecuador. Preliminary Results

DARÍO VEINTIMILLA[1], BALTAZAR CALVAS[1], REINHARD MOSANDL[2], BERND STIMM[2], PATRICK HILDEBRANDT[1], SVEN GÜNTER[3]

[1]*Technical University of Munich, Dept. of Ecology and Ecosystems Management, Germany*

[2]*Technical University of Munich, Inst. of Silviculture, Center of Life and Food Sciences Weihenstephan, Germany*

[3]*Thünen Institute, Institute of International Forestry and Forest Economics, Germany*

Forest plantations with exotic species in southern Ecuador have been characterised mostly by having negative externalities in both ecological and economic aspects. After 10 years of research in mountain forests in southern Ecuador on aspects of restoration and reforestation few native tree species with good growth response in comparison to exotic species have been identified. The knowledge transfer project New Forests for Ecuadoräims at testing the potential shelter effect of exotic *Pinus patula* plantations and natural stands of *Alnus acuminata* for natural regeneration and enrichment planting of native tree species in order to provide a tool for conversion of monocultures into mixed forests. 51 sample plots of 24×24 m of core area where established in eight different sites of *Pinus* and *Alnus* stands within the Province of Loja. The initial parameters (soil, mesofauna, mycorrhizae, light intensity and microclimate) were measured before applying silvicultural treatments. Silvicultural thinning treatments with three different intensities (reference, strong and slight intervention) were applied for *Pinus* stands, and two for *Alnus* stands (reference, strong intervention). Inside of each sample plot, nine native tree species were randomly planted and its growth was measured during one year. Preliminary results show a positive response to the canopy opening in *Pinus* and *Alnus* stands of four native tree species in terms of survival and growth. It is expected that the final results provide scientific basis for developing suitable tool for conversion of forest monocultures into mixed forests with higher ecological and economic values in mountain ecosystems of southern Ecuador.

Keywords: *Alnus acuminata*, mixed forest, natural regeneration, *Pinus patula*, reforestation, shelter effect

Contact Address: Darío Veintimilla, Technical University of Munich, Department of Ecology and Ecosystems Management, Munich, Germany, e-mail: darioalfredov@yahoo.com

Modelling Landscape Effects of Agroforestry on Watershed- and Ecosystem Functions in a Small Watershed in Nicaragua

ALEX POHL, CARSTEN MAROHN, BENJAMIN WARTH, GEORG CADISCH

University of Hohenheim, Inst. of Agricultural Sciences in the Tropics (Hans-Ruthenberg-Institute), Germany

Slash and burn agriculture without fallow in maize-bean systems of NW Nicaragua has led to severe soil degradation through soil organic matter (SOM) mining and erosion. SOM loss is aggravated through cattle grazing on harvested fields. Improved maize-bean rotation systems have been developed, namely Slashing & Mulching of Crop Residues (CR), which is current farmers' practice, and the Quesungual Slash & Mulch Agroforestry System (QSMAS), an agroforestry system based on permanent soil cover, absence of burning, minimal soil disturbance and efficient fertiliser use. Native trees conserved in cropping fields are heavily pruned twice a year, before maize and bean sowing to provide light, soil cover and litter. While CR and QSMAS do not differ in maize and bean yields, QSMAS is known for its potential to create important ecosystem functions (ground cover, nutrient cycling and soil moisture) through the provision of a mulch layer. However, fodder scarcity during dry seasons compels farmers to expand livestock grazing on QSMAS and CR plots, potentially counteracting systems benefits. Thus, a study using the spatially explicit and dynamic process based Land Use Change Impact Assessment model (LUCIA) was implemented to compare two QSMAS designs, which differed in species composition and pruning intensities, as well as the CR system regarding their effects on watershed functions under different management options.

Two landscape-scale questions were investigated: a) Potential effects of QSMAS and CR expansion into forests on watershed SOC stocks. Twenty year simulations suggest a strong depletion of landscape level carbon stocks under CR expansion (+2.4 %) but being less severe under QSMAS expansion (+0.5 %), compared to current baseline without any land use change. b) Recycling of dung depositions in corrals near homesteads as manure for vegetable production instead of current disposal into streams. Simulations suggest that matter fluxes off the plots, e.g. loss of SOM through grazing on agricultural land, could be partly compensated, once manure was returned to the farm system. Cash crops, like watermelons could profit from the additional organic inputs.

The study depicts scenarios, which possibly help in identifying key mechanisms to conserve watershed- and ecosystem services.

Keywords: Agroforestry, dynamic modelling, ecosystem services, Nicaragua, Quesungual

---

Contact Address: Alex Pohl, University of Hohenheim, Inst. of Agricultural Sciences in the Tropics (Hans-Ruthenberg-Institute), 70593 Stuttgart, Germany, e-mail: pohlalex@uni-hohenheim.de

ID 990

Screening Woody Species for Afforestation of Degraded Croplands in the Sudano-Sahelian Zone of Benin

FLORENT NOULEKOUN[1], JESSE B. NAAB[2], JOHN LAMERS[1], ASIA KHAMZINA[1]

[1] *University of Bonn, Center for Development Research (ZEF), Germany*
[2] *West African Science Service Center for Climate Change and Adapted Land Use (WASCAL), Burkina Faso*

In the Sudano-Sahelian zone of Benin, where deforestation and cropland soil degradation persist at alarming rates, the re-introduction of trees on degraded lands may offer great opportunities to sustain farming systems. To improve the understanding of the vital process of tree establishment and early growth, we conducted an afforestation experiment with five woody species on degraded cropland. The survival and growth response to manuring (1 kg plant^{-1}) and drip irrigation (0.5 liter of water sapling^{-1} day^{-1}) were monitored over the first 15 months, covering two growing seasons and one dry season. The overall high survival rates ($>60\%$) with a very low incidence rate ($<0.01\%$) indicated a successful establishment of all species, particularly *Jatropha curcas*, *Leucaena leucocephala* and *Moringa oleifera* which had the highest rates (67–100%). Supplemental irrigation reduced by ten-folds the mortality rate of the most drought-sensitive species *Parkia biglobosa* during the dry season. Significantly higher relative growth rates were recorded for *L. leucocephala*, *M. oleifera* and *J. curcas* (0.41-0.52 g g^{-1} month^{-1}) than for *Anacardium occidentale* and *P. biglobosa* (0.31 and 0.33 g g^{-1} month^{-1}). The plants responded to fertilisation and irrigation treatments by enhancing the shoot growth, as observed in both fast-growers (*L. leucocephala*, *M. oleifera* and *J. curcas*) and slow-growers (*A. occidentale* and *P. biglobosa*) during wet season. Increasing belowground development was observed in slow-growers during dry and wet seasons. Overall, the five examined species showed great potential for afforestation of degraded croplands, and manuring and irrigation were key for boosting and facilitating early growth and establishment of seedlings.

Keywords: Degraded cropland, morphological traits, multipurpose tree, northern Benin, survival rate

Contact Address: Florent Noulekoun, University of Bonn, Center for Development Research (ZEF), Walter-flex-Str.3, 0049 Bonn, Germany, e-mail: florentnoulekoun@yahoo.fr

Land Fragmentation and Agroforestry: Shifting Practices and Perceptions of Trees on Small Farms

LINE VINTHER HANSEN, LAXMI LAMA, MILAN MILENOVIC, IRIS RIOS
VARGAS, EDITH WELKER

University of Copenhagen, Department of Science, Denmark

In the central highlands of Kenya, decreasing farm size due to land fragmentation upon inheritance has the potential to threaten livelihoods and food security. Farmers are forced to prioritise food, fodder, cash crops, and trees to make the best use of limited space. The objective of this study was to investigate whether and how decreasing land size shapes agroforestry practices, as well as the effects of having trees on farms. In order to gain a holistic perspective on agroforestry practices and their impacts in the Othaya area, in Nyeri South District, a combination of social and natural science methods were used. These included field interviews, questionnaires, and focus group discussion, which were triangulated with analyses of soil, microclimate, and species richness.

Our findings show an increase in tree density as farm sizes decrease. For instance, farms of <0.5 ha have mean density of 187 trees ha^{-1}, while those >1 ha have mean density of 51 trees ha^{-1}. At the same time, 78 % of farmers report self sufficiency in fuelwood and timber, showing the subsistence value of trees. Farmers strongly prefer exotics also for timber and fruit for income. Species richness analysis revealed that fast growing exotic trees far outnumber indigenous. The cultural valuation of indigenous trees is simultaneously diminishing, potentially suppressed by economically-driven preferences. In addition, there is limited understanding of the potential ecological benefits of trees in farming systems. Multipurpose species, such as leguminous fodder trees, are underutilised, which may represent a missed opportunity for increased livelihood and farm system diversification.

The gap in farmer knowledge, as well as a lack of support for best practices, are key barriers to agroforestry in the Othaya area. With better understanding of trees' effects on crops, livestock, climate, soil, and water, it could be expected that systems would be more productive and resilient, in effect contributing to self sufficiency, increasing livelihood opportunities, and helping to mitigate the effect of land fragmentation.

Keywords: Agroforestry, barriers, crop-livestock systems, East Africa, Kenya, land fragmentation, land subdivision, multidisciplinary, multipurpose trees, smallholders

Contact Address: Milan Milenovic, University of Copenhagen, Department of Science, Taasingegade 29, 2100 Copenhagen, Denmark, e-mail: bhm989@alumni.ku.dk

ID 1064

Management of *Parkia biglobosa* in the Field of Farmers in Selected Sites in Burkina Faso

GUIBIEN CLÉOPHAS ZERBO[1], DAVID MILLOGO[1], BARBARA VINCETI[2], MOUSSA OUEDRAOGO[1], JÉROME DUMINIL[2], DJINGDIA LOMPO[1]

[1]*National Tree Seed Center, Burkina Faso*
[2]*Bioversity International, Italy*

Parkia biglobosa is ranked as one of the most important agroforestry multipurpose tree species in Sahelo-Sudanian zone. The National Tree Seed Center (CNSF) of Burkina Faso has been involved in a breeding programme of this species for many years and has already conducted several research activities (eg. germplasm collection, provenance trials establishment, selection of the best promising trees for propagation). To better conserve and guide the breeding program, it is important to understand how farmers perceive and manage the species in their fields. A survey was conducted in two villages in southern Burkina Faso to describe the farmers' practices with regard to encouraging regeneration of tree species in their fields, with a special emphasis on *Parkia biglobosa*. The survey targeted 150 people categorised by gender, ethnic group and status of residence. The results show that *Parkia biglobosa* is the most appreciated indigenous species across ethnic and gender groups. Its maintenance in the landscape is favoured by both the protection of spontaneous regeneration by farmers when they clear the land for agriculture, and by active planting. The species is valued both for its commercial use and human consumption in the household. The survey indicated a significant difference in the practices undertaken by women and men to safeguard regeneration. With regard to the preferred traits of *Parkia biglobosa* individuals, also some differences between genders emerge. The level of appreciation shown by farmers for *Parkia biglobosa* and the indications about what traits are most preferred are useful guidance in the identification of optimal sources of reproductive material to be made available to farmers through different channels. The results also indicated the need to couple the analyses of farmers' perception of trait variation among individuals with a systematic morphological characterisation of the various morphological types identified.

Keywords: Agroforestry, conservation, regeneration, selection

Contact Address: Guibien Cléophas Zerbo, National Tree Seed Center, Ouagadougou, Burkina Faso, e-mail: zercle@yahoo.fr

People's Forest Management on the Island of Java: How Have Changes Occurred after the Decentralisation Era?

WIENE ANDRIYANA, KARL HOGL, RALF NORDBECK

University of Natural Resources and Life Sciences (BOKU), Inst. of Forest Environmental and Natural Resource Policy (INFER), Austria

In Java, around 70 % of state-owned forests have been exclusively managed for more than 30 years by The State Forest Company (SFC). As with privately owned forests, the typical form of non-state forest management in Java is called a People's Forest (PF), which are usually managed in a non-commercial style. By regulation, the SFC is only authorized to manage state-owned forest in Java. However, since SFC was the only existing forest-related institution located at district level, for a long period of time SFC also had additional power to legitimize timber harvested from People's Forests. This means, without approval from the SFC, owners of People's Forests could not cut their trees to sell timber products in a legal manner. This complex administrative procedure has created disincentives for People's Forest development. This situation however has shifted since Indonesia's national decentralisation policy was introduced. This research analyses the extent and the causal pathways along which the practices of People's Forest management in Java have undergone changes after the decentralisation era. The research design builds on extensive review of policy and written documents and two major phases of fieldwork in two selected districts in Central Java. The expert interview was used to explore four dimensions of Policy Arrangement Approach (actors, rules, power and discourses) in the management of People's Forest. This study reveals that the People's Forest management scheme has been altered since the introduction of decentralisation policy by bringing a new actor into the playing field of People's Forest, namely the District Forest Authority (DFA). The DFA with its new power and authority as mandated by the decentralisation policy has to a large extent shifted the role and authority of the State Forest Company (SFC). Discourse surrounding People's Forests have also undergone changes, which later created incentives for land owners to invest in People's Forests. In summary, changes in the power structure, regulation, and actor constellation surrounding People's Forests have encouraged the way people frame People's Forests, which later contributed to the rapid development of People's Forests in Java.

Keywords: Decentralisation, forest management, people's forest, policy arrangement approach

---

Contact Address: Wiene Andriyana, University of Natural Resources and Life Sciences (BOKU), Inst. of Forest Environmental and Natural Resource Policy (INFER), Gustav Tschermakgasse 5-7, 1180 Vienna, Austria, e-mail: wiene.andriyana@gmail.com

ID 1128

Effects of Upland Immature Para Rubber Plantation on Erosion and Nutrient Losses in Northern Thailand

WANWISA PANSAK[1], JARUNTORN BOONYANUPHAP[2], NATTA TAKRATTANASARAN[3]

[1]*Naresuan University, Dept. of Agricultural Science, Thailand*
[2]*Naresuan University, Dept. of Natural Resources and Environment, Thailand*
[3]*Land Development Regional 1, Land Development Dept., Thailand*

Since 1989, rubber growing in Thailand has gradually shifted from its traditional area in the South to the North. Moreover, some original forests have been cleared for rubber tree cultivation. Intensive Para rubber plantation in upland areas is susceptible to soil erosion. Therefore, the objectives of this study were (i) to assess erosion and soil nutrient losses in upland rubber plantation and (ii) to assess the net present value (NPV) of soil nutrient losses by erosion. Data were collected from farmer trials in 2014 at Muab sub-basin of the Nan watershed (18°54'N, 100°54'E), with slope gradients ranging from 25 to >35 %. Five treatments consisted of 1) maize, 2) 3-year-old rubber plus bench terrace, 3) 3-year-old rubber, 4) 1-year-old rubber intercropping with maize and 5) 1-year-old rubber. Erosion is measured by Gerlach troughs with tipping buckets installed at the upper, middle and lower slopes of each plot. The total annual rainfall at the experimental site was 1,330 mm. The soil was classified as a fine, mixed, active, isohyperthermic Typic Haplustalfs with 39.5 % sand, 36 % silt, and a 24.5 % clay in the topsoil (0–25 cm). The topsoil had a pH of 4.5, organic matter of 0.3–1.8 %, P (Bray II) content of 2.8–7.0 mg kg^{-1} and K content of 99–149 mg kg^{-1}. The results showed significant differences in soil losses among treatments. The lowest soil loss was observed with the treatment 4: rubber plus maize (5.08 t ha^{-1} yr^{-1}). Runoff was highest in the 3-year-old rubber (31.98 % of total rainfall). Total N, P and K losses by soil loss did not significantly differ among treatments. The amount of nutrient losses by runoff including total N (1.52 – 3.41 kg ha^{-1}), P (3.45 – 9.11 kg ha^{-1}) and K (0.73 – 1.25 kg ha^{-1}) were not statistically significant. The calculated NPV for 20 years showed that rubber intercropping with maize treatment had the highest value (5,743 Euro ha^{-1}). Therefore, we conclude that immature rubber intercropping with maize is suitable systems which can reduce erosion and also the losses of nutrients by erosion in the upland rubber plantation.

Keywords: Erosion, immature Para rubber, northern Thailand, nutrient losses, upland

---

Contact Address: Wanwisa Pansak, Naresuan University, Dept. of Agricultural Science, 65000 Phitsanulok, Thailand, e-mail: wanwisapa@nu.ac.th

Water and soils

How Climate-Smart Are the GIZ Supported Soil Protection and Rehabilitation Technologies in Benin, Burkina Faso, Ethiopia, India and Kenya?

BIRTHE PAUL[1], CELINE BIRNHOLZ[1], JESSICA KOGE[1], AN NOTENBAERT[2],
JULIET BRASLOW[1], SUVARNA CHANDRAPPAGARI[1], BIYENSA GURMESSA[3],
ŠPELA KALČIĆ[4], ROLF SOMMER[1]

[1] *International Center for Tropical Agriculture (CIAT), Kenya*
[2] *International Livestock Research Institute (ILRI), Kenya*
[3] *International Center for Tropical Agriculture (CIAT), Ethiopia*
[4] *International Center for Tropical Agriculture (CIAT), Burkina Faso*

Agriculture is a significant cause of climate change, directly contributing an approximate 14 % of anthropogenic greenhouse gas (GHG) emissions, and indirectly another 17 % through land use change (mainly deforestation). Although climate smart agriculture aims at improving food security, adaptation and mitigation, it does not imply that every recommended practice should necessarily be a 'triple win'. Especially in developing countries, mitigation should be a co-benefit, while food security and adaptation are main priorities. Thus, climate-smartness underlines the importance of potential trade-offs between agricultural production and environmental impacts. Integrated *ex-ante* impact assessment can help policy and development decision makers in targeting and upscaling interventions and investments. This study presents results from a rapid *ex-ante* assessment of the climate-smartness of the technologies supported under the BMZ-GIZ programme on 'Soil Protection and Rehabilitation for Food Security' in Benin, Burkina Faso, Ethiopia, India and Kenya, which is part of Germany's special initiative 'One World – No Hunger'. In all countries, participatory stakeholder workshops identified four to six distinct farming systems that differed in terms of intensification, production orientation, commercialisation, agro-ecological potential and resource endowment. Stakeholders also shortlisted the most relevant soil protection and rehabilitation technologies promoted in the target sites, and estimated impacts on crop and livestock productivity. Subsequently, household interviews were conducted in representative farms of the identified farming system types. The data collected was used to assess baseline performance and tradeoffs, as well as changes in response to the soil technology scenarios in three indicators of climate-smartness: productivity (kcal ha^{-1} yr^{-1}), GHG emissions (CO_2-eq/ha/yr), and nitrogen balance (kg N ha^{-1} yr^{-1}). Recommendations resulting from this study will inform soil and climate policy development in each country, as well as BMZ/GIZ planning processes aiming to align the scope of the soil programme with goals of climate smart agriculture.

Keywords: *Ex-ante* impact assessment, farming systems research, trade-offs

Contact Address: Birthe Paul, International Center for Tropical Agriculture (CIAT), Tropical Forages Program, Nairobi, Kenya, e-mail: b.paul@cgiar.org

Assessment of Surface and Shallow Groundwater Resources for Small Scale Farming in Inland Valleys in Dano, Burkina Faso

MOUHAMED IDRISSOU[1,2], BERND DIEKKRÜGER[2], BERNHARD TISCHBEIN[1]

[1] *University of Bonn, Center for Development Research (ZEF), Germany*

[2] *University of Bonn, Dept. of Geography, Germany*

Dano is a rural area located in the South-East region of Burkina Faso. According to National Department of Statistics of Burkina Faso, approximately 57 % of the population lives with less than 1 Dollar a day. In the Dano catchment, as in many other rural areas in West Africa, many projects intend to reduce poverty through agricultural system improvement in inland valleys. Often they purely base on surface runoff either by constructing small dams or canalizing runoff directly to the fields. Although flooded in the rainy season, fields dry out quickly after the end of the rainy season so that crop growth is not possible without irrigation.

The aim of this research is to investigate surface runoff and shallow groundwater availability in order to support strategies for better utilisation of scarce water resources in small scale farming in Dano catchment. This paper examines the rainfall distribution at high spatial resolution using dataset of 10 rain gauges for a total study area of 65 km^2 in order to capture the spatial distribution of rain in the catchment. Its conversions into streamflow measured at 8 stream gauges were analysed based on hydrographs characterisation. Soil moisture spatial distribution measured at three different depths was analysed in order to understand the transfer of water between soil and shallow groundwater. The shallow groundwater table was determined from the measurements at 80 different locations in the study area. Its extension and continuity were determined by the analyses of electrical resistivity of the aquifer. Finally, water fluxes are modelled using the Water flow balance Simulation Model (WaSiM) and the main hydrological processes which control surface and shallow groundwater availability in inland valleys in the Dano catchment are determined.

Keywords: Hydrological processes analyses, inland valleys, small scale modelling, water balance, water resources availability

Contact Address: Mouhamed Idrissou, University of Bonn, Center for Development Research (ZEF), Walter-Flex-Str.-3, 53115 Bonn, Germany, e-mail: m.idrissou@uni-bonn.de

ID 421

Rainwater Harvesting as a Sustainable Alternative for Ensuring Food Security in Southern Kyrgyzstan (Central Asia)

AIPERI OTUNCHIEVA, SISIRA WITHANACHCHI, ANGELIKA PLOEGER

University of Kassel, Organic Food Quality and Food Culture, Germany

Rainwater harvesting (RWH) has been used since ancient times and gained popularity recently. As a simple, cost effective and sustainable alternative for securing food, RWH offers stability in terms of water availability for agricultural output for small scale farmers in arid and semi-arid areas. Although trivial forms of RWH exist in such areas, efficiency of water use might be doubtful. To be precise, poor water maintaining capacity, increased level of evaporation, absence of calculations of local precipitation levels and actual annual need for irrigation water weakens efficient use of this precious natural resource. Taking into account this assumption, the article presents practical solutions for food security in the absence of water system infrastructure in rural areas. Our hypothesis states that even with annual precipitation less than 300 mm, it is possible to ensure rainfed agriculture. This work serves as a continuation of the previous research completed in April 2015 on kitchen gardens in southern Kyrgyzstan (Central Asia). The four-day theory and practice-based training sessions will be provided for the farmers (representatives of 120 households) in the Shybran village of Batken province. It will take place at the end of dry and beginning of rainy season in the country. Within this framework, farmers will be informed about the chances to increase water supply, improve water use efficiency and employment of appropriate crops in terms of local climatic conditions. The results are about availability of RWH structures with efficient water use, its wider dissemination among rural farmers in southern Kyrgyzstan, insurance of water sustainability, increased reliance on self-grown food, and decrease youth migration from rural areas.

Keywords: Arid and semi-arid areas, food security, Kyrgyzstan, rainwater harvesting, water scarcity

---

Contact Address: Aiperi Otunchieva, University of Kassel, Organic Food Quality and Food Culture, Nordbahnhofstr. 1a, 37213 Witzenhausen, Germany, e-mail: aiperi3822@gmail.com

Emerging Erosion Risk in South-West Ethiopia: Farmers Prepardness and Soil Conservation Strategies

Vera Maria Haensel[1], Sebastian Arnhold[1], Thomas Koellner[1], Hans Hurni[2]

[1] University of Bayreuth, Ecological Services, Germany

[2] Bern University of Applied Sciences, Centre for Development and Environment (CDE), Institute of Geography, Switzerland

Soil erosion, a significant challenge of Ethiopian agriculture, has been intensively studied and addressed within the past decades. Efforts have mainly focused on areas with a long history of heavy agricultural pressure, namely the northern highlands of Ethiopia. In recent years government programs started to pay attention to other parts of the country that are increasingly affected.

One of those emerging risk areas is Kafa Zone in South-West Ethiopia. Until today it has a substantial forest cover of about 50 %, but erosion risk is rising due to expansion of agricultural activities. To analyse the preparedness of farmers in the region, erosion risk was modeled and interviews were carried out. The erosion risk of the study area and its administrative units was computed with the Unit Stream Power based Erosion Deposition Model (USPED), using parameters of the Universal Soil Loss Equation (USLE). Modelling was done in five different basic scenarios and additional sub-scenarios, to account for the uncertainty of the quality and quantity of existing soil conservation measures. Interviews were held with farmers and agricultural extension workers to evaluate existing knowledge and awareness, relevant farming practices and applied conservation measures in the context of soil erosion.

Interview results suggest that knowledge about soil erosion and potential soil conservation measures is relatively widespread in the area, while the implementation level of conservation efforts is low. Traditional and biological measures are predominantly seen as favourable options even though introduced physical measures are assessed as being more effective in reducing erosion. To increase the effectiveness of actions taken by the government, activities of the different sections of the agricultural offices could be further streamlined. Contextualisation of conservation measures could have a positive impact on the acceptance of conservation measures and their overall success.

Keywords: Ethiopia, farmers' awareness, soil conservation measures, soil erosion, USPED

Contact Address: Vera Maria Haensel, University of Bayreuth, Ecological Services, Destubenerstr. 57, 95448 Bayreuth, Germany, e-mail: haensel@posteo.de

ID 1043

Water Conservation Program and Practice in Irrigated Agriculture in Iran: A Case Study of Lake Urmia Basin

ASNA ASHARI FARAH

Ruhr-Universität Bochum (RUB), Institute of Development Research and Development Policy, Germany

Human and environmental demand for water resources across Iran are increasing while the water shortage in this semi-arid country is a serious problem. As agriculture is the main water user of all sectors (agriculture, industry and municipal supply), expanding efficient irrigation systems is a challenge for policy makers in Iran. Some parts of water shortage in traditional irrigation systems are due to lack of water conservation methods. The importance of farmers' roles as the main stakeholders in managing water resources cannot be exaggerated. This increases the pressure on farmers to use water as efficiently as possible.

This is a descriptive study to review the facts of water conservation application in Iran relying on a survey in Lake Urmia basin; one of the largest agricultural regions within the country. The survey was conducted in February to April 2013 in East Azerbaijan. Farmers were questioned about their water conservation practices and problems to enlighten the capacity for enhancing water and environmental sustainability programs in the region. About 20 percent of applied water conservation methods exist of proper watering techniques and irrigation system improvements. More than 50 % of the farmers stated that the main reason for not applying water conservation methods is the lack of financial means which put this problem on top of the list. Other reasons for sticking to traditional inefficient irrigation systems include a lack of knowledge and a lack of motivation. Small land size which makes using the techniques and tools costly is also a distinctive to conserve water.

Keywords: Agriculture, irrigation, sustainability, water conservation

Contact Address: Asna Ashari Farah, Ruhr-Universität Bochum (RUB), Institute of Development Research and Development Policy, Universitätsstr. 150 Gb 1 / 154, 44801 Bochum, Germany, e-mail: farah.asnaashari@rub.de

Spatial Variability of Soil Properties in the Floodplain of a River Oasis in the Mongolian Altay Mountains

SVEN GOENSTER-JORDAN[1], RAMIA JANNOURA[2], ANDREAS BUERKERT[1], RAINER GEORG JOERGENSEN[2]

[1] University of Kassel, Organic Plant Production and Agroecosystems Research in the Tropics and Subtropics, Germany

[2] University of Kassel, Soil Biology and Plant Nutrition, Germany

Owing to the fertility of alluvial soils, the leveled topography and the easy access to water, floodplains are favored areas for agricultural activities. These factors allow small-scaled cultivation of crops and hay even under the arid climate conditions in the floodplain of the river oasis Bulgan sum center located in the foothills of the Altay Mountains, Western Mongolia. Previous studies in the river oasis suggested a negative impact of agricultural land use on soil quality indicated by soil biological parameters which, however, were characterized by a high spatial heterogeneity. This study aims at a further characterization of the spatial variability of major soil properties within the floodplain of Bulgan sum center and the determination of factors responsible for the variation of soil biological properties.

In the framework of the IFAD-funded project WATERCOPE (grant I-R-1284), top-soil samples were taken every 20 m according to a grid sampling approach, covering a floodplain area of 4 ha. Samples were analyzed for physico-chemical (electrical conductivity (EC), inorganic carbon (C), pH, texture, total C) and biological properties (basal respiration, ergosterol, microbial biomass C). The coefficient of variation (CV in %) was calculated as a measure of spatial variability. Spearman correlations were computed between soil biological and physico-chemical properties.

While pH values were almost homogenous within the 4 ha (CV = 12 %), biological soil parameters were characterized by a relatively high variability (basal respiration: CV = 46 %, ergosterol: CV = 63 %, microbial biomass C: CV = 41 %). EC and inorganic C, however, were extremely variable within the area (CV = 86 % and 163 %, respectively). The variation of the biological parameters primarily depends on the spatial distribution of organic C (average r^2 = 0.62, $p < 0.01$), while for ergosterol and for microbial biomass C a positive relationship with EC (r^2 = 0.57, $p < 0.01$) and with the clay content (r^2 = 0.43, $p < 0.01$), respectively, was additionally observed.

In summary, presented variabilities confirm previous observations and are comparable to further floodplain studies. Results underline the significance of organic carbon to preserve the scarce and susceptible agroecological resources of river oases.

Keywords: Kriging, soil organic carbon, soil respiration, soil salinity

Contact Address: Sven Goenster-Jordan, University of Kassel, Organic Plant Production and Agroecosystems Research in the Tropics and Subtropics, Witzenhausen, Germany, e-mail: goenster@uni-kassel.de

ID 527

Water Resource Allocation for Optimal Selection of Agricultural Crops in Gezira Irrigation Scheme, Sudan

MOHAMED ELGALI[1], RAJAA MUSTAFA[1], SIEGFRIED BAUER[2]

[1] *University of Gezira, Agricultural Economics, Sudan*

[2] *Justus-Liebig University Giessen, Inst. of Farm and Agribusiness Management - Project and Regional Planning, Germany*

The Gezira Irrigation Scheme in Sudan, is with 880,000 ha one of the largest irrigation schemes on the African continent. Recently, under the reform process and privatisation of the scheme a new partnership for irrigation water has been established between the government and the farmers. Under the new arrangement, farmers are responsible for maintenance and operation of the water canals at farm level, while the government is responsible for managing water sources and main canals in the scheme.

The aim of this paper is to review the irrigation water partnership in the Gezira scheme. In addition a plan is set up for an optimal cropping pattern in the irrigation scheme under the new partnership and the water scarcity conditions. A non-linear programming model has been developed to suggest the optimal cropping pattern for maximizing net returns and ensuring efficient water use. The model also used to determine how much land should be allocated for each crop under available water resources. Data were collected from primary and secondary sources to derive the model's coefficients. The primary data were obtained through personal interviews using designed questionnaire covering 100 farmers who were selected randomly from different locations in the scheme. The model results showed that the optimal farm plan include non-traditional crops such as carrots and onions besides sorghum as a traditional activity in the scheme. The study recommends farmers in the Gezira scheme to take into consideration water scarcity when planning for selecting the optimal crop pattern for sustainable production.

Keywords: Gezira, non-linear programing, Sudan, water scarcity

Contact Address: Mohamed Elgali, University of Gezira, Agricultural Economics, Nishisheeba No. 25, 11112 Madani, Sudan, e-mail: moelgali@yahoo.com

Maize Relay with Legume without Residue Burning Impact on Soil Erosion and N Loss in Northern Thailand

ADIREK PUNYALUE[1], JEDSADA JONGJAIDEE[1], SANSANEE JAMJOD[2], BENJAVAN RERKASEM[2]

[1]Highland Research and Development Institute (Public Organisation), Department of Research, Thailand

[2]Chiang Mai University, Thailand, Agriculture, Thailand

Maize production in Thailand has expanded into the highlands, with land preparation by slash and burning residues from the maize crop. This has many detrimental effects on soil erosion and soil fertility, leading to reduction in maize yield and farmers' income, as well as adding to the haze problem in the lowlands. This study evaluated runoff, soil erosion, nutrient loss and maize yield on maize relay cropping with legumes without residue burning. The experiment was conducted in the rainy season of 2014 and 2015 in a highland field with 40 % slope at Santisuk district, Nan province in northern Thailand. There were 3 treatments consisting of the common farmer's practice of maize with residue burning, maize without residue burning and maize + lablab bean without residue burning, the measurement of runoff soil and N loss was based on three replicate 40 m^2 plots. Growing maize without residue burning reduced runoff, soil and N losses when compared with residue burning. Relaying legume into the maize crop further reduced runoff and soil loss. By the second year there was a small effect of not burning residues on maize yield, and significantly larger effect of adding a legume. Maize + lablab without burning yielded 22 % more maize grain than farmer's practice of residue burning, as well as an additional 0.77 t ha^{-1} of the lablab grain. Growing maize without residue burning land preparation practice and relay with a legume is promising as a method to reduce soil erosion and nutrients loss, increasing grain yields and farmers income, and lessening the impact on the haze problem. Further studies should explore more legumes for relaying and participatory research to determine the feasibility of how this practice may be adapted to management by highland farmers.

Keywords: Maize, N loss, runoff, soil erosion

Contact Address: Adirek Punyalue, Highland Research and Development Institute (Public Organisation), Dept. of Research, Chiang mai, Thailand, e-mail: adirek_p311@hotmail.com

ID 353

Impacts Assessment of Climate and Land Use Changes in Inland Valleys Agricultural Systems and Overview of Adaptation Strategies in Dano, West Africa

WENCESLAS SOMDA, BERNHARD TISCHBEIN, JANOS BOGARDI

University of Bonn, Center for Development Research (ZEF), Germany

Agriculture in West Africa is facing enormous challenges due to climate and land use changes. These challenges are driven by a high variability of rainfalls impacting the agricultural systems which are mostly rainfed, by the increasing pressure on the natural resources due to a growing population that is largely rural and dependent on agriculture and by the depletion of soil fertility.

Water management through the development of irrigation systems is therefore a necessity to intensify and to secure the agricultural production systems. Inland valleys are foreseen as a promising opportunity for adaptation to climate and land use changes thanks to their high and untapped potential in water and fertile soils. Different adaptation options exist as regards to infrastructures like the construction of reservoirs, to crops like the selection of more adapted varieties to dry and flooded conditions, to the management of land and water through resource-conserving techniques and supplemental irrigation inter alia. But there's a need for assessment of the impacts of climate and land use changes on these inland valleys and on the capacity of resilience from the different adaptation options cited above that is barely covered by literature.

The research focuses on five inland valleys in the Dano region in Burkina Faso. In order to observe different settings and improve appropriately their adaptation potential, two sites with reservoirs, two with partially controlled irrigation infrastructures and one with conventional farming were selected and monitored in rainy and dry seasons over two years. The water balance of these inland valleys have been set and irrigation systems performance indicators such as adequacy, productivity, sustainability and impacts on downstream areas of the catchment, have been applied under current and projected climate scenarios. Based on an understanding of the functioning of the hydro-agro-eco systems at the different sites, their evolution can be predicted and effective and site-specific adaptation strategies can be derived.

Keywords: Agriculture, climate change, inland valleys, water management

---

Contact Address: Wenceslas Somda, University of Bonn, Center for Development Research (ZEF), Walter-Flex-Str. 3, 53113 Bonn, Germany, e-mail: somda_wens@uni-bonn.de

Rapid Soil Mapping in Research for Development Projects: Combining Local Soil Knowledge and Gamma Spectrometry

NADJA REINHARDT, LUDGER HERRMANN

University of Hohenheim, Inst. of Soil Science and Land Evaluation, Germany

Unreliable rainfall and poor, degraded soils in central Tanzania lead to frequent food shortages, especially in rural areas. In the context of the TransSEC project (Innovating strategies to safeguard food security using technology and knowledge transfer: A people-centred approach) main food value chains were investigated in order to improve every step from soil preparation to product consumption. In the research strategy farmers were involved as decision makers and key informants as far as their domain was concerned. In order to improve local production systems, soil characterisation is of great importance as crop performance depends on the spatial distribution of soil properties. Suitable soil maps at sufficient resolution were not available. Unfortunately, soil mapping is costly and labor-intensive. Rapid and low-cost mapping approaches are required.

For this study, participatory soil mapping combined with gamma ray spectrometry was chosen for application in two villages of the Dodoma region in Tanzania. Both methods are known to deliver quick and valuable results. Participatory mapping, as basis to delimit the village territories and soil map units, applied focus group discussions, key informant interviews and transect walks. After discussions with the focus group members, reference profiles relating to typical soil units were chosen with the help of local farmers. Soil description followed FAO guidelines. Soil classification was done on the basis of the World Reference Base for Soil Resources. On transect walks, gamma radiation signatures were used to accurately allocate soil unit boundaries. With this approach, expensive and laborious chemical analyses for soil unit distinction on village scale became dispensable. Challenges during the map creation were posed by eroded and colluvial domains. In addition, terminological confusion arose from incorrect translation of tribal language terms and variable soil knowledge of focus group members and key informants. In the end, the combination of participatory mapping and gamma ray spectrometry led to sufficiently quick and reliable results with sufficient spatial resolution for site dependent cropping recommendations.

Keywords: Farmer stakeholder, natural radioactivity, participatory research, soil mapping methodology

Contact Address: Nadja Reinhardt, University of Hohenheim, Inst. of Soil Science and Land Evaluation, 70593 Stuttgart, Germany, e-mail: reinhardt.nadja.b@gmail.com

Impact of Soil Conservation Practices on Soil Health, Climate Smartness and Performance of Smallholder Farms in Western Kenya

ROLF SOMMER[1], JOB KIHARA[1], JOHN MUKALAMA[1], ANNE NJERI KARANJA[2], GEORGE AYAGA[3], JOHN NYAMBATI[3], BIRTHE PAUL[1]

[1] International Center for Tropical Agriculture (CIAT), Kenya
[2] Kenyatta University, Kenya
[3] Kenya Agriculture and Livestock Research Organization (KALRO), Kenya

Sustainable agricultural intensification is one of the major concerns to meet the growing demand for food, while conserving the natural resource basis for future generations. Undoubtedly, soils provide the fundamental basis for food production. The continued loss of soils and soil fertility is jeopardising the sustainability of agriculture in many parts of the world, and sub-Saharan Africa (SSA) in particular. Here, limitations in soil organic matter, the loss of soil health and key nutrients are major factors constraining agricultural productivity.

The poster provides first insights of an in-depth research on the impact of best-bet conservation practices (zero-tillage, residue retention, manuring, liming and mineral fertiliser application) on soil health, climate smartness and performance of smallholder farming systems in western Kenya. Therefore, a range of soil biological and soil health indicators of contrasting treatments (business as usual vs. best bets) were assessed in CIAT and KALRO long-term trials as well as on farmer's fields, such as the microbial diversity, structure and composition, and indicators describing nitrogen use efficiency, as well as greenhouse gas emissions from soil, in particular nitrous oxide, and soil organic carbon sequestration (potentials). These were compared against crop yields and other farm household performance indicators, to evaluate potential tradeoffs between ecological sustainability, resilience, income, workload and farmer's acceptance.

Insights from this study will help fine-tuning and guiding future implementation of soil protection and rehabilitation measures in Kenya under the BMZ/GIZ global programme on Soil Protection and Rehabilitation for Food Security, as part of the German One World — No Hunger initiative.

Keywords: Kenya, rehabilitation, smallholders, soil protection

---

Contact Address: Birthe Paul, International Center for Tropical Agriculture (CIAT), Tropical Forages Program, Nairobi, Kenya, e-mail: b.paul@cgiar.org

Soil Properties under Baobab Tree (*Adansonia digitata* L.) and their Influence on Fruit Nutrient Content

JAKUB HOUŠKA[1], MAKUEI AWUOL[2], JANA JAKLOVÁ[1], ONDREJ DRÁBEK[1], BOHDAN LOJKA[2], KATJA KEHLENBECK[3]

[1]*Czech University of Life Sciences Prague, Faculty of Agrobiology, Food and Natural Resources, Dept. of Soil Science and Soil Protection, Czech Republic*
[2]*Czech University of Life Sciences Prague, Fac. of Tropical AgriSciences, Dept. of Crop Sciences and Agroforestry, Czech Republic*
[3]*The World Agroforestry Centre (ICRAF), Kenya*

This study was conducted to determine soil properties under the baobab tree (*Adansonia digitata* L.) in Eastern and Coastal provinces of Kenya and to ascertain their influence on concentrations of baobabs' fruits nutrients. For this purpose 63 ICRAF baobab locations were used for collection of underlying soil. Chemical properties of the ICRAF baobab pulps (water content, ASCL, Total Acidity, Ash, Zn, Fe, Ca, Mg, K) were compared with the soil samples chemical composition to ascertain any relationships. Soil samples (Layer 1: 0–20 cm, Layer 2: 20–40 cm and Layer 3: 40–60 cm) were analysed for pH, cations in $BaCl_2$ solution using ICP measurement (Al, As, B, Ba, Be, Ca, Cd, Co, Cr, Cu, Fe, K, Mg, Mn, Na, Ni, P, Pb, S, Sb, Si, V, Zn) and plant available phosphorus according to Olsen. The statistical analyses PCA, RDA (Redundancy Analysis) and EFA (Exploration Factor Analysis) were performed. The results from PCA (with passively projected fruits parameters and locations) showed that high phosphorus concentrations (both in $BaCl_2$ and Olsen P) and pH in the main root zone are positively correlated with total acids concentrations in fruits whereas Fe and K correlate negatively. Ash is related to higher contents of Ca and S in Layer 3 and higher pH values in Layer 2. ASCL, water content and partly Fe in fruits show strong negative correlation to Sulphur in soils and positive correlation to Mn in both soil layers. Finally, Zn and Mg in baobab pulps are positively correlated to Fe and K (partly Cu) in Layer 3, while being negatively correlated with pH values. Similar results gives RDA (including Monte Carlo permutation test), where the soil properties served as environmental variables explaining the variability among fruits parameters. The statistically significant factors (with $\alpha = 0.05$) within the main baobab root zone were plant-avail. P, P (in $BaCl_2$), Si, K and pH. These findings are in agreement with the EFA. The study shows that fruits quality parameters are affected by soil chemistry, mainly phosphorus content (generally limiting factor in tropical soils) and properties related to bedrock type (silicates versus carbonates).

Keywords: *Adansonia digitata*, baobab, pulp chemistry, soil properties

Contact Address: Bohdan Lojka, Czech University of Life Sciences Prague, Fac. of Tropical Agri-Sciences, Dept. of Crop Sciences and Agroforestry, Kamýcká 129, 169 21 Prague, Czech Republic, e-mail: lojka@ftz.czu.cz

ID 1154

Climate change, remote sensing and GIS tools

High-Throughput and Homogeneous ^{13}C-Labelling of Plant Material for Fair Carbon Accounting in Maize Cropping Systems

JOHANNA I.F. SLAETS, CHRISTIAN RESCH, LEOPOLD MAYR, GEORG WELTIN, MARIA HEILING, ROMAN GRUBER, GERD DERCON

United Nations, Joint FAO/IAEA Division of Nuclear Techniques in Food and Agriculture, Austria

With growing political acknowledgement of the anthropogenic drivers and consequences of climate change, development of carbon accounting mechanisms is essential to distribute the burdens of greenhouse gas emission mitigation. Therefore, carbon storage and emission must be accurately quantified. Plant material labelled with ^{13}C can be used to measure carbon storage and carbon dioxide emission of various cropping practices under local conditions, both via *in situ* and incubation experiments. Such an approach, however, is only useful to stakeholders when plant material can be labelled homogeneously, cost-effectively and in sufficient quantity. Current pulse labelling methods often result in heterogeneous signatures and produce only limited amounts of material. We developed a high-throughput method in a walk-in growth chamber of 12 m^3, where ambient CO_2 concentration and isotopic composition are continuously monitored by an off-axis integrated cavity output spectroscope (Los Gatos Research), and are held at a δ^{13}C value between 350 and 400‰. Maize was chosen as a first test crop because of its global importance as cash crop and animal fodder, as well as the possibility to produce considerable amounts of biomass, yielding one kilogram dry matter of plant material per run. The resulting material showed a homogeneous isotopic labelling and variability in isotopic signature decreased with leaf age. Bottom leaves had an average δ^{13}C value of 277‰, with a 95 % confidence interval of [247, 307] whereas top leaves showed an average δ^{13}C value of 366‰, the 95 % confidence interval equalling [362, 370]. As C uptake by the plants in the initial growing phase is low, the effects of chamber leaking, although limited, were larger during this stage, which could be compensated for by having higher ^{13}C concentrations during early growth stages. Future steps of high-throughput ^{13}C labelling will focus on legumes and other cereal crops, opening research avenues for better understanding carbon dynamics in existing crop rotation systems. Furthermore, dual labelling with ^{13}C and ^{15}N would enable simultaneous accounting of not only CO_2 but also CO_2-equivalent emissions, such as N_2O. High-throughput isotopic labelling of plant material can thus provide accurate and cost-effective methods to establish fair plans for greenhouse gas emission reduction.

Keywords: ^{13}C, carbon accounting, CO_2, greenhouse gas emissions, stable isotopes

Contact Address: Johanna I.F. Slaets, United Nations, Joint FAO/IAEA Division of Nuclear Techniques in Food and Agriculture, Technikerstr. 8/7, 2340 Moedling, Austria, e-mail: hanna.slaets@gmail.com

Carbon Neutral Certified Coffee as an Innovation for Solidarity with Future Generations

ATHENA BIRKENBERG, REGINA BIRNER

University of Hohenheim, Inst. of Agricultural Sciences in the Tropics (Hans-Ruthenberg-Institute), Germany

Climate certifications are on the rise, but they have been doubted for their positive impact on the environment. This paper investigates the pioneer case of a Costa Rican coffee cooperative that produces the world's first coffee certified as carbon neutral by the independent international standard for demonstrating carbon neutrality, PAS 2060. It analyses on the one hand whether carbon neutral coffee is indeed more sustainable as expected by consumers. On the other hand, since pioneers often are successful where policies fail, this case-study considers the underlying success factors on Coopedota's way to carbon neutrality. The success factors are analysed not only qualitatively but also quantitatively using Social Network Analysis (SNA) and the Net-Map tool, a new way of visualising social networks. This paper finds that despite remaining challenges carbon neutral coffee can be more sustainable if the focus is placed on emission reduction instead of emission compensation. In this case, climate certification has the potential to mitigate climate change, motivate productivity and resource use efficiency and promote sustainability and solidarity with future generations at the same time. Past achievements in Coopedota's sustainability policy and strong actors that performed all necessary network functions were found as the most important success factor. Additionally we identified a success factor which has not been content of SNA in innovation systems so far: 'double linkages', meaning the provision of two different services between actors e.g. funding and advice. However the robustness and resilience of the innovation project might be threatened by the strong centrality structure of the network.

Keywords: Carbon neutral, coffee, Costa Rica, innovation systems, life cycle assessment, pioneer, social network analysis

Contact Address: Athena Birkenberg, University of Hohenheim, Inst. of Agricultural Sciences in the Tropics (Hans-Ruthenberg-Institute), Stuttgart, Germany, e-mail: a.birkenberg@uni-hohenheim.de

Towards Improved Land-Use Mapping of Irrigated Croplands: Evaluation of Field- and Pixel-Based Parametric and Non-Parametric Image Classification Algorithms

AMIT KUMAR BASUKALA[1], CARSTEN OLDENBURG[1], JÜRGEN SCHELLBERG[2], GUNTER MENZ[3], MURODJAN SULTANOV[4], OLENA DUBOVYK[2]

[1] *University of Bonn, Centre for Remote Sensing of Land Surfaces (ZFL), Germany*

[2] *University of Bonn, Inst. Crop Sci. and Res. Conserv. (INRES), Germany*

[3] *University of Bonn, Dept. of Geography, Remote Sensing Research Group, Germany*

[4] *Urgench State University, Uzbekistan*

An accurate agricultural land use map is an essential input for many agro-environmental applications such as crop land and water management. Enhancement of the accuracy of remote sensing based land use maps is still an ongoing process, since the development of the first classification algorithms for satellite datasets in the 1970s. With the rapid advances in computer technology, Earth Observation sensors and geographical information system (GIS), the field based (FB) and object based (OB) image analysis evolved along with the development of the machine learning algorithms. Studies showed that regardless of availability of different classification methods and algorithms no particular method has universal applicability and acceptability. This study aimed to compare different classification methods to provide recommendation on the choice of the suitable classification method for improved agriculture land use mapping of irrigated croplands. The comparison is made using two robust non-parametric machine learning algorithms, random forest (RF) and support vector machine (SVM), and a classical parametric algorithm, maximum likelihood (MLC) based on the multitemporal Landsat 8 OLI imagery. Accuracy assessment showed a significant higher overall accuracy (OA) of the machine learning FB-RF algorithm (87.69 %) and FB-SVM algorithm (89.23 %) over the PB-RF algorithm (78.28 %), PB-SVM (79.23 %) and PB- MLC (78.51 %). The lowest OA occurred with the FB-MLC (66.87 %). The kappa accuracy (KA) is also significantly higher for the FB parametric machine learning FB-RF algorithm and FB-SVM algorithm over the FB MLC and all PB algorithms based classifications. The FB-RF produced visually appealing real agricultural land use map of the area. Based on these results, we recommend the use of the FB based machine learning robust non-parametric algorithms for extracting land use information from satellite imagery captured over spatially heterogeneous irrigated croplands and imply them for further sustainable agro-environmental applications.

Keywords: Crop mapping, Landsat, maximum likelihood, random forest, support vector machine, Uzbekistan

Contact Address: Amit Kumar Basukala, University of Bonn, Centre for Remote Sensing of Land Surfaces (ZFL), Sebastian Str. 39, Bonn, Germany, e-mail: pblkamit@gmail.com

ID 595

Multi-Criteria, GIS and InVEST for Evaluation of REDD+: Case Study in Northern Thailand

GISELA QUAGLIA[1], MELVIN LIPPE[2], PRASIT WANGPAKAPATTANAWONG[3], GEORG CADISCH[1]

[1] *University of Hohenheim, Inst. of Agricultural Sciences in the Tropics (Hans-Ruthenberg-Institute), Germany*

[2] *University of Hohenheim, Inst. of Crop Science, Biobased Products and Energy Crops, Germany*

[3] *World Agroforestry Centre (ICRAF), Thailand*

The 'Reducing Emissions from Deforestation and forest Degradation' (REDD+) programme is promoted, in Southeast Asia and particularly in Thailand, as a cost-effective climate change mitigation option with co-benefits to improve food security, local livelihoods and to foster sustainable forest management. The needs of local communities are critical to develop REDD+ strategies that will be sustainable in the long run.

An integrated assessment framework for REDD+ and its effect on the social, environmental and economic aspects is presented for a case study area ($22.4\ \text{km}^2$) in Northern Thailand. Land use map and participatory approaches to develop scenario storylines based on local stakeholder opinions were combined in a GIS-based analysis to identify the most appropriate sites on a local scale. Spatially-explicit scenarios were developed using Multi-criteria Evaluation (MCE) by merging social and physical boundaries in combination with stakeholder interviews representing different levels of REDD+ knowledge, interest and influence as part of a suitability analysis. Field studies and aerial photos were employed to update and validate existing spatial land use information serving as further model input datasets. Model simulations with the Integrated Valuation of Ecosystem Services and Tradeoffs model (InVEST) were conducted to assess different stakeholder-driven future REDD+ scenarios to quantify environmental services and their tradeoffs.

Three REDD+ futures scenarios were obtained: 'Community', from interviews with community headmen, 'Compensatory' and 'Pragmatic' from the analysis of REDD+ factors as evaluated by key informant interviews. 'Compensatory' showed a higher preference of social over physical boundaries in MCE. Meanwhile, the physical boundaries such as distance to road, to community and slope were more relevant in 'Pragmatic'. The scenarios were evaluated with InVEST.

The participatory methods for scenario development can break down distances and incorporate community knowledge, hopes and perspectives into the REDD design process. This study illustrates a method for identifying and mapping landscapes for setting up a local REDD+ project. The framework and GIS tools demonstrated in the study could help policymakers, and project proponents to target projects considering multiple criteria that reflect the multiple expectations of REDD+.

Keywords: InVEST, multi-criteria evaluation, Thailand, participatory approach, REDD+

Contact Address: Gisela Quaglia, University of Hohenheim, Inst. of Agricultural Sciences in the Tropics (Hans-Ruthenberg-Institute), 70593 Stuttgart, Germany, e-mail: giselaquaglia@gmail.com

Urban Green Spaces Enhance Climate Change Mitigation in Cities of the Global South: The Case of Kumasi, Ghana

BERTRAND NERO, DANIEL CALLO-CONCHA, MANFRED DENICH

University of Bonn, Center for Development Research (ZEF), Germany

Urban green spaces (UGS) contribute to mitigate climate change impacts via carbon sequestration and offer several co-benefits in cities. This contribution, however, is omitted in most national and regional carbon stock estimates, and related literature in the global south is – at best – fragmentary. Therefore, this paper quantifies and maps the distribution of UGS above and below-ground carbon pools in Kumasi, Ghana. Vegetation carbon stocks were estimated using allometric equations for trees and destructive sampling for crops and other herbaceous plants. Soil organic carbon (SOC) was determined to a depth of 60 cm. Satellite imagery and GIS were used to map and extrapolate carbon stocks to a citywide scale.

In the metropolitan area of Kumasi, a total of 3,758 Gg of carbon is stored above-(vegetation) and below-ground (roots and soil). On average, 239 Mg C ha^{-1} is stored in trees and 81 Mg C ha^{-1} in the soil. Crops and herbs hold $<1\,\%$ of the total stock. There is no correlation between SOC and tree C stocks (r=0.1073, $p = 0.2982$). Vegetation carbon stocks differ among UGS ($p = 0.0071$). The highest SOC stocks are in cemeteries (111 Mg C ha^{-1}) and home gardens (105 Mg C ha^{-1}) while the lowest (46 Mg C ha^{-1}) occur under natural forest relics. No significant differences were observed in soils under all other UGS types. SOC stock dynamics within and between depths differ among UGS types ($p < 0.0001$).

Above and below-ground carbon stocks in Kumasi are quite enormous and sensitive to the UGS type. UGS should be accounted for in urban planning and included in national and regional carbon budgets. These findings complement the global carbon budget datasets and are relevant to urban climate change policy.

Keywords: Aboveground, allometric equations, belowground, carbon stocks, green spaces

Contact Address: Bertrand Nero, University of Bonn, Center for Development Research, Walter-Flex-Str. 3, D-53113 Bonn, Germany, e-mail: nerbefest@yahoo.com

The Role of Community Forests for Climate Change Adaptation in the Ayeyarwady Delta, Myanmar

MÉLANIE FEURER[1], JUERGEN BLASER[1], DAVID GRITTEN[2], MAUNG MAUNG THAN[2]

[1] *Bern University of Applied Sciences (BFH), School for Agricultural, Forest and Food Sciences, Switzerland*

[2] *The Center for People and Forests RECOFTC, Myanmar Country Program, Myanmar*

Community forests (CF) empower rural people to manage their own resources. In Myanmar's Ayeyarwady Delta, mangrove forests are important for communities' livelihoods. However, population growth, extension of rice production and unclear tenure rights are leading to deforestation and forest degradation. Additionally, in view of climate change, coastal communities are becoming more vulnerable. Experts predict sea level rise, irregular rainfall and more extreme weather events such as cyclone Nargis in 2008. As rice yields are declining, can mangrove restauration coupled with CF be a successful strategy to adapt to a changing climate?

This study aimed to assess communities' vulnerability and the potential of mangrove CF for climate change adaptation in the brackish water zone of Ayeyarwady Delta. Within four villages, 110 household interviews, 20 focus group discussions, key informant interviews and several participative research tools were applied. In addition 20 forest plots were analysed in terms of species composition and biomass density.

Major vulnerability factors are low education, tenure insecurity and depletion of natural resources. It was found that 25 % of total income in the study area is derived from CF products. The most important of those are crabs (80 %), which breed at the roots of mangrove trees. Income also comes from selling timber, fuelwood and Nypa palm. Other livelihoods consist of homegardens, small businesses, daily labour, long-term labour, livestock, remittances, fishing and farming, in that order. Apart from income opportunities, CF also provides housing material, fuelwood and a variety of food items. The communities are aware of changes in the climate. They already experience higher temperatures in summer, unpredictable rainfall and increased flooding, leading to salt intrusion on rice fields. During cyclone Nargis, however, community forests and homegardens proved to be more resilient than other land uses.

Summing up, the role of mangrove CF is crucial for livelihoods at present as well as in the future. A healthy forest which is managed sustainably has the potential to continuously provide goods for income generation and home consumption in addition to mitigating losses from extreme weather events. Thus, clear tenure rights and management principles through stakeholder dialogue are a must.

Keywords: Community forests, livelihoods, mangroves, Myanmar

Contact Address: Mélanie Feurer, Bern University of Applied Sciences (BFH), School for Agricultural, Forest and Food Sciences, Länggasse 85, 3052 Zollikofen, Switzerland, e-mail: melanie.feurer@bfh.ch

Collaborative Value Chain Innovation: A Partnership for Sustainable Intensification - The Case of Gusha Shinkurta Area, Awi Zone, Ethiopia

MISGANAW TESHAGER[1], GETACHEW ALEMAYEHU[1], ENYEW ADGO[1], YOSEPH
TEWODROS DELELEGN[2], JÖRN GERMER[3], FOLKARD ASCH[4],
BERNHARD FREYER[2]

[1]*Bahir Dar University (UBD), Ethiopia*

[2]*University of Natural Resources and Life Sciences (BOKU), Austria*

[3]*Sanergy, Engineering Office for Urban Sanitation and Energy Crop Cultivation in the Tropics and Subtropics, Germany*

[4]*University of Hohenheim, Germany*

In Ethiopia cash crop (maize, cereals, potato) based farm systems are widely promoted. To increase productivity and to better understand how to cope with climate change, this study presents a farmers value chain analysis to identify challenges and innovative practices, and viable adaptation options. Secondary documents were consulted to characterise, explore and analyse chain actors and linkages in the value chain. Qualitative interviews were held with ten respondents at regional, zonal and Woredas level, and 120 farmers were interviewed at Kebele level. Non-structured in-depth interviews were administered to 30 case farmers at the Kebele. Twelve focus group discussions composing 10-12 farmers were held. Moreover, a verification/validation workshop was held which drew participants from actors/partners in the chain to gain an understanding of prioritised needs and innovations. In the whole discourse farmers recognised the following agronomic practices as a possible adverse reduction measures to climate change: scheduling and optimising of sowing dates, appropriate planting methods like row planting which has a notable contribution to fertiliser management and weed management, lower planting density, organic matter fertilisation and crop residue maintenance, composts and farmyard manure, optimisation of crop rotation, replacing bare fallow with fallow crops, use of leguminous crops such as clover, lentil, pea, and bean inter-cropping, and supplement irrigation at critical growth stage of crops. The core challenges from farmer's perspective were: absence of irrigation scheme, lack of marketing cooperatives, inappropriate brokering, weak output market and absence of sustainable finance. From the market chain analysis it was found very little best practices to scale up, which is associated with farmer's unwillingness to cooperate, and untimely arrival of rainfall. Training, farm visits and workshops helped farmers to enhance their capacity in terms of selecting appropriate climate change adaptation options. The government with other relevant actors should establish farmers marketing and economic cooperatives to optimise farmer-market relations. An inclusive financial sector should be in place, promotion of the existing one (like micro finance) for accessing loan to the sustainably work of the value chain (e.g. energy saving stoves, vegetable farming), linking to service providers (e.g. improved seeds).

Keywords: Climate change adaptation, collaboration, innovation, value chain

Contact Address: Misganaw Teshager, Bahir Dar University, Disaster Risk Management, Bahir Dar, Ethiopia, e-mail: tmisganaw16@gmail.com

ID 964

Analysis of the On-Set of Seasonal Rainfall for Designing Climate Smart Strategies for Fair Use of Resources

PATRICK AWUOR OORO[1], RHODA BIRECH[2], JOYCE MALING'A[1], JÖRN GERMER[3], FOLKARD ASCH[3], BERNHARD FREYER[4], RAEL TAIY[5]

[1] *Kenya Agricultural and Livestock Research Organization (KALRO), Food Crops Research Institute-Njoro, Kenya*

[2] *Egerton University, Crops, Horticulture and Soil Chemistry, Kenya*

[3] *University of Hohenheim, Inst. of Agricultural Sciences in the Tropics (Hans-Ruthenberg-Institute), Germany*

[4] *University of Natural Resources and Life Sciences (BOKU), Division of Organic Farming, Austria*

[5] *Ministry of Agriculture, Livestock and Fischeries, Sector Development Support Programme, Uasin Gishu County, Kenya*

Kenya's climate is prone to extended rainfall deficits. In order to adapt to this, skilful prediction of seasonal (March-April-May) rainfall would bring sound strategies for the enhancement of food security to many regions of the country that depend on rainfed agriculture. Climate-smart agriculture (CSA) would help to address the challenges of meeting the growing demand for food among others. In trying to implement strategies for CSA there are many approaches that have been employed including the use of time of planting among others. Due to climate change the traditional time of planting has become more or less elusive. This therefore calls for the understanding of the long term statistics on the dates of the most probable time for on-set of seasonal rainfall. This study analysed long term rainfall data of Kenya Agricultural Research Organisation (KALRO) Njoro covering March-May (MAM) period between 1960 and 2014 using Instat computer package. The study generated information on the earliest start date, latest start date and mean start date for the on-set of rains in Njoro. Results indicate that there exists organised progression of the earliest start date for the on-set of rains (minimum of 20 mm consistently without dry spell within nine days) between 1960 and 2014 fell on the 2nd of March, the latest start date was on the 6 th July which was the 188th day (this means there was failure of the seasonal rains in 1961) whereas the mean start date for on-set of rains fell on 1 st April translating into failure of season in that year in Kenya. The information generated will be used for the design of CSA strategies using the mean start date for the on-set of rains to guide the farmers on fair and economical use of resources. At the same time the information will be used to make climate smart choices for the type of crops to plant at what time in Njoro.

Keywords: Climate change, climate smart agriculture, MAM

Contact Address: Patrick Awuor Ooro, Kenya Agricultural and Livestock Research Organization (KALRO), Food Crops Research Institute-Njoro, Nakuru-Njoro, 20107 Nakuru, Kenya, e-mail: paooro@yahoo.com

Greenhouse Gas Assessment of Soybean Biodiesel in Brazil

Xin You[1], Guilherme Silva Raucci[2], Carlos Clemente Cerri[2], Carlos Eduardo P. Cerri[2], Priscila Aparecida Alves[3], Francisco F.C. Mello[3], Leidivan de Almeida Frazão[2], Cindy Silva Moreira[3]

[1] *University of Hohenheim, Institute of Crop Science, Group of Biobased Products and Energy Crops, Germany*

[2] *University of São Paulo, Faculty of Agriculture Luiz de Queiroz, Brazil*

[3] *DeltaCO2 - Sustentabilidade Ambiental, Brazil*

Biodiesel has been playing an increasingly important role in Brazilian energy matrix and promoting the national bio-based economy. The biodiesel production in Brazil has grown from 736 m^3 in 2005 to approximately 4.4 million m^3 in 2014. Among all the inputs, soybean predominate the biodiesel production in Brazil with a share of 77.2% in 2014 and made Brazil the 2nd largest biodiesel producer worldwide. Current models used in energy balance reports have shown positive net energy ratio, indicating the renewability of soybean biodiesel. However, the environmental impacts and the fair use of this agricultural resource have debatably come to public attention. Consumers value more and more the environmental sustainability of agricultural products, with a particular interest in the greenhouse gas (GHG) emissions as a sustainability indicator. For policy and decision making processes, this sustainability indicator is also being progressively demanded. To assess the GHG emission of the soybean biodiesel production in Brazil, we used the data mainly from the Center West region and partly from the neighbour regions, which represent more than 70% of the whole soybean production in Brazil. A life cycle assessment (LCA) model from cradle to distribution was also integrated into our calculation and was divided into four stages: the field stage; the extraction stage; the production stage; the distribution and delivery stage. Carbon footprint through all stages are calculated and evaluated. Results show an average GHG emission of 316 g COeq kg^{-1} of soybean in agricultural stage. The largest source of GHG emission from the agricultural production in Brazil is the decomposition of crop residues (36%). Production stage contributes the highest amount of GHG emssion (52%) in a non-integrated system, which suggests the emerging integrated system (combined units from extraction and production) might have high potential in GHG emission reduction. The whole study with the integration of the four life cycle stages of soybean biodiesel will contribute to identify the main GHG emission source in the production chain of Brazilian soybean biodiesel and suggest the mitigation priority for policy and decision making.

Keywords: Carbon footprint, emission factors, life cycle stages

Contact Address: Xin You, University of Hohenheim, Institute of Crop Science, Group of Biobased Products and Energy Crops, Fruwirthstr. 23, 70599 Stuttgart, Germany, e-mail: Xin_You@uni-hohenheim.de

ID 995

Climate Change Awareness and Smallholder-Oriented Constraints and Opportunities in the Upper Rift Valley in Ethiopia

CORDULA WITTEKIND, FLORENS EWICH, KURT-JOHANNES PETERS

Humboldt-Universität zu Berlin, ADT-Institute of Agricultural and Horticultural Sciences, Germany

Climate change, its variability, interlinkages and effects on agriculture are manifold and will influence Ethiopia significantly. While climate model projections show increasing temperatures throughout the year for the entire country, precipitation projections are less conclusive, both in temporal as in spatial scale. Unreliable rainfall, growing water scarcity, failed harvests and the introduction of new pests are some of the factors that increase pressure on producers, especially small-scale farmers. Currently worsened by El Niño, these developments threaten wide parts of the country with famine. This paper presents results of a field study that has been conducted in September 2015 among vegetable growers and associated stakeholders to examine climate change awareness, as well as smallholder-oriented constraints and opportunities in the Upper Rift Valley in Ethiopia. The area is characterised by large surface water bodies, which are used for irrigation and therefore allow for the establishment of horticultural production. Through semi-structured interviews of stakeholders from government level to producers the importance of climate change, major challenges and already employed mitigation strategies were assessed and substantiated by literature research. In the course of the study, opportunities were identified that allow for decreasing the ramifications of climate change. Concerning government engagement, most actions are inadequate and fail to address the important issues for farmers, such as declining water resources, soil protection, climate information, production system adjustments, appropriate germplasm, phyto-health measures, market infrastructure and land tenure system. For farmers, restricted access to relevant knowledge, ignorance of water use efficiency, unsustainable, non-adapted farming techniques and little diversity of too water intensive crops are the biggest obstacles. Forward-looking research and institutional responsibility are absent. Irrigation is considered to be the most important measure for mitigating the effects of climate change, though not based on long-term hydrological evidence and prevailing widespread overuse of available water resources. As long as water resources are perceived to be available ad infinitum, irrigation will be seen as the sole mitigation strategy, prohibiting urgently required innovation.

Keywords: Constraints, enabling environment, Ethiopia, horticultural production, irrigation, mitigation, opportunities, Rift Valley, smallholder farmers, water

Contact Address: Florens Ewich, Humboldt-Universität zu Berlin, ADT-Institute of Agricultural and Horticultural Sciences, Otawistraße 23, 13351 Berlin, Germany, e-mail: florens.ewich@gmail.com

Sea Level Rise: Evaluating Adaptive Strategies and Options

RIDWAN BELLO

University of St Andrews, Department of Geography and Sustainable Development, United Kingdom

As the reality of climate change draws closer, discussions among scholars and policy makers are beginning to shift from climate change mitigation to adaptation. One of the climate change impacts that surely concerns millions of people living in coastal communities globally is sea level rise. Whether it is city planners in New York, coastal dwellers in Lagos or rice farmers in coastal Indonesian villages, the question of how to adapt to projected rise in future sea levels is an important one. Drawing upon a wide spectrum of existing literature, this study outlines the various typologies of adaptive strategies to sea level rise that have been proposed, and presents a comparative analysis of three adaptive strategies (retreat, accommodate and protect) which have thus far been the most accepted typology. In addition, the criteria that may be employed to evaluate alternative options when faced with the decision of choosing specific sea level rise adaptation measures are also discussed. The comparative analysis brings to light the merits and demerits of the retreat, accommodate and protect strategies. Each strategy was found to appeal to different social, economic, technological and ecological settings, and no single strategy fits into all kinds of settings. In terms of criteria for evaluating alternative adaptation options, five criteria namely effectiveness, efficiency, performance under uncertainty, sustainability and equity are proposed. This study concludes that the options available to coastal communities to adapt to sea level rise are many, but so are the factors to consider, and apparently the decision of which option(s) to apply will be far from simple or straight forward. It is the hope that the ideas discussed in this study will assist in making the decision-making process a little less cumbersome.

Keywords: Adaptive strategy, climate change, sea level rise

Contact Address: Ridwan Bello, University of St Andrews, Department of Geography and Sustainable Development, 5304 St Mary Street, KY16 8BP St Andrews, United Kingdom, e-mail: ridwanbbello@gmail.com

ID 148

The BOKU CO_2 Compensation System

DOMINIK SCHMITZ[1], THOMAS LINDENTHAL[1], FLORIAN A. PELOSCHEK[2]

[1] *Centre for Global Change and Sustainability, Austria*

[2] *University of Natural Resources and Life Sciences (BOKU), Centre for Development Research, Austria*

Climate mitigation projects can be carried out in different sectors, for example, the reforestation of fallow area with trees that absorb CO_2 from the air or the replacement of a diesel generator in a rural area by a photovoltaic system.

The core of the BOKU CO_2 compensation system are long term, innovative and participatory climate mitigation projects which are planned, funded, implemented and supported in host countries. Mostly BOKU staff had been involved in the area through joint research projects already prior to project intervention. The goal of BOKU mitigation projects is not only climate protection, but also the structural and sustainable change in the area! Therefore, the scientific CO_2 advisory board selects only those carbon offset projects which have a holistic approach e.g. through the cooperation of science and local population to develop comprehensive climate programs and which have varied positive benefits such as biodiversity, water and soil protection, gender equality, participation, education and training, entrepreneurship opportunities for the local economy.

The current BOKU climate mitigation projects are located in Ethiopia, Nepal and Costa Rica. The first project started 2012 in Ethiopia where suitable areas and tree species for afforestation had been selected in a participatory process with the local land users. This participatory process lasted more than a year and a joint Community Use Plan for the sustainable management had been agreed on. The permanence of the afforestation, the first 10.000 seedlings were planted in June 2015, can now be secured by a broad acceptance of the project by the land users.

The CO_2 price for BOKU climate mitigation project is between 22€ and 65€. The costs of the project represent the project development costs of each climate mitigation project. While a 5 % management fee for administration purpose is added. In addition to air emissions, companies or individuals can also compensate the CO_2 damage caused by its operations or specific products / processes emissions.

Keywords: Co-benefits, CO_2 compensation, financing CO_2 mitigation projects of BOKU

Contact Address: Dominik Schmitz, Centre for Global Change and Sustainability, Borkowskigasse 4, 1190 Vienna, Austria, e-mail: dominik.schmitz@boku.ac.at

Climate Impact Analysis and Adaptation Strategies to Climate Change on Peanut in Senegal

BABACAR FAYE[1], HEIDI WEBBER[2], THOMAS GAISER[2]

[1] University of Cape Coast, West African Science Service Center on Climate Change and Adapted Land Use (WASCAL), Ghana

[2] University of Bonn, Inst. Crop Sci. and Res. Conserv. (INRES), Germany

Climate change is projected to bring drier conditions to the western Sahel region, together with an increase of temperature and carbon dioxide (CO_2).

Our study was conducted in a part of this sub regional, assessed the impacts of climate change on peanut yield and proposed adaptation strategies for two sites in Senegal. Moreover, the effects of CO_2 variation on crop growth and yield were quantified under different climate change scenarios for four regional climate models. Biomass and seed yield were simulated for a present climate (1981-2010) and RCP4.5 and RCP8.5 scenarios (2016-2045) under dry season and rainfed conditions with and without irrigation. It was found that projected climate change without CO_2 elevation may impact negatively both biomass and seed yield for RCP4.5 and RCP8.5 in both seasons. For biomass the maximum change goes up to -12 % for RCP4.5 and 15 % for RCP8.5. While for seed, it goes up to -42.1 % for RCP4.5 to -55.8 % for RCP8.5. However, positive yield changes result when CO_2 concentration increase from 369 ppm to 439 pmm for RCP4.5 and 469 ppm for RCP8.5 for the scenario period of up to 5.4 % and 12.4 % for RCP4.5 and RCP8.5 respectively for biomass and for seed yield up to 9.6 % for RCP4.5 and 13.2 % for RCP8.5.

Under dry season conditions, where maximum air temperature are often higher than 36°C at these sites, the negative effects of climate change is greater than during the rainy season where maximum air temperature is typically lower than 35°C when air temperature is used in simulations. In addition, it was found that the greater the maximum air temperature is, the more the negative effects on yield record the higher values with is due to heat stress. Current sowing dates, in both sites, led to improved yield levels under climate change. Furthermore, short season varieties had greater relative yield changes and can therefore be recommended as adaptation strategy in these two sites to cope with the impact of early rain cessation. It is concluded that climate change will have positive impact on peanut yield in Senegal due to the elevated of CO_2 together with shorter season varieties.

Keywords: Adaptations, climate change, peanut, Senegal

Contact Address: Babacar Faye, University of Cape Coast, West African Science Service Center on Climate Change and Adapted Land Use (WASCAL), Cape Coast, Ghana, e-mail: bbcrfy@yahoo.fr

ID 372

The Collective Learning Community for Climate Change Adaptation in Mauche Ward of Njoro Sub-County, Kenya

Rael Taiy[1], Bernhard Freyer[2], Christopher Onyango[3], Agnes Nkurumwa[3], Rhoda Birech[4], Patrick Awuor Ooro[5]

[1]*Ministry of Agriculture, Livestock and Fischeries, Sector Development Support Programme, Uasin Gishu County, Kenya*

[2]*University of Natural Resources and Life Sciences (BOKU), Division of Organic Farming, Austria*

[3]*Egerton University, Agricultural Education and Extension, Kenya*

[4]*Egerton University, Crops, Horticulture and Soil Chemistry, Kenya*

[5]*Kenya Agricultural and Livestock Research Organization (KALRO), Food Crops Research Institute-Njoro, Kenya*

Participatory innovation in agriculture is key in enhancing food security in sub-Sahara Africa. The collective learning community (CLC) concept entails bringing people together for shared learning, discovery and generation of knowledge. It enhances formation of networks to promote continuous interaction and communication. Farmers in Mauche Ward of Njoro Sub-County depend on rain fed agriculture which is highly vulnerable to rainfall variability and the negative effects of climate change (CC). Smallholder farmers' Strategies to Cope with CC project established: CLC comprising of farmers and other potato value chain actors to exchange knowledge and collaboratively innovate for climate change adaptation. The Net-Map toolbox was used to assess the links between actors based on exchange of information, sharing of resources and influence. This enabled the CLC to clarify roles and power relations among the actors, and to identify weak points in the network that needed addressing. Chomosa farmers group was the centre of the project and focus of interventions on optimising the production to adapt to CC and storage of potato. The challenge was that there was no linkage between Chomosa farmers group and processors, and the share of income at the market was rather low. Currently the traders dominate the market. To negotiate with the local Njoro canning factory for potato selling, we co-opted the area chief, who has a lot of power and influence, into our CLC committee. As a result it was possible to negotiate a better potato price. The study recommends collective action for potato marketing, contract farming and involving of local leadership in CC adaptation initiatives for sustainability.

Keywords: Access to market, climate change adaptation, collective learning, food security, power relations

Contact Address: Rael Taiy, Ministry of Agriculture, Livestock and Fischeries, Sector Development Support Programme, Uasin Gishu County, P.O. Box 9361, 30100 Eldoret, Kenya, e-mail: raeltaiy@yahoo.com

Monitoring Soil Moisture Patterns in an Agriculturally Used Wetland in Central Uganda

Geofrey Gabiri[1], Bernd Diekkrüger[1], Constanze Leemhuis[2],
Frank Thonfeld[1]

[1] *University of Bonn, Dept. of Geography, Germany*
[2] *University of Bonn, Center for Development Research (ZEF), Germany*

The recent changes in temporal and spatial precipitation patterns in rainfed agricultural communities of East Africa, has tremendously affected the agricultural production in the region. Due to their prolonged plant water availability throughout the year wetlands among the marginal land areas are under intensive pressures for agricultural food production. Intensive cultivation of wetlands may alter their biophysical status hence affecting soil water availability and other water related ecosystem services across. Therefore, this study aims at understanding the spatial and temporal soil moisture variability of various hydrological regimes of an inland valley wetland (1100 m a.s.l.) in Uganda, East Africa. Land use related soil physical properties and spatial and temporal patterns of soil moisture dynamics are analysed. The inland valley wetland is mainly characterised by a mosaic land use pattern of upland crops, arrow roots with few plots left as fallows all year. Based on a Sentinel 2 satellite image from 2015 and ground truth data, a land cover map is developed. Since September 2014, soil moisture dynamics along four transects in the wetland covering three hydrological regimes (centre, middle, and fringe) are monitored using a frequency domain reflectometry (FDR) system. Furthermore, stream and groundwater levels are continuously measured for the same period. Anova test revealed significance difference ($p < 0.05$) in soil moisture between the fringe and the other regimes while no statistical significant difference in soil moisture between middle and centre is observed. Average soil moisture levels are relatively high throughout the observation period due to high shallow groundwater tables and lateral flows from the adjacent slopes. Land use systems significantly influence soil moisture as arrow roots and fallow plots generally maintain higher mean soil moisture levels compared to upland crops plots situated at the valley bottom of the wetland. Soil organic carbon and texture was significantly variable ($p < 0.05$) across all wetland transects. This research is part of the GlobE wetlands project providing sustainable and scientifically based guidelines for inland valley wetland management in East Africa.

Keywords: FDR, soil moisture, Uganda, wetland

Contact Address: Geofrey Gabiri, University of Bonn, Department of Geography, Meckenheimer Allee 166 53115 Bonn, 53115 Bonn, Germany, e-mail: geofreygabiri@gmail.com

ID 701

Detection of Land Cover Changes Using Multi-Temporal Satellite Imagery

WAFA NORI

University of Kordofan, Forest and Range Science, Sudan

Multi-temporal Landsat ETM+ and Aster data acquired on early dry season dates in 2003 and 2006 have been used for classification of land cover. Processing and classification of data for late rainy season which will extend the temporal series is currently underway. For temporal analysis, image calibration was necessary to reduce or eliminate differences due to atmospheric or sensor variations between the two dates. Absolute calibration using atmospheric corrections and sensor drift calibration was conducted by the software Geomatica. In order to enhance the image features a PCA fusion technique were applied by using the panchromatic and multispectral bands of Landsat ETM and Aster data, as a following step supervised maximum likelihood classification of PCA 2003 and 2006 scenes was conducted. In this study training data were selected in easily identifiable areas of the following four classes: grassland, closed forest, open forest and bareland. Following classification of imagery from the individual years, a post-classification approach comparing classification maps of 2003 and 2006 was applied. An advantage of the approach is that it provides "from-to" change information. As part of our analysis we have compared area estimates from the Landsat classifications with aster classification.

Results of supervised classification of ETM and Aster imagery have been evaluated for the study area. For Landsat ETM data of the year 2003, the Kappa coefficient indicates substantial agreement with values of 88.8 percent and the overall accuracy is 91.9 percent. For Aster data of the year 2006, the Kappa coefficient indicates substantial agreement by a value of 89.4 percent and overall accuracy with 92.1 percent. A post-classification result indicated that, closed forest and open forest are the most important change. From 2003 to 2006, closed forest increased by 8.9 %, or 9825 hectares and open forest increased by 9.1 % or 10074, while grassland decreased by 19.2 % or 21165 hectares and bareland showed very slight changes.

Keywords: Change detection, remote sensing

Contact Address: Wafa Nori, University of Kordofan, Forest and Range Science, Algama Street, 160 Elobied, Sudan, e-mail: waffanori@gmail.com

Estimation of Aboveground Volume, Carbon Stocks and NPP of Forests in the Amhara Region, Ethiopia Using Terrestrial and Satellite Data

Kibruyesfa Sisay[1], Christopher Thurnher[1], Beyene Belay[2], Tesfaye Teklehaymanot[3], Khlot Gebrehana[3], Sibhatu Abera[3], Hadera Kahesay[3], Hubert Hasenauer[1]

[1] University of Natural Resources and Life Sciences (BOKU), Inst. of Silviculture, Austria

[2] University of Natural Resources and Life Sciences (BOKU), Forest and Soil Sciences, Austria

[3] Amhara Agricultural Research Institute, Forestry Research Directorate, Ethiopia

In the last several years, the interest in forest productivity estimation has increased due to its importance for forest management, carbon stock, wood and other ecosystem services. However, no estimates of productivity, stored volume and carbon of different forest cover types exist throughout the Amhara region, Ethiopia. The objectives of this study are to estimate aboveground volume, carbon and net primary productivity (NPP) of the Amhara region. This will be done by (i) inventory, (iii) land cover classification and (iii) extrapolation of terrestrial estimates over the whole region based on the classified map. We collected inventory data from 5 forest regions (Ambober, Gelawdiwos, Katassi, Mahiberesilasse and Taragedam) with 4 natural forests, 2 plantation forests and 1 exclosure. The sites were selected to address the different forest types (natural forest, woodland and shrub land) in different agro-ecological zones of Amhara region. The terrestrial inventory data come from 220 sample plots. Individual tree parameters such as DBH, height, core increment samples, etc were collected to calculate the above ground volume, carbon and NPP for the 5 study regions. We obtained a land cover map from the Amhara Bureau of Agriculture and further regrouped it in to natural forest, shrub land, woodland and agriculture land in order to match with our inventory forest types. In the final step, we extrapolated our terrestrial volume, carbon and NPP over the entire region. The methodology presented here demonstrates the possibility of estimating forest volume, carbon stock and their productivity for the entire Amhara region. It can also be further improved by addressing more land cover types and integrating fine resolution land cover maps.

Keywords: Carbon, Ethiopia, land cover classification, NPP

Contact Address: Kibruyesfa Sisay, University of Natural Resources and Life Sciences (BOKU), Institute of Silviculture, Peter-Jordan-Straße 82, 1190 Vienna, Austria, e-mail: kibruyesfa.ejigu@students.boku.ac.at

ID 305

Estimation of Actual Evapotranspiration Using Remote Sensing Based Surface Energy Balance System at the Data Scarce Kabul River Basin of Afghanistan

FAZLULLAH AKHTAR[1], BERNHARD TISCHBEIN[1], USMAN KHALID AWAN[2],
UMAR WAQAS LIAQAT[3]

[1] *University of Bonn, Center for Development Research (ZEF), Germany*

[2] *International Center for Agricultural Research in the Dry Areas (ICARDA), Egypt*

[3] *Hanyang University, Dept. of Civil and Environmental Engineering, Republic of Korea*

Irrigated agriculture plays a vital role in providing food and economic gains to the people of Afghanistan. Winter snowfall in the upstream of the Kabul River Basin (KRB) is the only source of water supply to meet the water requirements of diverse crops. Mismanagement of the available water resources also triggers conflicts among the water users and adversely affects the ecosystem services in the KRB. For improved irrigation performance, accurate estimation of consumptive water use at a high spatial and temporal scale is key to strategic planning and operational water management. In this study the consumptive water use (actual evapotranspiration (AET)), an important irrigation performance indicator was estimated at the lower reaches of KRB (Nangarhar province). These estimations were undertaken at strategically important seasonal and annual time intervals, covering a period of 2003–2013 in the data-scarce environment of KRB. The Global Land Data Assimilation System (GLDAS) and Moderate-Resolution Imaging Spectroradiometer (MODIS) products were used as input parameters to Surface Energy Balance System (SEBS) for estimating AET. As a result, the annual average AET estimated was 552 ± 76 mm for the entire period while the minimum and maximum AET recorded was 428 ± 76 mm and 728 ± 76 mm in the year 2004 and 2006, respectively. The relatively lower AET in 2004 attests to the prevailing drought conditions in the country during that period. Similarly, the decadal average AET for winter (October-April) and summer (May-September) seasons were 215 ± 68 and 340 ± 29 mm respectively. The higher AET in summer season is due to the fact of dominant wheat and barley crops' cultivation over 10 % and 3.3 % of the land area of the Nangarhar province respectively. The decadal AET estimation at segregated spatial units as under this study can be efficiently utilised as an assessment marker of irrigation performance in sub-units of the large KRB. It provides guidelines for the regional water stakeholders to identify the bottleneck in water allocation for optimised strategic and operational performance.

Keywords: Actual evapotranspiration, data scarcity, surface energy balance system

Contact Address: Fazlullah Akhtar, University of Bonn, Center for Development Research (ZEF), Walter-Flex-Str. 3, 53113 Bonn, Germany, e-mail: fakhtar@uni-bonn.de

Assessment and Prediction of Unsustainable Land Use Practices Impact on Vegetation Degradation in Semi-Arid Sudan

ABDELNASIR IBRAHIM ALI HANO[1], ELMAR CSAPLOVICS[2]

[1]*University of Khartoum, Dept. of Conservation and Protection, Sudan*
[2]*Technische Universität Dresden, Inst. of Photogrammetry and Remote Sensing, Germany*

Vegetation cover is a critical key component of an ecosystem; particularly its importance is increasingly to get in arid land environments. Therefore vegetation degradation leads to environmental problems at local, national and international scale. Probably the unsustainable land use patterns which have been practicing in semi arid region of Sudan and most of the developing countries are considered the main causative vegetation degrading factors. Thus, the research aimed at assessing unsustainable land use patterns which were practicing in the past to link with the present and predicting the future. The methodology relied upon remote sensing and GIS technology supported by land survey for obtaining spatial and temporal information of 37 years (1972–2009) for the assessment. Then the extracted information was used as data, inserted in SSPS software for analysing and finding out SPSS- Pearson coefficient correlation matrix (PCM) results and multi-linear regression model for the prediction. The study was applied in Elgetiena Locality of White Nile State in Sudan. The findings revealed that a partial geospatial mutual conversion occurred between the vegetation cover (VC) and the LU activities which led to vegetation cover degradation during 1973 – 1986 and 1986 – 2009 respectively. The important PCM output depicted that: VC correlation with the fallow land was very strong and significant (0.995**). The resultant model of VC is VC = 735.519 – 1.105falow land – 3.357 residential area indicating that the fallow land and residential area will cause and determine VC in the future. The study is critical pre step for sustainable management of land use patterns and vegetation cover in semiarid land.

Keywords: Land use, remote sensing, semiarid, vegetation degradation

Contact Address: Abdelnasir Ibrahim Ali Hano, University of Khartoum, Dept. of Conservation and Protection, Ameen karib street, 13311 Khartoum, Sudan, e-mail: nasirhanno@gmail.com

 ID 884

Agrobiodiversity, ecology and ecosystem services

Driving Factors of Agrobiodiversity: Which Characteristics Influence Intra-Household Potato Diversity in the Peruvian Andes?

SOPHIA LÜTTRINGHAUS[1], SEVERIN POLREICH[2], WILLY PRADEL[3], VICTOR SUAREZ[3], STEF DE HAAN[3]

[1] *HFFA Research GmbH, Germany*

[2] *International Potato Center / CIM, Global Program of Genetic Resources, Peru*

[3] *International Potato Center, Peru*

Domesticated potatoes (*Solanum* spp.) originated in the Andes. Genetic hotspots of this important staple food exist throughout the mountain range. The conservation of potato diversity (and agrobiodiversity in general) is necessary to ensure functioning ecosystems and food security. Sufficient genetic material is the backbone of evolution and breeding. Despite agricultural modernisation (by e.g. introducing improved potato varieties), smallholder farmers continue to cultivate a large number of potato landraces. The initiative Chirapaq Ñan promotes *in-situ* conservation of such potato landraces and monitors some of their hotspots across the Andes. So far, the initiative's focus was cataloguing cultivated landraces and their genetic resources. Now, the better understanding of farmers' varietal choice is an additional aim. That is crucial to efficiently design and carry out *in-situ* projects. This study contributes to these efforts by assessing socioeconomic and environmental characteristics, which influence farming households' potato diversity. After literature review and expert interviews, eleven independent variables of the domains location, household assets, potato production and cultural factors were chosen. A binary dependent variable assigning farmers with up to three landrace varieties to the low potato diversity group and the spare to the high diversity group was created. Subsequently we ran a binary logistic regression model with household data from two Central Andean Peruvian provinces. The International Potato Center (CIP) collected these data in production year 2011/12. Results showed that four variables have a significant impact on intra-household potato diversity. These are the province in which farmers reside, their wealth (measured by cows per household), their level of technology adoption (number of improved varieties per household), and their participation in potato fairs. This study provides an overview of possible incentives and disincentives of potato diversity. Future research should apply a mix of quantitative and qualitative methods to better capture and analyse farmers' intrinsic value systems regarding agrobiodiversity and changing varietal preferences.

Keywords: Andes, food security, genetic hotspots, *in-situ* conservation, landraces, Peru, potato, smallholder farmers

Contact Address: Sophia Lüttringhaus, HFFA Research GmbH, Bülowstr. 66, 10783 Berlin, Germany, e-mail: sophia.luettringhaus@gmx.de

Biodiversity Assessment in Rubber Plantations – A Comparison of Different Species' Requests

INGA HÄUSER, MARC COTTER, FRANZISKA K. HARICH, PIA HE, ANNA C. TREYDTE, KONRAD MARTIN, JOACHIM SAUERBORN

University of Hohenheim, Inst. of Agricultural Sciences in the Tropics (Hans-Ruthenberg-Institute), Germany

Solidarity in a competing world can be seen from different perspectives. Looking from an intergenerational viewpoint, declining biodiversity may hamper potential options of future generations. Under intensive agricultural activities biodiversity is often declining rapidly, heating up the "sharing or sparing" discussion. Our study shows the impact of large-scale rubber plantations on biodiversity, represented by different plant and animal species. We used genuine data derived from up to eight years of multidisciplinary field research. Primary data on the distribution of vascular plants, pollinator species, ground beetles, ungulates and other selected mammals were collected in two study sites in Southwest China and Southern Thailand. The two sites shared similarities in land use and included intensively cultivated rubber plantations bordering protected areas. We supplemented these data with literature studies on the impact of rubber cultivation on the diversity of amphibians, reptiles and birds (all along mainland South East Asia). Based on this combination, we developed a classification scheme that enables the integration of different facets of biodiversity: 1) diversity of red list species representing a conservation approach (red list), 2) diversity as such representing intrinsic values of biodiversity (aggregated biodiversity), and 3) diversity of species with human use value (medicinal plants and bees) representing an anthropocentric approach (human use). Species diversity was normalised to show the impact rubber cultivation has on multiple levels of biodiversity. This resulted in a matrix of different land use types and their suitability as habitat for the respective species groups. The process presented allows for an application in the habitat quality model of InVEST (integrated valuation of ecosystem services and tradeoffs), using aggregated indices. Our results show that, compared with forest, the suitability of rubber plantations as habitat is 50–60 % less for red list species, 40–50 % less for aggregated biodiversity and 10–20 % less for species with human use values. The concept itself can be applied to a variety of land use systems and case studies, as well as to different magnitudes of data availability or spatial scales. Our approach will enable researchers and land use planners to estimate the impact that land use decisions can have on biodiversity.

Keywords: Ecosystem function, ecosystem services, Greater Mekong Subregion

Contact Address: Inga Häuser, University of Hohenheim, Inst. of Agricultural Sciences in the Tropics (Hans-Ruthenberg-Institute), Garbenstrasse 13, 70599 Stuttgart, Germany, e-mail: haeuser@uni-hohenheim.de

ID 753

Destructive Harvesting of Wild Honey in Miombo Woodlands Affects Keystone Elements in the Ecosystem

CHRISTOPH SCHRÖTTER[1], LALISA DUGUMA[2], LAURA SNOOK[3], JUDY LOO[3], TEREZA ALVES[4], CAMILA SOUSA[4], GEORG GRATZER[1]

[1] *University of Natural Resources and Life Sciences (BOKU), Department of Forest and Soils Sciences, Institute of Forest Ecology, Austria*
[2] *World Agroforestry Centre, Kenya*
[3] *Bioversity International, Forest Genetic Resources, Italy*
[4] *Instituto de Investigação Agrária de Moçambique (IIAM), Mozambique*

Protected areas cover 13 % of the world's terrestrial surface. With increasing demands on land and with challenges of land degradation and climate change, conflicts between conservation and use are on the rise, particularly in developing countries. Effective management of these conflicts requires viable livelihood options for local land users which are in line with nature conservation goals. Consolidation of nature conservation guidelines with local land use practices may be particularly challenging where keystone species are affected or where land uses have the potential for leading to ecosystem changes. This can be an issue even in ecosystems like savannahs, where fire largely defines ecosystem structure. The Miombo woodlands, covering around 2.4 million km² of land, harbour important diversity and are crucial for livelihoods of around 75 million people in southern Africa. As a result of various pressures, cover and biomass of Miombo woodlands are declining throughout their range.

Honey harvesting is an important land use in Miombo areas, both economically and culturally. Wild bees use cavities in trees for their colonies. Harvesting practices in some places include felling of trees with honeycombs to collect the honey and setting fire for pacifying bees. This leads to starvation and death of bee colonies. Given that most tree species are bee pollinated, trees with cavities colonised by wild bees can be classified as keystone elements in these ecosystems. Although ecologically far reaching, the effects of this harvesting practice on tree population structures in Miombo woodlands have seldom been studied. We characterised the ecological effects of destructive harvesting of wild honey on tree population structure and tree species distribution in Miombo woodlands in the Niassa wildlife reserve in Mozambique. The results show that forest structure and tree diversity differed along honey harvesting intensity gradients, with the highest number of fire tolerant tree species in areas with high honey harvesting intensity, which also showed the lowest tree regeneration density and Shannon diversity. Options for reconciling livelihoods with ecosystem maintenance do exist and include non-destructive harvesting based on climbing trees with locally produced ropes and leaving larval combs behind so the colony could continue to grow.

Keywords: Fire, honey harvesting, miombo, tree diversity

Contact Address: Christoph Schrötter, University of Natural Resources and Life Sciences (BOKU), Department of Forest and Soils Sciences, Institute of Forest Ecology, Geusaugasse 9/14, 1030 Wien, Austria, e-mail: christoph.schroetter@gmail.com

Genetic Diversity of Baobab (*Adansonia digitata* L.) Accessions along an Elevation Transect in Kenya

ANNA CHLÁDOVÁ[1], BOHDAN LOJKA[1], MARIE KALOUSOVÁ[1], BOHUMIL MANDÁK[2], JAKUB HOUŠKA[3], KATJA KEHLENBECK[4]

[1]*Czech University of Life Sciences Prague, Faculty of Tropical AgriSciences, Dept. of Crop Sciences and Agroforestry, Czech Republic*
[2]*Czech University of Life Sciences Prague, Faculty of Environmental Sciences, Czech Republic*
[3]*Czech University of Life Sciences Prague, Faculty of Agrobiology, Food and Natural Resources, Dept. of Soil Science and Soil Protection, Czech Republic*
[4]*The World Agroforestry Centre (ICRAF), Kenya*

Adansonia digitata L. (Malvaceae) is a huge multipurpose tree of the savannahs of sub-Saharan Africa, with high economic potential for local communities. The edible fruits and leaves are known for their high nutritional values and can be used fresh or processed. However, a high intra-specific variability regarding morphology, genetics and nutritional content of baobab and its products is documented for several African regions, while data for Kenya is largely lacking. This study aimed at documenting the genetic and morphological variability of baobab accessions in Kenya and at checking the presence of the newly described diploid baobab species Adansonia kilima. Samples were collected from 204 baobab trees from seven populations defined by geographical distance in South-eastern and Coastal Kenya at altitudes of 6–1,058 m asl. Leaf or bark samples for genetic diversity assessment were collected from all 204 trees, while leaves only from 65 and fruits from 76 trees (all in inland locations) for morphological analyses based on the publication 'Descriptors for Baobab'. Nine microsatellite loci were used to assess genetic variation and results analysed with specific software because of the tetraploid nature of baobab. Overall genetic diversity was high and all loci were polymorphic. The mean gene diversity was 0.803 and observed heterozygosity was 0.907. Analysis of molecular variance (AMOVA) revealed low variation among populations (12.4 %) and high variation within populations (87.6 %). Bayesian clustering and Principal Coordinate Analysis (PCA) divided the accessions into two clusters, one with only inland and one with coastal accessions. Although the presence of *Adansonia kilima* was previously postulated for Kenya, flow cytometry did not detect any among the analysed samples as only tetraploids were observed.Regarding morphological characteristics, no differences among the accession from inland populations were found (no fruits were collected in coastal areas). Leaf morphological data showed significant differences between inland and coastal populations with longest leaflets and leaf petioles in accession from the Coast, thus confirming the results obtained for genetic analysis. This study contributes to the overall knowledge of the genetic diversity of baobab in Kenya and can contribute to the development of germplasm conservation strategies and domestication programs for baobab.

Keywords: Conservation, domestication, genetic markers, microsatellites (SSR), morphological diversity

Contact Address: Anna Chládová, Czech University of Life Sciences Prague, Faculty of Tropical AgriSciences, Dept. of Crop Sciences and Agroforestry, Prague, Czech Republic, e-mail: anickachladova@gmail.com

Spatially Explicit Threat Assessment to Target Food Tree Species in Burkina Faso

HANNES GAISBERGER, BARBARA VINCETI, JUDY LOO

Bioversity International, Italy

There is a general agreement on the need to ensure the *in situ* conservation and availability of valuable genetic resources of wild species that are important for food security and nutrition. In order to be able to adopt adequate conservation measures a spatial assessment of their distribution and a sound analysis of the causes of and their sensitivity to threats is required.

The ADA funded project "Threats to priority food tree species in Burkina Faso: Drivers of resource losses and mitigation measures" gave us the opportunity to develop a spatially explicit threat assessment methodology with focus on expert feedback, as there is no comprehensive and standardised approach available at the moment. Relevant threats were identified jointly with regional project partners from INERA and CNSF during meetings in Ouagadougou in 2012 and 2013 and by means of a case study on farmers' perception. Once determined were the most important ones (overexploitation, overgrazing, fire, climate change, cotton production and mining) we identified openly accessible datasets suitable to represent the spatial patterns of threat intensities throughout the country. Now we needed to transform the threat intensities into potential impact over the target species distribution ranges.

To do so the distribution and threat sensitivity of 16 food tree species were assessed by 17 local and international experts by means of an online feedback survey that was specifically developed for this project. These experts were asked to rate on a five point scale different distribution models and the sensitivity to threats. The survey was analysed applying a consensus method to identify the most consistent distribution model and threat specific sensitivity rating on a species by species basis. The potential impact of climate change was modeled using Global Circulation Models (GCM's) deriving from the fifth assessment of the Intergovernmental Panel on Climate Change (IPCC5) in 2014.

The results were then used to calculate and create individual and combined threat potential maps that enable the identification of areas in Burkina Faso where species are highly threatened. The spatial patterns of the threat levels provides evidence to prioritise food tree populations with relative urgency for undertaking conservation actions.

Keywords: Assessment, Burkina Faso, climate change, cotton production, distribution modelling, fire, food tree species

Contact Address: Hannes Gaisberger, Bioversity International, Effective Genetic Resources Conservation and Use, Via Dei Tre Denari 472/a, 00057 Maccarese, Italy, e-mail: h.gaisberger@cgiar.org

Understory Tree Diversity and Regeneration Pattern in Four Land-Use Systems in Tropical Rainforests, Nigeria

JONATHAN C. ONYEKWELU, ADEOLA A. OLABIWONNU

The Federal University of Technology, Dept. of Forestry and Wood Technology, Nigeria

Biodiversity assessment in tropical rainforests has focused mainly on the overstory components with limited attention accorded to understory species. The diversity and composition of understory tree species and tree regeneration pattern were examined in four forest land-use systems: primary, degraded, enriched and *Gmelina arborea* plantation forests in Ondo State, Nigeria. Overstory species were inventoried in eight 400 m^2 temporary sample plots randomly laid across two hectare plots in each land-use system. Sapling and seedling species were investigated in 25 m^2 and 4 m^2 quadrants and sub-quadrants, respectively in all plots. Tree species totaled 53 in 25 families and disproportionately distributed among the land-use systems. The most important species were *Mansonia altissima, Cola gigantea, Bosqueia angolensis* and *G. arborea*, in primary, enriched, degraded and *Gmelina* plantation forests, respectively. The Shannon-Wiener diversity index of the overstory layers of the four forest land-use systems was higher than those of the sapling layers. A significant variation was observed in species diversity of understory species in the four land-use systems. Some abundant species in understory layers include *Strombosia* spp, and *Sterculia* spp, (primary forest); *Lecaniodiscus cupanioides* and *Carpolobia lutea* (enriched forest); *C. lutea*, and *Macaranga barteri* (*Gmelina* plantation); *S. pustulata*, and *Bridelia ferruginea* (degraded forest). The order of species richness in sapling layer is: *Gmelina* plantation (13) < primary forest (15) < degraded forest (16) < enriched forest (21) while it is enriched forest (18) = primary forest (18) < *Gmelina* plantation (24) < degraded forest (25) in seedling layer. When understory (seedlings and saplings) species richness was pooled together, species richness in the understories of the four land-use systems compared favourably with those of the overstories, except in *Gmelina* plantation, indicating the bright prospects of the ecosystems if degradation activities are minimised or halted. Knowledge of understory species diversity and regeneration pattern is essential in planning sustainable forest management and biodiversity conservation.

Keywords: Biodiversity, conservation, forest plantation, land-use system, natural forest, regeneration, understory species

Contact Address: Jonathan C. Onyekwelu, The Federal University of Technology, Dept. of Forestry and Wood Technology, P.M.B. 704, Akure, Nigeria, e-mail: onyekwelujc@yahoo.co.uk

ID 165

Assessing Forest Dynamics of Broad-Leaved Forest Ecosystems in the South-Central Part of Bhutan

JIGME TENZIN, HUBERT HASENAUER

University of Natural Resources and Life Sciences (BOKU), Dept. of Forests and Soil Sciences, Austria

Mountain forests are rich repositories of biodiversity. They are important for providing various ecosystem services which sustain the rural livelihoods and fuels the national development. However, as observed in other parts of the world, the mountain forests are now increasingly degraded as a result of unsustainable agricultural and forestry practices. A key to maintain these precious resources is to carefully manage them by having management plans based on proper resource assessment and volume increments derived from growth models. Bhutan is also one of the countries located in the mountain Himalayas with very limited scientific information on forest management especially with regard to broad-leaved forests. The purpose of the paper is to: (i) assess the forest dynamics of the broad-leaved forest ecosystems through forest inventory and (ii) understand the forest increment rates through study of growth rates of individual trees. The research was carried out in a watershed in the south-central part of Bhutan. We established 96 inventory points in a systematic grid of 800 m by 800 m covering an area of 6423 hectares of broad-leaved forests. Parameters such as DBH, tree height, horizontal distance from the centre, azimuth were collected for every tree and sapling for understanding the stand information. Increment cores to understand the growth rate of the trees for the last 10 years was collected from every plot. A total of 140 plant species was recorded indicating rich diversity of the watershed. The total mean basal area increment for the 2004–2008 and 2009–2014 were 3.13 ± 3.34 m^2 and 3.74 ± 4.06 m^2 respectively. The annual increment for the last 10 years was 0.69 m^2. The understanding of the forest dynamics and the available information of the forest increment rates is expected to further improve the sustainable forest management and avoid overexploitation of the resources. The results and recommendations from this study will be incorporated in to the watershed management plan which is currently being developed. The findings from this study will also be used in calibrating forest increment growth models for the broad-leaved forests of Bhutan.

Keywords: Bhutan, forest dynamics, growth model, increments, watershed

Contact Address: Jigme Tenzin, University of Natural Resources and Life Sciences (BOKU), Dept. of Forests and Soil Sciences, Peter-Jordan-Str.82 A-1190, 1190 Vienna, Austria, e-mail: jigmetenzin84@gmail.com

Measuring Leaf Area Index in Asian Rubber Plantations – A Challenge

MARC COTTER[1], ARISOA RAJAONA[2], SABINE STÜRZ[1], ALEXANDRA SCHAPPERT[1], FOLKARD ASCH[1]

[1] University of Hohenheim, Inst. of Agricultural Sciences in the Tropics (Hans-Ruthenberg-Institute), Germany

[2] Africa Rice Center (AfricaRice), Sustainable Productivity Enhancement, Madagascar

In order to estimate water use and water requirements of tropical plantations systems such as rubber it is adamant to have accurate information on leaf area development of the plantation as the main determinant of evapotranspiration. Literature commonly suggests a number of different methods on how to obtain leaf area index (LAI) information from rubber plantations. Methods include destructive measurements of leaf area at peak LAI, indirect methods such as gap fraction methods (i.e. Hemiview and LAI 2000) and radiation interception methods (i.e. SunScan) or litter fall traps. Published values for peak LAI in rubber plantation differ widely and show no clear trend to be explanained by management practices or the influence of local climate patterns. This study compares four methods for determining LAI of rubber plantations of different ages in Xishuangbanna, Yunnan, PR China. We have tested indirect measurement techniques such as light absorbtion and gap fraction measurements and hemispherical image analysis against litterfall data in order to obtain insights into the reliabiliy of these measuring techniques for the use in rubber plantation systems. In addition, we have tested the applicability of available satellite based remote sensing data.

The results that we are going to present here clearly show that there is no consistent agreement between the different measurements. Site, time of the day, age of the trees and incoming radiation all had a significant effect on the results depending on the device or the method.

This renders the data published so far doubtful as to their accuracy and their usefulness in estimating evapotranspiration from rubber plantations and the induced environmental effects.

Keywords: Leaf area index, methods, rubber

Contact Address: Marc Cotter, University of Hohenheim, Inst. of Agricultural Sciences in the Tropics (Hans-Ruthenberg-Institute), Garbenstr. 13, 70599 Stuttgart, Germany, e-mail: Cotter@uni-hohenheim.de

ID 501

Genetic Structure of the CITES-Listed Rosewood Species *Dalbergia oliveri* from Indochina: Implications for Conservation

Hoa Tran[1], Patrick van Damme[2], Alex Widmer[3]

[1] *Vietnam Academy of Agricultural Science, Institute of Agricultural Genetics; Forest Genetics and Conservation, Vietnam*

[2] *Ghent University, Dept. of Plant Production - Lab. for Tropical Agronomy, Belgium*

[3] *ETH Zurich, Institute of Integrative Biology (IBZ), Switzerland*

Forest genetic resources are threatened by a broad array of factors such as climate change, environmental pollution, habitat destruction and pest attacks. In developing countries, over-exploitation and the introduction of exotic species are often mentioned as decisive factors for the destruction of tropical forests. The capacity of forest trees to cope with these threats and to persist in spatially and temporally heterogeneous environments depends on their adaptive potential, which is determined by genetic diversity. This is why conservation strategies for forest trees should be based on an evolutionary approach and focus on the maintenance of within-species genetic diversity. High rates of deforestation and logging lead to local extinctions and have left a high number of tropical tree species threatened, among these the CITES-listed timber species *Dalbergia oliveri*. The aim of this study was to investigate genetic diversity in natural populations of *D. oliveri* in order to guide management plans for effective conservation of both natural populations and genetic resources for future breeding programs of the species. We collected seeds, leaf or cambium samples from 16 populations of *D. oliveri* across the entire distribution of area in Vietnam and genotyped them with 28 microsatellite markers (in 8 multiplex-sets). We found evidence that the species reproduces clonally by root suckers, and is capable of self-pollination at rates around 20–30 %. The level of genetic diversity was moderate (He=0.53) with high levels of diversity found in Chu Mom Ray National Park/mountain area (covering the combined Laos and Cambodia areas), and low diversity in the more peripheral populations in Laos and Vietnam. Genetic differentiation among populations was high (Gst=0.34), and strongly correlated to geographic distance between populations. Genetic clustering analysis showed a clear division of populations into five geographically defined groups. We recommend that (1) conservation plans should aim at conserving many different populations in order to maintain as much as possible the current genetic variation and (2) populations should be sufficiently large to minimise inbreeding and take into account the possible occurrence of clones.

Keywords: Conservation genetics, threatened species, timber species, tropical trees

Contact Address: Hoa Tran, Vietnam Academy of Agricultural Science, Institute of Agricultural Genetics; Forest Genetics and Conservation, Pham Van Dong Road, 10000 Hanoi, Vietnam, e-mail: tranthihoa@agi.vaas.vn

Flora and Vegetation of East African Wetlands in the Context of Land Use Changes

KAI BEHN, MIGUEL ALVAREZ, MATHIAS BECKER, BODO MÖSELER

University of Bonn, Inst. Crop Sci. and Res. Conserv. (INRES), Germany

Biodiversity and biomass are among the most important natural resources of wetlands worldwide. In East Africa, formerly undisturbed wetlands are increasingly used for agricultural production. Such changes occur at the cost of natural vegetation, impacting the biodiversity and biomass resources and hence the provision of related ecosystem services.

In order to assess the impact of long-term cultivation on wetland vegetation, we conducted a study in two different localities of East Africa, namely the inland valleys north of Kampala (Uganda) and the Kilombero floodplain, near Ifakara (Tanzania). Both study sites are mainly used for rice and vegetable cultivation, but differ strongly in their ecological properties and hence their potential natural vegetation. We sampled vegetation in a gradient of cultivation frequency from permanent croplands, to remaining areas of little disturbance. There we analysed species composition, structure, functional traits and potential uses. Additionally, we monitored the species turnover and biomass production after a strong disturbance event (tillage) in experimental plots.

Less disturbed vegetation in the Ugandan inland valleys is represented by marshes dominated by tall sedges, especially *Cyperus papyrus*, and swamp forests, while in the Kilombero valley the natural plant communities are tall grasslands of *Phragmites australis* and *Panicum fluviicola*. The dominating species of these communities can be sustainably used as resources for building or thatching material if their rhizomes and roots remain intact. The cropland flora consists to a large extent in pantropical weeds, often short-living sedges, while fallows often harbor some elements of regenerating natural vegetation. Plants used for food or medicinal purposes were found in all habitats. Invasive species such as *Mimosa pigra* and *M. pudica* were recorded at both sites, but they tend to be more frequent at the Ugandan study site. *Mimosa pigra* was frequent in fallows as well as in less disturbed sites.

Land use changes can increase the biodiversity of wetlands, because new habitats are emerging within the cultural landscape. These habitats are occupied by new species such as native pioneers or introduced or potentially invasive weeds. However, native species associated with undisturbed habitats are decreasing or even disappearing.

Keywords: Biodiversity, East Africa, ecosystem services, GlobE, land use changes, Tanzania, Uganda, vegetation, wetlands

Contact Address: Kai Behn, University of Bonn, Inst. Crop Sci. and Res. Conserv. (INRES), Nussallee 1, 53115 Bonn, Germany, e-mail: kaibehn@uni-bonn.de

ID 620

Seasonal Diversity and Abundance of Bee Pollinator Species in a Sudanese Agro-Ecological System (Burkina Faso, West Africa)

DRISSA COULIBALY[1], KATHARINA STEIN[2], SOULEYMANE KONATÉ[1], KARL-EDUARD LINSENMAIR[2]

[1]*University Nangui Abrogoua, Dept. of Research in Ecology and Biodiversity, Ivory Coast*

[2]*University of Wuerzburg, Theodor-Boveri-Institute of Bioscience, Dept. of Animal Ecology and Tropical Biology, Germany*

Bees are the most important pollinators of many crops and wild plant species. The ecosystem service of pollination provided by these insects is crucial to maintain overall biodiversity and to secure crop yields worldwide. Especially improving the livelihood of smallholders in developing countries through higher crop yields is essential for achieving global food security and poverty reduction. However, ecosystem degradation, depletion of plant species, habitat fragmentation, use of insecticides and global warming constitute severe threats to these organisms with some being clearly at risk of extinction. Despite the great ecological and economic importance of bees as pollinators hardly anything is known about the bee species in West Africa. The study aimed to assess bee communities of a Sudanese agro-ecological system in Burkina Faso. We investigated the diversity and abundance of bees in near-natural savannah habitats and in nearby fields of the main cash crops of this area (cotton, sesame). Bees were caught with 288 coloured pantraps for the duration of one year, covering the dry and rainy season. A total of 97 species of bees belonging to 31 genera and 4 families (Apidae, Megachilidae, Halictidae, and Colletidae) were determined.

The most diverse family with 37 wild bee species was Halictidae (sweat bees). Apidae (including honey bees, bumble bees and stingless bees) was the most abundant family including 92.57 % of specimen collected. The stingless bee *Hypotrigona gribodoi* was the most abundant species with 73.74 % of all specimen. During the dry season, bees were more abundant in the savannah habitats due to the flowering period of many wild plants, whereas more bees were recorded in fields during the flowering period of agricultural crops in the rainy season (availability of food resources). This study represents first insights into the West African bee diversity in relationship with the increasing pressure by human activities and climatic variability in the Sudanese area. The assessment of bee species and their seasonal distribution is an important scientific basis for the establishment of appropriate management strategies and can be used to create mutually beneficial scenarios between biodiversity and crop yields and hence human wellbeing.

Keywords: Abundance, bees diversity, pollination, Sudanese area

Contact Address: Katharina Stein, University of Wuerzburg, Theodor-Boveri-Institute of Bioscience, Dept. of Animal Ecology and Tropical Biology, Josef-Martin-Weg 52, 97074 Wuerzburg, Germany, e-mail: katharina.stein@uni-wuerzburg.de

Morphological and Genetic Diversity of Camu-Camu (*Myrciaria dubia* McVaugh) in Peruvian Amazon

Jan Šmíd[1], Bohdan Lojka[1], Marie Kalousová[1], Bohumil Mandák[2], Jan Bílý[2], Jakub Houška[3]

[1] *Czech University of Life Sciences Prague, Fac. of Tropical AgriSciences, Dept. of Crop Sciences and Agroforestry, Czech Republic*
[2] *Czech University of Life Sciences Prague, Fac. of Environmental Sciences, Dept. of Ecology, Czech Republic*
[3] *Czech University of Life Sciences Prague, Faculty of Agrobiology, Food and Natural Resources, Dept. of Soil Science and Soil Protection, Czech Republic*

Camu-camu (*Myrciaria dubia* McVaugh) is currently one of the most important fruit species that is grown in the Peruvian Amazon, as well as in Brazil, Colombia or Bolivia. Larger plantations were established only in the last two decades and a substantial part of the production is still obtained by collecting fruits from the wild. Domestication of the species is still at its very beginning; most of the farmers cultivate the plants without any breeding or just after simple selection. The aim of this study was to characterise the morphological and genetic variability of cultivated and natural populations of camu-camu in the Peruvian Amazon and also to compare the variability among and within these populations. In total we have sampled 13 populations; 10 wild populations in Iquitos region, three cultivated populations in Pucallpa in Peruvian Amazon. For genetic analysis, the leaf tissue samples were collected from ten individuals from each population (n=126), and for morphological data were collected from five trees of each population (n=65). To assess the genetic diversity, we used seven microsatellite primers that were developed from available DNA sequences. Using various genetic softwares, major indexes of variability were detected and dendrograms of relatedness of populations and individuals were created. The statistical analysis did not reveal statistically significant differences for most of the morphological descriptors, except for the fruit parameters. Surprisingly, the trees from wild populations had higher fruit and pulp weight and their fruits contained less seeds compared to cultivated populations. The observed heterozygosity was 0.347 and 0.404; expected 0.516 and 0.506; inbreeding coefficient was 0.328 and 0.200 for wild and cultivated populations, respectively. Wild populations could be divided according to the dendrogram into two completely different groups. In cultivated populations, their approximate origin was determined. All the results indicated a high genetic variability but also a high degree of inbreeding. This can be explained by isolation of the populations from each other or low number of individuals in the population. This high level of diversity can be explored for selection of superior individuals and further possibilities of breeding.

Keywords: Genetic diversity, microsatellites, morphological diversity, PCR, population genetics

Contact Address: Jan Šmíd, Czech University of Life Sciences, Fac. of Tropical AgriSciences, Dept. of Crop Sciences and Agroforestry, Prague, Czech Republic, e-mail: smidjancact@seznam.cz

ID 793

On-Farm Tree Diversity and Ecosystem Services at two Seasonally Dry Forest Sites of Nicaragua

VICTORIA VAGANAY[1], PABLO SILES[2], FALGUNI GUHARAY[2], CARSTEN MAROHN[1], GEORG CADISCH[1]

[1] University of Hohenheim, Inst. of Agricultural Sciences in the Tropics (Hans-Ruthenberg-Institute), Germany
[2] International Center for Tropical Agriculture (CIAT), Nicaragua

The Seasonally Dry Tropical Forest (SDTF) biome receives less research attention than the tropical rain forest although its biodiversity is under greater threat. Moreover, conservation of the dry forest is crucial in ensuring the provision of numerous ecosystem services. This study aims to identify opportunities to increase/maintain biodiversity at farm level using the circa situm conservation approach (farm-based conservation of tree species through use) to help farmers manage forest remnants sustainably. This study was carried out in two departments of Nicaragua nested in the SDTF biome, Chinandega and Matagalpa. Analyses were conducted to quantify vegetation composition and structure in different land-use systems and compare them between sites. Additionally, an ethnobotanical study using individual interviews and focus group discussions was carried out with farmers to consider their suggestions on ways to increase tree diversity within their farms. Results revealed strong dominance of a few selected tree species by farmers within agricultural land-uses, with a preference for multipurpose species performing distinct functions (economic/ecosystem). Analysis revealed that farmers participate in different ways to preserving tree cover. Two typologies were identified: planters and protectors, according to their strategies to ensure the sustainability of trees within their farms. Farm-size, farm location and social diversity of farmers exercised direct and interactive influence on farmers' perception about tree planting. Access to seeds, as well as markets and technical knowledge (extraction, germination) were the major constraints. Seeds, saplings and wire were needed by farmers regardless of their farm-size. Potential locations suggested by small farmers (< 4 ha) to increase on-farm tree diversity pointed to patios, live-fences and stream boarders; in contrast, larger farmers (> 7 ha) mostly suggested pastures and riparian areas. This study concludes that all these factors should be taken into consideration while developing conservation trajectories for the farms located in the dry forest. Furthermore, forest resources surrounding farms could be better protected if farmers were empowered with knowledge on natural regeneration and planting materials for urgent conservation of endangered species.

Keywords: Agroforestry, circa situm conservation, farmers' perception, Nicaragua

Contact Address: Victoria Vaganay, University of Hohenheim, Inst. of Agricultural Sciences in the Tropics (Hans-Ruthenberg-Institute), Stuttgart, Germany, e-mail: victoria.vaganay@gmail.com

How Quantitative Ethnobotany Involves Biodiversity Conservation: A Tested Approach on Wari Maro Forest Reserve (Benin)

CARLOS AHOYO[1], HOUEHANOU THIERRY[1], ALAIN YAOÏTCHA[1], MARCEL HOUINATO[2]

[1] *University of Abomey-Calavi, Laboratory of Applied Ecology, Benin*

[2] *University of Abomey-Calavi, Dept. of Sciences and Technics of Animal Production, Benin*

How quantitative ethnobotany researches can contribute to guide biodiversity conservation is questionable in developing countries these last decades. This study proposed an approach that can aid to identify priorities species for local conservation by combining the popularity, the versality and the ecological availability of the useful forest tree resources. Such approach has been applied on Wari Maro forest Reserve in Soudanian zone of Benin. Indeed, woody species of such forest are being hardly destroyed and needing development of biodiversity conservation strategies. Thus, the present study aims to: (1) establish the use pattern popularity of woody species of the forest, (2) evaluating the versality of most useful species (3) evaluate ecological availability of useful tree species and (4) establish the local priority conservation of useful tree species. Ethnobotanical surveys were conducted using individual interview with 149 surrounding people of the forest composed mainly of Nagots, Baribas and Fulani. Forty two (42) floristic surveys were conducted within the forest to assess the local ecological availability of used woody species. A Correspondence Canonical Analyze (CCA) was performed using the R software to establish the use patterns popularity of species in relation with ethnic groups. Afterwards a Principal Component Analysis (PCA) has been performed to characterise local conservation priority species using versatility and ecological availability indexes. In total 79 woody species have mainly been reported for six main types of use: timber (technology and construction) (48 %), traditional medicine (92 %), veterinary (16 %), food (30 %), forage (43 %), and energy (39 %).

The results of CCA showed a difference in the species use according to ethnicity. Among the most used species, *Adansonia digitata*, *Cussonia arborea*, *Kigelia africana*, *Milicia excelsa* and *Tamarindus indica* were not locally available. Also, *Khaya senegalensis*, *Afzelia africana*, *Daniellia oliveri*, *Annona senegalensis*, *Borassus aethiopum*, *Vitex doniana*, *Ceiba pentandra* and *Ficus* spp were much used with low local availability. Thus, by this ethnobotany approach the species such as *Adansonia digitata*, *Cussonia arborea*, *Kigelia africana*, *Milicia excelsa*, *Tamarindus indica*, *Annona senegalensis*, *Borassus aethiopum*, *Vitex doniana*, *Ceiba pentandra*, *Khaya senegalensis*, *Afzelia africana*, *Daniellia oliveri* and *Ficus* spp would be suggested to local priority conservation actions.

Keywords: Biodiversity conservation, ecological avaibility, popularity, quantitative ethnobotany, versatility

---

Contact Address: Houehanou Thierry, University of Abomey-Calavi, Laboratory of Applied Ecology, Cotonou, Benin, e-mail: houehanout@yahoo.fr

ID 813

Morphological Diversity of the Underutilised Fruit Species Guava (*Psidium guajava* L.) in Kenya

JOSIAH CHIVEU[1], MARCEL NAUMANN[1], ELKE PAWELZIK[1], KATJA KEHLENBECK[2]

[1] *Georg-August-Universität Göttingen, Dept. of Crop Sciences: Inst. Quality of Plant Products, Germany*
[2] *The World Agroforestry Centre (ICRAF), Kenya*

Guava fruit is highly nutritious and the tree occurs in a wide range of agro-climatic conditions in eastern Africa. Compared to other guava producing countries, the use of guavas for processing and product diversification is limited in Kenya due to lack of adequate agronomic information, poor integration of farmers into value chains and unawareness on the nutritional and economic potential of the species, among other reasons. Moreover, little is known about intra-specific variation in the available guava germplasm. The objective of this study was therefore to assess the morphological diversity in Kenyan guava germplasm. Four regions with diverse agroecological and edaphic conditions comprising of Western, Riftvalley, Eastern and the Coast were purposely chosen for sampling. In total, 105 trees were assessed in the field and 20 fruits from each accession collected for fruit trait assessments. Results indicate significantly higher diameter at breast height (DBH) of trees from the Riftvalley than the Coastal region (51.0 vs. 26.1 cm, respectively; $p = 0.003$). The mean fruits' pericarp thickness was slightly higher in fruits from the Coast (5.17 mm) than from the Eastern region (3.96 mm). Contrarily, mean pulp weight per fruit was significantly higher in fruits collected from the Eastern than from the Coastal region (19.0 vs. 10.9 g; $p = 0.001$). Mean proportion of seed weight from fruit weight was significantly higher ($p = 0.003$) in fruits from the Coast (10.7 %) and Western Kenya (10.6 %) than from the Riftvalley region (8.0 %). Fruit shapes included round (43 % of all 105 accessions), obovate (25 %) and ovate (14 %) among others. Majority (93 %) of all accessions had fruits with yellow-, orange- or reddish-coloured pulp, while 7 % had white fruit pulp. A combined cluster analysis of z-standardised qualitative and quantitative morphological variables using Ward's clustering method resulted in two distinct clusters, with lower values for pulp weight and fruit length, higher values for seed proportion and most accessions from Coast and Riftvalley found in cluster 1. Information on morphological diversity of guava can contribute to selecting suitable accessions for certain uses (e.g. fresh consumption or processing) and to identifying most promising mother trees for future guava breeding programs in Kenya.

Keywords: Guava, Kenya, morphological diversity, underutilised

Contact Address: Josiah Chiveu, University of Kassel / Georg-August Universität Göttingen, Crop Science, Carl-Sprengel-Weg 1, 37075 Göttingen, Germany, e-mail: josiah.chiveu@agr.uni-goettingen.de

Conservation of Genetic Resources through Multi-Level Initiatives in Eastern Ethiopia

ANDREA RUEDIGER

Oxford University, Bioversity International Research Fellow, United Kingdom

Agro-biodiversity - the genetic diversity of cultivated crops and crop varieties - is widely understood as an essential resource of small farmers to manage production risk and as a key factor for robust cropping systems. Genetic resources, however, can only be used effectively when they are accessible to small farmers. Consequently, there is a growing interest to improve access and conserve diversity *in situ* or on-farm. The highlands of Central Ethiopia as one of the world's eight centres of genetic diversity (for barley and durum wheat) have been subject to green revolution agricultural policies for the past decades. Genetic diversity has severely eroded through the introduction of high-input agriculture, including improved wheat varieties. Since the mid-1990s, remarkable efforts have been made in a multi-stakeholder initiative to reintroduce landrace wheat and barley varieties and conserve them in local gene banks. In this study we identify factors of success for two community gene banks located in East Shewa, eastern Ethiopia, which were initially funded through the Global Environmental Facility and established in 1996. 20 years later, the membership of the gene banks is steadily growing and they have achieved financial independence as well as a robust institutional set-up. Ethiopian non-governmental actors, governmental agencies like the Ethiopian Biodiversity Institute and Bioversity International as international actor continue to support local actors.

The case study is based on in-depth interviews with chairmen and committee members of the two gene banks as well as with representatives of all national and international stakeholders. The qualitative analysis is complemented by a comprehensive survey of 430 households allowing a comparison of the crop and varietal portfolio as well as characteristics of members and non-members of the community gene banks.

Keywords: Agro-biodiversity, Ethiopia, *in-situ*

Contact Address: Andrea Ruediger, Oxford University, Bioversity International Research Fellow, Somerville College, Woodstock Road, OX26HD Oxford, United Kingdom, e-mail: andrea.ruediger@gmx.de

ID 1145

Caught in the Act – Assessment of Intensity and Spatial Variation of Cattle Intrusion by a Network of Camera Traps in Tsimanampetsotsa National Park, Madagascar

Fidgerald Maeterlinck Ramananoro[1], Eva Schlecht[2], Pascal Fust[2]

[1]*consultant, Madagascar*

[2]*University of Kassel / Georg-August-Universität Göttingen, Animal Husbandry in the Tropics and Subtropics, Germany*

Population increase in Madagascar, especially in the surrounding of the Tsimanampetsotsa National Park in Southwest-Madagascar, in combination with the recent expansion of this park, has increased the local intensity of exploitation of natural resources. Since livelihood activities related to livestock keeping and the exploitation of forest resources are very important for the local population, we hypothesised that the intensity of livestock intrusion in the protected area for foraging purpose will be considerably high, in particular during the dry season, when foraging resources in adjacent rangelands get sparse. To quantify the intensity, timing and spatial variation in livestock utilisation of Tsimanampetsotsa National Park, we applied a network of camera traps. For a total period of five months during the dry season, thirty cameras were recording cattle movements along trails within the buffer and protected zone of the park. Throughout the study period (May – October 2014), 10'651 pictures of 4'943 animals and herders have been recorded by the camera traps, whereby pictures of 1'407 animals could be directly associated to accompanying herders. Sizes of animal groups recorded in consecutive photo captures ranged between one and 67 individuals. The similar ratio in movement directions into and out of the park of 48.3 % and 51.7 %, respectively, as well as the high percentage of records of free-ranging animals (71.5 %) indicate a more frequent use of the protected area for daily resource extraction than for traversing movements across the park for seasonal herd relocation. More than 19 % of all photo captures per month have been recorded inside the park's core zone, i.e. the area of strict protection, where theoretically any access and use of resources is forbidden by law. Applying spatial analysis, we were thereby able to map the most frequented livestock access trails into the park. The results of our study confirm that the pressure on the natural resources inside the protected area through herded and free-ranging cattle herds is substantial but shows a distinct spatial variability. Park management should particularly focus on the effective protection of easily accessible areas, where livestock intrusion was frequently recorded.

Keywords: Camera traps, cattle, intrusion, Madagascar

Contact Address: Eva Schlecht, University of Kassel / Georg-August-Universität Göttingen, Animal Husbandry in the Tropics and Subtropics, Steinstraße 19, 37213 Witzenhausen, Germany, e-mail: tropanimals@uni-kassel.de

Tree Diversity of Green Spaces in Kumasi, Ghana: Theoretical Model and Ecosystem Function

BERTRAND NERO

University of Bonn, Center for Development Research, Germany

Conserving biodiversity in cities is essential to halting global biodiversity loss. Nevertheless, there is paucity of data on the underlying mechanisms shaping species assemblages and species/trait diversity-productivity relationships in urban landscapes. The objectives of this study were to; 1) compile tree species diversity of different green space (GS) types, (2) describe the theoretical basis of species co-existence and 3) examine the links between species and life history trait diversity to GS and species productivity (carbon storage) in Kumasi, Ghana. Stratified sampling and species abundance models were combined in this study.

About 176 tree species in 46 families were recorded within Kumasi. About 96 species were in a natural forest located towards the outskirts of the city. Home gardens, institutional compounds, and public parks had the highest species richness of 76, 75 and 71, respectively while urban rangelands and farmlands were the least species rich with 6 and 23, respectively. Species richness (S) in the peri-urban (mean ndvi >0.2, S=142) and core urban (mean ndvi<0.2, S=108) areas were significantly different (X2 =15.7, $p < 0.0001$, n=1). Native species richness was lowest in the core urban area and highest in the neighbouring natural forest. There were moderate correlations between species richness and GS carbon storage ($p = 0.001$, r=0.57). Life history traits interacted antagonistically to affect the species carbon storage in the metropolis ($p = 0.02$; r=0.32). The geometric series model best fitted the tree assemblage of the city, depicting a species impoverished and environmentally hash landscape. Pioneers and anthropochory dispersed species were the most abundant suggesting that this urban landscape is shaped by both environment and social filters.

Plant species diversity and distribution depend on the type of GS and portray a perturbed landscape in early seres of succession with the overall ecosystem function sustained by both species and life history trait diversities.

Keywords: Geometric series, green spaces, species richness

Contact Address: Bertrand Nero, University of Bonn, Center for Development Research, Walter-Flex-Str. 3, D-53113 Bonn, Germany, e-mail: nerbefest@yahoo.com

ID 81

Organic agriculture and food systems

Organic farming systems

Tree Diversity Loss and Management Intensification: Implications for Coffee Performance in Agro-Forests in Kodagu, South India.

MAIKE NESPER, JABOURY GHAZOUL, CHRISTOPH KUEFFER

ETH Zurich, Environmental Systems Science (D-USYS), Switzerland

Kodagu in the Western Ghats is India's main coffee growing region. In this biodiversity hotspot, coffee is traditionally grown in very diverse agroforestry systems. In the past 40 years, coffee agroforestry has been expanding and intensified. Intensification happens at the level of the shade tree canopy (reduction in native tree diversity and planting of exotic timber tree *Grevillea robusta* [Proteaceae]) and the soil management system (conversion from organic [manure and compost] to conventional NPK-fertilisation). While it is hoped that intensification leads to economic benefits, resulting biodiversity loss and effects of different nutrient regimes on soils and coffee productivity and quality are not well understood.

We conducted an on-farm study to investigate the effect of different shade tree compositions and fertilisation treatments on coffee plant performance. It was hypothesised that shade tree diversity reduction affects biodiversity and multiple ecosystem services negatively, with conversion from organic to conventional soil management further aggravating these negative effects. Loss of ecosystem services is expected to counteract benefits of intensification. We selected 25 farms classified into three types: i) organic and native, multispecies shade tree canopy (9 replicates), ii) conventional and native, multispecies shade tree canopy (9), and iii) conventional and *Grevillea robusta* shade tree canopy (7).

As a result of a conversion from native-multispecies to *Grevillea* shade trees not only the native trees were replaced by *Grevillea* trees but among the remnant native trees diversity and number of red-listed species was additionally reduced. Ecosystem structure changed from few old trees in native-multispecies to many young trees in *Grevillea* plantations. Diversity loss led to a reduced and altered nutrient input through shade tree litter. Conversion from organic to conventional reduced the pH, soil organic matter and cation exchange capacity while fertilisation didn't improve leaf nutrient deficiencies. Coffee productivity wasn't affected by shade tree cover or fertilisation treatment but coffee plants in *Grevillea* plantations produced more single-seeded berries, and coffee beans suffered from higher coffee borer beetle (*Hypothenemus hampei*) attacks. In summary while we did not find substantial yield increase through intensification, several ecosystem qualities were negatively affect: tree biodiversity, soil quality, and resistance to pests.

Keywords: Agroforestry, coffee, diversity, intensification

Contact Address: Maike Nesper, ETH Zurich, Environmental Systems Science (D-USYS), Universitaetsstrasse 16, 8092 Zuerich, Switzerland, e-mail: mnesper@ethz.ch

Linking Land-Use and Product Quality: Do Micro-Environmental Growing Conditions Affect Cacao Bean Characteristics?

WIEBKE NIETHER[1], INGA SMIT[2], MONIKA SCHNEIDER[3], GERHARD GEROLD[1]

[1]*Georg-August-Universität Göttingen, Dept. of Landscape Ecology, Germany*

[2]*Georg-August-Universität Göttingen, Dept. of Crop Sciences, Quality of Plant Products, Germany*

[3]*Research Institute of Organic Agriculture (FiBL), Dept. of International Cooperation, Switzerland*

Global chocolate demand is increasing and also the demand on high quality cacao beans from geographical indication. Quality may concern commercial requirements and flavour, but also production conditions, i.e. ecological standards and certifications. The fermentation process is a very important factor for the structural development of cacao flavour, but little is known about the influence of micro-environmental conditions such as microclimate, light, and especially water availability during the ripening period of the cacao pods on bean quality. These conditions depend not only on the region but change over the harvesting period and differ within production systems. While cultivars are often selected by their agronomic performance, a selection according to their ability to cope with ecophysiological stressful conditions is also desirable.

Out of an experimental field trial in Alto Beni, Bolivia, cacao beans were sampled at the beginning and the end of the harvesting period from five production systems comprising full-sun and agroforestry systems under conventional and organic farming practices, and four cultivars. Micro-environmental conditions and soil moisture were measured. Beans were analysed according to their morphological traits including dry-bean-factor, 100-bean-weight, share of cotyledons, testa and radicle, fat content, and C/N ratio. Polyamines as a measure of systemic water stress response in the beans were estimated via HPLC-FLD.

Harvesting period prolonged over the dry season while water availability in the soil decreased. Cacao agroforestry systems provided a buffered microclimate for the understory cocoa in comparison to full-sun monocultures reducing transpiration. Finally, cultivars may have different strategies. Beans from different cultivars showed distinctions in their bean composition while polyamine content responded to the seasonal variation over the harvesting time in the production systems.

Enhancing knowledge about the ecophysiology of the cacao tree and responses to environmental conditions in the beans may help to support production systems that provide conditions in favour of the cacao performance and cultivation adapted to local and micro-environmental conditions. For small-scale farmers and cacao famers' cooperatives a stable cacao bean production over the season will improve their access and reliability on the chocolate market that asks for a constant supply and specific quality.

Keywords: Agroforestry, bean quality, soil moisture

Contact Address: Wiebke Niether, Georg-August-Universität Göttingen, Dept. of Landscape Ecology, Goldschmidtstr. 5, 37077 Göttingen, Germany, e-mail: wiebke.niether@geo.uni-goettingen.de

ID 438

Turnover of Soil Nitrogen in a Semi-Arid Tropical Soil: From Basic Research to Knowledge Application in Organic Agriculture

GUNADHISH KHANAL[1], MARIKO INGOLD[1], CHRISTINE WACHENDORF[2], ANDREAS BUERKERT[1]

[1] *University of Kassel, Organic Plant Production and Agroecosystems Research in the Tropics and Subtropics, Germany*
[2] *University of Kassel, Soil Biology and Plant Nutrition, Germany*

In the arid tropics, year-round high temperatures lead to fast mineralisation in irrigated agriculture which need quantification to develop management systems with enhanced nitrogen(N) use efficiency. In this context, the objective of this experiment was to investigate the loss of N_2O-N from ^{15}N labelled, soil incorporated manure in a laboratory incubation experiment. To this end male goats were fed ^{15}N incorporated (0.675 at %) or normal (0.369 at %) Rhodes grass (*Chloris gayana*) to produce labelled (M) and unlabelled (m) manure. This manure was subsequently applied at a rate of $210\,kg\,N\,ha^{-1}$ in experimental plots for two cropping seasons in 2013/14 and 2014/15. Soil samples labelled only in the first year (Mm), labelled in both the years (MM) and control soils (C) were collected at the end of the 2014/15 cropping season for the laboratory experiments. Four treatments, control (C), Mm + unlabeled manure (Mmm), MM + unlabeled manure (MMm) and MM + labelled manure (MMM) were replicated 4 times. 150 g soil was placed in air-tight 1.6-liter glass jars inside a thermostat chamber at 25°C for 31 days. The soil was reconditioned for 10 days (pre-incubation) at 50 % water holding capacity before manure (equivalent to $100\,kg$ $N\,ha^{-1}$) was applied. Gas samples were taken 15 times during the incubation period before and after flushing the jars with fresh air. N_2O and CO_2 were analysed by gas chromatograph (GC) and isotopic N was determined by mass spectrometry (MS). Cumulative N_2O-N emissions were 3.2, 12.1, 23.1 and 24.7 $\mu g\,kg^{-1}$ soil for C, MMM, MMm and Mmm, respectively, for the total period. N derived from labelled manure (N_2O-Nman) was lower in Mmm and higher in MMm and MMM. On the day of highest N_2O emissions Nman was 9 % for Mmm, 16 % for MMm and 61 % for MMM. During pre-incubation 7–15 % of N_2O -N emission was derived from manure applied two years ago and 9–10 % was derived from manure applied 1 year ago. Our study showed that even after two years, soil applied goat manure contributed to N_2O emissions.

Keywords: [15]N, N_2O, Oman

Contact Address: Andreas Buerkert, University of Kassel, Organic Plant Production and Agroecosystems Research in the Tropics and Subtropics, Steinstraße 19, 37213 Witzenhausen, Germany, e-mail: buerkert@uni-kassel.de

The Influence of Conventional and Organic Farming Systems on Soil pH and Organic Carbon Storage in Nitisols

NOAH ADAMTEY[1], DAVID BAUTZE[1], MARTHA MUSYOKA[1], EDWARD KARANJA[1], ANNE MURIUKI[2], MONICAH MUCHERU-MUNA[3]

[1] *Research Institute of Organic Agriculture (FiBL), Dept. of International Cooperation, Switzerland*

[2] *Kenya Agricultural Research Institute, National Horticultural Research Center, Kenya*

[3] *Kenyatta University, Environmental Sciences, Kenya*

Concerns about soil acidification, low soil organic matter content and the impact of climate change on food security in the tropics necessitated the search for farming systems that can improve crop productivity, profitability, environmental sustainability and increase soil carbon storage. The specific objectives of this study were to measure the effect of organic and conventional farming systems on soil pH and SOC storage or loss in the humid zone of the Central highlands of Kenya. Conventional (Conv) and organic (Org) farming systems were compared at Chuka on Humic Nitisols with high inherent soil fertility and rainfall; and at Thika on Rhodic Nitisols with low soil fertility and rainfall under two input levels. Under the high-input system (High), high amounts of fertilisers, pesticides and irrigation water was applied to mimic commercial-scale production; whilst in the low input system (Low) low amounts of fertilisers and pesticides was applied under rain-fed conditions to mimic smallholder production. The conventional systems received synthetic fertilisers and cattle manure, whilst the organic systems received compost, mulch and crop residues. The trials which started in 2007 consisted of a 6-season -3-year crop rotation. At the end of six years, Org-High raised soil pH from 5.80 to 6.96 and 5.32 to 6.32 at Chuka and Thika. Conv-High raised pH to 5.84 at Thika but reduces pH to 5.57 at Chuka. The pH of Org-Low and Conv-Low were similar (5.70 and 5.55). Though it was not significant about 11.3 t ha^{-1} of SOC was stored under Org-High at Chuka and this was 85 % higher than 6.1 t ha^{-1} stored under Conv-High. At Thika Org-High and Conv-High loss SOC but the loss was 32 % higher under Conv-High. On the contrarily, under Conv-Low about 8.8 t ha^{-1} of SOC was stored and this was 63 % higher than 5.5 t ha^{-1} stored under Org-Low. The study concluded that high input organic farming has the potential to improve soil pH and SOC in the tropics, but this is dependent on site conditions, the quality of organic input material and management practices in the organic system.

Keywords: Conventional farming, high and low input systems, organic farming, soil organic carbon storage, soil pH

Contact Address: Noah Adamtey, Research Institute of Organic Agriculture (FiBL), Dept. of International Cooperation, Ackerstrasse 21, 5070 Frick, Switzerland, e-mail: noah.adamtey@fibl.org

ID 1131

Influence of Conventional and Organic Agricultural Management Practices on Soil Microbiological and Biochemical Parameters–Evidence from Semi-Arid Tropics

AMRITBIR RIAR[1], NISAR BHAT[2], BHUPENDRA SISODIA[3], MAHAVEER SHARMA[4], AKETI RAMESH[4], SANJEEDA IQBAL[2], GURBIR S. BHULLAR[1]

[1] *Research Institute of Organic Agriculture (FiBL), Dept. of International Cooperataion, Switzerland*

[2] *Holkar Science College, Indore, India,*

[3] *Biore Association, India*

[4] *ICAR-Directorate of Soybean Research (DSR-ICAR), India*

Provisions for sufficient quantities of food and fiber at affordable prices to the ever-increasing global population is one of the greatest challenges facing mankind. Ongoing environmental changes and diminishing natural resources together with lessons learnt from the unwanted effects of the 'green revolution' technologies are evidence that continuing with the conventional farming practices is not a sustainable option, so the agricultural production needs to be increased in a sustainable manner without compromising the ecological balance of the planet. Therefore, it is imperative to identify and develop alternative production systems, which are highly productive, system efficient, ecologically compatible and sustainable in long run yet economically viable too. Organic farming systems seem to offer a suitable alternative. Growing evidence show that organic agriculture is economically viable and competes with modern conventional agricultural systems. Moreover, organic practices envisages improved soil health, nutrient recycling, higher microbial biodiversity and ecosystem. However particularly in semi-arid tropics, these evidences are scarce. Hence it is evitable to obtain plausible information and reliable evidence. To substantiate this, the Research Institute of Organic Agriculture (FiBL) Switzerland is running a long-term farming systems comparison (SysCom) programme in Kenya, India and Bolivia, which provide a unique opportunity to verify the above claims/hypothesis. Within the framework of this program, a field site in Vertisols was set up in Madhya Pradesh, central India, consisting two year crop rotation with Cotton-Soybean-Wheat. Field plots continuously receiving organic and conventional treatments on a fixed plot basis since 2007, provide a unique opportunity to verify the above claims. Studies were carried out during 2014–15 to determine the differences in soil biological properties and processes among different management practices taking place over time. From the analysis, the preliminary results indicates that soil microbiological and biochemical properties influenced due to soil management practices. By and large, organic practices showing encouraging evidence of improvement of soil quality parameters. The detailed results of the study will be presented. The results are expected to enhance our understanding of the relationships of soil biological properties with agricultural management and crop production.

Keywords: Organic agriculture, semi-arid tropics, soil biological properties, soil quality

Contact Address: Amritbir Riar, Research Institute of Organic Agriculture (FiBL), Dept. of International Cooperataion, Ackerstrasse 113 Postfach 219, 5070 Frick, Switzerland, e-mail: amritbir.riar@fibl.org

Agrodiversity in Urban Farming Sites in Havanna (Cuba)

CHRISTIANE RINGLER, FRIEDRICH LEITGEB, CHRISTIAN R. VOGL

University of Natural Resources and Life Sciences (BOKU), Dept. of Sustainable Agricultural Systems, Austria

By 2030 most of the world population will be living in cities and the sustainable supply of this growing population with fresh fruits and vegetables will be of major concern. Urban agriculture can contribute to ensure regional food security, reducing transportation and ameliorate the micro-climate in urban areas. The conservation and management of agro(bio)diversity in urban farming sites are major elements for a sustainable and resource sparing farming system, food diversity and food security. The aim of this research was to describe three selected elements of the concept of agrodiversity (agrobiodiversity, management diversity and organisational diversity) developed by Brookfield (2001) and their characteristics in Havanna (Cuba). Fifteen urban farms in the city were investigated in 2013 using a purposive judgement sample. The methods used were qualitative semi-structured interviews and an inventory of all agricultural crops and trees was carried out. Plant species diversity was measured using Shannon Index and Jaccard-coefficient. 130 different cultivars out of 65 plant families could be identified. The diversity of land management styles suggests a high awareness amongst farmers for the enhancement of soil fertility and a high diversity of agroecological land management styles were encountered. Regarding the organisational diversity a collectivistic approach towards leadership with profound exchange amongst farmers about agricultural topics was found. The Cuban government managed to build up a framework for the development of diverse urban farming systems. Potential for improvement can be found in-situ conservation of seeds representing one of the most important genetic resources and hence contribute to food sovereignty.

Keywords: Agrobiodiversity, agrodiversity, agroecology, organic farming, urban farming, urban gardening, urban agriculture

Contact Address: Christian R. Vogl, University of Natural Resources and Life Sciences (BOKU), Dept. for Sustainable Agricultural Systems, Gregor-Mendel-Strasse 33, 1180 Vienna, Austria, e-mail: christian.vogl@boku.ac.at

ID 1048

Growth and Productivity of Clover in Response to the Preceding Crops and Organic Matter Applications in the Highlands of Awi Zone of Ethiopia

AGEGNEHU SHIBABAW[1], GETACHEW ALEMAYEHU[1], BERNHARD FREYER[2]

[1]*Bahir Dar University, Agronomy, Ethiopia*

[2]*University of Natural Resources and Life Sciences (BOKU), Division of Organic Farming, Austria*

Erosion, low carbon and soil fertility status is one of the dominating challenges in Ethiopian agriculture since decades. Our research aim was therefore, to combine a clover crop rotation, with *Sesbania* mulching and farm yard manure to rebuild soil fertility. Hence, both station and on-farm experiments were conducted from 2013 to 2014 in Awi Zone/Ethiopia to evaluate the outcome of preceding crops and organic matter applications on growth and biomass yield of clover. On station, two levels of preceding crop (wheat and potato) and four different levels of organic matter applications (control; 5 t ha^{-1} farmyard manure (FYM); 2.5 t ha^{-1} fresh *Sesbania* manure (FSB); and 5 t ha^{-1} FYM combined with 2.5 t ha^{-1} FSB) were factorially combined and laid out under randomised complete block design (RCBD) with four replications. In the like style, the treatment combinations were applied at four different farmers' fields considering each on-farm site as a replication. Days to 50 % flowering, plant height, number of tillers plant^{-1}, number of nodules plant^{-1}, root biomass plant^{-1}, shoot fresh and dry biomass ha^{-1} of clover were considered as study parameters. The overall experimental results indicate that only the main effect of organic matter application showed a significant effect on the growth parameters and biomass yield of clover. The highest total dry biomass of clover (5.6 t ha^{-1}) was recorded on FYM at 5 t ha^{-1} combined with FSB at 2.5 t ha^{-1} followed by FYM at 5 t ha^{-1} (4.68 t ha^{-1}). The unfertilised control gave the lowest mean dry biomass (3.06 t ha^{-1}) of clover compared to all other treatments. FYM at 5 t ha^{-1} combined with FSB at 2.5 t ha^{-1} gave as much as 86.6 % biomass yield advantage over the unfertilised control. Thus, FYM at 5 t ha^{-1} combined with FSB at 2.5 t ha^{-1} could be recommended for better dry biomass yield of clover. The finding also bridges the gaps of chronic livestock feed shortage and green manure under sub-Saharan environmental conditions.

Keywords: Biomass yield, clover, organic matter application, preceding crop

Contact Address: Agegnehu Shibabaw, Bahir Dar University, Agronomy, Bahir Dar, Ethiopia, e-mail: agegnehus@yahoo.com

Wild Edibles and Organic Minor Crops for Household Food Security and Upkeep of Diversity

MAGDALENA WANAWAN

Cordillera Integrated Agricultural Research Center, Dept. of Agriculture, Philippines

Ensuring food security and maintaining biodiversity are part of the pressing concerns for a country with fast growing population. Edible wild plants and endemic minor crops offer a wide range of nutrients as well as interesting and distinctive flavours. Moreover, they are healthful since they are free from synthetic fertilisers and pesticides.

The study profiled 15 edible wild plants and 20 minor cultivated crops (including pulses) that are organically grown in eco-tourism towns in the Cordillera, Philippines. The profile included the physical description of the plants, their elevation habitat, peak harvest season, crop utilisation, and nutritional analysis. The richness of the wild and endemic crops in nutritional content implies that such plants could fill the nutrition gaps of rural household consumers during the growing stages of their cultivated crops when there is no harvest.

Alongside the issue of food sustenance is the preservation of biodiversity which should not be ignored in sustaining the ecosystems where food is produced or naturally present as in the case of wild edibles . Conserving or restoring key elements of biodiversity supports the production of food and sustains beneficial organisms. The study found out that tribal farmers preserve cultivated plant diversity within agricultural ecosystems. The practices of astute seed selection, proper seed storage, organic seed production and seed exchange have made the crops sustainable. Seeds of organic endemic plants are preserved through continuous seed production, seed exchange and proper storage in tightly covered containers using charcoal, ash, and pine wood chips as preservatives. The soil which cradles plant biodiversity is conserved through terracing, edge bordering, hedge row planting organic crop production, and canal installation to divert run-off water from washing out the top soil.

Such practices confirm a trademark of the organic farmers in the Cordillera which is the instinctive preservation of the natural ecosystem including nature's biodiversity endowments.

Keywords: Biodiversity, edible wild plants, food security, minor crops, nutritional content

Contact Address: Magdalena Wanawan, Cordillera Integrated Agricultural Research Center, Dept. of Agriculture, Sto. Tomas Road, 2600 Baguio City, Philippines, e-mail: ciarc_da@yahoo.com

ID 744

Growth Response of Ethiopian Kale (*Brassica carinata*) and Spider Plant (*Gynandropsis gynandra*) to Mulching

NAOMI KETTER[1], ODULA OSIA[1], JOHN WESONGA[2], HARTMUT STÜTZEL[1]

[1]*Leibniz Universität Hannover, Inst. of Horticultural Production Systems, Germany*
[2]*Jomo Kenyatta University of Agriculture and Technology, Department of Horticulture, Kenya*

Water shortage especially in the light of climate change is likely to limit crop production. Mitigation measures include growing crops that are adapted to low moisture such as African indigenous vegetables and use of water saving technologies such as mulching. Mulching reduces unproductive evaporation leading to reduced water loss and results in increased yields and quality of vegetables under limited moisture environment. A study was carried out from January to April 2016 in JKUAT farm in Juja, Kenya, to study the effect of mulching on growth and quality of Ethiopian kale and spider plant. Plants were grown under organic mulch, plastic mulch and no mulch replicated four times. Leaf length, plant height, shoot dry weight, root dry weight, leaf area index (LAI), leaf temperature and soil temperature measurements were measured. Data was subjected to analysis of variance and LSD used for means separation. Leaf expansion was characterised by an initial slow expansion rate followed by a fast expansion rate before leveling off with significant differences in effect of mulch for both vegetables ($p < 0.01$). There was a significant difference in plant height among the mulch type for Ethiopian kale ($p < 0.01$) and no significant difference for spider plant. The height of Ethiopian kale was 106 cm under organic mulch compared to 78 cm and 86 cm under polythene mulch and un-mulched respectively. The dry weights of shoots and roots, leaf area index and leaf temperature did not differ significantly among the mulch treatments in both vegetables. The soil temperature of organic mulch (22.7°C for kale and 24.1°C for spider plant) and plastic mulch (25.6°C and 27.9°C in Ethiopian kale and spider plant respectively) differed significantly ($p < 0.01$). The results showed that mulch type increases plants vegetative growth as a result of the temperature in the soil.

Keywords: Dry weight, leaf area index (LAI), leaf temperature, soil temperature, water

Contact Address: Naomi Ketter, Leibniz Universität Hannover, Inst. of Horticultural Production Systems, Herrenhäuser Str. 2, D-30419 Hannover, Germany, e-mail: naomichelimo@gmail.com

Agricultural Land-Use Change and Implications on Rural Livelihoods: A Case Study from Dagana, Bhutan

LUKAS GRIESBACHER

University of Klagenfurt, Institute of Social Ecology, Austria

Bhutan, a small land-locked country in the eastern Himalayas, well-known for its ambitious Gross National Happiness (GNH) concept, is undergoing a rapid change in society. Thereby, the land-use system and the use of natural resources, still providing livelihoods to over 55 % of the Bhutanese society, is also changing. The Bhutanese farming systems still build widely on traditional knowledge and low-input strategies. Nutrient transfers from forest to the agricultural systems and the usage of traditional plant varieties are still important elements of these farming systems. However, cash-crops gain increasing importance and represent a major transformation factor in the agricultural sector which has decreased in provision of livelihoods as well as the share of GDP over the years.

Having this in mind, this research builds on a case study that was conducted in a degraded watershed in the district of Dagana, in the southern part of Bhutan.

In order to shed light on the complex nexus between farmers' livelihoods strategies and social-, ecological and economical driving forces, a qualitative ethnographical study was conducted, using participant observation and qualitative interviews as the main methods during the fieldwork. The findings of this local study are discussed in relation to general theories on agricultural land-use change.

The research revealed critical points of intersection between national policies, general developmental processes of change, such as electrification and the construction of roads in the region, as well as farmers´ decisions about how to make their living. Cardinal points in this relation are a strong focus on cash-crops that goes along with a shift from traditional subsistence oriented agriculture towards a more money-oriented farming system, the country's vision in the agricultural sector to produce 100 % organic by 2020, and a strong rural-urban migration linked to the educational system that creates a lack of labour. These points shall open up important questions about sustaining a future of natural resources and rural livelihoods that are strongly interconnected with socio-cultural processes.

Keywords: Agricultural development, land-use change, rural livelihoods

Contact Address: Lukas Griesbacher, University of Klagenfurt, Institute of Social Ecology, Schrekergasse 38, 1160 Vienna, Austria, e-mail: lukgriesbacher@gmx.net

ID 561

Indicators for Carbon Cycling in Four Different Cacao Production Systems in Bolivia

ULF SCHNEIDEWIND[1], FLORIAN HACKMANN[1], FELIX HEITKAMP[1], MONIKA SCHNEIDER[2], GERHARD GEROLD[1]

[1]Georg-August-Universität Göttingen, Dept. of Physical Geography, Germany
[2]Research Institute of Organic Agriculture (FiBL), Dept. of International Cooperation, Switzerland

Carbon loss of tropical forests by land use change can be reduced by locally adapted agroforestry (AF) systems. Cacao AF systems have higher above- and below-ground biomass in comparison to monoculture systems. The opportunity to increase and sequester organic carbon depends on the composition of shade trees and system management.

A cacao long-term field trial in Bolivia by The Research Institute of Organic Agriculture (FiBL) is arranged in a block design with system and management as factors. The systems are agroforestry (cacao under shade trees) and monoculture (cacao under full sun). The management is divided into organic and conventional. In the organic managed plots compost is applied. While inorganic fertilisers are used in the conventional management.

Litterfall was sampled monthly using 0.25 m^2 circular litter traps. Monthly means were summed up to gain the annual litterfall for each plot. Litter decomposition of cacao and *Erythrina* leaves was measured by litterbags with a mesh size of 1.0 mm, which were placed onto the litter layer. The decomposition experiment was performed for a period of 10 months. Soil samples for microbial biomass were taken down to a depth of 25 cm.

The annual litterfall (1.3 to 2.3 Mg C ha^{-1}) was highest in conventional agroforestry systems. Cacao litter decomposed slower than legume tree litter, but there was no difference between system or management. Microbial carbon and nitrogen contents were mainly affected in uppermost layers by management with lowest values in conventional monoculture. Soil taken nearby legume shadow trees showed especially higher microbial nitrogen values. This effect tended to extent down to the B-layer.

Overall, the study showed that due to higher biomass in shade trees in agroforestry system the total carbon re-accumulation was highest in the initial phase. While soil organic carbon was highest in organic management. Over time, the balance between litterfall and decomposition will decide about changing carbon stocks in the soil compartment.

Keywords: Biomass, carbon stocks, leaf mass residuals, litter fall, microbial biomass, *Theobroma cacao*

Contact Address: Ulf Schneidewind, Georg-August-Universität Göttingen, Dept. of Physical Geography, Goldschmidtstr. 5, Göttingen, Germany, e-mail: uschnei@gwdg.de

Improving Resilience of Cities through Urban Farming

MICHAEL KIRYA, ESAU GALUKANDE

Kampala Capital City Authority, Directorate of Gender, Community Services & Production, Uganda

Statistics show that many of the poorest people living in Kampala City have moved there from rural areas to seek jobs and other opportunities, which are often not as available as expected. The poor in the city often struggle with food scarcity and malnutrition. Many households in the city that fail to get a source of income are turning to urban agriculture farming for survival in terms of nutrition and income generation. Given the role urban farming plays in addressing challenges of food and nutrition insecurity, Kampala Capital Authority (KCCA) is spearheading interventions to promote urban farming in Kampala city through dissemination of skills and knowledge on kitchen gardening and organic waste recycling.

The unique feature of Kampala's urban farming systems is that they are based on organic farming principles that prohibit the use of chemicals such as fertilisers, and pesticides. Among the services KCCA provides urban farmers practicing organic farming are plant clinics that support plant protection through identification of pests and diseases and recommendation on control methods that comply with organic farming principles. Studies are underway to understand how local ecosystems can be induced to provide biological control against pest and diseases.

Organic producers in Kampala are coordinated and supported by an umbrella organisation the National Organic Agricultural Movement of Uganda (NOGAMU) which provides certification services, extension services and linkages to niche markets. Use of organic waste for urban agriculture is viewed by KCCA as a sustainable management of waste because of its contribution to the resilience of the city through reduction of GhG emissions generated by the transport of food from outside the city, preserving and restoring soil organic structure and water holding capacity making urban farming more draught resistant and improved water infiltration in the soil to prevent floods. The major source of waste for making organic fertiliser is KCCA managed markets and city households but the safety and efficacy of this fertiliser for urban farming are still unknown thus throwing up a number of major research and innovation issues. Research findings on these issues can readily inform investment decisions on waste management systems.

Keywords: Kampala, urban agriculture

Contact Address: Esau Galukande, Kampala Capital City Authority, Directorate of Gender, Community Services & Production, Kampala, Uganda, e-mail: egalukande@kcca.go.ug

ID 782

Production and Distribution of Food Crop Diversity in Urban Horticultural Plots in Havana (Cuba)

MARIA LAVINIA MAYRHOFFER, FRIEDRICH LEITGEB, CHRISTIAN R. VOGL

University of Natural Resources and Life Sciences (BOKU), Dept. of Sustainable Agricultural Systems, Austria

Urban horticultural plots have been a major element of Cuba's national strategy to ensure food security for citizens. Urban horticulture in Havana has become an internationally recognised popular movement, especially since production focuses on local, self-sufficient and ecological approaches. This study explores production conditions of selected horticultural plots in Havana (Cuba). The plant species composition, yields, the management of the plots and socio-economic factors that influence production were examined. The selection of horticultural plots occurred via judgment sampling. In the year 2013, thirty structured interviews with producers, administrators and workers were conducted. On-site observation of work processes, direct marketing and visits to farmers' markets completed this data. The results show no significant differences in appearance (e.g. structure of the plant beds, fencing) of horticultural plots and their production methods (irrigation, plant protection, fertilisation, tillage), however, the size of the plots differ. All plots used agroecological cultivation methods. Specifically in 25 of 30 plots compost and so-called biopreparados (prepared from *Nicotiana tabacum, -rustica, Azadirachta indica* and agricultural lime) were applied. The diversity of food crops is high, 47 food crop species from 27 families were identified in all plots. Species grown provided yields from 4.5–348 tonnes ha^{-1} year^{-1} in total in all plots, with leafy-vegetables being the most cultivated species. Horticultural production in Havana exemplifies a system that generates high production volumes through relatively low input of production factors in urban land use. The variability of data obtained did not allow an economic benefit calculation of individual plots. Further studies will be required.

Keywords: Agrobiodiversity, agroecology, organic farming, urban farming, urban gardening, urban agriculture

---

Contact Address: Christian R. Vogl, University of Natural Resources and Life Sciences (BOKU), Dept. for Sustainable Agricultural Systems, Gregor-Mendel-Strasse 33, 1180 Vienna, Austria, e-mail: christian.vogl@boku.ac.at

ID 1040

Organic markets and certification

Livelihoods and Niche Markets: A Case Study of Kenyan Smallholder Bee Keepers in Mwingi

PETER MUSINGUZI, ASKE SKOVMAND BOSSELMANN, POULIOT MARIÉVE

University of Copenhagen, Department of Food & Resource Economics, Denmark

Honey is a product with quality premiums. Organic production is a quality parameter and thus niche markets have emerged with potentially large benefits to producers. Kenya is among East African countries with registered success in niche markets targeting smallholder farmers. However, the benefits to the smallholders depend on access to niche markets, functioning producer and organic farming support groups, extension personnel, skills and knowledge of organic farmers and government support. This study investigates contribution of certified organic honey production to the livelihoods of small scale beekeepers organised in a producer cooperative in Mwingi, eastern Kenya. Data were collected from December 2015 to February 2016 from 54 smallholder bee keepers' groups; 38 organic certified and 16 non-certified. Stratified random sampling was used and a total of 303 smallholder farmers (185 certified and 118 noncertified) were randomly sampled. Qualitative and quantitative data were collected for 2015 and 2008 (retrospectively) for purposes of comparing the before and after organic certification. The data were analysed using STATA. Results indicate no significant impact of certification on household incomes, quantity and price of honey produced and incidence of migration. The results further indicate that non certified smallholders were more diversified, food secure and sold less assets as compared to the certified organic farmers. Only 17 % of the certified smallholders attributed their wealth status to being organic certified. There are multiple reasons for lack of certification impact: i) no continuous support to certified farmers after initial phase as it is 100 % NGO supported, ii) low premium prices, iii) strong presence of middlemen, iv) lack of governmental support and iv) poorly managed Mwingi bee keepers and crops cooperative society where marketing of smallholders' organic honey is coordinated. This therefore calls for policy formulation that supports organic bee keeping for the benefit of organic farmers. Technical and financial support to the organic bee keepers' cooperative will be vital for marketing and adherence to organic standards. However, results indicate that certified organic bee keeping cannot single-handedly solve the livelihood challenges of smallholder farmers though it is vital for achievement of broad based rural development, sustainable livelihoods and conservation goals.

Keywords: Farmer cooperatives, Kenya, local certified organic production, niche markets, organic honey, rural livelihoods

---

Contact Address: Peter Musinguzi, University of Copenhagen, Department of Food & Resource Economics, Åkandevej 60, 3500 Værløse, Copenhagen, Denmark, e-mail: ktp990@alumni.ku.dk

Fairtrade Certification on Plantations: Household Welfare Implications for Hired Labour

KATHARINA KRUMBIEGEL, MEIKE WOLLNI

Georg-August-Universität Göttingen, Dept. of Agricultural Economics and Rural Development, Germany

About 500 million workers are employed on agricultural plantations world-wide. They are considered to be one of the most vulnerable groups in the global trade system. Recent developments such as the vertical integration of agri-food chains, access to international markets and rising consumer awareness have led to the increased adoption of sustainability standards, such as Fairtrade. While Fairtrade measures aim to ensure adequate employment conditions, collective action and fair wages its ultimate objective is to improve the socioeconomic well-being of workers' households and their communities. The question remains whether Fairtrade certification of large-scale plantations can contribute to decreasing workers' monetary and non-monetary poverty. This study therefore aims to assess whether Fairtrade can raise income levels of worker households and whether this may potentially lead to lower multidimensional poverty. The latter may be achieved through higher incomes but also other contributing factors, such as loan availability and permanent work contracts, which could help buffer shocks and support long-term planning. Service provisions like medical care and projects financed by the Fairtrade premium may lower expenditure requirements. For our study we use original survey data from 340 plantation workers and their households in the Ghanaian pineapple export sector. Our respondents are workers from four Fairtrade certified companies and four Non-Fairtrade certified companies. To address the research questions, we apply matching approaches as well as regression analysis, controlling for company level scale of production and productivity levels. Our findings confirm that Fairtrade workers have higher incomes due to higher wages on Fairtrade certified plantations. However, we find no evidence for lower multidimensional poverty. Here, indicators of multidimensional poverty do not point towards a consistent level of deprivation for either Fairtrade workers or Non-Fairtrade workers. Fairtrade workers are statistically significantly more deprived regarding food security, child mortality, adult education and flooring and Non-Fairtrade workers are more deprived in terms of electricity availability, access to clean drinking water and asset accumulation. We will further assess the pathways between higher income levels and poverty reduction and differentiate between rather short and more long-term poverty indicators.

Keywords: Agricultural labourers, asset accumulation, plantation agriculture

Contact Address: Katharina Krumbiegel, Georg-August-Universität Göttingen, Dept. of Agricultural Economics and Rural Development, Heinrich-Düker-Weg 12, 37073 Göttingen, Germany, e-mail: katharina.krumbiegel@agr.uni-goettingen.de

ID 578

Creating through Geographical Indication: Case of Kilimanjaro Coffee

INNOCENSIA JOHN[1], RAZACK LOKINA[1], HENRIK EGELYNG[2]

[1] *University of Dar es Salaam, Economics, Tanzania*
[2] *University of Copenhagen, Food and Resource Economics, Denmark*

As the demand for quality food increases in the global market, many developed countries like the EU countries have used geographical indication (GI) to protect the unique attributes linked to the area of production. GI not only provides consumers with quality food but also enables the producers of these products to earn a higher income of their product, protect the environment so they can maintain the quality of such products. Similar to the approach for wine in France and Italy, more and more coffee-producing countries try to establish appellation systems for coffee. Countries like Colombia and Ethiopia have already legally protected GIs for Coffee. The same can be done for the case of Tanzania that has a conducive environment for protecting its agricultural produce.

This paper aims to investigate the extent to which GI labeling could add value to the already created value of Kilimanjaro Coffee. It as well looks at the quality traits of the product that are linked to the environment, marketing, GI awareness and the institutional framework. A probit model based on a survey of farmers was developed to identify which factors influence the GI labeling and in turn increase farmer's benefits from coffee sales. A qualitative analysis of the product attributes was done from an in-depth interview with key informants.

Results from the fieldwork indicated that Kilimanjaro coffee organically grown below the rich volcanic soils of Mount Kilimanjaro, with unique aroma, rich in acidity and body, sweet taste with balanced flavours due to mineral nutrients from volcanic soils provides prospects for the product to be protected as a GI. The results of the regression analysis indicate that social and human capital variables significantly influence GI labeling of Kilimanjaro Farmers in adding value to their coffee produced.

Keywords: Coffee, geographical indications, probit analysis, quality traits

Contact Address: Innocensia John, University of Dar es Salaam, Economics, Dar es Salaam, Tanzania, e-mail: jinnocensia@gmail.com

Analysing Economic Efficiency in Organic and Fair Trade Cotton Production in Benin

DANSINOU SILVERE TOVIGNAN, ZAKARI F. TASSOU, S. PAUL HOUNTONDJI

Universty of Parakou, Fac. of Agronomy, Benin

Organic farming has been recognised as belonging to the most environmental friendly way of production and consumption. In particular, the adoption of such method in cash crop production in West African small scale system has reduced enormously farmers' reliance on synthetic chemical inputs. In order to enlarge the market outlets their organic cotton, farmers in West Africa use to get certified also for the fair trade standard in order to take advantage of its social benefits. In this regard, organic and fair trade certified cotton appears to be one important development tool for small producers and their communities. The present study investigates technical, allocative and economic efficiencies in organic and fair trade cotton (OFTC) production in Benin. Cross sectional data were collected from 96 OFTC producers randomly selected in Banikoara, Tanguieta (north) and Glazoue (centre). Stochastic frontier production and cost of Cobb-Douglas, was used to estimate production functions and costs, and served to assess the levels of technical, allocative and economic efficiencies. In order to identify the determinants of efficiency indices, a Tobit regression analysis has been performed.

The results show that organic cotton production is economically profitable. The estimated average profit per hectare is about 100 Euros with a return to capital of 2.15. In addition, the average indices of technical, allocative and economic efficiencies obtained are respectively 0.90, 0.60 and 0.54. This reveals that OFTC production is to a large extend efficiently using the production resources. The factors determining these levels of efficiencies of OFTC producers are among others: the number of training received, exercise of a secondary activity beside farming, frequency of contact with extension agents, the fertility level of the soil, size of livestock and practice of crop rotation with legumes. Therefore, these factors are necessary tools to improve the efficiencies of OFTC, basically, farmers training on production itinerary and improving capacity in terms of soil fertility.

Keywords: Benin, economic efficiency, fair trade cotton, organic cotton, stochastic frontier, Tobit regression

Contact Address: Dansinou Silvere Tovignan, University of Parakou, Faculty of Agronomy, Parakou, Benin, e-mail: tsilvere@yahoo.fr

ID 870

The International Soy Market - A Fair Production Alternative for Smallholders in Paraguay?

JOHANNES MÖSSINGER, MATTHIAS SIEBOLD

University of Hohenheim, Inst. of Agricultural Sciences in the Tropics (Hans-Ruthenberg-Institute), Germany

Ranking fourth in the list of soy exporters, behind the big global players Brazil, USA and Argentina, Paraguay is stirring up in the world of soy business. Currently Paraguay is reforming its policies for the agricultural sector to meet the demand of the global markets and to be part of the global bioeconomy. Its soy frontier is expanding, and processing facilities are installed to enhance the soy value chain. An international civil organisation, called Round Table on Responsible Soy, promises good agricultural practices and environmental responsibility. Smallholders, as a significant part of the Paraguayan agricultural sector, struggle to cope with the environmental damage caused by cash crop production for export, social conflicts related to land ownership, a lack of suitable cash crops alternatives and start to plant soy.

However, crucial questions still beg for answers: Does soy constitute a fair income alternative and is it the most attractive strategy for small-scale farmers to participate in upcoming bioeconomic markets?

This study investigates the social and economic conditions of the soy business in the district of San Pedro del Parana, Itapúa. The Net-Map tool illustrates the actors involved, their linkages and the decisive positions in the soy business. A farm-based mathematical micro-simulation model, based on representative crops and livestock production as well as own-consumption, is used to analyse data related to smallholder farm labour, costs and revenues. Gross margin opportunities of the soy business for smallholders are compared with actual production schemes and further bioeconomic crops, such as the multipurpose palm *Acrocomia totai*.

Preliminary results suggest a scenario where technological progress and the conditions of (inter-) national markets hits unprepared and weak social smallholder structures, which results in unfair deals and poor economic decisions.

The conclusions help to describe what economic and social barriers, smallholder farmers will have to overcome if they wish to participate in upcoming bioeconomic markets.

Keywords: Bioeconomy, mathematical programming, net-map, Paraguay, smallholder, soy

Contact Address: Johannes Mössinger, University of Hohenheim, Inst. of Agricultural Sciences in the Tropics (Hans-Ruthenberg-Institute), Wollgrasweg 43, 70599 Stuttgart, Germany, e-mail: moessing@uni-hohenheim.de

Ethical Certification and Sustainable Transformation of the Cocoa Value Chain: Insights from Ghana

FRANZISKA OLLENDORF

Justus Liebig University Giessen, Dept. of Political Science, Germany

This contribution explores the local and the governmental dynamics evoked by 3rd party ethical certification schemes in the global cocoa value chain through the lenses of a civic governance concept. It provides a comprehensive insight in the implementation processes and the outcomes of one project of UTZ certification in Ghana. The results shall inform the normative discussion on fair global food systems.

Increasing consumer awareness of serious grievances in the global cocoa value chain – like child labour, severe poverty and deforestation – led to a rising demand for fair and sustainable chocolate products. Additionally, the cocoa industry fears a future decline in cocoa production due to aging cocoa farmers and trees, and therefore is more concerned about the sustainability and the long term supply of cocoa. Hence, recently ethical certification schemes are introduced by the cocoa industry. However, being understood as a promising innovation for improved sustainability of the cocoa production and farmers' livelihoods, the actual local outcomes still have to be assessed. Furthermore, in order to evaluate whether these interventions lead to more fairness in the global cocoa industry, we also need to consider the implications for the governance of the cocoa value chain and to reflect on the political scope of industry-led certification programmes.

In Ghana, the world's second largest cocoa producer, four certification programmes are conducted: Organic, Fairtrade, Rainforest Alliance, and UTZ. Building on empirical data collected during fieldwork in Ghana in 2015, the study analyses one case of UTZ certification. The paper discusses effects at the institutional and at the local level. At the institutional level, a hybridisation of the sector governance caused by the implementation of certification projects can be observed. At the local level, we find immediate positive effects, particularly on the quality and quantity of cocoa beans. However, other findings reveal problematic developments, for instance, the creation of inequalities among the farmers, missing participation of the target groups in decision-making or an increasing lack of public capacity to regulate the sector. These tendencies should be addressed and analysed carefully before considering certification as the new panacea for a sustainable transformation of the cocoa sector.

Keywords: Certification, cocoa, Ghana, global value chains, governance, rural development

---

Contact Address: Franziska Ollendorf, Justus Liebig University Giessen, Dept. of Political Science, Karl Gloeckner Str. 21E, 35394 Giessen, Germany, e-mail: franziska.ollendorf@ggs.uni-giessen.de

ID 1056

Effects of Certification Schemes and Related Trainings on Sustainability on Small-Scale Tea Farms in Othaya, Kenya

IRENE VISSER[1], ANNE STINE HENRIKSEN[1], VILDE LAVOLL[1], SOFIE BUCH DALUM[2]

[1] University of Copenhagen, Natural Resource Management and Geosciences, Denmark
[2] University of Copenhagen, Anthropology, New Zealand

This report investigates how certification schemes and related Farmer Field School trainings are affecting the practices of small scale farmers in Othaya, Kenya. Mainstream sustainable development and the critique posed by political ecologists is used as a framework for analysing and discussing whether the local conditions of the tea farmers can be deemed sustainable.

The study identifies four main actors being the certifications schemes (Fairtrade and Rainforest Alliance), the Iriaini Tea Factory, Farmer Field Schools and the tea farmers, who all are especially influential when assessing the local sustainability. These actors represent differentiating structural positions and perceptions of sustainability, subsequently leading to a mismatch in how they see goals, strategies, challenges and outcomes in relation to sustainability.

Methods from the social sciences as well as the natural sciences have been adopted to investigate the processes, perceptions, experiences with and social, economic and environmental outcomes of sustainability. By understanding sustainability as more than an outcome and by including multiple actors that are affecting that process, a holistic picture has been created.

The report concludes, that especially economic sustainability in the area can be problematized, as most of the farmers included in the research did not consider the income from tea production satisfying in terms of sustaining themselves and their families. This is especially problematic since farmers' perception of sustainability is mostly voiced in economical terms. This contradicts the overall vision of Fairtrade and Rainforest Alliance and on this basis a critique of the overall visions behind mainstream sustainable development is posed.

Keywords: Certification, farmer field schools, sustainability, tea

Contact Address: Irene Visser, University of Copenhagen, Natural Resource Management and Geosciences, Rødovrevej 55, 2610 Rødovre, Denmark, e-mail: i.m.visser@hotmail.nl

Short Supply Chains of Organic Food: Socioeconomic Emancipation of Family Farmers

BRUNO JACOBSON DA SILVA[1], PAULINE DELTOUR[2], OSCAR ROVER[1]

[1]*Federal University of Santa Catarina, Laboratory of Commercialization of Family Farmer, Brazil*

[2]*Ghent University, Dept. of Crop Protection: Phytopathology Laboratory, Belgium*

Organic production of vegetables and fruits is assumed to be less harmful for the environment than conventional production and brings socioeconomic development for smallholder farmers. The distribution of organic products can be executed via the conventional chain or via alternatives, such as the short food supply chain, in which the intermediates between farmer and consumer are limited to maximum one. The relationship between farmers and retailers of short food supply chains can promote socioeconomic emancipation, although they might be as oppressing as conventional retailing in long chains. To gain inside in the relationships of farmers and short food supply chain retailers, an analysis of both actors was performed with regard to organic fruits and vegetables. One fair, one specialised organic shop and one supermarket were analysed on reciprocity in relationships and autonomy of the small holder farmers by surveys. The supermarket and the specialised shop were determined as canals with a considerable sales volume and great importance in the production flow, but showed asymmetric relations with the small holder suppliers. On the contrary, the fair revealed relationships with its suppliers which were far more symmetric, but accounted for a smaller sales volume. The fair resulted as the most democratic supply modality which offers the most autonomy to its suppliers. Due to the engagement of the fair in farmer organisations, farmers are involved in important decisions such as price setting. Moreover, the fair was, in comparison with the supermarket and the specialised shop, more efficacious in turning its objectives to face social, economic and environmental problems of commercialisation of organic products into action. Consequently, to promote a more correct and efficient market, it would be valuable to firstly, open new fairs which can bridge the gap in sales volume in the most symmetric way and secondly, stimulate supermarkets and specialised organic shops to invest in participation with the farmers.

Keywords: Autonomy of smallholder farmers, organic production, short retail chain

Contact Address: Pauline Deltour, Ghent University, Dept. of Crop Protection: Phytopathology Laboratory, Coupure Links 653, 9000 Ghent, Belgium, e-mail: pauline.deltour@ugent.be

ID 1035

Fair Trade and Institutions in Sustainable Value Chain Development for Cash Crops in Protected Landscapes

RAJESH S. KUMAR[1], NITY NISHANT[2], N.K. BINU[3], SHILPI KUNDU[4], RADHAKRISHNAN P.[5]

[1] University of East Anglia (UEA), School of International Development, United Kingdom
[2] University of Delhi, India,
[3] Kerala Agricultural University, Dept. of Tree Physiology and Breeding, India
[4] Sher-e-Bangla Agricultural University, Agricultural Extension & Information System, Bangladesh
[5] Periyar Tiger Conservation Foundation, India

Environmentally sustainable agricultural practices are integral to the policies and practices to realise sustainable development goals. The anchoring roles of fair trade and organic cultivation in building community-level environmental stewardship as well as livelihood security are reported from several parts of the world. However, organic production and fair trade of food materials by the resource dependent communities in forested landscapes surrounded by protected areas entail multiple challenges such as requirements of sustainability, the long-term viability of local biodiversity values and potentials, availability of options for socio-economic, political development of the local communities, etc,. The context therefore, calls for a synergistic integration of a spectrum of social, economic, ecological, institutional/political factors to build as well as to promote a sustainable base for production chains. The major dimensions that play critical roles in realising the dynamics in such production process are ecological knowledge, sustainable farming skills, economic viability, equity, institutional support/role of agencies etc,. However, policy positions and discourses for integrating food production, environment, and poverty reduction goals, biodiversity conservation, wildlife and ecosystem services in such landscapes are still evolving in different parts of the world. In this context, we have analysed the roles of fair trade as well as agencies/institutions in shaping eco-farming by the indigenous communities in the forested landscape in the Periyar Tiger Reserve in Kerala State, India to understand the dynamics of factors contributing to sustainable agriculture. We observed that organic farming can meet the requirements of eco-farming when challenges of sustainability are addressed at the landscape level along with equity and inclusivity in value chain development. We consider that the empirical evidence generated by the study validates the requirements of a much needed integrated policy for combining the synergy of nature conservation and sustainable agriculture for improved livelihood development and observed that fair trade and institutions play potential roles in realising that synergy. The case evidence depicts an encouraging scenario since, development and implementation of an integrated policy reconciling the development needs of indigenous communities, food security and livelihood protection whilst conserving wildlife and biodiversity resources in protected area landscapes, on ground, remains a major undertaking.

Keywords: Conservation agency, environmentally sustainable production, fair trade

Contact Address: Rajesh S. Kumar, University of East Anglia (UEA), School of International Development, 21 B Mary Chapman Court, NR3 3DX Norwich, United Kingdom, e-mail: rskumarifs@gmail.com

Coffee Farmers and Cooperatives Value Chain Coordination: Innovative Model for International Fair Trade Practices

LYLA RACHMANINGTYAS

Georg-August Universität Göttingen, Agriculture Economics and Rural Development, Germany

The structural change in agrifood products has developed the need for vertical coordination in value chains. Since agribusiness cooperatives are dealing with the internalisation of agrifood markets, cooperatives have internationalised their activities. Particularly, in coffee production, international sustainability practices for coffee products have structured the value chain in the highly brand oriented specialty sector. The impact of sustainability practices has changed the role of farmer cooperatives. In order to accomplish organic and fair trade certification, small farmers are required to form cooperatives for facilitating inspection and monitoring, and to conduct the various corporate codes. In the current value chain, cooperatives are a superior mode and are prioritised over traditional trade structures. However, it seems that many tensions have been created in local organisations. Coffee cooperatives that are dominated by small farmers face massive questions whether the fair trade practice will guarantee the farmers to receive premium price and better production or will it pull the farmers into tangled certification requirements and additional costs to guarantee the sustainability practices. A theory states that cooperatives are pooled interdependent organisations, characterised by a horizontal coordination mechanism, which is particularly true by standardisation of product quality. This research will elaborate a pooled interdependent organisation model and will view the parallel coordination on three dimensions: complementary (among service providers), horizontally (along farmers) and vertically (between farmers, buyers and end consumers). The model takes into consideration different value chain leaders, namely: farmer led model, trader-led model, processor led model and service provider led model. This research is basically based on literature determining and analysing the role of coffee farmers and cooperatives in value chain coordination to challenge international sustainability practices. At the end, this research will come up with an operational framework for farmers and cooperatives to maintain the innovative model for win-win strategy to deal with the international fair trade practices.

Keywords: Coffee farmers, cooperative, fair trade, value chain coordination

---

Contact Address: Lyla Rachmaningtyas, Georg-August Universität Göttingen, Agriculture Economics and Rural Development, Hermann Rein Strase 11, 37075 Göttingen, Germany, e-mail: lyla_rachmaningtyas@yahoo.com

ID 1117

Future Prospects of Camel Milk under Different Conditions in Sudan: A Source of Organic Food

IBRAHIM DOWELMADINA[1], IBTISAM EL ZUBEIR[2], OMER ARABI[3]

[1] *University of Gezira, Dept. of Genetics and Animal Breeding, Sudan*
[2] *University of Khartoum, Dept. of Dairy Production, Sudan*
[3] *University of Gezira, Dept. of Basic Science, Sudan*

The present study was designed to highlight the possibility of utilisation of camel milk as organic food. Camels are used traditionally as a source of food, in race and transportation of belongings when pastoral families relocate to new areas, and also in fetching water to pastoral homesteads for household utilisation. Camel milk is considered as one of the most valuable food sources for nomadic people in arid and semi arid zones. For centuries it has been consumed either fresh or fermented due to its nutritional values and medicinal properties. In Sudan, most camels are managed in traditional systems that include nomadic, transhumance or semi-nomadic systems and recently the sedentary or semi-sedentary systems, and intensive production systems. A field survey was conducted in two production systems in Sudan. The first was the dominant nomadic system that depend mainly on the grazing pasture, representing 40 % of the total camel milk production in Sudan. The second was the new semi-intensive system that was initiated with the objective of commercialisation of camel milk associated with harvesting of camel milk in pre-urban areas of Khartoum. The highest significant percentages of camel milk composition: protein, lactose, total solids, solids non fat, fatty acids and vitamins (A, E and C) levels were recorded for the camel in the traditional nomadic system compared to those from semi-intensive system. This paper recommended utilisation of camel milk, especially from traditional systems, as functional and organic food. It also suggests ways to harness the potentials of dromedaries to ensure organic food and environmental sustainability.

Keywords: Camel, food, management systems, Sudan

Contact Address: Ibrahim Dowelmadina, University of Gezira, Dept. of Genetics and Animal Breeding, University Street, 20 Wad Madani-sudan, Sudan, e-mail: camel2022@gmail.com

Transaction Costs in an Association of Organic Farmers in Goiania, Brazil

MARTA CLAUZET LEITE DE SOUZA[1], ALCIDO ELENOR WANDER[2]

[1] *Federal University of Goias (UFG), Brazil*

[2] *Brazilian Agricultural Research Corporation (EMBRAPA), National Rice and Beans Research Center (CNPAF), Brazil*

This study aimed to analyse the transaction costs of an association of organic farmers located in Goiania, Goias state, Brazil. We analysed the marketing and organisation relations based on data collected at the Association for the Development of Organic Farming in Goias state (ADAO/GO). This association exists since 2000. It brings together small farmers, technicians and consumers who practice organic farming and are organised to improve the marketing, disseminating production techniques, and encourage the consumption of organic products. Information were obtained through interviews with association leaders. The ADAO/GO association provides public places for direct to consumer marketing. Marketing through supermarkets and other retailers is discouraged because of their predatory pricing policy. Since the attribute of being organic is invisible to the consumer, to establish and to sustain a lasting relationship between farmers and consumers is a challenging issue. Certification is one possible strategy to reduce information asymmetry and overcome distrust of consumers regarding organic products. However, certification cost may be high and will only pay off if the costs of measuring an invisible trait, e.g. as being organic, are high enough. A label of the association exists and is used by all member farms. As long as all farmers follow the rules, the label will get stronger and its reputation may improve. If, for any reason, a member farmer decides to break rules of the certification scheme, the whole association will suffer the consequences. This is the main transaction cost related to the collective action of the association and its common certified marketing label.

Keywords: Certification, collective action, direct marketing, organic farming

Contact Address: Alcido Elenor Wander, Brazilian Agricultural Research Corporation (EMBRAPA), National Rice and Beans Research Center (CNPAF), Rodovia GO-462, km 12, 75375-000 Santo Antonio de Goias, Brazil, e-mail: alcido.wander@embrapa.br

ID 965

The Current Debate on Governance and the Regulatory Framework on Organic Farming in the European Union and for Actors Importing Organic Products into the European Union from the Global South

CHRISTIAN R. VOGL

University of Natural Resources and Life Sciences (BOKU), Dept. for Sustainable Agricultural Systems, Austria

Organic farming is a promising agricultural method with positive effects on the human ecological and social environment. Governments have taken over a major role in defining organic farming by creating legal standards. Many countries all over the world have established a certification and accreditation system in order to protect the justified expectations of consumers with regard to processing and controlling the product quality of organic goods and to protecting producers from fraudulent trade practices. As they are relevant to international trade, these standards do not only influence the organic farming movement on the national level but also have a converse impact across national borders. Organic farming was established in a bottom-up process as farmers aimed to design sustainable ways of using natural resources. Farmers' traditional knowledge and their awareness of ecological, as well as, of social affairs was the main base for the development of organic farming. Since public interest in organic farming has grown rapidly, the ownership on the process of defining organic farming is no longer in the hands of farmers and the original principles and aims of the movement seem to be threatened by a bureaucratic view of "recipe"-organic farming. However, unsolved problems also exist between the necessities of global harmonisation and the local adaptability of the standards on organic farming. This paper structures the current discussion on compliance, conformity and equivalence of standard, introduces the current debate on alternatives to third party certification such as participatory guaranteee systems or internal control systems and gives future prospects for potential topics of urgently needed research on governance in organic farming.

Keywords: Governance, organic farming

Contact Address: Christian R. Vogl, University of Natural Resources and Life Sciences (BOKU), Dept. for Sustainable Agricultural Systems, Gregor-Mendel-Strasse 33, 1180 Vienna, Austria, e-mail: christian.vogl@boku.ac.at

Organic strategies and policies

The Future of Smallholder Farms in Ethiopia

BERNHARD FREYER[1], JIM BINGEN[2], YOSEPH TEWODROS DELELEGN[3]

[1] *University of Natural Resources and Life Sciences (BOKU), Division of Organic Farming, Austria*

[2] *Michigan State University, Dept. of Community Sustainability, United States of America*

[3] *University of Natural Resources and Life Sciences (BOKU), Austria*

Ethiopian smallholder farmers face a long list of challenges. Is organic farming the solution? A conversion to organic confronts the following facts: Productivity is compromised by extensive soil erosion, soils pH below 5, low soil fertility. Farmyard manure is often burned; animal density is nearly 100% above the carrying capacity of the land; a decline of natural forests; lack of crop rotation, ploughing with oxen up to five times; low seed bed quality; no application of lime; harvest and post harvest losses up to more than 50%; inadequate or non-existent storage facilities and processing equipment. Land: farm size is limited with approx. 0,5-2,0 ha per farm; pressure on communal land through growing population and land grabbing; and finally, farmers' land rights are limited. Markets: weak value chains and linkages to markets; high fees demanded by market brokers; export crops like vegetables or flowers, or organic coffee or honey, currently do not offer an opportunity to seriously raise income.

This snapshot describes the living conditions of rural farm households and documents the dramatic situation of the agricultural sector in Ethiopia. Conversion toward organic is not a question of one farm but a regional challenge. Conversion means: to open a 'repair shop' for soils and biodiversity; to adjust pH, crop rotation, alley and tree farming, humus, nutrient and fodder balances, etc. - or in other words resetting the farming system. Beyond the farm boundaries, it demands a fundamental transformation of the local and international market - current organic and fair trade systems alone cannot stabilize the farm economy -, including broader rural and urban development policies, educational, training and research.

Based on this situation analysis, we discuss a series of systemically coordinated activities that could be established autonomously at the regional level and contribute to a more sound development of Ethiopians future agriculture. One part of this transformation will depend upon a fundamental change in international development aid and research that moves away from separate and individual donor projects to truly coordinated policies and programs.

Keywords: Ethiopia, organic farming, policies, smallholder, transformation

Contact Address: Bernhard Freyer, University of Natural Resources and Life Sciences (BOKU), Division of Organic Farming, Gregor Mendel Straße 33, 1180 Wien, Austria, e-mail: Bernhard.Freyer@boku.ac.at

Cuba's Agricultural Innovation System

FRIEDRICH LEITGEB, CHRISTIAN R. VOGL

University of Natural Resources and Life Sciences (BOKU), Dept. of Sustainable Agricultural Systems, Austria

Innovations are the driving force for agricultural development under present diverse situations of uncertainty. The innovation system perspective acknowledges the contributions made by all stakeholders involved in knowledge development, dissemination and appropriation. According to the specific agricultural production system, farmers adopt innovations, modify them or innovate on their own. This paper examines the role of farmers' experiments and innovations in Cuba's agricultural innovation and knowledge system (AKIS), identifies knowledge exchange encounters and describes some strategies implemented to institutionalize farmers' experiments and innovations. The research methods comprised 34 semi-structured interviews with agricultural experts from the science, administration and advisory system, and 31 free list questionnaires to assess the institutional influence on farmers' experiments and innovations. In addition, three case studies of outstanding farmers' experiments are presented, based upon extensive participant observation at their farms. The results suggest that the government's commitment to social participation in knowledge development provides the basic prerequisite for an effective integration of farmers' experiments and innovation in Cuba. The historically conditioned vertical structure of knowledge development and dissemination is gradually changing toward more horizontal procedures. The dynamic exchange of ideas at all kinds of interactive meetings, such as workshops or farmers' field schools, have favoured farmer to farmer learning as well as knowledge sharing with research, academic and extension officials. This multi-stakeholders' approach contributes to institutionalize farmers' knowledge. Farmers' experiments and innovations play a major role in improving farm management and thereby can contribute to build resilience at the farming system level as well as for the national agricultural system.

Keywords: Innovation, knowledge systems, organic agriculture, organic farming

Contact Address: Christian R. Vogl, University of Natural Resources and Life Sciences (BOKU), Dept. for Sustainable Agricultural Systems, Gregor-Mendel-Strasse 33, 1180 Vienna, Austria, e-mail: christian.vogl@boku.ac.at

ID 1058

Identifying the Barriers of Organic Crop Production in Hamedan, Iran

SOMAYE LATIFI[1], MICHAEL HAUSER[2], SARA KAWEESA[2]

[1]*University of Tabriz, Dept. of Extension and Rural Development, Iran*
[2]*University of Natural Resources and Life Sciences (BOKU), Centre for Development Research (CDR), Austria*

Organic farming was originally known as a form of agriculture that mainly relies on traditional production techniques, that is, without use of fertilisers and pesticides. However Organic farming has now evolved to mean that it can combine traditional knowledge, innovations and modern techniques that are backed by scientific research. It has also recently been introduced as one of the most sustainable and reasonable alternatives to conventional agriculture that can effectively improve food security and provide additional benefits. Nevertheless, farmers are reluctant to take up organic farming. Therefore, the main purpose of this study was to determine the factors that are hindering the growth of the organic production sector in the Hamedan province. We employed qualitative methods to gather data from key informants that were made up of experts and extension workers. A sample of 28 cases was determined using purposive sampling method. The interviews administered were guided by open-ended questionnaires. We also held two (2) separate focus group discussions each having eight (8) certified organic farmers. A total of 25 barriers were identified and put into five categories namely; financial, government support, technical and managerial, cognitive and emotional. The results from expert opinions also showed that lack of government support has the greatest importance in motivating conventional farmers to convert to organic farming. Other critical barriers included lack of experience in technology and management of weeds, pests and disease, lack of information, farmers' beliefs and attitudes, more resources in terms of time, energy and labour, the absence of specific markets, lack of special insurance services and uncertainty about economic returns when implementing organic farming practices. Understanding these barriers is critical for better policy and planning development in the country.

Keywords: Barriers, development, Hamedan province, Iran, organic crop production

Contact Address: Somaye Latifi, University of Tabriz, Dept. of Extension and Rural Development, No 7, Tohid Alley, Qiam Alley, Shahid Zamani Blv , 6517779369 Hamedan, Iran, e-mail: somaye.latifi84@gmail.com

Organic Agriculture in Bhutan - A Two-Edged Sword?
The Trade-Off Between Environmental Sustainability and Rice Self-Sufficiency

ARNDT FEUERBACHER, OLE BOYSEN, HARALD GRETHE

Humboldt-Universität zu Berlin, International Agricultural Trade and Development, Germany

Bhutan pursues an ambitious agricultural policy: by 2020 it intends to become the first nation to have fully converted to organic farming. Due to its benefits for environmental sustainability, organic agriculture is well aligned with Bhutan's philosophy of gross national happiness. In Bhutan, the cultivation of most crops is considered "organic by default", which does not hold for paddy cultivation. A recent field study in Bhutan has found that conversion to organic agriculture would increase the labour requirement for paddy production by 11 %, as agrochemicals have to be substituted by manual weeding and application of farmyard manure. Since paddy production is already highly labour intensive in Bhutan, a nationwide conversion to organic agriculture is likely to decrease farmers' competitiveness reducing the self-sufficiency in rice. Food self-sufficiency is, however, another priority of Bhutan's agricultural policy. The objective of this paper is to assess the trade-off between food self-sufficiency and achieving environmental sustainability through organic agriculture. As agriculture employs 57 % of Bhutan's labour force and due to the large relevance of rice as the major staple food, an economy-wide model is used to estimate the impacts of the organic agriculture policy. We use a recently developed social-accounting-matrix (SAM) for Bhutan based on 2012 within a single-country computable-general-equilibrium (CGE) model. The 2012 Bhutan SAM has a detailed depiction of the agricultural sector including farm inputs such as farm yard manure, crop residues and draught animal services. Two sets of scenarios are simulated. Within the first set, we simulate scenarios of government interventions that aim to increase food self-sufficiency resulting in varying degrees of self-sufficiency compared to the base. In the second set, we simulate the same government interventions as before, but now under a full conversion to organic agriculture. Comparing scenarios of the first and second set will allow to assess the trade-off between organic agriculture and different levels of self-sufficiency. Expected results are that the conversion to organic agriculture will result in lower self-sufficiency levels. Further, we expect to observe largest impacts in the paddy production sector, because of its relative high share of agrochemical input that needs to be substituted.

Keywords: Bhutan, food self-sufficiency, general equilibrium modelling, organic agriculture, policy analysis

---

Contact Address: Arndt Feuerbacher, Humboldt-Universität zu Berlin, International Agricultural Trade and Development, Unter den Linden 6, 10099 Berlin, Germany, e-mail: arndt.feuerbacher@hu-berlin.de

ID 1079

Factors Affecting the Adoption and Rejection of Organic Crops in the Khuzestan, Iran

FOROGH ALIGHOLI, AZIM AJILI, MASOUD YAZDANPANAH, MASOUMEH FOROUZANI

Ramin Agriculture and Natural Resources University (Khouzestan), Dept. of Agricultural Extension and Education, Iran

Although application of chemical inputs could affect the increase of agricultural crop yields positively, irregular usage of such inputs causes serious problems for human and environment. As such, persuasion of farmers as the key producers to organic farming in order to optimum usage of external inputs is of great importance. An organic crop is defined by the matter produced with least chemical input (fertiliser) in order to have no risk for consumers. In line with this, a study was done to investigate the factors affecting adoption and/or rejection of cultivating organic crops and to assign the best fitted model of adoption among vegetable growers in Khuzestan Province. The study was based on a survey using a non-proportional stratified random sampling in which 170 organic crop adopters as well as 170 non-adopters were selected. The needed data was gathered through a questionnaire. The results revealed that there was a significant difference between both groups in terms of using information channels and the number of visiting change agents. In addition, the adopters of organic crops had more favourite attitude towards environmental protection and low usage of chemical inputs. They also demonstrated more awareness of the disadvantages of conventional agriculture. The findings showed that the multiplicity model was the best fitted model which could well discriminate between adopters and non-adopters. The study recommends policy makers to apply the multi-dimensional (or multiplicity) model and to pay more attention to the quality of education and ratify the legal laws to support of organic crop producers

Keywords: Adoption, diffusion model, farm structure model, multiplicity model, organic crops

Contact Address: Masoud Yazdanpanah, Ramin Agriculture and Natural Resources University (Khouzestan), Dept. of Agricultural Extension and Education, Ahwaz, Iran, e-mail: masoudyazdan@gmail.com

Increasing Food Sovereignty with Urban Agriculture in Cuba

SARAH SCHNEIDER, FRIEDRICH LEITGEB, CHRISTIAN R. VOGL

University of Natural Resources and Life Sciences (BOKU), Dept. of Sustainable Agricultural Systems, Austria

Urban agriculture in Cuba has played an important role for citizens' food supply since the collapse of the Eastern Block. Through the land reform of 2008 and the Lineamientos of 2011, the Cuban government has aimed to support agriculture in order to increase national food production and reduce imports. However, the implementation of the designed measures faced obstacles. Therefore, the research objective was to display how the government's measures aiming to support domestic food production influenced urban agriculture. The qualitative research comprised semi-structured interviews with 15 urban farmers in Havana and revealed the respondents' experiences with the land reform and the Lineamientos and the potential of the reforms to implement food sovereignty. Findings show that the land reform has facilitated access to land for newcomer and existing farmers. However, availability of agricultural inputs has been limited and they were often expensive. Thus, urban farmers frequently produced farm inputs at their plots and applied sustainable farming practices to minimise their dependence on external inputs. The reforms have generated private marketing opportunities and have stimulated urban farmers to increase production. At the same time, subsidies have been reduced and consumers have faced increasing food prices. In conclusion, the land reform and the Lineamientos have created framework conditions for food sovereignty. However, the challenge is to increase the coherence of the theoretic aim and the practical implementation of the reforms. Cuba is known for its urbang agriculture but additional measures related to governance and policy could help amplyfing the already existing achivments in social, economic and ecological terms.

Keywords: Food sovereignty, governance, urban agriculture, urban farming, urban gardening

Contact Address: Christian R. Vogl, University of Natural Resources and Life Sciences (BOKU), Dept. for Sustainable Agricultural Systems, Gregor-Mendel-Strasse 33, 1180 Vienna, Austria, e-mail: christian.vogl@boku.ac.at

ID 1051

Farmer's Worlds of Justification for Conversion to Organic Farming

HADI VEISI[1], ALI ALIPOUR[2], ALIREZA SHOKRI[3], HOUMAN LIAGHATI[4]

[1] *Shahid Behehti University, Agroecology, Iran*

[2] *Zabol University, Agroecology, Iran*

[3] *Ministry of Agriculture, Iran*

[4] *Shahid Beheshti University, Environmental Sciences Research Institute, Iran*

Identifying and understanding the heterogeneity of the justifications of farmers is critical for designing better strategies to convert towards organic farming. The objective of this research is to identify and measure the motivations as justifications for conversion to organic farming in Iran. In this regard, the worlds of justification in convention theory i.e. 'market performance', 'industrial efficiency', 'civic equality', 'domestic relations', 'inspiration' and 'renown', more recently adding a seventh 'green-world', to explain the heterogeneity of reasons and motivations of farmers in organic agri-food system chain.

Survey data of 136 farmers was selected from the districts of Mashad village of Damadvan in Tehran Province and Gonabad of Khorasan Province. Analyses of data were accomplished using factor analysis, which was utilised to reveal the latent diminutions behind the motivations for organic production. Results suggest that economics motivations, health, safety concerns and environmental issues are the predominant justifications for conversion to organic farming, while social and ethical issues are of lesser importance. In conversation with the worlds of justification in convention theory, it can be argued that 'market performance', 'civic equality', 'green orders' are the most important of farmer's justifications for a conversion to organic food production. To prosper, the Iranian organic sector must consider these justifications in agricultural policy. Development of the alternative agri-food networks including farmers' markets and community supported agriculture (CSA) initiatives, sustainable procurement and informational strategies may help to encompass and address some of these justifications by providing more information to consumers and more support for farmers.

Keywords: Convention theory, conversion, justification, organic farming

Contact Address: Hadi Veisi, Shahid Behehti University, Agroecology, Velnjak, 19835-196 Tehran, Iran, e-mail: hveisi@gmail.com

Multi-Stakeholder Partnerships in Promoting Organic, Healthy and Sustainable Urban Communities

MA. CORAZON TAN

University of the Philippines Diliman, Dept. of Community Development, College of Social Work and Community Development, Philippines

Urban organic farming has become a viable strategy for many countries in Latin America, Africa and Asia for addressing urban poverty, food insecurity and for improving people's livelihoods. It has been proven to help provide accessible, diverse and healthy sources of food, accessible herbal medicines and supplementary sources of income for urban poor communities. Combining urban organic farming with urban resource and waste management could greatly enhance urban environmental management.

So that these interventions can create greater and sustainable impact, fair and just distribution of urban resources for public use (e.g. land) must be part of the social development policies and programs of local and national government. In the Philippines, there are existing policies that can support the practice of urban organic agriculture such as the Organic Act of 2010 and the Urban Agriculture Program. However, civil society organisations, NGOs and development practitioners must take an active part in advocating that sufficient urban resources be allocated for urban organic farming.

This presentation is based on the on-going study on multi-stakeholder partnership and building of solidarity between local governments, civil society organisations, NGOs and the academe in promoting urban organic farming and environmental management in cities in Metro Manila. Included in this initial study are initiatives by the local government of Quezon City in partnership with 34 villages that have started their urban organic farms. Another initiative is that of Marikina City wherein some public public primary and secondary schools have integrated into their curricular and extra curricular programs the teaching and actual practice of organic backyard gardening.

Organisations of poor urban communities and informal settlers must also play a key role in institutionalizing urban organic farming through the People's Plan, a plan formulated by the Beneficiary organisations of the local governments' programs for Socialized Public Housing. The People's Plans contain their plans for site development, self-help cooperatives and community livelihood projects. The People's Plan could be another entry point for institutionalizing urban organic farming as well as ensuring people's participation in the participatory development, management and governance of self-reliant,and sustainable urban communities and healthy urban eco-systems.

Keywords: Food security, multi-stakeholder partnership, social equity

Contact Address: Ma. Corazon Tan, University of the Philippines Diliman, Dept. of Community Development, College of Social Work and Community Development, 1101 Diliman, Quezon City, Philippines, e-mail: marionjimtan@yahoo.com

Promoting Green Economy in Hill Areas of Nepal

ASHMITA PANDEY, UJJAL TIWARI

Forum for Rural Welfare and Agricultural Reform for Development (FORWARD Nepal), Agriculture, Nepal

Green Economy is alluring for Nepal, as it aims at poverty reduction and sustainable development without impairing the nature and ensure reduced carbon emission, efficient use of natural resources, and better social equity. Nepal has immense potential to achieve a sustainable economic growth, as it has agriculture and natural resources-based economy, which accounts for one-third of the total GDP. However, the stable economic growth has been impeded by the political economy and unequal distribution of resources. The hill region shares 42 % of the total land area of the country, of which the forest blankets more than 50 %. Agriculture, livestock and forest resources underpin the livelihoods of rural people in hilly areas of Nepal, but still many areas of hills are food insecure, as the majority of households have marginal land holdings. The over dependency of poor and vulnerable communities on forest resources for food, fuel and fodder, and the dominance of shifting cultivation in hilly areas has threatened agrobiodiversity, which is further aggravated by the climate change impact. So, realising green economy as an approach to sustainable development, Nepal has adopted and promoted various green initiatives. Nepal has emphasised community and leasehold forests to maintain the balance between conservation and consumption, which promotes sustainable use of natural resources. Renewable energy as biogas plants, improved cooking stoves, and solar technologies are getting wider attention among the rural poor, as they are energy efficient, environment-friendly, and also creates green jobs. In true sense, green economy is not different to the practices adopted by the smallholder farmers in hilly areas of Nepal. However, the promotion of local level green initiatives along with integration and strengthening of existing green economy policies could lead transformational shift to low-emission and climate-resilient sustainable development. Various stakeholders as civil society, government line agencies, eco-clubs, and private agencies are upscaling the resource-conserving practices such as integrated pest management, integrated nutrient management, agroforestry, aquaculture, organic farming, water harvesting, waste recycling, crop and livestock integration, and integrated land use management along with the promotion of small and medium green enterprises, which could pave a path towards a greener economy.

Keywords: Climate change, green economy, natural resources, renewable energy

---

Contact Address: Ashmita Pandey, Forum for Rural Welfare and Agricultural Reform for Development (FORWARD Nepal), Agriculture, Kathmandu, Nepal, e-mail: apandey@forwardnepal.org

Opportunities for Mainstreaming Biodiversity for Food and Nutrition into Institutional Food Procurement Programs in Brazil

DANIELA MOURA DE OLIVEIRA BELTRAME[1], DANNY HUNTER[2], CAMILA NEVES SOARES OLIVEIRA[3], TERESA BORELLI[2], LIDIO CORADIN[1]

[1] Biodiversity for Food and Nutrition Project, Brazil
[2] Bioversity International, Nutrition and Marketing of Diversity Programme, Italy
[3] Ministry of Environment, Secretary of Biodiversity and Forests, Brazil

Brazil has a well-established political and regulatory framework aimed at promoting food and nutritional security. This framework represents an innovative and ethical social contract aimed at achieving social inclusion, sustainable livelihoods and citizenship. It includes the Food Acquisition Program (PAA) and the National School Meals Program (PNAE), institutional food procurement programs which provide equitable support to family farming by acquiring their products at a fair price and directing them to public schools, public programs and social organisations. PNAE and PAA have been identified by the GEF-funded Biodiversity for Food and Nutrition Project (BFN) as entry-points for potentially improving nutrition and livelihoods with links to native biodiversity. At least 30 % of the food purchased with federal funds through PNAE must be bought directly from family farmers. Both initiatives include ethical standards and incentives of up to 30 % in the price for organic or agroecological produce, prioritising purchases from quilombolas and indigenous communities, while also supporting family agriculture organisations to rescue, produce, store, and distribute seeds of local or traditional varieties. This creates new opportunities for the use of resources from Brazilian ecosystems, promoting institutional markets for biodiversity products while providing incentives for the management and sustainable use of agricultural biodiversity. However, assessments reveal that the proportion of food products from native biodiversity purchased overall by PNAE and PAA are low, which also reflects the current status of Brazilian agriculture, based mostly on exotic species. In order to better mainstream biodiversity into PNAE and PAA, the BFN Project in Brazil is working to increase awareness on the importance and nutritional value of native biodiversity species. Advocacy workshops, capacity building, as well as strategic alliances and partnerships with policy makers and other stakeholders are an important element of this, as are contributions to policy instruments that impact both programs. BFN also engages with Federal Universities, which are also collaborating centres for the implementation of PNAE, in research partnerships and activities to conduct analysis on the nutritional composition of 70 prioritised native fruit species and work with traditional communities to assess the knowledge and use of biodiversity foods.

Keywords: Biodiversity for food and nutrition, food procurement

Contact Address: Daniela Moura de Oliveira Beltrame, Biodiversity for Food and Nutrition Project, Sepn Quadra 505 W2 Norte, 70730542 Brasilia, Brazil, e-mail: dani.moura.oliveira@gmail.com

ID 467

Challenges and Constraints for the Adoption of Organic Farming Methods by Smallholder Farmers in Ethiopia

PIERRE ELLSSEL[1], MIA SCHOEBER[1], PAULA FLOTZINGER[1], BENJAMIN KLAPPOTH[2], SARAH OBERLÄNDER[3], ANNA PORCUNA[1]

[1] *University of Natural Resources and Life Sciences (BOKU), Dept. of Sustainable Agricultural Systems, Austria*

[2] *Universität für Bodenkultur Wien, Austria*

[3] *Justus-Liebig Universität Gießen, Dept. of Envrironmental Sciences, Germany*

Organic farming methods are not widespread neither well-known among a majority of smallholder farmers in Ethiopia; however, they bear great potential to improve productivity and efficiency while at the same time accomplishing sustainability goals such as protecting the soil and increasing resilience against drought - among many others. This study examines challenges and constraints for the adoption of organic farming methods among small scale farmers in Ethiopia. With the findings generated during a field visit in Ethiopia theses were elaborated and compared to findings from scholarly literature. Results show a variety of constraints, one being the deficit in knowledge about (the existence of) organic farming methods, as well as the perception of these techniques. Furthermore, a deficit in public support for research as well as effective and holistic support for smallholders poses a challenge for greater adoption. The availability of seeds and P-fertiliser as utilised in organic farming can be considered a further challenge. In addition, the strong increase in population leads to decreasing farm sizes which in return leaves less scope for the farmer to let land regenerate through e.g. fallows and growth of legumes. The consequences are non-sustainable land use with stagnating or decreasing yields. The widespread insecurity of land tenure is a further constraint that hinders investment into land. With the commitment of especially state actors many of the elaborated constraints might be properly addressed and eradicated. Strong support of research institutions, capacity building among extension services as well as farmers, farmer field schools and demonstration farms may be path-breaking.

Keywords: Capacity building, demonstration farms, Ethiopia, farmer field schools, organic farming, smallholder farming

Contact Address: Pierre Ellssel, University of Natural Resources and Life Sciences (BOKU), Dept. of Sustainable Agricultural Systems, Kröllgasse 27/8-9, 1150 Vienna, Austria, e-mail: pierree@web.de

Socioeconomics

Adoption, innovation and gender perspectives

"Being a Woman Farmer Is Like Being Cursed" - Gender Challenges in Horticultural Research in South Western Ethiopia

SARAH NISCHALKE[1], MULUNESH ABEBE ALEBACHEW[2], BENEBERU ASSEFA WONDIMAGEGNHU[2], TINA BEUCHELT[1]

[1] *University of Bonn, Center for Development Research (ZEF), Germany*

[2] *Food, Agriculture and Natural Resources Policy Analysis Network (FANRPAN), Nutri-HAF Project, Ethiopia*

Female farmers in the Global South are often overburdened with the multiple roles they inhabit in households, farming, childcare and the community. Horticultural projects that aim at improving nutrition and livelihoods usually address the women's domain of home gardens and vegetable farming. As a consequence interventions tend to increase the workload of female farmers and run the risk to negatively affect the well-being of women as well as the nutritional status of households. This paper explores gender challenges of horticultural research projects, using one example from Ethiopia, where an attempt is made to promote horticultural production in agroforestry systems without putting additional work on already overstrained women farmers. Data was collected through ethnography, 40 gender-disaggregated focus group discussions, 32 in-depth interviews and 13 key stakeholder interviews in four village sites in Oromia, Ethiopia. Research results showed a need for a critical reflection on the gender discourse in development. In Ethiopia, the government course of action on gender equality had as result that a gender and development rhetoric among male and female farmers was created, who predominantly assure that they control, access, share and decide everything equally. However, in reality, the underlying unequal power relations lead to a situation, where women are not relieved of work but work harder, because they face pressure and expectations to participate in male-dominated agricultural tasks. While men commiserate women with their workload, they do not take over female tasks. The research revealed that the new discourse in the scientific community on do-no-harm approaches in agricultural projects is more than relevant in the study region, where women already work at their limits. The paper investigates areas, where women farmers want and realistically could receive more support from male family members and it suggests strategies how to better involve men in the female domain of horticulture and nutrition in order to reduce the burden of women e.g. by saving time for firewood collection (cultivation of fast growing firewood trees) or through food processing techniques.

Keywords: Do-no-harm-approaches, gender, horticulture, nutrition, women's work burden

Contact Address: Sarah Nischalke, University of Bonn, Center for Development Research (ZEF), Bonn, Germany, e-mail: snischal@uni-bonn.de

ID 400

Access to Forest Resources: Women's Rights to *Parkia biglobosa* in Three Villages in Central-West Burkina Faso

CATHERINE A. K. PEHOU[1], HOURIA DJOUDI[2], BARBARA VINCETI[3]

[1] Center for International Forestry Research (CIFOR), Regional Office for West Africa, Burkina Faso

[2] Center for International Forestry Research (CIFOR), Head Office at Bogor, Indonesia

[3] Bioversity International, Italy

Parkia biglobosa, a NTFP tree species commonly known as "néré" is particularly important in the diet of rural and urban populations in the Sudano-Sahelian zone. The seeds are processed into a highly nutritious sauce, called "soumbala", combined with cereal dishes. While néré is very popular, its occurrence is declining because of various threats hindering its regeneration. In a condition of increasing scarcity of néré and increasing demand, changes in use and access rights, depending on the social status of harvesters, are taking place. Harvesting is an activity carried out by women. Although they depend on NTFP in general, and on néré in particular, to procure food for the household and for income generation, they have no secure access to tree resources. This study focused on the analysis of the dynamics of women's access rights and control over néré in three villages in Central-West Burkina Faso, inhabited by three ethnic groups (Nouni, Mossi and Fulani) with specific and differentiated modes of access to the land.

The approach adopted enabled to individually follow in the field each woman involved in the study and observe tree-specific conditions of access. Individual access rights of 180 women to 400 exploited trees were investigated. The findings indicate a different access for land and for trees. While access to trees and harvesting rights of women are stable and almost uniform in the land occupied by forest, within the boundaries of the household or within the territory attributed to a particular lineage, women are affected by gains or losses of rights to use néré that are highly dependent on changes in land tenure. These changes are associated with the transfer of land rights from a person to another through the processes of inheritance, renting, lending and sale. In addition, these access rights to néré are considerably differentiated based on a hierarchical system defined by ethnicity and position in the household. Understanding the differentiated tree tenure in a multi ethnical context of Burkina Faso will help to develop sustainable and equitable protection measures and policies, based on local management practices.

Keywords: Gender, NTFP, NTFP exploitation, *Parkia biglobosa*, tree access rights, tree tenure

Contact Address: Catherine A. K. Pehou, Center for International Forestry Research (CIFOR), Regional Office for West Africa, 01 BP 6828, Ouagadougou, Burkina Faso, e-mail: catherine.pehou@gmail.com

Economic Gain and Other Losses? Gender Relations and Matooke Production in Western Uganda

ANNE RIETVELD, SUSAN AJAMBO, ENOCH KIKULWE

Bioversity International, Uganda

Over the past decades cooking-banana (Matooke) has become increasingly important as food and especially as cash crop for farm households in Isingiro district in the western region of Uganda. High urban and regional demand for Matooke and dwindling Matooke productivity in other areas, drove expanded banana production and more intensive management. We hypothesised that the increased focus on Matooke by households in Isingiro, affected women and men both as individuals and as household members and affected gender norms on what constitutes a good wife or husband. Qualitative data from one community in Isingiro district was generated based on six in-depth Focus Group Discussions (FGDs), eight structured individual interviews and one community profile using the GENNOVATE method. Survey data with Matooke producers in Ishingiro (N = 51), FGDs with producers (3) and key-informant interviews (5) from a Matooke value-chain development project (ENDURE) was used to compliment and triangulate findings. Results show that the rapid expansion of Matooke cultivation has brought economic progress to many households and has markedly changed the physical landscape in the area. Ownership of a Matooke plantation is now among the most important criteria for determining male status and Matooke plantations are largely controlled by men. The focus of men on Matooke has made it easier for women to grow annual crops which increases their options of earning cash income. Women's access to land however is decreasing. Land is firmly in hands of men and with increasing land scarcity, they allocate less land, less often to their wives for cultivation. Women frequently rent land to cultivate but this is also becoming more expensive and less available. Although women spend a lot of time working in banana plantations, sales is exclusively controlled by men. Only women in female-headed households control sales from Matooke plantations, also because permanent cultures such as banana are not accepted on rented land. We conclude among others that the division of labour in Matooke production is highly gendered. Women in male-headed households benefit from increased revenue at household level but are limited in their options to engage in individual income-generating activities.

Keywords: Banana production, gender, intra-household relations, livelihoods, mixed methods, social norms, Uganda

Contact Address: Anne Rietveld, Bioversity International, Kampala, Uganda, e-mail: a.rietveld@cgiar.org

ID 542

The Socio-Ecological Impacts of Palm Oil Production in Rural Communities. A Regional MFA Study in the Micro-Region Tomé-Açu in Pará, Brazil

CHARLOTTE KOTTUSCH

Alpen-Adria-Universität, Inst. of Social Ecology, Austria

Pará is the largest palm oil producing state in Brazil, providing roughly 90 % of the palm oil produced nationally. In 2010, Lula da Silva, the former president of Brazil, initiated the PPSPO (Programa de Produção Sustenstável de Palma de Óleo), a government programme intended to foster a socially and environmentally sustainable production of palm oil by restricting the plantations to deforested and degraded areas in the Amazon, and by including small scale family farmers into the market.

In this work, the socio-environmental impacts of palm oil expansion in the micro-region Tomé-Açu are explored. Combining data driven analysis (regional material flow analysis (rMFA) and land use data) with qualitative work during research in the field, the study examines changes in the agricultural production in the region between 1990 and 2014, which produces 70 % of the palm oil in Pará.

Palm oil expansion influences land use interests as well as rural communities and their agricultural production patterns. One notable change is the increase of fallow land. A crucial fact is that this land type is regarded as degraded and thus suitable for palm oil plantations. A related development is a significant rise of land prices. Put together, these developments make it much more profitable to let these lands lie fallow and eventually sell them to palm oil companies than to use them for extensive cattle ranching. A second observable change is a decrease in production of certain local staples, especially cassava. Being a very price volatile crop, cassava production appeared less attractive compared to new employment opportunities or contract farming in the palm oil sector, pulling workforce out of small scale cassava production and thus leading to less production and higher prices of this important staple.

In summary, palm oil production pushes economic development in the region but leads to new risks in the competition for land and workforce resources. By describing and analysing these developments, the study contributes to a deeper understanding of socio-ecological impacts connected to palm oil production in Brazil that tries to cope with the challenge of producing palm oil in ecologically and socially sustainable ways.

Keywords: Brazil, cassava production, land use change, palm oil, regional material flow analysis, rural communities

Contact Address: Charlotte Kottusch, Alpen-Adria-Universität, Inst. of Social Ecology, Vienna, Austria, e-mail: Charlotte.kottusch@posteo.de

Multi-Stakeholder On-Farm Experimentation and Demonstration for Innovation in Argentinean Smallholder Livestock Production Systems

MARKUS FRANK[1], BRIGITTE KAUFMANN[1], MARCOS EASDALE[2], ANJA CHRISTINCK[3]

[1] German Institute for Tropical and Subtropical Agriculture (DITSL), Germany
[2] National Institute for Agricultural Technology (INTA), Rural Development, Argentina
[3] seed4change, Germany

Multi-stakeholder innovation approaches for on-farm experimentation, demonstration, monitoring and evaluation are widely used by AR&D institutions in the development of smallholder agriculture. Application of such approaches is highly dependent on site-specific conditions and frameworks. Therefore, it is necessary to analyse existing approaches and methods within their specific context of application, in order to assess their suitability to trigger self-driven change in practice and to derive relevant factors for improvements. Objectives of this study were to examine a multi-stakeholder demonstration farm approach for on-farm experimentation, monitoring, evaluation and diffusion of innovations, implemented by the National Institute for Agricultural Technology (INTA) in smallholder low-external input livestock production systems of northern Patagonia, Neuquén Province, Argentina, and to assess the collaboration processes and outcomes, based on the participants' perceptions in three selected cases of collaboration between livestock keepers' organisations, extension officers and researchers. A qualitative research approach was employed to gain insights into different perceptions of stakeholder interactions and activities for learning and innovation, emphasising i.) understanding of roles, ii.) expectations, iii.) costs and benefits, iv.) weaknesses and strengths, and vi.) ideas for improvements. During a four month field research stay (2014), semi-structured and narrative interviews were carried out, supported by visual tools as well as participant and activity observation. Collected material was examined and analysed by using qualitative content analysis. Results provide a detailed examination of the approach and methods used, indicating the predetermination of activities and methods by INTA, thus implementation of participatory principles for shaping collaboration processes, contents and outcomes were hardly found. The participants' assessment elucidates differentiated perceptions of livestock keepers, extension officers and researchers on the collaborative activities and proposed innovations. It was shown that livestock keepers' contextual knowledge and perceptions of innovations unfold substantial constraints and potentials for implementing innovations in restricted systems, which the employed monitoring system was not able to capture. The study highlights the importance of systematic integration of different knowledge systems and participatory construction of new knowledge in multi-stakeholder innovation approaches to open up multi-perspective views and shared understanding on context-specific problems, constraints and potential real-world solutions.

Keywords: Collaborative learning, demonstration farms, monitoring and evaluation, multi-stakeholder innovation, on-farm experimentation, smallholder livestock production systems

Contact Address: Markus Frank, German Institute for Tropical and Subtropical Agriculture (DITSL), Steinstraße 19, 37213 Witzenhausen, Germany, e-mail: m.frank@ditsl.org

ID 840

Fostering Collective Action in Sustainable Natural Resource Management with the Enabling Rural Innovation Approach

AMOS OWAMANI[1], THOMAS PIRCHER[2], MICHAEL HAUSER[3], ANN WATERS-BAYER[4]

[1]*Horizont3000, Enabling Rural Innivation East Africa Project, Uganda*
[2]*University of Hohenheim, Research Center for Global Food Security and Ecosystems, Germany*
[3]*University of Natural Resources and Life Sciences (BOKU), Centre for Development Research (CDR), Austria*
[4]*Agrecol Association, Germany*

The sustainable use of water and land resources for subsistence and commercial agriculture poses considerable challenges to farmers and development workers. This calls for collective action with farmers to help them conserve their natural resource base while becoming self-reliant entrepreneurs.

Since 2013, HORIZONT3000 has implemented the project "Enabling Rural Innovation in East Africa" (ERI–EA), which aims at enhancing and balancing food sovereignty and increasing incomes through market-oriented agriculture, while sustaining the natural resource base. It uses the Enabling Rural Innovation (ERI) approach developed in East Africa by the International Center for Tropical Agriculture (CIAT) to overcome the linear, top-down mode of technology development and market access in agriculture. In ERI–EA, community development facilitators in HORIZONT3000's partner organisations in Uganda and Tanzania trained farmer groups in their respective districts. The training comprised five modules: Participatory Diagnosis, Participatory Market Research, Farmer Participatory Research, Enterprise Development, and Participatory Monitoring & Evaluation. Project evaluations and field visits in 2015/16 showed that participating farmers were able to build strong groups that jointly manage material and knowledge resources for action. Within and across the farmer groups, collective action of pooling labour, financial resources (e.g. through savings and credit) and applied knowledge and skills (e.g. building energy-saving stoves in teamwork) enhanced their capacities for sustainable natural resource management (NRM). Through interacting with various market players, farmers were able to build profitable enterprises and negotiate fair prices and good terms of transaction for their products. As they know what the market needs are and what resources are required, farmers now invest part of their earnings in NRM to maintain steady production for the market. Farmer groups use an internal self-monitoring mechanism at group level that informs them about their progress toward self-set goals. By applying the ERI approach, farmers have demonstrated impressive development in terms of social organisation, group/individual marketing capacities, improved income and food security, and sustainable NRM.

Keywords: Collective action, farm investment, market access

Contact Address: Amos Owamani, Horizont3000, Enabling Rural Innivation East Africa Project, P.O. Box 9719, Kampala, Uganda, e-mail: amos.owamani@horizont3000.org

Participatory Climate Vulnerability Analysis of Watershed Communities: An Indicator Approach

ARCHANA RAGHAVAN SATHYAN[1], THOMAS AENIS[2], LUTZ BREUER[1]

[1] *Justus-Liebig University Giessen, Institute for Landscape Ecology and Resources Management (ILR), Germany*
[2] *Humboldt-Universität zu Berlin, Albrecht Daniel Thaer-Institute of Agricultural and Horticultural Sciences (ADTI), Germany*

Kerala state in India is severely threatened by vagaries of climate change because of its unique socio-economic, environmental and physical conditions such as high population density, mismanagement of water resources, encroachment of forests, wetland reclamations, peculiar slanting topography, humid tropical monsoon, excessive rainfall and hot summer. There is a strong decline in the groundwater level, change in rainfall patterns, deficit in monsoon rains and increase in temperature in recent years. Out of the total cropped area of the state, 86 % is under rainfed farming. Here, Watershed Management (WSM) programmes receive enormous attention due to their strategical approach and capacity to enhance production in rainfed agriculture, support livelihood system along with restoration of ecological balance and build adaptive capacity at community level. This study seeks to explore whether WSM does contribute in building adaptive capacities and thus reduce the vulnerability of local communities and ecosystems. The paper analyses the vulnerability vis-à-vis climate change at watershed community level of two micro watersheds (<1000 ha) in which the programmes have been implemented by two different agencies. The developed climate vulnerability indicator comprises of three dimensions of vulnerability: exposure, sensitivity and adaptive capacity and its ten major components: socio-demographic profile, socio-economic assets, agricultural, livelihood, social networks, health, food, water, climate variability and natural disasters. The approach combines both quantitative and qualitative methods with emphasis on participatory research tools. Data is collected using Rapid Appraisal of Agricultural Knowledge System methodology with main instruments such as household surveys, focus group discussions and key informant interviews.

The watershed programme implemented by the Local Self Government shows less vulnerability than the Non-Governmental Organisation (NGO) implemented programme. The results also show that the community more exposed to natural disasters does not experience a high vulnerability, due to its low value in subcomponents. Furthermore, the community more exposed to climate vulnerability does not overlap with lower adaptive capacity. The NGO implemented watershed could build higher adaptive capacity despite it becomes more vulnerable due to higher sensitivity and exposure. The results suggest location specific policies to address enhancement of socio-economic assets, improvement of livelihoods, sufficiency in food and water for resilient communities.

Keywords: Adaptive capacity, exposure, sensitivity, watershed management

Contact Address: Archana Raghavan Sathyan, Justus-Liebig University Giessen, Institute for Landscape Ecology and Resources Management (ILR), Heinrich-Buff-Ring 26-32, 35392 Giessen, Germany, e-mail: archanasathyan@gmail.com

ID 982

Participatory Research to Identify Irrigation Technologies for Women and Smallholder Farmers in Eastern Uganda

KATE M SCOW[1], ABRAHAM SALOMON[1], VICKI MORRONE[2]

[1] *University of California, Department of Land, Air and Water Resources, United States of America*

[2] *Michigan State University, Community Sustainability, United States of America*

Dry season vegetable production has been identified as a high priority in the largely rainfed (>97 %) agricultural systems of Uganda. Off-season vegetable supplies are currently inadequate to meet human nutritional needs. As rainfall patterns become increasingly unpredictable and rapid population expansion places more pressure on food systems, demand for vegetables will further outstrip supplies. This spin-off project convenes stakeholders from public and private sectors to develop innovations in small scale dry season vegetable production for women farmers in East Africa. We are using a participatory approach to research, design and implement dry season vegetable production and marketing schemes and our project builds on local capacity for irrigation and water management among farmer, university, extension, non-governmental, and private industry stakeholders in Eastern Uganda.

The project is working at 6 'innovation sites' throughout Eastern Uganda with a multi-disciplinary research team (farmers, research partners, Ministry of Agriculture, district staff, NGO partners, and university students) to co-develop technologies that will impact horticultural production, particularly by smallholder women farmers who are often excluded from irrigation and marketing developments. Innovations build on existing farmer knowledge as a foundation and combine with it in novel ways that are proving to be appropriate for small scale horticulture in the region (e.g. on-farm water storage, improved conveyance systems, drip irrigation, moveable sprinklers, managed infiltration/drainage, and irrigation strategies/schedules). Initial focus groups revealed that some concerns of women farmers were unique and needed to be considered in designing irrigation strategies and training. A gender sensitive framework is being developed for local public and private sector organisations to create, expand, and disseminate small scale irrigation systems. We are assessing agronomic and economic impacts and moving to further opportunities and education in marketing, nutrition, and assessing gender impacts of different innovations and developing scale-out options for the most promising technologies. Development of a co-innovation systematic approach for assessing and supporting innovations in dry season vegetable production will strengthen small scale farmer enterprises targeted to both local markets and family consumption.

Keywords: Agro-eco-zones, irrigation, uganda, vegetables, women empowerment

Contact Address: Vicki Morrone, Michigan State University, Community Sustainability, 480 Wilson Rd, Rm 303 , 48824 East Lansing, United States of America, e-mail: Sorrone@msu.edu

Agroecology in the Context of Rural Development Interventions in Burkina Faso: A Smallholders' Livelihoods' Catalyst?

DIANE KAPGEN, LAURENCE ROUDART

Université Libre de Bruxelles (ULB), Centre d'Études de La Coopération Internationale et du Développement (CECID), Belgium

Based on qualitative field research in Bilanga, eastern region of Burkina Faso, and on a thorough literature review about agroecology, we debate the effects of rural development programs implemented by a NGO under the umbrella of agroecology. We ask whether agroecology turns into just another imposed technical package or if it can sustainably improve smallholders' livelihoods as a whole.

Combining ecological and socio-economic principles, agroecology is an ambitious and complex transdisciplinary concept. In Bilanga, the local NGO ARFA – Association pour la Recherche et la Formation en Agro-écologie – introduced several agricultural techniques and field management strategies that should allow farmers to better cope with unpredictable rainfall patterns, soil degradation and loss of biodiversity. Our research results indicate that the adoption of these practices change farming systems towards meeting the ecological principles of agroecology and strengthen the natural capital base at the field and farm level. Farmer Field Schools and Farmer Groups organised by ARFA in the region's villages allow for transferring knowledge, creating social cohesion and providing access to farming tools and inputs and hence address some of the socio-economic principles of agroecology: the strengthening of social and knowledge networks, the development of market access and local production-consumption cycles and the socio-political empowerment of smallholders. But, looking closer, our data reveals unequal access to the groups and schools, material grabbing and misappropriation of funds by the groups' leaders, as well as top-down oriented knowledge diffusion processes.

As development projects are not power- and interest-free bubbles, but conflicted arenas where interests and visions of different actors enter into play, our original research enlightens the potential of agroecology in the context of rural development. In our case study, results demonstrate that the programmes risk creating new inequalities where more solidarity and fair access to resources were wished for, while not excluding potential pathways for more truly agroecology-based livelihoods.

Keywords: Agroecology, Burkina Faso, impact evaluation, livelihoods, rural development programs, smallholder farmers

Contact Address: Diane Kapgen, Université Libre de Bruxelles (ULB) (Free University of Brussels), Centre d'Études de La Coopération Internationale et du Développement (CECID) (Centre for Studies in International Cooperation and Development), Institut de Sociologie - 44 Avenue Jeanne - Cp 124, 1050 Brussels, Belgium, e-mail: diane.kapgen@ulb.ac.be

ID 296

Innovation Outcomes of Six Farmer Groups: Multiple Tools for Impact Assessment in Tanzania

ESTHER MIEVES, PAMELA NGWENYA, BRIGITTE KAUFMANN

German Institute for Tropical and Subtropical Agriculture (DITSL), Germany

Improving food security and livelihood conditions of vulnerable rural populations in Sub-Saharan Africa has been an on-going challenge particularly in light of climate change. Innovations, suitable to context-specific circumstances of small-scale farmers, are intended to reduce poverty and increase food security. Therefore, it is indispensable to collaboratively identify farmers' views about the factors that influence their action possibilities with regard to the adaptation and adoption potential of innovations. Within the frame of a transdisciplinary research project, focused on improving household food security in Tanzania, Trans-SEC, the aim of this research is to collaboratively assess the differences in farmers' experience regarding their innovation outcomes.

Field work took place from January to March 2016 in three large villages in the Morogoro (semi-humid) and Dodoma (semi-arid) regions, including six farmer groups that implemented different innovations. The participatory research comprised various qualitative tools and techniques, including: Most Significant Change (MSC), opinion line, outcome rating sensitive to socio-cultural factors, feedback sessions and semi-structured interviews. Advantages and constraints of these different impact assessment tools were reflected.

Even though the implemented innovations were diverse, some outcomes were similar across groups, such as: gaining knowledge (learning), additional income or money, time and labour saving. The open methods tools (such as MCS) allowed researchers to learn of diverse aspects regarding different innovation outcomes. It is demonstrated that multiple tools are necessary to reveal critical feedback from participants.

The elucidation of the farmers' perspectives concerning the relevance of certain innovation outcomes and the identification of those that are most important through collaborative assessment provide important information for up-scaling of the innovation processes. Critically, the results of this study can guide strategies for enhancing social inclusion and pro-poor innovation processes.

Keywords: Innovation, participatory impact assessment, qualitative tools and techniques, Tanzania, Trans-SEC

Contact Address: Brigitte Kaufmann, German Institute for Tropical and Subtropical Agriculture (DITSL), Steinstrasse 19, 37213 Witzenhausen, Germany, e-mail: b.kaufmann@ditsl.org

Expectations and Reality Check. Evaluation of Impact Assessments of Upgrading Strategies for Food Security

Enrique Hernandez L[1,2], Frieder Graef[2], Hannes König[2]

[1]*Humboldt-Universität zu Berlin, Albrecht Daniel Thaer-Institute of Agricultural and Horticultural Sciences (ADTI), Germany*

[2]*Leibniz Centre for Agricultural Landscape Research (ZALF), Germany*

Rural food insecurity continues to be an unfortunate shadow of many regions, such as semi-arid Dodoma and sub-humid Morogoro regions in Tanzania. In this sense, Trans-SEC project is oriented to understand and address this problem under the umbrella of a Food Value Chain approach. In this five years project, interdisciplinary groups of researchers alongside local rural stakeholders designed and evaluated strategies to enhance local food security. This paper will present the outcome of an *ex-ante* vs. *ex-post* mid-term evaluation, where local stakeholders scored the implemented strategies based on their personal experiences. Using a focus group discussion, nine different strategies were evaluated and scored under nine food securitycriteria, by a sample of implementers. The evaluation was then discussed in the focus group to gain insights on the "impact arguments" and story linesbehind seemingly odd scores. Later-on, the outcome of these evaluations was then compiled, compared and analysed within the village and in between villages and regions, thus gaining a deeper understanding on the reasons behind different outcomes. Results show expected differences between regions, but interestingly there are differences between outcomes that are not entirely related tobio-physical characteristics of the region. The qualitative analysis pointed at implementation status, engagement attitude, unexpected droughtconditions, and poor implementation. Whereas the analysis of determinants shows that there are context specific characteristics that influence, bothexpectations and impact results. Regarding the food security criteria there are clear differences within and between villages both in expectations andimpact results. Results signaled areas of improvement in project design, targeting and implementation practices.

Keywords: Food value chains, impact assessment, stakeholder evaluation, upgrading strategies

Contact Address: Enrique Hernandez L, Humboldt-Universität zu Berlin, Albrecht Daniel Thaer-Institute of Agricultural and Horticultural Sciences (ADTI), Hannoversche Str. 27, 10115 Berlin, Germany, e-mail: enrikke00@hotmail.com

 ID 752

Ex-ante Assessment of the Adoption Potential of Innovations in Rainfed Agriculture in South India

PIA FEHLE[1], DOMINIC BLÄTTLER[1], ALESSANDRA GIULIANI[1], S. MANJUBARKAVI[2], MANJULA MENON[3], RENGALAKSHMI RAJ[3], M. N. SIVAKUMAR[4]

[1] *Bern University of Applied Sciences (BFH), School of Agricultural, Forest and Food Sciences, Switzerland*

[2] *University of Madras, Department of Anthropology, India*

[3] *MS Swaminathan Research Foundation, Gender and Grassroots Institutions, India*

[4] *MS Swaminathan Research Foundation, Biodiversity Kolli Hills, India*

Small and marginal farmers in rainfed regions of South India are confronted with erratic rains, droughts, soil nutrient depletion, food and nutritional security issues and economic challenges. There is a need for innovations leading to more productive, sustainable, resilient and economically viable production systems. The BIOFI Network, a research project under the umbrella of the Indo-Swiss Collaboration in Biotechnology (ISCB), aims at the improvement of the rainfed production of two major local crops, namely finger millet (*Eleusine coracana*) and pigeon pea (*Cajanus cajan*), by developing and promoting a package of innovations called the BIOFI Package. The technology focuses on the aspects of biofertilisation and bioirrigation in a specified intercropping system of the target crops. An interdisciplinary approach is followed: while biotechnologists strive to optimise the Package on-station, socioeconomic researchers examine farmers' current practices and the adoption potential of the proposed innovations.

With the objective of identifying conducive and hindering factors for the adoption of the BIOFI Package, this study investigates on the existing finger millet and pigeon pea seed, cropping and farming systems in two semi-arid agroecosystems in South India and confronts the findings with different factors shaping the Package. For this purpose, a survey was conducted with 200 women and men farmers per site, amplified by a qualitative follow-up and a discussion with all researchers involved.

From an *ex-ante* perspective, the adoption potential of the BIOFI Package appears limited in both research sites. Conducive factors are among others the potential productivity increase and the high market potential of both target crops. Major hindering factors are the low relevance of one or both crops within the local farming systems, competing production branches and off-farm activities, limited market access, strongly differing agronomic practices and the relatively high complexity, cost and labour intensity of the BIOFI Package. Biofertilisers face the challenge of limited awareness, lack of information on use of or difficult access to the products. Based on these findings it is questionable whether marketing and extension can compensate for the obstacles identified. A reality-check in the field and a similar study in other locations are necessary.

Keywords: Adoption of innovations, biofertilisation, bioirrigation, climate change resilience, finger millet, interdisciplinary research, pigeon pea, rainfed agriculture, semi-arid agroecosystems

Contact Address: Pia Fehle, Bern University of Applied Sciences (BFH), School of Agricultural, Forest and Food Sciences, Länggasse 85, 3052 Zollikofen BE, Switzerland, e-mail: pia.fehle@bfh.ch

Institutional Learning in Conservation Agriculture Innovation: Evidence from Iran, Uganda and Burkina Faso

Sara Kaweesa[1], Somaye Latifi[2], Lorenz Probst[1]

[1] University of Natural Resources and Life Sciences (BOKU), Centre for Development Research, Austria

[2] University of Tabriz, Dept. of Extension and Rural Development, Iran

Conservation agriculture has been proposed as a strategy of sustainable intensification that can mitigate the effects of climate change and reverse land degradation. It has been introduced in a variety of countries spanning different agro-ecological zones such as Iran, Uganda, and Burkina Faso.

In Iran, Government interventions have promoted conservation agriculture mainly for sustainable management of soil and water. This intervention also leads to reduction in costs of production and increases productivity in dry lands and irrigated land. In Uganda and Burkina Faso, although in line with governmental policies, conservation agriculture has been promoted mainly by NGOs, development partners and research for development organisations.

Despite the differences in agro-ecological, social and economic environment, the adoption record of conservation agriculture remains weak in all of the studied regions. Much of earlier research and projects on conservation agriculture have targeted adoption barriers at a farm level. However, from an innovation systems point of view, we hypothesise that underlying institutional patterns, interests of different stakeholders and systemic constraints play a critical role in the innovation of conservation agriculture. We contrast preliminary findings from case studies in Iran, Uganda, and Burkina Faso to explore this hypothesis. Our methods include literature review, key informant interviews, and stakeholder mapping.

We conclude that the institutions, policy processes and promotion strategies related to conservation agriculture are site specific – the capacity to innovate conservation agriculture, however, is constrained by a lack of interaction and collaboration among stakeholders and their institutions in all sites. We thus suggest that interventions should shift their priorities towards facilitating institutional learning processes that first of all make the interests and constraints of different stakeholders transparent and explicit.

Keywords: Burkina Faso, conservation agriculture, innovation, institutional learning, Iran, Uganda

---

Contact Address: Sara Kaweesa, University of Natural Resources and Life Sciences (BOKU), Centre for Development Research, Borkowskigasse 4 1190, Vienna, Austria, e-mail: cdr@boku.ac.at

ID 742

Participatory Maize-Legume Experimental Trials as a Tool to Explore Social-Ecological Niches for Innovation Adoption in Small Scale Farming Systems

MARIA-VICTORIA ALOMIA[1], ERIKA N. SPEELMAN[1], ARUN THAPA[1], WEI HSIANG[1], ANDREW MCDONALD[2], PABLO TITTONELL[3,1], JEROEN C.J. GROOT[1]

[1]*Wageningen University and Research Centre, Farming Systems Ecology - Plant Sciences, The Netherlands*

[2]*International Maize and Wheat Improvement Center (CIMMYT), South Asia Regional Office, Nepal*

[3]*National Institute for Agricultural Technology (INTA), Natural Resources and Environment Program, Argentina*

Maize-legume mixed cropping is essential part of the farming systems in the mid-hills of Nepal. However, its productivity remains low. The low adoption of innovations are among the causes that condition the yield improvement of the systems. Therefore, we performed two years participatory on-farm trials with maize-legume crop combinations under best-bet management to determine their productivity, and the farmers' reasons of low innovation adoption. We also tested whether providing more information about innovations would influence farmer perceptions. Maize yielded on average $7\,Mg\,ha^{-1}$ in the intercrop, in comparison to $2\,Mg\,ha^{-1}$ under farmer practice. The intercrop under best-bet management showed higher land use efficiency and economy return. We involved farmers on field discussions during the duration of trials. In addition we assessed, by using a board impact tool, their perceptions about 1) technologies tested (mini-tiller, hybrid seeds and chemical fertilisers), and 2) improved cropping practices (optimal plant population in row arrangement). Farmers initially expected a high demand of labour for both row seeding and mini-tiller use before the trials, but this was adjusted to lower anticipated labour demand after the participatory trials. In contrast, the perception of high investment costs for both innovations persisted. By the second year of trials there was a relatively large percentage (17 %) of farmers that partially adopted the improved seeds and row seeding, the reasons for the non-adopters were the preference to consume local varieties and high labour at planting time for the row arrangement. The use of a mini-tiller was low (3 %) due to the low availability and the difficulty to take it to remote fields. The adoption rate of chemical fertilisers was low, because most of the households perceived the quantity of FYM they produced as sufficient, and perceived a risk of damaging soil if using chemical fertilisers without proper rainfall. Most of the early adopter farmers belonged to a medium to high resource endowment type and high caste. Our study shows that the participatory on-farm trials were effective to explore perceptions and preferences of farmers, and it increased understanding on targeting of innovations to achieve sustainable intensification in the mid-hills agroecosystems.

Keywords: Farmers perceptions, innovation adoption, maize-legumes inter-crops, participatory trials, small farming systems

Contact Address: Maria-Victoria Alomia, Wageningen University and Research Centre, Farming Systems Ecology - Plant Sciences, Droevendaalsesteeg 4, 6708 Wageningen, The Netherlands, e-mail: maria.alomiahinojosa@wur.nl

ID 780

Why Absence of "fihavanana" Is Limiting Agricultural Innovation Process in the Highlands of Madagascar?

Onjaherilanto Rakotovao Razanakoto[1], Rolland Razafindraibe[2], Lilia Rabeharisoa[3]

[1] University of Antananarivo, School of Agronomy, Madagascar
[2] National Center Research Applied to Rural Development, Dept. of Research - Development, Madagascar
[3] Laboratory of Radioisotopes, Service of Agronomy, Madagascar

Apart from institutional concern, human interaction between stakeholders merits to be considered in approaches related to development projects that provide innovations. Combining effort, pain, and gain are aspects of solidarity and cohesion concepts that Malagasy people consider in the term "fihavanana". Paradoxically, founding principles of Malagasy "fihavanana" are opposed to innovation initiative. "Fihavanana" concept is nowadays affiliated to rural people as farmers, the beneficiaries of most development projects. In contrast, many developers who are supposed to provide positive changes to beneficiaries are from the cities and are less connected to rural culture. Nevertheless, more than a mutual understanding is required to make innovative process effective. Synergetic mobilisation of human resources is also expected. This paper aims to demonstrate that the absence of "fihavanana" between implicated agents of innovation process conducts to its failure. Outcomes from PhD dissertation based on a literature review, on multi-site trials related to the improvement of rice yield and performed as a simulation of a development project, and on a household survey in two contrasted localities in the highlands of Madagascar show that stakeholders' objectives or activities inside innovation process do not converge. Developer and beneficiary diversely act relatively to their respective capacities and interests (effort and gain), even if participative approach is included. Moreover, each implicated agent is not able to overcome alone obstacles (pain) that constrain its own achievement. This paper suggests more consideration of cultural issues when designing development projects. The current strategy of development programme largely focuses on economical issues to cope with concerns such as reducing poverty or securing food in agrarian society. Combination of "fihavanana" with the innovation process conducted in Madagascar may be helpful to improve welfare and wellbeing of local population. These concepts may be compatible if we consider that both, "fihavanana" and innovation, cover almost the same social, cultural, environmental, technical, and economical dimensions.

Keywords: Agricultural research and development, behaviour, cultural concern, human resources, rice cropping systems

Contact Address: Onjaherilanto Rakotovao Razanakoto, University of Antananarivo, School of Agronomy, Ankatso BP 175, 101 Antananarivo, Madagascar, e-mail: ronjaheri@yahoo.fr

ID 549

Agricultural Cooperatives as Innovation Brokers: The Case of Climate Smart Agriculture in Uganda

MARLEEN POOT, GIAN NICOLA FRANCESCONI

Humboldt-Universität zu Berlin, Department of Cooperation and Cooperative Organizations, Germany

Climate Smart Agriculture (CSA) is thought to simultaneously tackle food insecurity and climate change. CSA is particularly important in the context of Sub-Saharan Africa. Here climate change and food insecurity poses more serious threats than anywhere else, affecting a myriad of rural smallholders. The dissemination and adoption of CSA in sub-Saharan African is however hindered by the limited accessibility of farm-households, who remain scattered over large and underdeveloped areas. The accessibility problem is well known to development experts, which have been trying to overcome it for more than a century, in order to scale up technological innovations for agriculture across the region.

Over time, agricultural cooperatives (agri-coops) and farmer organisations (FOs) have been largely used to aggregate and coordinate rural smallholders, and up-scale the adoption of agricultural innovations across Africa. Through agricultural advisory services and collaboration with government, civil society and research organisations, agri-coops and FOs can function as knowledge and innovation intermediaries, promoting and facilitating the adoption of improved farming practices, like CSA, among large numbers of smallholders. However, the sub-optimal performance of African agri-coops and FOs is attributed to: i) internal or organisational flaws, which leads to problems of side-selling and elite-capture, which in turn prevent them to sustain the costs related to input and extension service provision; as well as ii) external constraints resulting in imperfect information and bounded knowledge networks, which reduces the amount and quality of stakeholders, technologies and practices that are de-facto accessible.

This paper contributes to the literature by further investigating the potential role as innovation intermediaries that agri-coops can play in the up-scaling of CSA. It combines theory on innovation systems and knowledge networks with theory on cooperative organisational design, to find out which factors explain whether agri-coops and FOs provide climate-smart services to their members. Quantitative data from 99 agri-coops and FOs from Uganda are collected to perform organisational diagnostics. The main independent variable in this paper are access to information sources, relationships with other stakeholders, and knowledge inputs in the form of education and training, to analyze the influence of these variables on the provision of climate smart services to the cooperatives members as the main dependent variable. Additional case studies provide further evidence on how cooperatives channel climate smart information and knowledge between their members and other stakeholders, and how this can be either facilitated or hampered by the internal design characteristics of cooperatives.

Keywords: Agricultural cooperatives, farmer organisations, innovation network

Contact Address: Marleen Poot, Humboldt-Universität zu Berlin, Department of Cooperation and Cooperative Organizations, Eylauer Str. 3, 10965 Berlin, Germany, e-mail: mariannehelenapoot@hotmail.com

Influencing Factors for Adoption of Forage Technologies in Smallholder Dairy Systems in Lushoto, Tanzania

HYCENTH TIM NDAH[1,2], JOHANNES SCHULER[2], BIRTHE PAUL[3], BEATUS NZOGELA[3], WALTER E. MANGESHO[4], JULIUS BWIRE[4]

[1] *University of Hohenheim, Inst. of Social Sciences in Agriculture, Germany*
[2] *Leibniz Centre for Agricultural Landscape Research (ZALF), Inst. of Socio-Economics, Germany*
[3] *International Center for Tropical Agriculture (CIAT), Tropical Forages Program, Kenya*
[4] *Tanzania Livestock Research Institute (TALIRI), Tanzania*

The lack of sufficient quantity and quality of livestock feed on a consistent basis is often cited as a major constraint faced by dairy farmers in East Africa, especially during the dry season. However, new improved forage technologies often fail to be adopted for a variety of reasons. Within the frame of a BMZ/GIZ sponsored project we focus on exploring the adoption potential of these forage technologies following a case study based approach in two villages in North-Eastern Tanzania.

This contribution highlights first results derived from semi-structured qualitative explorative interviews and structured field observations - a follow-up inventory of farmers who had received planting material in 2014 and 2015. Main aim was checking sustainable adoption decision of farmers from first knowledge of improved forages to actual implementation. Specifically, the study unveils: triggering, sustaining and inhibiting forces towards further adaptation and adoption of these technologies from a farmer's perspective with its conceptual grounding on the theory of behaviour modification.

While the triggering factors were both related to shortage of feed and soil conservation problems, the expected economic advantages were not as dominant in the farmers' responses. Reasons for sustaining the practices of growing improved forages were the year round availability of fodder, increased fodder demand (due to higher livestock numbers) and accumulated benefits (e.g. increased animal numbers and forage yields). Soil conservation issues were mentioned less often, in contrast to their dominance in the triggering factors. According to the farmers, further upscaling needs now more support in animal breeding, provision of sufficient planting materials and the expansion of the programme to other farmers beyond the innovation platform. The change in the importance of triggering (esp. land conservation) and sustaining factors (e.g. constant availability of fodder) is an important lesson learnt from this survey.

These first results from the farmers' perspective will be further reflected when triangulated with findings from a multi-stakeholder workshop using a qualitative participatory expert-based assessment approach - QAToCA in order to clearly extract adoption constraints following a systems perspective.

Keywords: Adoption constraints, forage technologies, livelihoods, livestock systems

Contact Address: Hycenth Tim Ndah, Leibniz Centre for Agricultural Landscape Research (ZALF), Institute of Socio-Economics, Eberswalder Strasse 84, 15374 Müncheberg, Germany, e-mail: ndah@zalf.de

ID 725

Gender Disparities in Intra-Household Roles and Decision Making among Cocoa Producing Households in Nigeria

OLUWAFUNMISO ADEOLA OLAJIDE, DORCASS NGOZI ISHIE

University of Ibadan, Dept. of Agricultural Economics, Nigeria

The decision making landscape in rural households has been said to be dominated by men over the years. But could there be a difference in households where male and female members participate in production activities of major cash crops like cocoa? If there are, to what extent and what are the driving forces behind it? This study profiled cocoa households, examined the extent of men and women's participation in cocoa production and marketing activities, and the factors which influenced the decision to participate. Primary data were collected through interviews with structured questionnaires from 100 households which were randomly selected through a multi-stage sampling approach from a cocoa producing local government area of Osun state. The data were analysed using descriptive statistics and probit regression. The results show that over 80 percent of the decisions associated with cocoa production and marketing are made by men who are the household heads. In a few cases, joint decisions are made and in fewer cases the woman makes the decisions. It also shows that men and women participate effectively in the different activities from production through processing to marketing. Cultural norms/traditional belief systems, group membership and income are the constraints perceived to limit women's participation. Factors which drive the imbalance in decision making include education and extension training. The policy implication is that as Nigeria advances her match in cocoa expansion, women are likely to be excluded and left behind. The cocoa value chain needs to be made more gender responsive and the market development made more inclusive for different gender groups.

Keywords: Cocoa, households, inclusion, value chains, women

Contact Address: Oluwafunmiso Adeola Olajide, University of Ibadan, Dept. of Agricultural Economics, Faculty of Agriculture and Forestry, Ibadan, Nigeria, e-mail: preciousfunso@yahoo.com

Gendered Economic Strategies: Division of Labour, Responsibilities and Controls Within Households in Nyeri County, Kenya

KATHRINE DALSGAARD, GEORGIOS ORFANOS, CLARA ELIZABETH FOLKMANN VON STÖCKEN MUSAEUS

University of Copenhagen, Dept. of Anthropology, Denmark

In Central Highlands, Nyeri County, Kenya, the majority of people derive their daily livelihoods from agricultural activities. However, the sector exhibits distinct gendered asymmetries, which exist in regards to responsibilities, controls and tasks, both within and outside of the farm. Recently, with the reformation of the Kenyan Constitution in 2010, formal steps have been made to ensure a higher degree of gender equality. Nonetheless, land ownership and formal income generating activities are still prevailingly associated with men. In this study, we investigate the interrelation of gender roles and agricultural production analysed through the lens of Feminist Political Ecology. The objective of this paper is to link findings in division of labour among sexes with gendered household economics, which were collected during our fieldwork in Nyeri County. The focus of this analysis will be placed on household economics and hence we seek to expand the understanding of how formal and informal institutions affect gendered relations and accesses to different sorts of resources. Furthermore, we attempt to link our findings of women's active participation in self-help groups as well as their inclination towards keeping separate economic accounts with the concept of agency. Our analysis suggests that the gendered division of labour together with perceptions of crops and livestock as being associated with either men or women constitute the current asymmetrical gender structures. Men and women's separate agricultural activities, responsibilities and controls create different domains of knowledge, which constitute their different positions within the household and the farm. Consequently, men and women adopt different economic strategies and hence, use separate economic systems. We argue that women keep private savings, a practice passed on from mother to daughter, and engage in self-help groups, in a traditional *"Harambee"* spirit, in order to strengthen their agency and room for manoeuvre within societal structures. Moreover, we assert that these practices exhibit ways to get access into formal economic domains such as banks, otherwise primarily accessible by men.

Keywords: Agency, gender, household economics, Kenya

Contact Address: Georgios Orfanos, University of Copenhagen, Faculty of Science, Mantuavej 15, 2300 Copenhagen, Denmark, e-mail: georgeorphanos@hotmail.com

ID 589

Exploring Gender Differential in Adoption of Sustainable Intensification Practices in Northern Ghana

SHAIBU MELLON BEDI[1], BEKELE HUNDIE KOTU[2], GARDEBROEK KOOS[1], STEPHEN FRIMPONG[2]

[1] Wageningen University, Agricultural Economics and Rural Policy, The Netherlands
[2] International Institute of Tropical Agriculture (IITA), Ghana

Women contribute greatly towards most farming activities and family food security in Africa. Nevertheless, they are faced with many challenges such as lack of institutional support (e.g. extension services), lack of access to credit, lack of access to land, lack of education, and multiple family burden including domestic chores. Moreover, studies show that women have lower access to inputs and improved technologies which have placed them in a lower position as compared to men in terms of productivity and income. Therefore, improving women's livelihood requires a clear understanding of the situation of women in terms of these challenges and their potential to use existing opportunities. This study aims to explore gender differential in adoption of sustainable intensification practices thereby explaining income differential. We use the data collected for the purpose of monitoring adoption of sustainable intensification practices promoted by a research for development project known as "Africa Research in Sustainable Intensification for the Next Generation" (Africa RISING) in northern Ghana. Data were collected on application inputs and improved technologies, farming practices and output, socioeconomic characteristics, land and output allocation, and access to market and institutional services. We compare and contrast the adoption of sustainable intensification practices such as soil fertility management, cropping system diversification, and improved seeds between male and female plot managers and its effect on maize yields and income. A multinomial endogenous treatment effects model is used to explain adoption of SIPs, whiles Ordinary Least Square (OLS) and Instrumental Variable (IV) approaches are used to determine the impact of SIPs on maize yields and net income. Understanding plot level adoption decision pattern between men and women opens up new understanding about gender-technology gaps and offers an opportunity to both researchers and policy makers to identify key challenges associated with adoption of SIPs. This helps to develop specific extension strategies targeted to specific needs of both male and female farmers instead of just recommendation a single package for them.

Keywords: Gender, Ghana, multinomial endogenous treatment effects model, sustainable intensification practices

Contact Address: Shaibu Mellon Bedi, Wageningen University, Agricultural Economics and Rural Policy, Dijkgraaf 4-06B003, 6708 PG Wageningen, The Netherlands, e-mail: sbmellon2005@gmail.com

The Formation of Organisational Networks in Emerging Economy: The Case of Agribusiness Incubators

ANIKA TOTOJANI, CARSTEN NICO HJORTSØ

University of Copenhagen, Department of Food and Resource Economics, Denmark

Business incubators are mechanisms for promoting and supporting entrepreneurship, creating jobs opportunities, and giving rise to small and medium enterprises. The literature on incubation has shown that focus has shifted from a real estate provision to network access and resources provision. Although, scholars have identified the positive effect of networks on obtaining access to resources and for creating an enabling environment for future incubated enterprises, the business incubator literature rarely addresses social aspect at the incubator level. The purpose of this multiple-case study is to shed light on the process of network use and development during the initial phase of establishing four tripartite agribusiness incubators encompassing three major types of partners: universities, research organisations and private companies. We employ qualitative and quantitative data from Kenya, Uganda, and Zambia. Our findings illustrate that partners rely on previous relationships that they formalize when engaging in the incubators partnerships. Drawing on the social network theory, our findings show that partners of the business incubator draw on their social capital to establish the organisational network. The degree of partner's embeddedness in various organisational settings increase the diversity of contacts integrated into the incubator networks which will be used as potential resources for the incubated firms. In terms of the relational content, the partners of incubators have a tendency to consider ties as business, although the content can be different. The strengthening of relations is based on relationship formalisation and frequency of interaction. The study highlights the need to modify methodological approaches according to the cultural and institutional context in which they are used.

Keywords: Business incubator, partners, relational content & strength, resource acquisition, social networks

Contact Address: Anika Totojani, University of Copenhagen, Department of Food and Resource Economics, Rolighedsvej 25 Department of Food and Resource Economics, 1958 Copenhagen, Frederiksberg C, 1958, Denmark, e-mail: at@ifro.ku.dk

ID 544

Understanding System Innovation Adoption: Analysis of Integrated Soil Fertility Management Uptake in Ghana and Kenya

IVAN ADOLWA[1], STEFAN SCHWARZE[2], BOAZ WASWA[3], ANDREAS BUERKERT[1]

[1]*University of Kassel, Organic Plant Production and Agroecosystems Research in the Tropics and Subtropics (OPATS), Germany*

[2]*Georg-August-Universität Göttingen, Dept. of Agricultural Economics and Rural Development, Germany*

[3]*International Centre for Tropical Agriculture (CIAT), Kenya*

Sustainable intensification for improved productivity in African farming systems has been high on the agenda of research and development programs for decades. System innovations such as integrated soil fertility management and conservation agriculture have been proposed to tackle the complex challenges farmers face. In this study, we assess how different factors at the plot and farm level influence the adoption of integrated soil fertility management. We employed a stratified sampling approach to randomly select 285 and 300 farmers in Tamale, northern Ghana, and Kakamega County, western Kenya, respectively. These two sites were selected to understand the underlying reasons for their divergent adoption levels. Ordinal regression models were used to estimate adoption. In Tamale 5 % and in Kakamega 36 % of the farmers adopted improved seed and fertiliser whereas 3 % and 8 % of the respective farmers adopted improved seed, fertiliser, and the application of organic soil amendments. Lastly, improved seed, fertiliser, organic amendments, and local adaptation were adopted by 3 % of Tamale and 36 % of Kakamega farmers. Plot level variables such as soil carbon, clay content and pH had a significant effect on adoption at both sites. Among farm and household characteristics, number of adults, off-farm occupation, education, age of household head and livestock ownership significantly affected integrated soil fertility management adoption. The analysis infers that partial adoption predominates in Tamale, whereas Kakamega farmers opted for complete adoption of innovation packages. Key policy recommendations include improved access to credit for both sites as well as enhanced access to improved seeds in Tamale.

Keywords: Complete adoption, Integrated Soil Fertility Management (ISFM), partial adoption, system innovations

Contact Address: Ivan Adolwa, University of Kassel, Organic Plant Production and Agroecosystems Research in the Tropics and Subtropics (OPATS), Steinstraße 19, 37213 Witzenhausen, Germany, e-mail: ivan.adolwa@gmail.com

Impacts of Dairy Goat Production on Nutrition and Income Security of Smallholder Farmers in Tanzania

LUKE KORIR, MICHAEL KIDOIDO, NILS TEUFEL

International Livestock Research Institute (ILRI), Livelihoods, Gender & Impacts (LGI), Kenya

In Tanzania most goat production is extensive and aimed at selling live animals with limited direct impact on food security and nutrition. The Crop and Goat Project (CGP), implemented in Kongwa and Mvomero districts, aimed at improving income, food security and nutrition of poor households by promoting dairy goat production integrated with cassava and sweet potatoes. Within the project area, village leaders generated a list of 70 potential goat recipients in each of the 4 intervention villages, based on resources and capacity. Out of these, 108 households received a total of 229 dairy goats over the project period. The objective of this study is to evaluate the impacts of introducing dairy goats on income, assets and food consumption.

A baseline survey at project initiation was conducted among 552 households in 2012, including all households which later received goats. Out of these, 373 households were interviewed a second time in 2014. This sample includes 98 of the beneficiary households, 102 potential beneficiary households, not having received a project goat, and 120 non-potential households in project villages. Analysis of the baseline data revealed that beneficiary households were different to potential and non-potential households in terms of non-livestock assets and food consumption. Therefore, the study applies a difference-in-differences (DD) approach in combination with propensity score matching to overcome the observed bias for estimating the impact of the project intervention.

Results from the econometric analysis show the interventions had no significant effect on livestock or total income. Unsurprisingly, the project does appear to have significantly increased household ownership of small ruminants and total livestock. We also find a significant increase in the food consumption score of the survey respondent in project households, but no significant effect on the consumption score of the index child. Finally, we see a significant increase in the respondent's frequency of consuming dairy products, though none for the index child.

Results suggest that dairy goats in this context have a stronger impact on household nutrition than on income although a better understanding of intra-household food allocation is required to support child nutrition.

Keywords: Dairy goats, impact, income, nutrition, Tanzania

Contact Address: Luke Korir, International Livestock Research Institute (ILRI), Livelihoods, Gender & Impacts (LGI), Po Box 30709, 00100 Nairobi, Kenya, e-mail: l.korir@cgiar.org

ID 953

Harming Own Interests? Lessons Learned from Accompanying Villagers Change of Perceptions Regarding Innovative Improved Stoves

Götz Uckert[1], Harry Hoffmann[1], Johannes Hafner[2], Frieder Graef[1], Ogossy Gasaya Sererya[3], Anthony Kimaro[4]

[1] *Leibniz Centre for Agricultural Landscape Research (ZALF), Germany*

[2] *Humboldt-Universität zu Berlin, Albrecht Daniel Thaer-Institute of Agricultural and Horticultural Sciences (ADTI), Germany*

[3] *Sokoine University of Agriculture, Dept. of Forest Economics, Tanzania*

[4] *World Agroforestry Centre (ICRAF), Tanzania Country Programme, Tanzania*

Cooking energy is scarce in developing countries where a substantial part of the population strongly depends on woodfuels – particularly firewood and charcoal – to meet their energy demand as prerequisite for optimised calorie intake. The major part of the rural population is still applying inefficient traditional three-stone firewood cook stoves thereby likely increasing degradation of forest resources. Respective strategies counteracting damage of forests are non-existent leading to environmental damage. Since more than 30 years research and development projects aim on decreasing the energy input per cooking unit as well as emission quantity. The presented research design aimed at the adaptation, design and testing of improved cooking stoves and at creating a mutual process of knowledge exchange with the villagers to understand the up-grading-strategy of improved cooking stoves and the importance for their livelihoods. Training groups with about 100 farmers were organised to implement a specific technology (the "Salama improved stove"). This was realised via action-research integrated in the Trans-SEC project operating in four villages of Morogoro and Dodoma (Tanzania). Stove construction activities and the self-organised dissemination processes were monitored, which resulted in 125 additional households implementing the Salama stove. Data collection was carried out via a) focus group discussions to analyse variances between villages and general challenges of adoption and b) in-depth parameter testing of cooking and stove performance implemented in 80 households including emission tests in 24 households. Implemented stove models save about 50 % of fuelwood and reduces emission of GHGs by 65 % respectively, but they only are successfully implemented if wood resources are scarce. Users highly appreciated that the stoves were well insulated and safe in handling. They undertake design changes to allow improved simultaneous cooking with the two pots, leading to a 40 % reduction of overall cooking time. Concluding, it is substantial for successful implementation of improved cooking stoves that optimal engineering has to be accompanied by participatory exchange on users needs and perceptions. Subsequent up-scaling, further knowledge dissemination and increased local ownership will therefore carefully include improvements by the villagers diverting from the initial stove design including optimised combustion processes and heat transfer.

Keywords: Controlled cooking test, efficient cookstoves, energy access, firewood, household air pollution, kitchen performance test, Tanzania, technology adoption

Contact Address: Götz Uckert, Leibniz Centre for Agricultural Landscape Research (ZALF), Inst. of Socio-Economics, Eberswalder Str. 84, 15374 Müncheberg, Germany, e-mail: uckert@zalf.de

Cost Benefit Analysis of Seed Potato Replacement Strategies among Smallholder Farmers in Kenya

Bruce Ochieng Obura[1], Monica L. Parker[1], Christian Bruns[2], Maria Renate Finckh[3], Elmar Schulte-Geldermann[1]

[1] International Potato Center (CIP), Intergrated Crop Management, Kenya
[2] University of Kassel, Organic Farming and Cropping, Germany
[3] University of Kassel, Ecological Plant Protection, Germany

Potato yields of smallholder farmers in Kenya fall at 8 t ha^{-1} way below attainable yields of 35 – 40 t ha^{-1}, this is mostly due to a potent combination of inadequate supply of quality seed and limited awareness of better seed crop management practices. Most seed is informal, very often contaminated with seed borne diseases like Bacterial wilt caused by *Ralstonia solanacearum* and viruses in particular PVY and PLRV causing severe seed degeneration leading to yield and economic losses. The presented study aimed at providing smallholder potato farmers with information on how to increase their profit margin by choosing the best seed replacement strategy. In this respect a seed replacement strategy trial was set up at different on-farm sites in three counties (Kiambu, Nyandarua and Nakuru) in Kenya. The study employed a participatory approach at each site with an average of 15 farmers. The seed replacement strategies tested included: certified seed (CF), positive selected seed (PS), randomly selected farmers seed (RSFS), seed derived from bulking of small quantities of CF in small seed plot (SSPT) (5 % of the area demand bought in previous season for bulking) added with PS seed (5%SSPT+PS), or with RSFS (5 % SSPT+RSFS), 20 % CF seed combined with PS seed and RSFS respectively. Results showed significant difference in profit between the strategies used. Profit margins increased by 1200–3000 US$ compared to farmers seed qualities, however due to high investment cost for CF seed, profit margins of all integrated strategies with smaller CF seed influx quantities and PS were higher hence more likely to be adopted. Furthermore, to reach similar profit margins than with farm saved seed, farmers have to at least double their yields when using CF seed compared to only between 5 % (PS) to 22 % (20 % CF +PS) when using integrated seed quality improvement strategies. Best option in terms of profits at little risks of losing the investment have been the combination of SSPT and PS. The study recommends to promote integrated seed quality improvement strategies combining regular influx of small quantities of high quality seed with on-farm seed quality improvement methods adapted to smallholder farmers realities.

Keywords: Seed quality, seed-borne diseases, smallholder farmers

Contact Address: Bruce Ochieng Obura, International Potato Center - sub-Saharan Africa (CIP-SSA), Intergrated Crop Management, Old Naivasha Road Off Waiyaki Way, Nairobi, Kenya, e-mail: b.ochieng@cgiar.org

ID 946

Determinants of Multiple Adoption in Ethiopia and Effects on Income: A Double Selection Model

MARIKA E. RÖSEL, TIM K. LOOS

University of Hohenheim, Inst. of Agricultural Sciences in the Tropics (Hans-Ruthenberg-Institute), Germany

As most parts of the developing world, Ethiopia faces a fast growing population and the pressing need to increase agricultural production in order to be able to supply its people with sufficient and nutritious food. Land expansion is no option any more so that the focus lies on the intensification of production. While improved seeds and fertiliser are the traditional technologies of choice offered to the farmers by extension services, management practices like erosion prevention and conservation tillage have joined the circle of recommended innovations over the years. Numerous studies have tried to explain the mostly reluctant uptake by the smallholder farmers with results reaching from lack of information and access to all kinds of constraints, including lack of credit and insurance.

Adoption studies, however, mostly focus on a single technology, ignoring the fact that farmers are in reality facing a bundle of possible technologies among which they can choose from. Neglecting the simultaneity and interdependence of the adoption decisions leads to biased estimates. Even fewer studies investigate the effect of simultaneous adoption on outcome measures like income and thus inadequately check whether adoption indeed brought about the intended positive effect.

This paper models simultaneous adoption of five different technology types with a multivariate probit model and, in a second step, applies an elaborate double-selectivity model to answer the question of what the joint effects of sustainable soil management practices and improved seeds adoption on income are. Results show, first, that there is indeed a high interdependency of the adoption of the five technology types, namely that adoption of the different technologies have mutually encouraging effects. Second, factors encouraging (or discouraging) adoption vary between the technologies. And, third, in this case, adoption of soil management practices and/or improved seeds had no significant income increasing effects after controlling for the double selection bias.

Keywords: Adoption effects, agricultural technology, double selectivity correction, Ethiopia, multiple adoption, multivariate probit

---

Contact Address: Marika E. Rösel, University of Hohenheim, Inst. of Agricultural Sciences in the Tropics (Hans-Ruthenberg-Institute), Wollgrasweg 43, 70599 Stuttgart, Germany, e-mail: marika.roesel@uni-hohenheim.de

Agricultural Innovations in Family Farming: Case Study from Esmeraldas in Ecuador

Rawia Derbel[1], Narcisa De Jesús Requelme[2], Marco Moncayo Miño[3]

[1]*Agris Mundus, Tunisia*
[2]*Salesian Polytechnic University, Ecuador*
[3]*Technical University of Madrid, Spain*

In Ecuador, family farming (FF) is the predominant form of agriculture for food production as it represents 80 % of the agricultural employment of the rural population and provides almost half of the consumed basic food. This study deals with identification and characterisation of innovations in family farms and analysis of factors that affect their adoption. It values the strategic importance of the implication of innovations and technologies in FF in Ecuador. Results are based on an online survey applied with professionals from the three micro climate zones in the country; coastal plains, mountain chain and Amazonia. In order to get a general overview, an accurate territorial case study was carried out in Esmeraldas based on focus group discussions with farmers. They suggested a wide range of innovations that come to support public policiy makers and institutional frameworks in future strategies to let farmers produce competitively. The identified innovations have been classified according to multiple criteria: degree of novelty, nature and technological level. This generates eight types of innovations and an appraisal of fourteen typologies. A wide range of typologies has been evidenced in the field such as RaPcT that corresponds to radical process innovations based on generic technologies which modify profoundly the productive, environmental and economic parameters in production processes using existing technologies outside the local environment. However, to understand the social problematic of the adoption of innovations, factors have been pointed out from which the most important are economic, cultural, organisational and lack of technical information. To conclude, it has been evidenced that in FF in the Ecuadorian context, many innovations are considered because they modify and improve a production system and are adapted to territorial conditions. However, they cannot be considered as such in other production systems or territories. Therefore, state or private interventions must adjust to these realities. Furthermore the application of innovations in FF requires more than action by farmers alone, it involves the public sector, civil society and organisations in an innovation network to lead to a strong, competitive and sustainable FF.

Keywords: Ecuador, family farming, innovation

Contact Address: Rawia Derbel, Agris Mundus, Tunis, Tunisia, e-mail: rawia_derbel@yahoo.fr

Inhibiting Factors and Promotion Strategies for Increasing Adoption Levels of Improved Forages in Cattle Production

LISBETH ROCIO RUIZ[1], STEFAN BURKART[2], JHON JAIRO MUÑOZ QUICENO[1], KAREN ENCISO[2], JHON FREDDY GUTIERREZ SOLIS[2], ANDRES CHARRY[3], CRISTHIAN DAVID PUERTA RODRIGUEZ[2], NELSON JOSÉ VIVAS QUILA[1], NOÉ ALBÁN LOPEZ[1], SANDRA MORALES VELASCO[1], MICHAEL PETERS[2]

[1] University of Cauca, Dept. of Agricultural Sciences, Colombia
[2] International Center for Tropical Agriculture (CIAT), Colombia
[3] University of Hohenheim, Institute for Farm Management, Germany

In Colombia, cattle farming is the economic activity of greatest relevance in the rural environment, contributing to 53 % of the agricultural GDP and 1.3 % of the overall GDP. However, extensive management prevails, based on the use of native and / or naturalized pastures on soils of low to medium fertility, which limits the forage supply for prolonged periods of drought, leading to low productivity and increased production costs due to the additional use of concentrates and supplements.

Considering this problem, researchers from the University of Cauca and the International Center for Tropical Agriculture (CIAT) have been working for > 10 years in the Colombian Cauca Department on investigating processes of adoption, diffusion and transfer of improved forage technologies among small and medium scale livestock producers, which allow maintaining the feed supply in terms of quantity and quality throughout the whole year and contributing to the mitigation of greenhouse gas emissions, while also promoting socio-economic and environmental sustainability of the livestock production system. The results of these studies demonstrate the acceptability of improved forages among livestock producers, however adoption levels are still low.

For this reason and in order to identify strategies for adoption by small and medium scale livestock producers, between October and November 2015, a semi-quantitative study was conducted with 310 producers in the Colombian Cauca Department (Patía and Mercaderes Municipalities). In June 2016, participatory diagnostic workshops will be organised for gathering the perception of the participants related to improved grasses and legumes. The obtained information will be analysed and the hypothesis that the level of knowledge about the management and establishment of improved forages, as well as the access to resources (positively or negatively) influence the adoption level will be tested. Based on these results, factors that inhibit adoption will be identified and recommendations for both producers and regional authorities will be formulated to support the design of strategies for a wider adoption of improved forages, contributing to sustainable intensification of livestock systems, productivity increase and climate change mitigation.

Keywords: Adoption, cattle, climate change, improved forages

Contact Address: Stefan Burkart, International Center for Tropical Agriculture (CIAT), Tropical Forages Program, Km 17 Recta Cali-Palmira, Cali, Colombia, e-mail: s.burkart@cgiar.org

A Crowdsourcing Approach to Detect Farmers' Preferences: Evidences from Ethiopia for Adapting to Climate Change

Carlo Fadda[1], Chiara Mancini[2], Dejene Kassahun Mengistu[3], Yosef Gebrehawaryat Kidane[2], Matteo Dell'Acqua[2], Mario Enrico Pè[2]

[1] Bioversity International, Agrobiodiversity and Ecosystem Services Programme, Kenya
[2] Sant'Anna School of Advanced Studies, Life Science, Italy
[3] Mekelle University, Dept. of Dryland Crop and Horticultural Sciences, Ethiopia

Climate change is severely affecting production systems all over Africa. Ethiopia will face an increase in temperature and changes in rainfall patterns. One solution for long term management of climate related risks is to introduce new traits into production systems.

We present an approach to quickly deliver to farmers a selected number of preferred accessions of durum wheat using a crowdsourcing approach. After having completed a phenotypic and genotypic characterisation of 400 accessions of Ethiopian landraces and asked farmers to evaluate them, we distributed seeds of preferred varieties to a large number of farmers using a crowdsourcing approach.

In two sites representing different agroecological zones, we distributed 20 superior varieties and one check, an improved variety very common in both areas to 200 farmers in 12 villages per site, covering an area of roughly 350 km^2. We repeated the experiment for 2 years. Each farmer was given 3 blind varieties and the check, each variety being equally represented in the sample. In addition, in each village we included 2 i-buttons, measuring temperature and humidity every 3 hours throughout the growing season. This allowed to analyse the data on critical climatic parameters.

Results clearly indicate farmers' preferences: a) Landraces were preferred over improved varieties for their multiple uses; b) By considering farmers as citizen scientists, we have a better understanding of the criteria farmers use to select their preferred varieties (in our case straw and grain yield, drought tolerance, uniformity, long and dense spikes).

In conclusion:

• This process has been very effective in quickly disseminating seeds that match farmers' needs. After 2 years several hundred farmers can use better adapted material.

• It shows the potential of landraces to provide immediate option for managing climate related risks and calls for broader use of material conserved in gene banks.

• It indicates the need to strengthen local seed systems to better manage these resources.

• It indicates how farmers can provide very valuable scientific information that can be translated into research as well as development potential in other areas of research.

Keywords: Climate change, crowdsourcing, durum wheat, Ethiopia, farmers' participatory selection

Contact Address: Carlo Fadda, Bioversity International, Agrobiodiversity and Ecosystem Services Programme, Nairobi, Kenya, e-mail: c.fadda@cgiar.org

ID 803

Markets and value chain analysis

Population Increase and Market Development as a Peril for Traditional Home Gardens and a Promise for Khat in Southern Ethiopia

BEYENE TEKLU MELLISSE[1], GERRIE VAN DE VEN[1], KEN GILLER[1], ABEBE TESFAYE[2], KATRIEN DESCHEEMAEKER[1]

[1]*Wageningen University (WUR), Dept. of Plant Sciences, The Netherlands*
[2]*Hawassa University, Plant Sciences, Ethiopia*

Home gardens in southern Ethiopia are regarded efficient farming systems, allowing maximum interactions between the system's crop, tree and livestock components. However, these age-old traditional home gardens are subject to conversion processes linked to socio-economic change and biophysical conditions. Altered cropping patterns, farm size and component interactions may affect the systems' sustainability. Furthermore, home gardens exhibit a huge diversity in farms and farming systems, which needs to be understood in order to design adapted interventions for improvement. Two decade (1991–2013) dynamics of home gardens were studied based on a survey of 240 farm households and focus group discussions. Major trends in cropping patterns included an expansion of the cash crop khat and a consolidation of combined food and cash crop production. In the two market proximate districts the area share of khat per farm increased from 6 % to 35 % while the combined area share of enset and coffee decreased from 45 % to 25 % during the period of analysis. Cattle fell from 5.8 TLU to 3.9 TLU per household. In the other two less accessible districts, enset and coffee together maintained a share over 45 %. Farms were grouped into five home garden types: Khat-based, Enset-cereal-vegetable, Enset-based, Enset-coffee and Enset-livestock. Overall farm trajectories revealed a shift from food-oriented Enset-based, Enset-coffee and Enset-livestock systems to (1) cash crop oriented khat-based systems, and (2) combined food and cash crop oriented systems (Enset-cereal-vegetable). The strongest replacement of traditional home gardens based on combinations of enset, coffee and livestock by khat-based systems was observed within a radius of 36 km from major market areas. In these areas population density doubled, and the annual rate of decline in land holding per household increased from 0.5 % to 5.1 %. Easy transport and marketing of the perishable khat in combination with its cash-generating advantage over traditional crops boosts cultivation of khat among smallholders. However, increased vulnerability to shocks related to the decrease in diversity leads to concerns about the sustainability of these newly evolving systems. This study provided insights in trends, drivers and diversity that may help designing adapted interventions in the face of population increase and commercialisation.

Keywords: *Catha edulis*, commercialisation, cropping patterns, diversification

Contact Address: Beyene Teklu Mellisse, Wageningen University (WUR), Dept. of Plant Sciences, Bornsesteeg, 6708 GA Wageningen, The Netherlands, e-mail: beyene.mellisse@wur.nl

Investigating the Value Chain of African Indigenous Vegetables in Kenya from a Gender Perspective

RUTH GITHIGA, EMMA OKETCH

Humboldt-Universität zu Berlin, Dept. of Gender and Globalization, Germany

This paper aims at investigating the African Indigenous Vegetables (AIVs) value chain in Kenya from a gender perspective. In East Africa women significantly contribute to horticultural production; they are particularly involved in cultivating, harvesting, selling and preparation of AIVs. There is a trend of accelerating commercialisation of vegetable production, which comes along with value chain innovation and modernisation. The global value chain scholarship emphasises the importance of value chain modernisation and upgrading for reducing poverty in rural areas. However, the overall effects of value chain modernisation have to be critically assessed from a gender perspective: On one hand women get increasingly integrated into commercialised vegetable production, but on the other hand – due to existing gender norms and power relations within the society – there is a risk of deepening gender gaps and inequalities throughout the value chain.

This paper presents first findings of the HORTINLEA subproject "Gender Order: Embedding gender in horticultural value chains to close the productivity gap". The results are based on field research carried out in the rural, peri-urban and urban areas in Kenya. Qualitative methods of data collection such as semi-structured in-depth interviews and focus group discussions with male and female farmers and traders were applied. Qualitative content analysis (with MAXQDA) was applied for data analysis. Preliminary results show that women are the primary producers of AIVs but men are increasingly participating in AIV production due to increasing incomes because of commercialisation. This negatively affects women's share and participation in AIVs value chain. Further, women are disadvantaged in marketing, due to gendered asymmetries in bargaining power and their roles in social reproduction. The paper seeks to discuss policy innovations for making AIVs value chains more inclusive.

Keywords: African indigenous vegetables, commercialisation, gender asymmetries, gender order, gender perspective

Contact Address: Ruth Githiga, Humboldt-Universität zu Berlin, Dept. of Gender and Globalization, Berlin, Germany, e-mail: githigaruth@gmail.com

ID 532

The Contribution of Agricultural Value Chain Promotion to Food Security – Evidence from German Development Cooperation

SABINE BRÜNTRUP-SEIDEMANN[1], MARCUS KAPLAN[1], MARTIN NOLTZE[1],
SIMON BETTIGHOFER[2]

[1]*German Institute for Development Evaluation (DEval), Germany*
[2]*World Health Organization (WHO), Switzerland*

The promotion of agricultural value chains is currently perceived as one of the most promising approaches in international development cooperation. Proponents claim that the promotion of value chains contributes to poverty reduction and food security for smallholders and rural labourers. Yet, there is only limited evidence in how far and through which pathways the promotion of agricultural value chains contributes effectively to these prominent development goals. This is due to methodological challenges when evaluators have to disentangle the multiple cause and effect issues in systemic and complex sector environments.

We used a mechanism-centered approach to investigate the impact of agricultural value chain promotion on food security using the case of German Development Cooperation in two partner countries. Adopting a theory-driven approach, four case studies were carried out, including maize and pineapple value chains in Ghana and rice and cashew chains in Burkina Faso. The case studies are accompanied by a literature and a portfolio review as well as expert interviews.

The evaluation identifies positive food security effects for both export crop and staple food crop promotion. However, the impact pathways are different. The promotion of export value chains addresses the access to food through higher farm profits which may translate into increased food consumption. However, the results also show that export chains are prone to price and production volatilities in global food markets posing an economic risk to value chain actors. On the contrary, the support of staple food chains addresses the access to and the availability of food at national markets. This is particularly decisive for countries with reduced food availability and non-functioning food markets. Lower profits for staple food chains are partly offset by fewer risks due to international price fluctuations. In both cases, entry barriers hinder the successful inclusion of the less market-oriented and resource-endowed producers. The authors conclude that successful support strategies have to be case- and context-specific taking both staple food crop and export crop promotion into consideration. Moreover, the findings suggest that combined approaches may come with additional positive effects with regard to economic risks, food availability and food access.

Keywords: Agricultural value chains, evaluation, food security, German Development Cooperation

---

Contact Address: Sabine Brüntrup-Seidemann, German Institute for Development Evaluation (DEval), Fritz-Schäffer-Straße 26, 53113 Bonn, Germany, e-mail: sabine.bruentrup-seidemann@deval.org

Traditional Markets for Poverty Reduction and Food Security: Exploring Policy Options in Honduras and Nicaragua

Matthias Jäger[1], Irene van Loosen[1], Byron Reyes[2], Marco Vasquez[3], Francesca Larosa[2], Lorena Gomez[2], Milagro Espinal[3], Jennifer Wiegel[4], Ivan Rodriguez[3], Mark Lundy[1]

[1]*International Center for Tropical Agriculture (CIAT), Colombia*
[2]*International Center for Tropical Agriculture (CIAT), Nicaragua*
[3]*Swisscontact, Honduras*
[4]*Lutheran World Relief, Nicaragua*

Much of the current research on value chains and market linkages focuses on formal markets, such as linking farmers to supermarkets, while less attention is given to traditional markets. This tendency leads to a bias in the design of policy interventions that benefit the formal private sector, while the lives of many smallholders, processors, traders, and poor consumers could be improved by researching their needs and implementing appropriate, actor-tailored market policies.

A 2015 project funded by the Ford Foundation aimed to better understand the traditional market channels for agricultural goods in Honduras and Nicaragua in order to identify policy options to increase the value that these markets offer to producers and poor consumers. The study examined the existing rural-urban linkages between small producers and other low-income actors through a representative food basket including red bean as an index for basic grain crops, plum tomato representing vegetables, and dry/semi-dry cheese as a representation of animal protein. In both Honduras and Nicaragua, traditional markets (i.e. wholesalers, retailers and farmers' markets) play a major role in the distribution of agricultural products to the consumer, especially for those consumers with limited purchasing power. Applying a range of quantitative and qualitative methods, it was found that the competitiveness of businesses in traditional markets for basic grains, vegetables and cheeses in Honduras and Nicaragua is negatively affected by the occurrence of poor food safety, post-harvest losses, seasonal price fluctuations and a reduction of sales. These factors lead to a contraction in demand and may force poor consumers to purchase their goods in more expensive markets, reducing their food security.

Public policies that implement health and safety regulations in traditional markets, improve product quality and food safety, and stimulate efficient production, processing, sorting, transport and storage practices should be introduced or reinforced, while taking into account the different needs of each group of value chain actors linked to the traditional markets of Honduras and Nicaragua. Additionally, the establishment of a collective action platform convening key stakeholders from traditional markets and the public sector could help to inform and ultimately influence public policy and decision making.

Keywords: Food security, market policy, rural-urban linkages, traditional market, value chain governance

Contact Address: Matthias Jäger, International Center for Tropical Agriculture (CIAT), Cali, Colombia, e-mail: m.jager@cgiar.org

ID 936

Horticulture Value Chains in Ethiopia: Opportunities for Better Nutrition and New Market Access?

AKALU TESHOME[1], JOCHEN DÜRR[2]

[1] *NutriHAF Project, Value Chain, Ethiopia*
[2] *University of Bonn, Center for Development Research (ZEF), NutriHAF Project, Germany*

Fruits and vegetables are the most important source of micronutrients and are essential for a balanced and healthy diet. Diversifying and increasing horticulture production can help to overcome malnutrition and poverty by augmenting household consumption and also create new market access for smallholders. Moreover, horticulture value chains can offer new income and employment opportunities in trading and processing sectors. The present research uses a nutrition-sensitive value chain approach for horticulture development in the Yayu biosphere reserve in Ethiopia. To identify possible diversification and/or intensification strategies, we mapped the already existing value chains and assessed market opportunities for new products, including the most important actors along the whole chain. The main drivers, bottlenecks and potentials for the intensification and/or diversification of fruit and vegetable production include: on the supply side, seasonal constrained production systems, competition with cash crops (mainly coffee), crop damages through wild animals, lack of nutrition-sensitive farming systems, gender division in horticultural production, lack of research and extension supports, marketing problems and non-availability of improved technologies; on the demand side, lack of awareness for nutritional issues, existence of underutilised crops, reluctance to consume indigenous fruits and vegetables and low purchasing power; and on the intermediation side, technical problems with storage, processing and packaging, existence of weekly markets in the nearby towns but with inadequate infrastructure for perishable products, seasonal unavailability of products in the market. Thus, nutrition-sensitive horticulture value chain development may need a multi-dimensional strategy of awareness creation between all stakeholders, specific nutrition-sensitive extension services, infrastructural and technical improvements and market development as well as political support from the local to the national level.

Keywords: Diversification, fruits, intensification, nutrition, value chains, vegetables

---

Contact Address: Akalu Teshome, NutriHAF Project, Value Chain, Addis Ababa, Ethiopia, e-mail: akalu_firew@yahoo.com

Improving Market Access for Smallholder Rice Producers in the Philippines

Ekkehard Kürschner, Daniel Baumert, Christine Plastrotmann, Anna-Katharina Poppe, Kristina Riesinger, Sabrina Ziesemer

Humboldt-Universität zu Berlin, Center for Rural Development (SLE), Germany

In the Philippines, rice is one of the main agricultural commodities that not only supports the livelihoods of around 45 % of Filipino farm households but also serves as the country's main food staple. Thus, political efforts are split between simultaneously securing remunerative farm gate prices and affordable consumer prices. However, comparatively high production costs and inefficient rice marketing render this a difficult task. Consequently, improving market access for smallholder farmers in the Philippines is assumed to bridge the gap between affordable consumer prices for food security and remunerative farm gate prices for poverty reduction.

This study analyses market access constraints of smallholder rice producers in the Philippines in order to identify entry points for development interventions. It combines elements of value chain and of livelihood analysis with a multi-dimensional definition of market access. Therefore, the study was able to take smallholder heterogeneity into consideration and to develop context-specific recommendation.

Results indicate that the varying asset endowment of smallholder farm households determine the use of marketing opportunities and the access to support services. This is based on a typology of smallholders' marketing practices taking the time of transaction, the number of marketing outlets accessed and the freedom to choose the trading party into account. Three distinct marketing practices were identified. By grouping the smallholders accordingly and by examining the differences of the asset endowments across groups, the most significant differences were noted with regard to market-related knowledge, dependencies, the type of production financing, and access to post-harvest facilities and farm machinery. The study concludes that development interventions which aim at improving the market access of smallholders have to address the group-specific needs when targeting these aspects. Smallholders can only be empowered to freely choose from existing marketing opportunities and to freely decide upon the time of transaction when access to financial capital, to post-harvest facilities and to information is being improved. Interventions have to follow a multi-dimensional approach targeting, at the same time, individual farmers and farmer organisations as well as the entire value chain.

Keywords: Agricultural development, livelihoods, market linkages, staple food

---

Contact Address: Daniel Baumert, Humboldt-Universität Berlin, Center for Rural Development (SLE), 12053 Berlin, Germany, e-mail: daniel.baumert@hotmail.de

ID 454

Does Improved Market Access for Smallholders in Bhutan Affect Food Self-Sufficiency?

KIRAN SUBEDI[1], TIM K. LOOS[2], ARNDT FEUERBACHER[3], HARALD GRETHE[3]

[1] *Ministry of Agriculture and Forests, Department of Agriculture, Bhutan*

[2] *University of Hohenheim, Inst. of Agricultural Sciences in the Tropics (Hans-Ruthenberg-Institute), Germany*

[3] *Humboldt-Universität zu Berlin, International Agricultural Trade and Development, Germany*

In Bhutan, a country with extreme mountainous geography, a large share of the rural and dispersed population has poor access to markets. As this impedes agricultural development, the construction of farm roads became a key priority of Bhutan's government during the last decade. This study investigates how the construction of farm roads between 2009 and 2012 has affected farmers' land use, marketing of output, income and food self-sufficiency. The underlying hypothesis is that improved market access leads to increased output of cash crops and a simultaneous decline in cereal output. This would contradict the policy objective of achieving higher levels in rice self-sufficiency, another key political priority. Employing propensity score matching (PSM) techniques, socio-economic data of 834 farming household collected in 2013 was analysed and supplemented by qualitative information from expert interviews and field observations in 2015. The findings of this study suggest that the short-term impact of farm roads has resulted in significantly increased cultivation of cash crops, while the cultivation of rice, the most relevant and highly valued cereal, did not decrease. In contrast, however, cultivation of low value cereals such as maize and wheat declined. Bhutan's land use policies, which constrain farmers to convert wetland used for paddy to dryland used for the cultivation of cash crops, could be a possible explanation of these mixed results. This is supported by the finding that dryland left fallow has significantly decreased, while wetland left fallow was not impacted by improved market access. Overall, the study concludes that the construction of farm roads does not contradict the policy objective of rice self-sufficiency. Further research could assess the economic efficiency of farm road construction based on village specific cost-benefit analysis. Long-term impacts of farm roads may be analysed in the future, particularly with regard to the adoption of improved technology and effects on rural labour markets through an increased rural-urban migration.

Keywords: Bhutan, food self-sufficiency, propensity score matching, road infrastructure, rural development

Contact Address: Arndt Feuerbacher, Humboldt-Universität zu Berlin, International Agricultural Trade and Development, Unter den Linden 6, 10099 Berlin, Germany, e-mail: arndt.feuerbacher@hu-berlin.de

Decoding Fairness in the Value Chain of the Tagbanua Wild Honey Community Forestry Enterprise

DENISE MARGARET MATIAS

University of Bonn, Center for Development Research (ZEF), Dept. of Ecology and Natural Resources Management, Germany

Indigenous Tagbanuas in the Philippines are one of the hunter gatherers of the non-timber forest product wild honey in the country. The Tagbanuas have been gathering honey from giant honey bees (*Apis dorsata*) since time immemorial for personal consumption. When a market for wild honey has opened in the early 1980s, they started to gather wild honey for the purpose of selling. This practice has been formally organised into a community forestry enterprise through the help of non-government organisations (NGO). The Tagbanua community of Aborlan is one of the biggest suppliers of wild honey combs to the NGO Nagkakaisang mga Tribu ng Palawan (United Tribes of Palawan). NATRIPAL buys the honey combs from the indigenous Tagbanua and thereafter processes the honey combs into filtered honey and beeswax blocks which they sell on both wholesale and retail bases. One of the sustainability research questions for the wild honey enterprise is the quality of its economic contribution to the lives of indigenous Tagbanua. A value chain analysis of the 2015 harvest and sales record of the Tagbanua was conducted vis-à-vis a qualitative assessment of the value addition functions of each actor in the value chain in order to understand which value chain actor or value addition function captures the most economic value. This mixed methods research provided substantial insight on how fairly or unfairly compensated each of the value chain actors was. Preliminary results show that the compensation for indigenous honey hunters is not commensurate to their intensity of work compared to the other value chain actors. This presentation argues that the principle of fairness in a rural enterprise must not only be analysed within the context of horizontal actors but also with vertical actors.

Keywords: Forest honey, indigenous honey hunting, non-timber forest product, value chain analysis

Contact Address: Denise Margaret Matias, University of Bonn, Center for Development Research (ZEF), Dept. of Ecology and Natural Resources Management, Walter-Flex-Str. 3, 53113 Bonn, Germany, e-mail: denise.matias@uni-bonn.de

Kilimanjaro Origin Sugar: A Tanzanian Pathway to Green Inclusive Growth

INNOCENSIA JOHN[1], HENRIK EGELYNG[2], RAZACK LOKINA[1]

[1] University of Dar es Salaam, Economics, Tanzania
[2] University of Copenhagen, Food and Resource Economics, Denmark

The increasing attention to develop the sugar sector in Tanzania to protect its local industries paves way to create a market in which geographical indication (GI) can play a useful role. This paper investigates whether unique attributes of Tanganyika Planting Company (TPC) represent a potential for registration with protected geographical indication, protected denomination of origin and/or traditional specialty guaranteed. From a preliminary study of products, TPC-produced sugar from the slopes of mountain Kilimanjaro may be worth protection.

The paper aims at looking at the unique attributes of sugar from Kilimanjaro and its potential for GI registration. Further, it explores the institutional conditions under which the Tanzanian sugar producers currently market their products. A qualitative analysis is presented reporting the estimated gains the Tanzanian economy could harvest by valorizing its sugars through geographical indications, and assessing the producers perception of territorial qualities of sugars and feasibility of their business strategy.

The study used in depth-interviews with sugar producers, stakeholders, key informants and sellers of the Kilimanjaro region. The results show that Kilimanjaro sugar has potential for protection using GI since it has some unique attributes and in turn protects the environment through a better cultivation method. The study revealed from the origin food producer how value addition by incorporating territory specific cultural, environmental and social qualities into marketing, production and processing of unique local, niche and specialty products could be shaped. The case investigated has prospects for Tanzania to advance in exports of geographical indicated sugar, and allows to create employment and build monetary value, while stewarding local food cultures and natural environments and resources, and increasing the diversity of supply of natural and unique quality product.

Keywords: Geographical indication, green growth, qualitative analysis, sugar

Contact Address: Innocensia John, University of Dar es Salaam, Economics, Dar es Salaam, Tanzania, e-mail: jinnocensia@gmail.com

Regional Market Integration and Price Transmission in Supply and Consumer Markets

SCHOLASTICA LEAH MUSYIMI, SIEGFRIED BAUER

Justus-Liebig University Giessen, Inst. of Farm and Agribusiness Management - Project and Regional Planning, Germany

The study gives an overview of spatial market integration investigated for grain white maize markets in Eastern Africa, namely Kenya, Tanzania and Uganda. Following food surges, prices of most staple food commodities in most developing countries mirrored the surges suggesting global price transmission. However, volatile prices act as disincentives for producers' agricultural investment and consumers purchasing decisions with impact on sustainable agricultural productivity. The study seeks to explore market failures, investigated whether prices in rural and urban deficit and surplus markets of selected countries of Eastern Africa are co-integrated. Despite maize being staple food commodity and the most traded, in Kenya its demand outweighs supply due to increasing population and climatic impacts contributing to food insecurity and poverty. In food policy, economic theory affirms that markets allocate scarce resources from surplus to deficit regions absorbing demand and supply shocks arising from uncertainties. Eight markets were selected for the study from three countries based on data availability of monthly wholesale white grain maize prices and the correspondence CPI and exchange rates for the period between 2006 and 2014. Using bivariate equation, threshold error correction model was used to investigate consumer and supply price responses within and across selected Eastern Africa markets. Prices were found to be volatile in the region whereby Kenyan markets had highest wholesale prices while Uganda had the least, suggesting possibility of high transaction costs. The study also found out that rural and urban consumer and supply markets are co-integrated in Eastern Africa with estimated price shock adjustments between surplus and consumer markets ranging between 2 to 11 weeks. However, the study found economic agents respond faster in case of demand shock compared to supply shock. In the short run, the study gives useful insights for production and consumption decisions. In the long run, to lower transaction costs, policy formulations in Kenya should promote investment in infrastructure, mainly road network, agriculture, marketing and information for sustainable agricultural productivity and economic growth.

Keywords: Deficit, grain white maize, price transmission, regional market integration, rural, spatial, surplus, urban

---

Contact Address: Scholastica Leah Musyimi, Justus Liebig University Giessen, Agricultural Economics and Related Sciences, Giessen, Germany, e-mail: scholaleah@yahoo.com

ID 1046

Market Constraints and Opportunities for Cassava Products in Tamil Nadu, India: A Value Chain Analysis

RILEY LINDER[1], ALESSANDRA GIULIANI[1], KR ASHOK[2]

[1] Bern University of Applied Sciences, School of Agricultural, Forest and Food Sciences, Switzerland

[2] Tamil Nadu Agricultural University, Economics, India

Cassava (*Manihot esculenta* Crantz), renowned as a highly productive tropical tuber crop, known to support rural communities for its high caloric value and vast industrial application uses, supports over 10,000 smallholder farmers in Tamil Nadu. To support this large community of smallholder farmers, the Indo-Swiss Collaboration in Biotechnology (ISCB) has established a project aimed to develop cassava varieties to overcome the negative impact on production yields associated with the Cassava Mosaic Disease (CMD).

To support ISCB project objectives for improving food security and rural development, socioeconomic research tools were used. A value chain analysis was conducted to understand market structure, supply, demand and trends of production for cassava in Tamil Nadu. This information serves to develop an understanding of market constraints and opportunities that exists amongst value chain actors. In 2015 and 2016, two field surveys were conducted in Tamil Nadu, utilising purposive sampling to conduct interviews and group discussions. Quantitative and qualitative data were collected from actors and key informants along the industrial cassava value chain.

Clear constraints were observed influencing market functions and actors. The cassava industry is undergoing continual transition amidst pressure in an unregulated and highly fluctuating marketplace, further constraining demand trends. The industrial market, composed of highly diverse production units relative to size and economical value, has become very competitive, resulting in constraints relating to product quality, environmental practices, and production methods. These constraints have a direct impact on farmers, who often take the greatest economical risk along the value chain.

The findings show that socio-economic and market interventions are of crucial importance in addition to the varietal development of cassava. Key recommendations resulting from this research include: establishing government imposed minimum support prices, establishing industrial production standards, further development of industrial quality and safety standards, and the introduction of improved marketing methods. Essential to these recommendations is a collaborative effort towards innovation along the value chain, as growth will need to be pursued collectively in order to ensure sustainable market function. These solutions serve to benefit continued production of an essential crop supporting the smallholder farmer community.

Keywords: Agribusiness, market access, rural development, smallholder farmers

Contact Address: Riley Linder, Bern University of Applied Sciences, School of Agricultural, Forest and Food Sciences, Länggasse 85, 3052 Zollikofen, Switzerland, e-mail: riley.linder13@gmail.com

Economic Returns and Smallholder Participation in High-Value Markets for African Indigenous Vegetables in Rural Kenya

Dorcas Jalang'o, David Otieno, Willis Oluoch-Kosura

University of Nairobi, Agricultural Economics, Kenya

The existence of effective markets holds potential for maintaining a consistent supply of produce in rural areas and possibly ensuring adequate surplus for trade. This is critical in promoting the transition from subsistence production to vibrant commercial farming. In recent literature and policy debates, much focus has been on the growth of supermarkets, particularly in developing countries. However, there is limited documentation of the extent of penetration of and farmers' participation in other emerging high-value agri-food markets such as schools, hospitals and restaurants in the rural remote areas. In order to address this critical knowledge gap, this study analysed the effectiveness of such markets for African indigenous vegetables in Siaya county; a relatively remote lake-side rural area of western Kenya. The findings of the study revealed that less than one-tenth of the smallholder farmers sell their vegetables in high value markets. Surprisingly, the high-value markets have a marketing margin of over 60 %, but smallholder farmers' share of this margin is less than one-third. Comparatively, traditional open-air markets have marketing margins of less than 30%; but this is fairly distributed as the farmers who supply open-air markets receive more than two-thirds of this margin. The findings from this study call for interventions that seek to improve the distribution of market margins along high-value markets so as incentivize smallholder farmers to supply their produce to these channels. Alternatively, it looks plausible to accelerate infrastructural investments in value-addition facilities in open-air markets so as to improve the commodity prices, enhance shelf-life and assure better quality to consumers. This would in turn guarantee better returns to smallholder farmers. It is envisaged that spending resources in making markets work for smallholder farmers will ultimately contribute to welfare improvement and development of the rural economic base.

Keywords: High-value markets, indigenous vegetables, Kenya, smallholder farmers

---

Contact Address: Dorcas Jalang'o, University of Nairobi, Agricultural Economics, 29053 Upper Kabete, 00625 Nairobi, Kenya, e-mail: jalango88@yahoo.com

ID 370

Exploring Potentials of the Bamboo Sector for Food Security and Sustainable Livelihoods in Ethiopia: An Institutional and Market Analysis of Bamboo-Based Value Web

JESSIE LIN, SAURABH GUPTA

University of Hohenheim, Social and Institutional Change in Agriculture Development, Germany

Effective management of natural resources and forest produce is very important for enhancing the livelihoods of smallholders in resource rich but economically poor countries like Ethiopia. Bamboo is one of the more important natural resources in Ethiopia with potential usages in construction, furniture and handicrafts, floor boards, incense sticks, paper and energy supply (bamboo-based charcoal), among others. While the country is the largest producer of bamboo in Africa, the existing utilization of bamboo-sector in Ethiopia remains under-developed with little value addition. As a result, Ethiopian bamboo-growers continue to suffer from food insecurity and seasonal vulnerabilities. What are the governance and institutional challenges in the development and growth of bamboo sector in the country? How can Ethiopian bamboo growers as well as traders and processors benefit from the development of the sector? These are the main analytical questions addressed in this paper.

The main objective of theis research entailed in the paper is to provide insights into the current status and future potentials of the bamboo sector in order to enhance sustainable livelihoods and to improve food security for smallholders in Ethiopia. Owing to the multiple usages of the same crop, which limits the adoption of value chain study, this research adopts the "value web" approach to assess the potentials of different product lines that create the bamboo value web. The study utilizes qualitative data collection methods, in particular in-depth interviews, focus group discussions and participatory net-mapping with important stakeholders, including government officials, policy makers, development organisations, processing companies, traders and sub-traders, and bamboo growers . The output from this demand driven research can be used as an input to update the future strategies to develop the sector; will bring together different stakeholders; and generate scientific work that has direct policy relevance for strengthening the potential of bamboo sector.

Keywords: Bamboo, Ethiopia, food security, natural resource base, sustainable livelihoods, value chains

Contact Address: Jessie Lin, University of Hohenheim, Social and Institutional Change in Agriculture Development, 70593 Stuttgart, Germany, e-mail: jessie.lin9@gmail.com

Adapted Institutional Environment and Sustainable Resource Access for Co-Developing Brazil Nut Value Chains in the Amazon?

MARCELO CUNHA

Freie Universitaet Berlin, Geography, Germany

The potential of sustainable use and commercialisation of non-timber forest products (NTFPs) – as a means for forest dependent smallholders to make a living while contributing to biodiversity conservation – has not yet been fully harnessed in Brazil's environmental agenda.

In the frame of inclusive sustainable rural development, key determinants of the access to natural resources and markets of Brazil nut (BN) value chain (VC) actors are analysed based on a bottom-up research approach to provide input for policy making. Within the Lower Amazon basin, Brazil, focus is laid on the Trombetas River Biological Reserve – a Protected Area (PA), which was established in 1979 in territories that have been traditionally occupied by 'Afro-Brazilians' for over a century. Established in 2012, the 'Term of Compromise' ('ToC', based on a Decree), and related limited institutional environment for gathering and marketing of BN is analysed, as is its purpose of overcoming conflicts concerning the access to BN and markets among traditional populations and the responsible branch of the country's Ministry of Environment.

The central research question was: "How do rules regulating BN gathering and marketing formalised per ToC affect the position of BN gatherers vis-à-vis local buyers within the VC?" Qualitative and quantitative data were collected from 2012–2014, including a survey with 185 households as well as key-informant interviews from national to community level. An analytical framework was developed for combining conceptual analysis with evidences as an input for co-developing BN VCs, which can be applied to other VCs elsewhere.

Findings indicate: (i) importance of sustainable BN and market access, given 13 % of smallholders' income; (ii) formal environmental rules (ToC – Clause 10) enabled the exclusion of external buyers, which led to local oligopsonies and cartel building within the PA while it institutionalised the dependency of BN gatherers from established buyers and limited their bargaining power as well as market outlets; (iii) self-sustaining inclusive BN VC development depends on 'locally desired adaptation' of the ToC combined with socioeconomic upgrading of the position of BN gatherers while enabling their participation in shaping formal institutions for democratic environmental governance.

Keywords: Amazonia, forest conservation, formal institutions, livelihood strategies, local markets, non-timber forest products, production networks, resource access, sustainable development, value chains

Contact Address: Marcelo Cunha, Freie Universitaet Berlin, Geography, Berlin, Germany, e-mail: marcelocunha@zedat.fu-berlin.de

ID 410

Institutional Challenges in an Emerging Bio-Economy: A Case Study of Maize Value-Webs in Nigeria

AYOBAMI ADETOYINBO[1], SAURABH GUPTA[1], VICTOR OKORUWA[2], REGINA BIRNER[1]

[1] *University of Hohenheim, Inst. of Agricultural Sciences in the Tropics (Hans-Ruthenberg-Institute), Germany*
[2] *University of Ibadan, Dept. of Agricultural Economics, Nigeria*

Growing challenges of sustainable development require a shift in the conventional thinking of considering agricultural sector as only the supplier of food. It is increasingly becoming a "supplier of biomass", which caters to multiple demands of food and non-food purposes. Traditionally, the analysis of biomass sector has been dominated by value chain studies. Recent advances suggest that it is pertinent to look beyond conventional value chains to a more holistic "value web" because the same crops find diverse usages in the biomass-based economy. The value web approach adopted in this study helps in identifying the potential opportunities in the maize sector beyond the focus on food. Maize is one of the most important cereal crops in Nigeria. It is particularly important for the poorer citizens and smallholders for food security purposes. The study employs focus group discussion and uses innovative participatory net-mapping tool to elicit information on how maize biomass flows and the institutional environment governing the sector. The value web also helps to show how maize is used locally by households as well as industrial sector, and the disconnects in the flow due to the current institutional structure. The study found that marketing problem arising from pest and chemical residues *e.g.* aflatoxin is a major constraint for maize utilization by industries producing human consumables. Food and drink industries source for maize grains only from the northern part where aflatoxin infestation is minimal. Inconsistent financial support to the national research institutes and Agricultural Development Program (ADP) is a major problem affecting the sector's institutional structure. Extensive means of disseminating information to smallholders is through ADP and Maize Association of Nigeria (MAAN). However, smallholder farmers who are not linked to MAAN are disadvantaged. The study suggests that government should consistently finance ADP and national research institutes. Research effort into aflatoxin eradication and local use of maize biomass should be increased. Linkages between state governments and national research institutes as well as between small-scale farmers and MAAN should be made stronger.

Keywords: Institutional challenges, participatory net map, smallholder farmers, value-webs

Contact Address: Ayobami Adetoyinbo, University of Hohenheim, Inst. of Agricultural Sciences in the Tropics (Hans-Ruthenberg-Institute), Wollgrasweg 43, 123, 70599 Stuttgart, Germany, e-mail: acubed_101@yahoo.com

Do Unique Farmer Trader Relations Enhance Resilience: Case of Green Gram Markets in Mbeere County, Kenya

ESTHER KIHORO, PATRICK IRUNGU

University of Nairobi, Dept.of Agricultural Economics, Kenya

This study sought to contribute to a better understanding of market dynamics of green grams (*Vigna radiata*) as a traditional crop within a resource poor producer community in Mbeere South sub-County, Kenya. The study aimed to characterise the green gram marketing channels and to evaluate the factors that influence the choice of green gram marketing channel by the producers. Further the study sought to assess farmer-trader relationships that enhance resilience. A multinomial logit model was estimated through data from households growing green grams. Results show that 70 percent of farmers in the study site grew green grams. On average, each household has 1 to 2 acres of land under green grams production each year. Farmers used three marketing channels, rural retailers (58 percent), wholesalers (14 percent) and assemblers (26 percent). The multinomial results showed that age of the farmer ($p = 0.06$), access to credit ($p = 0.065$), price of green grams ($p = 0.079$), and selling as individuals ($p = 0.000$) positively influenced the choice of rural assembler marketing channel. Gender of the household head ($p = 0.001$), production cost ($p = 0.000$) and use of mobile phone to access marketing information ($p = 0.019$) positively influenced the probability of choosing rural retailer over wholesaler marketing channel. In conclusion, farmers prefer marketing channels where they incur low production and transport costs and that offer higher prices to maximise profits. The study also shows farmers prefer selling to traders where they have repeat visits and establish trust. The study recommended first, identification and prioritisation of unique farmer-trader relations that enhance adaptive resilience and increase farmers marketing options. Secondly, interventions to enhance market-based signals e.g. price should be reinforced.

Keywords: ASALs, green grams, market signals, marketing channels

Contact Address: Esther Kihoro, University of Nairobi, Dept.of Agricultural Economics, 573, Nairobi, Kenya, e-mail: emkihoro@gmail.com

 ID 554

Oil Palm Tree (*Elaeis guineensis*) Value Chain in South-South – Nigeria: Opportunities for Food Security

DAMIAN AGOM[1], EDDY ATTE ENYENIHI[2], EKAETTE UDOH[1]

[1]*Akwa Ibom State University, Dept. of Agricultural Economics and Extension, Nigeria*
[2]*University of Uyo, Agricultural Economics and Extension, Nigeria*

The Oil palm tree (*Elaeis guineensis*) is a major tree resource in the southern part of Nigeria and has both indigenous and improved varieties; the tree stands out with social, cultural and economic significance on the lives of the people. The palm tree has special adaptation to survive even when the environment is harsh. This paper examined the tree ownership structure, various uses to which the tree is put in the area, compares the returns from each of these uses and the potential of the value chain for increased income and food security. Data was collected from community members on the ownership rights of this tree, the various uses to which it is put, as well as returns from the various uses; this was complemented with data from secondary sources on tree potential, growth rate and processing possibilities. The study used descriptive statistics as well as budgetary analysis to fulfil its objectives. The results show that the oil palm tree has multiple ownership structure that varies from one community to another especially for wild trees. The uses to which the tree products can be put are multiple and sometimes mutually exclusive, the uses have both cultural and or economic significance to the people. The processing into palm oil, palm kernel oil, palm wine, gin, broom, furniture/building, cages, contributed in that order to income and food security in the area. There was high variance between the outputs from the indigenous and improved varieties. The potential of waste recycling needs to be tapped in the area for increased utilisation of the products from the oil palm tree. The oil palm tree still holds the key to not only individual and community cash flow but also national economic development and food security.

Keywords: Cash flow, food security, oil palm tree, value addition, value chain

Contact Address: Damian Agom, Akwa Ibom State University, Dept. of Agricultural Economics and Extension, Obio Akpa, Nigeria, e-mail: agomd@yahoo.com

Sustainable Milk and Beef Production in Nicaragua: Actions and Opportunities for an Inclusive Value Chain

REIN VAN DER HOEK[1], MARTÍN MENA[1], ROLDAN CORRALES[2], MARIA ALEJANDRA MORA[1], JULIE OJANGO[3]

[1] International Center for Tropical Agriculture (CIAT), Nicaragua

[2] National Agrarian University (UNA), Integral Systems of Animal Production, Nicaragua

[3] International Livestock Research Institute (ILRI), Kenya

In Nicaragua the cattle sector accounts for 36 % of agricultural exports and presents an important opportunity for smallholder farmer livelihoods. Current extensive dual-purpose (milk and beef) cattle production leads to soil degradation, deforestation, high levels of greenhouse gas (GHG) emissions per unit of product, and a shift of the agricultural frontier towards the vulnerable Caribbean region. The CGIAR Research Program on Livestock and Fish is implementing activities to make the dual-purpose cattle value chain more efficient, competitive and inclusive, with a specific focus on gender equality. Feed and forages work has improved the productivity of forage-based livestock production (up to 100 % in terms of kg milk/ha), increased carbon accumulation and at the same time reduced its ecological footprint (by over 50 % in terms of GHG emissions per unit of product) as part of LivestockPlus. This concept addresses sustainable intensification in three ways: socioeconomic – market opportunities and policy application; ecological – improved farm and natural resource management practices; and genetic – improved forage cultivars. Work on genetic improvement of cattle has included establishing an information, input, and service data platform linked to breed improvement in a wider farm-household context. It involves continuous monitoring and assessment of the performance of the predominant breed-types reared by 155 farmers in central Nicaragua as an initial step towards informing development of breeding strategies for dual purpose cattle in mixed farming systems. In collaboration with a farmers cooperative, capacity development in Farmer Field Schools and on-farm research involving 1000 farmers has resulted in increased productivity (milk by 40 %, liveweight by 70 %), income (by 20 %) and natural resource integrity (establishment of 4,000 ha of silvopastoral systems). Strategic alliances have been developed between value chain actors (farmers' organisations, NGOs, research, private sector with a focus on value addition to livestock products while increasing gender equity. In general, however, adoption of improved technologies and practices is still low. There is therefore a strong need for an increased policy incidence on sustainable livestock development and incentive mechanisms for farmers and other value chain actors, including certification of sustainable livestock products.

Keywords: Dual-purpose cattle, genetic improvement, Nicaragua, value chain

Contact Address: Rein van der Hoek, International Center for Tropical Agriculture (CIAT), Central America, Managua, Nicaragua, e-mail: r.vanderhoek@cgiar.org

ID 625

Micro-economics and livelihoods

Alternative Food Sources When Living in the City: Coping with Rising Food Prices in Kampala

Eefke Mollee[1,2], Morag McDonald[1], Anders Ræbild[2],
Katja Kehlenbeck[3]

[1] *Bangor University, School for Environment, Natural Resources and Geography (SEN-RGy), United Kingdom*

[2] *University of Copenhagen, Dept. of Geosciences and Natural Resource Management, Denmark*

[3] *Rhine-Waal University of Applied Sciences, Fac. of Life Sciences, Germany*

With some of the highest urbanisation rates in the world, sub-Saharan Africa is facing serious challenges in providing sufficient and healthy foods for its growing urban populations. Fresh fruits and vegetables at urban markets are often too expensive for the poor. Alternative food sources can provide solutions to a rising urban demand for healthy, nutrient-dense foods, but only if recognised and treated as a fair alternative practice. In many countries urban agriculture is still considered controversial and non-metropolitan. Additionally, collection of edible wild species as an alternative food source in urban and peri-urban areas has only received scant attention in natural resource studies and development projects. Consequently, data on the importance of these alternative food sources for food security of urban communities are largely missing. This study aimed at assessing the extent and importance of urban agriculture and wild food sources for poor residents in Kampala, Uganda. A total of 98 urban and peri-urban households with gardens were purposively selected, food plants in the gardens inventoried and respondents interviewed on socio-economic data, household food security levels, plant uses and food sources. In addition, respondents were asked about wild collection behaviour, in both urban and rural areas, as well as dependency on rural connections. Kampala's gardens can be considered highly diverse, with 75 edible plant species found, including 24 vegetable, 24 fruit, 14 condiment, eight root/tuber, four legume and one sugar/syrup species. At least a third of the identified species can be considered indigenous, species that are often underutilised yet can have important nutritional properties to enhance food and nutrition security. Furthermore, 25 % of the respondents reported collecting edible species from the urban environment, 23 % reported collecting in rural areas, and 33 % reported being sent farm produce from relatives in rural areas within the six months preceding the interview. These findings indicate that wild and farm plant resources play an important role in the lives of Kampala's residents, which means that in order to ensure fair access to alternative food sources policy makers and urban planners need to be aware of diverse land use types and incorporate them in future development plans.

Keywords: Food security, natural resource management, nutrition, Uganda, urban agriculture, wild food plants

Contact Address: Eefke Mollee, Bangor University, School for Environment, Natural Resources and Geography (SENRGy), Deiniol Road, LL57 2UW Bangor, United Kingdom, e-mail: e.mollee@bangor.ac.uk

ID 984

The Influences of Contract Farming on Small-Scale Household Performance in Developing Countries: A Modelling Approach

LE NGOC HUONG, LUDWIG THEUVSEN, VERENA OTTER

Georg-August-Universität Göttingen, Dept. of Agricultural Economics and Rural Development, Germany

Under the pressure of globally increasing demand for food, the expansion of agricultural production and consumption has received remarkable attention. In this regard, the need for higher productivity, increasing economies of scale, gains in efficiency and sustainability in agricultural production are considered to be very important. In order to deal with these needs, the market accesses for small-scale farmers in stable supply chains of agricultural products is considered to be a key factor. Therefore, contract farming is generally associated with opportunities for farmers in rural areas of developing and emerging countries to overcome market barriers and improve farming efficiency. This is also assumed to be true for Vietnam as a developing country with more than 70% of the population working in the agricultural production. In this country, rice is one of the most important agricultural products making it the second largest exporter worldwide mainly based on small-holder production. Thus, this study addresses the influence of contract farming on small-scale farmers' performance in the export rice sector in Vietnam. In order to obtain quantitative cross-sectional data 266 export rice farmers were surveyed in the Mekong River Delta of Vietnam, where 90 percent of the national export rice is produced, using a structured questionnaire. In order to analyze the data, first a binary probit model was applied to examine the probability to participate in rice contractual arrangement of farmers and Ordinary Least Squared (OLS) regression to estimate the influence of contract farming on household income. The OLS-model was estimated in combination with the propensity score matching (PSM) procedure for identifying the income differences between the treatment (contract-farmers) and the comparison group (non-contract-farmers) to deal with the problem of sample selection bias. The results of the probit model show that determinants such as income, rice farming experience, community relationship, world price information and extension service access were the main factors leading to the households' marketing decision and, thus, influence the probability of contract participation. The OLS regression and the descriptive statistics illustrate that the contract participants have higher income, approximately 15% more than non-contract participants. Moreover, it becomes evident that there is a positive relationship between farm income and the duration of contract participation. In detail, households marketing export rice through contracts for more than 3-years achieve a 20% higher income than households marketing through contracts for less than 3-years. Based on the empirical results, policy implications are derived regarding the development of supporting programs for farmers and agribusiness.

Keywords: Contract farming, developing countries, farmer performance, Mekong river delta, Vietnamese export rice sector

Contact Address: Le Ngoc Huong, Georg-August Universität Göttingen, Agricultural Economics and Rural Development, Göttinger Sieben 5, 37073 Göttingen, Germany, e-mail: huongln65@gmail.com

Women and Power in the Market: A Case Study of Market Queens in Ghana

Lilli Scheiterle, Juliet Kariuki, Regina Birner

University of Hohenheim, Inst. of Agricultural Sciences in the Tropics (Hans-Ruthenberg-Institute), Germany

Markets in Ghana are largely managed by women traders organised into groups according to commodity. These associations are headed by a leader called *ohemma* which can be translated into queen mothers or market queens (MQ). MQ therefore represent a relevant female-led institution. Although much emphasis has been placed on strengthening women-led agricultural institutions more broadly, little attention both in the literature and within local structures has been focused on MQ. The neglect of MQ is surprising despite their important and unique role in Ghana's agricultural value chain. The scant existing literature on MQ reflects a largely negative connotation associating MQ with characteristics akin to market-led cartels. Our study contributes to this limited body of knowledge by exploring the extent to which MQ access and utilise power within Ghana's agricultural markets. We applied a theoretical sampling technique through the use of in-depth interviews with MQ and traders of plantain, cassava and maize to empirically assess their source and use of power. Our findings show that MQ are nominated into power either by existing traditional leaders or market traders. Contrary to current literature, our results reveal that MQ do not leverage their power to set market prices, but instead to provide an important informal safety net for group members - especially rural women. These findings are important as they challenge the negative representation of MQ and highlight the need for systematic support of women-led organisations in rural areas of Ghana. We conclude therefore that failure to comprehensively account for the role of MQ will limit any efforts seeking to address the challenges faced by agriculturally-dependent women in Ghana.

Keywords: Ghana, institutions, market queens, power, women

Contact Address: Lilli Scheiterle, University of Hohenheim, Inst. of Agricultural Sciences in the Tropics (Hans-Ruthenberg-Institute), Wollgrasweg 43, 70599 Stuttgart, Germany, e-mail: lilli.scheiterle@uni-hohenheim.de

ID 1075

The Future of Smallholder Societies in the Okavango Basin - Socio-Economic Transitions in Three Case Studies

BENJAMIN KOWALSKI, STEPHANIE DOMPTAIL

Justus-Liebig University Giessen, Agricultural and Environmental Policy, Germany

The Okavango River Basin (ORB) is a sparsely populated nearly pristine water-based environment shared by three countries of southern Africa: Angola, Namibia and Botswana. Population growth and a general desire for a consumption-based lifestyle lead to changes in resource use and rural livelihoods, as farming is the main livelihood source and land use in the ORB. Empirical analyses of farming systems and socio-ecological societies were conducted for three case studies, one in each country. We aim to understand from a transition perspective what characterises the current systems, which factors may shape their transition pathways, and towards which state they may develop under the current conditions. Data was collected from 2011 to 2013 at the household level using household surveys and explorative farmer interviews and at the basin scale via stakeholder interviews following a stakeholder analysis. Methods of analysis comprise livelihood analysis, farming system analysis and in the case of Botswana and Angola Material-&-Energy-Flow-Accountings. Results show that stratification among rural households of the ORB increases with population density and cash availability. Furthermore, relative household wealth is a decisive determinant of farming strategies and for reaching food self-sufficiency. Poorer households are dependent upon agricultural production and have to invest their scarce resources primarily into farming. For them, increasing crop failures resulting from soil degradation lead to an increasing danger of falling into a poverty trap. In addition, the societies in all case studies are at a point of transition. In the next decades and resulting from population growth, increasing environmental degradation and cash market integration, both the Angolan and Namibian case studies may turn to more intensive forms of agriculture. A comparison of agricultural efficiency indicators reveals that Conservation Agriculture may be a solution for sustainable intensification for Namibian but, due to unfavourable input-output relations relative to the traditional systems, not for Angolan smallholders. In the Batswana research area, the advent of a tarred road may spur economic diversification and the abandonment of arable agriculture by many households. Our results suggest that without policy intervention, societies within the ORB may continue on a pathway of gradual resource degradation.

Keywords: Degradation, farming system analysis, smallholder farming, socio-ecological transitions, Southern Africa, sustainable intensification

Contact Address: Benjamin Kowalski, Justus-Liebig Universität Gießen, Chair of Agricultural and Environmental Policy, Senckenbergstr. 3, 35390 Giessen, Germany, e-mail: benjamin.kowalski@agrar.uni-giessen.de

Changing Livelihoods in Rural Cambodia: Evidence from Panel Household Data in Stung Treng

Rasadhika Sharma, Thanh Tung Nguyen, Ulrike Grote, Trung Thanh Nguyen

Leibniz Universität Hannover, Inst. for Environmental Economics and World Trade, Germany

Analysis of livelihood strategies can aid to understand and resolve problems associated with vulnerability to poverty and food security. This paper aims to identify and describe the changes in rural livelihood activities by using household data for 2013 and 2014 collected in Stung Treng, Cambodia. We use the same variables and estimate different clusters for both the years. The paper concludes that despite the lag of only one year, there are noticeable changes in livelihood strategies. Firstly, we find a group of transition farmers in 2014 that is composed of households that are witnessing a shift towards commercialisation. They invest and consume more than subsistence farmers. Secondly, there is a greater diversification in activities amongst the various groups. Most households practice multiple activities. Lastly, with regards to self-employment, there has been a shift from agriculture and the production sector to services and crafts. All of the above changes can be deemed as positive as there is a gradual movement away from more vulnerable sectors. Accordingly, households that participate in livelihood activities related to agriculture and natural resource extraction are most affected by shocks and face the highest vulnerability to poverty. The paper additionally highlights some concerns such as a decline in availability of extracted products such as the fish stock which are expected to negatively impact on these more vulnerable rural households in the medium and longer term. Furthermore, the state of education is dismal and needs attention. Therefore, policy makers need to consider these issues while addressing rural poverty.

Keywords: Cambodia, cluster analysis, diversification, livelihoods, rural poverty

Contact Address: Rasadhika Sharma, Leibniz Universität Hannover, Inst. for Environmental Economics and World Trade, Königsworther Platz 1, 30167 Hannover, Germany, e-mail: sharma@iuw.uni-hannover.de

ID 778

Rural Land Management: Challenges for Family Farming and its Contribution to Food Production in Argentina

MARIANA ARZENO, FRANCISCO FERNÁNDEZ ROMERO, EMANUEL ALBERTO JURADO, LUCILA MUÑECAS, AYMARA ZANOTTI

Universidad de Buenos Aires, Emerging Geographies Research Group: policies, conflict and socio-spatial alternatives, Argentina

In the past decade, public policies concerning family farming promotion have been developed in Argentina and the rest of Latin America with the goal of contributing to local food supply and, ultimately, food sovereignty. However, these policies are geared toward rural and peri-urban areas where, at the same time, other government actors encourage commodity production and tourism and real-estate business endeavours which reproduce unfavourable conditions for small agricultural development. In particular, the expansion of activities mobilised by large companies exerts pressure on land access, resource use, and alternative types of production and commercialisation with regards to family farming. In this context, territorial analysis is key to understand and account for conflicts and different actors' strategies in the pursuit of imposing their own projects.

Our ongoing research is based on a perspective which centres the political dimension of territorial production; that is, the different ways in which power is exercised over territory, which are manifested not only by hegemonic actors' practices of government but also by the resistance practices which question them. Our overall purpose is to identify and analyse the land management process configured by the practices of state and non-state actors in rural areas where family farming is prevalent, through observing the disputes around territorial control and management. Specifically, the main questions which guide our inquiry are: Through which mechanisms and instruments do state and non-state actors reproduce, modify or dispute the established territorial order? What socio-spatial inclusions or exclusions do they entail for the family farming sector?

Our analysis centres on case studies in different Argentinean provinces, which represent land management issues in which family agriculture and food production are threatened by the revaluation of agricultural spaces for the purpose of real-estate development, by the development of tourism and/or by the expansion of economic activities aimed at foreign markets.

Keywords: Argentina, family farming, food production, rural land management

Contact Address: Emanuel Alberto Jurado, Universidad de Buenos Aires, Emerging Geographies Research Group: policies, conflict and socio-spatial alternatives, Remedios Escalada de San Martín 867 1a, 1416 Caba, Argentina, e-mail: emanueljurado@hotmail.com

Forest Resources and Rural Livelihoods: Evidence from Chobe Enclave, Botswana

HESEKIA GAREKAE[1], OLEKAE THAKADU[1], JOYCE LEPETU[2]

[1]*University of Botswana, Okavango Research Institute, Botswana*

[2]*Botswana University of Agriculture and Natural Resources, Crop Science, Botswana*

For centuries, developing countries have being immensely dependent on environmental resources, forests included. Forests have been considered essential to livelihoods of communities living adjacent to them. Despite the contribution of forests to livelihoods, the level of community's reliance on forest resources, their uses, and value in household economies has not been adequately explored in Botswana. This paper assessed the extent of household's reliance on non-timber forest products and their contribution towards livelihoods of Chobe enclave communities. Primary data were collected through administration of survey instrument to 183 households, randomly selected from three communities adjacent to Chobe Forest Reserve. Complementary in-depth interviews with selected key informants were conducted. Descriptive and inferential statistics were used to analyse the data. The results show that on average, households were generally dependent on forest resources for their sustenance, as evidenced by the mean forest dependency index of .50 (SD = .41). The results also indicate that several forest products contributed substantially to rural livelihoods. Among them, firewood (85.8%, n = 157) was predominate while fodder (2.7%, n = 5) was the least. Consequently, forest products provided both subsistence and cash income towards household economies. The annual direct-use value per household per year was USD347.25 (SD = 284), ranging from USD28.75 to USD1 677.24. Based on the foregoing, forest resources are particularly important in rural livelihoods diversification. Since households are reliant on forest resources, conservation programmes which tend to jeopardise the inextricable links between the local people and their environment may culminate into a series of people-park conflicts. That being the case, protection and improvement of local livelihoods and ecological conditions should be the cornerstone for sustainable conservation programmes. Therefore, integrative policy approaches which facilitate both equitable resource use and conservation of forests are necessary.

Keywords: Botswana, Chobe Forest Reserve, non-timber forest products, rural livelihoods, safety net

Contact Address: Hesekia Garekae, University of Botswana, Okavango Research Institute, Private Bag 285, 0000 Maun, Botswana, e-mail: garekae@yahoo.com

ID 54

Micro-Level Impacts of Private Sector Investments in the Agriculture and Food Sector in Sub-Sahara Africa

CHRISTINE HUSMANN, ANNAPIA DEBARRY

University of Bonn, Center for Development Research (ZEF), Germany

Our study presents a review of empirical literature on the impacts of private sector investments along agricultural value chains in Africa on the local population. Processes of liberalisation and globalisation have led to profound market transformations including growing export orientation, the consolidation of processing and retailing along with related organisational and institutional changes. These changes were accompanied by a rising importance of foreign direct investments into the African food and agriculture sector. While the negative attitude towards the engagement of private companies has changed at least partly, private sector investments still face severe criticism regarding potential negative consequences for smallholder farmers, local communities, or environmental damages. Against this background, our study aims to illustrate what is really known about these impacts. Based on a conceptual framework covering the potential impacts of private sector investments, we review studies with primary data collected since 2000 using different search engines and the snowball method. Much of the empirical literature focuses on the production level (in particular contract farming), whereas other parts of the value chain are found to be neglected research areas. At the production level, the findings of our review show that benefits mainly arise via labour and product market channels. Positive impacts on the incomes of contract farmers, outgrowers and employees are found. Access to contracts is often biased to better-off households. However, the study also identifies severe research gaps on other levels of the value chain. For instance, the role of private sector investments in the seed and fertiliser sector, or in the food processing industry. Little is also known about the impacts of private sector investments on public goods and resources such as infrastructure, land, water and ecological impacts. Further research on institutional arrangements is required to be able to relate observed impacts to the institutional setting of the investment projects.

Keywords: Impacts, investments, private sector, sub-Sahara Africa

Contact Address: Christine Husmann, University of Bonn, Center for Development Research (ZEF), Walter-Flex-Str. 3, 53113 Bonn, Germany, e-mail: husmann@uni-bonn.de

Assessment of Household Food Security through Crop Diversification in Natmauk Township, Magway Region, Myanmar

CHO AME, TUN OO AUNG, STIJN SPEELMAN

Ghent University, Department of Agricultural Economics, Belgium

This study examines the crop diversification levels and determinants of crop diversification and assesses food security status of the farm' households in Natmauk Township, Magway region, Myanmar. The study was carried out in March 2015 and data were collected by using structured questionnaires. A total of 80 farm households were randomly selected from four villages in Natmauk Township. The study uses Simpson's index of diversification (SID) to measure the extent of crop diversification among the farmers in the study area while censored Tobit regression model was used to determine the factors affecting crop diversification. The study revealed that mean computed crop diversification index was 0.54. High crop diversification indexes were found among 32.5 % of the sampled farm households. About 5 % of households practised very low crop diversification while the same proportion diversified their crops very highly in their farms. The study further revealed that farming experience, education level of household heads, farm size, access to irrigation and access to credit positively and significantly affected crop diversification while age of household heads, non-farm/off-farm income and distance to market negatively and significantly affected crop diversification among the farmers. Majority of the households reported that market purchase is the main source of foods for them. Based on the Household Food Insecurity Access Scale (HFIAS) categories, 31 % of the households were food secure while 35 % mildly food insecure, 25 % moderately food insecure and 8 % were severely food insecure. According to correlation analysis, it was observed that HFIAS score is negatively correlated with Household Dietary Diversity Score (HDDS) and crop diversification. Correlation was significant at 0.01 level and the strength of the correlation is strong. The findings clearly indicate that better food security is associated with crop diversification in the study area. Therefore, the study recommended that the farmers should be encouraged to improve the right selection and cultivation of different crop types on their farms, which will eventually lead to increase in crop outputs and otherwise, improve food security.

Keywords: Crop diversification, food security, Simpson's index of diversification, Tobit regression

Contact Address: Cho Ame, Ghent University, Dept. of Agricultural Economics, Waarschootstraat 1, 9000 Ghent, Belgium, e-mail: amecho717@gmail.com

Challenges and Prospects of Farm and Non-Farm Livelihood Strategies of Smallholder Farmers in Yayu Biosphere Reserve, Ethiopia. A Qualitative Analysis

BENEBERU ASSEFA WONDIMAGEGNHU[1], SARAH NISCHALKE[2], MULUNESH ABEBE ALEBACHEW[1], TINA BEUCHELT[2]

[1] Food, Agriculture and Natural Resources Policy Analysis Network (FANRPAN), Ethiopia

[2] University of Bonn, Center for Development Research (ZEF), Germany

The study aimed at analysing the challenges and prospects of farm and non-farm livelihood strategies of smallholder farmers taking Yayu Biosphere reserve in Ethiopia as a case study site. 28 focus group discussions, 6 key informant interviews, and participant observation were employed to collect in depth gender disaggregated qualitative data from four sampled sites. Data was analysed by summarising narrations and further doing triangulations to explain and justify findings of the research in the course of analysis. The research found out that farming remains an important livelihood strategy among smallholder farmers despite facing a number of challenges. The findings indicated that farming is a demanding job with challenges such as low price for commodities, inaccessibility and unaffordability of agricultural inputs, fragmentation of farmland as a result of population pressure, wild animals' attacks and crop diseases. In addition, non-farm activities such as petty trade, daily labour, local brewery, low-skill formal employment, firewood and charcoal sale, food preparation and sale, handicraft, carpentry and rendering transportation services were found to be the main non-farm livelihood diversification strategies. However, the study found out that these activities are not common among land owners and have long been anticipated to be "low-skill" and "low-paying" jobs. Land owners involve in these activities as a coping mechanism during adverse conditions and to cover minor expenditures of their families particularly during off-seasons where there is no active agricultural activity. On the contrary, non-farm activities are found to be the main livelihood strategies for landless households along with sharecropping. The findings show that farmers lack other better livelihood alternatives, and they are losing hope in taking up farming as a main means of livelihood due to the challenges they are facing on farming. This has created a gloomy feature on the future prospects of farming and calls for the urgency of integrated development interventions. These include interventions that focus on improving the resource management capacity of smallholder farmers and reducing pressure on land by designing capacity building programs to enable them fit to better paying non-farm employment opportunities.

Keywords: Farm livelihoods, income diversification, non-farm livelihoods

Contact Address: Beneberu Assefa Wondimagegnhu, Food, Agriculture and Natural Resources Policy Analysis Network (FANRPAN), NutriHAF Project, P.O. Box 2289, Bahir Dar, Ethiopia, e-mail: benassefa2006@gmail.com

Irregular Migration and Agricultural Production among Smallholder Farmers in Kasulu District, Tanzania

JUSTIN KALISTI URASSA[1], SAMWEL ROBBY MAGWEIGA[2]

[1]*College of Social Sciences and Humanities, Sokoine University of Agriculture, Department of Policy, Planning and Management, Tanzania*

[2]*Ministry of Home Affiars, Imigration Department, Tanzania*

Despite the fact that irregular migrants (IRMs) have often been facing a lot of challenges in sustaining their livelihood in Kasulu District, yet in recent years, there has been an increase of IRMs from within and outside Kasulu District in search of casual labour in the local community. The study therefore was undertaken in four villages in Kasulu, Kitanga, Kagera-Nkanda, Mvugwe and Nyachenda to determine the contribution of IRMs into the growth and prosperity of smallholder farmers. Specifically, the study aimed to determine the driving factors of irregular migration, to assess smallholder farmer's attitude towards IRMs, to compare agricultural related benefits among smallholder farmers, and finally, to identify factors affecting both IRMs and smallholder farmer interaction. A cross-sectional research design was adopted for the study in which a simple random sampling, purposive and snowball sampling techniques were employed to select 120 respondents. Data were collected using a variety of methods namely questionnaire survey, key informant interviews, focus group discussions (FGDs), direct observation, reviewing of secondary sources and tape recording. In addition data were collected using various tools, these include, questionnaires, checklists, camera, tape recorders and secondary sources of data. Quantitative data were analysed using statistical package for social science (SPSS) by adopting, descriptive, gross margin analysis. While qualitative data were analysed using content, discourse and narrative analyses. The results showed that the profit margin for smallholder farmers employing IRMs was higher with 926 925 Tanzanian Shillings (Tsh) and 924 375 Tsh from maize and bean production respectively, as compared to smallholder farmers not using IRMs, whose margin was 289 200 Tsh and 223 170 Tsh, respectively. Social, cultural, economical and political factors have an influence in triggering irregular migration, which indirectly compel smallholder farmers to employ or not employ IRMs.

Keywords: Irregular migrants, Kasulu, smallholder agriculture

Contact Address: Justin Kalisti Urassa, College of Social Sciences and Humanities, Sokoine University of Agriculture, Department of Policy, Planning and Management, P. O. Box 3035 Chuo Kikuu, Morogoro, Tanzania, e-mail: urassa@suanet.ac.tz

ID 524

Impacts of Rice Contract Farming System on Smallholders in Myanmar

AYE MOE SAN, SIEGFRIED BAUER

Justus-Liebig University Giessen, Inst. of Farm and Agribusiness Management - Project and Regional Planning, Germany

Myanmar government has encouraged the rice sector development along the supply chain with the investment of private rice specialisation companies (RSCs) with the resource providing contract system at major rice production areas since 2008. The activities of RSCs are providing seasonal loans, credit in kind in terms of quality seed and fertilisers, extension services and farm mechanisation services, purchasing paddy at the prevailing market price, and providing milling and trading facilities. Cross-sectional data from 220 contract smallholders and 183 non-contract smallholders was collected in Pyay and Danuphyu townships where two RSCs are actively implementing contract farming scheme during 2014-2015 rice production season. Endogenous switching regression model was applied to simultaneously estimate the decision to participate contract scheme and its implication on annual farm and household incomes of smallholders. The age and education level of household head, production shocks during last five years, participation into farmer organisation, and frequently contact with extension services were influencing the decision of smallholders to participate contract scheme. Statistically significant value of region dummy also showed the contract participation decision would be significantly different between two study townships. The correlation coefficients for contract smallholders (ρCF) and noncontract smallholders (ρNCF) were both positive but only (ρCF) were statistically significant, indicated that there were self-selection among contract smallholders. The significance of the likelihood ratio tests for independence of equations also indicated that the participation in contract scheme had joint dependences with annual farm and household incomes for smallholders. The average treatment effects of contract participation on annual farm and household incomes for contract smallholders (ATT), 0.23 and 0.17 respectively and those for non-contract smallholders (ATU), 0.12 and 0.09, respectively indicated that contract farming would increase 23 % annual farm income and 17 % household income for contract smallholders and 12 % annual farm income and 9% household income more for non-contract smallholders if they join the contract scheme. The base heterogeneity effects showed that there were some important factors that skilled the actual contract smallholders even if they were without contract system had better conditions than the non-contract smallholders, and these factors could have also influenced on the contract participation decision. Transition heterogeneity effects also revealed that contract smallholders achieved significantly higher impacts of contract system on their annual farm and household incomes compared to non-contract smallholders. Overall findings indicated that contract farming had positive and significant impacts on livelihood of smallholders.

Keywords: Contract farming, endogenous switching regression model, farm income, household income, Myanmar, smallholders

Contact Address: Aye Moe San, Justus-Liebig University Giessen, Inst. of Farm and Agribusiness Management - Project and Regional Planning, Senckenbergstr 3, 35390 Giessen, Germany, e-mail: ayemoesan.2010@gmail.com

What Works Where for Whom – Identifying Farm Household Strategies for Food Security Across Uganda

JANNIKE WICHERN[1], MARK VAN WIJK[2], KATRIEN DESCHEEMAEKER[1], JOOST VAN HEERWAARDEN[1], ROMAIN FRELAT[3,2], KEN GILLER[1]

[1]*Wageningen University (WUR), Plant Production Systems, The Netherlands*
[2]*International Livestock Research Institute (ILRI), Livestock Systems and the Environment, Kenya*
[3]*International Maize and Wheat Improvement Center (CIMMYT), Sustainable Intensification and Socioeconomics programs, Mexico*

East Africa's smallholder agriculture is expected to be strongly affected by climate change, which, together with a growing population and pressure on natural resources, will result in an increasing challenge to achieve food security for households and regions. Policy makers need information on what works where for which farmers in order to guide their decision making and prioritise investment for agricultural interventions to increase food security. For this, we must better understand how smallholder farm strategies for achieving food security differ across regions and farm types and what drives these strategies.

In this study we present new analyses at country and farm household level that quantify drivers of productivity and food security, and that can be used to prioritise agricultural interventions. Uganda was chosen as a case study because of data availability but the approach can be applied to other countries in sub-Saharan Africa.

First, we quantified how food security and farm types varied across Uganda, and which key factors drive this variability. We used household level data from the Living Standard Measurement Study – Integrated Survey on Agriculture (LSMS-ISA) of the World Bank and developed an approach to map and quantitatively explain food security and agricultural land use across Uganda. The resulting maps showed where which crops and livestock activities are important for which types of farm households. Subsequently, the effects of agricultural interventions on food security of different farm types were assessed.

Second, we used this information to select contrasting sites and farm households for detailed interviews, which aimed at identifying drivers of farmers' decision making, assessing farmers' vulnerability to climate change and how proposed interventions match with the farmers' socio-ecological niche.

The spatial approach we developed is a novel way to use farm household level information to generate country-wide patterns in farming systems and their productivity. It generates useful information for a quantitative assessment of what might happen to the food security of smallholder farmers in Uganda under climate change and for a country-wide targeting of agricultural interventions that aim at mitigating the effects of climate change.

Keywords: Climate change, East Africa, farm strategies, food security, spatial, Uganda

Contact Address: Jannike Wichern, Wageningen University (WUR), Plant Production Systems, Droevendaalsesteeg 1, 6708 PB Wageningen, The Netherlands, e-mail: jannike.wichern@wur.nl

ID 601

Perception of Genetic Modification Technology among People in South-Western Nigeria

BUNMI OLASANMI, GRACE OLASANMI

University of Ibadan, Dept. of Agronomy, Nigeria

Genetic modification (GM) technology has great potential to solve some of the food security and nutrient deficiency (hidden hunger) problems globally. The controversy surrounding adoption of the technology in some countries due to lack of awareness and misconception among the consumers may hinder the adoption of the technology leading to great loss. This problem may be more in Africa and Asia considering the level of education of the populace. The perception of farmers and consumers in southwestern part of Nigeria on GM technology was investigated using structured questionnaires. A total of 121 respondents in Osun and Oyo states were interviewed using the questionnaires. The study also examined the position of the respondents on signing of biosafety bill in the country, potential benefits and possible challenges of the technology. The result showed that about 55 % of the respondents were aware of the availability and potentials of GM crops while about 54 % were aware that GM crops are already being cultivated in some African countries. About 43 % of the respondents have not heard about the technology before. The study also revealed that 70 % or more of the respondents would support approval of the bill for biosafety in the country, consume, cultivate/allow cultivation of GM crops and recommend products from GM crops to others. Most of the respondents admitted that adoption of GM technology will result in increased income, improved food quality, availability of more food and job opportunities. Some of the challenges envisaged by the respondents are high production cost, long-term health implications, need for technical know-how, poor awareness, illiteracy and unstable government policies. Therefore, there is need to educate the populace on the cost implication, profitability, environmental-friendliness, safety and simplicity of application of the technology. There is also need to put in place good, stable and practicable policies that will ensure beneficial utilisation of GM technology in the region.

Keywords: Food security, genetic modification, GM technology, hidden hunger, perception

Contact Address: Bunmi Olasanmi, University of Ibadan, Dept. of Agronomy, No. 23 Adegboyega Shiyanbola Street, Orogun, 200284 Ibadan, Nigeria, e-mail: bunminadeco@yahoo.com

Expanding to Wetlands in Beninese Family Farms: A Trade-Off Between Collective and Individual Development Opportunities

LISE PARESYS[1,2], ERIC MALÉZIEUX[2], JOËL HUAT[3,2], MARTIN KROPFF[4], WALTER ROSSING[1]

[1] *Wageningen University (WUR), Farming Systems Ecology, The Netherlands*

[2] *French Agricultural Research Centre for International Development (CIRAD), UPR HORTSYS, F-34398 Montpellier, France*

[3] *Africa Rice, Sustainable Productivity Enhancement Program, Benin*

[4] *International Maize and Wheat Improvement Center (CIMMYT), Mexico*

Agricultural production in sub-Saharan Africa is mostly upland-based. Indeed, wetland potential for rice and market gardening production is currently underexploited. Opportunities for greater provision of year-round food are expected from utilising these land and water resources. Wetland crops are, however, labour-demanding crops. Besides, in some smallholder households, labour is already distributed between family fields intended for collective profit and individually managed fields intended for individual financial benefit to the women or men. Changes in crops and cropping calendars may thus interfere with intra-household labour distribution. Our objective was to investigate differences in the uptake of wetland crops among smallholder households in relation to intra-household labour distribution.

Smallholder households were described in a functional farm typology for two villages where rice fields and market gardens co-occurred in wetlands; Zonmon in the southern part of Benin and Pelebina in the north-western part. Larger areas under wetland crops were found for farm types with more available labour. However, among the farm types with greater labour availability, the extent of wetland crops depended on the labour distribution between upland fields and wetland fields as well as between family fields and individual fields.

Granting individual fields may be a strategy to secure a fair remuneration for work and freedom of initiative. The extent of the expansion to wetlands may be the result of a trade-off between collective interest and individual interest. Just as increasing the area farmed in family fields in wetlands may conflict with fairness associated with individual development opportunities, increasing the area farmed in individual fields in wetlands may conflict with fairness associated with collective development opportunities. Unlocking the potential of wetlands therefore requires insight in practices at the level of the farm and the level of the workers within the farm.

Keywords: Farm typology, intra-household labour distribution, wetland crops

---

Contact Address: Lise Paresys, Wageningen University (WUR), Farming Systems Ecology, Droeven-daalsesteeg 1, Wageningen, The Netherlands, e-mail: lise.paresys@wur.nl

ID 629

Family Farming in Urban and Peri-Urban Tamale, Northern Ghana

EILEEN BOGWEH NCHANJI[1], IMOGEN BELLWOOD-HOWARD[1], NIKOLAUS SCHAREIKA[1], TAKEMORE CHAGOMOKA[2]

[1]Georg-August-Universität Göttingen, Social and Cultural Anthropology, Germany
[2]AVRDC - The World Vegetable Center, Mali

Farm succession and inheritance interacts with land policy in ways that resonate across continents, cultures and post-colonial policy environments. Land scarcity has not historically constrained African family farming. However, recently, lucrative land markets have changed this, especially in urban and peri-urban agriculture. Rapid urbanisation implies land-use competition for industrial, residential and agricultural purposes. This paper draws on empirical ethnographic data collected from Tamale, northern Ghana to explain the challenges of family farming and its future.

Overlaps and contradictions between customary and state land governance has shaped and is still reshaping farm succession, inheritance and retirement in different Ghanaian land scenarios. We consider three situations - farming on community land, government irrigation sites and interspaces. The latter refers to undeveloped patches within the urban landscape. Farmers have usufruct rights over plots they use on community land, traditionally passing these to their heirs. This pattern is the norm in northern Ghana, where farming, the default livelihood activity, is intertwined with cultural identity, and persists in low-income urban contexts. However, farmers farming on community land cannot indefinitely stay in the family. The traditional customary custodians ultimately decide who should use these lands and for how long. In government irrigation sites, farmers are expected to hand over land to irrigation officers after retirement for reallocation to other interested farmers. In practice, they assume the same system as on traditional lands, passing usufruct rights to junior relatives. In interspace farming, the legal owner of the land is often a private individual who has purchased it in a market or undeveloped government land. Usufruct of these spaces depends on a good relationship with the owner, but construction and urbanisation makes access to them less secure.

Land policy is changing. Planners are attempting to form new solutions that legitimise urban farming, limiting yet respecting the role of traditional chiefs and to some extent restraining the booming land market. These different scenarios show how confluences of land governance regimes and differential implementation of land policy by various actors' influences farm succession, inheritance and retirement in Tamale. We recommend that government provides affordable public land to poor urban dwellers.

Keywords: Family farming, land governance, policy, urban agriculture

Contact Address: Eileen Bogweh Nchanji, Georg-August-Universität Göttingen, Institute for Social and Cultural Anthropology, Theaterplatz 15, 37073 Göttingen, Germany, e-mail: eileen-bogweh.nchanji@sowi.uni-goettingen.de

ID 689

Impact of Livestock Production on Rural Poverty and Income Inequality: Evidence from Vietnam

TRUONG LAM DO, TRUNG THANH NGUYEN, ULRIKE GROTE

Leibniz Universität Hannover, Inst. for Environmental Economics and World Trade, Germany

Livestock production has been an important source of income and a means of livelihoods of rural households in developing countries. The study assesses the roles of livestock production in reducing rural poverty and income inequality in Vietnam. The data used in this paper are obtained from surveys conducted in three provinces of Vietnam, Ha Tinh, Thua Thien Hue, and Dak Lak in four years, 2007, 2008, 2010 and 2013 under the Project "Impact of shocks on the vulnerability to poverty: consequences for development emerging Southeast Asian economies". 2200 households in 220 villages of these provinces were randomly selected and interviewed. The study uses the difference-in-differences method and the propensity score matching to estimate the Average Treatment Effect on the Treated that measures the impact of livestock production on poverty and income inequality reduction, and a dynamic econometric model to examine the response of livestock assets to shocks. The findings show that livestock production reduces the income poverty by about 13 to 20 % and income inequality by 3 %. Livestock assets are negatively impacted by the number of shocks that households have faced during the last three years, though the impacts are different for different types of livestock. Large animals are mostly affected by demography shocks while climatic shocks mostly impact small animals. Other factors affecting livestock assets include access to credits, farmland size, labour, number of owned motorbikes, education of household head, and membership of a social or political group. The study suggests that promoting rural credits and education as well as capacitating rural households to cope with shocks could contribute to improve the welfare of rural households.

Keywords: Inequality income, livestock, poverty, shocks, Vietnam

Contact Address: Truong Lam Do, Leibniz Universität Hannover, Inst. for Environmental Economics and World Trade, Königsworther Platz 1, 30167 Hannover, Germany, e-mail: lam@iuw.uni-hannover.de

ID 715

Irrigated Family Farming as a Livelihood Potential for Rural Populations in Semi-Arid Northeast Brazil

HEINRICH HAGEL[1], REINER DOLUSCHITZ[2]

[1] *University of Hohenheim, Food Security Center, Germany*
[2] *University of Hohenheim, Dept. of Computer Applications and Business Management in Agriculture, Germany*

In the recent decades, Brazil's government intensified the promotion of irrigated agriculture in the country's semi-arid northeast to combat the negative impacts of severe droughts to the rural population. Since the 1980s, constructions of dams for hydropower generation facilitated constant availability of irrigation water leading to the establishment of several public irrigation schemes along the lower-middle São Francisco River. Despite economic growth in the region, as in the surroundings of the three public irrigation schemes around the Itaparica Reservoir, many smallholders cannot generate sufficient farm income to provide an adequate livelihood to sustain a family. Based on a dataset of 60 expert interviews and 192 farm household interviews, the income distribution between the three public irrigation schemes was analysed. A linear programming (LP) farm optimisation model was developed to identify potential farm incomes, and the optimal allocation of land, water, and labour. The model included two different producer price scenarios and considered local smallholders' farming objectives. Results show a high variability of farm income between the irrigation schemes. Farm income depended rather on appropriate crop choice and availability of irrigable land, than on socio-economic status of the farm household head. Annual high risk and labour-intensive crops were highly competitive towards perennial low risk banana and coconut crops. In general, given a favourable land allocation, a farm size of four hectares could provide an adequate livelihood. Technical assistance, combined with investments in infrastructure to improve the smallholders' access to markets and information, is highly recommended to increase the income opportunities for poorer and often less educated smallholders. Especially improved market access seems crucial to guarantee an adequate farm income on the long-term, considering the extremely low producer prices in the region compared to the national or even northeastern average. Volumetric water pricing may serve as a suitable tool to reduce the excessive consumption in the irrigation schemes. However, smallholders should be compensated for their income losses. Compensations may consist of a monetary part and a non-monetary part such as agricultural consultancy, education, and the improvement of the local infrastructure to increase smallholders' market access.

Keywords: Farm income, irrigated agriculture, linear programming, northeast Brazil

Contact Address: Heinrich Hagel, University of Hohenheim, Food Security Center, 70599 Stuttgart, Germany, e-mail: hagel@uni-hohenheim.de

Income Risk and Coping Strategies of Small-Scale Vegetable Farmers in the Central Rift Valley, Ethiopia

Gerlinde Behrendt, Nora Boehm, Kurt-Johannes Peters

Humboldt-Universität zu Berlin, Albrecht Daniel Thaer-Institute of Agricultural and Horticultural Sciences (ADTI), Germany

Due to its relatively high income generating potential horticultural production offers opportunities for poverty alleviation in the developing world and can be an attractive business, particularly for small-scale farmers. Yet, compared to the production of staple crops it increases income risk due to the perishable nature of horticultural crops, considerable price volatility and higher production costs. An enabling environment which ensures reliable market conditions as well as the individual ability of farmers to cope with the increased income risk are crucial for small-scale farmers' realisation of the income generating potential of horticultural production. A field study based on literature research and semi-structured interviews was conducted in September 2015 with small-scale vegetable farmers and other stakeholders of the Vegetable Value Chain in the Ethiopian Central Rift Valley to analyse the impact of vegetable price volatility on small-scale farmers' income situation and potential coping strategies. The Ethiopian enabling environment of vegetable production fails to contribute to a dependable market situation. Traders and brokers, though providing a vital service linking producers and consumers, benefit from farmers' lack of access to reliable market information. Small-scale farmers perceive their income situation as fluctuating and unstable. They are aware of the need to develop coping strategies in order to decrease the risks associated with vegetable production. Therefore, the interviewed farmers engage in income diversifying activities, such as non-agricultural income generating activities, rely on subsistence farming and make use of financial services, i.e. credits and savings. However, present conditions do not allow all vegetable farmers to create a complex set of income-securing activities, leaving them vulnerable to price volatility and other effects of the existing information and knowledge asymmetry. Farmers generally attribute the risks of vegetable production to market failure and less to their individual shortcomings regarding production planning. Our research suggests that, given the weak enabling environment and underdeveloped market linkages, in the short term small-scale vegetable farmers should not rely on government institutions to solve their problems. Rather they are well advised to assume responsibility for their fates, e.g. by self-organising in local networks to reduce their individual income risk.

Keywords: Central Rift Valley, Ethiopia, income diversification, income risk, price volatility, small-scale farmers, vegetable production

---

Contact Address: Gerlinde Behrendt, Humboldt-Universität zu Berlin, Albrecht Daniel Thaer-Institute of Agricultural and Horticultural Sciences (ADTI), Berlin, Germany, e-mail: behrendtgerlinde@web.de

 ID 862

Evaluating Irrigation Investments in Malawi: Economy-Wide Impacts under Uncertainty

FRANZISKA SCHUENEMANN[1], JAMES THURLOW[2], STEFAN MEYER[3], RICHARD ROBERTSON[2], JOAO RODRIGUES[2], MANFRED ZELLER[1]

[1] *University of Hohenheim, Inst. of Agricultural Sciences in the Tropics (Hans-Ruthenberg-Institute), Germany*

[2] *International Food Policy Research Institute (IFPRI), United States of America*

[3] *IFPRI, Environment and Production Technology Division, Malawi*

Africa is rapidly becoming the developing region where food insecurity and extreme poverty are concentrated, making irrigation crucial to increase crop yields and mitigate effects from climate change. However, there is still very little irrigation use despite a large potential in terms of water resources. One reason for this is that returns are often too low to cover the costs of infrastructure investment, because the various impact channels are not considered. Benefits from irrigation arise directly at the household level and indirectly from multiplier effects on the rest of the economy. Higher agricultural productivity and higher cropping intensity directly increase incomes and economy-wide output. Through minimising risks from weather variability, irrigation reduces vulnerability to climate change. In addition, agronomic linkages through the interaction between water and nutrients determine the profitability of irrigation. While irrigation studies have examined one or more impact channels, an assessment and decomposition of the combined benefits is still missing.

Our paper closes this research gap on the potential value of irrigation beyond measuring direct effects using an integrated modelling framework on the example of Malawi, whose government launched a major irrigation investment plan to increase land under irrigation substantially. To assess the economy-wide effects of irrigation expansion we develop a computable general equilibrium (CGE) model of Malawi extended with irrigated agricultural sectors. The CGE model is linked to a process-based crop model that simulates yield effects due to irrigation considering historical climate data and agro-ecological conditions. We model the effect of higher cropping intensity by introducing a second season and estimate the additional benefit accruing from agronomic linkages as well as the impact of irrigation on risk reduction. We find that if the joint benefits of the varying impact channels are considered the returns to irrigation exceed the costs. Moreover, our results emphasise that irrigation can make a decisive contribution to food security and poverty reduction for the whole economy and simultaneously mitigate effects from climate change calling for intensive investments in irrigation in Africa.

Keywords: Africa, climate change, food security, irrigation, poverty

Contact Address: Franziska Schuenemann, University of Hohenheim, Inst. of Agricultural Sciences in the Tropics (Hans-Ruthenberg-Institute), Wollgrasweg 43, 70599 Stuttgart, Germany, e-mail: franziska.schuenemann@uni-hohenheim.de

TransRe: Building Resilience to Climate Change through Migration and Translocality

Harald Sterly[1], Patrick Sakdapolrak[2]

[1] *University of Bonn, Dept. of Geography, Germany*
[2] *University of Vienna, Geography and Regional Research, Austria*

The paper presents an overview of the TransRe project and it's findings of the first project phase. The project explores the contribution of migration and translocal linkages to improved household and community resilience in rural Thailand. It takes the perspective that migration already is and will continue to be a major phenomenon as well as a driver of global change, and that through migration a multitude of translocal practices and networks are induced. Migration can thus lead to profound changes in a place's demography – and the often mentioned brain and labour drain – but is also connecting people, facilitating flows of knowledge and resources, and creating networked and interconnected translocal spaces. This intensifying translocal connectedness, the paper argues, has the potential to increase the ability of households and communities to respond to risks and to enhance their livelihoods and well-being – that is, their social resilience. The project focuses especially on climate and climate change related risks that smallholder farmers face in rural Thailand.

The research design follows place-based as well as multi-sited fieldwork approaches and seeks to generate empirical evidence based on case studies carried out in Thailand and in the places of destination of migrants, urban places in Thailand as well as international destinations such as Singapore or Germany.

The paper addresses findings in four interconnected fields: first of translocal networks of support and innovation, second of the related practices of migrants and the connected non-migrants in the places of origin and destination, third the changes in household and community resilience in the three dimensions of coping, adaptation and transformation, and fourth the governance of the nexus of climate change adaptation and migration.

Keywords: Climate change, resilience, smallholder farmers, Thailand, translocality

---

Contact Address: Harald Sterly, University of Bonn, Dept. of Geography, Meckenheimer Allee 166, 53115 Bonn, Germany, e-mail: sterly@giub.uni-bonn.de

ID 1104

Agricultural Commercialisation and Species Diversity of Urban Livestock in Bamako

JENNIFER PROVOST[1,2], EVA SCHLECHT[2], STEPHAN VON CRAMON-TAUBADEL[3], HAMIDOU NANTOUMÉ[4], REGINA RÖSSLER[2]

[1] Georg-August-Universität Göttingen, Sustainable International Agriculture, Germany

[2] University of Kassel / Georg-August-Universität Göttingen, Animal Husbandry in the Tropics and Subtropics, Germany

[3] Georg-August-Universität Göttingen, Dept. of Agricultural Economics and Rural Development, Germany

[4] Institut d'Economie Rurale (IER), Laboratory of Animal Nutrition (Sotuba), Mali

This paper studies agricultural commercialization and production patterns of urban and peri-urban livestock-owning households in Bamako, capital of Mali. Since almost forty percent of the country is already urbanized and livestock in Bamako alone represents 28 % of the domestic national stock, it is of great interest to study urban and peri-urban agriculture (UPA) as a food insecurity and poverty alleviator. Research was conducted from 11/2015 to 01/2016 in the framework of the BMBF-funded project UrbanFoodPlus and with support of the "Institut d'Economie Rurale du Mali". A total of 198 semi-structured questionnaires were completed in livestock-keeping UPA households. Their location matched population densities and was randomly fixed ex-ante, with 30 points in urban and 30 points in peri-urban areas.

Farmers have on average 12 years of experience in livestock management. Poultry and sheep, present in 74 % and 72 % of households, respectively, are by far the most popular species. In contrast, cattle and goats are owned by only a quarter of interviewed households. Most households manage two species (29 %), but this is barely above the 27 % of farms that keep only one species, which is sheep for more than half the cases.

In terms of market orientation, most households do not sell any livestock, and if they do, they sell small numbers. For instance, 48 % of households sold a ruminant in the last year. More importantly, 83 % of those ruminants' sellers sold less than 10 heads, resulting in a median of 3 ruminants sold per year. For poultry, 39 % of households sold chicken (either exotic or local breed), but 81 % thereof sold less than 100 birds per year (median 10). Commercialisation of animal produces is also limited. Out of the farmers who keep track of their hens, only 14 % sell the eggs. Additionally, zero goat owners marketed milk, even though one liter can be sold for 1000 Francs CFA (€ 1.52) in comparison to 400 FCFA (€ 0.60) for cow milk. Thus, there is a considerable potential for cash earning through UPA livestock activities in Bamako, which is yet not very much exploited.

Keywords: Commercialisation, food security, species diversity, urban livestock, West Africa

Contact Address: Jennifer Provost, Georg-August-Universität Göttingen, Sustainable International Agriculture, Hannoversche Str. 102, 37077 Göttingen, Germany, e-mail: jennifer.provost25@gmail.com

Governance, policy, strategy and macro-economics

Yield Gap Analyses to Inform Policy on Crop Intensification Pathways in Uganda

WILBERFORCE WALUKANO[1], PIET VAN ASTEN[1], D. NANFUMBA[2], A. ARINAITWE[2], D. BASALIRWA[1], R. ASIIMWE[1], PAMELA PALI[1]

[1]International Institute of Tropical Agriculture (IITA), Research for Development, Uganda
[2]Kachwekano Zonal Research and Development Institute, Uganda

Crop yields of smallholder farming systems in Uganda are low, but highly variable between farmers and sites. Development and policy actors wish to intensify crop production systems to, (i) reduce poverty and (ii) keep up food supply with population growth. Policy Action for Sustainable Intensification of Cropping systems in Uganda (PASIC) tries to understand constraints for crop intensification at plant, plot, household, community, and institutional level. Agronomic yield gap studies were conducted on potato in southwestern highlands and rice cropping systems in the eastern plains to stimulate policy action in crop intensification. Agronomic study was undertaken in 2014–2015 in a total of 333 households surveyed for: production and crop management, access to services and technologies. Data on soil properties, crop yields and plant nutrition were also collected at: vegetative, flowering and maturity stages. Households were selected using stratified cluster sampling based on exposure and use of improved technologies. Yield data obtained was compared to on-station yields under best management practices and modelled potential yield to establish the yield gap. Preliminary results show large yield gaps (60–80 %) exist between average farmer and best on-station yield using SPSS version 20. The results suggest that seed is the major limiting constraint in potato cropping systems. Households using good quality seed potato obtained an average 14 t ha^{-1} versus 6.2 t ha^{-1} for those using poor quality seed. On-station yields reach 25 t ha^{-1}. Poor disease and pest management practices are negatively related to yield. In the rice cropping systems however, pest management is the leading cause of yield gap. Households managing pest obtained an average 4.2 t ha^{-1} versus 2.9 t ha^{-1} for those not managing pests. On-station yields reach 6.5 t ha^{-1}, and it causes a gap of 3.6 t ha^{-1}. From the preliminary results, it can be concluded that Uganda has the potential to more than double the yield if an enabling environment of increasing access to quality seed for potato is created and if rice farmers improve adoption of improved pest and soil management practices and illustrate that investments for intensification have to be location and crop specific.

Keywords: Uganda, yield gap

Contact Address: Wilberforce Walukano, International Institute of Tropical Agriculture (IITA), Research for Development, plot 15 Naguru East Road, Upper Naguru., Kampala, Uganda, e-mail: W.Walukano@cgiar.org

ID 1149

The Impact of Changing Livelihoods on Micro Water Basins in Esmeraldas, Ecuador

MARIE HERMAN

Protos, Ecuador

This study discusses the challenges faced by the canton of Rioverde in Esmeraldas, Ecuador in terms of integrated water management. Furthermore, it develops a methodology for the setting up of water management plans. Review of secondary information, interviews with authorities and local organisations as well as a set of focus group discussions with inhabitants revealed the environmental degradation taking place in the area. Chemical analysis of water samples showed a deterioration of water quality in the different micro basins. Factors impacting the micro basins' water quality were found to be mainly of local anthropogenic origin: bathing of cattle in the river, cleaning of laundry, discharge of excrements and sewage water in water sources, agrochemicals used for agriculture and for capturing shrimps, disposal of garbage and cleaning of spray devices and chainsaws directly in the river as well as soil erosion, contamination and alterations in the hydrological cycle linked to land use changes (e.g. deforestation). Results evidence that this environmental deterioration is related to rapidly changing lifestyles and immigration in the zone combined with a lack of mitigation and control measures by local authorities as well as a limited access to basic services. The change of livelihoods from mainly subsistence oriented activities in the 80s to cash generating activities was promoted by the credit scheme of the Ecuadorian Government 'Fondo de Fomento Popular' which encouraged inhabitants to raise cattle for commercialisation, eased by the introduction of technology and driven by market demand. The study highlights the influence of policies and changing paradigms on environmental conservation and the challenges to counter environmental degradation in the area.

Keywords: Environmental conservation, Esmeraldas, integrated water management, livelihood changes, water basin

Contact Address: Marie Herman, Protos, Luis Tello E Hilda Padilla 902, 080107 Esmeraldas, Ecuador, e-mail: marie.ingrid.herman@gmail.com

Policies for a Sustainable Biomass Energy Sector in Malawi: Enhancing Energy and Food Security Simultaneously

Franziska Schuenemann[1], Siwa Msangi[2], Manfred Zeller[1]

[1] *University of Hohenheim, Inst. of Agricultural Sciences in the Tropics (Hans-Ruthenberg-Institute), Germany*

[2] *International Food Policy Research Institute (IFPRI), United States of America*

Biomass energy in the form of firewood and charcoal still dominates the energy sector in sub-Saharan Africa, in particular as the main cooking energy source in rural and urban areas. These strong linkages between energy, food security and the environment place biomass at the heart of sustainable development, especially since biomass is inherently renewable. However, population and GDP growth are exacerbating already existing supply-demand imbalances in highly populated countries such as Malawi, making it imperative to identify policy interventions that promote sustainable biomass energy while simultaneously considering the linkages with other sectors.

Our study thus analyses how the biomass energy sector in Malawi will evolve in the coming years and which policy measures could ensure sustainability. We use new data on demand and supply for biomass energy in Malawi and develop a model that estimates fuelwood demand based on actual diets and cooking habits and project future demand considering GDP and population growth. The model is expanded to simulate how demand side interventions in the form of improved cookstoves affect biomass demand. Moreover, we develop a behavioural model for agroforestry adoption considering constraints of rural households to analyse the potential of agroforestry for promoting a sustainable biomass energy sector in Malawi.

Without any change in cooking habits, household demand for biomass energy almost doubles within 20 years. Even with the most optimistic assumptions of sustainable biomass yields, demand in 2030 is one third above sustainable supply. Our findings show that policy measures aimed at increasing cooking efficiency reduce demand for cooking energy initially, but are not enough to establish a sustainable biomass energy sector due to high population growth. Supply side interventions like agroforestry on the other hand will not only increase sustainable supply substantially, but can also enhance food security and protect the environment. Since trees take time to grow, it is imperative to start investing in reforestation and agroforestry now to save Malawi from more forest degradation. In regions with large supply-demand imbalances and high population growth, however, a faster development of modern energy is highly desirable.

Keywords: Agroforestry, biomass energy, food security, Malawi, sustainability

Contact Address: Franziska Schuenemann, University of Hohenheim, Inst. of Agricultural Sciences in the Tropics (Hans-Ruthenberg-Institute), Wollgrasweg 43, 70599 Stuttgart, Germany, e-mail: franziska.schuenemann@uni-hohenheim.de

ID 571

Are Large-Scale Land Investments Only for Food Production? An Investigation of the Determining Factors and Sectoral Allocation of the Investments

OLAYINKA KAREEM

University of Marburg, Marburg, Chair of Development and Cooperative Economics, Faculty of Business Administration and Economics, Germany

The economic potentials of countries in part depend on their natural resources endowment and productive utilisation. Land remains invaluable natural resource that is precious to man, but it is non-renewable. The non-renewability of land and the scarcity of fertile, arable and productive land led to its increasing demand. A lot of people in developing countries, particularly in Africa, depend on land for their economic activities and/or livelihood. This is due to the fact that, it is from it that food is provided, shelters are constructed, infrastructures are laid and other valuable minerals are found. Recent economic events, particularly the commodity crisis of 2007–2008, have shown that there had been increasing demand for land in the global south, especially in Africa, which affected the availability of fertile and arable land. It is on this basis that this study investigates whether the motivation for the global land rush in Africa is mainly for food production purposes or otherwise. This study adopts a selection bias model with firms' heterogeneity using a negative binomial estimator to find that the acquisition of large-land is not solely for agricultural food production but also for forestry, conservation, renewable energy and tourism. The findings also indicate that the propensity to acquire land is determined by the availability of arable land, economic size of the investors' countries, institution capacity, governance and security and safety in the destination countries. However, at the intensive margin, economic size does not stimulate land investment, so also trade, population density, institutions and security of life and property. The availability of arable land, good governance and adequate precipitation are the land investment-enhancing factors.

Keywords: Africa, firm heterogeneity model, food production, land resource, negative binomial

Contact Address: Olayinka Kareem, University of Marburg, Marburg, Chair of Development and Cooperative Economics, Faculty of Business Administration and Economics, Am Plan 2 D-35032 Marburg Germany, 35032 Marburg, Germany, e-mail: olayinkaidowuus@yahoo.com

Policy Options for Improving Drought Resilience and Implications for Food Security: The Case of Ethiopia and Kenya

Daniel Tsegai[1], Michael Bruentrup[2], Mesay Kebede Duguma[1]

[1]United Nations Convention to Combat Desertification (UNCCD), External Relations, Policy and Advocacy (ERPA) Unit, Germany

[2]DIE-German Development Institute, Competitiveness and Social Development, Germany

Drought in the arid and semi-arid land of the Horn of Africa (HoA) is one of the most serious and permanent threats to food security. Despite the efforts by the governments and the international community, serious famines have been registered in the past decades. Assessing the impacts of droughts, and investigating the risk profile of vulnerable communities as well as identifying the challenges at all levels is a fundamental task before remedial measures are proposed for enhanced drought resilience. This will require the involvement of various actors from different strands of governments, civil society, international organisations and - more importantly- the affected people themselves.

This joint study conducted by the UNCCD Secretariat and the German Development Institute aims to synthesize lessons learnt from past drought events, policy adjustments and presents proposals for improved policy options for drought resilience and food security in the dry lands. Research questions include:

1. What are the remedial measures/policy options to enhance drought resilience and thus food security at sub-national and national levels Ethiopia and Kenya? What are the challenges and opportunities?

2. What were the impacts of the 2011 drought in Ethiopia and Kenya? What are the reasons behind the scale of drought impact observed? How did the National Systems at various levels perform? What has changed since then?

3. What are the roles of other factors including 'state fragility', 'land degradation' and 'political setup' in mitigating or exacerbating drought impacts?

We are conducting interviews with policy makers, NGOs, donors and intergovernmental organisations both in Ethiopia and Kenya. The study is expected to be finalized in June 2016.

Keywords: Drought, Ethiopia, food security, Kenya, policy

Contact Address: Daniel Tsegai, United Nations Convention to Combat Desertification (UNCCD), External Relations, Policy and Advocacy (ERPA) Unit, Bonn, Germany, e-mail: dtsegai@unccd.int

ID 334

Governance Challenges in an Emerging Bio-Economy: A Case Study of Maize Value-Webs in Nigeria

AYOBAMI ADETOYINBO[1], SAURABH GUPTA[1], VICTOR OKORUWA[2], REGINA BIRNER[1]

[1]*University of Hohenheim, Inst. of Agricultural Sciences in the Tropics (Hans-Ruthenberg-Institute), Germany*

[2]*University of Ibadan, Dept. of Agricultural Economics, Nigeria*

Maize is one of the most important cereal crops in Nigeria. It is particularly important for the poorer citizens and smallholders for food security purposes. Agricultural policies in Nigeria have conventionally focused on enhancing food production. However, growing challenges of sustainable development require a shift in the conventional thinking of considering agricultural sector as only the supplier of food. It is increasingly becoming a "supplier of biomass", which caters to multiple demands of food and non-food purposes. Recent advances suggest that it is pertinent to look beyond conventional value chains to a more holistic "value web" because the same crops find diverse usages in the biomass-based economy. As a result, recent governmental policies have been geared towards increasing the production of priority crops like maize in the country. For this, the government has employed the innovative Growth Enhancement Support (GES) scheme as a means of eliminating governance challenges in the procurement and distribution of inputs to smallholder farmers. The study employs focus group discussion and uses innovative participatory process net-mapping tool to elicit information about GES and found that governance challenges still persisted, preventing fair utilisation of resources made available by the government to the smallholder farmers. The study also found that corruption and leakages are rampant between redemption centres and before targeted farmers use the inputs. The study, therefore, suggests a more consistent support from both the federal and state governments to the sector and to the GES scheme. The study also suggests that the government should continue with the GES scheme while endeavouring to make consistent periodic reviews to block points of corruption and leakages. The Government should also provide more incentives for targetted smallholder farmers to use these resources.

Keywords: GES, governance challenges, participatory process net map, smallholder farmers, value-web

Contact Address: Ayobami Adetoyinbo, University of Hohenheim, Inst. of Agricultural Sciences in the Tropics (Hans-Ruthenberg-Institute), Wollgrasweg 43, 123, 70599 Stuttgart, Germany, e-mail: acubed_101@yahoo.com

Persistence of Food Price Shocks and Domestic Market Performance in Ethiopia

DEGYE GOSHU HABTEYESUS

Haramaya University, Agricultural Economics and Agribusiness, Ethiopia

Persistence of food price shocks is an overriding challenge faced by consumers in Ethiopia. The empirical evidence on the dynamics of relative price convergence of commodities and the persistence of price shocks is crucial to capture the policy effects of domestic market intervention measures and for designing marketing channel development and price stabilisation objectives with optimum policy costs. To investigate the problem of food price convergence and persistence of price shocks, a panel dataset of 18-year monthly price series of nine agricultural commodities widely traded and consumed in seven regions and cities was used. To analyse the dynamic process of food price convergence and persistence of shocks, the period was divided into two sub-periods (1996–2004 and 2005–2013). The first period was characterised by depressed food prices and the second by food price inflation in Ethiopia. To estimate the rate and speed of relative price convergence of commodities in the two periods, two panel unit root tests (LLC and IPS), fixed-effects, and half-life methods were employed. The empirical findings markedly indicate that rate and speed of relative price convergence of food commodities were considerably low, suggesting that higher proportion of food price shocks was persistent among regions and markets. Domestic market interventions undertaken by the government were less effective in adjusting food price shocks among regions and over time, leading to higher consumer price risks in Ethiopia. The results generally suggest the need to design relevant and proactive market policy interventions in improving convergence of food prices and adjustment of price shocks among regions and markets in Ethiopia.

Keywords: Ethiopia, fixed-effects, half-life, persistence, price convergence

Contact Address: Degye Goshu Habteyesus, Haramaya University, Agricultural Economics and Agribusiness, 05 Haramaya, Ethiopia, e-mail: degyeabgos@yahoo.com

ID 127

Factors Affecting Fertiliser Use Intensity among Farm Size Groups: Perception about Fertiliser Subsidy Policy in Bangladesh

MAHMUDA NASRIN, SIEGFRIED BAUER

Justus-Liebig University Giessen, Inst. of Farm and Agribusiness Management - Project and Regional Planning, Germany

The major objectives of the paper are to explore farmer's perceptions about fertiliser subsidy policy and to estimate the influence of determinants that affect farm level fertiliser usage in Bangladesh. Primary data were collected from three regions of the country. In total, 299 respondents were interviewed who were classified in four groups according to farm size i.e., marginal, small, medium and large. Both descriptive and econometric analyses are done to achieve the objectives. Fertilisers play an important role in achieving improved agricultural productivity in Bangladesh. As such, government implicitly subsidises fertiliser market to keep price within the purchasing capacity of farmers. In spite of universal subsidy policy setup, a wide variation in fertiliser use intensity is observed across different farm size groups. Financially constrained farmers are using lower amounts of fertiliser in their crop fields which implied the relative distribution of benefits of this subsidy among medium and large farmers as revealed from field survey. With regard to farmer's perception, about 72 percent sampled marginal farmers are unaware that government is providing huge subsidy on the fertiliser market. Instead, they claim that they are getting no help from government to bear the rising costs of rice production. This is mainly due to ineffective extension services in survey areas. Overall, only 31 percent farmers were satisfied with current policy and market prices which also highlights uneven distribution of subsidy benefit. Ordinary least square regression indicates that output prices relative to fertiliser price received by the farmers, off-farm income, labour use and extension services are significantly affecting fertiliser use intensity of different farm size groups. Farmers' financial conditions and their purchasing capability are crucial in deciding about the amount of fertiliser to be used. Moreover, farmers are more concerned about the output prices that they received instead of fertiliser prices that they paid. On the basis of these findings, the authors recommend that policy makers should revise the subsidy policy in order to reduce the distortions of resource allocation and also to secure the welfare of the farmers.

Keywords: Fertiliser use intensity, subsidy

Contact Address: Mahmuda Nasrin, Justus-Liebig University Giessen, 35392 Giessen, Germany, e-mail: namsa2505@gmail.com

Bilateral Aid Drives Formal Development Goals or Informal Interests? Insight from Forest Development Aid in Bangladesh

MD SAIFUR RAHMAN, LUKAS GIESSEN

Georg-August-Universität Göttingen, Section Forest and Nature Conservation Policy, Germany

Why aid allocation? Does it serve the informal self-interests of donors or simply extend the formal development goals of the recipient countries. The formal goals are exposed developmental goals of donors offer for the recipient country, and are inscribed in formal strategic documents. In contrary, the informal interests are largely unrevealed. However, it renders political action that is assessable, nonetheless its apparent diversity. As forest produce diverse utility, actors' interest is diverse who are really associated with it. In a developing country like Bangladesh, the utilisation of donors' aid in the forestry sector has rarely been explored. Here, forestry, as a development sector, has been received various levels of substantial development aid in the form of projects, because the significance of forests has been changed over time considering the increased importance of community-based forest management and climate change. In this context, the research aims to analyse the formal development goals as well as informal interests of foreign donors induced by the bilateral development project aid in forest development cooperation policy in Bangladesh. The analytical framework combines concepts from bilateral development cooperation policy, bureaucratic politics theory, and concepts of actors' interest in the policy field. Methodologically, a full quantitative survey of all bi-governmental donor funding projects and subsequently, quantitative analysis of fund flow against various items of activities from the project was carried out. Before that, a qualitative expert interview in order to have an overview and perceptions of the informal interests of donors was made. The analysis indicates that United States Agency for International Development (US-AID) allocated much aid in the activity area – 'consultancy' and 'collaboration and networking' that relish their economic and political interest. The allocation of aid in self-interest area is higher than real developmental intervention. In contrary, German Federal Enterprise for International Cooperation (GIZ) and the European Union (EU) allocated major aid in recipient developmental intervention; nevertheless the activity area demonstrates that they minutely gain economic and political interest as well. Future studies with other big sectors (e.g. infrastructure, power), and even including informal interests of multilateral donors would generate added research interest.

Keywords: Bi-governmental donors, development aid, development project, donor interest, forest sector

Contact Address: Md Saifur Rahman, Georg-August-Universität Göttingen, Section Forest and Nature Conservation Policy, Büsgenweg 3, 37077 Göttingen, Germany, e-mail: saifur69@yahoo.com

　　　　　　　　　　　　　　　　　　　ID 302

Impact of Presidential Cassava Initiative on Cassava Productivity: Implication for Food Security and Economic Development

EMMANUEL DONKOR[1], STEPHEN ONAKUSE[1], JOE BOGUE[1],
IGNACIO DE LOS RIOS[2]

[1] *University College Cork, Dept. of Food Business and Development, Ireland*
[2] *Technical University of Madrid, Higher Technical School of Agronomic Engineers, Spain*

Governments in sub-Saharan Africa have devised a number of agricultural interventions to stimulate economic development. One of such interventions is the presidential cassava initiative (PCI) in Nigeria, implemented during the period 2002–2010. The intervention aimed at promoting cassava production, alleviating rural poverty and promoting national food security. Although there are claims about the positive outcomes of this intervention, there is limited empirical evidence to prove the extent to which the intervention has impacted on cassava production and food security. Therefore, this study examined the impact of the intervention on productivity of cassava and its implications on food security and economic development using a system of multivariate linear regression models. Smith and Blundell approach was used to address endogeneity problems in the food security and food production models. The study employed a time series data from 1961–2013. The time series data consisted of cassava production, land area under cassava production, fertiliser, agricultural machinery, food production index and food adequacy index. Food adequacy index was used as a proxy for food security. The empirical findings from the study showed that the implementation of presidential cassava initiative increased cassava productivity by 17.6 %. Moreover, fertiliser application and agricultural mechanisation were found to promote production of cassava. Food production in general appeared to have gone higher during the period of PCI. The food production in turn increased the national food security level. The main conclusion drawn from the study is that government interventions that seek to promote agricultural development are critical to enhancing national food production, food security and economic development as a whole.

Keywords: Economic development, food security, multivariate regression, presidential cassava initiative, productivity

Contact Address: Emmanuel Donkor, University College Cork, Dept. of Food Business and Development, Cork, Ireland, e-mail: edonkor.knust@gmail.com

Large-Scale Land Based Investments and Employment in Nigerian Communities

FELICIA OLOKOYO[1], EVANS OSABUOHIEN[2], IBUKUN BEECROFT[2], UCHENNA EFOBI[3], PAUL ADEKOLA[4]

[1]*Covenant University, College of Development Studies, Nigeria*
[2]*Covenant University, Economics and Development Studies, Nigeria*
[3]*Covenant University, Accounting, Nigeria*
[4]*Covenant University, Demography and Statistics Studies, Nigeria*

African countries have been undergoing some measures of transformations in the last decade while recording commendable economic growth. Among the key driving factors include natural resources, technological innovation and adoption, and the transformation of the agricultural sector. Some of the major expectations in the acclaimed agricultural transformation include: the provision of more employment, integration and development of rural communities, provision of social amenities especially in peri-urban and rural areas, and so on. However, a pertinent question is - to what extent has the existence of Large-scale Land Based Investments (LLBIs) in host communities in Nigeria delivered on their promises to the households in such communities in relation to employment? Thus, this study is motivated with the aim of examining how the presence of LLBIs in a community will provide a more comprehensive outcome – in terms of employment. The study utilises data from the Living Standards Measurement Study-Integrated Study on Agriculture, which is a survey conducted by the World Bank in collaboration with Nigeria's National Bureau of Statistics. In this dataset, the communities with the occurrence of LLBIs are identified using the Land Matrix Global Observatory Dataset, which is complemented by field visits in the areas. The relationship between employments of household members in the community and the presence of LLBIs as well as a number of other household characteristics is modelled in the study. This is estimated by employing the tenets of impact evaluation based on the propensity score matching (PSM) approach. A significant effect of LLBIs on the employment levels in the host communities in Nigeria is anticipated. A significant difference is also expected between the employments across different strata. These associated differences are expected to be informed by the strength of the indigenous institutions in the respective communities.

Keywords: Agricultural transformation, employment, host community, large-scale land based investment, welfare

Contact Address: Felicia Olokoyo, Covenant University, College of Development Studies, Canaanland, Km 10 Idiroko Road, 112001 Ota, Nigeria, e-mail: felicia.olokoyo@covenantuniversity.edu.ng

Decision-Oriented Research for Development – Making Best Use of Existing Information and Closing Critical Knowledge Gaps

EIKE LUEDELING[1,2], KEITH SHEPHERD[2]

[1]*Center for Development Research (ZEF), Germany*
[2]*World Agroforestry Centre (ICRAF), Kenya*

Agricultural development is a complex challenge. The resilience of landscapes and livelihoods and the success of innovations depend on many factors, spanning the social, economic and ecological domains. Decision-makers in agricultural development, e.g. policy-makers or development professionals, have to – or should – consider all these factors. Ignoring the target group's cultural preferences can hamper the impact prospects of technologies; and ignoring off-site environmental impacts can threaten sustainability. Impact-oriented research should support decision-makers, because decisions are critical junctures in most pathways through which research can effect change. However, information on many critical aspects is often limited, and where data are available, they have often not been collected from the location of interest. Impact-oriented researchers needs smart ways of combining the best local expert knowledge and broader global knowledge on all important factors to make the best possible recommendations to decision-makers. Structured decision analysis can assist in combining disparate sources of knowledge and data and help set priorities for research. Decision analysis aims to support risky decisions on complex systems under uncertainty, which is quite precisely the challenge that development decision-makers face. It produces models that fully represent specific decisions, considering all factors of relevance. Models consider all available evidence, and they draw heavily on the knowledge of experts, stakeholders and the decision-makers themselves. Analysts quantify the current state of knowledge about all uncertain factors in the model, which they express as probability distributions. Once a model has been generated through participatory interactions between experts, stakeholders and decision analysts, probabilistic simulations produce projections of the plausible range of decision outcomes. This range is typically wide, providing limited immediate guidance to decision makers, but Value of Information analysis can highlight those knowledge gaps that most limit the decision-maker's ability to make a well-informed choice. After further information collection on high-value variables, a preferable choice emerges. Decision analysis can help development researchers realise the ambition to study agricultural decisions in a holistic manner that does justice to the complexity and multidimensionality that characterises most development contexts. It can provide a transdisciplinary umbrella for systems research that allows identification of pressing research needs.

Keywords: Complexity, transdisciplinary, uncertainty, value of information

Contact Address: Eike Luedeling, World Agroforestry Centre (ICRAF) and Center for Development Research (ZEF), Walter-Flex-Str. 3, 53113 Bonn, Germany, e-mail: e.luedeling@cgiar.org

Governance Challenges in the Liberalisation of the Commercial Maize Seed System in Africa: A Case Study of Ghana

Adu-Gyamfi Poku, Saurabh Gupta, Regina Birner

University of Hohenheim, Inst. of Agricultural Sciences in the Tropics (Hans-Ruthenberg-Institute), Germany

The liberalisation of African commercial seed systems has largely been seen as an essential means of improving agricultural productivity. Nonetheless, upstream activities such as varietal development and source seed production principally remain the domain of public sector agencies with wide reaching implications for varietal adoption and seed quality. The paper analyses the governance challenges in the transition towards a more effective privatized maize seed system using Ghana as a case study. Ghana recently passed a new seed law that aims to give the private sector greater opportunities in the seed value chain. Similar to most African countries, maize is the predominant crop in Ghana's commercial seed system in terms of volume of seed production. However, there has been a chronic lack of varietal diversity as an open pollinated variety released in 1992 called Obatanpa, continues to overwhelmingly dominate commercial seed production. The paper uses a participatory mapping technique known as Process Net-Map and in-depth interviews with different stakeholders to investigate the institutional bottlenecks that result in the observed lack of varietal diversity. The empirical evidence reveals the problem of limited involvement of poor farmers by the public research institutes in setting breeding priorities, making varietal development a "hit or miss" exercise. Restricted private sector participation in source seed production has also led to a limited number of varieties made available by the public sector for commercial seed multiplication. Furthermore, mandatory seed certification by an under-resourced public regulatory body has proved ineffective in ensuring high seed quality. Overdependence on a weak public extension system to promote improved varieties has also contributed to the enduring problem of low adoption rates. The study concludes that commercial seed sector development is dependent on increased private sector involvement at all stages of seed production, with the public sector concentrating more on an oversight role.

Keywords: Agricultural innovation system, Ghana, governance challenges, maize seed system, seed production, varietal development

Contact Address: Adu-Gyamfi Poku, University of Hohenheim, Inst. of Agricultural Sciences in the Tropics (Hans-Ruthenberg-Institute), Wollgrasweg 43, 70599 Stuttgart, Germany, e-mail: adu-gyamfi.poku@uni-hohenheim.de

ID 463

How Does Implementation of the Nagoya Protocol on Access and Benefit-Sharing Affect Biodiversity Research?

MAARTEN VAN ZONNEVELD[1], JUDY LOO[2], SILVANA MASELLI[3], JULIO JAVIER MADRID[4], MICHAEL HALEWOOD[2], JOSÉ LUIS ECHEVERRIA[5]

[1]*Bioversity International, Costa Rica*
[2]*Bioversity International, Italy*
[3]*Valle University of Guatemala, Guatemala*
[4]*Association of Community Forestry Organizations in the Petén (ACOFOP), Guatemala*
[5]*National Counsil of Protected Areas (CONAP), Guatemala*

In 2014 the Nagoya Protocol on Access and Benefit-sharing took effect and is being implemented by countries. This is important for fair and equitable sharing of benefits derived from genetic resources. However, scientists are concerned about its effect on non-commercial research, which has scientific, societal and environmental benefits beyond commercial gains. Such research may be delayed by cumbersome procedures and hampered by poor understanding of its scientific purposes and research requirements. Such delays negatively affect both biodiversity conservation and sustainable development.

A test case in Guatemala revealed how the Nagoya protocol functions in practice for non-commercial genetic research. We piloted the steps required for the national authority to approve a request for genetic material to be extracted and shipped out of the country for analysis as part of a research project on conservation genetics. We draw lessons for improving the Nagoya process in subsequent cases. This study focused on understanding the impact of timber harvesting on the regeneration of the most valuable timber species, mahogany, in community-managed forests in the Maya Biosphere Reserve.

Our request to collect and analyse seeds and leaves was approved after 1.5 years. As this was the first study to be reviewed considering the Protocol in Guatemala, there were no standard criteria or procedures. This pilot provided valuable lessons to the national authority for standardising and shortening procedures. These procedures should be based on national regulations, which are currently under development.

Good communication by scientists is vital because many people may not understand what genetics studies mean nor realise their potential benefits for communities and society. In our case, the forest communities, who were consulted at the start, supported the study after they understood that this investigation is seeking evidence of their sustainable management.

When implementing Nagoya, we encourage governments to establish committees including scientists, community representatives and other stakeholders to advise them. This helps to build trust among actors and ensure that different viewpoints are reflected in the codes of conduct. We encourage scientists to reach out to non-scientists to demonstrate to governments, local communities and society the relevance of their research.

Keywords: Conservation genetics, Guatemala, mahogany, Nagoya protocol on access and benefit-sharing, prior informed consent, science communication, sustainable forest management

Contact Address: Maarten Van Zonneveld, Bioversity International, Turrialba, Costa Rica, e-mail: m.vanzonneveld@cgiar.org

Competing Policy Consulting and Science in Establishing a Fair Use of Natural Resources – The Case of Pu Luong – Cuc Phuong Limestone Landscape Conservation in Vietnam

HUONG THI DO, MICHAEL BÖCHER, MAX KROTT

Georg-August-Universität Göttingen, Section Forest and Nature Conservation Policy, Germany

Establishing a fair use of natural resources is a great challenge for politics, especially in developing countries. Competing interests like nature conservation, hunting, tourism etc. have to be managed and collectively binding rules have to be established. But already the advice provided by external sources, like international donors or consultants differ substantially promoting biased solutions serving stronger powerful users than supporting a fair distribution. We analyse by the example of Pu Luong – Cuc Phuong Limestone Landscape Conservation in Vietnam how different actors and sources compete in delivering external advice. On the one hand, there is advice based on scientific research, dealing with species conservation and requirements for nature protection and ecotourism. On the other hand policy consulting by actors like the World Bank provides suggestions for establishing management plans or hunting regulations that are not clearly based on scientific evidence. Our contribution analyses the influence of these different kinds of expertise on national regulation by using the research (R), integration (I), and utilisation (U) model of scientific knowledge transfer (RIU model). The research question is how these competing sources of advice influence Vietnamese policy and to which degree scientific advice becomes influential under the condition of competition with policy consulting. The interactions between the different actors relevant for nature protection in this area will be analysed based on the RIU model of scientific knowledge transfer. Different activities between research, integration, and utilisation are revealed in order to show how different kinds of expertise compete with each, win actors as allies and lead to political decisions regarding the management of a fair use of natural resources in this area.

Keywords: Fair use, natural resource, policy consulting, Pu Luong – Cuc Phuong, RIU model

Contact Address: Huong Thi Do, Georg-August-Universität Göttingen, Section Forest and Nature Conservation Policy, Büsgenweg 3, 37077 Göttingen, Germany, e-mail: dohuongnlkh@gmail.com

ID 512

Do Energy Policies Work? Empirical Evidence from Targeted Fuel Subsides in the Agricultural Sector, Iran

Masoumeh Forouzani, Masoud Yazdanpanah, Negar Rahmkhoda, FatemehZahra Romina

Ramin Agriculture and Natural Resources University (Khouzestan), Dept. of Agricultural Extension and Education, Iran

Energy efficiency policy has been followed by Iran's government system during recent years as the main approach to access sustainability. Targeted fuel subsidies law constitutes a substantial part of this approach. The main premise of this law is to generate additional income for government to spend on other social assistance and anti-poverty family focused policies such as cash transfers; public works programs; provision of basic social services, and hygiene or health programs or subsidies. Agriculture sector as one of the major consumers of oil fuels has benefitted greatly from implementing fuels price reforms. As such, the opinions of producers in the agricultural sector in southwest Iran were investigated to find out if the mechanism applied to implement targeted fuel subsidies law is satisfactory in terms of reaching equal resources distribution, accessibility, optimal usage of fuels, and avoiding illegal jobs like fuel smuggling. A random sample of 160 farmers who use fuels for their various farm operations such as pumping ground water, moving agricultural equipment and vehicles were surveyed. The findings revealed that all of the respondents evaluated the targeted fuel subsidies law as a moderately successful programme in optimal usage and equal distribution of fuel, convenient access to assigned portion of fuels, and also avoiding fuel smuggling. There were also significant differences between farmers' attitude on these four aspects, depending on their monthly fuel consumption. Those who consume less than 1000 liter fuels per month believed that the targeted fuel subsidies law has been more successful compared to those who consume more. Farmers who poses large farmland and use more farming equipment which needs huge amount of oil fuels are dissatisfied with the implementation of the law. The study followed by presenting specific recommendations to improve and facilitate the mechanism of fuel distribution and further inter-organisational coordination.

Keywords: Agricultural fuel consumers, energy resources, Iran, targeted fuel subsidies law

Contact Address: Masoumeh Forouzani, Ramin Agriculture and Natural Resources University (Khouzestan), Dept. of Agricultural Extension and Education, Ramin, Iran, e-mail: m.forouzani@yahoo.com

Better Environmental Governance for Mitigation of Environmental Pollution - A Case Analysis of the Emerging Cities in South Asia

Shilpi Kundu[1], Rajesh S. Kumar[2], Nity Nishant[3], N.K. Binu[4]

[1] Sher-e-Bangla Agricultural University, Agricultural Extension & Information System, Bangladesh

[2] University of East Anglia (UEA), School of International Development, United Kingdom

[3] University of Delhi, India,

[4] Kerala Agricultural University, Dept. of Tree Physiology and Breeding, India

As more than half of the world population is already living in urban areas and since several locations in Asia are among the fast urbanizing part of the globe, it is very necessary to ensure better environmental conditions to secure health and wellbeing of dwellers in these high density urban agglomerations. The multiple environmental determinants of health operating in such environs are also reported to adversely affect human health as well as leads to development of several chronic and lethal diseases impacting human health and longevity. The reports of various studies in the domain have already identified the strong linkage between the operation of various environmental determinants and disease prevalence in urban areas. Several cities have dealt with the unprecedented wave of urbanisation in differing degrees and in many a cases the scenarios resulted in heavy environmental pollution, poor urban sanitation, high incidences of diseases linked to environmental pollution, water quality, etc. In several of the instances, the causes behind negative operation of various environmental determinants have been linked to poor environmental governance. In the current paper we have attempted to approach the issue by analysing the urban environmental governance prevailing in two of the actively expanding cities in South Asia fraught significantly with environmental pollution viz. Dhaka and New Delhi. In the case analysis we have approached the scenario analysis with the principles of good governance and attempted to describe the prevailing governance patterns in the study cities as well as made suggestions for further improvement of governance model for urban environmental pollution management. The output of the current study is expected to find potential applications for improvement of urban environmental governance in urban agglomerations with similar features while contributing to the overall mission of securing urban health as well as knowledge holding in the domain.

Keywords: Environmental determinants, environmental governance, environmental pollution, South Asia

Contact Address: Shilpi Kundu, Sher-e-Bangla Agricultural University, Agricultural Extension & Information System, Sher-e-Bangla Nagar, 1207 Dhaka, Bangladesh, e-mail: shilpi.agro@gmail.com

ID 633

Marginal Willingness to Pay for Indirect Procurement Programme Attributes

FREDDY NOMA[1], AFOUDA JACOB YABI[2], RANGANATH LAKSHMAIAH[1], SIEGFRIED BAUER[1]

[1]*Justus-Liebig Universität Gießen, Institute of Farm and Agribusiness Management, Germany*

[2]*University of Parakou, Dept. of Agricultural Economics and Rural Sociology, Benin*

Since the world food crisis of 2008–09, West-African countries have re-launched procurement programs and rebuilt food stocks. State interventions on markets are known to lead to distortions. But the food crisis has revealed free economy limits to provide food for all citizens and to handle shocks. Then, states and free economy cooperation is advocated to overcome these challenges. Indirect procurement policy is implemented in Benin, under a Public-Private Partnership (PPPs) agreement. The study proposes designs to improve PPPs agreement to strength its actors' loyalty. Data were collected on three agricultural markets in northern Benin for a total of 210 respondents in the discrete choice experiment (DCE). Hypothetical policies have some attributes already existing (price information, prices, payment delay); but improvements are introduced in their levels. Two new were added: "supply chain" attribute, referring to the number of links and type of traders involved in the partnership. It has three levels: link1 (L1) for assemblers, only; link2 (L2) for assemblers + small-whole sellers; and link3 (L3) for assemblers + small-whole sellers + whole sellers. The second attribute is "transport" offered by the program. Six attributes were used: 1 of 3 levels, 2 of 2 levels and 2 of 4 levels. The full-factorial design ($31 \times 22 \times 42$) gives 192 profiles, reduced to 16 profiles, using main effects orthogonal design. Choice cards present two alternatives (Pa and Pb) and "free market", which captures respondents not interested to participate. Mixlogit model estimates were used to evaluate willingness to pay for change in attributes levels. Note that, traders are paid for maize delivered. If not interested, they request higher price as compensation. Otherwise, they are willing to accept lower price. Regarding supply chain, traders will require 0.42 FCFA kg^{-1} and 3.15 FCFA kg^{-1} more to join PPPs for supply chains "L1" and "L2", respectively. But they accept 5.25 FCFA kg^{-1} less for "L3". They accept lower prices for price information (-2.68 FCFA kg^{-1} and transport means (-1.97 FCFA kg^{-1}). For longer payment delay, traders will require 1.47 FCFA kg^{-1} more. Considering "free market", traders will require 39.41 FCFA kg^{-1} more to quitt or not to join the agreement.

Keywords: Discrete choice experiment, indirect procurement programme, marginal willingness to pay

Contact Address: Freddy Noma, Justus-Liebig Universität Gießen, Institute of Farm and Agribusiness Management, Giessen, Germany, e-mail: orounoma@yahoo.fr

What Can Ethiopia Learn from the Brazilian Sugarcane Sector Development?

Tim K. Loos[1], Lilli Scheiterle[1], Alina Ulmer[2]

[1] University of Hohenheim, Inst. of Agricultural Sciences in the Tropics (Hans-Ruthenberg-Institute), Germany
[2] University of Hohenheim, Chair of Economics and Innovation, Germany

Shifting from a fossil based economy to a biomass based economy is becoming a major strategic concept for many countries. A key aspect of this shift includes the fuel sector and in particular, establishing a sustainable ethanol production. Brazil may be considered a successful pioneer in the holistic use of sugarcane for various products ranging from sugar, ethanol, and energy to various industrial uses of by-products. Despite its agro-ecological potential, Ethiopia on the other hand, currently cannot reach sugar self-sufficiency. Further, the country depends fully on fuel imports to cover national demand. In order to close the demand gap, the Ethiopian government defined the sugarcane sector as a priority for the second growth and transformation plan. Considering the similarities between these two countries, it is surprising that so far only few lessons from the Brazil experience were applied to the Ethiopian or other African country contexts. This study aims at comparing the characteristics of the sugarcane sectors in two sugarcane producing countries regarding key stakeholders, institutional settings, and policies that contribute to the development of the industry. Based on Porter's diamond framework, we use secondary and primary data collected with qualitative research methods such as in-depth interviews, net-maps, and focus group discussions so as to assess the sectors. Results indicate that the sectors vary substantially. Brazil shows a decentralised and dynamic structure with numerous actors involved, which developed during the military dictatorship with the goal of being independentfrom imports. Targeting a comparable goal, Ethiopia is currently structured around the Ethiopian Sugar Corporation, a government corporation that almost exclusively influences the development of the sector. Ethiopia may learn from the Brazilian experience how to avoid economically inefficient stages and jump directly to a holistic, efficient and sustainable use of sugarcane in the whole value web. Drawing conclusions from this comparison could help to understand the challenges and opportunities for an upcoming bioeconomy in Ethiopia.

Keywords: Bioeconomy, Brazil, Ethiopia, sugarcane

Contact Address: Tim K. Loos, University of Hohenheim, Inst. of Agricultural Sciences in the Tropics (Hans-Ruthenberg-Institute), Wollgrasweg 43, 70599 Stuttgart, Germany, e-mail: timloos@uni-hohenheim.de

ID 763

Farmland, Family Farms and Food Security in Ethiopia: The Case of Farming Families Around Yayu Coffee Forest Biosphere Reserve

GIRMA KELBORO, TILL STELLMACHER

University of Bonn, Center for Development Research (ZEF), Germany

Ethiopia leads a dominantly agrarian economy with about 85 % of its population practicing family farming. Land, the underlying resource for farming, however, is a limiting and increasingly contested factor for family farming households. The average landholding of a family farm in Ethiopia is about 1 hectare, and continues to shrink due to increasing population. Landless family farms are a relatively new but fast growing concern. This study investigates the dynamics of land access in and around the Yayu Coffee Forest Biosphere Reserve, Oromia Regional State, and the mechanisms and strategies used by family farms to adapt to the challenges in their efforts to gain or maintain food security. Data was collected through a combination of quantitative and qualitative methods. For household survey, 300 randomly selected family farm households in 8 kebeles were interviewed. Key informant and expert interviews, focus group discussions and guided farm observations were applied to collect qualitative data. Our findings show that informal arrangements among farmers play a key role to gain and maintain access to land. For 57 % of the interviewees, the land holding they have is insufficient to produce enough for their families; 20 % do not have cereal producing area; 6 % have no coffee land. They fill in the land shortage or landlessness through sharecropping (30 %), land contract (12 %), and a combination of sharecropping, contract, and entering into forest (31 %). Based on the data, we conclude that shortage of land or landlessness is not an end to family farms thanks to informal arrangements. The informal arrangements of access to farmland should be considered in institutional support to strengthen the efforts of farming families in the process of securing food for their households.

Keywords: Biosphere reserve, family farms, food security

Contact Address: Girma Kelboro, University of Bonn, Center for Development Research (ZEF), Walter-Flex-Str. 3, 53113 Bonn, Germany, e-mail: Girma75@yahoo.com

The Dynamics of Land-Use Change in Kilombero Valley Floodplain Wetland: An Agent Based Modelling Approach

BISRAT HAILE GEBREKIDAN, THOMAS HECKELEI, SEBASTIAN RASCH

University of Bonn, Institute of Food and Resource Economics, Germany

Floodplain wetlands, such as those of the Kilombero Valley Floodplain (KVFP), are endowed with a productive natural resource base, fertile land, reliable water availability and extensive pastures. Shared by Kilombero and Ulanga districts, the valley supports a plethora of socio-economic activities. It also remains the major focal area for the Tanzanian government particularly in its bid to transform the farming system and eradicate poverty in the country. However, in recent decades, prompted by different economic, social and environmental disturbances, land-use change through rapid expansion of crop-land and grazing-land (especially, after the immigration of agro-pastoralists with their oxenisation technology) and commercial agriculture endeavours at the expense of wetlands is threatening the stability of the system and triggering recurrent conflict of interest between different users.

Arguably, the observed dynamics of land-use and land cover change in KVFP is the result of the interplay of individual decision making and the natural systems that operate across a range of temporal and hierarchical spatial scales. Given this complexity, we are developing an Agent Based Model (ABM) that integrates both the agent's decision making mechanism and biophysical process of wetlands through specification of feedback and interdependencies among agents and their environment at landscape and regional scale.

Herein, as the first step in system conceptualisation of ABM, we present the empirical characterisation of agents and their behaviour. Agricultural Sample Surveys and individual interviews with 304 farmers and other stakeholders are used to elucidate agents' land-use decision-making architecture and a set of rules governing their strategy when allocating means of production to alternative land-use options. Although agents are diverse in terms of experiences, preferences, objectives, abilities, and resources, agent typologies were created to simplify their diversity and reduce decision making complexity at regional scale. More so, we show, once finalized, how the ABM serve as a virtual laboratory to experiment the effect of different policy interventions, management options and climate change on heterogeneous agents, their land-use and the resilience of the wetland landscape of which they are part.

Keywords: Agent based modelling, agent typology, decision making, floodplain wetland, resilience

Contact Address: Bisrat Haile Gebrekidan, University of Bonn, Institute of Food and Resource Economics, Nussale 21, 53115 Bonn, Germany, e-mail: bisrat.gebrekidan@ilr.uni-bonn.de

Measuring Rice Competitiveness: New Evidence Using an Extension of the Policy Analysis Matrix

FAZLEEN ABDUL FATAH, STEPHAN VON CRAMON-TAUBADEL

Georg-August-Universität Göttingen, Dept. of Agricultural Economics and Rural Development, Germany

The advent of free trade agreements, including the Asean Free Trade agreement (AFTA) and WTO accession, pose challenges for the Malaysian rice sector as it must compete with low-cost exporting countries. This implies not only structural changes in trade, but also adjustments at the farm level to improve efficiency and competitiveness. Further developments in the rice sector will therefore depend on the availability of sufficient, relatively low-cost and high-quality rice, or in other words, on the competitiveness of rice production. In this paper we aim to improve our understanding of the forces that drive the competitiveness of rice production in Malaysia. We use an extension of the Policy Analysis Matrix proposed by Monke and Pearson (1989). This extension allows us to take farm-level heterogeneity into account and draws distribution of competitiveness scores for each rice farm. The results demonstrate that more than 50 % of farmers produced rice competitively in the main and off seasons over the period 2010-2014 and these competitive farms produced a disproportionately large number of the total rice production in each year. Additionally, we briefly note the contrast between the distributions of using disaggregate social cost benefit (SCB) and average SCB that would result from the use of aggregated data. In a second stage analysis, we use dynamic panel regressions methods to examine factors influencing rice competitiveness. We conclude that participation in farmers' organisation, gender and total farm size are the major determinants of rice competitiveness, while the distance to the rice mills, off-farm income and the use of hired labour are the main constraints that reduce competitiveness. Finally, the dynamic system generalized method of moment (SGMM) estimates provided in this paper reveal that the provision of input subsidies and bonus payments in the previous period have no strong effects on the current competitiveness. This suggests a better understanding of the agricultural policy reform, which allows better targeting of policies in order to enhance the competitiveness of the rice sector.

Keywords: Competitiveness, dynamic panel, Malaysia, rice farming, subsidies

Contact Address: Fazleen Abdul Fatah, Georg-August-Universität Göttingen, Dept. of Agricultural Economics and Rural Development, Platz der Göttinger Sieben 5, 37075 Göttingen, Germany, e-mail: fazleen_abf@yahoo.com.my

Estimating Farmers' Willingness to Protect Export Crops as Geographical Indication in Kenya: Choice Experiment Analysis

FREDAH MAINA, JOHN MBURU

University of Nairobi, Dept. of Agricultural Economics

In Kenya, coffee and tea are major export products that are sold raw. Buyers demand for the products is mainly linked to their high quality compared to similar products from other parts of the world. The quality of the two crops are attributable to the handling at both farm and processing levels as well as geographical characteristics according to focused group discussions with producers and key informant interviews. These characteristics require environmentally sustainable practices, which in turn are compromised when returns to farmers' investments decline. Geographical indications have been used to differentiate products where unique characteristics are essentially attributable to the production region, and ensuring environmental sustainability of production. In Kenya, this remains a new area with the geographical indications bill still being in draft form. The objective of this study was to apply choice experiments to assess farmers' willingness to protect their tea and coffee as geographical indications. The study was conducted among 127 and 132 producers from Kirinyaga County for tea production and Muranga County for coffee production respectively. Data was analysed using latent class model in the NLOGIT software package. Latent class model enables identification of heterogenous segments in the population who value GI components of the crops differently. For each crop, two segments were identified and willingness to pay for different attributes determined. The attributes for both crops were (i) time information on price is received (beginning of season, before or after selling), (ii) level of protection (factory, county or regional), (iii) having minimum guaranteed returns; and (iv) approximate cost (per household) of registering the product. The positive and significant coefficients for the attributes show that tea producers are willing to protect their products as geographical indications in line with the various attribute levels. The choice experiment results are important for policy makers and implementers of geographical indications for export crops in designing implementation programs that provide information for producers but do not increase their costs substantively.

Keywords: Choice experiments, coffee, geographical indication, Kenya, producers, tea

Contact Address: Fredah Maina, University of Nairobi, Dept. of Agricultural Economics, Nairobi, Kenya, e-mail: fredah.maina@yahoo.com

ID 1022

Knowledge, participation, stakeholders and social networks

Activity and Knowledge Analysis of Small-Scale Milk Traders in Nakuru County, Kenya

ANNE EMDEN, MARIA JOSE RESTREPO RODRIGUEZ, MARGARETA LELEA, BRIGITTE KAUFMANN

German Institute for Tropical and Subtropical Agriculture (DITSL), Germany

Small-scale milk traders in Kenya, who market the large majority of milk produced, are facing significant restrictions related to financial capital, knowledge, and political context. Reasons are that little is known about their system, neither in the research, nor in the political area. This explains why the 'informal' market, to which small-scale milk traders are attributed, is often accused of low quality milk — although scientific findings show that milk quality in the informal is not worse than in the formal market. This study aims at contributing to an understanding of the traders' activity system, their context-specific knowledge and the overall importance of their business in Nakuru County, Kenya. By conducting an activity and knowledge analysis using second-order cybernetics, rules that underlie routine and problem-solving actions of the traders can be made explicit and improvement strategies can be derived.

Field data was collected in two study sites during May and September 2015 by applying an actor-oriented approach using different qualitative methods such as semi-structured (n=8) and narrative (n=3) interviews, participant observations (n=7), focus groups (n=3 with 2, 2 and 4 participants) as well as group meetings (n=15 with 3-12 participants each).

Results show that small-scale milk traders manage their system through a wide range of routine and problem-solving actions which enable them to pursue their overall goal of gaining a stable income from the business and several sub-goals such as ensuring quality milk, reducing losses and involvement in sound relations with different stakeholders. Problems encountered by traders in their activities were made explicit. Based on these outcomes, traders identified improvement strategies that they could pursue self-reliant such as testing milk quality with Alcohol tests and others that required collaboration with other stakeholders of the milk supply chain, such as workshops on hygienic milk handling with primary or meetings with secondary stakeholders on political regulations.

With their context-specific knowledge, small-scale milk traders guarantee supply of quality milk at affordable prices and increase market access for smallholder dairy farmers. Reconstruction of the traders' routine and problem-solving rules shows that they adapt their decisions to their business-related, environmental and political-framework conditions.

Keywords: Kenya, RELOAD, second-order cybernetics, small-scale milk traders

Contact Address: Anne Emden, German Institute for Tropical and Subtropical Agriculture (DITSL), Albanikirchhof 1a, 37073 Göttingen, Germany, e-mail: emdenanne@gmail.com

Farmers Organisations' Position in the Development of Sustainable Agriculture Practices in Burkina Faso

ABOUBAKAR IYABANO[1,3], GUY FAURE[2], LAURENS KLERKX[3]

[1] *SupAgro-CIRAD, France*

[2] *CIRAD, Innovation, France*

[3] *Wageningen University and Research Centre, Knowledge, Technology and Innovation, The Netherlands*

The concept of sustainable agriculture aims to address the drawbacks of conventional agriculture by employing a systems approach. A systems perspective is essential to understanding sustainability, by giving the tools to explore the interconnections between the social and ecological system of the farming environment. In recent decades, a range of sustainable agriculture practices (such as soil and water conservation, intercropping and the use of organic inputs) have been promoted by many development actors in Burkina Faso in order to adapt to the increasing environmental and climatic variability. Farmers Organisations (FOs) are portrayed as key drivers in this process; due to their position as an intermediary organisation between rural farmers and institutions.

Several studies have been done with regard to the role of FOs in agricultural and rural development, but little is known on how they position themselves in the sustainable agriculture paradigm. This research addresses this gap and explores the diversity of FOs involved in sustainable agriculture practices in Burkina Faso, in order to build a typology based on their position into this paradigm. It consisted of case studies of twenty FOs by using a triangulation of research methods: document analysis, observation, surveys and in-depth interviews. The main indicator for the definition of sustainable practices of FOs' members is the integration of ecological principles into agricultural management in order to reduce dependency on external inputs and/or increase the productive capacity of their farming system.

The findings show that, FOs can have three main positions regarding the sustainable agriculture paradigm: minor position (sustainable practices concern a few farmers), average position (sustainable practices vary per types of crops grown) and major position (where sustainable practices are the dominant system for the majority of farmers). Further, the results indicate that the degree of involvement of FOs in the sustainable practices varies according to their origin. FOs with internal origins are much more involved in the sustainable practices as compared to those with the external origins. This points to the need to look at the potential roles that these FOs could provide to their members in the promotion of sustainable practices.

Keywords: Ecological principles, farmers organisations, intermediary organisation

Contact Address: Aboubakar Iyabano, SupAgro-CIRAD, 73 Avenue Jean François Breton, 34 398 Montpellier, France, e-mail: iyabano1aboubakar@yahoo.fr

ID 428

Area Closure Management in Ethiopia: Social and Socio-Economic Aspects of Common Pool Resource Activities

MAXI DOMKE, JÜRGEN PRETZSCH

Technische Universität Dresden, Inst. of International Forestry and Forest Products: Tropical Forestry, Germany

Climate hazards, population growth and mismanagement accelerate the problem of natural resources degradation. To break the circle, actions are required that lead to positive ecological and socio-economic outcomes. Area closures (AC) as common pool resource activity ideally lead to environmental rehabilitation under community participation. Ethiopia has a long history of AC activities. Applied under different management and conditions their performances varies. This study aims to assess social and socio-economic factors contributing to efficient and sustainable AC management in Ethiopia. The objectives are to (1) determine the institutionalisation with relevant stakeholders, structures and processes, (2) investigate the level and motivation of community participation, (3) comparing the ACs' management performances and their potential contribution to local environment and livelihood. The explorative study was carried out in 2014/2015, following a multiple case design: five ACs in two districts in Amhara and Oromia Region. Data were collected by reviewing official documents, conducting semi-structured and key informant interviews with 112 local community members and 40 representatives from state and civic entities. Findings show that communities endorse the closed areas, based on observations of rehabilitated parts and water generation. Besides using grass in selective cases, benefits for livelihood support and knowledge about it are sparse. Existing income generating activities are externally induced and funded. Their effect is limited as they are not strongly linked with the AC and timely restricted. Continuous technical training and support is desired by the community. Experience sharing shows to be an efficient and appreciated method by the farmers taking up their way of learning. But benefits are not accessible for all. People are excluded through the incapability to financially contribute or being outside decision making bodies. The institutional collaboration on ACs is not clearly determined, impeding essential information flow and holistic implementation. Additionally, the performance of AC depends on the individual context of the located area: severity of environmental hazards, level of degradation and land pressure, traditional lifestyles and agricultural knowledge. To achieve rural development and environmental protection on a long term, individual conditions in a social-ecological system have to be pre-assessed, knowledge and responsibilities equally distributed and individual benefits balanced.

Keywords: Area closure management, common pool resources, Ethiopia, multiple case design, social-ecological system

Contact Address: Maxi Domke, Technische Universität Dresden, Inst. of International Forestry and Forest Products: Tropical Forestry, Pienner Straße 7, 01737 Tharandt, Germany, e-mail: maxi.domke@tu-dresden.de

Participation in Water Management in the Mena Region – Perspectives from Refugee-Hosting Communities in Rural Jordan

RAND ABU AJAMIA, MICHELA CANNOVALE-PALERMO, DANIEL NAEK
CHRISENDO, KIM EDOU, KATJA GEORGE, SUSANNE HOFMANN-SOUKI,
MARGARITA KABAKOVA, EMILY NACHTIGAL, STRAHINJA SAVIC, ELENA
SCHAEGG, JAKOB SEIDLER, MITJA SEYFFERT, JOHANNA STRIECK, NATALIYA
STUPAK, ANTONIA ZAMPA

Humboldt-Universität zu Berlin, Dept. of Agricultural Economics, Germany

At an annual water supply of 145 m^3 per capita, Jordan is categorised by the UN as a country with extreme water scarcity. The ongoing influx of refugees from Syria into Jordan is placing a heavy burden on its already strained water resources. This brings existing deficiencies in water supply to the forefront, leading to frequent, sometimes aggressive protest among the population – refugees and Jordanians alike. The Jordanian Ministry of Water and Irrigation and GIZ have initiated a project which should introduce participatory elements into local water management processes, hoping that this might channel the populations' discontent into collaborative improvement efforts. The northern Jordanian villages of Samar, Kharaj and Foa'rah had been chosen for testing the new approaches and hence for this preparatory study. Main objectives are an understanding of stakeholders' current practices and experiences in water management as well as proposing suitable forms of public participation as an approach to increase the satisfaction of water users. A special focus is on vulnerable groups (e.g. women, people with special needs). 71 semi-structured qualitative interviews and transect walks through the villages have been conducted. Refugees, local community members and representatives from the local water company were interviewed. Particular attention, also during analysis, is given to understanding social relations within the communities, water supply and demand, as well as people's willingness and capacities for participation in water management, or limitations thereof. The tailor-made analytical framework has been developed based on Esser's adaptation of Coleman's Macro-Micro-Model, integrating elements of Ostrom's CPR theory as well as theories social capital and public participation. Research results show that strong family ties are central in community life and in dealing with problems, including those related to water. Syrian refugees often remain outside these connections for various reasons. Water shortage is perceived as a major issue and refugees are particularly vulnerable to it. Jordanians use personal relationships to employees of the water company for pressing their issues. Experience with public participation is minimal. However, possible strategies for future public participation were identified within the existing social structures. Conditions for their implementation and possible limitations are discussed, too.

Keywords: Institutions, Middle East, natural resource management, public participation, water governance

Contact Address: Michela Cannovale-Palermo, Humboldt-Universität zu Berlin, Dept. of Agricultural Economics, Jablonskistrasse 24, 10405 Berlin, Germany, e-mail: michela.cannovale@gmail.com

ID 651

Complex Systems - Simple Solutions? The Importance of Social Context for Sustainable Intensification.

Mirja Michalscheck[1], Bekele Hundie Kotu[2], Iddrisu Baba Mohammed[2], Irmgard Hoeschle-Zeledon[3], Jeroen C.J. Groot[1]

[1] *Wageningen University and Research Centre (WUR), Farming Systems Ecology Group, The Netherlands*
[2] *International Institute of Tropical Agriculture (IITA), Ghana*
[3] *International Institute of Tropical Agriculture (IITA), Nigeria*

Smallholder farming systems in northern Ghana exhibit low adoption rates of measures for sustainable intensification (SI). Measures are only meaningful if they match with people's livelihood strategies, gender roles and human capital (knowledge, habits). Smallholder systems are complex 'businesses' where intra-household differences in roles, objectives and power positions strongly influence farm management decisions and therewith the adoption behaviour. For the Africa RISING project, we investigated smallholder farm and farmer diversity in northern Ghana with the aim to better understand technology adoption for SI. We generated and combined statistical and participatory typologies to capture local smallholder diversity. We then collected bio-economic information of each farm type to describe and explain the current system as well as to evaluate and explore alternatives for SI using the whole farm model Farm DESIGN. The whole farm modelling was performed at household level since the farm household forms a strong unit of agricultural production, with tight interdependencies in decision making, exchanging and sharing resources like land, tools, labour, capital, inputs (fertilisers, seeds) and outputs (food, income). However, different fields, crops and livestock types are typically managed by different household members with different individual objectives and hence different interests and viewpoints on 'improved farm technologies'. In our interviews, we hence went beyond the usual consultation of a single 'representative' household member by interviewing all members with 'own' fields. We found that technologies for SI had different impacts and received different evaluations by the different household types and household members. The combination of whole-farm modelling and social contextualisation revealed that technologies such as a systematic integration of maize and legumes seem technically simple and economically promising, but are difficult to implement if the crops are traditionally grown by different household members and on different fields. We further identified the need to distinguish between technologies and techniques: While technologies are more technical (inputs, machinery) techniques are more managerial (behaviour change) making them differently attractive and feasible for low and high resource endowed farm types. Analyzing the social context of measures for SI significantly improved our understanding of challenges and opportunities for SI in smallholder systems in northern Ghana.

Keywords: Farmer and farm typology, gender, Ghana, intra-household differences, smallholder, sustainable intensification, technology adoption, whole farm model Farm DESIGN

Contact Address: Mirja Michalscheck, Wageningen University and Research Centre (WUR), Farming Systems Ecology Group, P.O. Box 430, 6700 AK Wageningen, The Netherlands, e-mail: mirja.michalscheck@wur.nl

Networking, Information and Technology Adoption: A Social Network Analysis of Colombian Small/Medium Scale Cattle Producers

CRISTHIAN DAVID PUERTA RODRIGUEZ[1], STEFAN BURKART[1], KAREN ENCISO[1], ANDRES CHARRY[2], JHON FREDDY GUTIERREZ SOLIS[1], JHON JAIRO MUÑOZ QUICENO[3], LISBETH ROCIO RUIZ[3], NELSON JOSÉ VIVAS QUILA[3], NOÉ ALBÁN LOPEZ[3], SANDRA MORALES VELASCO[3], MICHAEL PETERS[1]

[1] *International Center for Tropical Agriculture (CIAT), Colombia*
[2] *University of Hohenheim, Institute for Farm Management, Germany*
[3] *University of Cauca, Department of Agricultural Sciences, Colombia*

Social networks are an important strategy in helping people to cope with challenging conditions such as a lack of basic services or inputs. The worse the conditions are and the more difficulties exist in the access to resources, more likely people will protect themselves by forming social networks. In many cases, social networks replace formal services and input providers, relying on the delivery of informal financial services, extension services and problem solving assistance. Small and medium scale cattle producers in Colombia are facing difficult conditions, which not only comprise climate change related production constraints, market or credit access, but also the access to technical information (e.g., feeds, animal production, marketing). In this paper, an analysis will be carried out in order to understand how social networks function as assets for small and medium scale cattle producers in the Colombian Cauca Department. Precisely, the authors will test the hypothesis that a strong social network has a positive influence on the adoption of improved forages in cattle production. Data was obtained in October 2015 through 308 semi-structured questionnaires with randomly selected small and medium scale cattle producers and is currently being analysed for network density, actor betweenness and actor centrality by applying UCINET as an analysis software for social network studies. These indicators will be statistically correlated with socio-demographic information and forage adoption levels to test the hypothesis.

Based on a similar study conducted for small scale pig and chicken producers in the same region, where significant relationships were found between social networking and the access to credit, the authors expect that cattle producers' social networks are an important asset and that they also have significant influence on the access to technical information, helping producers to make a decision on the adoption of improved forages and to take advantage of their benefits, which include e.g., climate change mitigation and adaptation potential or increased livestock productivity. In addition to that, this study will provide valuable information on the key actors of the network, which could play an important role in the dissemination of scientific findings and new technologies facilitating up- and out-scaling processes.

Keywords: Access to information, social network analysis, technology adoption, tropical forages

Contact Address: Stefan Burkart, International Center for Tropical Agriculture (CIAT), Tropical Forages Program, Km 17 Recta Cali-Palmira, Cali, Colombia, e-mail: s.burkart@cgiar.org

Nikinake – An Agricultural Extension Campaign for Resource Management and Food Security: The Case of Bako and Yem, Southwestern Ethiopia

GERBA LETA[1], GIRMA KELBORO[1], ANNA-KATHARINA HORNIDGE[2], KRISTOF VAN ASSCHE[3], TILL STELLMACHER[1]

[1] University of Bonn, Center for Development Research (ZEF), Germany
[2] Leibniz Center for Tropical Marine Ecology (ZMT) & University of Bremen, Germany
[3] University of Alberta, Planning, Governance and Development, Canada

Participatory Extension System (PES) is one of the approaches developed and used in Ethiopia to nurture farmers' involvement in agricultural innovation dissemination and scaling-up for resource management, food security and rural development. To reinforce the scaling-up process and enhance adoption of best agricultural practices, the regional government jointly with district stimulate the implementation of agricultural extension. The approach is called *"Nikinake"* meaning movement. The process and effectiveness of such an agricultural extension approach has not been given sufficient attention in research. Therefore, our study aimed at filling in this gap by taking Bako and Yem *woredas* in Southwestern Ethiopia. We generated empirical data through participant observation, key informant interviews, expert interviews and informal group discussions in the year 2015/2016. Based on our findings, this presentation will shed light on how *Nikinake* is coined, organised, empowered and accelerated implementation of land management activities. The result show that *Nikinake* is a joint architecture of *aketatay sened* (a "fueling document") by regional bureaus of agriculture in collaboration with regional administration, and the *Nikinake* organizing committees. Implementation of *Nikinake* initiated with a regional training workshop in which heads of zone and *woreda* sector offices participate. Following the training, each of the stages in the government administrative ladder commits to its implementation. Similarly, the *woredas* execute *Nikinake* with participation of *kebele* cabinets and relevant lower level development actors. In the two *woredas* we studied, all the farmers were brought on-board the implementation process. However, the implementation modalities of *Nikinake* differ between the two *woredas*. In general, *Nikinake* has an added value in improving farmers' participation and promotion of collective learning and action mainly on the dissemination of innovation and scaling-up of resource management practices. Nevertheless, the process can be improved and long-term viability of achievements of *Nikinake* can be realised by devising strategies to facilitate participation of farmers in the planning process to change the hitherto top-down model with an agenda coming as a surprise to the local level with a requirement for participation in implementation.

Keywords: Agricultural extension, rural development, southwest Ethiopia

Contact Address: Gerba Leta, University of Bonn, Center for Development Research (ZEF), Political and Cultural Change, Walter-Flex-Str. 3, 53113 Bonn Bonn, Germany, e-mail: gerbaleta@yahoo.com

Agricultural Management Strategies to Enhance Family Farming in Brazil

ANA PAULA TURETTA, RAFAEL TONUCCI, LUCIANO MANSOR DE MATTOS

Brazilian Agricultural Research Corporation (EMBRAPA), Brazil

Family farms in Brazil produce 70 % of the food consumed nationwide and its production is primarily designated for urban populations. Therefore, these farms do play a major role in food security. However, it is necessary to improve agricultural management in this sector, in order to enhance the food production, to ensure ecosystem service (ES) provision and to offer better life conditions for rural population.

Brazil is a huge country, with differences in natural characteristics and cultural aspects. For this reason, it is not proper to recommend a unique model for family farm management. So, in this study, we present a framework to identify the weaknesses and potentialities of agroecosystems in three study areas, each one located in different biomes in Brazil: Atlantic Forest, Cerrado and Caatinga. The aim is to recommend more appropriate agricultural practices that are able to improve food production in a sustainable way.

The proposed framework establishes the link between agroecosystems and ES provision, considering the criteria of management and agroecosystem establishment in each study area. A set of soil parameters that can be used as indicators to monitor the changes in the agroecosystems is also considered in this framework. The criteria for the agroecosystem development were based on existing knowledge of the biomes associated with gathered information through interviews with farmers and further stakeholders, and small field studies on social, economic, environmental and agricultural aspects. In each study area these criteria for deployment and management of agroecosystems were validated with representatives of agricultural entities and farmers. In a next step, the same group systematised the information and defined the agroecosystems priorities for their area. As a result, sustainable alternatives for agricultural management were identified in order to improve the output of the agroecosystems, considering the specific biome characteristics as well as the community necessities. For instance, "no fire use" and "agricultural consortium" were the main criteria for the deployment and management of agroecosystems with a higher potential for increasing ES provision, and biomass stock in soil and litter were the related soil parameters to be used as indicator to monitor the impact.

Keywords: Ecosystem services, multiple agricultural system, tropical farming

Contact Address: Ana Paula Turetta, Brazilian Agricultural Research Corporation (EMBRAPA), Soils, Rua Jardim Botanico 1024, 22460000 Rio de Janeiro, Brazil, e-mail: ana.turetta@embrapa.br

ID 1127

Local Understandings of Soil Fertility, Rainfall and Conservation Agriculture in Laikipia, Kenya: A Qualitative Analysis

JOANA SOUSA[1], GOTTLIEB BASCH[1], PAULO RODRIGUES[1], PETER KURIA[2], SAIDI MKOMWA[2], KALIFA COULIBALY[3]

[1]*Universidade de Évora, Instituto de Ciências Agrárias e Ambientais Mediterrânicas (UE/ICAAM), Portugal*

[2]*African Conservation Tillage Network (ACT), Kenya*

[3]*Université Polytechnique de Bobo Dioulasso, Institut du Développement Rural (UPB - IDR), Burkina Faso*

Conservation Agriculture (CA) is mostly referred to in the literature as having three principles at the core of its identity: minimum soil disturbance, permanent organic soil cover and crop diversity. This farming package has been described as suitable to improve yields and livelihoods of smallholders in semi-arid regions of Kenya, which since the colonial period have been heavily subjected to tillage. Our study is based on a qualitative approach that followed local meanings and understandings of soil fertility, rainfall and CA in Ethi and Umande located in the semi-arid region of Laikipia, Kenya. Farm visits, 53 semi-structured interviews, informal talks were carried out from April to June 2015. Ethi and Umande locations were part of a resettlement programme after the independence of Kenya that joined together people coming from different farming contexts. Since the 1970–80s, state and NGOs have been promoting several approaches to control erosion and boost soil fertility. In this context, CA has also been promoted preferentially since 2007. Interviewees were well acquainted with soil erosion and the methods to control it. Today, rainfall amount and distribution are identified as major constraints to crop performance. Soil fertility is understood as being under control since farmers use several methods to boost it (inorganic fertilisers, manure, terraces, agroforestry, vegetation barriers). CA is recognised to deliver better yields but it is not able to perform well under severe drought and does not provide yields as high as 'promised' in promotion campaigns. Moreover, CA is mainly understood as "cultivating with chemicals", "*kulima na dawa*", in kiswahili. A dominant view is that CA is about minimum tillage and use of pre-emergence herbicides. It is relevant to reflect about what kind of CA is being promoted and if elements like soil cover and crop rotation are given due attention. CA based on these two ideas, minimum tillage and use of herbicides, is hard to stand as a programme to be promoted and up-scaled. Therefore CA appears not to be recognised as a convincing approach to improve the livelihoods in Laikipia.

Keywords: Adoption constraints, conservation agriculture, farmers' perception

Contact Address: Gottlieb Basch, Universidade de Évora, Instituto de Ciências Agrárias e Ambientais Mediterrânicas (UE/ICAAM), Largo dos Colegiais n.º2 , 7002-554 Évora, Portugal, e-mail: gb@uevora.pt

Towards Resilient and Profitable Farming Systems in Central Mozambique Using an Open Innovation Platform Approach

SABINE HOMANN-KEE TUI[1], MICHAEL HAUSER[2], CARLOS QUEMBO[3], CLAUDIO GULE[4], FERNANDO ASSANE[4], FELICIANO MAZUZE[3], JULIO ONOFRE RAINDE[5,3], CLAUDIO SIXPENCE[5,3]

[1] International Crops Research Institute for the Semi-Arid Tropics (ICRISAT), Zimbabwe

[2] University of Natural Resources and Life Sciences (BOKU), Centre for Development Research (CDR), Austria

[3] Agricultural Research Institute of Mozambique (IIAM), Mozambique

[4] Provincial Livestock Department Tete (DPASA), Mozambique

[5] International Crops Research Institute for the Semi-Arid Tropics (ICRISAT), Mozambique

Despite growing local and regional markets for crop and livestock products, farmers in Central Mozambique do not benefit adequately. Innovation Platforms help to address some of the intertwined ecological, economical, social barriers, but do not tackle the root causes impeding the transition from subsistence to sustainable, market-oriented farming. In this study, therefore, we develop a methodology for facilitating open innovation niches in dryland and semi-humid ecosystems. We describe lessons from this work, and outline how to engage multiple actors in two different environments. In semi-arid Marara and higher-rainfall Manica, respectively, the niches provide space and momentum for multiple development outcomes: 1. Market oriented goat and common bean value chains providing short-term profits: in Marara registration as association was most important towards empowerment of farmers in market processes; in Manica better organised farmers more than doubled their revenues from common beans; 2. Biomass enhancing technologies tailored to farm types and their capacity to diversify: 60 farmers hosted on-farm food-feed crop demonstrations, illustrating mitigation of dry season feed shortages and increased crop production, enabling greater participation in markets and reduced risk; 3. Mechanism for strengthening longer-term resilience: associations gained tenure security over 13,000 ha land and representatives urged investments in road and market infrastructure and seed quality control; 4. Learning based value, beliefs and behavioural change: inviting a wide range of actors influenced establishment of 4 new associations and influenced more than 1,500 farmers; and 5. The niches created momentum as inclusive and effective drivers for rural change, government expressed will to mobilise resources for support. The integration of actors and their objectives at large scale turned out the single most important success factor. Such integration created a sense of unity, ownership and connectedness. Better self-organisation resulted in new partners and investments. Communities tracking their own progress and presenting advances and challenges to outsiders, such as policy makers or support organisations, strengthened their ability to claim and negotiate. We are developing this approach further, and through multi-level institutional learning build agency for actors themselves to influence the conditions for farming.

Keywords: Innovation platforms, mixed farming systems, Mozambique, profitability, resilience, social capital

Contact Address: Sabine Homann-Kee Tui, International Crops Research Institute for the Semi-Arid Tropics (ICRISAT), PO Box 776, Bulawayo, Zimbabwe, e-mail: s.homann@cgiar.org

ID 848

Assessment of Participatory Monitoring and Evaluation Systems for the Effectiveness of Innovation Processes among Tanzanian Smallholder Farmer Groups

PRAMILA THAPA[1], MARIA JOSE RESTREPO RODRIGUEZ[2], PAMELA NGWENYA[2], BRIGITTE KAUFMANN[2]

[1] *Georg-August-Universität Göttingen, Dept. of Agricultural Economics, Germany*
[2] *German Institute for Tropical and Subtropical Agriculture (DITSL), Germany*

Participatory assessment of rural innovations self-chosen and adopted by smallholder farmers enhances both reflection on their activities and learning for further improvement. As social diversities within farmer groups can affect such assessments, taking them into consideration when designing monitoring systems may enhance effective functioning of innovation processes. This study aims to assess how the facilitation of a participatory monitoring and evaluation (PM&E) system enhance innovation processes.

As part of a transdisciplinary research project, Trans-SEC, we worked with four farmer groups from August to November 2015 in two regions of rural Tanzania. These farmer groups had implemented the following innovations: soap making and commercialising, construction of improved cooking stoves, bicycle renting-out business, and irrigation. We facilitated the development of group-specific 'PM&E systems' and group-assessments of these systems following implementation. Motivations to join the PM&E team, factors influencing PM&E systems, and results of the systems were assessed. Semi-structured interviews (n=25) and group sessions for SWOT analysis (n=4), cost-benefit analysis (n=4), in-depth PM&E follow-up (n=4) and feedback sessions (n=4) were conducted.

Being introduced to the importance of PM&E with examples of success stories, group members became motivated to form a monitoring team. Main motivations were related to their willingness to see the innovation process more transparent, accountable and successful. Those who chose not to participate in the PM&E teams cited old age and other time commitments as factors. In all four groups, the established PM&E systems enabled accountability and transparency among group members for the group resources and responsibilities. The PM&E systems promoted learning among group members by reflection on their action plan and outcomes of innovation processes, which in turn resulted in corrective actions through collective decision making. In implementing PM&E systems, level of education, experiences, gender, time commitment and trust on the monitors played a role.

PM&E systems allowed to assess the innovation specific to their group and revealed to what extent the goals had been achieved. Functioning of the PM&E systems is influenced by group dynamics of each specific case. Hence, efforts should be made to consider such diversities while implementing the PM&E systems.

Keywords: Corrective actions, group dynamics, innovation processes, participatory monitoring and evaluation

---

Contact Address: Pramila Thapa, Georg-August-Universität Göttingen, Dept. of Agricultural Economics, Robert-Koch-Strasse-38, 37075 Göttingen, Germany, e-mail: thapa.prami@gmail.com

Gender-Sensitive Stakeholder Characterisation and Analysis of the Pineapple Supply Chain in Uganda

KATHARINA BITZAN[1], KATHARINE TRÖGER[2], MARGARETA LELEA[1,2], BRIGITTE KAUFMANN[1]

[1]German Institute for Tropical and Subtropical Agriculture (DITSL), Germany
[2]University of Kassel, Agriculturtal Engineering, Germany

Stakeholder identification and characterisation is an important pre-requisite for effective participatory stakeholder processes integral to transdisciplinary research. In food systems research, applying an actor-oriented, gendered lens for this process is necessary to provide insight into the complex interplay between gender and the socio-ecological context in which actors maneuver. In this study, gendered stakeholder analysis of the pineapple supply chain with regard to roles and activities influencing participation in the chain are compared between two districts in Uganda. Within the frame of a transdisciplinary research project that seeks to reduce losses and add value in small-scale East African food chains (RELOAD), this study aims to investigate how women and men actors experience the supply chain in similar and contrasting ways, regarding several factors including their function, activities, and challenges. Qualitative data was obtained during fieldwork in Ntungamo and Masaka Districts in Uganda between July – September 2015. Identification and characterisation of the actor landscape was carried out through semi-structured interviews (n=112) and a combination of mixed and single-gender group sessions (n=22) in which participatory tools were applied including value chain mapping, focus group discussions and fuzzy cognitive mapping. Pineapple supply chains in Ntungamo and Masaka differ in their structure with gender-divisions established more rigidly in Masaka, yet in both gender is found to be an important organising principle, influencing actors' functions, activities and challenges in the chain. Women are more likely to carry out retail, local trading and on-farm supporting roles, whereby it is more likely that owners of pineapple farms are men, and men are also more likely to be involved as traders, brokers, and transporters. Some actors are better able to negotiate constraints placed upon them by gender-related social norms, because of their endowment with different forms of capital (e.g. financial, physical, human) and by leveraging social capital. Gender is shown to influence actors' participation in pineapple supply chains to differing extents in Ntungamo and Masaka, confirming the importance of addressing gender during the process of initiating and establishing stakeholder processes for collaborative learning.

Keywords: Food systems, gender, small-scale agriculture, transdisciplinary

Contact Address: Katharina Bitzan, German Institute for Tropical and Subtropical Agriculture (DITSL), Witzenhausen, Germany, e-mail: katharinabitzan@gmail.com

ID 1002

Building Trust and Collaboration through Co-Learning - Multi-Stakeholder Platforms for Sustainable Intensification of Smallholder Farming in Tanzania

PER HILLBUR[1], CAITLIN MCCORMACK[2]

[1] *Malmö University, Sweden, Dept. of Science, Environment, Society, Sweden*
[2] *SLU, Urban and Rural Development, Sweden*

This presentation focuses on an evaluation of the organisation, functioning and long-term sustainability of Research-for-Development (R4D) platforms established by the USAID Feed the Future programme Africa RISING (Research in Sustainable Intensification for the Next Generation). The case presented here is from Babati District in north-central Tanzania.

Strategies for sustainable management of agricultural resources by rural communities and farmers must be tailored to local conditions and should foster communicaton, collaboration and trust between stakeholders on the ground. This is particularly important for reaching groups with limited access to resources, including women and youth. Furthermore, programmes must be able to incorporate local knowledge and consider the particular challenges in specific contexts in order to design effective interventions and build the trust required to introduce them in local communities. This process of co-learning between local stakeholders and programmes needs to be initiated at an early stage.

R4D platforms were initiated as a model for such institutional collaboration and co-learning for Africa RISING in 2014 and formally launched as the district level platform JUMBA (Jukwaa la Utafiti kwa Maendeleo wilaya ya Babati) in April 2014. This initiative summons all major stakeholders in agricutural development in Babati District and functions as a strategic body for coordination of research and development activities on crop and livestock farming and natural resource management in the district.

One of the challenges is how to follow up and measure the progress and impact of such R4D platforms. Long-term benefits will require strong commitment in the form of local ownership and leadership that fosters mutual trust between stakeholders and a commitment to the sustainability of farming into the future. However, solidarity and trust between stakeholders are seldomly measured in terms of development outcomes. What are the success criteria? For what kind of interventions are platforms suitable or necessary? We consider these aspects in an evaluation of the JUMBA platform based on interviews with key stakeholders in the process.

Keywords: Co-learning, platforms, smallholders, sustainable intensification, Tanzania

Contact Address: Per Hillbur, Malmö University, Sweden, Dept. of Science, Environment, Society, Mandelpilsgatan 31, 212 31 Malmö, Sweden, e-mail: per.hillbur@mah.se

Stakeholders' Participation in Innovation Platforms of Humidtropics in West Africa: Implications on Livelihood Outcomes

Latifou Idrissou[1], Herve Bisseleua[2], Adebayo Ogunniyi[3], Djana Mignouna[1], Peter Olurotimi[4], David Obisesan[1]

[1] International Institute of Tropical Agriculture (IITA), Nigeria
[2] World Agroforestry Centre (ICRAF), Kenya
[3] University of Ibadan, Dept. of Agricultural Economics, Nigeria
[4] Obafemi Awolowo University, Dept. of Agricultural Economics, Nigeria

Key to improving livelihood outcomes is implementation of innovations target at boosting productivity and income of concerned households. This attempt informed a CGIAR research programme with a focus of provision of integrated innovation platforms to enhance improved livelihoods.The programme is designed to work in divers selected agro-ecologies, market conditions, and farming systems to develop innovations, integrating increased productivity, improved market performance, and sustainable management of the natural resource-base in the region. We assessed livelihood outcomes of stakeholder participants and non-participants in the Innovation Platforms established by Humidtropics, a CGIAR research programme on integrated systems for the humid tropical region in Nigeria. A multistage random sampling technique was used to select 200 stakeholders comprising 93 participants and 107 non-participants. Data were collected using structured questionnaire on socio-economic characteristics and five livelihood asset capitals (social, natural, financial, human and physical) of the stakeholders. The data collected were analysed using descriptive statistics and sustainable livelihood model. The results showed that the livelihood asset of the participants (0.72) was found to be significantly higher ($\chi 2 = 3.732$, $p < 0.10$) than that of the non-participants (0.45). The results further revealed remarkable increase from 0 to 0.77 and 0.33 to 0.82 for human capital and social capital respectively, as stakeholders participate in Innovation platforms for research and development. The policy message from this revelation is simply succinct: further investment should be made in the establishment and strengthening of innovation platforms that enable the development, effective dissemination and adoption of agricultural innovations, thus fostering improved livelihood, alleviate poverty and reduce food insecurity.

Keywords: Humidtropics, innovation platforms, livelihood outcomes, participation, West Africa

Contact Address: Latifou Idrissou, International Institute of Tropical Agriculture (IITA), Ibadan, Nigeria, e-mail: L.Idrissou@cgiar.org

ID 1103

Social Capital and Efficiency in Resource Utilisation among Cassava-Based Farmers in Southwestern Nigeria

KEHINDE OLAGUNJU[1], ADEBAYO OGUNNIYI[2], LATIFOU IDRISSOU[3]

[1] *Szent Istvan University, Inst. of Regional Economics and Rural Development, Hungary*
[2] *University of Ibadan, Department of Agricultural Economics, Nigeria*
[3] *International Institute of Tropical Agriculture (IITA), Nigeria*

Despite Nigeria's leading position in world cassava production, the quantity of cassava produced has not reached a level to meet both the demands of local and international markets neither has it attained the much desired potential productive capacity which was attributed to inefficiency in resource use. A number of economic approaches has been put together in various research outputs, unfortunately, few or none examined the potential impact of social capital on optimisation of resource use which necessitated this study.

This study examined the effects of social capital on resource use efficiency in southwestern Nigeria. The data for the study were collected from 390 households in 8 local government areas (LGAs) using probability proportionate to size of the residence in the LGAs. Data analysis was done using descriptive statistics, social capital indices, marginal value product-marginal factor cost approach and ordered probit regression technique. The average cassava farming household size was 5.0 ± 3.7 persons belonging to at least 4 associations, while the average age of the cocoa farming household head was 44 ± 9.8 years. Cassava farming households have meeting attendance index of 65.42 % and decision making index of 7.30 % in the associations. Index of heterogeneity as 58.40 % in association, while, cash and labour contributions were 13.45 % and 10.12 %, respectively. The aggregate Social Capital Index was 23.76 % in association indicating low level of social capital among the cassava farming households. Furthermore, the study reveals that there is under utilisation of all the production inputs under consideration. Specifically, a unit increase in social capital would increase optimum utilisation of resources of cassava farmers by 0.36 %. Social capital was truly exogenous to resource utilisation with no reverse causality. Although, cassava farming households have good meeting attendance, poor decision making and cash contribution in associations however, affected their resource use optimisation. The study concludes that social capital positively affect resource use optimisation; it was therefore recommended that government should create an enabling environment for the emergence of local organisations in terms of their registration and the constitution governing formation of such.

Keywords: Nigeria, participation, resource utilisation, social benefit, social groups

Contact Address: Kehinde Olagunju, Szent Istvan University, Inst. of Regional Economics and Rural Development, 1 Pater Karoly, 2100 Godollo, Hungary, e-mail: olagunjukehindeoluseyi@gmail.com

Trust as Integral to Multi-Stakeholder Processes for Dairy Value Chain Improvement

JOANA ALBRECHT, MARGARETA LELEA, BRIGITTE KAUFMANN

German Institute for Tropical and Subtropical Agriculture (DITSL), Germany

Multi-stakeholder platforms for agricultural value chain improvement do not often focus on primary stakeholders in small-scale food sectors. As the small-scale sector supplies the majority of milk in Kenya, where about 70 % of total milk is produced by smallholder farmers and more than 80 % of the marketed milk is transported by mobile traders, improving the chain requires their collaboration. In the framework of the project RELOAD, this study analyses the process of establishing "bottom-up" multi-stakeholder processes with a focus on the role of relationships between different stakeholder groups with an example from Nakuru County, Kenya.

Primary stakeholders such as smallholder farmers, mobile traders and micro-processors from different parts of the county, as well as secondary stakeholders such as county-level government officials, were invited to engage in multi-stakeholder processes. Data was collected in narrative and semi-structured interviews (n=34), intra-stakeholder meetings (n=6/75 participants) inter-stakeholder meetings (n=5/20 participants), and multi-stakeholder platform meetings (n=6/30 participants). Additionally narrative interviews from continued research by our team in 2016 supplement the data with reflection on the group dynamics that were initiated in 2015.

Coding this qualitative data offers results about relationships, including cooperation and conflict, between different stakeholder groups, as well as how they perceive each other. In the initialisation phase of this action research, trust was required between the prospective participant and the researcher tempered by issues related to past experiences and interests. Those who chose to engage in the multi-stakeholder processes, were later able to gain trust, even among stakeholders who initially may have had negative perceptions of each other. During the multi-stakeholder processes trust was strengthened enabling further collaboration such as exchange of knowledge about feeding cows, and more options for milk marketing. Multi-stakeholder platform meetings allowed for dialogue about how to improve communication and cooperation such as between primary and secondary stakeholders.

Conclusions reveal the importance of trust as a necessary precondition for the successful establishment of multi-stakeholder platforms. The growing trust in the group changed the relationships between participants, creating new possibilities to improve the dairy value chain.

Keywords: Kenya, multi-stakeholder platform, Nakuru County, small-scale dairy, trust

Contact Address: Joana Albrecht, German Institute for Tropical and Subtropical Agriculture (DITSL), Steinstr. 21, Witzenhausen, Germany, e-mail: joana.albrecht@t-online.de

ID 1053

Participatory Assessment of Institutional and Operational Challenges Affecting Small-Scale Dairy Chain Actors' Market Participation in Kenya

FELIX KRAUSE[1], MARGARETA LELEA[2], BRIGITTE KAUFMANN[2]

[1]Georg-August Universität Göttingen, Germany
[2]German Institute for Tropical and Subtropical Agriculture (DITSL), Germany

The dairy sector in Kenya is characterised by the dominance of small-scale actors. Although usually labelled as the informal chain compared to milk trade and processing conducted by large scale operators, small-scale actors increasingly fulfil formal requirements such as paying taxes and acquiring health certificates. However, they still face constrained market access due to lack of adequate information, infrastructure, and financial and human capital endowment, so that there is a need for an integrated assessment of the dairy system. This paper deals with the institutional and related operational challenges of the small-scale dairy sector through a participatory analysis with both primary (e.g. farmers, transporters, retailers) and secondary stakeholders (e.g. government officials) in Nakuru County, Kenya.

The Institutional Analysis and Development (IAD) Framework serves as the theoretical background on which the process of milk production and marketing, and the outcomes obtained by the different actors are analysed using a participatory action research approach. Semi-structured interviews with stakeholders, as well as multi-stakeholder exercises to map stakeholder relations and challenges along the value chain provided information to analyse the institutional environment. Multi-stakeholder processes with the primary stakeholders are facilitated to co-identify entry points for a socially inclusive market development.

Institutional challenges in forms of deficient input and service provision, high transportation costs, and substantial milk price fluctuations raise the need for increased coordination among primary stakeholders. In this regard, the multi-stakeholder processes revealed several entry points for collective action as a promising approach of economic organisation and smallholder advocacy. Furthermore the need for increased harmonisation among research, training, and extension services, as well as among law and enforcement was revealed. As some milk transporters can already afford to shift towards use of aluminium cans, and as some milk retailers are in the position to purchase milk pasteurisers, public and private support to such gradual harmonisation towards formalisation within the institutional environment can enable greater social inclusion of the more vulnerable actors along the chain. Context-specific and demand driven input and service provision, aligned with investments in infrastructure in the remote areas are some of the recommendations that emerged from this participatory assessment.

Keywords: Dairy, IAD framework, Kenya, smallholder market participation, value chain development

Contact Address: Brigitte Kaufmann, German Institute for Tropical and Subtropical Agriculture (DITSL), Steinstrasse 19, 37213 Witzenhausen, Germany, e-mail: b.kaufmann@ditsl.org

The Impact of Farmer Field School Training on Productivity and Crop Income: Evidence from Smallholder Maize Farmers in Oromia, Ethiopia

ADMASSU TESSO HULUKA

Association for Strengthening Agricultural Research in Eastern and Central Africa (ASARECA), Capacity Building and Knowledge Transfer Theme, Ethiopia

This study examines the impact of Farmer Field School (FFS) training programme on productivity and the net crop income of the smallholder farmers. The FFS programme was sponsored by the Ethiopian government and launched in 2010. The study aims to compare the impact of the training on productivity and net crop income of those FFS graduate sand non-FFS graduate maize farmers in Oromia, Ethiopia. For this, panel data were collected in two rounds from 446 randomly selected households of three districts consisting of 218 FFS graduate farmers and 228 non-FFS graduate farmers. The analytical procedure has involved three stages: in the first stage, descriptive analysis was used to detect existence of difference in the outcome indicators between the two farmer groups. In the second stage, a semi-parametric impact evaluation method of propensity score matching with several matching algorithms was applied. In the third stage, difference-in-difference was used as robustness check in detecting causality between programme intervention and the change in outcome indicators. The result shows that the crop productivity growth rate of the FFS graduate farmers was statistically lower than those of non FFS graduates. However, net crop income growth rate of the FFS graduate farmers was not statistically different from those of non-FFS graduates. In most cases, FFS graduate farmers became heavily involved in various mandatory meetings and other activities thereby reducing the time they had for their agricultural activities. Consequently, FFS graduate farmers allocated statistically less family labour per hectare than non-FFS graduates. Following these findings, a number of policy recommendations are suggested.

Keywords: Crop economic income, difference in difference, impact evaluation, productivity, propensity score matching

Contact Address: Admassu Tesso Huluka, Association for Strengthening Agricultural Research in Eastern and Central Africa (ASARECA), Capacity Building and Knowledge Transfer Theme, Cheleleki, Nekemte, Ethiopia, e-mail: admassutesso@gmail.com

ID 318

Collective Action Effects on Farm Productivity and Efficiency of Rice Producers in Vietnam

THAI THUY PHAM, LUDWIG THEUVSEN, VERENA OTTER

Georg-August-Universität Göttingen, Dept. of Agricultural Economics and Rural Development, Germany

Rice is an important staple food in Vietnam. Increasing productivity and efficiency of its production could therefore reduce poverty and food insecurity among the rural farmers. Despite the extensive literature on efficiency and productivity determinants of rice production, empirical work on effects of collective action has remained under-represented so far. To close this research gap, we analyse effects of collective action on productivity and technical efficiency from a sample of 280 specialty rice (SR) farmers randomly selected from the Red River Delta in Vietnam, consisting of 170 producers in specialty rice farmer associations and 110 non-members producers. The results reveal that expenditure on labour and chemicals variables positively contribute to specialty rice productivity while expenditure on other costs has a negative sign. Estimates of the stochastic frontier analysis show an average technical efficiency of 77 %, implying that specialty rice production could potentially be increased by 30 % without raising the current inputs levels. The average technical efficiency of specialty rice producers ranged between 50.4 % and 97.8 %. With regard to the SR farmer associations the average technical efficiency are 79.4 % and 73.5 % for members and non-members respectively. Furthermore, specialty rice association membership has a positive significant effect on farmers' technical efficiency, however the magnitude is small: 9.4 % ($p < 0.01$). That might be due to the fact that many members do not fully respect the technical protocol of their specialty rice associations. Other factors such as planted area under specialty rice, gender and off-farm employment of the household head, and rice farming experience significantly contribute to specialty rice production efficiency ($p < 0.05$), whereas advancement in age of household head reduces production efficiency ($p < 0.1$). There is need to develop and enhance specialty rice farmer associations to increase producers' efficiency. Based on the empirical findings, other wider policy recommendations are proposed.

Keywords: Collective action, specialty rice, stochastic frontier analysis, technical efficiency, Vietnam

Contact Address: Thai Thuy Pham, Georg-August-Universität Göttingen, Dept. of Agricultural Economics and Rural Development, Heinrich-Düker-Weg 12, 37073 Göttingen, Germany, e-mail: pthai@gwdg.de

How Do Local Agro-Pastoralists Judge their Forage Resources?: Using Quantitative Ethnoecological Approach in West Africa

JOHN-BAPTIST S. N. NAAH

University of Cologne, Institute of Geography, Germany

A profound local ecological knowledge (LEK) of natural resources is a prerequisite for a sustainable land management among local farmers in subtropical savannahs, where unpredictable precipitation regimes may negatively influence the quality and quantity of forage resources for livestock production. Notwithstanding, little is still known about LEK of forage resources in the study area. This paper therefore presents quantitative ethnoecological evidence on how local agro-pastoralists judge their forage resources for different livestock types and seasonal regimes in the face of climate change and variability. Using a stratified random sampling, we performed 526 ethnobotanical interviews across three dominant ethnic groups and a steep climatic gradient in Ghana and Burkina Faso. We specifically asked informants to separately list five most important forage resources for dry and wet seasons, and different livestock types (cattle, goats and sheep). Weighted ranks of forage resources were calculated via cognitive salience indices (CSI) using ANTHROPAC 1.0. Our findings revealed that ca. 72.62 % of local agro-pastoralists regarded herbaceous forage plants to be very palatable for livestock consumption in rainy season, but became less relevant (ca. 10.27 %) in dry season, representing a decline of ca. 62.35 %. In contrast, woody vegetation and crop-related forage plants were rather perceived to be more important to domestic livestock in the dry season than in the rainy season. In terms of livestock-specific preferences, herbaceous forage plants were most important to cattle (ca. 45.63 %), while crop-related forage plants were highly ranked for goats (ca. 43.35 %) and sheep (ca. 48.67 %) as compared to other forage plants, irrespective of seasonal type. For instance, *Pennisetum pedicellatum* Trin was adjudged the most salient forage species for cattle and during rainy season, and *Arachis hypogaea* L. was recorded as the most salient species for goats and sheep and in dry season. This study thus throws more light on how local land-users perceive and utilise their forage resources in both periods of abundance and scarcity, and the need for integrated feeding mechanism for sustainable subsistence agriculture and rural livelihood security.

Keywords: Agro-pastoralists, ethnoecological approach, forage resources, local ecological knowledge, West Africa

Contact Address: John-Baptist S. N. Naah, University of Cologne, Institute of Geography, Otto-Fischer Str. 4., D-50674 Cologne, Germany, e-mail: jeanlebaptist@yahoo.co.uk

Multi-Stakeholder Analysis in the Implementation of Upgrading Strategies (UPS) for Enhancing Food Security in Tanzania: Regional Differences between Morogoro and Dodoma

ESTEPHANIA E. DELGADILLO JAIME[1], ERNESTINE MEFOR HALLE[2], FRIEDER GRAEF[3], BARBARA SCHRÖTER[3]

[1] *Technical University of Munich, Faculty of Forest Science and Resource Management, Germany*

[2] *University of Hohenheim, Inst. of Agricultural Sciences in the Tropics (Hans-Ruthenberg-Institute), Germany*

[3] *Leibniz Centre for Agricultural Landscape Research (ZALF), Germany*

The challenges of the current food systems in Tanzania are given mainly by the increasing food demand, unpredictable climate and rural poverty. There is a strong need to improve the current smallholder agricultural production system in order to increase the system´s resilience against future hazards and to improve rural livelihood. This can be done by adapting local agricultural systems through the implementation of upgrading strategies. The Trans-SEC project aims to improve the food situation of the rural poor population by implementing food securing upgrading strategies (UPS) along local and regional food value chains through a participatory platform. The UPS are presently being tested and adjusted to site-specific settings in four villages of two districts, which are located in two different regions in Tanzania. The success of the UPS to a major extent relies on the interactions among the stakeholders. The aim of this study was to understand the stakeholders' social relations that enhance the success of the different UPS. We present the outcome of a social network analysis among the different stakeholders in the different UPS groups. Individual interviews were carried out with different stakeholders followed by the application of the Net-Map tool. Interviews were carried out across the 24 UPS groups; participants were selected through group specific criteria in order to represent the most relevant stakeholders of the groups. Focus group discussions were implemented on each group to jointly discuss the outcomes of the Net-Maps, getting additional insights of the group. Our results explain the roles of the stakeholders, their motivations and relationships. These results are compared between the regions and case study villages in order to further understand the regional differences and driving forces in the performance and success of the UPS. Understanding these relations enables the enhancement and success of long-lasting sustainable UPS solutions.

Keywords: Net-Map, social mapping, upgrading strategies

Contact Address: Estephania E. Delgadillo Jaime, Technical University of Munich, Faculty of Forest Science and Resource Management, Munich, Germany, e-mail: esteph.delgadillo@tum.de

Operational Context as a Driver for Post-Harvest Product Handling Practices: The Case of Pineapple Value Chain in South Western Uganda

Collins Sebuuwufu, Grace Kagoro

Mbarara University of Science and Technology, Biology, Uganda

The pineapple post-harvest system in SW Uganda is characterised by a wide variety of goal oriented product handling practices, in which the value chain actor seeks to regulate the activity system through reflexive observation of his actions, learning and setting handling rules, in order to gain the most income from his engagement in the value chain. The chain actor's capacity however, to effectively direct the post harvest activity system towards the direction he desires, is dependent upon the specific characteristics of the contextual frame in which that activity system is functioning.

The operational context usually consists of a wide range of infrastructural, institutional, financial, technical, knowledge and expertise aspects, all of which provide either opportunities for or constraints to the chain actor successfully influencing the activity system into a direction that ensures that his goal for performing a particular post-harvest product handling practice is effectively achieved.

A context with more opportunities, adequate packaging, storage, processing and transport infrastructure, access to credit, ready market and up to date market information, extension support, facilitates the value chain actor to stay in control and more effectively utilise the activity system to achieve his desired goal. On the other hand, an operational context with more constraints, rudimentary packaging, storage, processing and transport infrastructure, limited access to credit, ready market and market information as well as extension support, greatly limits the capacity of the controller to effectively regulate the system. The chain actor's product handling practices in this case are performed as a way of adapting to the unfavourable context, and much of the sought after benefits are not accrued to the actor.

Keywords: Activity system, constraints, operational context, opportunities, post-harvest product handling practice, value chain actor

Contact Address: Collins Sebuuwufu, Mbarara University of Science and Technology, Biology, P.O. Box 1410, Mbarara, Uganda, e-mail: collinsinno@yahoo.com

ID 84

Relearning Traditional Knowledge to Achieve Sustainability: Honey Gathering in the Miombo Woodlands of Northern Mozambique

Laura Snook[1], Tereza Alves[2], Camila Sousa[2], Judy Loo[1], Georg Gratzer[3], Lalisa Duguma[4,3], Christoph Schrötter[3], Natasha Ribeiro[5], Rosalina Mahanzule[2], Feliciano Mazuze[2], Esmeraldina Cuco[2], Marlene Elias[6]

[1] Bioversity International, Forest Genetic Resources Programme, Italy

[2] Instituto de Investigação Agrária de Moçambique (IIAM), Mozambique

[3] University of Natural Resources and Life Sciences (BOKU), Dept. of Forest and Soils Sciences, Austria

[4] World Agroforestry Centre, Kenya

[5] University Eduardo Mondlane, Mozambique

[6] Bioversity International, Malaysia

Mozambique's Niassa Reserve contains Africa's best preserved miombo woodlands. Half of the households there gather wild honey from natural hives for consumption and income. However, most collectors used destructive techniques: setting fire to the grasses under the hive tree to create smoke and then felling the tree. Cutting trees to obtain honey was the principal source of tree mortality. Trees grow very slowly, about 0.25 cm diameter at breast hight [dbh] per year, meaning an average hive tree was nearly 200 years old. Furthermore, of the trees $> 20\,cm$ dbh of species important for nectar and hives, only about 15 % had cavities. Although fire is intrinsic to miombo woodlands, the increased frequency resulting from anthropogenic sources impedes regeneration of some tree species as well as affecting bees, other wildlife and villages. A few people in the reserve had learned from earlier generations how to gather honey in a non-destructive way, using certain plant species to keep bees from stinging and climbing the trees using ropes to take the honeycombs out of the hives. Traditional practices included leaving the larval combs behind so the colony continued to grow. Previously, the older men who had this knowledge had not been willing to share it with younger men. The project arranged for one of the traditional honey hunters to participate in an international conference on honey collection with other indigenous collectors from around the world. This helped him recognise the value of his knowledge. The project team then arranged for him to demonstrate these traditional techniques to groups of honey hunters in nine communities within the reserve. A year later, monitoring revealed that many collectors had adopted these nondestructive techniques. They found them less time consuming, and appreciated that they allowed collectors to return to the same trees repeatedly to obtain honey. Sharing traditional knowledge made honey hunting compatible with the conservation of miombo woodlands.

Keywords: Bees, conservation, fire, miombo woodland, protected areas, sustainability, traditional knowledge, wild honey

Contact Address: Laura Snook, Bioversity International, Forest Genetic Resources Programme, Rome, Italy, e-mail: l.snook@cgiar.org

The Role of Cooperatives in Serving Farmers within Solidarity: Case of Dire Dawa Multipurpose Cooperative in Eastern Ethiopia

ABDULKADIR WAHAB AMAN

Yildiz Technical University, Economics, Turkey

Dire Dawa is one of the biggest cities in Ethiopia located in the eastern part of the country. With 8 urban and 38 rural kebeles (localities or districts) around 97.73 % of its size is located in a rural area in which 32.5 % of the population lives. The two main ethnic groups claiming the ownership of the city are the Oromo and So-mali. The main sources of income for the farmers of these rural areas are mainly from producing vegetables, fruits, cereals (maize, sorghum) and livestock (camels, cattle and small ruminants). However, these rural areas have dry weather and it af-fects the productivity of the farmers. To reduce such challenges and enhance their market bargaining power, the farmers have organised many cooperatives. These agri-cultural cooperatives, mainly from the main two ethnic groups in the rural areas, help the farmers and pastoralists minimise their socio-economic problems and technolog-ical access limitation. To enhance such benefits, these primary cooperatives formed a multipurpose cooperative union in 2009. This union was formed by 38 primary agricultural cooperatives with more than 6,000 farmers and pastoralists. The major objectives of the union are to encourage internal saving and credit among members, assisting farmers in accessing and using modern technology (for production, process-ing, and marketing), creating better markets and building the capacity of members through training. Currently, the union is one of the most successful cooperatives in the country. It mobilised the farmers and pastoralists together forgetting their ethnic or economic differences. Within the last few years, the number of members reached above 10,000 and its capital is multiplied by five times. It also helped to bring the in-habitants together and get better services from governmental programs and projects. In this study, the successful journey of this cooperative union will be assessed. The way how the union created the solidarity of competing groups will be presented.

Keywords: Cooperative, Ethiopia, solidarity

Contact Address: Abdulkadir Wahab Aman, Yildiz Technical University, Economics, 50. Yil Mah, 2017 Sok. No: 33-35, D:11, Istanbul, Turkey, e-mail: abdiscoop@gmail.com

 ID 699

Stakeholder Analysis in Support of Joint Land Use Decision Making: Case from Xishuangbanna, Southwest China

JUE WANG, THOMAS AENIS

Humboldt-Universität zu Berlin, Albrecht Daniel Thaer-Institute of Agricultural and Horticultural Sciences (ADTI), Germany

The Chinese-German project SURUMER aims at developing integrative, applicable land use options for "Sustainable Rubber Cultivation in the Mekong Region". It is intended to develop complex solutions which improve ecological sustainability of the biodiversity hotspot region but not impair smallholder farmers' livelihoods. For this purpose, land use changes are being analysed, and consequences of different scenarios are being modelled with respect to ecosystem services and trade-offs. From the beginning, stakeholders on different levels of decision-making (village heads, prefecture bureaus, companies) have been involved. Ongoing dialogues are seen as crucial in order to validate the resulting set of options (land use measures and policies), thus increase the likelihood of implementation.

This presentation discusses the role of stakeholder analysis in a broader sense. It describes the whole approach, presents its results and application in the context of the transdisciplinary process, and discusses opportunities and constraints. The approach itself can be characterised as "participatory learning and action": Qualitative data has been collected with a triangulation of empirical methods, analysed by the researchers, and fed back into stakeholder dialogues and inner-consortium discussions, iteratively and reflexively. The whole process includes three pillars: 1) Identification and engagement of key stakeholders; 2) Scenario discussions with information gathered during open and in-depth interviews; 3) Analysis of power structures and communication networks to provide information on framework conditions for further implementation.

Analysis shows that stakeholders are aware of the problems caused by current land-use systems. However, these problems seem not be the prior according to stakeholders' agenda and they are lack of motivation to initiate changes. This implies that linking sustainable land-use with stakeholders' interests and objectives could increase their motivation, e.g. including regional governmental development plan into the scenarios. In addition, external supports could be incentives for them as well, e.g. farmers welcome alternatives with financial or technical supports, and regional authorities are interested in the concrete research results and techniques. In general, stakeholder analysis is beneficial to joint land use decision making. In future it would be good to start as early as possible with adequate time and resource inputs.

Keywords: Decision making, land use, stakeholder analysis, sustainability

Contact Address: Jue Wang, Humboldt-Universität zu Berlin, Agricultural Extension and Communication Group, Luisenstr. 53, 10099 Berlin, Germany, e-mail: jue.wang.1@agrar.hu-berlin.de

Youth and Agriculture in the Drylands: Realities, Aspirations, Challenges of Rural Youth in Midelt, Morocco

Sebastian Mengel[1], Alessandra Giuliani[1], Courtney Paisley[2]

[1]*Bern University of Applied Sciences (BFH), School of Agricultural, Forest and Food Sciences (HAFL), Switzerland*

[2]*Young Professionals for Agricultural Development (YPARD), Italy*

The province of Midelt, Morocco is located between the High and Middle Atlas. Traditional nomadic and sedentary pastoralism and annual and perennial crops play a vital role for farmers' subsistence and income. The study, supported by the Drylands CGIAR Research Program and YPARD, aims at providing a diagnostic analysis to take into account the specific situations of rural youth engaging in the agricultural livelihood systems of dry areas: 'irrigated', 'rainfed' and 'pastoral'. In 2015 and 2016, a group of researchers conducted a survey comprising 106 in-depth interviews with youth and 28 key informant interviews (parents, teachers, employers, associations and Agricultural Research for Development (AR4D) organisations. Focus group discussions gave youths the opportunity to visualise the 'village of their dreams'. In areas where food security was assured, youth raised first the issue of primary needs which are not yet fulfilled, i.e. access to education, health care, sanitation and other basic infrastructure. Excessive degradation of natural resources strongly affects local livelihoods. Many youths are illiterate, own no land, little livestock, and are cut out of job opportunities. Young women are in even more unfavourable positions. Their choices and desires are strongly influenced by their fathers or husbands; their level of education is lower than that of their male peers. The use of information and communication technology (ICT) is limited to mobile phones; internet use is not widespread. Training on agricultural practices is required as the present system of associations fails to include youth. Value added activities in agriculture are limited and migration to urban areas is a controversial issue. Many young people expressed their wish to stay in their villages. However, the difficult conditions of establishing their own independent livelihood in their current place may force many of them to leave their homes in search of a better life. This is why it is so crucial to better understand the realities and needs of rural youth in agriculture. Increased attention is required from the perspective of AR4D, and a better focus and collaborative action from different stakeholders must ensure youth do not remain the neglected group that they were in the past.

Keywords: Migration, Morocco, pastoralism, rural youth, youth aspiration

Contact Address: Sebastian Mengel, Bern University of Applied Sciences (BFH), School of Agricultural, Forest and Food Sciences (HAFL), Blumenstrasse 6, 3052 Zollikofen, Switzerland, e-mail: sebastian.mengel@students.bfh.ch

ID 552

Community-Based Development of Agricultural Activities Aiming to Improve Dietary Diversity in Western Kenya

JULIA BOEDECKER[1], CÉLINE TERMOTE[1], GINA KENNEDY[2]

[1]*Bioversity International, Healthy Diets from Sustainable Food Systems, Kenya*
[2]*Bioversity International, Healthy Diets from Sustainable Food Systems, Italy*

This research examines the suitability of community-based participatory workshops for developing agricultural activities in order to diversify diets. The study represents the second phase of a project consisting of a diagnostic phase covering agricultural biodiversity, diets and nutrition (phase I), participatory development of community activities (phase II) and a participatory implementation of the activities (phase III). The project is part of the nutrition cross-cutting cluster work within Humidtropics, a CGIAR research programme (CRP).

A series of six participatory workshops was carried out in five sub-locations of Vihiga County in Western Kenya. The workshops aimed to raise awareness on nutrition, to discuss the results of the diagnostic phase (phase I) and to identify and plan community activities to improve nutrition. Per sub-location, 36 men and women were selected to participate in the workshops.

In order to diversify diets in their communities, all sub-locations decided to plant vegetables and legumes and to raise poultry. The participants developed community action plans specifying how these activities are going to be realised. In addition, they chose local funding mechanisms to finance the actions and developed a budget. The groups also succeeded in organising an event to officially kick-off their activities and thereby reaching out to other community members.

Except for one less successful sub-location, the workshop groups well developed agricultural activities for improved nutrition. Harmony within the group was a crucial factor for good performance. Sensitivity to group dynamics is thus very important for participatory development of community activities. It was observed that the continuous workshops built trust between researchers and participants and that ownership was developed among the groups. These findings are in line with similar studies on participatory intervention development in Africa. Other related projects in low-income countries stress the importance of community-based approaches in improving nutrition and livelihood outcomes.

Keywords: Agrobiodiversity, community-based participatory approach, dietary diversity, intervention development, nutrition

Contact Address: Julia Boedecker, Bioversity International, Healthy Diets from Sustainable Food Systems, c/o ICRAF, P.O. Box 30677, 00100 Nairobi, Kenya, e-mail: j.boedecker@cgiar.org

Towards Effective Communication between Smallholder Farmers and Village Extension Workers in the MENA Region

NAGWA HASSAN, THOMAS AENIS

Humboldt-Universität zu Berlin, Albrecht Daniel Thaer-Institute of Agricultural and Horticultural Sciences (ADTI), Germany

All over the Middle East and North Africa (MENA) Region, Extension work for agricultural and rural development at village level is lacking effectiveness due to top-down hierarchies and a lack of involvement of farmers in provision of extension. A general lack of communication between smallholder farmers (SF) and village extension workers (VEW) seems to be a crucial problem hindering success of extension.

This case study in Menoufia Region, Egypt,was conducted in order to identify the main reasons and constraints towards effective communication from the users (SF) perspective. Furthermore, suggestions to improve the communication between SF and VEW are deduced. Data was gathered using a questionnaire as a starting point for more in-depth questions. 142 SF in two districts were interviewed by the author who originates herself from an Egyptian smallholder family.

Results showthat nearly half of the farmers complained about non availability of the VEW, one-third didn't know a VEW at all. Information of VEWs is valued generally as insufficient. Regarding extension messages and channels, the majority of respondents stated that they do not play any role in increasing production or solving other problems. Farmers do not even know how to get the extension message. Education level, farm size, participation in extension activities, size of responsibility of respondents and communication with VEW are closely correlated.

Effective communication at village level requires, not surprisingly, first and foremost an increased number of VEWs which receive better qualification, *i.e.* continuous and ongoing provision of training. A focus may be laid on methodology - such as monitoring and evaluation of the extension process and its results - and knowledge exchange between VEW and SF. VEWs need to be able and motivated to set up dialogues with smallholder farmers using individual and group methods, especially field visits; to build social relationship and mutual trust and, to jointly analyse and understand farmer's needs, problems, and livelihoods. A positive attitude is of utmost importance: VEWs should define their own role positively: to help farmers to improve their livelihoods.

Keywords: Agricultural extension, communication, smallholder farmers

Contact Address: Nagwa Hassan, Humboldt-Universität zu Berlin, Albrecht Daniel Thaer-Institute of Agricultural and Horticultural Sciences (ADTI), Unter Den Linden 6. Sitz: Luisenstraße 53, 10099 Berlin, Germany, e-mail: nagwa.hassan1@yahoo.com

ID 453

Improving the Impact of Horticultural Research through Transdisciplinary Knowledge Exchange

EMIL GEVORGYAN[1], STEFAN SIEBER[2], NANCY MUNYIVA LAIBUNI[1], SUSANNE NEUBERT[1], TUROOP LOSENGE[3], MARLEN BACHMANN[1]

[1]*Humboldt-Universität zu Berlin, Albrecht Daniel Thaer-Institute of Agricultural and Horticultural Sciences (ADTI), Germany*

[2]*Leibniz Centre for Agricultural Landscape Research (ZALF), Inst. of Socio-Economics, Germany*

[3]*Jomo Kenyatta University of Science and Agriculture, Horticulture, Kenya*

The uptake and utilisation of horticultural research results by farmers is often problematic since academic top-down research approaches generating only knowledge from selected disciplines have reportedly failed to provide smallholder farmers with affordable, practical and readily available solutions to their problems. Transdisciplinary research approaches often provide platforms to address real-world problems by involving academic and non-academic actors into the research process, thus integrating local knowledge and creating better ownership for the expected research outputs.

This paper presents a research framework that holistically analyses horticultural knowledge generation, exchange and adaptation process in Kenya and bordering regions of Tanzania and Ethiopia using an inclusive transdisciplinary knowledge exchange framework. As case study, novel empirical results will be presented using the transdisciplinary knowledge exchange approach that the multi-stakeholder German-Kenyan research project HORTINLEA (Horticultural Learning for Improved Livelihood and Nutrition in East Africa) aims to support and participate in. It particularly focuses on underutilised African Indigenous Vegetables which represent a great potential in terms of workplaces and income opportunities, the delivery of vital micronutrients for combatting malnutrition and, not least, a raised diversity of agricultural production systems. To promote the transdisciplinary knowledge exchange and sustainable uptake of research results, the expected HORTINLEA-innovations have been analysed and broadly classified in five categories (i) technological, (ii) institutional, (iii) health and environmental, (iv) social, (v) culture and educational. This categorisation has been done based on the results of an systemic assessment of all relevant actors their interactions and relationships, as well as factors from the general political, cultural and socio-economic context, such as institutions, laws, perceptions, business practices and cultural values that affect the sector and its actors' innovative potential. The paper concludes with recommendations in order to further enhance the practice of transdisciplinary research on food and nutrition security through inclusive and sustainable knowledge exchange.

Keywords: African indigenous vegetables, East Africa, food and nutrition security, horticultural research, innovation, Kenya, transdisciplinary knowledge exchange

Contact Address: Emil Gevorgyan, Humboldt-Universität zu Berlin, Albrecht Daniel Thaer-Institute of Agricultural and Horticultural Sciences (ADTI), Robert-Koch-Platz 4, 10115 Berlin, Germany, e-mail: emil.gevorgyan@agrar.hu-berlin.de

World Café: A Key Method to Link Disciplines in International Research

KATHARINA LÖHR[1], MICHAEL WEINHARDT[2], STEFAN SIEBER[1]

[1]*Leibniz Centre for Agricultural Landscape Research (ZALF), Inst. of Socio-Economics, Germany*
[2]*Bielefeld University, Sociology, Germany*

Interdisciplinary research has become a key principle in research on real-world problems such as food security and climate change adaptations, integrating the knowledge and skills of scientists of multiple disciplines, institutes and cultures in order to find viable solutions. Usually a participatory research approach is applied in order to also ensure stakeholder involvement.

While participatory research methods are manifold, few methods such as interviews and focus groups are highly popular to obtain stakeholder knowledge. We introduce and discuss the 'World Café' as additional research method. While the 'World Café' is widely used as an assessment tool in community development and organisational change processes, it certainly has not found its way into standard text-books of qualitative research.

We introduce the 'World Café' as a participatory method of data collection for a large group of participants and discuss potential strengths and weaknesses in comparison to other well-established methods in the qualitative research tradition: semi-structured interviews and focus groups. We link our research to the food security project Trans-SEC that aims to improve the food situation for the most vulnerable rural population in Tanzania, and targets a variety of local and regional key stakeholders. The project consortium is composed of more than 100 scientist and non-scientists from different institutions and countries.

As key result, we evaluated 'World Café' as a method that complements other research methods. It helps exploring and innovating as well as verifying themes with a large number of participants and it is therefore ideal for the field of interdisciplinary and international agricultural research. Furthermore, it is a method that does not only produce data for the researcher but also benefits the participants as it facilitates dialogue and mutual learning.

Keywords: Food Security, interdisciplinary research, participatory research, qualitative research, World Café

Contact Address: Katharina Löhr, Leibniz Centre for Agricultural Landscape Research (ZALF), Inst. of Socio-Economics, Müncheberg, Germany, e-mail: katharina.loehr@zalf.de

ID 504

Role of Chiefs in Managing and Resolving Resource Conflicts between Farmers and Pastoralists in Ghana

KADERI BUKARI[1], PAPA SOW[1], JÜRGEN SCHEFFRAN[2]

[1] University of Bonn, Center for Development Research (ZEF), Germany

[2] University of Hamburg, Institute of Geography, Germany

With increase in the value of land in Agogo-Ghana through commercialisation, commoditisation and expansion in agricultural activities, different resource users are all scouting for resources (land). These actors include local farmers, migrant farmers, Fulani pastoralists, and tree plantation and agro companies. Farmers and pastoralists in particular have engaged in violent conflicts in many parts of Ghana as a result of competition for land resources (farming land, pasture land water) resulting in several deaths, injuries and destruction of farms and killing of cattle. The Agogo area remains the 'hub' of these conflicts with more than 50 media reports of violent clashes in the first quarter of 2016 alone. Traditional chiefs and chiefs of Fulani pastoralists have played active roles in preventing, managing and resolving resource conflicts between farmers and pastoralists. Traditional chiefs in particular who are managers of communal resources have power to mediate between conflict parties over the use of resources as well as decide who is allocated resources. Using interviews and focus group discussions, this study examined the role of chiefs in managing violent resource conflicts between farmers and pastoralists in Agogo in the Ashanti Region of Ghana. The study found that while many farmers and local community members are suspicious of traditional chiefs in their allocation, lease and sale of land and use of resources to pastoralists, farmers and community members nonetheless see traditional chiefs as important in managing conflicts over land disagreements, land allocation and leases and mediating and adjudicating pastoralists' payment of compensation to farmers for crop destruction. Pastoralists' chiefs and cattle owners are also seen as crucial in restraining herders organised attacks and also mediating with farmers over the destruction of crops and use of resources such as land for pasture and water bodies.

Keywords: Chiefs and conflict resolution, farmers, Ghana, pastoralists, resource conflicts

---

Contact Address: Kaderi Bukari, University of Bonn, Center for Development Research (ZEF), Walter Flex Str.3, Bonn, Germany, e-mail: bukarinoagah@yahoo.com

Food and nutrition security and engineering

Food security and nutrition

Fighting Hidden Hunger: Diversity, Composition and Nutrient Adequacy of Diets of Lactating Mothers in Southwest Ethiopia

Sirawdink Fikreyesus Forsido[1], Tefera Belachew[2], Oliver Hensel[1]

[1]*University of Kassel, Agricultural and Biosystems Engineering, Germany*

[2]*Jimma University, Dept. of Population and Family Health, Nutrition Unit, Ethiopia*

Optimal nutrition during lactation is important for the well-being of the mother and the infant. Studies have shown that access to nutrient-rich foods during lactation is critical as inadequate stores of micronutrients can have adverse effects. We assessed the diversity, composition and nutrient adequacy of diets of lactating mothers in Southwest Ethiopia. Community based cross-sectional survey was carried out in three districts of Jimma Zone from March to May, 2014. A multistage stratified sampling technique was used to select 558 lactating mothers. Data were collected using structured interviewer administered questionnaires. Dietary diversity score (DDS) was calculated by summing the number of food groups consumed over the last 24 hours from a scale of seven food groups. The DDS was converted into terciles. The proximate, mineral and anti-nutritional compositions of 12 commonly consumed foods were analysed using standard methods. Nutrient adequacy ratio (NAR) was calculated as the ratio of subject's intake of a nutrient (per day) and recommended daily allowance of the nutrient. The mean ($\pm$SD) DDS of the study participants was 4.51 ($\pm$1.1). The prevalence of "low DDS" was significantly ($p < 0.05$) higher among informally educated, rural mothers, who reside in poor households and cereal producing district. The proximate composition and calorific value of the sampled foods ranged between 24.8–65.6%, 7.6–19.8%, 2.1–23.1%, 2.0–27%, 1.0–21.2%, 0.9–45.8%, 124.5–299.6 Kcal/100g for moisture, protein, crude fat, crude fiber, total ash, total carbohydrate and energy content, respectively. The mineral contents ranged between 9.5–52.5 mg, 2.2–4.2 mg, 42.6–318.2 mg, 150.7–379.9 mg for iron, zinc, calcium and phosphorus, respectively. The anti-nutritional factors contents ranged between 11.1–178.9 mg for phytate and 3.7–315.9 mg for tannin. All the commonly consumed maternal foods were not sufficient to meet the energy, fat and protein requirements, (NAR<1). However, all diets provided adequate iron and majority of the cereal based foods provided adequate carbohydrate and minerals. The overall nutrient adequacy was below the cut-off point for all food types. The diversity and nutrient adequacy of diets of lactating mothers in the study area were below the recommendations. A community based nutritional education based on multi-sectoral approach is needed to curb the problem of malnutrition among lactating mothers in the study area.

Keywords: Dietary diversity score, mean adequacy ratio

Contact Address: Sirawdink Fikreyesus Forsido, University of Kassel, Agricultural and Biosystems Engineering, Nordbahnhofstr. 1a, 37213 Witzenhausen, Germany, e-mail: sirawdink.forsido@student.uni-kassel.de

ID 100

Seasonal Food Availability Calendars for Designing Nutrition-Sensitive Agriculture in Ethiopia

GUDRUN B. KEDING[1], ADMASSU TESSO HULUKA[2], SIMONE KATHRIN KRIESEMER[3]

[1] University of Bonn, Center for Development Research (ZEF), Germany
[2] Association for Strengthening Agricultural Research in Eastern and Central Africa (ASARECA), Capacity Building and Knowledge Transfer Theme, Ethiopia
[3] University of Bonn, Horticulture Competence Centre, Germany

While cropping calendars are a common tool in agricultural production, seasonal food availability calendars are less used. Yet, they could contribute to agricultural production in a more nutrition-sensitive way as they show when which food is actually available for consumption. This includes the time when food is available fresh, from the market, or from storage. The latter in turn reveals whether storage facilities or preservation techniques are successfully used to make food available during all seasons. The NutriHAF project on "Diversifying agriculture for balanced nutrition" in the Yayu Coffee Forest Biosphere Reserve, Ethiopia, collected baseline information through five focus group discussions, one with female and four with male farmers from two different *woredas* (districts). A calendar showing the availability of typical foods within eight different food groups for each month was generated, including foods from own production and the market. The calendars show differences for the two *woredas* situated in the same agro-ecological zone suggesting that markets might source food from different areas. In Hurumu, there were hardly any availability gaps for fruits and vegetables. Yet, less starchy roots and tubers were available from March to September while cereals were less available in July/August. Pulses were available to a lesser extent from April to November except for faba beans. Within Yayu, there was a gap for vegetables from December to March and for fruits from August to October. Pulses were hardly available from May to October, starchy roots and tubers less from June to November and cereals, similar to Hurumu, had an availability gap from June to August. An additional survey within the project is exploring the subspecies level to determine whether different cultivars might be available during different months of the year; and the exact source of the food (own production or market) and the food condition (fresh, from storage or preserved). The final calendar will show during which months certain food groups providing a unique combination of nutrients are lacking. Strategies for filling these seasonal gaps, e.g. through preservation, improved storage facilities or adding late/ early maturing varieties, are available but not yet consequently pursued and applied.

Keywords: Food availability gaps, fruits and vegetables, market, nutrition

Contact Address: Gudrun B. Keding, University of Bonn, Center for Development Research (ZEF), Walter-Flex-Straße 3, 53113 Bonn, Germany, e-mail: gkeding@uni-bonn.de

Exploring the Potential of Wild Sorghums in Sudan as Sources for Improving Grain Minerals and Protein Concentrations

TILAL ABDELHALIM[1], AMRO B HASSAN[2], NAHID ABD ALFATAH KHALIL[3], AMANI ELTAYEB[4]

[1]*Agricultural Research Corporation (ARC), White Nile Research Station, Sudan*
[2]*National Center for Research, Environment and Natural Recourses and Desertification Research Institute (ENDRI), Sudan*
[3]*Dongola University, Agronomy, Sudan*
[4]*Sudan University of Science and Technology, College of Agricultural Studies, Agronomy, Sudan*

Micronutrient malnutrition, and particularly deficiency in zinc (Zn) and iron (Fe), afflicts over three billion people worldwide, and nearly half of the world's cereal-growing area is affected by soil Zn and Fe deficiency. In the case of cultivated modern sorghums, the variation in zinc and iron concentrations in seeds is relatively small. Wild sorghums might serve as an important source of new genetic material for increasing mineral nutrients and protein contents. Exploiting the genetic variation of wild sorghum collections in Sudan for their grain minerals and protein concentration might attract special interest for several reasons. Since Sudan is within the geographical range where sorghum is postulated to be domesticated for the first time, and where the largest genetic variation exists. To investigate this, we studied the variations in zinc, iron, calcium concentrations and protein contents in seeds of 10 wild sorghums, 2 landraces and 4 released sorghum cultivars namely Tabat, Butana, AG-8 and Elwafir. Across all genotypes tested, zinc concentration of the seeds varied from 3.9 to 8.7 mg kg^{-1} with an average of 6.03. The wild sorghum accessions exhibited higher grain iron concentration (15 mg kg^{-1}) and superimposed the released sorghum cultivars and landraces by 74 and 41 %, respectively. The highest concentration of iron was found in the seeds of *S. bicolor* var arundinaceum collected from Elmahkara area (40.3 mg kg^{-1}). The overall average protein contents of wild sorghum accessions were superior to that of released cultivars by 15 %. The highest calcium concentrations were recorded in the seeds of the Safra (296.7 mg/100g) followed by Adar Umbatikh-buda resistance (276.7 mg/100g). It could be concluded that *S. bicolor* var arundinaceum collected from Elmahkara, PQ-434 and Safra could be used as potential sources for iron, protein and calcium biofortification, respectively.

Keywords: Biofortification, malnutrition, micronutrients, sorghums

---

Contact Address: Tilal Abdelhalim, Agricultural Research Corporation (ARC), White Nile Research Station, 300 Kosti, Sudan, e-mail: tilalkosti@yahoo.com

ID 1047

Dietary Exposure to Mycotoxins and Risk Assessment for Adult Consumers of Locally Processed Rice from Nigeria

ROFIAT B. ABDUS-SALAAM[1], OLUSEGUN O. ATANDA[2], MICHAEL SULYOK[3], MARTIN E. KIMANYA[4], RUDOLF KRSKA[3], CYNTHIA A. CHILAKA[5]

[1] *Federal University of Agriculture, Dept. of Food Science and Technology, Nigeria*
[2] *Mcpherson University, Dept. of Biological Sciences, Nigeria*
[3] *University of Natural Resources and Life Sciences (BOKU), Dept. of Agrobiotechnology, Austria*
[4] *Nelson Mandela African Institution of Science and Technology, School of Life Sciences, Tanzania*
[5] *Michael Okpara University of Agriculture Umudike, Dept. of Food Science and Technology, Nigeria*

Exposure to mycotoxins is associated with life threatening disease conditions. In this study, locally processed rice collected from five agro-ecological zones (AEZ) of Nigeria were analysed for some important mycotoxins by a liquid chromatography tandem mass spectrometric method. The data obtained was subsequently used to determine the probable dietary intakes (PDIs) and to carry out a risk characterisation of the mycotoxins. The range of mycotoxin contamination was between $0.27\,ng\,g^{-1}$ for sterigmatocystin and $464\,ng\,g^{-1}$ for zearalenone. The PDIs of the mycotoxins varied significantly ($p < 0.05$) across the zones and the mean national PDIs for total fumonisin (FBT), ochratoxin A (OTA), deoxynivalenol (DON), zearalenone (ZEA), sterigmatocystin (STE), beauvericin (BEA), nivalenol (NIV) and moniliformin (MON) was estimated to be 19.13, 1.50, 5.97, 157.36, 24.85, 15.19, 20.81 and $39.77\,ng\,kg^{-1}\,BW\,d^{-1}$ respectively while that of aflatoxins was $5.20\,ng\,kg^{-1}\,BW\,d^{-1}$. The mean national margin of exposure (MoE) to aflatoxin was 42.78 which was below 10000, thus indicating a public health concern. The co-occurrence of ZEA, STE, BEA and MON occurred most frequently and was about three and a half times more than the maximum % relevant tolerable daily intake (TDI). The study showed that daily intake of mycotoxins especially aflatoxins and zearalenone from the locally processed rice may predispose consumers to harmful health effects of mycotoxins. The continual monitoring of mycotoxin levels in rice will have significant impact on intervention strategies along the value chain.

Keywords: Aflatoxin, agro-ecological zone, probable daily intake, rice, zearalenone

Contact Address: Olusegun O. Atanda, Mcpherson University, Dept. of Biological Sciences, Seriki Sotayo, Nigeria, e-mail: olusegunatanda@yahoo.co.uk

Smallholders and Quality Infrastructure. Safeguarding Quality of Agricultural Products and Natural Resources by Ghanaian Farmers

MILICA SANDALJ[1], EDDA TREIBER[1], THOMAS PFEIFFER[2], NICO WILMS-POSEN[1], DAVID BEXTE[1], ERIK DOLCH[1]

[1] *Humboldt-Universität zu Berlin, Centre for Rural Development (SLE), Germany*

[2] *Mastering aid, Consultant, Germany*

Global consumers of agricultural products are disconnected from food growers. Food safety and quality of products are commonly assured through Quality Infrastructure (QI) services. Assured quality enables agricultural producers to access new markets, beyond the local level. Examples of QI services include the use of laboratory tests, universal measurements, and certification schemes. Ninety percent of Ghana's agricultural sector is characterised by smallholder production. Do smallholders have equal chances to engage in product quality assurance as do large farmers? Is there a need to examine soil properties in times of growing land pressure? These and other questions guided this research commissioned by the National Metrology Institute of Germany. The study looked into the utilisation of QI by maize and pineapple smallholders. In the maize value chain some analysed aspects included the use of laboratory services and test field kits to determine grain moisture and mycotoxin levels. The pineapple value chain was analysed with respect to, amongst others, the utilisation of soil testing and weighing scales on farm level. Main study sites were in Ghana's capital Accra, Brong-Ahafo, a maize growing region, and the emerging pineapple growing Volta region. A qualitative methodological approach consisting of 137 extensive semi-structured interviews, 7 focus group discussions and a workshop allowed interviewing 105 farmers and 137 representatives of ministries, traders, scientists and other stakeholders. Additionally, four soil analyses were performed to assess soil profiles and estimate the need for good soil management. Benefits of fertiliser interventions were assessed with the help of cost benefit analyses. The results showed that very few smallholders use QI services. In contrast, products from large scale farmers undergo food safety and quality tests which allow them to access export and processing markets. Further findings revealed that incentives to use QI for reducing economical, health and environmental pressures need to be linked with other identified obstacles. Such obstacles include lacking market connections, storing facilities and access to finances for smallholders. Soil analyses showed soil deterioration. With the help of QI, soil fertilisation can be improved with relatively low costs, thus contributing to ensuring food safety in times of rising demand for land.

Keywords: Maize, pineapple, quality infrastructure, rural areas, value chains

Contact Address: Milica Sandalj, Humboldt-Universität zu Berlin, Centre for Rural Development (SLE), Hessische Str. 1-2, 10115 Berlin, Germany, e-mail: milicasandalj@yahoo.com

ID 529

Natural Preservatives Minimizing Products Waste in the Supply Chain of the Future

FATANEH YARI

Iranian Research Organization for Science and Technology (IROST), Dept. of Agriculture, Iran

The global population is expected to increase from 7.3 billion in 2015 to around 9 billion by 2050. As a result world demand for food is expected to be 70 % higher in 2050 compared to 2015, mostly in developing and emerging economies in Asia. In recent decades, there has been much research into innovative food preservatives and packaging technologies and solutions. This includes research aimed at reducing the need for chemical preservatives while maintaining the nutritional and sensorial properties of food and increasing the shelf-life of products. Essential oils are a good source of several bioactive compounds, which possess antioxidative and antimicrobial properties; they can extract from different non-edible parts of plants; which are considered as agricultural wastes. Efficient use of natural preservatives has an important role on prevention of losses in supply chain. In this regards, Sour orange old leaves and sour lemon peels were considered as essential oils resource. Following oil extraction, one of the Iranian native citrus (*Citrus sinensis*) treated with different concentration (0, 250 and 500 μll^{-1}) of essential oils to prevent of spoilage and mold growth during storage period; than fruits stored in the passive MAP condition. Treated oranges were evaluated for post-harvest quality after 30 days of 4°C storage. The quality parameters included: weight loss, loss in firmness, colour change, total soluble solids, acidity, and percentage of spoilage. It was found that all treatments have significant effects on various parameters of citrus fruit. Independent of treatments, total sugars and organic acids decreased continuously with increasing storage duration. Packaging provided protection against weight loss and loss of firmness; although delaying the rate of colour change in compare to control was observed with high concentration of sour orange oils. Regarding antifungal activity, the results were satisfactory against gray and green mold growth which varied significantly ($p < 0.05$) with respect to concentration of sour orange oil treatments versus sour lemon. This data allowed deduction to be made fruit and vegetable waste is recycled through essential oils and minimising the amount of product losses and increasing the fair use of resources.

Keywords: Essential oils, natural preservatives, product losses, waste

Contact Address: Fataneh Yari, Iranian Research Organization for Science and Technology (IROST), Dept. of Agriculture, P.O. Box 3353-5111, 3353136846 Tehran, Iran, e-mail: fataneh.yari@gmail.com

The Role of Urban Livestock Keeping in Household Food Security in Bamako, Mali

AZIN SADEGHI[1], MEIKE WOLLNI[2], HAMIDOU NANTOUMÉ[3], EVA SCHLECHT[1]

[1]*University of Kassel / Georg-August Universität Göttingen, Animal Husbandry in the Tropics and Subtropics, Germany*

[2]*Georg-August-Universität Göttingen, Dept. of Agricultural Economics and Rural Development, Germany*

[3]*Institut d'Economie Rurale (IER), Laboratory of Animal Nutrition (Sotuba), Mali*

As the urban population continues to grow, a trend in practicing agriculture, including livestock keeping, has been observed since a few decades both in and within the vicinity of many cities in West Africa. One of the main topics associated with urban agriculture has been the issue of food security. The involvement in urban agriculture can theoretically improve the household's food security through increasing the income as well as enhancing its members' direct access to nutritious food.

The current study aims at accessing the role of livestock keeping in urban and peri-urban settings for household food security status. Data on household food security status as well as livestock-related features were collected for 187 households in urban and peri-urban areas of the Malian capital, Bamako. The household food insecurity status was computed and categorised based on the Household Food Insecurity Access Scale Score (HFIAS) and Household Food Insecurity Access Prevalence (HFIAP).

The descriptive statistics indicate that on average each household comprises 14.93 heads to feed. According to HFIAP, 63.15 % of households are food insecure, of which 24.73 % fall under the category of moderately food insecure and the rest are mildly food insecure. A moderately food insecure household has to sacrifice quality and occasionally reduce the quantity of the food consumed, whereas a mildly food insecure household worries often about access to adequate food and rarely cannot afford the desired food. On average, a food secure household owned 9.37 tropical livestock units (TLU), which was 2.14 units higher that the average number of TLU owned by mildly food insecure households and 3.46 units more than moderately food insecure households. The data on TLU ownership of households shows over-dispersion with many families owing only few animals and some owing a very large number of animals. A negative binomial regression is conducted to check for possible correlation between HFIAS and TLU ownership. The regression results indicate that the coefficient for logarithm of number of the animals owned by households is significant at alpha= 5 % level.

The data thus indicates that a household's involvement in livestock keeping does not totally annihilate the threat of food insecurity in Bamako, even though the size of livestock possession (TLU) is positively related to food security.

Keywords: Household food security, tropical livestock unit, urban and peri-urban livestock, West Africa

---

Contact Address: Azin Sadeghi, University of Kassel / Georg-August Universität Göttingen, Animal Husbandry in the Tropics and Subtropics, Göttingen, Germany, e-mail: azin.sadeghi@stud.uni-goettingen.de

ID 839

Aflatoxins in Dairy Cattle Feed in Senegal

KAREN MARSHALL[1], AYAO MISSOHOU[2], STANLY FON TEBUG[1], IRENE KAGERA[1], DELIA GRACE[1], JOHANNA LINDAHL[1]

[1]*International Livestock Research Institute (ILRI), Kenya*
[2]*Inter-State Veterinary School of Dakar, Animal Production, Senegal*

Aflatoxins are toxic byproducts from moulds, especially *Aspergillus flavus*. These moulds grow on crops, and in particular maize and ground nuts are often contaminated. In humans, aflatoxins cause rare, high case fatality outbreaks (acute aflatoxicosis) while long term consumption leads to hepatocellular cancer (globally, around 20,000 deaths annually). Aflatoxins are also associated with childhood stunting, although a causal relation is not yet proven. Humans are exposed through the consumption of contaminated foods, including cereals, legumes and human and animal milk (as aflatoxins are excreted in milk). Similarly in livestock, aflatoxins cause hepatic disease, immunosuppression and reduced productivity. In tropical and sub-tropical developing countries, aflatoxins are common and 4.5 billion people are chronically exposed. In addition to the burden of this exposure, the reduction in livestock productivity impacts food security and trade and hence increases aflatoxins' total burden.

Knowledge about aflatoxins in Senegal is scarce, especially in relation to the dairy cattle value chain. In this pilot project we measured aflatoxin B1 levels in dairy cattle feeds. Feed samples were obtained from low-input cattle farms in two regions in Senegal (the Thies and Diourbel regions) in August 2015, with between 16 and 36 samples per feed type. Aflatoxin levels were determined by a commercial competitive ELISA. Feeds with the highest levels of aflatoxin were purchased concentrate (with an average of 50 ppb, and a range of 0 to 305 ppb), ground-nut cake (45ppb, 0 to 187ppb) and millet bran (37ppb, 0 to186 ppb). A number of other feeds tested contained aflatoxins at lower levels, namely cornmeal (18ppb, 0 to 104 ppb), wheat bran (9ppb, 0 to 41 ppb) and rice bran (7ppb, 0 to 58ppb). The percentage of feed samples that were above the World Health Organisation's recommended limit for aflatoxin in animal feed (of 5ppb) was high, for example 96 % for ground-nut cake, 80 % for millet bran, and 69 % for concentrate. Although, the aflatoxin levels reported may not significantly affect herd productivity, their impacts on susceptible livestock and carry-over to animal source food may be problematic. Overall, these results suggest the need for further investigation on aflatoxin in Senegal dairy.

Keywords: Feed safety, food safety, food security, mycotoxin

Contact Address: Johanna Lindahl, International Livestock Research Institute (ILRI), Nairobi, Kenya, e-mail: j.lindahl@cgiar.org

Fungal Pathogens Associated with Stored Maize and Nutritional Quality Losses along Supply Chain in Southwestern Ethiopia: Implication for Food Security

CHEMEDA ABEDETA GARBABA[1], FIKRE LEMESSA OCHO[2], OLIVER HENSEL[1]

[1] *University of Kassel, Agricultural and Biosystems Engineering, Germany*
[2] *Jimma University, Horticulture and Plant Sciences, Ethiopia*

Food security and economic well-being of Ethiopia in general depend on agriculture. Maize is considered amongst the top commodities which serve as food security due to its wide adaptability, high production, productivity and relatively cheap calories compared to other cereals. As a result it is included in the national food security strategy. However, maize postharvest losses are tremendous, leading to quantity and quality losses but these are poorly addressed. Therefore, this study was initiated to assess fungal pathogens associated with stored maize and nutritional quality losses along maize supply chain in southwestern Ethiopia. Multistage sampling technique was employed to select five districts that represent different agro-ecologies and major maize producers for fungi mycoflora assessment. Three districts out of five were purposely considered for nutritional and anti-nutritional analysis. In each district different actors along the supply chain were randomly selected for sample collection. Data collection was carried out monthly for fungal damage assessment, and every second month for nutritional analysis till six month storage period. Fungal identification was done by means of morphological characterisation. Nutritional and anti-nutritional analysis was carried out following international standard of Association of Analytical Chemists methods. Collected data were analysed using appropriate software including SAS (version 9.2) general linear model (GLM). Fungal pathogen incidence and severity significantly ($p < 0.05$) increased throughout the study period. *Fusarium* spp., *Penicillium* spp., *Aspergillus* spp., *Phoma* spp., *Geotricum* spp., *Cladosporium* spp. and *Drechslera* spp. were genera isolated. However, *Fusarium*, *Penicillium* and *Aspergillus* spp. which are able to produce mycotoxins were the most dominate fungal genera identified. Crude protein, crude fat, carbohydrate, caloric value and phosphorus content were significantly ($p < 0.05$) decreased as the storage duration increased. But, fiber, ash and major minerals (Ca, Zn and Fe) content were increased along the storage period. This implies the storing maize under traditional storage conditions leads to high damage by fungal pathogens and negatively affects the nutritional content. It has great implication on nutrition insecurity and hidden dietary hunger for the society. Thus, there is a need to develop and disseminate appropriate storage technologies that minimise quantity and quality loss in the store.

Keywords: Agro-ecology, fungi, nutrition loss, storage duration, stored maize

Contact Address: Chemeda Abedeta Garbaba, University of Kassel, Agricultural and Biosystems Engineering, Nordbahnhofstraße 1A, 37213 Witzenhausen, Germany, e-mail: chemedaa@yahoo.com

Assessment of Food Loss and Waste (FLW) Associated with the Cassava (*Manihot esculenta* Crantz) Root Value Chain in Southern Ethiopia

ADITYA PARMAR[1], BARBARA STURM[2], OLIVER HENSEL[1]

[1]*University of Kassel, Agricultural and Biosystems Engineering, Germany*
[2]*Newcastle University, School of Agric., Food and Rural Developm., United Kingdom*

The lack of data on the occurrence of food loss and waste (FLW) prevents governments, research institutes and other stakeholders from realising its socio-economic, nutritional and environmental significance. The awareness of where and how much FLW occurs can help develop better food loss reduction and waste management strategies. The cassava value chain was evaluated in three districts of southern Nations Nationalities and People's Region, Ethiopia, in the purview of GlobE project RELOAD. The objective was to identify hot-spots and causes of FLW demanding strategic intervention. The food (edible parts) loss and waste (inedible parts) were quantified in the framework of the recently developed FLW protocol from WRI (World Resource Institute), which is a multi-stakeholder accounting and reporting standard. Field measurement (direct weighing) and survey (semi-structured questions) were selected as assessment tools from the list of possible quantification methods. In total 200 stakeholders were surveyed with cluster sampling and three replicas of measurements were taken. The food losses were observed in the cassava value chain during peeling and chopping (2.6 %), drying (0.2 %), storage (up to 30 %) and milling (2 %). Losses during storage were highest, primarily due to storage insects. Four insects were identified in the cassava storage systems: *Rhyzopertha dominica*, *Sitophilus zeamais*, *Gnatocerus cornutus* and *Heterobostrychus brunneus*. The predominant use of cassava is in the form of a composite flour of teff, cassava and maize which is further processed into staple flat bread. The waste associated with 100 kg of fresh unpeeled cassava during processing was mostly peels (21.8±4.2 kg). However, cassava production results in considerable amounts of stem cuts wood (9.2 t ha^{-1}) and leaves (2.2 t ha^{-1}) during harvest. Lastly 100 kg of dried cassava flour results in 3.5±0.5 kg fibrous material after sieving. The peeling and chopping is carried out by woman with local knives which is labour intensive (8 hours/100 kg fresh cassava). Sun drying of cassava chips takes up to 14 days depending on weather conditions which adds the risk of fungal growth, soil contamination and pilferages. Interventions with simple technologies at processing and storage stages can lessen the drudgery particularly of woman workers, improve the quality of the final product and reduce the food losses.

Keywords: Cassava, food loss, storage insects, waste

Contact Address: Aditya Parmar, University of Kassel, Agricultural and Biosystems Engineering, Nordbahnhofstrasse 1a, 37213 Witzenhausen, Germany, e-mail: aparmar@hotmail.de

Traditional Foods Contribute to the Minimum Dietary Diversity Score of Indigenous Woman in Guasaganda, Ecuador

DOLORES PENAFIEL[1], CARL LACHAT[2], RAMON ESPINEL[3], PATRICK VAN DAMME[1]

[1]Ghent University, Dept. of Plant Production, Belgium
[2]Ghent University, Dept. of Food Safety and Food Quality, Belgium
[3]Escuela Superior Politecnica del Litoral, Life Science, Ecuador

The objective of this study was to document the intake of traditional foods by indigenous women in Guasaganda, central Ecuador, and evaluate the nutrient adequacy of the diet and the nutrient contribution of the consumed traditional foods.

Therefore a two-step cluster design was used. Initially, 18 villages were selected from a list retrieved by the Ecuadorian Institute of National Surveys (INEC) using probability proportionate to size. Then households were selected at random using a list of household identified by GPS points. The intake of traditional foods was recorded during 2 visits using a 24 hour recall (n=260).

The intake of energy, protein, total fat, carbohydrates total, carbohydrates available, dietetic fibre, calcium, iron, zinc, vitamin A and vitamin C was documented. Also, the intake of the 15 most consumed foods was listed. To evaluate the adequacy of the diet the Mean Adequacy Ratio and the Women Dietary Diversity Score were reported. Summary statistics were used to report the nutrient intake of studied women. To report the Mean Adequacy Ratio, nutrient adequacy ratios of 10 nutrients were calculated. Additionally, the Multiple Source Method was used to reduce interpersonal variability using the two visits.

The results show that the studied diet is adequate for most of the macro- and micronutrients, with a Women Dietary Diversity Score higher than 5 (7) and a Mean Adequacy Ratio close to 1 (0.79). The consumption of traditional foods contributes to 80 % of the Recommended Nutrient Intake for protein, 52 % for fat and 40 % for carbohydrates. The Recommended Nutrient Intake for Vitamin C is fully reached by the consumption of local foods. Plantains, milk, banana, papaya and oranges are the most consumed local foods.

Traditional foods are important contributors of nutrients to indigenous peoples' diets. Promoting the consumption of the former is key of future food-sovereignty interventions.

Keywords: Diet, Ecuador, indigenous people, women

Contact Address: Dolores Penafiel, Ghent University, Dept. of Plant Production, Coupure Links 653, 9000 Ghent, Belgium, e-mail: doloresdaniela.penafielanchundia@ugent.be

ID 558

An Agro-Climatic Zone Perspective of Factors Influencing Stunting among Children in Rural Tanzania

HADIJAH MBWANA[1], JOYCE KINABO[1], CHRISTINE LAMBERT[2], HANS KONRAD BIESALSKI[2]

[1] *Sokoine University of Agriculture, Food Science and Technology, Tanzania*

[2] *University of Hohenheim, Inst. of Biological Chemistry and Nutrition, Germany*

This paper uses household cross-sectional survey from a sample of 120 households from rural Dodoma and Morogoro regions in Tanzania to analyse factors influencing stunting in children residing in rural areas of differing agro-climatic conditions in Tanzania. Demographic, socioeconomic and mothers/caregivers' knowledge in nutrition and kitchen gardening information was collected using a semi structured questionnaire. Nutritional status was assessed by measuring the weight, height and haemoglobin level of children and their mothers or caregivers. The paper uses logistic regression models to establish relationships between stunting and multiple categorical variables. The study finds out that the prevalence of stunting and severe stunting in children was 41 % and 21 % respectively while 11 % of women had Body Mass Index of below 18.5. Results also indicate that 17 % and 16 % of children and women were anaemic respectively. Determinants of child stunting in Dodoma are sex and age of the child, duration of breastfeeding, household size, use of iodized salt and the distance to a water source. In Morogoro child's age, duration of breastfeeding, literacy status of mother and Body Mass Index of mother predict stunting. Evidence that factors causing malnutrition vary according to different agro-ecological conditions was clearly indicated in this study. Therefore, we conclude that agro-climatic variations somewhat predict the variation in child stunting. It is therefore recommended that nutrition interventions should not be too general but specific to various agro-climatic environments. Implementing agro-climatic sensitive well thought actions may help to reduce undernutrition and food insecurity in specific areas. There is also need to improve access to portable water: provision bore-wells that can provide drinking and household consumprion water to residents in areas whether there is a need of walking of 60 minutes or more to fetch water.

Keywords: Agro-climatic, anaemia, kitchen gardening, nutritional status, rural, stunting

---

Contact Address: Hadijah Mbwana, Sokoine University of Agriculture, Food Science and Technology, Morogoro, Tanzania, e-mail: hadija27@yahoo.com

The Role of Biodiversity and Natural Resource Management in Food Security in South Eastern Madagascar

NARILALA RANDRIANARISON[1], SARAH NISCHALKE[2], SECONDE FRANCIA RAVELOMBOLA[1]

[1]University of Agricultural Sciences, NutriHAF Project, Madagascar
[2]University of Bonn, Center for Development Research (ZEF), Germany

Madagascar still ranks low on the HDI (rank 151) and about one third of the population is undernourished. South Eastern Madagascar with its rich biodiversity has the highest rate of food insecurity (64 %) and the largest proportion of households with a poor diet with regard to quantity and quality.

This study aims at exploring consumption behaviour of rural populations and understanding the reasons for poor nutrition and micronutrient deficiencies in the area. The role of biodiversity for the diversity of diets is investigated and assessed along with natural resource management practices and usage of ecosystem services with regard to contribution to diet diversity, livelihoods as well as their sustainability.

The data for this study was collected through ethnography, 16 gender-disaggregated focus group discussions and about 300 in-depth interviews with smallholder farmers as well as key stakeholder interviews in two village sites in Atsimo Atsinanana Region in South Eastern Madagascar.

The research showed that food consumption is characterised by a high priority for staple foods, so that three quarters of the daily calorie intake is covered through rice, cassava or maize. Despite the high biodiversity in the region people do not consume a balanced diet. Whereas fruit consumption is relatively high, perception and consumption of vegetables is low ("vegetables" are considered as green leaves). Eating fish is not common and meat is not affordable for most, so consumption is also not meeting nutritional needs. Especially the poorest people in the region highly depend on hunting, fishing and gathering of wild foods from their surroundings to supplement their deficient diets. Hence, a healthy ecosystem plays a vital role in diversification of diets of the people and in providing additional livelihood sources (e.g. material for basketry). Through that they maintain a close relation with nature and the environment.

The paper will also look into how sustainable such practices are and what effects established collective rules (*dina*) for natural resource management by local authorities (*Ampanjaka*) have. Apparently they are respected well. In a last step, recommendations are given how interests of conservation and utilisation can be harmonised.

Keywords: Balanced diet, biodiversity, food insecurity, natural resource management

Contact Address: Sarah Nischalke, University of Bonn, Center for Development Research (ZEF), Bonn, Germany, e-mail: snischal@uni-bonn.de

ID 1077

Dietary Contribution of African Indigenous Vegetables to Rural and Peri Urban Households in Kenya

OCHIENG RONALD MWANGA, SINDU KEBEDE, WOLFGANG BOKELMANN

Humboldt-Universität zu Berlin, Albrecht Daniel Thaer-Institute of Agricultural and Horticultural Sciences (ADTI), Germany

Food security is a serious recurrent problem in developing countries. Contemporary research on food security has reached consensus that food security has four components namely availability, access, utilisation and stability (continuity). We focus on the access and availability dimensions to determine the adequate dietary intake of nutrients. Population explosion and climate changes call for novel agricultural based hunger eradication strategies.

We argue that incorporating African Indigenous Vegetables (AIVs) in daily diets is a key step in ensuring food security. They contain high levels of vitamin A, C, iron, calcium, magnesium and protein and are a valuable source of nutrition in rural areas. Production of AIVs does not require much capital investment, involves short labour-intensive production systems and low level of purchased inputs. This makes it relatively easy for resource poor households to plant them in their backyards or inter-crop them with staple crops such as maize.

The above characteristics of AIVs have important implications to the contribution of AIVs to food security. On the one hand, because of the macro and micronutrients that AIVs contain, they are the closest solution to the 'hidden hunger' dimension of food security. On the other hand, because of their production characteristics, they become handy in filling the food insecurity problem of poor and vulnerable population.

We use data from the HORTINLEA survey collected on 1232 AIV producers in rural and peri-urban areas of Kenya in 2014 by Humboldt University of Berlin in collaboration with Egerton University. We analyse the five priority indigenous vegetables namely amaranth, cowpeas, African nightshade, spider plant, and the Ethiopian kale. Quantitative analysis is conducted using food security indicators produced by ADePT-Food security Module (ADePT-FSM) data analytical software.

Our findings indicate that, consumption of AIVs provides a maximum of 48.6 Kcal day^{-1} which covers estimated 2.3 % of the total energy requirement. The AIVs contain significant protein content that add variety to staple diets at comparatively low median dietary unit values. They cover up to 48 % of additional protein requirement for vulnerable groups like pregnant and lactating mothers. Therefore, efforts to enhance AIVs consumption should be sustained through research, awareness and policy formulations.

Keywords: African indigenous vegetables, food security, nutrients

Contact Address: Ochieng Ronald Mwanga, Humboldt-Universität zu Berlin, Faculty of Life Sciences, Oberfeldstrasse 132, 12683 Berlin, Germany, e-mail: rnldmwanga@yahoo.com

The Role of Edible Aroids in the Elimination of Hunger and Poverty in Sub-Saharan Africa

KARIN VANEKER[1], BAMWESIGYE DASTAN[2], ERWIN SLAATS[3]

[1]*Independent researcher, The Netherlands*

[2]*Mendel University, Fac. of Regional Development and International Studies, Czech Republic*

[3]*Lekker Ontwerpen, The Netherlands*

Aroids or taro (L. Araceae) are the world's most ancient food crops. Their antiquity and central role in agriculture and food cultures is underlined by the symbolic meaning and cultural value of the plants, plant parts and numerous dishes. Since times immemorial, aroids have been maintained in a wide range of agro-ecologies. In the tropics, elephant ear (L. *Alocasia*); elephant foot yam (L. *Amorphophallus*) and swamp taro (L. *Cyrtosperma*) are of importance, but taro (L. *Colocasia*) and tannia (L. *Xanthosoma*) are the most widely cultivated and consumed aroids. All plant parts are eaten and nutritious, but they are foremost cultivated for their starchy underground parts.

In sub-Saharan Africa (SSA) taro and tannia are important food crops and wild-harvested plants that make a valuable contribution to the rural and urban diet. Although the scope and scale of cultivation for local and home consumption is unknown, it is estimated that SSA accounts for three-quarters of the global production of taro and tannia roots and tubers, often referred to as cocoyams. Because they are mostly grown by small and subsistence farmers that rely on infertile and marginal soils for food, income and employment, cocoyams are often nicknamed a food security and poor man's crops.

Currently most of the world's poorest nations are located in SSA, a region faced with chronic food insecurity, climate change, loss of biodiversity and soil degradation. Even though cocoyams grow well in marginal, often harsh and complex environments not well suited for intensive agriculture and conventional staple crops such as wheat, corn and rice, schemes to address a fair use of resources hardly incorporate cocoyams. The authors will examining the role of cocoyams in SSA farming systems, cuisines and cultures, and show that there are practical, cultural, and moral grounds to optimise the cultivation and utilisation of cocoyams.

Keywords: Aroids, cocoyams, cuisine and culture, food insecurity, small farmers, soil degradation, sub-Saharan Africa

Contact Address: Karin Vaneker, Independent researcher, Zuideinde 71, 1511 GB Oostzaan, The Netherlands, e-mail: karinvaneker@braitman.com

ID 534

Edible Insects of Ghana: Opportunities for a Food Secure World

JACOB ANANKWARE PAARECHUGA[1], DANIEL OBENG-OFORI[2]

[1]*Aspire Food Group, Research and Production Unit, Ghana*

[2]*University of Energy and Natural Resources, Dept. of Horticulture and Crop Production, Ghana*

A survey was conducted to identify and taxonomically classify the major neglected and underutilised edible insects of Ghana in order to assist in developing programmes for their enhanced utilisation. Two thousand questionnaires were administered using key informant interviews, focus group discussions and direct observation to randomly selected respondents in all the ten regions of Ghana. A total of nine different species of major edible insects belonging to four orders were identified. The nine edible insects in Ghana are: palm weevil (*Rhynchophorus phoenicis* Fabricius) larvae, termites (*Macrotermes bellicosus* Smeathman), ground crickets (*Scapteriscus vicinus* Scudder), field crickets (*Gryllus similis* Chapman), house cricket (*Acheta domesticus* Linnaeus), grasshopper (*Zonocerus variegatus* Linnaeus), locust (*Locusta migratoria* Linnaeus), shea tree (*Cirina butyrospermi* Vuillot) caterpillar and scarab beetle (*Phyllophaga nebulosa* Harris) larvae. The scarab beetle (2 %), field cricket (5 %), shea tree caterpillar (8.7 %), ground cricket (9.5) and the locust (10) were the least consumed insects whereas palm weevil larvae (47.2 %), termites (45.9 %), house cricket (33.3 %) and grasshopper (30.5 %) were the most consumed insects in Ghana. Northern Ghana currently dominates in entomophagy; especially the Upper West and Upper East regions where eight out of the nine identified insects are consumed. Whereas the honey bee and termite were consumed in all the ten regions of Ghana, the palm larva was consumed mainly in the middle belt and southern Ghana; where the palm tree thrives. The other insects are consumed mainly in the northern part of Ghana. Termites, field crickets, ground crickets, house crickets, grasshoppers and locusts are consumed by almost all tribes in Ghana.

Keywords: Classification, edible insects, identification, palm weevil larva, termites

Contact Address: Jacob Anankware Paarechuga, Aspire Food Group, Research and Production Unit, Kings Cottage Chapel, Denkyemouso, Kumasi, Ghana, e-mail: anankware@yahoo.com

Identification of Species and the Traditional Uses of Edible Insects by Indigenous Communities Awajún in Peruvian Amazon

RUBEN CASAS REATEGUI[1], ZBYNEK POLESNY[1], PABLO PEDRO VILLEGAS PANDURO[2]

[1]*Czech University of Life Sciences Prague, Fac. of Tropical AgriSciences, Dept. of Crop Sciences and Agroforestry, Czech Republic*

[2]*National Intercultural University of the Amazon, Dept. Agroforestal Acuicola, Peru*

Currently, insects are a resource exploited as food by indigenous communities in the Peruvian Amazon as important source of protein for these populations.The proposed study was conducted in four Awajun communities of the district of Cenepa in Northwest of the Peruvian Amazon. The main objective was to document the traditional knowledge on usage and collection patterns of edible insects in Awajum communities. Secondary objectives were to determine species/taxonomic of edible insects. Samples of insects used as food were collected and preserved in vials with 70% alcohol. For the identification and characterisation of the collected insects published keys were used. A consolidated list of edible insects used in the four indigenous communities Awajún has been prepared. The list is based on thorough, semi-structured field-interviews with 44 informants of each communities. At least 10 insect species, belonging to two orders were considered edible. Coleoptera (05) *Metamasius hemipterus* (Picudo Rojo), *Rhynchophorus palmarum* (Suri), *Rhinostomus barbirostris* (Suri blanco) of the Curculionidae family; *Stenagostus rhombeus* (Chuu) of the family Elateridae; *Megaceras crassum* (Papaso) of the Scarabaeidae family and Hymenoptera (05) *Cephalotes atratus* (Dakerae), *Crematogaster sordidula* (Hormiga), *Atta cephalotes* (Siquisapa), *Agalaia pallipes* (Avispa amarilla), *Mischocyttratus* spp. (Huayranga) of the Formicidae family. As far as usage and collection of insects are concerned, food insects are chosen by members of the communities according to taste, as well as regional and seasonal availability. Depending on the species, only certain, but sometimes all, developmental stages are consumed. The preparation of the food insects for consumption involves mainly roasting, boiling or covering these with leaves.

Keywords: Awajún communities, edible insects, entomophagy, forms of consumption, traditional knowledge

---

Contact Address: Ruben Casas Reategui, Czech University of Life Sciences Prague, Fac. of Tropical AgriSciences, Dept. of Crop Sciences and Agroforestry, Kamýcká 129, 165 21 Praha 6 Suchdol, Czech Republic, e-mail: rcasasr@yahoo.com

Consumer Preferences and Market Segmentation for Differentiated Beef with Less Environmental Impact

KAREN ENCISO[1], STEFAN BURKART[1], ANDRES CHARRY[2], CRISTHIAN DAVID PUERTA RODRIGUEZ[1], JHON JAIRO MUÑOZ QUICENO[3], LISBETH ROCIO RUIZ[3], JHON FREDDY GUTIERREZ SOLIS[1], NELSON JOSÉ VIVAS QUILA[3], NOÉ ALBÁN LOPEZ[3], SANDRA MORALES VELASCO[3], MICHAEL PETERS[1]

[1] International Center for Tropical Agriculture (CIAT), Colombia
[2] University of Hohenheim, Institute for Farm Management, Germany
[3] University of Cauca, Department of Agricultural Sciences, Colombia

Environmental awareness is increasing globally and this leads to a segment of consumers willing to pay a higher price for products developed under more environmentally friendly conditions. In Colombia, beef production is specifically characterised by extensive management, with low levels of productivity and a significant negative environmental impact. Taking into account this problem, the International Centre for Tropical Agriculture (CIAT) and the University of Cauca in Colombia have worked during the last decade on the development of new alternatives for livestock production, such as improved forages, farming practices and silvo-pastoral systems, which generate significant benefits for the environment (e.g., reduction of greenhouse gas emissions, protection and maintenance of soil fertility, biodiversity conservation) while also improving productivity levels (load capacity and weight gain). However, the implementation of these new technologies often requires high levels of initial investment, which detains producers from adoption. Thus, identifying a segment of consumers willing to pay for beef produced with less environmental impact would create an incentive for producers to invest in new technologies and result in higher levels of adoption.

This study aims to determine the relevant consumer segment for beef produced with less environmental impact. For this purpose, a consumer characterisation will be performed in order to know the preferences, buying habits and consumption of beef and its main substitutes (chicken, fish, pork). As a result, a market segmentation based on variables of socio-economic and demographic character will be conducted. The methodology consists of a descriptive analysis using contingency tables and relative frequencies, and an analysis of market segmentation using a CHAID algorithm and association tests (X2). Information was collected in April 2016 through personal interviews, with a pre-structured questionnaire for consumers directly responsible for buying meat. Research areas are the cities of Cali and Popayan, and the municipalities of El Patía and El Bordo, all in the Colombia Cauca and Cauca Valley Departments. Data analysis will take place in May 2016 testing the hypothesis that level of income, education, age and gender are significant determinants for identifying the segment of potential consumers of differentiated beef with less environmental impact.

Keywords: Beef, CHAID algorithm, Colombia, consumer preferences

Contact Address: Stefan Burkart, International Center for Tropical Agriculture (CIAT), Tropical Forages Program, Km 17 Recta Cali-Palmira, Cali, Colombia, e-mail: s.burkart@cgiar.org

Willingness to Pay for Beef with a Reduced Environmental Footprint in Cali and Popayán, Colombia

Andres Charry[1], Stefan Burkart[2], Manuel Narjes[1], Karen Enciso[2], Cristhian David Puerta Rodriguez[2], Jhon Jairo Muñoz Quiceno[3], Lisbeth Rocio Ruiz[3], Jhon Freddy Gutierrez Solis[2], Nelson José Vivas Quila[3], Noé Albán Lopez[3], Sandra Morales Velasco[3], Michael Peters[2]

[1] University of Hohenheim, Institute for Farm Management, Germany
[2] International Center for Tropical Agriculture (CIAT), Colombia
[3] University of Cauca, Department of Agricultural Sciences, Colombia

Cattle production contributes with nearly 15 % of all human induced greenhouse gas emissions, but given its current conditions it is a sector with high potential for mitigating the negative environmental impacts of human activity. In countries with extensive livestock systems (such as Colombia) the emissions per unit of production may be particularly high due to, among others, low productivity. The International Center for Tropical Agriculture (CIAT) and the research group for agricultural nutrition of the University of Cauca work on developing a combination of improved forages and management practices that substantially reduce the livestock sector's carbon footprint. These technologies and practices also allow for an increase in livestock productivity but require significant setup investments. For being able to motivate livestock producers in investing in such technologies, the market potential for a differentiated final product has to be known and communicated.

This study will provide a market assessment in order to identify potential consumers of beef with a reduced environmental footprint and to determine their willingness to pay for such a product. In detail, this study will assess the state of the art of the consumers' knowledge about the environmental footprint of beef production, identify consumer segments that are willing to pay a price premium for a more eco-friendly beef, and determine the extent of such a price premium. This information will help in connecting livestock producers that are willing to produce under more environmentally friendly conditions, with emerging markets for such niche products. Research area will be Popayán and Cali, two of the most important cities in the southwest of Colombia. Data will be obtained from April to July 2016, through a series of focus group discussions followed by a discrete choice experiment (DCE). The authors will test the hypotheses that the current consumers' knowledge of the negative impacts of livestock production is low, and that increasing income and education are significant factors for determining the consumer segment that may be willing to pay a price premium for beef with a reduced environmental footprint.

Keywords: Discrete choice experiment, improved forages, livestock production

Contact Address: Andres Charry, University of Hohenheim, Institute for Farm Management, Stuttgart, Germany, e-mail: charryandres@gmail.com

ID 220

Development of a Sustainable Intensification Indicators Framework: Reports from the Frontline in Mali and Malawi

SIEGLINDE SNAPP[1], PHILIP GRABOWSKI[1], MARK MUSUMBA[2], CHERYL PALM[2], REGIS CHIKOWO[1], MATEETE BEKUNDA[3]

[1] Michigan State University, Plant Soil and Microbial Sciences, United States of America
[2] Columbia University, Earth Institute, United States of America
[3] International Institute of Tropical Agriculture (IITA), Tanzania

An emerging area of science is 'Sustainable Intensification', with a focus on efficient use of resources for agriculture, with attention to equity and environmental services. Our multidisciplinary team is assessing the view of practioners using sustainable intensification indicators framework for agricultural research in development. Documentation was through semi-quantitative interviews and systems dynamics exercises conducted during site visits with Africa RISING farming systems researchers in Mali and Malawi. The protocols in use by scientists were collected and assessed to document types of sustainable intensification indicators and metrics. A systems dynamic exercise was introduced as a means for researchers to consider all five domains. We evaluated metrics in use by researchers in relationship to sustainable intensification indicators and metrics that were developed through literature review and a consultative process as a living document, as a sustainable intensification framework. The sustainable intensification framework includes systematic consideration of five domains: production, economics, environment, social and human. A comparison was conducted of metrics in use and how these could be expanded or refined. At all locations production and economic sustainable intensification indicators were being used in assessment of technology performance and farming systems outcomes, whereas at some sites environmental indicators were monitored as well. The domains of social and human capacity building were rarely considered in a systematic manner, such as metrics for nutrition and equity status. The later indicators were judged by many participants to provide new insights into aspects of sustainable intensification. Overall, the sustainable intensification indicators framework provided a systematic means to consider tradeoffs and opportunities for sustainable intensification.

Keywords: Agriculture development, environment, equity, farming systems, indicator, metric, sustainable intensification

Contact Address: Sieglinde Snapp, Michigan State University, Plant Soil and Microbial Sciences, 1066 Bogue St., 48824 East Lansing, United States of America, e-mail: snapp@msu.edu

Smoking of Milk Containers Improved Microbiological and Organoleptic Quality of Fermented Milk

ALEMAYEHU TADESSE[1], VEERLE FIEVEZ[2], FRANS SMEULDERS[3], BRUNO GODDEERIS[4], JOZEF DECKERS[5], NIGSTI HAILEMARIAM[1], MARK BREUSERS[6]

[1]Mekelle University, Animal, Rangeland and Wildlife Sciences, Ethiopia
[2]Ghent University, Animal Production (Lanupro), Belgium
[3]Green Watt, Biogas Plants Fitting Your Wastes, Belgium,
[4]KU Leuven, Biosystems, Division Gene Technology, Belgium
[5]KU Leuven, Earth and Environmental Sciences, Belgium
[6]KU Leuven, Faculty of Social Sciences, IARA, Belgium

The effect of fumigating milk containers was examined by smoking, using wood from one of the three following tree species (*Acacia etbaica*, *Olea europaea* ssp. *cuspidata* and *Cadia purpurea* vs. a non-smoked control) on biochemical, microbiological and organoleptic quality of milk, traditionally fermented for 0, 48, 96 or 144 hours. A plastic milk container of 1.2 liter capacity was fumigated by inverting it over smoking chips of 5 g of the specific tree species until the smoke died out (about 2–3 minutes). About 700 ml of milk were stored in this container at ambient room temperature of $24\pm0.8°C$ for the respective fermentation period. The change in pH, titratable acidity (TA %), standard plate count (SPC) and coliform count (CC) of the fermented milk from each treatment was determined. Organoleptic quality parameters (aroma, flavor, appearance and overall acceptance) of the fermented milk were evaluated by 10 panelists based on a 5 point hedonic scale. An interaction effect of container smoking and fermentation period ($p < 0.05$) was observed for TA, SPC and CC values. SPC and CC values tended to increase till 96 hour fermentation period in all treatment groups and slightly reduced thereafter. A rapid drop of pH was observed in the first 48 hours incubation. The SPC of milk samples stored in the smoked containers ranged between 6.84–7.53 log CFU ml^{-1} as compared to non-smoked container (7.66 log CFU ml^{-1}). TPC and CC in milk fermented for 48 and 96 hour stored in a container smoked with *Acacia etbaica* were reduced by 1.39 and 0.87 log CFU; and 0.98 and 1.09 log CFU as compared to their respective values in the non-smoked containers, respectively. Furthermore, flavor, appearance and overall acceptance scored better in smoked as compared to non-smoked containers.

Keywords: Coliform count, pH, smoking, titrable acidity, standard plate count

Contact Address: Alemayehu Tadesse, Mekelle University, Animal, Rangeland and Wildlife Sciences, Mekelle University Endayesus Campus, 231 Mekelle, Ethiopia, e-mail: alextmu@yahoo.com

ID 1070

Extraction, Characterisation and Application of Pectin from Indian Mango (*Mangifera indica*) Peels

GERALDINE GANTIOQUE[1], MA. CRISTINA GRAGASIN[2], DARENE CARGO[1], MING VINCENT DELA CRUZ[1], JERALD PUZA[1]

[1] *Central Luzon State University, Dept. of Food Science and Technology, Philippines*
[2] *Philippine Center for Postharvest Development and Mechanization (PHILMECH), Bio-Process Engineering Division, Philippines*

A valuable by-product that can be obtained from fruit wastes is pectin. This study focuses on the extraction, isolation and characterisation of pectin from Indian mango (*Mangifera indica* L.) peels based on their degree of ripening. Dried peels from Indian mangoes were obtained by drying the fresh peels at 60°C for a couple of hours depending on the volume being dried. To extract pectin, dried peels were cooked in acidified water (pH 2) for 1h, filtered using satin cloth to obtain pectic liquor, and precipitated in 95 % ethyl alcohol for 12h. The extracted pectin was dried for 1h at 105°C and pulverised using mortar and pestle. Physical properties (colour, pH, % moisture content, viscosity and total soluble solids) and chemical characteristics (% methoxyl content, % degree of esterification, % galacturonic acid, setting time and temperature and gel grade) of produced pectin were analyzed. The resulting Indian mango peel pectin was applied in a yogurt for sensory evaluation in comparison to Carabao mango peels (control).

Results showed that half-ripe Indian mango peel pectin contained relatively higher amounts of galacturonic acid, methoxyl content, degree of esterification and pectin yield ($p < 0.05$) in comparison with full-ripe mango peel pectin. These physico-chemical characteristics of mango peel pectin were within the accepted limit of good quality pectin.

Consumer acceptability testing (n=50) of yoghurt mixed with Indian mango peel pectin showed no significant difference ($p > 0.05$) in acceptability level with the control in terms of aroma, taste, mouthfeel, thickness and overall acceptability except for colour. Penalty analysis showed no significant drop in overall acceptability since majority of the respondents ($>70\%$) perceived that the sensory attributes of the yoghurt mixed with Indian mango peel pectin and the control was 'just about right'. Indian mango peels can be a rich source of pectin with good physicochemical characteristics with potential application to various food products.

Keywords: Galacturonic acid, indian mango peels, methoxyl content, pectin extraction

Contact Address: Geraldine Gantioque, Central Luzon State University, Dept. of Food Science and Technology, College of Home Science and Industry, Central Luzon State University, 3120 Science City of Munoz, Philippines, e-mail: geraldine.gantioque@gmail.com

Evaluation of Fruits and Vegetables as Phytonutrients Potential in Jordan

YONNA SACRE[1], MICHAEL BÖHME[1], RACHAD SALIBA[2]

[1]*Humboldt-Universität zu Berlin, Dept. Horticultural Plant Systems, Germany*
[2]*Lebanese University, Lebanon*

Fruits and vegetables (FV) are known to contain considerable amounts of vitamins and minerals in addition to phytonutrients and bioactive compounds having many positive health effects in the prevention of diseases.in the frame of a project related to status of human nutrition in the East Mediterranean the consumption of FV as sources of phytonutrients was studied in Jordan. A cross sectional analysis of 144 Jordanian individuals aged between 20 and 65 years old living in Amman and the surrounding, was conducted. Sociodemographic, lifestyle, eating behaviour, food frequency questionnaire (FFQ) and awareness information were collected through a questionnaire. Statistical analysis was carried out and multivariate models were used in order to evaluate the association between fruits and vegetables consumption and different independent criteria.the FV consumption among the Jordanian population was not as high as expected according to the international recommendations, even though these produces are highly available in the country. Regarding vegetables, 38.0 % of the Jordanian respondents, showed a medium level of consumption versus 29.3 % having a low level of consumption. Related to fruit consumption, 36.8 % Jordanian respondents consuming low level of fruits compared to 31.9 % of the Jordanian respondents, showing a high fruits intake. Furthermore, it was observed that the majority (54 %) of the study population was highly aware of the importance of phytonutrients in FV and were willing to increase their consumption of FV so they can benefit from more phytonutrients. The FV consumption was the most associated with age, education level, employment, salary ranges, expenses on a monthly basis assigned for FV and herbs consumption.the findings stated that the most frequently consumed produces were cucumber, tomato, sweet potato, apple, orange, banana, olives, mint and thyme, and the consumption of FV in Jordan is low to medium, due to the effect of several socio demographic and lifestyle factors. Future governmental or national programs and interventions could be settled to encourage and increase the FV consumption among all the population age levels. Furthermore, laboratory analysis would be recommended in order to determine the exact amount of phytonutrients in the more frequently consumed FV, therefore, the proper recommendation regarding the quantities and types could be settled.

Keywords: Awareness, bioactive compounds, health, phytonutrients, vegetable

Contact Address: Yonna Sacre, Humboldt-Universität zu Berlin, Dept. Horticultural Plant Systems current address: PO Box 40230, Baabda, Lebanon, e-mail: yonna.sacre@gmail.com

ID 424

Orange Fleshed Sweet Potato Adoption Improved Dietary Quality: Evidence from Women and Children in Western Kenya

TEMESGEN FITAMO BOCHER[1], TAWANDA MUZHINGI[2], JAN LOW[1]

[1] International Potato Centre, Sweetpotato Action for Security and Health in Africa (SASHA), Kenya

[2] International Potato Center, Food Processing, Peru

This study aims at understanding the influence of OFSP (Orange fleshed Sweet Potato) adoption and its intensity (share of OFSP area in sweetpotato area) in improving women and children dietary diversity and intake of vitamin A rich foods. Data were analysed from the endline study of a five-year integrated agriculture-health project in western Kenya. The project linked access to OFSP vines to public health services for pregnant women. In total, 2,269 mother-child pairs (children <24 months of age) were randomly selected in four intervention areas and four control areas. Two-stage instrumental variable and ordered logit regression models were employed to test effect of adoption on diet quality. Diagnostic tests for endogeneity and misspecification were conducted to confirm model validity. Two indices were identified: dietary diversity food groups consumed in pervious 24 hours,and the frequency of consumption of vitamin A-rich foods during the seven days prior to the interview. Not surprising, staple foods are the dominant food group, with less frequent consumption of nutrient-rich fruits and vegetables. The surveyed households reported consuming starchy staples (91 %), dark green leafy vegetables (80%), fruits and vegetables rich in vitamin A (26 %), other fruits and vegetables (58 %), organ meat (2 %), meat and fish (32 %), eggs (11 %), legumes (31 %), and milk products (80%). Women and children in households growing OFSP have 15 % and 18 % higher diet diversity scores, respectively, than those not growing OFSP. Similarly, the index capturing frequency of intakes of vitamin A rich foods was 10 %, and 20 %, higher for women and children in OFSP growing households, respectively, than those who not grow. Head age, mother's education, wealth index, and the sweetpotato plots have a positive effect on the dietary diversity and frequency of vitamin A intake. Households with limited access to a health facility, larger household size, and mother engaged in casual labour have less diversified diets and lower frequencies of consumption of vitamin A rich foods. Both OFSP adoption and the share of OFSP area have positive influence on dietary diversity and vitamin A intake for both women and children under two years of age in western Kenya.

Keywords: Adoption, children, malnutrition, OFSP, women

Contact Address: Temesgen Fitamo Bocher, International Potato Centre, Sweetpotato Action for Security and Health in Africa (SASHA), Old Naivasha Road, 25171-00603 Nairobi, Kenya, e-mail: t.bocher@cgiar.org

Exploring the Effectiveness of a Rapid Participatory Method in Mapping the Role of Agricultural Biodiversity in Local Food Systems to Identify Potential Entry Points to Improve Peoples' Capabilities to Be Nutrition Secure

MOLLY AHERN[1,3], JESSICA RANERI[2,3], PASQUALE DE MURO[1], GINA KENNEDY[3]

[1] *Università Degli Studi Roma Tre, Fac. di Economia, Italy*

[2] *Ghent University, Belgium*

[3] *Bioversity International, Healthy Diets from Sustainable Food Systems, Italy*

Vietnam has improved its food security situation at the price of losing traditional varieties adapted to local tastes and conditions due to increased production and use of high-yield crop varieties (mainly large scale mono-cropping). Decreased diversity of foods is a growing issue, and the existence of malnutrition in regions where staple crop production and food availability are sufficient highlights the necessity for a multidisciplinary approach to design interventions that target the four dimensions of food security - availability, access, stability and utilisation, of a diverse group of locally available nutritious foods.

This paper demonstrates the use of the Four Cell Approach to participatory research to rapidly identify trends in a) species and food usage in a landscape and b) the dynamics of the food system which may contribute to, or be leveraged to improve, peoples' capabilities to be nutrition secure. In the case of Son La Province, Vietnam, explored in this paper, it is possible to conclude a positive relationship between increased production diversity and dietary diversity, and highlight the importance of markets for diffusion of diverse foods. Diversification of species production and consumption has a positive effect on resilience during the off-season, and diversification of coping mechanisms utilised by communities can build resilience for future shocks. Food-based approaches that promote diversified production and consumption of locally available nutritious foods that local people value, while ensuring access to markets, have the potential to improve capabilities of local people to provide nutritious foods for themselves and their communities while improving resilience to be food and nutrition secure at all times.

Keywords: Capability approach, food, nutrition, food security

Contact Address: Molly Ahern, Università Degli Studi Roma Tre, Fac. di Economia, Rome, Italy, e-mail: mahern0115@gmail.com

Optimum Food Consumption Can Save Natural Resources

TSIGE-YOHANNES HABTE, MICHAEL KRAWINKEL

Justus-Liebig University Giessen, Inst. of Nutritional Sciences, Germany

Adequate nutrition refers to the consumption of diverse food groups that meet the nutrients requirement for growth, body maintenance, physical activities and health of people. Optimal nutrition satisfies daily nutrient-requirement and controls excess and unhealthy food consumption. The lack of optimal nutrition leads to either nutrients deficiency or overweight and obesity with subsequent health and environmental problems.

The quantification of the effects of undernutrition and nutrients deficiency in terms of change to natural resources is unknown. However, body growth, strength, energy utilisation, cognitive ability, motivation, immune system and health are negatively influenced, affecting seriously the productive performance of people. It is recorded that child undernutrition in Africa is associated with losses in health, education and productivity and cost Egypt, Ethiopian and Uganda 1.9, 16.5 and 5.6 % of their GDP, equivalent to 3.7, 4.7 and 0.9 billion USD/year respectively.

The total food energy cost for global overweight and obesity in 2015 is estimated at 659.445 Billion Mcal. Based on this, the global food expended for the development of global overweight and obese weight is 261.684 million tons. The global food energy cost for the maintenance of excess weight is estimated at 239.8 Billion Mcal/year. This accounts to 95.07 million tons of food per year. Land area equivalent to 100.26 million hectares is used to produce enough food to meet the cost of global excess body weight whereas additional 36.43 million hectares/year is required to meet the requirement for maintenance.

In general, optimal nutrition can save 137 000 000 ha land from the change of land use by cultivation. This can limit the loss of biodiversity, soil erosion, soil biology- and nutrient depletion, as well as greenhouse gas emission. Water volume of about 355 km^3 that might be needed to cultivate the excess land area can be saved. An estimated amount of nitrogen fertiliser equivalent to approximately 20 Mt season^{-1} usable to fertilise the excess area of land remains undistributed. This controls the use of fossil oil for N-fertiliser production, subsequent gas emission, and the loss of nitrogen compounds to the atmosphere and hydrosphere.

Keywords: Natural resources, nutrient deficiency, obesity, optimum food consumption, overweight

Contact Address: Tsige-Yohannes Habte, Justus-Liebig University Giessen, Inst. of Nutritional Sciences, Wilhelmstrasse 20, 35392 Giessen, Germany, e-mail: tsige-yohannes.habte@ernaehrung.uni-giessen.de

Traditional Enset (*Ensete ventricosum*) Fermentation Process in Gamo Highlands of Ethiopia

FEKADU ADDISU[1,2], WOLDESENBET FANTAHUN[2], KAREN VANCAMPENHOUT[3,1], LEEN VAN CAMPENHOUT[4,1]

[1]*KU Leuven, Dept. of Microbial and Molecular Systems, Belgium*
[2]*Arba Minch University, Dept. of Biology, Ethiopia*
[3]*KU Leuven, Dept. of Earth and Environmental Sciences, Belgium*
[4]*KU Leuven, Food Science and Nutrition Research Centre, Belgium*

Enset (*Ensete ventricosum* (Welw.) Cheesman, Musaceae) is one of the most important food security crops for about 20 million Ethiopian people. It is a multipurpose crop, used as human food, animal forage, fiber source and medical purposes. Enset is fermented to produce kocho, the main food product obtained by fermenting the mixture of the scraped pulp of the pseudostem and corm. The aim of this study was to investigate the traditional enset fermentation process in Gamo highlands of Ethiopia. A detailed survey and field observations were conducted to generate information on traditional enset fermentation practices, storage conditions, the use of a starter culture, length of fermentation time, sensory properties of the fermented enset and major tools used to process enset. The study revealed that enset processing practices are carried out in enset farms at the backyard of the farmer home. The traditional enset fermentation process is characterised by a wide variety of processing techniques and storage conditions across different districts. But in all cases, the first phase involves scrapping of the pseudostem with a sharp edged bamboo split to extract the long fibres. The scrapped pseudostem is squeezed using a clean cloth or sack. The squeezed liquid is decanted and the starch residue (bulla) is wrapped with enset leaves and kept inside a quantity of fermenting enset. The corm part is also scrapped and mixed with the squeezed pseudostem. In a first phase of the fermentation, the mixture is placed under wilted enset leaves and stored for fifteen to twenty one days. During the second phase, the mixture is transferred either into a fermentation pit or into a specially designed storage device (Erosa) or it is packed into small parts using wilted enset leaves. It was stored for a minimum of one month without disturbance. In the survey, the sensory quality of the fermented enset was found to be very poor. The survey also showed that the length of fermentation time varied greatly depending on the altitude of the district, the season and the volume of enset to be fermented. However, the majority of the respondents mentioned that a minimum of two month is required for complete fermentation. None of the respondents use any traditional or standard starter culture for enset fermentation. The survey further revealed that indicators like smell, colour change and elasticity were used to check the completion of the fermentation process. The enset fermentation process in Gamo highlands is an old-age technique. There is a need to optimise the fermentation process by developing a starter culture and by introducing appropriate modern processing technology.

Keywords: Corm, enset, fermentation, pseudostem, starter culture

Contact Address: Fekadu Addisu, KU Leuven, Dept. of Microbial and Molecular Systems, Leuven, Belgium, e-mail: addisufkd@gmail.com

ID 1118

Determinants of Household Drinking Water Quality in Rural Ethiopia

MUHAMMED USMAN, NICOLAS GERBER, EVITA HANIE PANGARIBOWO

University of Bonn, Center for Development Research (ZEF), Germany

Safe and adequate water supply is a vital element to preserve human health; however, access to clean water is limited in many developing countries. Furthermore, improved water sources are often contaminated with fecal matters and consumption of unsafe water poses a great public health risk. This study seeks to identify determinants of microbial contamination of household drinking water in rural areas of Fogera and Mecha districts of Ethiopia. In this analysis, a random sample of 454 households was surveyed from February to March 2014, and water samples from community sources and storage containers were collected and tested for fecal contamination. The number of *Escherichia coli* colony coliform counts per 100 ml (cfu/100 ml) water was used as an indicator of fecal contamination. The results show that 50 % of households used protected water sources, 38 % used unprotected sources and 12 % used surface water sources. However, water microbiological tests demonstrated that 58 % of household storage water samples and 74 % of water sources were contaminated with *E.coli*. After controlling for household sanitary factors, high level of *E.coli* coliform colonies were observed in unprotected water compared to surface water and protected wells/springs sources. To ensure the quality and safety of water stored in the household, our findings suggest that point-of-use water treatment, safe water handling and storage, proper hygiene practices such as washing hands after critical times and proper disposal of household garbage should be promoted. On-site water wells should be properly designed to prevent seepage from unhygienic household pit latrine. Furthermore, community water sources should be adequately protected and sanitary measures should be undertaken regularly to reduce contamination from human and animal waste.

Keywords: Drinking water quality, *Escherichia coli*, rural Ethiopia, sanitation and hygiene, water source

Contact Address: Muhammed Usman, University of Bonn, Center for Development Research (ZEF), Dept.of Economic and Technological Change, Walter-Flex Str. 3, 53113 Bonn, Germany, e-mail: mabdella@uni-bonn.de

Engineering aspects

A Comparative Analysis: Impacts and Sustainability of Rural Small Wind Electrification Programmes

Philipp Schaube[1], Jon Sumanik-Leary[2], Luciana Vanesa Clementi[3]

[1] *Wuppertal Institute for Climate, Environment and Energy, Future Energy and Mobility Structures, Germany*

[2] *Loughborough University, Low Carbon Energy for Development Network, United Kingdom*

[3] *National University of Central Buenos Aires, Center for Latin America Social Studies, Argentina*

This paper offers a comparative analysis of two small wind electrification programmes targeted at remote sheep farming households in two of the windiest regions of the world, Argentine Patagonia and the Falkland Islands/Islas Malvinas. In Argentina the research was carried out in different districts of the province of Chubut: Tehuelches, Paso de Indios and Rawson. Chubut is a province in southern Argentina which rural areas are characterised by a significant presence of indigenous communities, a very low population density rate and a lack of social infrastructure and facilities, due to the long distances between settlements. Within the Chubut region following the latest statistical records currently approximately 1.490 households do not have access to electricity. Despite comparable environmental conditions and local livelihoods, the impact of these two electrification programmes in the Argentine Patagonia and the Falkland Islands/Islas Malvinas was vastly different. A socio-technical systems approach was adopted to gain a deeper understanding of the local context and development dynamics. This study identifies the critical success factors that have contributed to these two distinct outcomes, drawing out those that can inform the design of future initiatives. The research is based upon a series of semi-structured interviews with key stakeholders (households, community leaders, maintenance providers, programme designers, small wind turbine manufacturers and national small wind experts), observational field visits (to remote farms, service centres and local authorities) and the review of project reports. Taking a user centred approach that tailors each energy system to the needs of that particular household and establishes ownership was found to be one of the most important considerations, alongside consistent institutional support, a strong and accessible service network and the successful integration of maintenance practices with the local way of life.

Keywords: Argentina, Falkland Islands, Islas Malvinas, rural electrification, small wind

Contact Address: Philipp Schaube, Wuppertal Institute for Climate, Environment and Energy, Future Energy and Mobility Structures, Doeppersberg 19, 42107 Wuppertal, Germany, e-mail: philipp.schaube@wupperinst.org

Solar Powered Milk Cooling System for Small Dairy Farmers in Kenya

ANA SALVATIERRA, VICTOR TORRES TOLEDO, KLAUS MEISSNER, JOACHIM MÜLLER

University of Hohenheim, Inst. of Agricultural Sciences in the Tropics (Hans-Ruthenberg-Institute), Germany

Dairy industry in Kenya is relatively well developed compared with other countries in sub-Saharan Africa. Milk production in Kenya covers 70 % of the total milk production in the country, despite poor handling of milk at the farm and longer distances to the market. Moreover, under warm climatic conditions, the maximum bacterial count in raw milk usually exceeds the threshold established by food safety regulations. Therefore, milk management needs to be better addressed in milk production chain to guarantee high quality and minimise losses. As a response an innovative milk cooling system, developed and tested by the University of Hohenheim, was transferred to Kenya by the Program of Accompanying Research for Agricultural Innovation (PARI) and it is currently tested. The system is based on commercially DC-refrigerator powered by photovoltaic modules which has a control unit to customize the availability of solar energy. The freezer has a volume of 166 l and is capable of producing 8–13 kg of ice per day. The system comes with 25 reusable ice tins of 2 kg capacity and two isolated milk cans with removable ice compartment. Every isolated milk-can is able to cool down 30 l milk from 36°C to 15°C with help of 6 kg ice. At this temperature, good milk quality is assured for 4 h after milking. By adding 4 kg ice, the temperature of the milk decreases to around 8 °C assuring good milk quality for at least 12 h more. The system is able to run autonomously for up to 5 days during periods of extreme low solar radiation and high ambient temperatures due to the ice storage (50 kg) inside the freezer. The introduction of this promising technology gives access to a business opportunities based on higher milk quality and farm productivity. An on-field assessment will provide value information of the potential social and economic costs and benefits which might flow from the implementation of the small-scale solar milk cooling system.

Keywords: Cooling efficiency, dairy farm, milk quality, solar energy

Contact Address: Ana Salvatierra, University of Hohenheim, Inst. of Agricultural Sciences in the Tropics (Hans-Ruthenberg-Institute), Garbenstrasse 9, 70599 Stuttgart, Germany, e-mail: Ana.SalvatierraRojas@uni-hohenheim.de

ID 934

Improving On-Farm Water Management by Introducing Wetting Front Detectors to Small Scale Irrigators in Ethiopia

PETRA SCHMITTER[1], AMARE HAILESLASSIE[1], YIGZAW DESALEGN[2], AMENTI CHALI[2], SEIFU TILAHUN[3], SIMON LANGAN[1], JENNIE BARRON[4]

[1] *International Water Management Institute (IWMI), Ethiopia*

[2] *International Livestock Research Institute (ILRI), Animal Science for Sustainable Productivity (ASSP) - LIVES Project, Ethiopia*

[3] *School of Civil and Water Resources Engineering, Bahir Dar Institute of Technology, Ethiopia*

[4] *International Water Management Institute (IWMI), Sri Lanka*

Smallholder irrigation to improve food security in the dry season as well as economic and demographic growth within Ethiopia is developing rapidly. However, the long term sustainability of increased irrigated production, together with degradation of soils (and associated water bodies) may be irreparably damaged by inappropriate watering schedules. In irrigation schemes, over-irrigation results in periodic water scarcity issues and in some cases sodicity. The aim of the study was to evaluate whether using wetting front detectors (WFD), a simple mechanical irrigation advice tool, would give farmers the right knowledge on when and how much to irrigate. Therefore, improving sustainable on-farm water management without negatively affecting crop and water productivity while fostering a more equitable water distribution within the scheme. The study, conducted in different regions of Ethiopia, covered various agro-ecological zones and soil conditions with over 200 farmers irrigating cereals or vegetables. Farmers and water user associations were trained on using the WFD to irrigate and distribute water within the scheme. Irrigation and crop performance was evaluated against control plots, having the same crop variety and management but traditional irrigation practices. Reduction in applied irrigation volume due to the WFD differed within and between sites due to furrow length, soil texture and farmer experience. Although yield increases were highly variable between farmers due to differences in farm management and crop variety cultivated, there was a positive effect of WFD on water productivity. Water productivity on average increased by 9 % whereas yields for the different crops increased between 13 and 17 %. In some cases the volume of water saved could double the cropped area. The reduction of irrigation events, when using the WFD, led to labour saving (up to 11 working days per ha) and fuel saving (between 50 and 150 US$ per ha). In both sites, farmers positively evaluated the scheduling tool, acknowledging that they learned to save water without negatively impacting crop productivity. The study showed that by providing access to when and how much to irrigate, farmers can positively adjust their on-farm water management resulting in more sustainable usage of their natural resources.

Keywords: Ethiopia, irrigation, water management, water productivity, wetting front detector

Contact Address: Petra Schmitter, International Water Management Institute (IWMI), Nile Basin and East Africa Office, c/o ILRI-Ethiopia Campus P.O.Box 5689, Addis Ababa, Ethiopia, e-mail: p.schmitter@cgiar.org

Bio-Oil from Pyrolysis of Cashew Nut Shell: A Near New Value Chain in Benin

THIERRY GODJO

Université de Lokossa, Benin

Benin is one of the African producer countries of cashews (*Anacardic occidental* L). Unfortunately most produced cashew nuts (95%) are exported unprocessed. This makes losing great value to the country. In order to increase the rate of cashew nuts processing in Benin several researches were carried out. The processing of Cashew Nut Shells (CNS) in bio-oil is an example. Indeed, biomass in the form of CNS represents a renewable and abundant source of energy. In this research, CNS obtained from two local cashew nut processing plants (Kake-5 and Nad & Co) were pyrolysed in a Pyrolysis Reactor (PR) designed by Cefrepade and fabricated at University of Lokossa. About 500 kg of the CNS were used in the PR. The PR (400–500°C) is connected to a condensing unit, in order to effectively recover the exhaust gases. The temperature of the PR and that of the exhaust gas stream were measured and recorded at regular intervals. The volatiles which condensed at the condensing unit were collected, the heating was stopped when no significant changes in temperature and gas condensates was observed. The mass of pyrolysis oil produced was determined by mass balance calculation of the whole recovery system, before and after the experiment. The pyrolysis vapours were condensed to get a combustible oil fraction: bio oil. This oil is tick dark brown and represents 20% of the hull mass processed. The detailed chemical compositional analysis (moisture content, specific gravity, viscosity, saponification value, Iodine value, acid value, pH, calorific value) of the oil was carried out. The pyrolysis oil was found to be a renewable natural resource and marked absence of anacardic acid. Also, the oil has been found to be fairly stable. The oil was completely miscible in diesel.

Keywords: *Anacardium occidentale*, Benin, cashew nut, energy recovery, pyrolysis oil, value chain

Contact Address: Thierry Godjo, Université de Lokossa, B.P. 133, Lokossa, Benin, e-mail: thierrygodjo@hotmail.com

ID 1116

Concept Design for a Biochar Sanitation System in Kivalina, Alaska

THERESA THEURETZBACHER[1,2], BRIAN VON HERZEN[2],
GÜNTER LANGERGRABER[1]

[1] University of Natural Resources and Life Sciences (BOKU), Inst. for Sanitary Engineering and Water Pollution Control, Austria

[2] The Climate Foundation, United States of America

Residential homes in Kivalina, an Inupiat village located on a barrier island in Alaska North of the Arctic Circle, lack toilets and running water. Residents use honey buckets (paint buckets lined with plastic trash bags) as toilet replacement to collect human waste.

A concept design for a sanitation system that converts human solid waste into biochar will address key public sanitation issues in Kivalina. The various infrastructural, climatic, economic, environmental, and social contexts were researched and a feasibility study was performed for the planning and implementation of the future Kivalina biochar sanitation system.

During the site visit to Kivalina in fall, 2014 rapid rural appraisal (RRA) and participatory rural appraisal (PRA) as methodologies were applied to collect information about community village sanitation and waste management economics. The survey data was statistically, numerically and graphically analyzed.

Two installation types of the selected UDDT (Urine Diverting Dry Toilet) model Villa 9210, were developed. One version is an underfloor collection system (37 houses) for houses on piles to collect human solid waste outside the home. The alternative is an in-home collection system (48 houses) for houses where underfloor collection is not possible for architectural reasons. A pilot toilet trial in Kivalina to test the operability and function of UDDT technology showed that only minor adaptions on the toilet interface are necessary.

Mapping of local waste management economics revealed, that the current hauling system is socially not fair; wealthier families have to pay less than poorer families. The financial analysis showed that using the UDDT model Villa 9210 is 30 % cheaper than using a honey bucket. The total operational costs of the toilet, hauling system and the biochar reactor are 40 % higher than using honey buckets. The total capital costs of the biochar sanitation system are only 10 % of the capital costs of conventional wastewater treatment systems in Arctic villages.

The proposed biochar sanitation system will reduce handling and open storage of human feces, decrease rates of waterborne diseases and the contamination of aqueous and terrestrial habitats in Kivalina. Further, it will decrease the need for additional village infrastructure and individual investments.

Keywords: Affordability, Arctic, biochar, honey bucket, urine diverting dry toilet

Contact Address: Theresa Theuretzbacher, University of Natural Resources and Life Sciences (BOKU), Inst. for Sanitary Engineering and Water Pollution Control
current address: Vognstølen 10b, 5096 Bergen, Norway, e-mail: theuretzbacher@gmail.com

Strength and Disintegration Characteristics of Compost Pellets from Urban Waste in Sri Lanka

LAKSHIKA HETTIARACHCHI[1], JOHANNES PAUL[2], SUDARSHANA FERNANDO[2], NILANTHI JAYATHILAKE[2], SANJA GUNEWARDENA[1], FELIX GRAU[3,2]

[1]*Moratuwa University Sri Lanka, Dept. of Chemical & Process Engineering, Sri Lanka*
[2]*International Water Management Institute (IWMI), Resource Recovery and Reuse (RRR), Sri Lanka*
[3]*University of Applied Sciences Osnabrueck, Fac. of Agricultural Sciences and Landscape Architecture, Germany*

Recovering resources from urban organic wastes can serve agricultural production as well as provide cost savings through volume reduction. However, in both liquid and solid waste management, the magnitude of planned resource recovery so far remains restricted in low-income countries, although the agricultural value of both resources is well recognised.

In Sri Lanka, urban waste composting is well known, but marketing is poor and so is Word-of-Mouth promotion as standard compost receives limited attention from farmers.

To address this issue, the IWMI implemented a resource recovery treatment project based on co-composting of nutrient rich fecal sludge and organic municipal solid wastes. The project looks at the safe production of co-compost, compost blending and pelletizing, its agricultural application, and the economic viability of the whole process. This paper summarises results on the pelletizing process which makes compost transport, storage and application easier, and also allows to influence nutrient release.

Pelletizing increases the density of the compost material by 30 %. In general, compost-pelletizing process consists of compost drying and pulverisation prior to pelletisation. This research confirmed that the above two steps can be successfully eliminated while reducing energy consumption and process cost.

With the right pressure and humidity, compost pellets can also be produced without binding agent. However, binding agents can increase pellet strength, as compared to pellets without binders. Most importantly, pellets without binding agent did not disintegrate in immersed water for a testing period of one month. Rice flour binder added by 3 % was able to achieve a quick pellet disintegration within 3 days. Evidence proved that careful selection of binding agent could control the time for disintegration while enabling the production of a tailor made fertiliser for crop type, depending on the crop nutrient demand. In addition, "roller and die" pelletizer appears more suitable in compost pelletizing, compared to 'extruder' models.

This research is supported by the German Ministry for Economic Cooperation and Development (BMZ) through GIZ/CIM.

Keywords: Co-composting, pelletisation, resource and nutrients recovery, urban waste

Contact Address: Johannes Paul, International Water Management Institute (IWMI), Resource Recovery and Reuse (RRR), 127 Sunhil Mawatha Pelawatta, Battaramulla, Colombo, Sri Lanka, e-mail: j.paul@cgiar.org

ID 422

Hydraulics and Uniformity Performances of an Innovative Bamboo Drip System

HERNAUDE AGOSSOU, JANOS BOGARDI, BERNHARD TISCHBEIN

University of Bonn, Center for Development Research (ZEF), Germany

With respect to technical performance, drip irrigation is the most promising approach to raise irrigation efficiency and thus improve productivity of growing crops. But in West-Africa as in many developing regions in the world, the lack of financial resources for establishing, operating and maintaining drip systems is the main reason for their non-adoption by smallholder farmers. A promising attempt to step out of this dilemma is an innovative bamboo-drip system that would have the advantages of conventional plastic systems, but be less costly. This study was initiated to support that option, and aimed at assessing hydraulics and uniformity performances of that system. To construct the bamboo-drip system, bamboo culms were harvested in the wild, 20 cm internodes cut and their inner part slightly coated with candle wax to reduce friction head loss. Conventional glue was used to join the internodes and form bamboo pipes. Emitters were hand-made and of ball-pen ink tube. Laboratory tests were carried out at 80, 60, 40 and 20 cm pressure heads, to determine inherent variabilities in hydraulics and emitter flow uniformity in the bamboo system. For inherent variabilities in hydraulics, Coefficients of variation of emitter flow were determined with regards to the bamboo material, emitter precision and emitter plugging, and compared to ASAE EP405.1 standards. This revealed that emitter plugging, due to singularities in bamboo segments, is the most important factor causing emitter flow to vary in the bamboo system. For flow uniformity test, Christiansen uniformity coefficient was determined. Comparisons with ASABE EP458 standards revealed that emitter flow uniformity in the bamboo system is at least fair; but at 20 cm head, performance in terms of uniformity becomes poor. The test revealed that creating pipes with more uniform internodes is a promising approach to reduce emitter flow variation and improve uniformity. As a consequence, this highlights the fact that bamboo cultivation in a uniform environment is the prerequisite for bamboo-drip introduction in rural and peri-urban West-Africa.

Keywords: Flow, irrigation, uniformity, variation

Contact Address: Hernaude Agossou, University of Bonn, Center for Development Research (ZEF), Am Jesuitenhof 1, D-53117 Bonn, Germany, e-mail: agossouhernaude@yahoo.fr

Production of Biogas as an Alternative Fuel for Domestic Use

OSAMA OSMAN ALI[1], BASHEER MUSBAH ABDELHAKEEM[2], EL BASHIR ALI
HAMMAD[1], ABOUBAKAR AGHMARI ALAMIN[2], HAMED ABDULGADIR
MOHAMMED[2]

[1]*Alneelain University, Dept. of Agricultural Engineering, Sudan*
[2]*Sebha University, Dept. of Agricultural Engineering, Libya*

An experiment was conducted in the Faculty of Agriculture, Sebha University, Libya during 2014/2015 to study the production of biogas as an alternative fuel for domestic use in the surrounding areas. Relative amounts of biogas producible from remnants (dung, dropping) of cows, camels, sheep, chickens and damaged fruit (fruit waste) were investigated.

A special steel tank (biogas digester) allowed fermentation of the experimental materials and the collection of the produced biogas. The remnants were mixed with water and added to the steel tank (calculated amount). A gas flame test was done to test ability of gas inflammation by using a burner. The actual gas production started three weeks after putting the remnants in the tank.

Also a laboratory assay was used to measure the gas volume by using three measuring cylinders: one of these cylinder received a waste - water mix, the second cylinder was packedwith water and the third cylinder was left empty.

Biogas produced from the dung of cow, camel, sheep, chicken and fruit waste was found to average 320.6 cm^3 kg^{-1}, 342.32 cm^3 kg^{-1}, 316.64 cm^3 kg^{-1}, 486.68 cm^3 kg^{-1} and 483.32 cm^3 kg^{-1}, respectively.

Chicken manure gave the highest gas production per kg, followed by fruit waste, while dung of camels, sheep and cows recorded the lowest production. This could be due to a longer fermentation time needed for these remnants as compared to chicken dung and fruit waste.

On the base of this result we conclude that animal and plant waste could be used efficiently and environmental friendly for gas production.

Keywords: Biogas, domestic, environment, fermentation, waste

Contact Address: Osama Osman Ali, Alneelain University, Dept. of Agricultural Engineering, 11121 North Khartoum, Sudan, e-mail: osama12660@hotmail.com

Smart Power Management for Improved Energy Performance of an Inflatable Solar Dryer

ANA SALVATIERRA, MARCUS NAGLE, JOACHIM MÜLLER

University of Hohenheim, Inst. of Agricultural Sciences in the Tropics (Hans-Ruthenberg-Institute), Germany

Post-harvest losses are an important factor that influence the production cycle of many crops. Research is required to support initiatives which improve processing and storage, since inadequate technologies, improper practices and lack of knowledge are currently causing considerable qualitative and quantitative post-harvest losses. Drying is a critical post-harvest process during which the end product can be significantly affected. Sun drying is commonly practised in tropical regions, despite leading to higher losses. As an alternative, an innovative solar drying technology has been developed. The Inflatable Solar Dryer (ISD), a further development of the solar tunnel dryer Hohenheim type, is made out of plastic films and is inflated using two ventilators. The ISD does not need any solid structure as the ventilators inflate the dryer forming a tunnel, thus it is collapsible and can easily be transported. The ventilators are driven by a photovoltaic system for off-grid operation. Further improvement on the power system/ventilators was required to optimise the energy consumption accordingly as drying is performed. Digital implementation presents a possibility to control and monitor processes via proportional integral derivative controller (PID). These controllers are commonly used in many applications to reduce costs, time and to better handle energy supply/consumption. A PID control with digital signals was developed to manage the energy consumption of the ventilators in the ISD, lowering the energy consumption. The regulation system used a micro-controller, which read analog signals from temperature and relative humidity sensors integrated in the ISD. Output signal was transformed to digital signals in order to adjust the speed of the ventilators based on the control signal. The principle relays in controlling the ventilators via pulse width modulation (PWM). The interface has been written using wiring-language in Arduino software. To investigate and demonstrate the effectiveness of the proposed approach, the PID controller is presented together with initial results.

Keywords: Automatisation, energy efficiency, PID control, solar dryer

Contact Address: Ana Salvatierra, University of Hohenheim, Inst. of Agricultural Sciences in the Tropics (Hans-Ruthenberg-Institute), Garbenstrasse 9, 70599 Stuttgart, Germany, e-mail: Ana.SalvatierraRojas@uni-hohenheim.de

Explosive Decompression Pretreatment in Lignocellulosic Ethanol Production

MERLIN RAUD, JÜRI OLT, TIMO KIKAS

Estonian University of Life Sciences, Institute of Technology, Estonia

The pretreatment is essential step prior to the conversion of the lignocellulosic material to ethanol which could be used as a liquid fuel in engines. However most traditional pretreatment methods have low efficiency, use chemicals or vast amount of energy and therefore, these processes might not be economically feasible. A novel biomass pretreatment method will be presented which opens up the biomass structure for more efficient enzymatic hydrolysis. No catalysts or chemicals are used in the process thereby, making it economically and environmentally attractive.

In this method the biomass is exposed to a high pressure using different gases, and temperature where the cells of the lignocellulosic biomass are filled with a solution saturated with dissolved gases. When the pressure is suddenly released, the feedstock is exposed to an explosive decompression and the dissolved gases are released from the solution. Sudden change in the volume breaks the cell walls and opens the biomass structure resulting in increased surface area of the substrate for enzymatic hydrolysis. In this paper two gases nitrogen and compressed air are utilised for pressure generation where range of different pressures (1–60 bar) and temperatures (25–175°C) were applied to barley straw to evaluate the efficiency of the pretreatment. The pretreatment was followed by enzymatic hydrolysis and fermentation. Resulting glucose and ethanol concentrations were measured to estimate the most suitable set of pretreatment conditions.

Results show that the highest glucose yield was gained when nitrogen gas was used (at 150°C 278 to 338 g kg^{-1} depending on the pressure). The results with compressed air were almost the same as those gained in autohydrolysis pretreatment, where no added pressure was used in addition to elevated temperature. The fermentation efficiency was lower at higher temperatures, however, in spite of the decrease in ethanol yield when pretreatment temperature was increased, the highest ethanol yield was gained at 150°C and in 10–30 bars with nitrogen explosion since the high glucose yield at pretreatment temperature 150°C enables to gain high ethanol yields in further process.

Keywords: Bioethanol, biofuels, biomass pretreatment, explosive decompression, lignocellulosic ethanol

Contact Address: Merlin Raud, Estonian University of Life Sciences, Institute of Technology, Kreutzwaldi St 56, 51014 Tartu, Estonia, e-mail: merlin.raud@emu.ee

ID 196

On-Farm Maize Storage Systems and Rodent Postharvest Losses in Maize Growing Agro-Ecological Zones of Kenya

Kukom Edoh Ognakossan[1,3], Hippolyte D. Affognon[2], Daniel N. Sila[3], Soul-Kifouly G. Midingoyi[1], Willis Omondi Owino[2], Christopher Mutungi[1], Oliver Hensel[4]

[1] International Centre of Insect Physiology and Ecology (ICIPE), Kenya

[2] International Crops Research Institute for the Semi-arid Tropics (ICRISAT), Technology Uptake, Mali

[3] Jomo Kenyatta University of Agriculture and Technology (JKUAT), Dept. of Food Science and Technology (JKUAT), Kenya

[4] University of Kassel, Agricultural and Biosystems Engineering, Germany

Rodents are one of the major postharvest pests that affect food security in impacting food availability and safety. However knowledge of the impact of rodents in the on-farm maize storage system in Kenya is limited. A survey was conducted in 2014 to assess the magnitude of postharvest losses in on-farm maize storage systems in Kenya, and rodents contribution to the losses. A total of 630 farmers spread across the six maize growing agro-ecological zones (AEZs) were interviewed. Insects, rodents and molds were the main storage problems reported by farmers. Storage losses were highest in the moist transitional and moist mid-altitude zones, and lowest in the dry-transitional zone. Rodents represented the second most important cause of storage losses after insects, and were ranked the main storage problem in the lowland tropical zone, while insects were the main storage problem in the other AEZs. Where maize was stored as cobs, the total storage losses were $11.1 \pm 0.7\%$, and rodents contributed up to 43%. Contrastingly, where maize was stored as shelled grain, total losses amounted to $15.5 \pm 0.6\%$ with rodents accounting for 30% of the losses. Regression analysis showed that rodents contributed significantly to total storage losses ($p < 0.0001$), and identified rodent trapping as the main storage practice that significantly ($p = 0.001$) lowered the losses. Together with insecticides, rodent traps were found to significantly decrease total losses; it was concluded that the proper application of these practices needs to be strengthened to effectively mitigate losses in on farm-stored maize.

Keywords: Food security, Kenya, maize, on-farm storage, post-harvest losses, rodents

Contact Address: Kukom Edoh Ognakossan, International Centre of Insect Physiology and Ecology (ICIPE), ICIPE Kasarani, Nairobi, Kenya, e-mail: kukom.edoh@gmail.com

Addressing Post-Harvest Losses During Traditional Banana Fermentation for Increased Food Security in Southwest Uganda

CORY WHITNEY[1,4], EDIE MUKIIBI[2,3], CAROLYNE NAKAKETO[3], JENS GEBAUER[4], ANNE RIETVELD[5], KATJA KEHLENBECK[6,4]

[1] University of Kassel, Fac. of Organic Agricultural Sciences, Germany
[2] Slow Food International, Italy
[3] Slow Food Uganda, Uganda
[4] Rhine-Waal University of Applied Sciences, Fac. of Life Sciences, Germany
[5] Bioversity International, Uganda
[6] The World Agroforestry Centre (ICRAF), Kenya

Postharvest losses (PHL) destroy 20-60 % of the food production in East Africa, exacerbating already severe regional food insecurity. Fermenting perishable foods such as fruits may reduce PHL while providing nutritional enrichment, improving shelf-life and food quality, and addressing seasonality in food supply. Fermented banana products have been refined and diversified in Uganda over generations to make the greatest use of available food resources, but still parts of the raw material are being lost during processing. This study aimed at exploring existing traditional methods and efficiency of fermentation of *Musa* (AAA-EAHB) 'Mbidde' in southwestern Uganda. The study gathered information through participatory explorations (working with brewers) on banana juice (lightly fermented beer with < 1 % alcohol content [n=20 brewers]), *tonto* (turbid beer with ~4% alcohol [n=20]), and *amarwa* (smoky spirit with ~40% alcohol [n=20]). Brewers mentioned several losses of material during harvest and processing. Harvesting bananas requires felling the plant causing ripe fruit damage, particularly during harvest for processing banana juice (loss from fresh bananas=6.4% $\pm$ 8.8%) or *amarwa* (loss=9.3% $\pm$ 9.5%). Second, losses occur when brewers squeeze juice from the raw banana pulp using stems of *Imperata cylindrica*, which is then discarded or fed to animals together with the adherent fruit pulp (losses from raw banana juice=50.6% $\pm$ 0.2%; from *tonto* 39.2% $\pm$ 21.4% and *amarwa* 47.6% $\pm$12.5%). Other causes of PHL during processing are excessive peeling for *tonto* processing (loss of banana flesh=18.6% $\pm$ 5.8%) and losses of intermediate products during distillation of *amarwa* (loss=75.9% $\pm$ 1.3%). Total losses of banana products during processing were rare and caused by sabotage (mostly by children), mistakes in the brewing process (e.g. addition of too much water), using bananas of wrong ripening stage, and equipment failure (e.g., burst or leaking drums in distillation equipment). Other non-PHL challenges include Banana Xanthomonas Wilt (BXW) and bad weather (up to 50% losses in the field).

Despite the general efficiency of traditional fermentation practices, significant portions of fruit are still lost. Reduction in PHL can complement, both culturally and nutritionally, the role that fermented banana products play in Ugandan food systems and contribute to regional food security. Collaborative mechanisms for PHL reduction should target the cited sources of PHL.

Keywords: Banana beer, indigenous knowledge, *Musa* spp., postharvest losses (PHL), traditional knowledge

Contact Address: Cory Whitney, University of Kassel, Fac. of Organic Agricultural Sciences current address: Marie-Curie Str. 1, 47533 Kleve, Germany, e-mail: cory.whitney@hsrw.eu

ID 465

Special programmes and visiting CGIAR centre

Research for development - innovative partnerships in Africa, Central Asia and Southeast Asia (BMBF)

The Uptake of Nicotine from the Soil: An Example for the "Horizontal Transfer of Natural Products"

DIRK SELMAR

Technical University Braunschweig, Plant Biology, Germany

Within the last decade numerous contaminations of plant derives commodities with problematic natural products such as nicotine, pyrrolizidine or tropane alkaloids have been reported by the European Food Safety Authority (EFSA). Until recently, the sources of these contaminations were unknown.

The goal of our current project "Nicotine contaminations in plants derived foods and commodities" funded by German Egyptian Research Fund (GERF - 01DH14019) was the identification of the potential sources of nicotine contamination in spice and medicinal plants. The centre of focus corresponds to the question, whether or not the uptake of the alkaloid from the nicotine contaminated soils could be responsible for the observed contaminations. The results shall contribute to avoid - or at least to minimise – such contaminations in the future.

Together with our cooperation partners in Egypt from Kafrelsheikh University we were able to document that – at least in part – the uptake of nicotine (i.e. leached out from cigarette butts) is responsible for the observed contaminations, which are thought to be problematic for human health.

Based on the results of our studies the concept of "Natural Product transfer" was established: plants take up substances from the soil, which previously have been leached out from rotting plant materials. This novel discovered phenomenon opens new doors for many further practical approaches. In this sense, new projects had been outlined for further funding. Together with the AGERI (Cairo) we will analyse, to which extent the horizontal transfer of natural products represents a general source for contaminations in plants derived foods and commodities. Another project is scheduled as cooperation with Mansoura University. This approach is aimed to investigate to what extent the horizontal transfer of natural products could be the basis for the production of functional plant derived foods.

Keywords: Soil contamination

Contact Address: Dirk Selmar, Technical University Braunschweig, Plant Biology, Mendelssohnstraße 4, 38106 Braunschweig, Germany, e-mail: d.selmar@tu-bs.de

Agricultural Restructuring, Water Scarcity and the Adaptation to Climate Change in Central Asia: A Five-Country Study (AGRIWANET)

NODIR DJANIBEKOV[1], MARTIN PETRICK[1], DAUREN OSHAKBAYEV[2], ROMAN MOGILEVSKII[3], KHODJAMAKHMAD UMAROV[4], GURBANMYRAT OVEZMYRADOV[5], YULIY YUSUPOV[6]

[1] *Leibniz Institute of Agricultural Development in Transition Economies, Germany*
[2] *Applied Research Center Talap, Kazakhstan*
[3] *University of Central Asia, Inst. of Public Policy and Administration, Kyrgyzstan*
[4] *Tajik National University, Tajikistan*
[5] *NGO Natural Energy, Turkmenistan*
[6] *Center for Economic Development (CED), Uzbekistan*

The experience of the five post-Soviet Central Asian (CA5) countries in restructuring attempts and outcomes in agriculture, policy formation to address water-related problems, and strategies to tackle climate change provides a fertile ground for comparative analysis to address general issues in agricultural development. Two decades after national independence, research on water-climate-farm restructuring nexus in the CA5 region has progressed slowly due to little exchange of researchers in the region, a lack of a centralised database, and focus of existing studies on technical solutions. The project's objective is to provide an analytically sound and policy-relevant understanding of the CA5 climate-water-restructuring nexus by investigating the vulnerability of certain organisational forms of agricultural production to water availability, and causal relations between agricultural restructuring and climate resilience. To support this objective, the project consolidated a unified database of regional patters of production, restructuring, water use and climate change, and produced policy chronicles of each CA5 country. Within its capacity building and networking objectives, the project organised trainings and networking events for the CA5 researchers. The project's international socioeconomic research consortium unites IAMO, Martin Luther University Halle-Wittenberg, Kazak Applied Research Center Talap, University of Central Asia in Kyrgyzstan, Tajik National University, Turkmen NGO Natural Energy, and the Center for Economic Development in Uzbekistan. The consortium conducted several summer schools, workshops, conference sessions and an international conference jointly with the International Association of Agricultural Economists (IAAE). The consolidated database, policy chronicles and country reports will be made publicly available. The first results indicate various challenges for the regional sustainable development caused by the heterogeneity of national approaches in agricultural reorganisation. These approaches juxtapose the evolution of farm structures with the shifts

Contact Address: Nodir Djanibekov, Leibniz Institute of Agricultural Development in Transition Economies (IAMO), Theodor-Lieser-Str. 2, 06120 Halle (Saale), Germany, e-mail: djanibekov@iamo.de

in production portfolio and have particularly strong implications in irrigated areas. Based on the project results, the consortium will continue to update the cross-country expertise and expand its academic value addition such as via a new CA-focused AGRICHANGE project, and target additional EU research funds for CA5-related research topics. The study results will be consolidated into policy briefs and serve to institutionalise the Central Asia platform on agricultural development coordinated in Germany.

Keywords: Climate change, water scarcity

Scientific Cooperation to Face International Challenges — Short Rotation Coppice Development for the Provision of Firewood and Hydrothermal Carbonisation of Water Hyacinth for Hydrochar Production in Myanmar

TOBIAS CREMER[1], THIDA SWE[2], JORGE DE VIVO[3], DIETER MURACH[1], JAN-PETER MUND[1]

[1] *Eberswalde University for Sustainable Development, Department for Forest Utilization and Timber Markets, Germany*

[2] *Forest Research Institute, Myanmar*

[3] *Universidad de la República, DETEMA Facultad de Química, Uruguay*

Due to a still growing need for firewood and construction timber, the pressure for utilisation on Myanmars remaining natural forests is steadily increasing. Furthermore, water hyacinth (*Eichhornia crassipes*), one of the most invasive species worldwide, is becoming more and more of a challenge in valuable ecosystems of Myanmar like the Inle-Lake.

The overarching goal of this project therefore is, to build an international network that specifically addresses these challenges, by linking scientists and young researchers of both countries, active in the field of short rotation coppice (for an utilisation as firewood to decrease pressure on natural forests) and hydrothermal carbonisation (as one possible way to gain positive value from fighting water hyacinth, i.e. production of hydrochar for combustion and/or fertiliser for short rotation coppice plantations from the process water).

Together with the Forest Research Institute in Yezin, Myanmar, two short rotation coppice plantations for firewood are established and managed on their local research stations, to gain experience on suitability, growth and yield of two native fast growing tree species (*Gmelina arborea* and *Acacia catechu*). A test design for the plantations was developed in the first workshop phase, possible sites were visited and preparations for the planting were made. Furthermore, a large sample of water hyacinth was already harvested and transported to Germany, to do basic tests on its suitability for hydrothermal carbonisation in a larger technical scale, together with the company AVA-CO2, Karlsruhe. First results regarding its carbonisation behaviour are promising.

These results will be analysed and discussed in detail with all partners in the remaining two workshop phases.

Beyond BMBF funding, it is planned, to intensify the cooperation in additional joint research and development activities – a sound basis could already be laid in this first phase of the current project. More disciplines, especially GIS and remote sensing, e.g for the monitoring of plantations or to estimate future expansion of water hyacinth shall be included. Additional contacts, e.g. with the University of Forestry, Yezin, could be established as well and future cooperation in terms of curricula development and revision is expected.

Keywords: Firewood, natural forests, water hyacinth

Contact Address: Tobias Cremer, Eberswalde University for Sustainable Development, Department for Forest Utilization and Timber Markets, Alfred-Möller Str. 1, 16225 Eberswalde, Germany, e-mail: tobias.cremer@hnee.de

Development of Grain Drying Facilities That Use Superabsorbent Polymers (SAP) to Optimise Drying and Control Aflatoxin Contamination in Kenya

FRANZ ROMÁN[1], OLIVER HENSEL[1], DUNCAN MBUGE[2]

[1] University of Kassel, Agricultural Engineering, Germany
[2] University of Nairobi, Dept. of Environmental and Biosystems Engineering, Kenya

Maize is the most important staple food in Kenya but is highly susceptible to aflatoxin contamination. Chronic exposure to aflatoxins from maize is prevalent in a high percentage of the Kenyan population and fatal outbreaks from acute exposure have also been reported in the past. Aflatoxin producing species are also cause of economic losses by spoilage, reduced prices and the effects on animals fed with contaminated maize. A condition to stall postharvest aflatoxin contamination of maize is to store it with a low enough moisture content. This, however, is seldom possible, especially for small-scale farmers who rely on sun drying for it and are instead faced with rains during harvest. This project aims to address this problem using superabsorbent polymers (SAP) to assist maize drying where fossil fuels or electricity are not available. These materials can adsorb a relatively high amount of water vapour, and preliminary studies on laboratory scale showed that they can be effective for drying and aflatoxin control in maize if present in sufficient proportion. The main objective of the project is to produce forced-convection drying and storage structures that incorporate SAPs and to test their performance in field conditions. Research partners working in the project are the Department of Environmental and Biosystems engineering at the University of Nairobi (Kenya), the Department of Agricultural Engineering at the University of Kassel (Germany), the Food and Soft Materials Laboratory at the ETH Zürich (Switzerland), and the Department of Agricultural and Rural Engineering at the University of Venda (South Africa). First results showing the high water vapour adsorption capacity, the adsorption kinetics, and the regeneration properties of the SAP, as well as the simulation model of the heat and mass transfer in the system are presented and discussed.

Keywords: Aflatoxin, maize, post-harvest

Contact Address: Franz Román, University of Kassel, Agricultural Engineering, Nordbahnhofstr. 1a, 37213 Witzenhausen, Germany, e-mail: franz.roman@uni-kassel.de

ID 1159

Partnership in Fisheries – ZMT Projects along the West African Coast

AGOSTINO MERICO, WERNER EKAU

Leibniz Center for Tropical Marine Ecology (ZMT), Ecology, Germany

The fisheries along the West-African coast is focused on small pelagic species of the upwelling ecosystem of the Canary current, especially off the Mauritanian and Senegalese coasts. The interplay between climate change, the potential adaptation of species, and the impact of fisheries on the coastal and offshore resources is only partially understood. Fisheries is an important source of income in the West African countries and understanding the factors driving changes in the coastal ecosystems is essential for the sustainable management of this resource. The Leibniz Center for Tropical Marine Ecology participates in several bi- and trilateral projects and activities to provide a scientific basis for the resource management in the region. In this talk we will present our current projects AWA and HARVEST. AWA (Ecosystem Approach to the management of fisheries and the marine environment in West African waters) is a trilateral project among German, French and West African institutions to investigate the stocks of small pelagic fish species in the Canary Current. In the Sine Saloum we analyse the combined effects of reduced freshwater inputs, intense evaporation, and a low gradient in the lower estuary on the nursery function of this estuary for coastal fishes. We combine these land-based investigations with ship-based expeditions (FRV Walther Herwig in 2014 and 2015, and RV Meteor in August 2016) to assess the outreach of shallow water areas such as the Banc d'Arguin and the Sine Saloum estuary to shelf waters. HARVEST (Harvest behaviour in common pool resource systems: data analysis and modelling of dynamic decision making) is a cooperative project with the African Institute for Mathematical Sciences (AIMS) in Mbour, Senegal that aims at (1) conducting a series of human behavioural experiments with a new, state-of-the-art mobile application to identify relevant factors influencing fish harvest behaviour and (2) develop and apply a traitbased model to describe adaptive human harvest following a dynamic tradeoff between current and perceived future harvest.

Keywords: Climate change, fisheries, modelling

Contact Address: Agostino Merico, Leibniz Zentrum für Marine Tropenökologie, Bremen, Germany, e-mail: agostino.merico@leibniz-zmt.de

Impact of Water Quality on Aquaculture: Target and Non-Target Analysis of Trace Organic Substances and their Transformation Products

IAN KEN DIMZON[1], ANN SELMA MORATA[2], JANINE MÜLLER[1], ROY KRISTIAN YANELA[2], HEIKE WEIL[1], TERESITA PEREZ[2], FABIAN M. DAYRIT[2], THOMAS P. KNEPPER[1]

[1]*Hochschule Fresenius, Fac. of Chemistry and Biology, Germany*
[2]*Ateneo de Manila University, Dept. of Chemistry and Department of Environmental Science, Philippines*

Aquaculture is a major source of livelihood in the Philippines. Foods derived from aquaculture have high market share and has a lot of export potential. However, aquaculture is under threat due to the deteriorating water quality and pollution from various sources. The situation of the Seven Lakes of San Pablo in Laguna Province exemplifies the problems and efforts being undertaken to maintain water quality for sustainable fresh water aquaculture.

Our research focuses on the target and non-target analysis of trace organic substances and their transformation products in three of the Seven Lakes: Palakpakin, Sampaloc and Pandin. We also study the entry and the elimination of the compounds to and from the lakes. Fish antibiotics sulfadiazine and sulfamethoxazole, and hypertension drug telmisartan were found at concentrations 126, 175 and 76 ng/L, respectively in Lake Sampaloc. Due to the presence of rice fields and fruit plantations in the surrounding area, pesticides like chlorpyrifos, cyprodinil, disulfoton, endosulfan-B, fenoxaprop-ethyl, pendimethalin, picolinafen and quinoxyfen were found in the lake water samples taken during the rainy season (July – October 2015) at concentrations between 40 to 110 ng L^{-1}. Insect repellant diethyltoluamide (DEET), and phosphate-based fire retardants were also detected. The fire retardants were also found in the materials from the houses in the lakes' coast. The pesticides, fire retardants and DEET were all below the limit set by the US Environmental Protection Agency for bodies of water or by the World Health Organisation for safe drinking. Biodegradation tests using the fixed-bed bioreactor are being done to study the elimination of representative pollutants by the natural microorganisms of Lake Palakpakin.

Emerging organic pollutants including microplastics will be determined in future studies. The impact of these organic pollutants on aquaculture and on the health of people living in the vicinity of the lake (for example, toxicity) will additionally be assessed. This collaborative work of Hochschule Fresenius and Ateneo de Manila University with the help of the German Federal Ministry for Education and Research is part of a bigger interdisciplinary project that aims to develop holistic, science-based and sustainable methodologies for the fishing communities, especially in the tropical regions.

Keywords: Aquaculture, water quality

Contact Address: Ian Ken Dimzon, Hochschule Fresenius, Fac. of Chemistry and Biology, Limburger-str. 2, 65510 Idstein, Germany, e-mail: dimzon@hs-fresenius.de

ID 1161

BMEL: Diversified agriculture and nutrition

Diversified Agriculture for a Balanced Nutrition in Sub-Saharan Africa – Projects Supported by the Federal Ministry of Food and Agriculture, BMEL

HENNING KNIPSCHILD, ARIANA BYSTRY

Federal Office for Agriculture and Food (BLE), International Cooperation and Global Food Security 323, Germany

With the funding instrument "Research Cooperation for Global Food Security and Nutrition" The Federal Ministry for Food and Agriculture (BMEL) strengthens the contribution of Germany's agricultural and nutritional research to the development of an efficient food system in partner countries, by building long-term partnerships between agricultural and nutritional research institutions in Germany, Africa and Southeast Asia.

Two calls for proposals have been published since 2013 focusing on diversified agriculture for nutrition-sensitive food production and on improved processing of local food to reduce seasonal food insecurity as well as food and nutrient losses.

Funding agency is BLE.

The BMEL session at Tropentag 2016 seeks to present the consortia and their projects funded within the frame of the first call on diversifying agriculture and the ERA-Net ERA-ARD II:

1. BAOFOOD - Enhancing local food security and nutrition through promoting the use of Baobab (*Adansonia digitata* L.) in rural communities in Eastern Africa, coordinator: Rhine-Waal University of Applied Sciences (HSRW). Participation: Justus Liebig University of Giessen (JLU).

2. Urban farming in Southern Africa – improved food safety and income options for urban disadvantaged communities (UFISAMO), coordinator: Humboldt University of Berlin (HU Berlin). Participation: Free University of Berlin (FUB).

3. Crops for Healthy Diets: Linking Agriculture and Nutrition (HealthyLAND), coordinator: Justus-Liebig University Giessen (JLU). Participation: University of Hohenheim (UH).

4. Diversifying agriculture for balanced nutrition through fruits and vegetables in multi-storey cropping systems (NutriHAF), coordinator: The Center for Development Research (ZEF).

5. Scaling-Up Nutrition: Implementing Potentials of nutrition-sensitive and diversified agriculture to increase food security (Scale-N), coordinator: Leibniz-Centre for Agricultural Landscape Research (ZALF). Participation: University of Hohenheim (UH).

Contact Address: Henning Knipschild, Federal Office for Agriculture and Food (BLE), International Cooperation and Global Food Security 323, Deichmannsaue 29, 53179 Bonn, Germany, e-mail: henning.knipschild@ble.de

6. ERA-ARD II (co-fund with BMLFUW): Smallholder Farmer Strategies to cope with Climate Change (SMACC), coordinator: University of Hohenheim (UH). Participation: University of Natural Resources and Life Sciences (BOKU).

Keywords: Climate change, diversification, nutrition-sensitive agriculture, research cooperation, sub-Saharan Africa

Urban Farming in Southern Africa – Improved Food Safety and Income Options for Urban Disadvantaged Communities (UFiSAMo)

HEIDE HOFFMANN[1], KARIN FIEGE[2], CARSTEN PÖTZSCH[3], SAMUEL QUIVE[4],
ANTONIO PAOLO[5], DANIEL TEVERA[6], ABDULRAZAK KARRIEM[7], CHRIS
D'AIUTO[8], MAXIMILIAN BAUMANN[9], PETER-HENNING CLAUSEN[10],
DOREEN SPARBORTH[11]

[1]*Humboldt-Universität zu Berlin, Albrecht Daniel Thaer Institute of Agricultural and Horticultural Sciences, Germany*

[2]*Humboldt-Universität zu Berlin, Centre for Rural Development, Germany*

[3]*Frankenförder Forschungsgesellschaft mbH, Germany*

[4]*University Eduard Mondlane, Faculty of Literature and Social Sciences, Mozambique*

[5]*Technical Secretariat for Food Security and Nutrition, Mozambique*

[6]*University of the Western Cape, Department of Geography, Environmental Studies & Tourism, South Africa*

[7]*University of the Western Cape, Institute for Social Development, South Africa*

[8]*Abalimi Bezekhaya, South Africa*

[9]*Freie Universität Berlin, FAO Reference Centre for Veterinary Public Health, Department of Veterinary Medicine, Germany*

[10]*Freie Universität Berlin, Institute for Parasitology and Tropical Veterinary Medicine, Germany*

[11]*Frankenförder Forschungsgesellschaft mbH, Germany*

The aims of this project on urban farming (UF) are to contribute to the improvement of urban food security, nutrition and food safety. To do this, we will investigate possible means to increase availability, consumption and marketing of diverse, safe and nutritious foods through improved production and marketing of crops and animal products in disadvantaged communities of Maputo, Mozambique and Cape Town, South Africa.

The expected outcomes for the main user groups are:

I. Policy stakeholders:

1. Sensitised for importance of UF for food security
2. Development of recommendations for the integration and improvement of UF in urban development

II. Universities:

1. Integrate UF in curricula and promote UF research (Research and Education Network)

III. Implementing agencies (NGOs, farmers' cooperatives, etc.)

1. 1. Better assessment of risks and benefits of UA

Contact Address: Carsten Pötzsch, Frankenförder Forschungsgesellschaft mbH, Potsdamer-Str. 18a, 14943 Luckenwalde, Germany, e-mail: carsten@potzsch.eu

2. Use of "best practices" for quality production (production, processing, marketing)

We will assist in improving the operational framework for UF through the project network, and will strengthen research on UF and the sustainable application of the project results from grass root to upper policy levels.

Objectives

Objectives 1:

- To study food habits, consumer behaviour and current systems of UF, and analyse UF value chains in disadvantaged urban areas of Maputo and townships of Cape Town. Based on the results, explore value-adding options through improving and diversifying the UF systems.

Objectives 2:

- To investigate the benefits and risks to human health and food safety of crop and animal UF.

Objective 3:

- To extend the current agricultural research and education network of the partner universities to the area of UF for all Mozambican, South African and German project partners.

Objective 4:

- To assist the sustainable implementation of project results from grass root to upper policy level and enhance local capacity building.

  Coordination and control

The project is financially supported by the German Federal Ministry of Food and Agriculture (BMEL) based on a decision of the Parliament of the Federal Republic of Germany through the Federal Office for Agriculture and Food (BLE) (Duration: 2016–2019) and will be controlled and coordinated in network coordination, which interacts between all partners and to BLE. Yearly workshops in project areas serve as ongoing control of successful project management and specification of upcoming work- and research plan. The documentation of successful project phases is based on milestones.

Keywords: Crop cultivation, livestock farming, Southern Africa, urban farming, value chains

The Baofood Project: Enhancing Local Food Security and Nutrition in Eastern Africa with the Baobab Tree

KATHRIN MEINHOLD[1], YAHIA OMAR ADAM[2], MUNTHALI CHIMULEKE[3],
ESTHER EVANG[4], JENS GEBAUER[1], TSIGE-YOHANNES HABTE[4], KATJA
KEHLENBECK[1], MICHAEL KRAWINKEL[4], FLORIAN KUGLER[1], TARIG ELSHEIKH
MAHMOUD[5], NYORI JEREMIAH MBUGUA[6], DAGMAR MITHÖFER[1], KAVOI
MUTUKU MUENDO[6], ANTHONY MAINA NJIRU[7], WILLIS OMONDI OWINO[6],
FREDAH KARAMBU RIMBERIA[6], EL AMIN SANJAK[2], MARTIN SCHÜRING[8],
MUNEER ELYAS SIDDIG[2,5], ARTHUR STEVENS[9], MOHAMED EL NOUR TAHA[5],
ANDREAS TRIEBEL[10], DIETRICH DARR[1]

[1] Rhine-Waal University of Applied Sciences, Fac. of Life Sciences, Germany
[2] University of Khartoum, Fac. of Forestry, Sudan
[3] Mzuzu University, Fac. of Environmental Sciences, Malawi
[4] Justus-Liebig Universität Gießen, Germany
[5] University of Kordofan, Gum Ararbic Research Center, Sudan
[6] Jomo Kenyatta University of Agriculture and Technology, Kenya
[7] Wild Living Resources, Kenya
[8] ttz Bremerhaven, Germany
[9] PhytoTrade Africa, United Kingdom
[10] Baobab Social Business gGmbH, Germany

The baobab tree (*Adansonia digitata* L.) is found throughout the drier parts of sub-Saharan Africa. Particularly though the use of its highly nutritious fruits, but also its leaves and other parts of the tree it can make a positive contribution to family nutrition and food security — either directly or indirectly though income generation. The latter pathway is receiving increasing attention, following the acceptance of baobab fruit pulp as a novel food ingredient in both the US and Europe. In addition, baobab food products are of significant and increasing importance in a number of local African markets. These growing markets may offer additional income opportunities for baobab producers throughout Africa. However, in Eastern Africa, particularly Kenya and the Sudan, the opportunities baobab trees offer to improve local nutrition and livelihoods have largely been neglected.

The BAOFOOD project, which is funded by BMEL under its "Research Cooperation for Global Food Security and Nutrition" and runs from 2016 to 2019, aims at promoting the domestication, market development, processing and consumption of baobab for the improvement of food security, nutrition and rural livelihoods in these target countries. Addressing the identified bottlenecks of inconsistent quality in plant materials, lack of cultivation and processing technologies or underdeveloped market chains research activities will touch on all parts of the value chain. The geograph-

Contact Address: Dietrich Darr, Rhine-Waal University of Applied Sciences, Faculty of Life Sciences, Marie-Curie-Str. 1, 47533 Kleve, Germany, e-mail: dietrich.darr@hochschule-rhein-waal.de

ical range of baobab as well as phenological variations are being assessed in order to preserve and protect the baobab tree as a natural resource while simultaneously developing viable recommendations for the sustainable cultivation and domestication of these trees. The nutritional value of baobab fruit and leaves are being analysed and the effect of baobab products on the food supply and the economic situation of local populations investigated in order to predict how increased commercial use will impact the project region. Extensive target group and market analyses in Kenya and Sudan are planned to explore the market demand and potential for new baobab-based products. The ultimate goal is to then produce those products with the most demand and potential in a local pilot production facility.

Keywords: Baobab (*Adansonia digitata*), food security, Kenya, nutrition, Sudan, underutilised plant species

Crops for Healthy Diets: Linking Agriculture and Nutrition (HealthyLAND)

IRMGARD JORDAN[1], JAN WELSCH[1], ANNA RÖHLIG[1], SAHRAH FISCHER[2], SAMWEL MBUGUA[3], JULIUS TWINAMASIKO[4], PAUL FALAKEZA FATCH[5], MICHAEL KRAWINKEL[1], JULIUS MASINDE[3], LYDIAH WASWA[3], JENINAH KARUNGI[4], GABRIELLA CHIUTSI PHIRI[5], ERICK MAINA[3], ELIZABETH MBUTHIA[3], JOHNNY MUGISHA[4], CHARLES MASANGANO[5], THOMAS HILGER[2], ERNST-AUGUST NUPPENAU[1]

[1] *Justus Liebig University Giessen, Germany*

[2] *University of Hohenheim, Inst. of Agricultural Sciences in the Tropics (Hans-Ruthenberg-Institute), Germany*

[3] *Egerton University, Human Nutrition, Kenya*

[4] *Makarere University, Uganda*

[5] *Lilongwe University of Agriculture and Natural Resources, Malawi*

East Africa shows relatively high rates of malnutrition and low dietary diversity. Our goal is to discover to what extent and how a more diverse farming system contributes to diverse diets and nutrition security.

The research aims at contributing to the discussion on nutrition oriented agriculture and capacity building. The focus will be on knowledge exchange, fostering nutritional health between consumption and production units using a trans-disciplinary approach, in which crop scientists, agronomists and nutrition experts work together with farmers, households and re-tailers.

We hypothesise that improvements in farming systems, based on ecologically oriented farming, impact positively on food diversity and nutrition security. Expected outcomes are: a comparison of nutritional status, level of dietary diversity and agrobiodiversity and choice of crops among resource poor households in Kenya, Uganda and Malawi. The target sites are currently following carbohydrate based survival strategies.

Cross-sectional surveys were carried out in May and June 2016 among farm families with chil-dren below five years in Kapchorwa District (Uganda) and Teso South Sub-County (Kenya). Focus group discussions, a farming system analysis, observations, collection of soil and crop samples to assess level of degradation complemented the baseline data collection. The information will be used to identify agricultural interventions and nutrition education messages that are likely to improve the nutrition security of households. In Malawi data collection will start in October 2016.

Land productivity appears to be poor and the sites fit into the frame of hypothesised degradation, low-diverse monoculture, and nutrition problems. Kitchen gardens were

Contact Address: Irmgard Jordan, Justus-Liebig University Giessen, Center for International Development and Environmental Research, Gießen, Germany, e-mail: Irmgard.Jordan@ernaehrung.uni-giessen.de

available in 74 % and 73 % of the farm households in Teso (n=418) and Kapchorwa (n=454). In Teso, they were mainly used to produce vegetables only (89 %) and rarely to produce both, fruits and vegetables (8 %). Crop rotation (39 %), intercropping (12 %), permanent crops (13 %), crop pure stand (14 %) or fallowing (10 %) were main practices in Teso.

Stunting levels were 14 % in Teso and 29 % in Kapchorwa. First results indicate that family nutrition is a challenge and need further investigation. In both areas the interventions will focus on linking nutrition messages and agriculture innovations to improve the food systems for nutrition security.

Keywords: Agriculture innovations, agro-biodiversity, dietary diversity, nutrition - agriculture linkages, nutrition education

Scaling-Up Nutrition: Implementing Potentials of Nutrition-Sensitive and Diversified Agriculture to Increase Food Security

Constance Reif[1], Hadijah Mbwana[2], Wolfgang Stuetz[3], Michelle Bonatti[1], Stefan Sieber[1]

[1] Leibniz Centre for Agricultural Landscape Research (ZALF), Inst. of Socio-Economics, Germany

[2] Sokoine University of Agriculture, Food Science and Technology, Tanzania

[3] University of Hohenheim, Inst. of Biological Chemistry and Nutrition, Germany

Food and nutrition security is still one of the most pressing challenges to constantly growing populations in Sub-Saharan Africa. The nutritional situation in Tanzania has only slightly improved in the last decade despite high rates of economic growth.

Scale-N aims at ameliorating the critical food security situation and nutritional status of the rural poor in Tanzania by implementing nutrition-sensitive agricultural innovations and nutrition education. Following the core principles of participatory and collaborative research, the project design includes the following steps (i) analyses of the food and nutrition situation; (ii) application of nutrition-sensitive interventions; (iii) measurements of impacts of the interventions on the nutritional status, livelihoods, and food security and (iv) up-scaling of successful interventions at farm-, policy-, and educational levels.

To identify the baseline situation of the local population, Scale-N conducted a household survey including the following core topics: (1) socio-economics; (2) disease history and medical conditions; (3) home gardening; (4) nutrition knowledge attitudes, perception and practices; (5) food production, distribution and consumption; (6) problem perception and community drivers; (7) measurement of nutrition status of mother-child-pairs: More than 650 households (mothers) from four different study sites were interviewed and anthropometrics and haemoglobin of mother-child-pairs were measured on study sites; blood samples were drawn for further analysis on iron status (serum ferritin, sTfR), infection markers (CRP, AGP), vitamin A status (serum retinol, RBP, pro vitamin A carotenoids) and zinc status (plasma zinc).

Outcomes of the survey and the nutrition value chain analysis will be evaluated to design a tailored education programme for local target groups on a household level and a specific training programme for facilitators will be set up. In this participatory approach, local population will be involved in learning processes to develop and improve nutritional knowledge of local nutrient-dense foods and optimised post-harvest treatments.

Keywords: Food and nutrition security, nutrition education, nutrition value chains, participatory action research

Contact Address: Constance Reif, Leibniz Centre for Agricultural Landscape Research (ZALF), Inst. of Socio-Economics, Eberswalder Str. 84, Müncheberg, Germany, e-mail: constance.reif@zalf.de

Progress and Experiences of the NutriHAF-Africa Project

Jochen Dürr

University of Bonn, Center for Development Research (ZEF), NutriHAF Project, Germany

In the framework of the "Research Cooperation for Global Food Security and Nutritionfunded by the BMEL, the NutriHAF-Africa project explores and integrates appropriate fruit and vegetable crops into multi-storey cropping systems to increase (micro-) nutrition security in order to diversify and intensify agriculture and thus to reduce pressure on natural habitats in biodiversity hotspots in Ethiopia and Madagascar. NutriHAF is a research and capacity building project. The research will enable poor male and female smallholders to increase sustainably their agricultural productivity and species diversity by integrating fruits and vegetables into existing multi-storey cropping systems. This is achieved by increasing knowledge about appropriate fruits and vegetables for multi-storey cropping systems and by improving knowledge on food behaviour and adoption constraints. Capacity building will increase the awareness and knowledge of farmers, consumers and decision takers about balanced diets, nutritional values of different foods, fruit and vegetable production and processing, food preparation and quality.

The project consortium consists of thirteen partners from Germany and Africa that are partly research organisations, partly international, regional and national research and development networks and partly capacity building and implementing organisations.

Progress and results

After one year of research first results and the progress of the project will be presented. The presentation will share experiences from a successful participatory crop selection process and other activities. It will reflect on opportunities and challenges in project implementation that are relevant for the practice in the region and other African countries. The three main opportunities for the project are: the promising marketing potential for (indigenous and other) fruit and vegetables in the area, a long lean period of local vegetables and a high interest in and little knowledge on postharvest techniques. Challenges included the dominance of administrative structures during the implementation stage and highly overloaded female farmers (the vegetable cultivators) who have little time for trainings and vegetable cultivation in the distanced forests. Finally, attention will be drawn to the importance of training extension services and doing policy advocacy in order to support the project outcome.

Keywords: Biodiversity, diversification, multi-storey cropping systems, nutrition-sensitive agriculture, research cooperation, sub-Saharan Africa

Contact Address: Jochen Dürr, University of Bonn, Center for Development Research (ZEF), NutriHAF Project, W.-Flex-Str. 3, Bonn, Germany, e-mail: jduerr@uni-bonn.de

ID 1172

Improving Rural Livelihoods in Sub-Saharan Africa: Sustainable and Climate-Smart Intensification of Agricultural Production (SMACC)

BERNHARD FREYER[1], FOLKARD ASCH[2], GETACHEW ALEMAYEHU[3], ENYEW ADIGO[3], RHODA BIRECH[4], JOYCE MALING'A[5], JOACHIM MÜLLER[2], JÖRN GERMER[2], TILAHUN TADDESE[6], AGEGNEHU SHIBABAW[6], MISGANAW TESHAGER[3], PATRICK AWUOR OORO[5], RAEL TAIY[7], YOSEPH TWODROS[1], CHADWICK DIGO[4]

[1] *University of Natural Resources and Life Sciences (BOKU), Division of Organic Farming, Austria*

[2] *University of Hohenheim, Inst. of Agricultural Sciences in the Tropics (Hans-Ruthenberg-Institute), Germany*

[3] *Bahir Dar University (UBD), Ethiopia*

[4] *Egerton University, Crops, Horticulture and Soil Chemistry, Kenya*

[5] *Kenya Agriculture and Livestock Research Organization (KALRO), Food Crops Research Institute, Kenya*

[6] *Amhara Regional Agricultural Research Institute (ARARI), Ethiopia*

[7] *Ministry of Agriculture, Livestock and Fischeries, Sector Development Support Programme, Uasin Gishu County, Kenya*

The project is aimed at providing sustainable field-to-market strategies on production intensification of selected key crops that are adapted to help sub-Saharan regions to cope with climate change. To achieve the targeted goal, the research project was conducted by multidisciplinary consortium consisting of European Universities (BOKU and UHOH) and African Universities and Agricultural Research Institutes (Bahir Dar, Ethiopia; Egerton, Kenya; and ARARI (Ethiopia) and KARI (Kenya)). Hence, the entire research project was divided into five work packages.

The project, ERA ARD (2013–2016) financed by KEF, BMLFUW (Austria) and BMEL (Germany) addressed the improvement and sustainability of rural livelihoods in Sub-Saharan Africa through adaptation of sustainable and climate-smart intensification of agricultural systems. The indended project output was to foster sustainable farming practices, economic and social development and help to reduce negative CC impacts on livelihoods in rural areas.

Main project results are that with a combination of clover, green manure from alley farming as well as the addition of farm yard manure, cash crop yields can be increased. However a longer period is needed to show the effects of organic manure management. At household level we identified a set of activities that help to optimise the efficiency of the energy and water system. The research process was supported

Contact Address: Bernhard Freyer, University of Natural Resources and Life Sciences (BOKU), Division of Organic Farming, Gregor Mendel Straße 33, 1180 Wien, Austria, e-mail: Bernhard.Freyer@boku.ac.at

through intense communication between researchers, advisors, farmers and other representatives of the region, continuously observing and discussing the findings through field walks and workshops. This also helped building trust between the actors, which we identified as one key factor for the dissemination of the findings.

Keywords: Alley farming, climate change, market strategy

Impact of Food Knowledge and Social Structures on Educational Program Development in the Scale-n Project in Rural Tanzania

MICHELLE BONATTI[1], CONSTANCE REIF[1], STEFAN SIEBER[1], HADIJAH MBWANA[2], WOLFGANG STUETZ[3]

[1] Leibniz-Centre for Agricultural Landscape Research (ZALF), Germany
[2] Sokoine University of Agriculture, Food Science and Technology, Tanzania
[3] University of Hohenheim, Inst. of Biological Chemistry and Nutrition, Germany

Food and nutrition security is still one of the most pressing challenges to constantly growing populations in Sub-Saharan Africa. The Scale-N project aims to safeguard food and nutrition among Tanzania's local poor by supporting the development of sustainable agriculture and local knowledge integrated education programme on nutrition. Within the Scale-N education programme the role of food knowledge and social structures in critical food security situation as well as the driving forces for food adoption of the local population in food insecure situations will be assessed. Methodological steps to assess interlinkages between traditional knowledge and social structures on the behaviour in food insecure situations will include (1) exploratory expeditions (2) participant observation (3) household surveys focusing on problem understandings and food perceptions and (4) focus groups. In total 650 households at four different study sites are involved in project activities. Exploratory expeditions and participant observations showed that despite the influence of biophysical environmental conditions (i.e., drought, lack of infrastructure) the patrons of sociocultural structure plays a fundamental role in critical food security situations (scoping strategies for adaptation, routine of child feeding, consumption practices, gender relations of food sharing). Next, in-depth information will be generated (3 and 4) about local knowledge on the driving forces for food adaptation strategies of the local population in food insecure situations. Scale-N project findings will target to inform the national policy planning sectors of food security to develop livelihood adoption strategies and to implement key finding to improve future school and university curricula.

Keywords: Food adoption strategies, food perception, nutrition education

Contact Address: Michelle Bonatti, Leibniz-Centre for Agricultural Landscape Research (ZALF), Eberswalder Str. 86 , 15374 Müncheberg, Germany, e-mail: michebonatti@gmail.com

Scaling-Up Effects of Food Value Chain Upgrading Strategies: Opportunities for Optimised Nutritional and Food Security for Local Food Systems in Tanzania

CHARLES PETER MGENI[1,2], KLAUS MÜLLER[1,2], STEFAN SIEBER[2], CONSTANCE REIF[2], ANJA FASSE[3]

[1]*Humboldt-Universität zu Berlin, Albrecht Daniel Thaer-Institute of Agricultural and Horticultural Sciences (ADTI), Germany*

[2]*Leibniz Centre for Agricultural Landscape Research (ZALF), Inst. of Socio-Economics, Germany*

[3]*Leibniz Universität Hannover, Institute for Environmental Economics and World Trade, Germany*

Achieving food security is one of the most pressing challenges, particularly in developing countries. Food security is achieved when all people at all times have access to sufficient, safe, nutritious food to maintain a healthy and active life. Effort on tackling these challenges, differ among the affected individual countries, and much depend on the policies adopted to counteract them. Across the developing world, the majority of the poor and most of the hungry live in rural areas, where farming and smallholder agriculture are prevailing. Policies geared towards agriculture have profound impacts on the opportunities and constraints that affect food systems. However, many countries in the developing world including Tanzania, lack the required capacities and data to provide evidence-based policymaking. This study uses a village Social Accounting Matrix (SAM) as a tool to provide evidence-based information for stakeholders. The study uses Dodoma region in Tanzania, which is semi-arid with its food system, is primarily based on sorghum, millet, and sunflower which are adapted to drought conditions, and farmers practicing agroforestry cropping system as a climate adaptation strategy. Nevertheless, Dodoma region face food insecurity. Specific objective of this study is to assess the effects of sunflower value chain and agroforestry for rural economy in Tanzania: using a selected village with high potential for sunflower and practicing agroforestry. The research question is whether the sunflower value chain or agroforestry cropping system can substantially improve the livelihood of the rural poor and how positively contribute to stabilise food security? Hence we answer this question by analysing household specific labour effects applying sunflower value chain and agroforestry cropping system in comparison to other crops and the effects of increasing exogenous demand for sunflower if has contribution to income of village households using a case of Idifu Village in Dodoma, Tanzania.

Keywords: Food security, value chain, village SAM

Contact Address: Charles Peter Mgeni, Leibniz Centre of Agricultural Landscape Research, Institute of Socio-economics, Eberswalder Straße 84, Müncheberg, Germany, e-mail: chrlsmgeni099@gmail.com

ID 1170

Bioversity International (CGIAR centre)

Seeds of Resilience: Novel Strategies for Using Crop Diversity in Climate Change Adaptation

RONNIE VERNOOY[1], CATHERINE KIWUKA[2]

[1]*Bioversity International, Italy*

[2]*National Agricultural Research Organisation (NARO), Plant Genetic Resources Centre, Uganda*

Findings from the field point to a decline in diversity of local varieties in many countries. Future impacts of climate change are expected to become more pronounced in many parts of the world forcing farmers to change their practices and find crops and varieties better adapted to new weather dynamics. Providing farmers with better access to crop and varietal diversity can strengthen their capacity to adapt to climate change. Under supportive policy and socioeconomic conditions, such strengthened capacity could contribute to greater food availability throughout the year, the production of more nutritious and healthy crops, and income generation. Bioversity International and national research partners are implementing a comprehensive seed resilience strategy allowing farmers to access and use plant genetic diversity more effectively in the context of climate change adaptation. The strategy combines the use of climate and crop modelling tools and participatory research methods. The strategy has eight steps:

1. Situational analysis and planning
2. Data preparation and selection of software
3. Climate change analysis and identification of germplasm
4. Germplasm acquisition
5. Field experimentation
6. Germplasm conservation
7. Participatory evaluation
8. Knowledge sharing and communication.

In Uganda, a team of scientists and extension agents used the strategy to diversify farmers' access to beans, one of the country's key crops for food security. Using climate change scenario analysis, DIVA-GIS and crop suitability modelling the team identified bean accessions with good climate adaptation potential from three sources: (i) the national gene banks in Rwanda and Uganda, (ii) communities in both countries and (iii) international genebanks. In 2014, the first phase of participatory field trials with farmers was realised using materials from the national genebank and locally adapted varieties. In addition, accessions from international genebanks were requested and then tested in the field in 2015. A third source of novel germplasm are farmers' own varieties. Based on an exchange visits between farmers of community seed banks in Uganda Rwanda, a number of varieties of beans were identified and tested in 2016.
Resources: http://www.seedsresourcebox.org

Keywords: Adaptation, climate change, crop and variety diversity, resilience, seeds

Contact Address: Ronnie Vernooy, Bioversity International, Via Dei Tre Denari 472/a, 00057 Maccarese, Italy, e-mail: r.vernooy@cgiar.org

ID 1179

Index of Authors

Index of Keywords

Abstract IDs

A